Meeting the Basic Needs of the Rural Poor

Pergamon Titles of Related Interest

Cole/Lucas   MODELS, PLANNING AND BASIC NEEDS
Goodman/Love   MANAGEMENT OF DEVELOPMENT PROJECTS
Goodman/Love   PROJECT PLANNING AND MANAGEMENT
Morris   MEASURING THE CONDITION OF THE WORLD'S POOR
Nelson   WHY HAS DEVELOPMENT NEGLECTED RURAL
   WOMEN?
Salas   INTERNATIONAL POPULATION ASSISTANCE
Stepanek   BANGLADESH — EQUITABLE GROWTH?

Related Journals*

BUILDING AND ENVIRONMENT
PROGRESS IN PLANNING
REGIONAL STUDIES
SOCIOECONOMIC PLANNING SCIENCES
WORLD DEVELOPMENT

*Free specimen copies available upon request.

PERGAMON
POLICY
STUDIES

ON INTERNATIONAL DEVELOPMENT

Meeting the Basic Needs of the Rural Poor

The Integrated Community-Based Approach

Edited by
Philip H. Coombs

A Report of The International Council
for Educational Development

Based on a research project supported by
the Ford Foundation, Rockefeller Foundation,
Charles E. Merrill Trust, International Planned
Parenthood Federation, Netherlands Department of International Technical Assistance,
U.S. Agency for International Development,
and Save the Children Federation.

Pergamon Press

NEW YORK • OXFORD • TORONTO • SYDNEY • PARIS • FRANKFURT

Pergamon Press Offices:

U.S.A.	Pergamon Press Inc., Maxwell House, Fairview Park, Elmsford, New York 10523, U.S.A.
U.K.	Pergamon Press Ltd., Headington Hill Hall, Oxford OX3 0BW, England
CANADA	Pergamon of Canada, Ltd., Suite 104, 150 Consumers Road, Willowdale, Ontario M2J 1P9, Canada
AUSTRALIA	Pergamon Press (Aust.) Pty. Ltd., P.O. Box 544, Potts Point, NSW 2011, Australia
FRANCE	Pergamon Press SARL, 24 rue des Ecoles, 75240 Paris, Cedex 05, France
FEDERAL REPUBLIC OF GERMANY	Pergamon Press GmbH, Hammerweg 6, Postfach 1305, 6242 Kronberg/Taunus, Federal Republic of Germany

Library of Congress Cataloging in Publication Data

Main entry under title:

Meeting the basic needs of the rural poor.

(Pergamon policy studies on international development)
"A report of the International Council for Educational Development."
Includes index.
1. Social work, Rural—Asia—Case studies.
2. Rural poor—Asia—Case studies. I. Coombs, Philip Hall, 1915-   II. International Council for Educational Development. III. Series.
HV376.M43   1980   362.5'8'095   80-19838

ISBN 0-08-026306-2

Printed in the United States of America

Contents

Chapter

Acronyms and Glossary

ORGANIZATIONAL ACRONYMS

AI   Agricultural Institute at Kosbad Hill, India
APHA   American Public Health Association
BAPPENAS   Indonesian National Development Planning Board
BKKBN   Indonesian National Family Planning Coordination Board
BRAC   Bangladesh Rural Advancement Committee
CBFPS   Community-Based Family Planning Service, Thailand
C-BIRD   Community-Based Integrated Rural Development Projects,
            South Korea
CDF   Community Development Foundation, USA and South Korea
CIDA   Canadian International Development Agency
FFWP   Food-for-Work Program, Bangladesh
GBSK   Gram Bal Shiksha Kendra, Kosbad, India
GK   Gonoshasthya Kendro (People's Health Centre), Bangladesh
IBRD   World Bank
ICED   International Council for Educational Development
IKIPs   Teacher Training Institutions, Indonesia
IPPA   Indonesian Planned Parenthood Association
IPPF   International Planned Parenthood Federation
IRDP   Integrated Rural Development Program, Bangladesh
KNPI   National Youth Committee, Indonesia
LHDP   Lampang Health Development Project
NCERT   National Centre for Educational Research & Training, India
NESDB   National Economic & Social Development Board, Thailand
NFPCC   National Family Planning Coordinating Committee, Thailand
PENMAS   Indonesian National Community Education Program
PKBI   Indonesian Plaanned Parenthood Association
PNPK   National Population Education Project, Indonesia
PPAT   Planned Parenthood Association of Thailand
SCF/CDF   Save the Children Federation/Community Development
            Foundation, U.S.A.
STCCA   Sulla Thana Central Cooperative Assoc., Bangladesh
SWRC   Social Work and Research Centre, India
UHSPH   University of Hawaii School of Public Health

GLOSSARY OF LOCAL TERMS

Adivasi   Aboriginal tribal people in India
Amphoes   Thai districts
Ashram   Residential primary school with attached farm, India
  shala
Ayurvedic   Traditional medicine practiced in India
Balsevika   Preschool teacher in India
Balwadi   Indian child care center similar to kindergarten
Bhagat   Tribal medicine man in India
Bidan   Midwife in Indonesia
Bor   Native berry
Bupati   Indonesian district head
Camat   Indonesian subdistrict head

vii

Chagwag | Thai province
Dais | Insian traditional birth attendants
Daktarnee | Bangladesh lady doctor
Death Aid Society | Traditional mutual help group, Sri Lanka
Dokabu | District doctor in Indonesia
Dukuns | Traditional birth attendants, Indonesia
Gono-kendro | Community center in Bangladesh
Gonoshasthya kendro | People's health center, Bangladesh
Gotong-royong | Traditional mutual help in Indonesian villages
Grama sevaka | Chief government age in Sri Lankan villages
Gromdaya Mandala | Sarvodaya village council
Gramodaya | Stage of "village awakening" under Sarvodaya
Gram Sabha | Local village organization, India
Gram-sevak | Village level worker or extension agent, India
Gun | South Korean county
Gun-chong | County administrative office, South Korea
Hectare | Equals 2.5 acres
Kabupaten | Indonesian district
Kecamatan | Indonesian subdistrict
Kharif | Summer monsoon crop season
Khas | Public land, Bangladesh
Kota-madya | Municipality in Indonesia
Lakh | One hundred thousand, India
Maul Kumgo | Micro bank, South Korea
Mubans | Thai villages
Myon | South Korean township or subcounty
Myong chang | South Korean subcounty chief
Pada | Indian hamlet or group of huts
Panch | Member of village council, India
Pramuka | Indonesian scounting organization
Puskesmas | Indonesian community health center
Rabi | Winter crop season, after kharif
Ri | Administrative village, South Korea
Saemaul Undong | New Community Movement, South Korea
Sarpanch | Chairman of village council, India
Savkar | "Moneylender" or "landlord-cum-moneylender", India
Scheduled castes | Officially classified lower castes in India
Shramadana | Sarvodaya work camp
Tahsil | Also Taluka or Taluq: administrative division between village & district level, India
Tambol | Thai subdistrict
Thana | Bangladesh subdistrict
Warka | Uncultivated grassland, India
Warli | Specific Indian tribal group in Maharashtra
Wechakorn | New type of paraphysician in Thailand

CURRENCY EQUIVALENTS (1978)

Bhat (Thailand) | 20 bhats | = US$1.00
Rupee (India) | Rs. 8.58 | = US$1.00
Rupee (Sri Lanka) | Rs. 7 | = US$1.00
Rupia (Indonesia) | Rp. 388 | = US$1.00
Taka (Bangladesh) | Tk. 16 | = US$1.00
Won (South Korea) | 500 won | = US$1.00

Preface

The nine case studies in this volume, and the introductory chapter that highlights some of their important findings, are end products of an international research project that was unusual in several respects.

First of all, unlike most research projects, the impetus for this one, and the key questions it addressed, did not come from researchers but from a variety of development practitioners in developing countries and external assistance agencies who felt the need for help on coping with some new and difficult operational problems. Accordingly, the main purpose of this report is to assist all such practitioners--including future ones now being trained or yet to be trained.

The second special feature is that able local researchers in each country played a major role in preparing the case studies, in close partnership with ICED, thus giving the reports a valuable local perspective and flavor and incidentally enhancing the capacity of each country to do similar studies in the future. As explained in the Editor's Notes, these local partners became the principal authors of several of the case study reports. Important contributions were also made by officials and staff members of the projects and programs examined and by numerous villagers and local leaders who viewed them from the grassroots level.

Third, the case studies themselves are unusually comprehensive and critically analytical. They examine the evolution of each project, including critical incidents along the way, and they candidly identify both the achievements and shortfalls that may hold useful lessons for others. They also cut across a variety of sectors, disciplines and professional fields that have traditionally been dealt with separately by both operating agencies and researchers. Thus, for example, they probe into activities relating to health and family planning, nutrition and food production, rural industry and employment, improving the status of women and young children, and into a variety of educational, organizational and financial issues that permeate all of these. And they draw upon the special insights of such diverse disciplines and professions as rural sociology, economics, education, cultural anthropology, political science and development administration.

Finally, the project was co-sponsored and funded by an unusual combination of private and official organizations, including: three private foundations, the Ford and Rockefeller Foundations and the Charles E. Merrill Trust; two voluntary international organizations, the International Planned Parenthood Federation and the Save the Children Federation; and two official bilateral aid agencies, the Department of International Technical Cooperation of the Netherlands Ministry of Foreign Affairs, and the United States Agency for

International Development. In addition, these and several other organizations including the United Nations Children's Fund, the World Health Organization, the United Nations Fund for Population Activities and the Population Council, provided valuable information, suggestions and logistical support.

The International Council for Educational Development welcomes this opportunity to express publicly its warm gratitude to all of the above individuals and organizations for their generous and valuable assistance. It should be added, however, that these contributors-- both individuals and organizations--share no responsibility for what is said in this volume; that responsibility rests solely on the ICED and the authors of the various chapters.

I also take this opportunity, as director of the project, to extend both professional credit and my personal appreciation to my ICED colleagues whose efforts made this volume possible. Dr. Manzoor Ahmed, deputy director of the project, helped to plan and manage it from the outset, wrote the two case studies from Bangladesh (his own country), and organized and followed through on three others from Thailand and Indonesia. He has since moved on from research to practical operations and presently heads UNICEF's mission in Ethiopia.

Dr. Pratima Kale, the other key member of ICED's professional team on this project, was principal author of one of the reports from India (her own country) and also organized and backstopped two other studies in India and Sri Lanka. Another ICED researcher turned "operator", she now directs the Asian program of the Save the Children Federation/Community Development Foundation. Dr. Lyra Srinivasan joined ICED as a consultant late in the project and made important contributions to the comparative analysis of the case studies that is reflected in the introductory chapter. My special thanks go to Frances O'Dell, a charter member of ICED's staff, who performed with extraordinary efficiency all those unspectacular but crucial tasks that are so essential to the success of a complex project of this kind-- from making travel arrangements and keeping financial accounts to backstopping her wandering colleagues in far away places and finally typing the "camera ready" copy for this volume. My thanks also go to Fessenden Wilder who periodically interrupted the serenity of his retirement to assist in editing the case studies, and to Dr. Julie Fisher who uncomplainingly took on the task of preparing the index to this volume.

                                        Philip H. Coombs
May 1980   Vice Chairman and
Essex, Connecticut USA   Director of Strategy Studies, ICED

1 What it Will Take to Help the Rural Poor

Philip H. Coombs

The new international consensus on rural development that grew out of the radical changes in development thinking in the 1970s offers bright promise of a better life for the millions of rural families living in extreme poverty throughout the developing world. But what will it take to deliver on this promise? This introductory chapter suggests some partial answers, based on the case studies that follow.*

This new international consensus calls for a massive, multi-faceted rural development effort aimed at meeting the "basic needs" of the rural poor, with special attention to disadvantaged women, young children and minorities; at increasing rural employment and the productivity of small farmers and other rural workers; and at the full participation of all rural people in the development process, and equitable distribution of its benefits. The unorthodox strategy advocated by the new consensus for achieving these ambitious goals differs drastically from the fragmented sector-by-sector, top-down strategy that has been universally followed ever since the short-lived "community development" boom of the 1950s; the new strategy calls for an "integrated" approach, combined with extensive "community participation".

There can be little question about the necessity and timeliness of these new goals and strategy. But the question still up in the air is how to convert these good intentions into effective deeds. The sobering truth is that the new consensus has confronted policymakers,

---

*This new international consensus is not inscribed in any single international accord. It is widely reflected, however, in strikingly similar language, in fresh policy statements by virtually all multi-national development agencies (subscribed to by the great majority of their member states) and by most bilateral assistance agencies of OECD countries. It also finds strong support in the writings and discussions of numerous leading development experts, many of whom espoused quite different views earlier.

planners and program operators in developing countries and external
assistance agencies with a bewildering array of agonizing implementation problems to which there are no easy solutions. This is not to
suggest that the new goals and strategy cannot be implemented, but
rather to emphasize that it will be a far longer and more difficult task
than one might suppose from the easy rhetoric.

PURPOSE AND BACKGROUND OF THE RESEARCH

The aim of the case studies in this volume is to shed helpful
light on how to cope with these implementation problems. The case
studies grew out of an international research project undertaken in
the late 1970s by the International Council for Educational Development with the encouragement and cooperation of officials in a variety
of developing countries and external assistance agencies.

The project focuses on the rural *family* as the basic social unit
and on the community as its basic habitat. Hence the study cuts
across all types of rural services directly related to the basic needs
of rural families and communities, including such diverse fields as
education, health, nutrition, agriculture, family planning, occupational skill training, child care and women's programs--fields usually
treated separately by planners, operating agencies and researchers.

The study is addressed in particular to the following questions
most frequently raised by operators in their discussions with ICED:

1) What does *integration* actually mean and what practical steps
    can we take to achieve it?

2) What different forms can *community participation* take; how
    can it be brought about and organized; and what measures
    can be taken to insure that the poorest members of rural
    communities are included?

3) How can appropriate *educational components* be developed
    and incorporated in various programs for improving the
    quality of rural family life?

4) How can the unique flexibility of *voluntary organizations* be
    more fully utilized to help larger scale government programs
    to serve more people more effectively at affordable costs?

5) What are the *financial* and *organizational* implications of all
    the foregoing?

The project began with the premise that many useful lessons
relevant to the above questions were buried away in the accumulated
experiences of a number of on-going innovative rural programs, and
that it would be helpful to dig them out. Thus the basic research
strategy adopted was, first, to identify an appropriate sample of
such programs; second, to examine each one systematically and
critically with a view to extracting pertinent lessons (both positive
and negative) from their experiences; third, to make a comparative
analysis of the findings of the various case studies to discover significant commonalities that might suggest widely applicable general
principles and useful operational guidelines; and finally, to write up
the findings in straightforward, jargon-free language and disseminate
them to operators, training organizations, researchers, and others

who could put them to practical use.

The main criteria used in selecting the cases were that each should (1) have as a primary objective, *improving the conditions of poor rural families*; (2) be employing an *integrated approach* encompassing two or more important facets of rural family life; (3) include a substantial element of *community participation*; and (4) contain significant lessons about *education*.

Finding a good sample of cases was not easy; numerous possibilities in many countries were screened before the nine presented here were chosen. Three additional ones were also chosen but had to be abandoned along the way because of bureaucratic snags or political upsets in the host countries. The initial hope was to secure an equal mix of governmental and private programs. But finding government programs that fitted the criteria proved very difficulty, for although many governments had recently committed themselves to move in these new directions, few had yet created programs with sufficient operating experience to warrant examination. Thus most of the selected cases involve voluntary organizations, but fortunately most of these, contrary to tradition, contain significant elements of collaboration with government agencies, thus enhancing their potential for beneficially affecting larger scale government programs.

Some readers may wonder why all the cases were chosen from Asia rather than from all developing regions. One reason is because it was logistically easier and less expensive to concentrate on one region. But a more important reason is because it became clear, after exploring a wide diversity of situations in various regions and completing two trial case studies in Asia, that developing countries everywhere, despite their many individual differences, face much the same fundamental problems in trying to improve rural family life, and that the same basic principles involved apply regardless of country and regional variations. In any event, it would be hard to find a more heterogenous set of countries than the six Asian ones covered by these case studies. They include Bangladesh, India, Indonesia, Sri Lanka, South Korea and Thailand.

In addition to the nine "full blown" case studies presented in this volume, the project also examined, though in less depth and breadth, numerous other pertinent projects and programs--including some in Africa, the Caribbean and Latin America--on the basis of available documentation, interviews and occasional on-the-spot observations. The project also benefitted from ICED's earlier field investigations of diverse rural programs and nonformal education in some two dozen countries scattered across all the main developing regions.[1]

---

[1]See (1) *Attacking Rural Poverty: How Nonformal Education Can Help*, P.H.Coombs with M.Ahmed, Johns Hopkins University Press, Baltimore, 1974, an ICED report prepared for the World Bank; (2) *New Paths to Learning: For Rural Children and Youth*, P.H.Coombs, R. Prosser and M.Ahmed, ICED, Essex, Conn., 1973, an ICED report prepared for UNICEF; and (3) *Education for Rural Development: Case Studies for Planners*, M.Ahmed and P.H.Coombs, Praeger, N.Y., and ICED, Essex, Conn., 1975.

The information sketched in Chart 1 provides a rough idea of the size, age, sponsorship, major and minor program objectives, and certain noteworthy features of the nine case studies. This chart is intended not only to provide a general profile of the sample but to help readers to select the particular cases that may be of greatest interest to them. Those especially concerned with health and family planning, for instance, will find the first five cases listed in Chart 1 particularly pertinent.

It should also be emphasized at this point that this volume does not have to be read like a novel or textbook, page by page from beginning to end. The headings and sub-headings are meant to assist the reader in locating those portions that coincide with his or her main interests.

Each case study involved extensive field work by ICED in part- nership with able local researchers. The principal investigators and authors of most of the cases are citizens of the countries concerned. ICED prepared a general set of guidelines designed to make all the studies as comparable as possible, then worked out more detailed plans for each study in cooperation with its local partners after joint visits to the program sites. Draft reports of the case studies were submitted for critical review by the managers of the programs examined and other interested parties, then put in final shape for publication by ICED.

It should be made clear that the aim of the project was *not* to discover "success cases" that could be recommended as "models" for others to emulate. Past experience teachers clearly not only that success is a highly relative commodity but that transplanting identi- cal program models from one country to another generally creates more problems than it solves. Developing countries can certainly benefit from the operational lessons of each other's experiences-- negative as well as positive--but in the end each country must fashion its own programs to fit its own circumstances and preferences. Thus ICED felt that, in contrast to simply trying to give an overall "success" rating to each case, it would be far more useful to try to discover what concrete factors within each program and its environment had helped or hampered the achievement of its objectives, and to what extent similar positive and negative factors turned up repeatedly in different program contexts. This, in brief, is the basic rationale and objective of the case studies.

Although the case studies reveal many useful clues and guides, this report makes no pretense of providing full and definitive answers to the five earlier questions posed by the operators. There is much still to be learned from experience and further research. It should also be said that there are notable exceptions to most of the general- izations made below, reflecting the wide differences among individual countries and programs. Moreover, these generalizations vary con- siderably in the strength of their evidential foundations; some, based on hard and extensive evidence, are beyond dispute whereas others are necessarily more impressionistic and subject to revision in the light of better future evidence. Despite these qualifications, how- ever, there is good reason to believe, based on encouraging reactions

TABLE 1: A GUIDE TO THE CASE STUDIES

Name & Characteristics	Types of Activities*	Interesting Features
SAVAR: *Gonoshasthya kendro* (People's Health Centre) Bangladesh (started 1972) Indigenous voluntary rural development organization that evolved from wartime relief work. Service area includes 100 villages with 100,000 population.	Initial focus on HEALTH CARE & FAMILY PLANNING, but has gradually added nutrition, food production, functional education for children and adults, occupational training for youth and women, etc.	A multi-pronged rural development program, with special emphasis on destitute women and children. Uses itinerant paramedics (mainly young women), and *dais* (indigenous midwives) as local health workers and family planning motivators. Has innovative health insurance scheme and employs unconventional training methods.
LAMPANG HEALTH DEVELOPMENT PROJECT in Thailand (started 1974). Experimental project of National Ministry of Public Health. Covers entire Lampang Province with population of 600,000.	PRIMARY HEALTH CARE, including preventive, promotive and curative services, nutrition, maternal and child care and family planning.	Large scale effort to establish a horizontally and vertically integrated rural primary health care system, based on village health workers supported by new type paramedics in nearby rural clinics, who in turn are supported by hospital-based physicians.
CBFPS: *Community-Based Family Planning Service*, Thailand (started in 1974). Indigenous voluntary org. (cooperates closely with Ministry of Public Health). Serves 10 mil. (23% of national pop.) in 113 (out of 600 districts) and 12,000 (out of 45,000) villages.	FAMILY PLANNING, community-based motivation and contraceptive distribution; also health promotion.	A uniquely vigorous, innovative and well-managed national network of community distributors, supervised by government health officers and CBFPS field staff. Is now experimenting with a much broader approach linking family planning with agricultural input, credit and marketing services for small farmers, and other practical rural services.

*Major activities shown in capital letters.

Table 1: Guide to Case Studies (continued)

Name & Characteristics	Types of Activities*	Interesting Features
SWRC: *Social Work & Research Centre*, Tilonia, Rajasthan, India (started 1972). Indigenous voluntary org. Main service area: 80,000 population. Satellite programs in four other areas.	WATER DEVELOPMENT, AGRICULTURE, HEALTH, EDUCATION; also child care, rural industry, craft training & production for women; new experimental programs for settling landless families on newly cleared farm land.	Based on 3-tier partnership between urban university-trained "specialists", SWRC-trained rural "professionals", and village level "field workers". Village health system based on locally chosen Village Health Workers & midwives, trained and supervised by Health Centre staff. SWRC has close working relations with various government services and seeks to become self-supporting.
BRAC: *Bangladesh Rural Advancement Committee* (started 1972). Indigenous voluntary rural development organization that evolved from a wartime relief agency. Main project area plus two others have total population of about 250,000.	Main activities in AGRICULTURE, HEALTH, FAMILY PLANNING, ADULT EDUCATION; also occupational training and cooperatives for women; youth activities; construction of community centers and infrastructure; creation of community-based organizations.	Health services use itinerant paramedics, village women health workers and family planning auxiliaries; health insurance scheme helps finance service. Tailoring of local activities to fit special needs and interests of particular groups (e.g., destitute women). Program strong on improving status of women.
SARVODAYA SHRAMADANA MOVEMENT, Sri Lanka (started 1958). Indigenous voluntary organization. Covers 2,000 villages (in varying degrees) throughout Sri Lanka.	Activities vary according to village interests, needs and leadership; most include PRE-SCHOOLS, community kitchens for CHILD NUTRITION, and MOTHERS' GROUPS; other typical activities include YOUTH VOCATIONAL TRAINING in agriculture & fishery; development of rural industry & village infrastructure.	Main focus on poorest families & villagers. Based on Buddhist philosophy of helping the needy and Gandhian values of cooperation & self-help. Encourages formation of village self-help organizations for various sub-groups. Extensive use of urban volunteers. Leadership provided by trained Sarvodaya extension workers & local monks or priests.

*Major activities shown in capital letters.

Table 1: Guide to Case Studies (continued)

Name & Characteristics	Type of Activities*	Interesting Features
C-BIRD: *Community-Based Integrated Rural Development* projects in So. Korea. Non-governmental multi-village development organization in 7 "impact" areas, each covering 7 to 21 villages with populations ranging from 2,000 to 9,000.	LOCAL INFRASTRUCTURE (Community Centers, roads, bridges, telephones, banks, etc.; AGRICULTURAL DEVELOPMENT: HOUSEHOLD IMPROVEMENTS; also social services (child care centers, limited health services); rural industry.	Unusual example of community-based development planning and implementation, flexibly linked with national government rural development program (*Saemaul Undong*). Especially effective on income-increasing projects.
IPPA Youth Projects: Indonesia (started in 1975). Pilot project of Indonesian Planned Parenthood Assn. supported by International Planned Parenthood Federation.	Dissemination of POPULATION EDUCATION AND INFORMATION in rural areas by members of existing voluntary youth organizations.	An interesting effort by a specialized voluntary agency (IPPA) to use voluntary youth organizations as vehicles for propagating the "population" message.
AI: *Agricultural Institute* at Kosbad Hill, Maharashtra, India (started 1949). Non-governmental training & research institution serving agricultural development in large areas of Maharashtra State. Case study focuses on AI's special development program involving about 750 tribal families around Kosbad.	AGRICULTURAL research, training, and technical assistance to improve PRODUCTIVITY & HOUSEHOLD conditions of Warli tribal families. Also provides PRIMARY & SECONDARY EDUCATION & FARMER TRAINING schools for tribal children and youth.	AI's special interest in helping neighboring tribal families reflects its origins in the Indian Independence Movement; its many years of effort show the limitations of a purely technical approach to altering deep-rooted cultural traits of the Warli tribals.

*Major activities shown in capital letters.

Table 1: Guide to Case Studies (continued)

Name & Characteristics	Types of Activities*	Interesting Features
GBSK: *Gram Bal Shiksha Kendra* at Kosbad Hill, Maharashtra, India (started in 1957. Non-governmental institution for preschool and elementary education. Case study focus is on GBSK's activities directed at children and mothers of 750 tribal families close to Kosbad village.	EDUCATION and SOCIAL SERVICES for preschool and elementary age tribal children; works with mothers; also trains preschool teachers for rural areas elsewhere in India.	GBSK also grew out of the Indian Independence Movement and has devoted itself to improving the lives of disadvantaged children, particularly in rural areas, through early childhood education. It exerts strong national leadership in preschool education through its research, teacher training, production of materials and publications.

*Major activities shown in capital letters.

to the case studies thus far, that the results of this project can be helpful to today's and tomorrow's operators, to those involved in training them, and to researchers anxious to lend a hand to these operators in meeting the challenges of implementation they face.

THE GENESIS OF THE NEW CONSENSUS

To appreciate the nature of these implementation problems it is helpful to look briefly at why the new consensus came about. By the early 1970s there was rapidly growing skepticism and disenchantment among development experts and authorities with the conventional theories that had dominated national and international development strategies, organizations and programs for over 20 years. The new facts available by then made it clear that the impressive economic growth achieved by many developing countries over the previous two decades had been accompanied by a very lopsided and inequitable pattern of development. These disturbing revelations--including the jolting discovery that 600 to 800 million people, about 40 percent of the total population of the developing world, were living in "absolute" poverty--called into serious question the following implicit assumptions that often underlay the old GNP/economic growth concept of development:

1) That by concentrating development efforts on the modernization and industrialization of major urban centers, shockwaves would soon radiate out across the countryside, triggering a dynamic and self-sustaining process of rural development and thereby minimizing the need for direct government intervention and investment in rural areas.

2) That agricultural development (measured mainly in terms of increased output of export and other commercial crops) was the essence of rural development and should be given top priority in any rural investments.

3) That *economic* development and *social* development were distinct and separate processes, and that sizeable progress on the former must precede any significant progress on the latter.

4) That villages and villagers were all more or less alike, hence solutions appropriate for one would be appropriate for all.

5) That the most efficient and effective way to organize and deliver rural services was by separate specialties, each having its own independent "delivery system" running downward to the rural areas from each specialized ministry and its sub-divisions in the capital city.

The new evidence that became available in the 1970s demonstrated beyond any doubt that these earlier assumptions, though perhaps valid in some degree, were seriously flawed. Urban-rural disparities, by any measure, had grown enormously, reflecting a fundamental imbalance in overall national development. It was clear that without strong and expanding rural markets, further growth of urban industry would be seriously hobbled. Moreover, the economic and social disparities between the strong and the weak *within* rural areas were also widening. The number of rural families living in absolute poverty was increasing rapidly, with no let-up in sight. There could also be no doubt that the earlier neglect of rural "social services"--such as health, nutrition, family planning, maternal and child care, and programs to improve the status and productivity of rural women--had become a major handicap to economic development, not only in rural areas but, by extension, in urban areas as well.

The conventional piecemeal, top-down approach to delivering "specialized" rural services, one by one, had also proved to be seriously flawed, on several scores:

1) It resulted in costly bureaucratic competition and duplication of effort, and in major absorption of limited resources by heavy administrative superstructures, leaving far too little for use at the village level where it really counted.

2) It resulted--from the vantage point of the rural families on the receiving end--in a bewildering fragmentation of disconnected, ill-fitting and often contradictory "messages" and advice on how to run their lives.

3) It resulted in the benefits of government programs--such as agricultural extension and credit, health, and primary schooling --accruing largely to the stronger and better off members of rural communities, by-passing the weaker and most needy members.

4) The inflexibility and excessive standardization of these highly centralized services--including the uniformity of the "messages" and advice they delivered--ignored important differences in conditions and priorities between different local areas, and between the needs of different subgroups within the same community.

5) The authoritarian stance and "father-knows-best" tone of voice of these top-down delivery systems tended to foster a sense of dependency rather than self-reliance on the part of villagers.

6) The costs per family served were so high under this top-down, single-purpose approach that the central government in any low income country would find it economically impossible in the foreseeable future to accommodate a sizeable majority of all rural families.

This is not to say that government rural services have had no useful impacts. Agricultural extension,credit and input services, for example, have sometimes been of substantial help to larger and more progressive commercial farmers, but they have generally been of far less help to small subsistence farmers, many of whom have lost their land in the process. Again, rural health services have brought benefits to many families--particularly the campaigns to stamp out major diseases such as cholera, smallpox and malaria; but they have typically been very weak and incomplete services, often accessible to less than 20 percent of the rural population, and least of all to the poorest members. In most developing countries family planning services until recently have been largely clinic-based and urban-bound, and even where they have sought to reach out to rural areas their strident, single-purpose message has often met a deaf

ear from the poorest families, whose private logic on how many
children to have conflicted sharply with the logic of national population policy. Conventional "women's programs" in home economics
have sometimes proved attractive and useful to the elite women of
the community, but irrelevant for the poor ones, whose first need is
to earn some income. Nutrition programs have often fallen between
the stools of health and agricultural services, with nutritionists
telling mothers what they should feed their children but not how to
grow it, and with agricultural advisers pressing for market-oriented
crops that sometimes had severe nutritional side-effects on the family.

As a result of this critical reexamination of earlier assumptions
and approaches, and the shock effect of the gross inequalities that
had been unmasked, by the mid-1970s the GNP had been dethroned
as the cardinal definition and measuring-rod of national development
in favor of a much broader, more humanistic and more egalitarian
view that defined development in terms of meeting the "basic needs"
and "improving the quality of life" of the people themselves,
especially the most disadvantaged. The discredited "trickle-down"
approach to rural development, and the artificial dichotomy between
economic and social development, were discarded in favor of the
view that the two were interdependent and therefore a combined
attack on the economic and social roots of rural poverty was imperative. Recognition of the severe shortcomings of conventional rural
delivery systems led to the demand for a more "integrated" and more
"community-based" approach to rural development.

By the end of the decade the new consensus on the goals and
strategy of rural development had found expression in a host of new
policy statements and initiatives by various multilateral and bilateral
development agencies and voluntary organizations, and by a growing
number of developing country governments. To cite but a few
examples: during the 1970s the World Bank moved strongly into the
areas of population and health and initiated   new-type "integrated
rural development projects" that sought to combine the previously
fragmented elements of agricultural production systems. By the
late 1970s the World Health Organization in concert with the United
Nations Children's Fund was vigorously advocating a new type of
rural "primary health care system", based on community health
workers and combining such previously scattered elements as nutrition, clean water, maternal and child care, family planning, sanitation, and curative services. The International Planned Parenthood
Federation and the United Nations Fund for Population Activities
abandoned their earlier allegiance to the "single-purpose", clinic-
based and medically dominated approach to family planning in favor
of an "integrated" approach tied to other basic family services.
UNESCO began promoting "life-long" education and a broader
concept of adult education that extended well beyond literacy classes,
and urged its member states to give greater attention to "nonformal"
education.

The bilateral aid agencies of most OECD countries similarly
realigned their policies and strategies in conformity with the basic
principles and goals of the new consensus. The British Ministry of
Overseas Development issued a White Paper that assigned a new
priority to rural development; the American Congress established

"New Directions" for the U.S. Agency for International Development,
aimed at improving the lot of the rural poor; the bilateral aid programs
of Sweden and the Netherlands placed new emphasis on encouraging
community-based self-help efforts and a more integrated approach to
rural development. Meantime, voluntary organizations such as OXFAM,
Save-the-Children Federation, CARE, various church affiliated groups
and many others were quietly shifting emphasis from purely relief
efforts to innovative community-based rural development projects
that could have a more lasting impact on improving the welfare of the
rural poor.

By the close of the 1970s the new rhetoric of the new consensus
had become common coinage throughout the world. It included such
phrases as "meeting the basic needs of the rural poor", "growth with
equity", "community participation", "integrated approach", "improving
the status of women", "protecting the welfare of young children",
"helping the small farmer", "reducing family size", "primary health
care", "generating rural employment", and spreading "basic education".

For the most part, however, the new policy commitments were still
at the rhetorical stage as the 1970s ended. Here and there concrete
actions had been put underway, but these were exceptions to the
general rule; the old order still dominated the action. Hence the
hard task of implementing the new consensus was carried over into
the 1980s, and it was clear by then that to set the new policies in
full motion would require major changes of many sorts--not least of
all in organizational structures, styles and attitudes. It would also
require a great deal of discovery, trial and error and new learning on
the part of program designers and operators--not to mention a good
deal of *unlearning*. This is where, it is hoped, the present case
studies can make a useful contribution.

What follows is a summary of some of the conclusions that derive
from a comparative analysis of these studies. They are only one
person's interpretation, of course, and readers are encouraged to
draw their own conclusions from a reading of the cases.

GETTING TO KNOW THE RURAL POOR

One important conclusion from the case studies is that the first
"must" for anyone desiring to help the rural poor is to *get to know
them*--to appreciate not only their physical circumstances and needs
but their social and political environment; their beliefs, traditions,
values and psychological outlook; their life style and the daily
demands upon their time and energies. This may seem self-evident,
yet many well-intentioned schemes have foundered for lack of sufficient understanding of the people they were intended to benefit.

Bloodless statistics flowing into an urban-based planning office
cannot produce such understanding, nor can tidy sociological and
political theories born in academe. There is no substitute for meeting
the rural poor face-to-face where they live, observing their conditions
and behavior, and listening carefully and patiently to what they have
to say--*before* deciding on what specific program approach to adopt
to meet their needs.

Another important requirement is to *focus on the family*--the *whole* family. Western-educated planners, reared in individualistic societies, are prone to think in terms of helping "the individual"--the young child, the out-of-school youth, the woman, the small farmer. But the case studies emphasize that the poverty syndrome is not an individual affair; it permeates entire families and whole groups of similarly situated families, and for this reason is perpetuated from one generation to the next. For this reason also, rural poverty must be attacked by a combination of measures aimed at all members of the family, not simply the head of the household, or the children or the women. What affects one member inevitably affects all. And for many purposes the corrective measures must be aimed at changing the whole community, because it is the social, economic and political structure and environment of the whole community that breeds and perpetuates poverty among its members.

Bare statistics conceal the inner feelings and true condition of these unfortunate people: the deep sense of fatalism and hopelessness that dominates their lives, that shapes their image of themselves and of the world around them; the gnawing hunger and chronic ill-health that constantly saps their energy to work and inhibits their capacity to learn; their high vulnerability, particularly the young children and mothers, to natural and manmade disasters; the economic inability of small farm families to take even modest risks (such as trying out a promising new high-yielding variety) lest the vagaries of nature or the market or their own miscalculation should wipe out their livelihood and even their children; their perpetual dependency on the larger neighboring farmer, storekeeper, and moneylender; and not least of all their deep-rooted fear of "getting out of line" that so often keeps these poverty stricken people from reaching out to help themselves, even when opportunities are available.

As noted earlier, these destitute families--often comprising over half the local population and sometimes an entire village--get few benefits from whatever rural services the government may provide, not necessarily by design but by the natural play of forces in such situations. Small subsistence farm families, for example, usually get little or no help from the agricultural extension and credit services or from cooperatives because they do not "qualify" and because the technical "messages" are tailored to more affluent commercial farmers. The women are generally left out, even though they do a sizeable portion of the farming--especially producing the family's own food--because these services are usually run by men and cater only to men. The thinly spread rural health services never even reach a good many villages, and the poorest members lack the means to transport themselves to the nearest clinic, often miles away. Without the indigenous medicine man, healer and midwife, many villages would be utterly devoid of health services.

It is largely the children of the poorest families who lie behind those shockingly high statistics of non-schoolgoers and early dropouts that show up in Unesco reports. The cash costs of school fees, uniforms and books, even though they may seem small to middle class urban dwellers, are often prohibitive for the poor rural family. And once the muscles of their children grow strong enough to help with the family's chores and survival, the opportunity costs of their spending time in a classroom become even more prohibitive.

THE DIFFICULTIES OF REACHING THE POOREST

It is not enough simply to understand the individual family; it is also important, as the case studies show, to get to know the community as a whole--its socioeconomic and political features, its culture and traditions, its leadership and power structure, its economic potential, how its resources are distributed, and the nature of its local institutions and decision-making processes. All these are major determinants of what strategies will work, and not work, in any effort to help the poorest members.

The penalties of poverty are heaviest, and the opportunities for escape most limited, in rural areas that are economically static and where even the relatively well-to-do are prisoners of chronic poverty. In such situations strengthened social services may provide a modicum of temporary relief, but without the creation of a fresh economic dynamic bringing new employment possibilities, additional income, and enhanced mobility, there is little chance for substantial improvements in the quality of family life, above all for the marginal families on the outside looking in. Their best hope is to move to a more promising area, but the options here are often extremely limited, especially in the land-scarce countries of Asia.

In more favorably endowed areas--with good land, water, climate and markets--the prospects for stimulating a new dynamic are, of course, much better. However, it is one thing to assist the general development of a particular rural area--for example, by a World Bank-supported agricultural development project--but quite another thing to help the poorest families within that area to participate equally in the development process and benefits. Just as the pattern of national economic growth and income distribution in most developing countries has been very lop-sided as between urban and rural areas, so also has rural development been very lopsided as between the strong and the weak *within* each rural area.

This inequality problem is rooted partly in the poor themselves-- in their fatalistic acceptance of their miserable circumstances, in their pervasive sense of impotence and hopelessness, and in their fear of treading on forbidden social territory lest they offend the "higher classes" and the patron on whom they are dependent. But these attitudes did not come with their genes; they were nurtured and are perpetuated by the kind of social, economic and political environment in which they find themselves.

The rural areas of developing countries, as the case studies bring out so vividly, are typically characterized by highly uneven access to productive resources such as land, water and capital; by traditional social stratification and division based on caste, lineage, religion, and sex; and by political and economic institutions and practices that reinforce the existing structure of privileges, exploitation and inequalities. Those who are well placed in the hierarchy, who are better educated and endowed, (and who themselves are often quite poor by urban middle class standards), generally get the lion's share of whatever new opportunities, inputs and services become available in the area, leaving only scraps for the poorest segment. Those in power are naturally fearful of any intrusion or innovation that might upset the *status quo* at their expense.

Any outside agency that ventures blindly and innocently into such a milieu, bent on helping the poorest of the poor toward a more decent and dignified life, can soon find itself frustrated and even in serious trouble. The case studies are replete with examples of this sort.

The unavoidable conclusion to be derived from them is that reaching the poorest families in rural areas and drawing them into the mainstream of development is undoubtedly the single most difficult task of rural development. This is not to say that it cannot be done or that much greater efforts should not be made in this direction. It is simply to emphasize that success requires more than noble rhetoric, laudable intentions and a warm heart. It also requires a realistic appreciation of the socio-economic and political structure, institutions, attitudes, and pattern of human relationships of each village, a knowledge of the real and potential leaders, a wise sense of tactics, and above all an abundance of patience, persistence and courage. Neat technocratic schemes designed in central ministries or in distant external assistance agencies cannot possibly take these critical factors into account. They can only be seen and dealt with at close range.

This brings us to a close range view of how to get started toward better program integration, increased community participation, and effective educational provisions--all of which, as will be seen, have far-reaching organizational implications.

THE MEANINGS OF INTEGRATION

The case studies help de-mystify this ambiguous term by providing concrete examples of five varieties of integration, namely: (1) integrated national planning for rural development; (2) integration of the essential components of a particular program; (3) integration of related activities conventionally dealt with in separate programs; (4) horizontal and vertical integration; and (5) integration of efforts between separate organizations.

Before looking at these it will be useful to introduce a few basic concepts and ways of looking at integration. Broadly defined, integration in all these examples means essentially: combining naturally related parts into a more cohesive and unified whole in order to enhance their collective cost-effectiveness. The best way to seek out opportunities for fruitful integration is to visualize and analyze any project or program as a productive "system" or "sub-system". Any such system is intended to accomplish certain specified *objectives* in a particular setting; but to do so it must have an appropriate *process* made up of a suitable combination of inter-acting, mutually supporting components; and to fuel this process the system requires sufficient resource inputs of the right kind and combination. This easily applied type of "systems analysis" (not requiring any mathematical model or difficult quantitative measurement) focuses attention on the critical *functional relationships* between the components within any particular program, or between two or more closely related programs, and between any program and its intended beneficiaries and their socioeconomic milieu. If any of these crucial relationships are malfunctioning, or if any important component is missing, the efficiency and cost-effectiveness of the whole system is bound to suffer.

Take the example of an agricultural extension service--viewed as a major component of an "agricultural knowledge delivery system" whose basic purpose is to help farmers increase their productivity and income. If the work of the research components of the same system, which are supposed to generate timely and relevant technical "messages" for delivery to the farmers, are in fact seriously out of tune with the real needs and concerns of the farmers, then the extension component will misfire (as is often the case, unfortunately). Similarly, single-purpose family planning programs frequently misfire because their "I,E & C" (information, education and communication) components are disconnected from one another and from the supply and service components--leaving the so-called "target audience" confused and unmoved. In both these examples, better integration among the parts would obviously improve their effectiveness.

Many rural programs have low effectiveness because they are *incomplete* systems, much like an automobile lacking spark plugs, or a wheelbarrow without a wheel. A common example of this is when a visiting engineer helps a village to install a safe water supply, but no one explains convincingly to the villagers what they must do thereafter to keep it safe. A month later the engineer returns to find the fence down and the bullocks once again polluting the "protected" water supply. Another example of an incomplete system is the health service--and unhappily there are many like this--that concentrates on curative services and neglects preventive and promotive health measures. Without attacking the root causes of illness and disease, such a system can never catch up with the mounting curative load.

The above "system" concepts are useful in examining the five varieties of integration listed earlier.

(1) *Integrated national planning for rural development.*

Although ICED's overall project and the case studies are mainly concerned with the operational integration of action programs as they function at the *local* level, it should be noted that integration at this level can be greatly facilitated by integrated thinking and planning at the national level. This is especially true if it leads to a greater decentralization and devolution of certain specific responsibilities and detailed decisionmaking to lower echelons, thus providing more latitude and encouragement for more realistic and effective local planning and greater local initiative on the part of government field agents, working with each other and in concert with each community.

Integrated rural development planning at the national level requires *joint* planning of national policies and programs, cutting across all relevant "sectors," with a view to weaving them into a cohesive and unified strategy within which all sectors become mutually reinforcing. This is in sharp contrast to the usual practice of planning each sector independently, then giving each its separate budget and its own chapter in the published National Plan (whose

chapters often have little or no connection with each other). Under
such piecemeal planning, for example, the Ministry of Agriculture may
be mainly concerned (as is often the case) with maximizing production
of selected commercial crops for urban and export markets, in which
event the pressing food and nutritional problems of the rural poor,
and the problems of small non-commercial farmers, are likely to get
short shrift.

Similarly, if everyone expects the family planning organization to
manage the "population problem" all by itself, then other important
measures conducive to smaller family size--such as improved educational and employment opportunities for women, and better health
care for young children--are likely to be neglected.

Broadscale integrated rural development planning at the national
(and international) level can be very helpful in overcoming this piecemeal kind of thinking and programming. Its effectiveness, however,
depends on how deeply the planners, top administrators and operating
personnel of each specialized agency become genuinely imbued with a
broader and more cohesive vision of rural development and convinced
that their own special objectives will be better served by a more
integrated approach. *It should be a major objective of all staff
training programs in all specialized fields to promote this broader
perspective and way of thinking*, and not simply the limited concepts
and methodologies of the particular specialty.

One of the case studies, which focuses on *local* level integrated
planning in several *Community-Based Integrated Rural Development
(C-BIRD)* projects in South Korea, happens also to include a good
example of national level integrated planning for rural development,
known as Saemaul Undong (meaning roughly "New Community Movement"). One of the challenges to the C-BIRD project managers was
to get their own local planning and activities effectively integrated
with the nationwide Saemaul Undong.

(2) *Integration of the components of a particular program.*

Most of the case studies provide examples of this type of
integration, but it will suffice for the moment to cite two illustrations
from the *Social Welfare and Research Centre (SWRC)* in Rajasthan,
India.

SWRC, among other activities, organized a "social education"
course for destitute women that gave primary emphasis to literacy but
also included craft training. The literacy part failed (for all the
usual reasons) but the craft training proved popular. Once the women
had mastered the craft skills and could produce marketable end products, however, it became evident that the training was useless
unless the women had access to simple equipment, raw materials,
credit and a profitable market. SWRC was ingenious enough to take
the necessary steps to "complete the system" by arranging for these
missing components, and the women soon began earning some much
needed cash.

Many well-intentioned skill training programs in developing
countries over the past 25 years have not had such happy results.
They provided only the skills, without the complementary system

components, naively assuming that the market would automatically absorb and reward them. The lesson here (which applies to a wide
range of situations) is that skill training *per se* is only one piece of
an employment and income generating "system"; if the other pieces
are missing the training is likely to go to waste.

SWRC also pieced together, quite pragmatically and without any
advance plan, a system to restore the livelihood of destitute low caste
leather tanners who had lost their market due to the poor quality of
their product. In this instance the tanners already possessed the
necessary skills but their technology was deficient. A leather research
expert, visiting SWRC, was pressed into service and demonstrated a
better technology that made sense to the experienced tanners and
they readily adopted it. But to complete the system they still needed
credit to build better "pits" and to purchase appropriate chemicals.
SWRC helped them to fill in these missing links and also to organize
their own small cooperative, and soon the tanners were back in business. The resulting improved supply of good quality leather at
reasonable prices, plus some help from SWRC on product design and
marketing, also enabled skilled traditional leather-craft workers
(women) in the area to revive their local industry and to bring in
desperately needed cash.

All the above examples were on a small scale, but they demonstrate
some basic principles that could be applied on a much wider scale.

(3) *Integration between separate programs.*

This important type of integration is perhaps best illustrated
by the health improvement activities that were a central element in
several of the case study programs. Their combined experience offers
a variety of useful lessons to those concerned with developing
community-based rural primary health care systems. Readers interested in rural health--including family planning--will find particularly
pertinent the case studies on the *Bangladesh Rural Advancement
Committee (BRAC)*, the *SAVAR (People's Health Project* in Bangladesh,
the *Social Work and Research Centre (SWRC)* in India, the *Community-
Based Family Planning Service (CBFPS)* in Thailand, the *Lampang
Health Development Project* in Thailand, and the section on health in
the *C-BIRD* case study in South Korea.

One of the central lessons coming out of these projects is the
importance of combining within a single integrated service the various
essential health measures and services that are typically scattered
among several different organizations (most of them sub-divisions of
the Ministry of Health). It is little wonder that rural families are
often bewildered by the many different messages and voices telling
them how to stay healthy; in the course of a month they may hear
(by radio if not in person) from the sanitarian, the nutritionist, the
family planning worker, the cholera worker, the malaria worker, the
maternal and child care specialist, and perhaps still others, all talking
a different language and sometimes giving conflicting advice. Yet the
chances are that when a member of the family is seriously ill or
injured there is no adequate medical service within physical or affordable reach.

The case study programs listed above, each in its own way, sought to consolidate at least some of thes e basic preventive, promotive and curative services and to bring them either directly into each village or within feasible reach.

(4) *Horizontal and vertical integration.*

The case studies demonstrate that both horizontal and vertical integration are essential to the effective operation of any "community-based" program. There is need, on the one hand, to tie together *horizontally* at the individual community level certain closely related activities impinging on basic family needs and interests. An infant and child care program, for example, must be linked to nutrition, and nutrition must be linked to the raising, preservation and preparation of family food. It must also include systematic health monitoring at the village level, protective innoculations against major diseases, and above all, the education of mothers on how to avoid or to cope with such common but frequently serious ailments as diarrhoea and scabies. Experience in the case study programs and elsewhere has shown that family planning programs are often rejected by poor and uneducated villagers unless they are horizontally integrated with other services of more immediate and compelling interest to local families--such as child health care and ways of earning some extra cash.

Vertical integration is indispensable to the successful operation of community-based programs because villagers cannot do everything on their own; their efforts must be integrated with selective help from outside the village. The sustained motivation, credibility and effectiveness of community health workers, for example, is dependent on their getting common medical supplies from outside sources, on supervision, assistance and training from more highly trained health personnel at higher echelons in the system, and on their being able to refer difficult cases rapidly to a clinic or hospital.

The same principles apply to local workers and programs in any other important sector of rural life--they need selective assistance from the outside to augment and facilitate their own resources and efforts.

(5) *Integration of efforts by different organizations.*

This type of integration, which overlaps with the third type described above, does not come easily because it requires close collaboration between separate organizations that are usually accustomed to working independently. It also involves more than simply "coordination", a term that often means in practice arriving at a mutual agreement between parallel organizations to stay off each other's turf, in the name of avoiding wasteful duplication and bureaucratic conflict. This kind of "coordination", however, results in quite the opposite of integration, by keeping the activities of neighboring organizations sharply divorced rather than working hand and glove together.

Contrary to the traditional strong desire of most voluntary organizations to remain at arms' length from government and even from each other, the voluntary organizations in ICED's sample made a concerted effort to develop cooperative relations and a productive division of labor with particular government agencies, usually with useful results and without compromising their independence.

The SWRC (Social Work and Research Centre), for example, adopted as a basic rule that it would never try to go-it-alone on any activity; it would always seek to join forces in a complementary way with some other voluntary organization or educational institution or government agency with similar interests. In line with this policy, its water survey and development program, run by a small and competent energetic staff, was financially supported by government irrigation and electrification agencies, and these agencies then used the results of SWRC's surveys as a basis for sizeable government investments in irrigation and rural electrification in the area that would probably have been delayed for years in the absence of SWRC's initiative.

SWRC's community health program, centering in its own health center and involving local SWRC health workers chosen by each village, became integrated in several specific ways with the state government's health service, which was unable to serve all villages by itself. Government health officers, for example, participated in the training of SWRC's local health workers and dais (indigenous midwives). These local workers in turn helped to organize their communities for eye clinics and similar health events conducted by visiting government health officers. They were also able to refer difficult medical cases to government health centers where these were closer than the SWRC center or sub-centers. SWRC also secured its medical supplies from the government at low prices.

State agricultural officers regularly participated in SWRC's farmer training programs and supplied experimental seeds and plants for distribution to small farmers by SWRC workers. At the time of the case study, SWRC was in process of working out, in cooperation with the agricultural services of the State of Rajasthan, a complex experimental program for assisting small farmers on marginal land.

SWRC also carried out a radical experiment in elementary school reform with the professional and financial support of the National Ministry of Education and Culture and the help of a state teacher training college. And on frequent occasions SWRC enticed technical specialists and other experts from government research institutions, universities, and the private sector to serve for a brief stint on some cutting edge of SWRC's evolving program (as in the case of the leather workers noted earlier).

There was no apparent sign that SWRC had compromised its independence and freedom to take unconventional initiatives because of these close governmental ties. On the contrary, the evidence indicates that innovatively-minded government officers (and there usually are some, everywhere) actively encouraged SWRC to take on important tasks and experiments that would not have been possible for their own official agencies.

There are numerous other examples in the case studies of the integration of government and voluntary efforts, taking many different forms. The CBFPS (Community-Based Family Planning Service) in Thailand, which has an impressive record of accomplishment with its community-based system of contraceptive distribution, coupled with health promotion, has worked closely with the Ministry of Health from the start and has contributed to some important breakthroughs in the government's larger scale family planning program. It is also noteworthy that CBFPS was given an experimental role in the government's Lampang Health Development Project.

An example of integrated efforts between voluntary organizations is provided by the case study on the Indonesian Planned Parenthood Association's experimental youth project, in which the IPPA sought to incorporate a population education component with the ongoing recreational and other activities of several voluntary youth organizations in the project area. Though the results were not all that had been hoped for, partly because the funds ran out but apparently also because of interorganizational differences, some valuable lessons for the future were nevertheless learned about the essential conditions for effective collaboration between voluntary agencies.

The impression should not be left that all these efforts at interorganizational integration were easy or necessarily successful. One would have thought, for example, that the SAVAR People's Health Program and the Ministry of Health in Bangladesh were natural allies; yet for a number of years the Ministry frowned on the voluntary organization's good works and declined offers to cooperate--apparently because SAVAR's unorthodox practices, such as the use of young paramedics to perform certain functions customarily reserved to fully trained doctors, violated the mores of the orthodox medical establishment. One of the most difficult and delicate tasks of the Lampang Health Development Project was to persuade key members of the urban-oriented, hospital-based medical profession to team up with the public health profession in an integrated attack on widespread rural health problems, embracing preventive and promotive health services along with access to curative services.

Some general observations on integration

It may be useful at this point to sum up a few broad practical conclusions regarding integration that come from ICED's case studies and appear to have wide applicability.

First, integration is not an all-or-none affair; it is a matter of degree. It cannot suddenly spring full-blown on the local scene from the brow of an inspired distant planner or program designer, nor are there any pat formulas for achieving it. It must be a step-by-step evolutionary process, generally starting small and then, if conditions are favorable, gradually broadening to a wider area of activities. It is also a highly pragmatic process, responding to opportunities and necessities as they arise, and it is bound to progress unevenly in different geographic areas depending on a variety of variables, not least of which is the calibre, courage and ingenuity of the leaders on the scene.

Second, the main obstacle to effective integration is usually not the villagers, for to them an integrated approach generally makes better sense than a fragmented one because it fits their own unified view of their family-life. The main obstacle is usually the specialized bureaucracies and specialists whose job is to serve the villagers. The reasons are quite understandable. These organizations and specialists, by the very nature of their mandate and training, are prone to take a narrow view of development in which their own

specialty (whatever it may be) is seen as the hub around which all
else revolves. It is basically these narrow perceptions and the attitudes they breed--plus the natural competitiveness and pride and the
often perverse system of incentives that govern the behavior of
bureaucracies--that constitute the more serious deterrents to a more
integrated approach.

To break out of these habits of mind the first requirement, as
suggested earlier, is for the various specialists and administrators
to acquire a broader and more unified view of rural development, and
of how their own particular piece fits into the larger whole. Only
when they become intellectually convinced that their own efforts and
those of others working in the same vineyard can be mutually reinforcing, and therefore more effective if they all work in close partnership, are they likely to abandon their natural compulsion to go it
alone. This intellectual and attitudinal transformation, of course, does
not happen easily, and for some it probably can never happen. But
the process can be greatly accelerated if the top political leaders and
the heads of these organizations become overt and enthusiastic
advocates of a more integrated approach, and if every staff training
program provides clear guidance on how to go about it.

Third, another basic requirement for achieving better integration
is a larger measure of organizational decentralization and devolution
of responsibilities that gives all workers close to the scene of action
wider latitude for taking initiatives, for cooperating with other
services, and for working more closely with each community in
designing and implementing action plans that conform to general
national policies and priorities but are also tailored to fit the peculiar
needs and circumstances of each area. In the case of national
programs, nothing could be more helpful for a starter than for each
central ministry to inform its lower echelon staff and agents that
they have a green light and are positively encouraged to collaborate
with the agents of other ministries.

It should be cautioned, however, that decentralization, like integration, is neither an all-or-none proposition nor a panacea. It is a
matter of striking a good balance between central control and local
intiative and latitude. And for such a balance to work well there must
be personnel at lower echelons capable of exercising responsibility and
managing local activities. There must also be safeguards against
decentralized programs being captured by local vested interests to
their own advantage.

Integration is usually more easily achieved at the lower echelons
of the hierarchy than at the top because the local representatives of
different central organizations are all looking closely at the same
realities in the same place and are thus more disposed to collaborate
in tackling them. They are also in the best position to devise and
implement practical and productive ways to integrate their efforts.
But this, of course, is quite the opposite of how things normally work
in hierarchical single-purpose organizations; the field agents are
trained to stick closely to "the book" and to their "own business",
and failure to do so may jeopardize their career.

Fourth, as a general rule progress toward better integration is easier where all or most of the relevant components are under the jurisdiction and control of the same organization. Even then, however, the various semi-autonomous subdivisions of a large organization, such as a ministry of health or of agriculture, may stoutly resist any move that seems to violate their particular philosophy or threaten their independence. It takes strong and persuasive top leadership, more interested in helping the people than preserving an empire, to overcome these internal bureaucratic resistances.

Smaller voluntary organizations have the advantage of not having to cope with these divisive bureaucratic problems, and this helps give them their unique flexibility to pioneer in fresh directions and develop significant lessons that may later be adopted by larger scale government programs to extend their own effectiveness. But even voluntary organizations, as they expand and mature, are not immune to excessive centralization and to "hardening of the categories". The authors of the Sarvodaya case study in Sri Lanka felt that this dynamic and rapidly expanding organization, whose record of helping the rural poor is outstanding, might be suffering from a touch of these classic bureaucratic infirmities.

Developing country organizations, of course, have no monopoly on resisting a more integrated approach that might jeopardize their bureaucratic autonomy. In this respect, larger external assistance agencies are a mirror image of the organizational structures in developing countries. Most of them, both bilateral and multilateral, have been finding it very painful to apply to their own organizational arrangements and practices the message of "integration" they are preaching to others. It is still rather rare, for example, to find the agricultural or health or population staffs in these categorically structured organizations turning to the education staff for help on designing effective and low cost training and learning components for inclusion in their "sectoral" projects. Perhaps a good motto to hang over the door of each sectoral office in such organizations would be: "Integration, like charity, must begin at home".

Toward Greater Community Participation

The ICED case studies strongly support the proposition that extensive community involvement and self-help are indispensible to the success of any broad-gauged effort to transform a rural society and to meet the basic needs of its poorest families. One reason is because central government treasuries simply cannot marshall sufficient resources to do the job alone. But an equally important reason is because authentic rural development requires extensive changes in the rural people and communities themselves--changes of a kind that even the strongest government is powerless to bring about by fiat.

The case studies also make clear, however, that creating and organizing extensive community involvement, where it does not already exist, is far more complicated than many ritual advocates of "community participation" apparently realize.

The difficulties are to be found mainly in the hierarchical social, economic and political structures of most villages; in the highly uneven distribution of productive assets, income and power; in the patterns of dependency, exploitation and rivalry among different sub-groups; and in the lack of viable democratic local institutions. It should be added, however, that villages are by no means all alike; they differ enormously from place to place in many respects, which is one reason why identical models and standardized solutions are so often out of kilter with local realities. Few if any, however, fit the romantic image that some people still cherish of villages as little self-reliant democratic societies brimming with brotherly love and ready to respond eagerly to any external intervention designed to help the people help themselves.

Any intervention from the outside, however well intentioned, is likely to misfire if it does not take sensitive account of the attitudes, sociology, cultural traditions, politics and economics of the particular community, and of the differing circumstances and needs of various subgroups within the community, as *they* see their needs. It is important especially to realize that many villages are actually not "communities" in the unified sense; they are frequently loose federations of rival sub-communities of various castes, kinship or other groupings, each with its own loyalties and traditions and its own stake, status and role in the local scheme of things.

The mistaken assumption that underlies many top-down programs is that villagers, because they are illiterate, are unintelligent and must be treated like children. Hence the "message" devised by experts at higher echelons often tend to talk down to the rural people, telling them what is "good" for them (without really explaining *why*) and urging them to abandon various traditional practices in favor of innovative ones the experts consider better. But in reality most rural people, far from being stupid, have acquired considerable wisdom through years of struggling for survival. They may cling to certain ill-founded myths and taboos that do them more harm than good, but they also have a very practical sense and a great fund of local knowledge that exceeds that of the outsider. Their cautiousness about accepting advice from "outsiders" is usually well founded; they have been burned too often before. They may listen politely to them but are unlikely to heed their advice--for example, to alter their diet or to adopt modern family planning methods or some agricultural innovation--until and unless they are convinced in their own mind and by their own logic that it is in their own best interest to do so. They are far more likely to accept the advice of a respected neighbor whom they consider the local expert on a particular matter than to follow the advice of outside specialists. Thus, much of the impetus for change must come from *within* the community. The problem is how to spark this impetus and then how to get the community effectively organized for self-help, self-direction and broad-scale change.

Another common error is to overestimate the potentialities of a single project--particularly one of those standard projects whose outside support disappears after three to five years--to bring about fundamental and permanent changes in a rural area. A well conceived "project" may well improve conditions in a village, but it would be naive to suppose that it can transform that village's deeply-rooted traditions, values and human relationships all by itself. Only powerful and fundamental nationwide social, economic and political changes can do this, as the C-BIRD case study from South Korea explains so convincingly.

Different forms of participation: Standing alone, "community participation" is just as ambiguous a term as "integration". It acquires concrete meaning only when viewed in a specific context. There are numerous types and degrees of community participation, ranging across a wide spectrum. At the one extreme, villagers may participate negatively, as they did at first in the SWRC program by actively resisting the overtures of strangers from the city whose offers of help they instinctively mistrusted. Or they may participate passively in a purely top-down program by listening politely to its "messages" and accepting any hand-outs, but without altering their customary views and behavior. Standing at the other extreme is the village that has organized itself democratically to examine its needs and options, to make decisions and plans to mobilize its own resources, and to seek specific kinds of help from outside sources to fill gaps and break bottlenecks beyond its own capacity. Most villages seem to fall between these extremes.

Listed below are a number of different types and forms of community participation that are illustrated by the case studies.

(1) *Local "specialists" in a community-based program* who render particular services to their neighbors, with backstopping from specialists and institutions outside the village. Examples are: the local health and family planning workers and indigenous midwives in BRAC and SAVAR (Bangladesh) and in SWRC (India); the local ladies in Sri Lanka who operate Sarvodaya's community kitchens and nurseries; the locally-based contraceptive distributors and motivators in the CBFPS program in Thailand; the multi-purpose local "Health Post Volunteers" and the "Health Communicators" in the Lampang Project; and the volunteer "population communicators" in IPPA's Youth Project in Indonesia.

It is generally a sure sign of serious community commitment and involvement wherever one finds local "specialists" and volunteers with limited training seriously carrying out important grass-roots operational responsibilities in a vertically integrated program, especially if there is also a representative local committee that selects the local workers and supports and oversees their activities.

(2) *Local contributions of money or labor and materials* to help defray the costs of a service or project. Examples here include the SAVAR and BRAC health insurance schemes and the family health fees paid to SWRC; the local contributions of labor in bridge-building and other construction projects in the C-BIRD villages in South Korea; and contributions of food to the Sarvodaya community kitchens. These types of contributions, involving sacrifices of personal goods and time, are also usually a sign of serious local commitment to the idea of self-help and self-reliance.

(3) *The creation or strengthening of self-run local institutions and mechanisms* to carry out important functions beneficial to particular needy sub-groups. Examples of this type include the cooperatives created under BRAC for fishermen and for women handicraft

workers; the mothers and small farmers groups organized with the help of Sarvodaya; the leather tanners' cooperatives under SWRC; and the Mothers' Clubs in South Korea.

(4) *The creation of broader community-wide mechanisms for selecting priorities and for planning and implementing local development projects*, including the identification of specific kinds of assistance required from outside sources to supplement local inputs. The most striking example of this among the ICED cases is the local planning and implementation system established in the C-BIRD project areas in South Korea. Each project area includes several neighboring villages, each of which elects members of an overall council who in turn elect a smaller executive group headed by a chairman (who spends a high proportion of his time as general manager of the planned development schemes). Another example is the Village Reawakening Council in the Sarvodaya Movement which considers communitywide problems and serves as an umbrella for other local organizations involving particular subgroups such as children, youths, mothers, farmers and elderly people.

(5) *The formation of local pressure groups* to bring about structural changes and reforms, to achieve a more equitable sharing of the benefits of development, to demand better services from government agencies, or to exercise a larger voice in policy and program decisions affecting their lives. Such examples are relatively exceptional, in part because the poorest and most vulnerable rural people are generally hesitant to organize themselves for political action. But it appears to be happening increasingly as disadvantaged people become more aware of the causes of their poverty and of their own innate power to do something about it, and as the notion spreads that distributive justice and not simply a higher GNP is a major objective of development.

The above list by no means exhausts the possible forms that community participation can take, but it suggests some of the important clues to look for in assessing and improving any existing rural development program and some important possibilities to consider in designing new ones.

Getting the process started: All villages, even the poorest, have considerable potential for helping themselves and improving the condition of their members, but to realize this potential they may require initial stimulation and substantial assistance from the outside --not just any kind of assistance but the right kind at the right time, rendered in a way that will strengthen rather than inhibit their spirit of self-reliance and self-determination.

A village that is already in motion, that is internally organized and reasonably unified and that has confidence in its ability to improve itself based on previous accomplishments, is far easier to assist toward further accomplishments than one that is static, unorganized, and divided. One detects significant differences in this respect, for example, between many villages in Indonesia, with their long tradition of internal cooperation (*gotong royong*) and many in Bangladesh that seem almost devoid of community institutions or traditions around which local self-help efforts might be organized. The latter type situation, which unfortunately is still very common, presents the most difficult and delicate challenge to well-intentioned outsiders.

The experience of programs such as BRAC, SAVAR, SWRC and Sarvodaya make it clear that the most important and often most difficult task for outsiders approaching a rural community for the first time is to win their trust and acceptance by convincing all segments of the community that the outsiders genuinely have the community's own interests at heart and are not there as exploiters; that they are willing and able to provide certain types of needed help over a *sustained* period; and that the community itself will have a major voice in deciding what activities will be undertaken and in carrying them out.

This introductory phase can often be very time consuming, and very frustrating for the outsider who thinks he already has the answers and is anxious to get on with the action--if only to prove to his own headquarters or funding source that he is getting "concrete results". It is important for all concerned, especially outside funding agencies, to realize that short circuiting this initial process or hurrying it unduly can be self-defeating. Desirably, this first phase requires sparking a process of self-examination by all groups in the community, designed to elicit their candid views on their priority needs, problems and the roots of these problems, and on possible alternative ways to tackle them with their own efforts, supplemented by selective outside help. Vogueish "base-line surveys" and household interviews are no substitute for this kind of communitywide introspection and dialogue.

In the course of this exploratory phase the outsiders will have an opportunity to size up the local situation--the economic conditions and potentialities, the social patterns, power structure and kinds of leadership, the various sub-groups and divisions within the population, and the general climate of attitudes and opinions. These insights into the "chemistry" of the community can provide invaluable guidance on what kinds of initial actions to undertake, how to go about them, and what to avoid.

Various "coping techniques". Obviously there can be no fixed formula for all situations, but the experiences of the programs examined in the case studies suggest a number of "coping techniques" worth considering.

1) Making positive use of traditional local values and forms of cooperation, and building wherever possible on existing local institutions of various kinds. Sarvodaya, for example, embraced the traditional Buddhist values of charitable works to help the less fortunate and the Gandhian values of community self-help.

2) Starting off with one or more activities that are directly addressed to locally expressed priority needs, that can show relatively quick and visible results, and that are clearly beneficial to the elite as well as to other segments of the community in order to win support of the "powers that be", or at least to forestall their immediate opposition. (The initial water development activities of SWRC were criticized by some for benefitting mainly the larger farmers, but they undoubtedly helped to avert

their opposition to later projects designed specifically to benefit the poorest community members. SWRC's health program, which benefitted all members of the community, was also helpful in this respect.)

3) Working with different sub-groups having similar needs and interests, rather than directing all projects at the community as a whole, so as to encourage freer participation in small peer group settings and to adapt the activities to the special circumstances of each group.

4) Initiating as soon as feasible viable income-generating projects tailored to the needs of particularly disadvantaged sub-groups and helping them develop the required institutional base for effective self-management.

5) Using educational processes to increase people's awareness of their inherent capacity to effect change and improvement in their own condition, even starting from bare subsistence levels.

6) Finding ways to mobilize and upgrade existing special talents in the community--such as local religious leaders, teachers, traditional birth attendants and other health practitioners, organizational leaders, progressive farmers, and so forth.

7) Seeking ways to broaden the leadership base of the community by developing leaders for new types of organized activities and especially by encouraging the development of youth leaders and women leaders and organizations for rendering constructive services to the community.

8) Encouraging traditional cultural and recreational activities--such as festivals, fairs, exhibitions and contests--that subordinate class distinctions and invite community-wide participation.

9) Setting good personal examples by involving able and respected urban participants in the program, but under village austerity conditions, to demonstrate the value attached to serving the cause of the rural poor.

10) Developing local competencies to plan and manage projects on a village-wide or multi-village basis.

THE IMPORTANCE OF FRONT-LINE WORKERS

A switchover by any government to a more integrated, community-based approach to rural development--for example in the health area--will inevitably require the recruitment, training and effective back-stopping of large numbers of front line workers. These include particularly: (1) resident village *workers*, often volunteers, who serve as the main link between their neighbors and vertical delivery systems and (2) *para-professionals* who are full time employees, based within close range of a set of villages, who function as the main supervisors and supporters of village workers and as their liaison with the rest of the delivery system. The basic role of all other professionals and administrators at higher echelons of a community-based system is to stimulate, guide, and support these front-line workers. In other words, they play primarily a *facilitating* role in contrast to their predominantly *directive* role under a typical top-down system.

Several of the case studies demonstrate vividly that the ultimate efficiency and effectiveness of any community-based system depends heavily on the functions and responsibilities entrusted to these grass-roots workers and how well they   carry them out. This in turn depends on how well the front-line workers are selected, trained and supported, and what incentives and motivations they have for doing their best. As a general rule, the more serious the responsibilities given them, the more seriously they and the community are likely to take their work. By the same token, however, the more essential it is that they be given strong and continuous support and super-vision from the outside in order to sustain their competence, morale, credibility and effectiveness in the community. A community-based health or family planning program, for example, that is not adequately tied in with and supported by higher levels of the system *could* be worse than no locally-based program at all. It would be a deceptive sham, perhaps good for national and international public relations but quite unfair to the rural people.

A number of practical questions arise with respect to these front-line workers. What functions and responsibilities should they be given and *not* given? Should they be single or multi-purpose workers, and if the latter, how much can they handle without becoming over-loaded? What qualities and qualifications should they have? How should they be recruited, selected and trained? What should be done about personnel turnover? What incentives do they need to take their responsibilities seriously, to stay with the job, and to put forth their best efforts? What sort of supervision and continuing support and follow-up training do they require?

The case studies shed considerable light on these and similar questions, at the same time demonstrating, however, that there are no pat answers to fit all situations. They also support the following widely applicable propositions.

First, village workers and paraprofessionals can effectively carry out more important responsibilities than many highly trained professionals, particularly in the medical field, are willing to concede --*provided* (and this is a crucially important proviso) they are properly selected and trained and are given steady and adequate supervision and support by more highly trained personnel. The impressive performance of the paramedics in the SAVAR Project and the Lampang Project, and of SWRC's village health workers and indigenous midwives, are good examples of what is possible. The less impressive performance of the local "health post volunteers" and "health communicators" in the Lampang Project, on the other hand, offers a stern warning of what happens when too little attention is given to training and backstopping local workers.

Even with good backstopping from the outside, however, care must be taken not to impose too many different functions and responsibili-ties on individual local workers, lest they end up doing none of them adequately. Again the problem is one of striking a balance between giving them too little and too much to handle. There is no univer-sally valid formula; the best solution must be found to fit each set of circumstances. As a general rule, however, it usually is better to confine a local worker to a few closely connected activities--rela-ting say, to the care and feeding of young children plus family planning--than to give them more diversified assignments cutting across such different sectors as health, agriculture, skill training and rural industry.

Second, selection of the right types of candidates at the outset is fundamental. It is generally helpful if the local community plays a significant role in selecting them. Village workers should desirably possess the right values and motivations, a strong sense of community service, good intelligence, and the ability to take initiatives, accept responsibility and follow instructions. For some functions they should also be sufficiently literate to be able, for example, to read a health or agricultural manual and to keep simple records; but to insist on some minimum number of years of formal schooling, such as a secondary school certificate, may be self-defeating. No amount or type of formal training can, by itself, create the above qualities; but good training can enhance and channel them where they already exist.

Third, "good training" constitutes much more than a one-shot, pre-packaged intensive "training course" extending over a few days or weeks. The basic competencies, skills, attitudes and insights that are needed by front-line workers can only be acquired through practical experience on the job, in close association with more experienced people and under their guidance and supervision. The apprenticeship approach used by SAVAR, BRAC and SWRC, not simply to "train" but to "develop" their local workers and parapro-fessionals, placed a sizeable burden on more highly trained staff but paid large dividends. Structured and highly compact training courses, such as those relied on by the Lampang Project for training "health post volunteers" and "health communicators" can be useful if they are well designed and well carried out, but they must be followed up with frequent field contacts and informal on-the-job training (which was missing at Lampang). The common tendency of program designers and managers to put their full faith in one-shot pre-service training courses and to neglect the need for subsequent training experiences invariably leads to disappointing results.

Finally, it is also important that more highly trained personnel in the system treat local workers not simply as common errand boys but as professional colleagues. Only in this way can they gain the self-respect, personal satisfaction and community appreciation so essential to growing on the job and "keeping up the good work".

EDUCATING VILLAGERS FOR CHANGE

If the training of front-line "operators" often tends to be neglected by program designers and managers, the education of the "users" is neglected even more. During the 1970s, for example, the World Bank gave increasing attention (though often not enough) to including "training components" in their projects for those involved in operating them, but no comparable attention was given to educating the intended "users" on how to take full advantage of the new services.

The point was made earlier that rural people themselves must be the *real* change agents and that to play this role they require education of many sorts, not only to give them new technical information and skills but new insights into their own lives and surroundings leading to changes in their outlook and behavior. To meet these essential learning needs requires a broad and flexible view of education, one that extends far beyond schooling or formal training courses and equates education with *learning*, taking many different forms.

Professional educators (especially adult educators well versed in the techniques of nonformal education) as well as information and communication specialists have important contributions to make in this area. But they cannot do the job alone, and they will fail if they try to. Virtually everybody involved in the operation, but especially the village workers and paraprofessionals who are closest to the villagers, have important educational roles to play.

The very process of development is itself an important educational experience. The health worker doing his or her rounds, the midwife conferring with pregnant women, the paraprofessional visiting a village, are not simply technicians but teachers. A preventive and promotional health program is 90 percent an educational effort--an effort to give people not only "information" but a better *understanding* of the causes of their health problems, of what they can do to correct them, and of how and why they must change their own practices in order to improve the health status of their children. Such under- standing is better achieved through demonstrations and practical actions--such as a baby "weighing program"--than through abstract lectures or hortatory slogans. Such understanding, in personal terms, is similarly essential to the success of family planning programs. Access to contraceptives is not enough (notwithstanding the contrary claims of some advocates); the potential users will only use the contraceptives if they come to see clearly for themselves that it is in their own best interest to do so. And sometimes it is not.

In short, rural people are not sheep who can be led blindly. They generally do not respond well to preaching and propaganda that fail to give them convincing reasons and new insights into *why* they should change their customary behavior and practices. This is the fundamental difference between an *educational* strategy and a simplistic *propaganda* strategy that underestimates the intelligence and psychology of rural people.

Unfortunately, the bureaucratic world of specialization is generally ill-equipped to infuse appropriate learning (educational) elements into various development activities. Educators are expected to do all the educating and other specialists are expected to stick to their own last. But all too often education specialists design "education" components for rural development programs in the image of formal schooling and operate them in isolation rather than making them an integral part of other development activities. Frequently their inclination is to start out (as happened with the SWRC, for example) by launching a conventional adult literacy campaign (which almost invariably fails). While the education specialists preoccupy themselves with literacy, "social education", "home economics" and similar conventional "education" classes, other types of specialists-- for example, in agriculture, health, family planning and sanitation-- are left to their own devices to improvise the essential training and learning components for their particular programs (though they usually do not think of this as "education"). Sometimes they find good solutions, but sometimes not. It is not unusual for specialists in agricultural production, medicine and other fields, to regard education as something to keep the educators busy but as quite peripheral and unimportant to the achievement of *their* objectives.

Communications specialists, who are knowledgeable about important educational tools, endeavor to provide "communications support" for various sectoral programs, sometimes to very useful effect. However, they too usually think of themselves as a separate professional breed from the educators, and many are narrowly wedded to one or another particular medium or technology rather than being *multi*-media and *multi*-method generalists. Thus they may tilt strongly toward using radio or TV, or film strips or some other favorite audio-visual aid, to the neglect of traditional local media, such as folk singers and entertainers that are lower cost, more adaptable to local conditions and more convincing to local people. Some of them also lean heavily toward advertising and propaganda techniques rather than authentic educational efforts.

Although most of the case study programs started off with these stereotype views of education, they gradually moved toward a more flexible, functional and integrated view of education (and training), with correspondingly better results. Their experience leaves unanswered, however, an important question that will face all rural development programs increasingly: where does one turn for help and competent personnel to insure that appropriate and affordable learning components get built into family improvement and other rural development services? Most educational research institutes, teacher training colleges and ministries of education are hardly the place, because their interest, knowledge and methods are tightly tied to *formal* education, which is a quite different affair. Adult education institutes come closer, but even they are often too much the prisoners of formal education thinking and practices, and of a narrow "literacy tradition". There is an important vacuum here that needs filling.

NEW ROLES FOR VOLUNTARY ORGANIZATIONS

Voluntary organizations--both religious and secular--have long been active in many developing countries in providing social services to the rural needy. Generally they operated on a modest scale in a limited geographical area and kept their distance from government agencies and other voluntary organizations. Although they frequently benefitted the population in a limited area, only rarely did their influence spread to other areas or programs, least of all to governmental programs. Moreover, because they usually confined their efforts to purely social services and relief activities without attempting to strike at the economic roots of social problems, their efforts generally failed to create a self-sustaining process of development managed by the people themselves.

In recent years, however, important changes have been occurring. A growing number of voluntary organizations have begun to shift their emphasis from relief and limited social services to more fundamental development efforts. Also a new brand of indigenous secular voluntary organizations has begun to appear that is strongly committed to integrated, community-based, long term development and to cooperating with government agencies and other private organizations in order to enhance their mutual effectiveness.

The voluntary organizations examined in ICED's case studies fall largely into this new category. Their collective experiences demonstrate the following specific ways by which voluntary organizations can effectively augment government efforts by doing things that are more difficult for government agencies to do themselves:

1) By helping rural communities to organize themselves to plan their own development projects and programs and to identify specific kinds of help they need from the government and other "outsiders" for carrying out these local plans (e.g., C-BIRD).

2) By conducting local studies (e.g., of water development and agricultural potentials) that can pave the way for broader investment and actions by appropriate government agencies (e.g., SWRC).

3) By using their special training facilities and techniques and their capacity for creating effective training materials to assist in training government staff for rural work (e.g., the Kosbad Institutes, BRAC and C-BIRD).

4) By undertaking relatively radical experiments (for example, in rural elementary education, or in using local health and family planning auxiliaries, or in settling landless families on new land) that can provide useful lessons and guidance for larger scale government programs (e.g., CBFPS and SWRC).

5) By developing community-based mechanisms that can help to coordinate and integrate the development contribution of various available government services to the community (e.g., Sarvodaya, BRAC and C-BIRD).

6) By conducting experiments and research whose results can be applied by government agencies and private organizations in other parts of the country (e.g., the Kosbad Institute's work in agricultural research and preschool education for tribal children).

With the increased interest today on rural development and helping the rural poor, a number of governments--India, is an example--are turning more seriously to voluntary agencies for help. The voluntary agencies in turn are working more closely together toward common objectives.* Among the case study programs, BRAC is providing

---

*An encouraging example is the *Agricultural Development Agencies in Bangladesh (ADAB)* which provides clearing house, consulting, publication and other services, as well as forums and seminars, for some 50 voluntary agencies working in Bangladesh on agriculture, rural industry, irrigation, fisheries, cooperatives, etc. It also publishes the monthly *ADAB NEWS*, packed with pertinent information, technical reports, etc., of value to its members and others, and has produced a "Ready Reference Directory" with useful details on more than 150 voluntary and governmental agencies involved in various aspects of rural development.

Another significant example is the long-time work of the Kenya

staff training services and materials for other voluntary groups; the
Gram Bal Shiksha Kendra (GBSK) at Kosbad Hill (India) is training
preschool teachers for other organizations; the IPPA's Youth Project
on population education (Indonesia) involved an integrated effort with
voluntary youth organizations; and other examples could be cited.

International voluntary organizations such as International
Planned Parenthood Federation, OXFAM, the Boy and Girl Scouts,
YMCA, Save the Children Federation, the 4-H Club Foundation, and
various church groups, have long given encouragement and support
to local affiliates and indigenous voluntary groups in developing
countries. Their collective efforts appear to have been growing in
recent years, with increased emphasis on basic rural development and
diminished emphasis (in the case of church-connected groups) on
proselytizing. Without such private external help, many indigenous
voluntary groups in developing countries would find it difficult to
survive. This applies to most of those covered by ICED's case
studies, though it is noteworthy that virtually all of them are
endeavoring, with some success, to reduce their dependency on
foreign sources of finance.

Ironically, most of the official aid agencies--especially the multilateral ones--that have been vigorously promoting the goals and
strategies of the new international consensus on rural development
have done little to assist indigenous voluntary organizations, which
are uniquely suited to help along these lines. There are notable
exceptions, however; some bilateral aid agencies, such as those of
the Netherlands, the Federal Republic of Germany, and the United
States, have channeled substantial funds to voluntary groups in
developing countries through their own national voluntary organizations. The Inter-American Foundation, funded directly by the
U.S. Congress, is a quite unique organizational innovation in this
respect; it concentrates exclusively on assisting promising indigenous
voluntary groups in Latin America and the Caribbean and has
achieved an impressive record. There would appear to be a useful
place for similar organizations serving other developing regions.

This is not to suggest, of course, that voluntary agencies should
take over the responsibilities of governments or, conversely, that
governments should dominate the voluntary agencies (which could
quickly destroy their independence and unique flexibility and utility).
Nor is it to suggest that governments can replicate on a large scale
various innovative program models developed by voluntary organizations, for this in most instances would be patently impossible because
of the very nature of large government organizations. However, this
by no means rules out, as the case studies demonstrate, abundant
possibilities for well-conceived and well-managed voluntary programs
to assist and supplement governmental rural development efforts in
a variety of significant ways, even if on a modest scale.

Christian Council in analyzing critical problems--such as that of
unemployed school leavers--and facilitating a coordinated attack on
such problems by various voluntary organizations.

WILL IT BE POSSIBLE?

It is clear from the evidence examined in these pages that the effective pursuit of the new goals and strategies of rural development, which have now been widely endorsed in principle throughout the international community and by leaders in the majority of developing countries, will be far more difficult than the attractive rhetoric suggests. Our purpose in highlighting these difficulties, however, has not been to sound a note of discouragement but rather to make a plea for realism, particularly on the part of official external assistance agencies whose bold proclamations and "targets" so often dwarf their resources and their capacity to act, and whose own organizational behavior so often contradicts their "integration" advice to developing countries.

To progress toward these new goals with the necessary dispatch will require far-reaching changes in existing organizational structures, procedures, attitudes and operational styles, at *all* levels. It will also require an enormous increase in resources for all the main aspects of rural development, including a much enlarged flow of resources from rich to poor countries.

It must also be borne in mind that the family life improvement measures examined in this study--health, nutrition, family planning and so forth--though crucially important, do not in themselves comprise a total rural development strategy. They must be part of a broader strategy that includes strong measures for accelerating rural economic growth (both agricultural and non-agricultural), for generating increased rural employment and boosting productivity, and for achieving a more equitable distribution of the benefits of development.

All this will require major structural changes, both economic and political, for so long as the rural poor are economically impotent and politically voiceless they can hardly be expected to be self-assertive and self-reliant and to help themselves toward a better life.

Undoubtedly the most fundamental requirement for building a strong momentum in these new directions is strong and enlightened political leadership at all levels, genuinely dedicated to these humanistic goals, and a unified sense of direction and urgency on the part of the general public, including the general public in the industrialized nations. For it must be better understood in the richest nations as well as the poorest that without a more equitable sharing of the world's goods--both within nations and between them--the security, stability and progress of *all* nations is in jeopardy.

Obviously each country must find its own best way to bring about these fundamental changes, but no country can with impunity ignore the urgent need for them. It is not simply a question of one brand of ideology versus another, for the simple reality is that, whatever a nation's professed ideology may be, the kinds of necessary changes sketched above have become imperative to its continuing overall development and its future political viability.

Will it be possible to effect these changes and to implement the goals and strategies of the new consensus? The born optimist and the glandular pessimist will give very different answers, but obviously no one really knows and only time will tell. But there are at least two substantial grounds for encouragement. The first, which is often forgotten in our preoccupation with the formidable unresolved problems that still lie ahead, is the quite remarkable, and for most earlier prognosticators, the quite inconceivable, overall record of progress attained by many newly developing nations over the past 25 years--notwithstanding their enormous handicaps, frequent disappointments and serious political and economic disruptions. The second, also often overlooked, is the enormous body of instructive development experience that has been built up, the hard way, over the past 25 years and that simply was not available earlier. Some of this experience can tell us what works and why under certain conditions; some of it can tell us what will *not* work under almost any conditions.

Development agencies, both national and international, have always been so busy with the next crop of "projects" on their drawing board that they have found little time to look back critically and analytically at their earlier projects to learn important lessons from them. The most important lesson taught by the modest sample of case studies in this volume is that future progress can be made more quickly, efficiently and smoothly, and many needless failures and misfires avoided, if more attention is paid to ferreting out these valuable lessons of experience and to putting them to practical use in future actions.

NEXT STEPS FOR DEVELOPMENT AGENCIES

If bilateral and multilateral development assistance agencies are to pursue their announced rural development goals effectively they must first put their own house in order. They must, for one thing, find ways to shift their emphasis from the sector-by-sector approach to a broader and more cohesive *problem* approach. For another, they must develop more adequate ways to size up individual rural areas and to tailor projects to fit the needs and circumstances thus revealed. They must also learn to exploit more fully the valuable but frequently neglected lessons of their own past experience and that of others.

These changes cannot be brought about simply by altering the boxes and labels on the organization chart. The basic requirement is to alter and broaden the thinking, attitudes and working styles of the specialists occupying these boxes. This can only be done by getting them into more frequent and closer dialogue and collaboration with each other--in short, by breaking the bureaucratic sound barriers. This applies not only *within* complex agencies dealing with a variety of sectors but *across* specialized single sector agencies all working on different facets of rural development.

Some of the able and occasionally frustrated members of such assistance agencies who reviewed an earlier draft of this chapter urged us to add some concrete suggestions of "next steps" these agencies might usefully take to move more quickly and effectively in these new directions. The suggestions we therefore offer below are only illustrative of a wide range of possibilities and will not fit every situation. Most of them, however, are based on steps that some agencies have already initiated.

1. *Breaking the bureaucratic sound barriers.*

This will inevitably require a *combination* of steps, such as those listed below.

-- *Create a strong Rural Development Working Group* composed of able and analytically-minded staff members from different sectors and disciplines who are given a top-level mandate: (a) to explore in depth selected crucial cross-cutting problems, obstacles and opportunities involved in implementing the agency's official rural development objectives and priorities; (b) to assess candidly and realistically both the agency's special strengths and its inherent limitations for promoting these objectives (insofar as they coincide with priority objectives of individual countries); (c) to recommend specific arrangements--such as special operational teams and intersectoral task forces, that would enable the agency to bring its various strengths to bear on a particular need or problem with maximum impact; and (d) to develop guidelines for preparing, implementing and evaluating rural development projects that can be useful to all sectors.

-- *Assignment of several broad-visioned and creatively minded specialists to work with other sectors;* for example, a nutritionist to work with agriculture, an agriculturist with the health and population group, and a few unconventional educators to assist several different sectors with their training and education components.

-- *Establish a series of intersectoral staff seminars* that focus on common issues and project case studies that transcend different sectors.

-- *Modify the bureaucratic incentive and disincentive structure* to reward rather than inhibit intersectoral collaboration and the rendering of technical assistance by one sectoral group to another.

-- *Make a concerted effort to breed and recruit more "generalists"* who can play important catalytic roles and help knit together the strengths of different specialties and disciplines.

-- *Recruit and infiltrate into various bureaus some operationally-minded rural sociologists, cultural anthropologists and political scientists,* and include them on field missions.

2. *Capitalizing on Past Experience.*

One often hears the complaint that "Our development agency has no memory. We frequently start from scratch as if nothing ever happened before. We are under such pressure to produce new projects that we have no time to go back and learn important lessons from the old ones."

This is a valid and serious criticism; most agencies literally throw away many of the valuable and costly lessons of their own experience that could improve their future operations. When they do evaluate a "completed" project it usually takes the form of a management-type post audit to determine whether the project kept to its original work plan and schedule, stayed within its budget, and achieved its initial objectives. Only rarely is it a case study type of evaluation aimed at discovering not only what overall success and impact the particular project had but what the main factors were that either facilitated or handicapped its performance. Such knowledge and insights drawn from a variety of projects and programs can be especially useful at this time when many agencies are venturing into broader and more complex types of rural development projects. They need all the help they can get from actual grassroots experience.

The cost in money and manpower of such evaluative case studies is minor compared to the investment already made in the projects, and the future benefits are likely to far outweigh the cost. Not every past project needs to be evaluated; the effort should be concentrated on a relatively limited number that hold the greatest promise of yielding valuable lessons *for the future*. Three different ways to go about it, separately or in combination, can be suggested.

-- *Set up an independent evaluation unit within the agency,* with a small staff and sufficient funds to engage consultants as needed.

-- *Contract the work to an independent group of well-qualified outside analysts* (being sure, however, that there is a clear meeting of minds at the outset on what kinds of evidence they will seek and what key questions they will try to answer).

-- *Send out small ad hoc "mixed teams" of regular staff members,* temporarily released from their usual duties in different units of the agency, to conduct an on-the-spot examination of one or two selected projects, resulting in a candid and objective report that will circulate widely in the agency (and even outside). The members should be free of any present or previous association with the particular project they are evaluating and should be firmly instructed to call a spade a spade. Over a period of time numerous staff members could be sent out on such short term evaluation missions.

Of these three approaches, we would particularly encourage agencies to experiment with the third, mainly because it provides an excellent and highly relevant and usable training experience for staff members and because the lessons they bring home are more likely to permeate the agency's thinking than a packaged report from outsiders. But whatever approach is used, the full payoff will come only when a series of such field evaluation studies are subjected to careful comparative analysis aimed at discovering important common factors and experiences that turn up repeatedly in different contexts and therefore suggest widely applicable operational guides for future use.

3. *Designing Rural Projects to Fit the Realities.*

One of the clearest lessons to emerge from ICED's case studies is that the success, impact and survival of virtually any rural development project is determined not only by economic factors but by deep-rooted social, cultural and political factors in its environment, and all these factors vary considerably from one rural area to another. A further important lesson is that a new project, service or program introduced into a village or larger rural area has a greater chance of having a substantial impact and of surviving long after the project is "completed" if it is linked in with well accepted existing organizations already serving the area, including especially home-grown local institutions, and makes a serious effort to mobilize and involve local resources of various kinds, particularly residents with special talents and leadership capacity.

These influential realities are often recognized by project designers and sponsors too late--after the new project has already been designed and put in motion. Even then they often go unrecognized as major causes of difficulties encountered by the project. It is vitally important, therefore, to develop project preparation procedures that will identify and make provision for such influential factors in advance, and to design each project to take account of them and to be sufficiently flexible to be able to adapt to unforeseen obstacles and opportunities that inevitably arise. It is also essential to design such projects from the outset to maximize their chances of ultimate replication on a larger scale with the country's own resources.

A good many rural projects in the past have fallen short of expectations because they did not honor these basic criteria. Some of the steps that can be taken to improve the "fitness", cost-effectiveness and durability of future projects include:

-- *Preparation of a checklist of important items to be considered in "sizing up" any rural situation--before* fixing the design of a new project. Such a list would include, for example: important divisions and potential conflicts within the local population; cultural factors affecting their perceptions, values, attitudes and motivations; social and economic relationships between different sub-groups; the pattern and sources of leadership and decisionmaking in the community on different matters; a simple inventory of both outside and local institutions, "specialists", and other potential resources that might help (or hamper) the project's success; and information on what important experiences--both good and bad--the people in this area have had with outside agencies and projects over the past 10 years that could substantially color their response to this new one.

This kind of preliminary "sizing up" diagnosis does not require elaborate social science "surveys", base-line studies or large teams of researchers. Basically it requires two or three people with a substantial understanding of rural societies, a good pair of eyes and ears, an empathetic personality, and a knack for getting people to "open up". While a certain amount of quantitative data can be very useful (if available), some of the most important findings of this preliminary diagnosis will necessarily be qualitative and judgemental. It may seem crude alongside the elaborate quantitative data and methodologies preferred by many social scientists, but it is far more feasible and less expensive to apply, it will call attention to critical factors that elude quantitative measurement, and it will avoid venturing blindly into a new area with a prefabricated project design that looks good on paper but may be a serious misfit in that particular situation.

To avoid the embarrassing situation where an externally-supported project succeeds impressively on its own terms so long as the outside support lasts, but then has little prospect of spreading or even surviving once this support vanishes, it is vitally important to consider from the outset what essential conditions must be met to maximize its chances of surviving and being replicated. This requires:

-- *Building in a contingency plan for success.*

Three of the important factors to consider here are: the eventual cost of keeping it going and replicating it with indigenous resources; the extent to which the government and local people see it as *their* project and give it a high priority; and whether it is the kind of activity that the country's own existing bureaucratic machinery, given its strengths, weaknesses and style of operation, could reasonably be expected to absorb and manage effectively.

-- *Taking account of implementation requirements in shaping the project.* Some projects have been destined to fail, predictably, before they even got underway, because the planners failed to pay sufficient attention to what it would take to implement it and whether it would be feasible in the particular circumstances to satisfy these requirements. One often hears complaints from assistance agencies, for example, that a project never blossomed due to the lack of competent local management personnel. There is often some truth to this assertion, but the question that must be asked is whether the shortage of such management personnel could not have been foreseen in the planning stage and remedial provisions made for breaking this bottleneck. Some of the time often spent in the project preparation stage on making refined equipment lists and cost-benefit calculations could better be spent anticipating various implementation problems and finding ways to avoid them.

4. *Cooperating with other Official Agencies and Voluntary Organizations.*

Our final suggestion is that official development agencies seek further ways to cooperate with each other and to work more closely with experienced voluntary agencies (which some are already doing to advantage).

Certain voluntary organizations (not all) can be helpful in a variety of possible ways, such as recounting their own significant experiences in certain developing countries, making pertinent suggestions from their special vantage point on how an official agency might be more useful and effective in certain respects, and in performing particular functions in selected rural situations for which they have special capabilities not possessed by government agencies or external assistance agencies. Some good ways to get started are these:

-- Get better informed about the activity record, special competencies and areas of operation of selected voluntary agencies reputed to be doing especially effective work.

-- Invite their representatives to a meeting to exchange ideas and to explore possible opportunities and methods of future operations. Discuss with them the rural development objectives of your agency and some of the problems and needs it is encountering, and invite their suggestions on these matters.

-- Consult with government officials in selected developing countries on how they feel about voluntary agencies and whether they would like to make greater use of them.

-- Look for good opportunities for voluntary organizations with appropriate capabilities to fill important gaps in rural programs that match their special competence.

What goes for voluntary organizations also goes for official development agencies. In both instances the essential objective is to share the pertinent information and experiences and to pair up the unique capabilities of different organizations--including especially those of both governmental and private organizations within the developing countries concerned--with a view to enhancing their collective efforts and impact. Admittedly it is often difficult for different organizations to work together and there are limits to what is feasible or even desirable. But within those limits many untapped opportunities still remain that are well worth exploring and exploiting.

2 The Savar Project: Meeting the Rural Health Crisis in Bangladesh
Manzoor Ahmed

EDITOR'S NOTE

Gonoshosthya kendro (People's Health Centre), located in Savar 10 miles northwest of Dacca, had its origin in the Bangladesh war of liberation and has since evolved into a major indigenous voluntary primary health care and rural development program.

The main focus of the Savar Project has been health care and family planning, but a distinctive feature of the project is its efforts to relate the health and family planning activities with other basic essentials for improving the welfare of rural families, such as growing subsistence food, raising women's social status and income-earning capacities, and expanding the opportunities for basic education. The project has also attempted to put into practice the principle of mobilizing community resources and involving the beneficiary population in various meaningful ways in the implementation of the project. All these features of the project make it a repository of significant experience and lessons useful for other voluntary and government health care and rural development efforts in Bangladesh and other developing countries.

Manzoor Ahmed, deputy director of the ICED project and a citizen of Bangladesh, prepared this report with generous help from Dr. Zafrullah Chowdhury, the founder and guiding spirit of the project, Dr. A. Quasem Chowdhury, the Project Director, and other members of the SAVAR staff.

The methodology of the study laid stress on the use and analysis of readily available evidence from existing documentation, supplemented by direct field observations and extensive unstructured interviews, rather than on generating new quantitative data from costly and time-consuming "surveys". This in the author's judgment was the most efficient and effective way to arrive at an objective assessment of the project's experiences and to shed useful light on the kinds of operational questions addressed by the study--some of the most important of which do not lend themselves to quantitative treatment. In keeping with this research strategy, available project documents such as service records, periodic reports, articles and papers written by project personnel, and financial data were used extensively. In addition the writer visited many of the project sites, joined the daily cycle of activities of some of the field workers,

*and spent long hours interviewing and interrogating field workers
and the project leaders. In the field visits, the writer was accompanied by Saleh Chowdhury, a journalist with advanced training in
social work and an intimate knowledge of rural areas.*

*A preliminary draft of the report was reviewed by the project
leaders who corrected factual oversights and errors, brought the
project story up-to-date with additional information, and added their
own commentaries to those of the writer. Responsibility for the end
product, however, including especially the interpretations   and
evaluative judgments, lies solely with the author.*

INTRODUCTION

On January 1, 1972, within weeks after the conclusion of the
war of liberation in Bangladesh, a group of Bengali physicians and
lay volunteers, who had set up and run a field hospital for the
liberation fighters, launched what was then known as the Bangladesh
Hospital and Rehabilitation Centre. The Centre occupied a cluster of
makeshift huts and tents, erected by volunteers on a piece of recently cleared land along the North Bengal highway, twenty miles west of
Dacca.

As Dr. Zafrullah Chowdhury, the director and guiding spirit of
this *Savar* Project, wrote at that time:

> The purpose of our project is to evolve some system by
> which the medical care of the whole population of a particular
> area can be undertaken efficiently and effectively with the
> minimum expenditure and maximum benefit with the employment
> of limited medical manpower.[1]

The project later became known as the Gonoshasthya Kendro
(People's Health Centre, henceforth referred to as the Kendro or the
Centre); in the five years since its inception it has developed a low-
cost partially self-supporting primary health care and family planning program for 100,000 people in about 100 villages covering one-
half of Savar thana.[2] It has also begun exploring ways of improving
the nutritional balance and food production in the villages, raising
the social status and earning capacity of women, launching functional
education programs for children and adults, and creating local
institutional structures for a greater local control over all
of these efforts as well as for their better integration and
management. The significance of the Savar Project lies in
the pioneering effort it (along with a number of other nongovernment

---

[1] Proposal by the Bangladesh Hospital and Rehabilitation Centre,
February 1972 cited in W.B.Greenough III and Richard A. Cash, "Post-
Civil War Bangladesh: Health Problems and Programs" in Lincoln C.
Chen (ed.), Disaster in Bangladesh: Health Crises in a Developing
Nation, New York, Oxford, 1973, p. 252.

[2] An administrative unit with an average population of 200,000.
There are over 400 thanas in Bangladesh, about 350 of which are
rural.

projects) has initiated to develop an affordable health care and family planning service and to ensure its effectiveness by linking it with a multifaceted rural development effort. In the following pages we will examine the results of these endeavors and try to identify the lessons it teaches for programs designed to raise the level of welfare of rural families in Bangladesh and other developing countries.

Background of the Project Area

Savar thana, twenty miles north west of the capital city of Dacca, covers an area of 134 square miles and includes over 300 natural villages. The population of the thana according to the census taken in 1974 was 205,000.

Being close to the capital, Savar is the location of a number of enterprises not found in rural areas--a residential university, a large government dairy farm, an agricultural farm run by the military, and a small number of industrial plants (two small cotton mills, a cigarette factory, a brick factory, and a chemical industry plant under contruction). These enterprises, however, remain as small modern enclaves in the sleepy rural communities and paddy fields of Savar without affecting very much the rural life, except for taking away some of the village land from its traditional agricultural use and offering unskilled laborers' jobs to a small number of villagers.

One special government project that is aimed at helping the rural people is a demonstration project run by the Bangladesh Agricultural Development Corporation for deep tubewell irrigation and horticulture. Partly by the effort of this project, cooperative irrigation groups have been formed and over 200 diesel-operated deep tubewells have been installed in the thana and the local farmers have taken up vegetable cultivation in the dry season. Deep tubewell irrigation and horticulture are not, however, unique features of this area, as these are found to some extent in other rural thanas, and the overall agricultural productivity is not considered to be significantly different in Savar from other rural areas.

Pertinent socioeconomic data for the thana were not available, but the overall estimate for rural Bangladesh will be sufficiently indicative of the situation in the thana. The per capita yearly income for the country is estimated at about US$70.00, but in the rural areas it may be only one-half of this amount. In an agriculture-based economy, access to cultivable land is the most important factor in determining the level of welfare enjoyed by a rural family. A recent sample survey of households revealed that 70 percent of the workers in the rural areas relied for their livelihood either entirely (42 percent) or partially (28 percent) on agricultural labor. However, 38 percent of the rural households had no land available for farming (either by ownership or by rent), only 5 percent of the households rented out all or part of their farm land, and

11 percent of the households were able to rent in farm land. (Therefore,
46 percent of the households farmed their own land without renting in or
out.)[1]

The heavy pressure on land use and the primitive agricultural technology result in extremely low agricultural productivity. The same sample
survey indicates that slightly over 4 percent of the households produced
a marketable surplus of foodgrain, and little over 9 percent of the households could be considered self-sufficient. As high as 62 percent of the
households harvested less than three months' food needs from their own
production.[2] The result is that more than half of all families were below
the acceptable calorific intake, while more than two-thirds were deficient
in proteins and vitamins.[3] Estimates of unemployment and underemployment
range from one-quarter to one-third of the labor force.[4]

The health and population situation reflects mass poverty of the rural
areas. The overall deathrate is estimated to be 17 per thousand. Particularly vulnerable groups are infants (about 13 percent deaths among the
live births), children between one and five years (about 2.6 percent)[5],
and pregnant women (27 percent of all deaths of females between age 10 and
49 years were birth-related).[6]

A prime factor in the poor health situation is the rural sanitary and
hygiene condition. The household survey mentioned above showed that 63
percent of the rural households did not have ready access to or use of
pure drinking water or covered latrines.

The crude birthrate in the country, estimated to be around 47 per
one thousand people, resulted in a population growth rate of about 3 percent.

[1]Integrated Rural Development Program. Problems of Rural Development:
Some Household Level Indicators, Benchmark Survey Report Series No. 2,
Dacca, October 1976.

[2]Ibid.

[3]World Bank estimates. See also Irwin H. Rosenberg, "Nutrition:
Food Production, Dietary Patterns, and Nutritional Deficiencies," in Chen,
op. cit., pp. 31-51.

[4]World Bank estimate.

[5]Five year average for 1966-67 to 1970-71 in one thana with exceptionally well-recorded vital statistics. Cited in George T. Curlin, et
al, "Demographic Crisis: The Impact of the Bangladesh Civil War (1971)
on Births and Deaths in a Rural Area of Bangladesh," Population Studies,
30:1, 1976. Table 5, p. 97.

[6]Lincoln Chen, et al, "Maternal Mortality in Rural Bangladesh,"
Dacca, Ford Foundation, 1974.

In the Savar thana, all of the government rural health facilities found in many other parts of the country, such as rural health centres and general preventive and curative services, do not exist. The health service in the thana consists of a thana health administrator and about thirty health workers engaged in malaria and smallpox surveillance and prevention. The facilities for a thana health complex under the standard government plan were under construction in late 1976. (See Appendix II)

The old-style government family planning service in the thana, with a Family Planning Officer and a part-time male Family Planning Organizer in each union and part-time village-based female workers (dais) as motivators and distributors of contraceptives, has existed in Savar for many years--without any significant impact. A reorganized family planning program separate from the health service (according to the national pattern) has been launched in December 1976. A staff of fourteen male Family Planning Assistants and twenty-one female Family Welfare Assistants has been recruited and has undergone a one-month orientation course at the thana center. The main tasks of the family planning workers are to educate and inform the population about family planning, organize the distribution of contraceptives, provide advice about maternal health and child care, and recruit candidates for such terminal birth control measures as tubectomy and vasectomy. These cases are sent to a family planning clinic in Dacca. The impact of the reorganized service is yet to be seen.

The overall literacy rate among adults in Bangladesh is estimated to be around 20 percent. The level of actual functional and usable literacy skills in rural areas is much lower than this rate would suggest. The household sample survey cited above revealed that in 65 percent of the rural households all members were illiterate. Females are especially disadvantaged in their access to educational opportunities. In six primary schools of Savar thana, out of ninety-nine fifth class students in 1975 only fourteen were observed to be girls.[1] In Savar thana there were ninety-two primary schools with an average enrollment of 200 each, twenty-two secondary schools with an average of 250 students in each, and one four-year college in 1976. In addition there were forty primary-level religious madrassahs.

---

[1] Data collected by Nurun Nahar of Gonoshasthya Kendro.

CHAPTER 2

THE HEALTH CARE AND

DEVELOPMENT APPROACH

The Health Delivery Problem

As in the rest of rural Bangladesh, the basic health care service in Savar is utterly inadequate, inaccessible, and costly for most of the people in the area. Even if the government health service were to function perfectly in the thana, the rural families would at best receive vaccination, inoculation, vitamin A pills, and some general health advice from the Family Welfare Workers, who might pass by the village once or twice a month. For the most common sickness the villager has to travel up to ten miles on foot to see one practising health service doctor and spend the better part of a day waiting for a free prescription. Or he can go to one of the half-dozen qualified physicians in the thana and pay him a substantial fee. The only other recourse is to visit one of the quacks or the practitioners of traditional ayurvedic or hakimi medicine.

The health problem of the area manifests itself in a limited number of common disease symptoms--diarrhea, dysentery, fever and cold, scabies, anaemia, and any or all of these compounded by malnutrition. The health situation in the area could be dramatically improved if an approach were found to deal with these common symptoms effectively. It is evident that one qualified physician cannot by himself take care of 30,000 to 40,000 people, even if the services of all the qualified physicians in the thana were distributed evenly among the people. Nor can most of the rural people afford to bear the time and cost of visiting the physician; consequently they avoid treatment until the illness causes serious physical disability or becomes life-threatening. The problem, therefore, can be tackled only by taking the treatment for the common diseases to the doorstep of the villagers, and that would have to be done at a cost that is affordable to both the nation and the individual rural families.

The Paramedic Solution

Drawing upon lessons learned in providing medical care with hastily trained lay volunteers on the battle front during the liberation war of Bangladesh and from programs of rural health care with paramedics and "barefoot doctors" in other countries, the Centre decided that the only feasible method of making basic health care available to the villagers would be through rural youths--boys and girls with some education (usually not beyond secondary education and sometimes only primary education)-- trained to serve as paramedics for diagnosing and treating the most common half dozen diseases in the village.

The paramedics would provide treatment from fixed locations ("clinics") within a reasonable walking distance from each village and, in addition, the paramedics would literally take their service to the village doorsteps by making regular rounds of home visits.   The paramedics, it was envisaged, would refer the more complicated or less common illnesses requiring special care to qualified physicians and hospitalization facilities located in the Centre.   (The plan for a well-equipped indoor patient facility at the Centre was later abandoned on the ground that the costs were not justified in terms of the needs and that a small indoor facility for emergency and surgical patients would suffice. The relatively few cases requiring prolonged hospitalization are sent to the hospitals in Dacca.)

Family planning is viewed by the Centre as an essential part of the basic health care service for the rural people. Providing information and motivation for family planning, advising on appropriate contraceptive methods and carrying out the necessary preparatory checking, distributing the supplies, advising on and treating side effects, and providing general follow-up service are tasks that could be performed by the paramedics in the usual course of providing the other health care services. To the extent that safe child delivery and child survival were considerations in limiting births, it was felt that family planning belonged to the package offered by the paramedics. On the other hand, well-spaced and fewer births had direct favorable health effects on mothers and children. A pregnancy-related complication was the single most important killer of women of child-bearing age.

As in the case of disease treatment, the clinical services associated with family planning (such as male and female sterilization, menstrual regulation, and the insertion of contraceptive devices) suffer from the absence of qualified physicians. It is paradoxical that the government should insist on the use of physicians, or other personnel with high formal qualifications, for the clinical services when they are in such short supply. Applying the same logic as for the common diseases, it was reasoned in the Kendro that paramedics could be trained for performing the surgical procedure involved in tubectomy (suprapubic minilaparotomy), a relatively simple permanent measure considered to have high potentiality. According to the Director of the Centre:

> Tubectomy is a family-planning method with great potential for developing countries: in many traditional societies a method for women is, at present, more acceptable than a method for men, and a permanent measure is desired by a large proportion of clients who have completed their families. Further, follow-up and additional services are unnecessary once the wound is healed-- an important consideration in areas without an established medical service.[1]

---

[1] S. Chowdhury and Z. Chowdhury, "Tubectomy by Paraprofessional Surgeons in Rural Bangladesh," Lancet, September 27, 1975, pp. 567-9.

Moreover, according to the Centre, the measure would be more acceptable
to rural women if they were to submit themselves to a female paramedic
for treatments, probably a familiar face from earlier home visits,
rather than to a male doctor (female doctors being even scarcer).

Integrated Rural Development

Although it may not have been adequately developed and articulated
at the outset, there is now a high level of awareness at the Centre
that health and population problems are rooted in the total socioeconomic
situation of the population and are not isolated symptoms to be treated
with specific therapies. The common diseases in the area--the most
common being malnutrition and related symptoms--are basically caused by
the poverty and ignorance in which the people live. The recurrence of
the diseases can be prevented only by actions that change the conditions
that breed disease and ill-health. More food, better shelter, pure
drinking water, proper latrines, knowledge about balanced diets and
basic hygiene would have a greater impact on the health situation than
all the curative services that can be made available.

The same reasoning applies to population control. As stated in the
Centre Progress Report for 1974-75:

> ...population growth is only one symptom of the poverty
> syndrome. Are we poor because we are overpopulated, or
> overpopulated because we are poor? Is it just a coincidence
> that we are also illiterate and unemployed?... If, then, the
> demand for family planning in the village is limited, this is
> for definite reasons, and reflects the general problem of
> rural backwardness which we must tackle.... In practice, we
> find that a demand for family planning does already exist,
> which has nothing to do with the persuasive powers of FP
> workers but is due to the villager's own thinking.[1]

As the Centre sees it, the existing national family planning program
is not able to deliver the services even at the present level of demand,
and hence the need for trying a new delivery approach at the Centre.
Ultimately, however, improvement of the health situation as well as the
acceptance of a norm of small and planned families are linked up with
how the general socioeconomic situation can be improved and how the
"syndrome of poverty" can be tackled.

The People's Health Centre (the name betrays its original narrow
focus on health), recognizing the interdependence of health and family
planning and socioeconomic development, is beginning to move towards a
broadening of its objectives and scope of activities. From the practical
necessity of supplementing its resources and indeed as an expression of
identity with the rural people, all of the Centre's staff from the director to the custodial personnel work every day in the morning and the evening on the grounds of the Centre producing a substantial part of their
own grains and vegetables. These fields and the pond on the grounds
now have become an informal agricultural deomonstration project and a

---

[1]Gonoshasthya Kendro, Progress Report No. 5, April 1975.

means for the staff to have practical lessons in agriculture. It is
envisaged that a new group of field workers to be known as para-agros
will provide extension service on agriculture and, in cooperation with
the paramedics, on nutrition for the villagers who are also the clients
of the health and family planning service.

A small program of functional education and vocational skill training has been in operation in the Centre for over two years. Future
plans include extension, through multipurpose subcentres, of the educational program into villages for women and other groups and the establishment at the Centre of an experimental program of basic education
for children and youth. A nucleus of a rural technology development
program has been initiated at the Centre under the direction of an
interested mechanical engineer.

There is now increasing attention at the Centre on institutional
development in the villages. The informal involvement of the villagers
and their participation through the insurance scheme (see section on
finances and costs) in the health program are important features of the
Centre. Just as essential is the more systematic and somewhat institutionalized participation of the villagers in management and planning of
the health, family planning, and other activities in their own areas.
Committees formed for a group of villages, it is foreseen by the Centre,
will be involved in planning all the activities in and around a subcentre;
first, to ensure that the obligations and duties of the communities
served by the subcentre are fulfilled, and, second, to mobilize support
and resources for the program from the local communities.

Organization and Staff

The emphasis of the project so far on health and family planning and
the relatively small geographical coverage have permitted a simple organizational structure and staffing pattern. Until early 1975 the project's organizational structure did not show any functional or territorial subdivisions, and the whole project was run, by and large, directly
by the Project Director.

Staff.

The project staff as of April 1975 totaled fifty-six persons and
included the following: the Project Director, the Executive Director,
the Coordinator, two Accounts Officers, two Stores Officers, five doctors, one medical record keeper, one sewing instructor, one jute handicrafts instructor, one works inspector, two drivers, four guards, one
agricultural labourer, thirty-one paramedics (nine male and twenty-two
female), and two para-agros. There were also four foreign volunteers.

The organization has become somewhat more complicated with the
Centre's efforts to broaden its activities. The activities are now
(end of 1976) organized as three projects: Project I--health, family
planning and nutrition in Savar, Project II--education, women's vocational training and workshop, and Project III--Jamalpur family planning
and mother and child health project. Each of the projects is directed
by an experienced old timer who has been with the Centre from its inception. The director of Project I is a qualified male physician while

the two other projects are headed by experienced women workers who had
begun their association with the Centre as volunteer nurses and later
became paramedics.[1]

Centre-based activities.

Except for the Jamalpur Project, located about a hundred miles away
from Savar and launched as a special project under UNICEF auspices, much
of the Kendro activities have been centered in the physical facilities
located in Savar. A large part of the staff except those based in subcenters reside in dormitories in the Kendro and board at a subsidized
price in a common kitchen facility. Many of the agricultural production
and demonstration activities are confined to the Kendro. The women's education and vocational training activities are also mostly held in   the
Kendro. The main medical facilities are, of course, located here too.
Two of the weekly clinics for the villages are held in the Centre.   The
visits (the interval between village visits is, in principle, one week
but it may be considerably longer before an individual family gets   a
return visit) to the villages carry the services to the villages, but
the visits do not really establish a "presence" of the Kendro in   the
village and it therefore does not become a part of the rural community
except in the vicinity of the subcenter.

Subcenter.

The Kendro has adopted a plan of establishing up to six subcenters
covering the hundred-odd villages it serves at present. Some progress
has already been made in implementing this plan and three subcenters
have been opened. In each of three locations one-third of an acre of
land has been donated for the purpose by well-to-do villagers.   Altogether 19 paramedics (and one educational worker in one subcenter) have
been resident in the three sites with responsibility to guide the health,
family planning, and educational work in a cluster of villages around
each subcenter. The subcenter is visited at least once a week by a qualified physician from the Kendro to care for the referral cases and to provide supervision and guidance to the paramedics.

Eventually, it is envisaged, a subcenter for each union (covering
10-20 villages) in the thana will be set up that will establish a tangible presence of the Kendro in the village, will become a support base
for the well-known health and family planning services as well as other
new development activities in the area of education, agriculture, nutrition, and women's economic skills. Through local management committees
for the subcenter and through participation in planning and managing
various subcenter activities the local people will have a meaningful
form of involvement in the whole effort. The expectation is that ultimately the administration of the subcentres and the associated activities will be taken over by the subcenter staff and the local people,and
the Kendro would cease to be directly responsible for the management of
the subcent   activities. All this is, of course, yet to be shaped and
unfolded in the future.

---

[1]In a communication on September 23, 1977 the Project Director informed us that "Now Projects I and II have been combined and the whole
Project has been divided into 5 sections, each with a section chief--
Health and Family Planning, Education, Agriculture and Nutrition, Vocational Training, and Research and Evaluation."

Auxiliary village-based workers.

The idea of another layer of workers below the paramedics to be based in individual villages and serving up to a maximum of 200 families (roughly a population of 1,000) is being currently explored in the Kendro as well as by several other voluntary health care projects in Bangladesh. The reasoning behind this thought is that even a subcenter in each union combined with home visits at certain intervals does not really ensure ready accessibility of primary health care to the individual village. Moreover, family planning motivation, service, and follow-up and mother and child health care call for a more intensive contact and communication with villagers than is possible through a visitor to the village from a certain distance--especially if such a visitor has the responsibility for at least 5,000 people (the standard population-to-paramedic ration). The full-time availability of a person in the village within close proximity of every household is, therefore, considered necessary. Such a person would normally be a woman from the village, preferably literate, who would be trained for performing a limited number of tasks--diagnosing and treating a few of the common symptoms (diarrhea, cough and cold, anaemia, scabies, worms); supply oral contraceptives and conduct follow-up of clients; educate her clients on general hygiene, sanitation, nutrition, and disease prevention; probably help keep records of births, deaths and morbidity; and do common inoculation and vaccination. She could be a part-time or full-time worker, but would always be under the close supervision of the paramedics. Her work and home visits are not expected to substitute for the regular rounds and other duties of the paramedic in the village.

The Kendro has already started using some of the village-based dais (traditional birth attendants) for keeping and distributing contraceptives and has attempted to upgrade their traditional skills so that they can serve as effective auxiliary nurse-midwives in their own villages. The training of the dais is considered important because of the high incidence of birth-related female mortality and tetanus deaths of both mothers and infants.

The staff of the Kendro for all of its activities rose by the end of 1976 to about seventy-five with the addition of fifteen trainee paramedics, one workshop engineer, two apprentices (with the aim of exploring the rural technology area and developing a male vocational training program), and one person with specific duties in connection with the present limited and exploratory functional education activities.

Women staff.

There is a ratio of one to four between male and female paramedics in the Kendro (counting those in training at the end of 1976). The premises are that girls can be more effective than men in serving women and children (the most numerous victims of the health hazards), that girls can reach and communicate easily with rural families (particularly the housewives and mothers), and that the most numerous clients for various family planning services are women. There is no policy to exclude males in the recruitment of paramedics, but there is a definite preference for girls, although it is recognized that often a combination of boys and girls is needed especially in making village rounds.

One factor that has contributed to the present Kendro-based nature of the activities is the preference for girls as paramedics. Most of the female staff members come from other districts, rather than from the locality, and a dormitory-like arrangement in one installation is the most practical solution for residential accommodation.

For some reason, not fully understood, female education is lower in Savar thana than in neighboring thanas, and the rural families are relatively less inclined to let their girls take up a role outside the home. But this situation is changing, partly by the example of the female paramedics from the Kendro.

Immediately noticeable to a visitor to the Kendro is the absence of hierarchical relationships and neat organizational divisions among the personnel. There is an atmosphere of camaradarie--no doubt, the result of communal living and of shared experiences in a common endeavor beginning from the days of the liberation struggle. If there is a loss of efficiency in the informal organizational style, that is probably compensated by the sense of personal commitment and dedication that can exist only in a close-knit group.

Staff Training

Besides the administrative staff, the main body of personnel of the Kendro consists of the paramedics. The paramedics, with educational backgrounds varying from incomplete primary education to years of college education, but with no special preparation for their tasks in the Kendro, develop the required skills and knowledge for their multifunction role as Kendro workers through in-service training.

Emphasis on supervised practice.

The general training for paramedics is highly unstructured, does not follow a rigid timetable, though a systematic body of knowledge is sought to be transferred to the trainees. The basic approach is supervised practical experience given to the trainees by pairing them up with experienced paramedics as they perform their normal duties in the clinics or in village rounds. The usual practice in training programs of teaching theory first and then giving some practical experience is reversed in the training of the paramedics. As the trainee accompanies the experienced paramedic, he observes the procedures and actions of his senior colleague, receives an explanation of what is happening, and asks questions. Often at the end of the day a review of the day's activities takes place for the benefit of the trainees. Slides, wall-charts, and models are used as teaching aids.

After this apprenticeship and a thorough exposure to the health problems of the people in the area, and how the general socioeconomic situation affects health and welfare of the rural families, the trainees attend a series of somewhat formal instructional sessions guided either by a physician or an experienced paramedic. The topics covered in these sessions are body structure and function (basic anatomy and physiology), common disease symptoms, communicable diseases, inoculation and vaccination, common drugs and toxicity, personal hygiene and sanitation, nutrition and food habits, child care and common children's diseases, pregnancy and lactating mothers, and family planning.

The instructional sessions are held in the late afternoon or evening. Having been involved in practical work, the trainees usually have many questions to ask the instructors at the end of the day; they become active participants rather than the passive listeners of lectures. The instructional sessions are held two or three times a week for about six months, the frequency and number being determined by the rate of progress of the group.

There is no formal examination to pass at the end of training.[1] From the very beginning the trainees start to help their senior colleagues in their daily activities and gradually assume greater responsibilities. Ultimately, after a period that may vary from six months to one year for different individuals, the trainees are judged by their senior colleagues and the physician supervisor to be fit to make independent home visits and take clinic responsibilities. In principle, the training of the paramedic never ends, because the physician at the Kendro or in weekly clinics is on call for referral and for answering the paramedic's questions.

Training for special tasks.

Besides undergoing general paramedic training, a number of female paramedics, selected for their special interest and aptitude, are trained for performing tubectomies, menstrual regulation, and abortion. The training for tubectomy is described in the British medical journal, Lancet:

> The young women who are given tubectomy training are selected from a larger number of female paramedics who have already gone through a basic in-service training of at least six months as medical auxiliaries. Most of them have had 10 years of school education and have passed matriculation, although this is not a formal requirement: one trainee is essentially illiterate and has, up to now, performed 77 successful tubectomies.

> Apart from the experience gained through daily work in outpatient clinics, the sickroom, and home visits in the villages, the basic training includes classes in gross anatomy, selected topics in physiology, common drugs, and simple pathology.

> The tubectomy training is conducted by a qualified physician with 10 years of surgical experience. Eventually, perhpas, experienced paramedics may train new recruits, but this is not feasible at present. So far, 14 women have been trained, all

---

[1]As the Project Director remarked, "We do not have a formal final examination, but we do have several oral, practical, and written tests throughout the training period, which coupled with careful observation of performance, help us to evaluate an individual more fully than any final exam ever would."

have performed several tubectomies, themselves, but only 6 have
gained sufficient experience to operate independently. Out of
the 600 tubectomies reported here, 366 were performed by paramedics and the rest by qualified physicians.

The tubectomy training itself begins with learning to
sterilise linen and instruments, followed by circulating assistance in the theatre. During this initial period the trainee
learns the function of the different instruments and memorises
their names. It is an advantage that the method requires only a
few types of unfamiliar instruments--blades, scissors, and non-
tooth forcepts are already known to most trainees from their
daily lives. Later on she is instructed in scrubbing-up and the
correct handling of sterile garments and gloves. She assists in
several tubectomies before being allowed to handle the knife
herself. As far as possible, explanations are given with objects
and actions already familiar to the trainees. For example, the
necessity for catheterisation of the bladder is explained by
describing the bladder as a balloon-like organ which collapses
when empty and can thus be removed from the field of operation.
The ovary has to be identified on both sides without fail (this
is easy, owing to the distinctive appearance of the organ) and
both the trainee and her assistant have to ascertain that the
same tube runs between ovary and uterus: this ensures that the
fallopian tubes rather than the round ligaments are excised.
The first 10 to 15 tubectomies of each trainee are performed
under close supervision, which is relaxed only when she has gained
sufficient self-confidence and skill. A qualified physician is
always on call.

The period of training varied greatly with availability of
cases and individual aptitude of the trainee but, given both,
training can be completed within six weeks.[1]

A number of other paramedics have become adept in the use of the
microscope and other simple procedures for common pathological diagnostic
tests of blood, stool, urine, and sputum. A physician with pathological
training and a volunteer laboratory technician from Australia have helped
to train the paramedics for the common pathological procedures.

The traditional midwife or dai serves as a distributor of contraceptive pills, offers information and reassurance on the side-effects
of pills, makes referral to clinics when necessary, and provides advice
on diarrheal diseases of children and malnutrition of mothers and children. She receives short informal training on her assigned role from the
paramedics at the Kendro or the subcenter.

---

[1]"Tubectomy by Paraprofessional Surgeons in Rural Bangladesh," The
Lancet, September 27, 1975, p. 567-9.

CHAPTER 3

MAJOR PROJECT ACTIVITIES

As noted already, health and family planning dominate the services provided by the Kendro. Essentially as complement to the health and family planning program, there are some activities in the area of nutrition, crafts training, and literacy lessons for women. Family planning and mother and child care clinics in collaboration with the local family planning program of the government constitute a special UNICEF-sponsored project only in Jamalpur.

Health Care

About 100,000 people in roughly 100 villages in the western part of Savar thana are served by the health care efforts of the Kendro. The health care activities, carried out by four doctors (including the Project Director) and forty paramedics (including fifteen halfway through their training at the end of 1976) are the following: clinical services including pathological tests, home visits and treatment of common illnesses, emergency hospitalization, referral to Kendro physicians or Dacca hospitals, emergency outdoor treatment, inoculation and vaccination, nutritional advice, and dissemination of information about hygiene and sanitation.

The clinics are held once a week for a cluster of villages. Two of the clinics are held in the Kendro itself for neighboring villages; four others are held on a mobile van or on existing or future subcenter locations. A physician is either present or on call at the clinics to assist the paramedics. A pathological laboratory at the Kendro provides the essential diagnostic testing and analysis service. A pathological kit is carried in the mobile van to perform the basic tests for stool, blood, urine, and sputum.

In each of the clinics which are held for four to six hours a day--the time it takes to take care of all the patients that show up--100 to 300 men, women, and children are treated. The total number treated through the clinics in a year between April 1975 and April 1976 was over 48,000 patients. This was about 100,000 more than the number treated during the previous year.

The main function of the paramedics, besides conducting clinics under the physician's supervision, is to visit every home in order to carry medical service directly to the source of need. They make diagnoses and provide drugs and advice for such common symptoms as primary malnutrition, diarrhea, dysentery, fever and cold, scabies, and anaemia. They also provide basic information about hygiene, sanitation, and healthful living; but in the absence of any systematic health education effort, hygiene appears to receive only casual attention. For cases beyond the paramedic's competence, the patient is referred to the physician at the weekly clinic

Each paramedic in principle, is responsible for home visits to about 400 families (a population of 2,500). If twenty families are covered in a day (the maximum reported to be actually covered) and home visits are made four days a week, it would take five weeks before a return visit is made to a home. In practice, the villages under the insurance scheme receive more frequent visits from the paramedics than the villages not in the scheme.

Nutritional deficiencies are often detected by paramedics during their visits and advice is provided about remedial measures. Incidentally, the agricultural activity and the raising of fish and ducks at the Kendro, besides providing food for the Kendro, are intended to serve as an informal demonstration of means by which nutritional deficiencies and imbalance are overcome. The rural families are encouraged by the paramedics, when the occasion arises to discuss nutritional deficiencies, to grow more vege- tables; raise fish, poultry and ducks, and to cultivate new types of protein rich crops suitable for the land in the area, such as soybean. Such encouragement and advice, however, are secondary tasks for the para- medics, who are not prepared by their training for this function. Their preo-cupation with basic health care tasks leave them little time for the educational function. The Kendro has helped to introduce soybean in the area. It also distributes on a limited scale vegetable and fruit seeds and small plants of fruit and vegetables. Nutritional advice is focused on meeting the needs of children, pregnant and lactating mothers, and convalescing patients. Examples include encouraging solid food for infants and children instead of prolonged reliance on a diet of just milk, encouraging breast feeding, and overcoming the belief that diarrhea and fever patients should be fed only liquid or near-liquid food.

Inoculations and vaccinations are given in clinics and during home visits to those who need them. BCG and Triple Antigen (diptheria, whoop- ing cough and tetanus), the supply of which is limited, are provided only to children.

The Kendro has emergency surgical and hospitalization facilities that are available at a reduced price for insured clients and at cost to others. Simple surgery and the cleaning and dressing, etc. of wounds are also done at the subcenters and in the mobile clinics. Both emergency and non-emergency patients are admitted to the 12-bed residential ward at the Kendro. However, the project emphasizes domiciliary care and tries to educate people to treat early symptoms before the cases become compli- cated. It is believed that most rural patients would recover better in their own homes if advice regarding care of patients and necessary follow- up at home are provided. Serious cases requiring special equipment and facilities such as general anaesthetics are referred to hospitals in Dacca.

Family Planning

The family planning services include motivation and education of eligible couples, distribution of contraceptives, follow-up of the ac- ceptors, and clinical services.

The motivational work is carried out mainly through village rounds by paramedics for general health care purposes. It is the premise of the Kendro, as noted earlier, that there is already a demand for family planning among the rural people that is not being met adequately. More-over, there is a latent demand which can be tapped if the basic health care situation and the general economic level improve and the family planning services are made easily accessible. It is stated in the 1975 Kendro progress report, "As we expected, once they had a taste of the new freedom--freedom from childbirth--many women were keen to try a more permanent method of birth control."

The distribution of contraceptives (oral pills) is done through a village-based agent--usually a traditional birth attendant (dai) who is also used for reinforcement of the motivational work done by the para-medics, follow-up of pill-acceptors, and identification of candidates for terminal methods. As a part-time worker she is paid a monthly al-lowance ranging from Tk 30 to 50. About twenty dais served as many villages in late 1976. In addition to maintaining a stock of contracep-tives with the village-based dais, the paramedics carry supplies in their village rounds and these are, of course, available from the mobile clinics and subcenters.

The emphasis in contraceptive method has shifted in 1975 from oral pills to Depo Provera injections (a long-acting Oestrogen, one shot ef-fective for three months). The shots are given by paramedics who indivi-dually maintain records of their own clients and ensure that the repeat shots are given on time. Altogether 2,560 women received the injection since a small-scale beginning of the experiment in April 1974. In Decem-ber 1976 about 1,500 were practising the method. About one-half of the clients were acceptors for six months or less. The positions of acceptors in April 1975 and December 1976 were as follows:

April 1975		December 1976	
		(approximate figures)	
Total acceptors	2,700 (approx.)	Total acceptors up to that point	5,000
On injection	245	On injection	1,500
On pills	1,271	On pills	400
Tubectomy	96	Tubectomy	500
Drop out	1,100 (approx.)	Drop out	2,600

The injection is reported to have side-effects less widespread than pills, but it can have relatively serious side effects in some cases, including total halt to menstruation, heavy bleeding, and spotting (irregular bleeding). There have also been some reports of reduced breast-milk flow. The results of the experiment, therefore, are not conclusive yet, but there appears to be an inclination in the Kendro to favor the injection because of the convenience of the once-in-three months treatment. The Kendro, therefore, has reached roughly one-quarter of the eligible 20,000 couples in the village served by its activities and has been able to maintain an acceptor rate of about 12 percent of the eligible couples. The Kendro, instead of offering cash incentives for accepting family planning, makes a charge for all supplies--0.25 Taka for a cycle of oral pills, Tk 2 for De Provera shots (Tk 1 for insured clients),   Tk 6 for tubal ligation,   Tk 20 for men-strual regulation for both insured and uninsured clients and Tk 15 for both

tubal ligation and menstrual regulation at the same time as an
indirect inducement for ligation.

The clinical family planning services offered by the Kendro
are especially the following: tubectomy, vasectomy, fitting
diaphragm and intrauterine contraceptive devices, menstrual
regulation, and abortion.

Tubectomy, performed usually by paramedics (with a physician
available on call), is the most emphasized clinical service. Women
with at least three children requesting a permanent method of birth
control are permitted to have tubectomy. Most frequently the candidates for tubectomy are recruited by the dais and the clients are
generally found to progress from a temporary contraceptive method
such as oral pills or the De Provera injection to this method. A
total of 1,086 minilaparotomy tubectomies were performed in Savar
and Jamalpur between August 1974 and January 1976. Of these operations, 744 were performed by paramedics and the remaining 342 by
doctors. The infection rate in operations carried out by paramedics
was 5.37 percent, in those carried out by physicians it was 5.84
percent. All infections ultimately healed completely. (Total
tubectomies by the end of 1976 numbered about 2,000, most of the
increase during the year coming from Jamalpur.)

The tubectomy process in the Kendro is described as "while-you-
wait" minilaparotomy under local anaesthesia. The whole process from
preliminary shaving to discharge of the patient, takes about two hours,
and the patient walks home. The patient has to return after seven
days to have the stitches removed. Contrary to local medical custom
antibiotics are used only if an infection occurs (about 5 percent).
This practice reduces the cost of tubectomy significantly.[1] Patients
are advised to report any complication and home visits are made by
paramedics if any post-operative difficulty is reported. A very small
number of vasectomies (about 10) has been performed at the Kendro.
Although it is a simpler type of surgery than a tubectomy, it has
become very difficult to make this method popular in a male dominated
culture.

Menstrual regulation (abortion within first few weeks of conception) and abortion are infrequently applied techniques for birth control at the Kendro, because of the uncertain legal status of abortion
in the country. (Abortion is not legal, but a doctor can perform it
on the ground that the mother's or a child's health is in question).
About a hundred cases of this type are handled by the Kendro in a
year. Again the paramedics are trained for the task, and over a
third of the cases during the past year have been handled by the paramedics with doctors being present or on call.

---

[1]Project Director's communication of September 23, 1977 noted,
"Every tubal ligation patient gets tetanus toxide before the operation. Now we are giving TT to all women aged 15-44 at the village
level and therefore, in time, pre-operative dispensing will not be
necessary."

Agriculture and Nutrition

As noted above, the agricultural work undertaken so far is a marginal activity. It is viewed as a means of improving the nutritional situation of the area and making some contribution to the Kendro's own resources. As the Project Director explained the role of agricultural work:

Gonoshasthya Kendro does not think that health care can be separated from the socioeconomic context of people's lives. Our paramedics are trained to realize that good health is not a function of drugs, but nutrition, and to motivate villagers accordingly. Our evolving emphasis on agriculture (both demonstration at the project and via credit to landless and land-poor families) underlines this.

Agricultural work is undertaken in the Kendro by all of the staff, and several crops are gown including high yielding aman and baro rice and several crops new to the area--soybean, pulses, and vegetables. Soybean is considered particularly suitable for the relatively high and dry land and is a good source of protein. Attempts to introduce soya flour in food items in the Kendro has had success. Chappattis made of a mixture of soya flour and wheat flour, soya flour biscuits, and soymilk as a drink by itself or with tea sell well in the Kendro canteen. The local farmers have become interested in the commercial prospects of the soybean crop. But its spread among the farmers is handicapped by the difficulties in grinding the beans into flour by the local flour mills because of the high oil content of the beans. Extracting oil from the beans is a capital intensive proposition requiring relatively heavy investment in equipment. An attempt to prepare a milk substitute from the beans has proved to be technically possible but not yet a commercially viable idea. The success of the soybean venture, it is evident, is dependent on solving the processing and marketing problems of the crop.

The Centre distributes on a very limited scale fruit and vegetable seeds to the local farmers at cost. The Kendro site includes a dug reservoir which supplies some irrigation water for the rice field. It is stocked with fish and accommodates a flock of cross-bred ducks.

The Kendro's plans include subcentre-based agricultural extension into the villages along with its expanding health and education work. However, it reports problems in finding workers for this effort. Its attempt to recruit personnel for agricultural work, as related in Progress Report No. 5 is instructive and bears quoting here at length:

We advertised in several newspapers for an experienced, practical man to supervise farming work at our centre. 40 applicants arrived for interview. All but two were agriculture graduates (one with a double first class), and four had training abroad. Instead of a simple interview, we had a practical exam, followed by a written test, and finally a viva-voce.

In the practical exam, the candidates were asked to plant a coconut seedling and prepare a vegetable seed bed. Almost all were unsure of which tools they should use. Some made holes too big or too shallow for the seed coconuts. They then had

to identify a number of samples of seeds, fertilizer and
insecticide. Although with the exception of soybean, all
the items were in common use in Bangladesh (any "uneducated"
farmer would have got full marks), none of our candidates
scored more than 65%. Not one of them could recognize the
common insecticide Malathion. In the written test, the applicants were asked to say what was needed to improve agriculture
in Bangladesh. Remembering what they had been taught in
college, all gave the stock answer: mechanization. But
when, in the viva examination, they were asked about particular machines, it came to light that only one of them had
ever driven a tractor; none could repair one; some could
not distinguish between a tractor and a power tiller;
few had seen more than a couple of deep tubewells in their
life; none had any clear ideas regarding servicing and fuel
supply for machines in rural areas, or about the cost-effectiveness of these machines in comparison with traditional
methods.

We appointed the man who seemed least remote from the
realities of farming. He left us after a few weeks, saying
he couldn't stand working such long hours outside in the sun.[1]

Women's Vocational Training and Education

The educational program of the Kendro, as of December 1976, consists essentially of crafts training and literacy for about forty women at the Narikendro (Women's Centre). The rationale behind the women's program is to "strengthen their position in the home, give them
some respite from exploitation, and enable them to enlarge their spiritual, as well as economic contribution to the community." A graphic
description of the women's lot in the villages in a Kendro report
shows the urgent need for the effort towards social and economic
emancipation of rural women:

> We have admitted to our sickroom, in the last 18 months,
> 11 cases of attempted suicide by married women. Sociologi-
> cally, these cases are highly significant. They represent
> an uncounted number of village wives whose position drives
> them to despair.

> If she has a considerate husband and a fair mother-in-
> law, a wife in a Bangladesh village may be no worse off than
> a housewife anywhere. But her husband and in-laws can, if they
> wish, treat her as a free servant; in that case, she may find
> nobody to turn to. The dutiful wife is held up so much as an
> ideal that any woman who tries to resist the tyranny of her
> husband is likely to become an outcast. She can flee to her
> father's home, but her father will not welcome her: a woman

---

[1]Gonoshasthya Kendro, Progress Report No. 5, April 1975, p. 4.

separated from her husband is abhorred, irrespective of her reasons for leaving him, and brings disgrace on her parents. Trapped between the cruelty of her husband and the lashing tongue of society, many a wife finds no way out but death....

At the root of the weak position of women in our village society is their dependence on father or husband for their daily food. A degree of economic independence would greatly improve their lot. This is the thought behind our vocational training programme.[1]

In December 1976, about forty women from the neighboring villages were participants of vocational training and education at the women's Centre. Of these, eleven had been in training since the beginning of the program three years ago and have acquired skills in jute work, bamboo and reed crafts, and tailoring. They have not been able, however, to use their skills to launch independent enterprises of their own. Therefore they continue to work in the Centre earning a piece-rate wage for making handicrafts, which the Centre tries to market. Another twenty women joined the training in early 1976 and have so far completed the jute work skills (making jute bags, pot-hangers, mats and toys). They also work for the Centre and earn a small wage. Ten more women have started the training in November 1976.

The first group started with thirty participants, of whom about one-half survived long enough to acquire a sufficient level of proficiency in the crafts. Only three of these trainees, besides the eleven working at the Centre, are able to supplement their family income by tailoring and making jute handicraft products. Some bamboo and reed products are probably made for use in the women's own households--this already being a traditional women's chore in the villages.

The women trainees of the Centre are from very poor families and about one-third are widowed or divorced. They are initially paid Tk 25 per month for the first six months to cover the transportation cost. After the initial stage, they are paid Tk 10 per month plus a wage based on pieces of work completed. Average earning comes to Tk 60 per month. All raw materials and equipment for the crafts work are provided by the Centre.

Marketing of the Centre's products is done by supplying small orders from Dacca and abroad. Some jute handicrafts have been shipped to Canada and Holland. Enquiries have been received from the United States, France, and England. In addition to these sales, the tailoring needs of the Kendro (staff clothing, draperies, etc.) are also met by the Centre.

The Centre is under the direction of one of the senior paramedics, who is assisted by two women specially trained in the crafts from a crafts centre in Dacca.

---

[1]Ibid., p. 6.

The Kendro has plans to broaden the educational effort by adding
general functional education and children's and youth's educational
programs appropriate for the rural areas. All of the trainees for the
crafts are given a literacy course based on the functional educational
materials used by Bangladesh Rural Advancement Committee (BRAC). An
experimental primary level school for children and youth is expected
to be opened in early 1977 at the Kendro. The school will be based on
a curriculum that will combine the usual primary education objectives,
social development, and useful rural skills. It is expected to serve
as a prototype for rural primary schools.[1] Functional education programs combining literacy and the creation of critical consciousness
about the rural situation is also expected to be initiated around the
subcenter program of health and other services.

Workshop.

A workshop managed by a mechanical engineer (and assisted by a
British VSO volunteer, who is a former steel fabricator, and two
apprentices) has been opened in late 1976. The workshop is expected
to serve the general aims of vocational training for rural youths, to
improve rural technologies, and to contribute towards making the project self-sufficient. How exactly these aims are to be served, what
specific activities the workshop and its staff should engage in, and
what personnel and facilities are needed remain to be fully worked out.
The shop and its staff at the moment are occupied with the slow and
laborious task of fabricating a steel surgery table with simple hand
tools. This will serve the immediate need of the Kendro and may
serve as a prototype for operating tables in the country's other
medical facilities--thus replacing expensive imported equipment and
creating employment for a certain number of metal workers. Another
VSO Volunteer with experience in appropriate technologies for rural
Africa is expected to join the workshop in 1977.[2]

The Jamalpur Project

In the wake of severe flooding and famine condition in parts of
Bangladesh, UNICEF launched in February 1975 a project to help destitute women in the Jamalpur subdivision of Mymensingh district (120

---

[1]We have been informed in September 1977 that the school had been
already in operation with eight teachers and 110 children, aged 4-12,
from the poorest families in the nearby villages.

[2]In a communication to the writer on September 23, 1977 the
Project Director observed:

[Hand-fabrication of OT tables] is laborious to a person who
thinks of production only as capital-intensive factories. But
each OT table produced incorporates the training of apprentices
and the foreign exchange earnings you note. We have produced 25
such tables and have orders for another 100.... OT tables at one
level can be seen to serve the rural people and therefore to be
"rural technology." At another level, the training village boys
and girls receive in such projects can be applied to more directly
"rural" technology (e.g., making agricultural implements).

miles northwest of Dacca) by employing them in the production of new drought-resistant crops while paying them in kind with wheat from the World Food Program. A family planning and child care program was also started for the women, and in this effort Gonoshasthya Kendro's assistance was sought.

The Kendro set up tubectomy and vasectomy services in Jamalpur, using paramedics under a physician's supervision. Motivation and location of clients were performed by the thana family planning staff of the government and village dais. In a period of six months (March-September, 1975), 634 tubal ligations were performed (110 among a total of over 800 women in the project and 534 among their relatives and neighbors). Oral pill distribution among the women and their relatives was added to the project in October 1975.

After the harvesting of the crops in June, the women became participants in a functional education program conducted with the help of Bangladesh Rural Advancement Committee (BRAC). Along with the educational program, a child care program was started to take care of the children when their mothers were in the classroom.

A similar but expanded "food-for-food" program was initiated again in January 1976 with 18,000 women in twenty-seven sites. The family planning service assisted by the Kendro spread to five thanas in the subdivision. Clientele as of October 1976 (since January 1976) were:

Tubal ligation	203
Vasectomy	96
IUD	488
Oral pill	953
Foam	138
Menstrual regulation	11
	1,889

The Kendro paramedics provided clinical services in five centers while motivation, distribution of contraceptives, and follow-up were accomplished by government family planning staff.

Child care service, also assisted by the Kendro, was provided in thirty-four locations for under-five children and mothers. In seven of these centers government Family Welfare Visitors (FWV) provided basic health care, including treatment of such complaints as diarrhea and fever (in contrast to normal government insistence on a qualified physician for all treatments and prescriptions), and immunization under the supervision of Kendro paramedics. The paramedics also helped train the FWVs (who already had eighteen months of mother and child health care training).

The project plans calls for an expansion, with Kendro assistance, of the approach using FWVs for mother and child care including treatment of common diseases through the child care centers. The Kendro is also looking into the prospect of reviving the traditional services of dais and upgrading them into village-based auxiliaries for health care, nutrition, family planning, and mother and child health services. Sixty such <u>dais</u> are being trained by the Kendro for this purpose.

The functional education components, agricultural demonstration work, as well as various small-scale joint economic ventures by women, are also planned to be expanded or added to the project.

In the Jamalpur project, the Kendro has become involved in a relatively broad-range effort to improve the socioeconomic condition of a disadvantaged group of people. The Kendro's own contribution is confined to health, family planning, child care, and nutrition. It has, however, the opportunity here to test and implement its own health care approach in a new setting and in close collaboration with government health and family planning services. There is also an opportunity to explore the interaction and forge the links between health and family planning efforts and other development activities, while concentrating on the needs of a specially deprived group of people. The prospect, however, for using Jamalpur as a testing ground is uncertain through no fault of the Kendro or its approach.[1] The problem lies in the economic feasibility of the total project and the logistical and other difficulties in dealing with multiple national and international bureaucratic structures. More information about the Jamalpur Project is given in Appendix I.

-----

[1]We have been informed in September 1977 that the project in Jamalpur had been terminated and the activities had been shifted to Bhatsala union in the neighboring Sherpur thana. An "integrated health and rural development programme" with fourteen trained and six trainee paramedics had been initiated in the new location.

CHAPTER 4

IMPACT OF

PROJECT ACTIVITIES

The workers of Gonoshasthya Kendro felt that collecting and recording benchmark socioeconomic data, compiling adequate service statistics, and measuring the results of effort were serious distractions from the main task of providing services to the people. There were urgent needs to be met, and all of the energies and resources of the program should be applied directly to meeting these needs. However, the managers of the program now see that certain information about the clientele and the results of program efforts need to be systematically collected and recorded; otherwise it is not possible to know if the right services are being provided or if there are other more efficient ways of delivering the services. The Kendro intends to give more attention to the recording of benchmark data and the evaluation of results. In the meantime, however, this case study has to rely on the fragmentary information available from the program and the judgment of the writer after making a few short field visits and talking with the program personnel.

The impact of the Kendro's activities may be best discussed in relation to the major program efforts--curative health care, preventive health care and nutrition, family planning, education and training, and the creation of an institutional structure for health care and rural development.

Curative Health Care

Curative care, of necessity, is a major element of the program and is provided through the twice-a-week clinic at the Kendro and weekly clinics at the subcenter for outpatients as well as through home visits by paramedics.

In the weekly clinics held in five different locations, drugs and medical advice were given to 48,786 patients from April 1975 to April 1976. During their appointed rounds in the villages the paramedics also treated patients or referred them to the clinics. It is estimated that paramedics home treatments took care of another 6,000 patients in the same year. Approximately 10 percent of the visits resulted in prescription of drugs or referral to the clinic. The total number of homes visited by paramedics in a year is estimated to be 60,000 including repeat visits. The total number of times villagers benefited from the curative services in one year, therefore, was about 55,000.

How intensive and adequate is this curative service coverage? Analysis of patients in terms of age, sex, economic status, and place of residence is not available. After separate discussions with the paramedics and the directors of the program the writer believes that age, sex, and

economic status are not important factors in acceptance of the clinical
services of the Kendro. The low charge for outpatients, especially when
it is compared to the costs for any available alternative, makes it possible for most rural families to take advantage of the service. The program personnel pointed out, however, that distance of the village from
the location of the weekly clinics is the most important factor in determining the intensity of coverage of the villages. Program personnel agree
that most of the patients in the clinics are from villages within a radius
of one and a half miles of the clinic site. The farther away the village,
the fewer is the number of those attending clinics.

A rough measurement of the adequacy of curative coverage may be
derived from a comparison of the number of times curative service is
actually provided with the number of times such service is really
needed by a given population. According to Gonoshasthya Kendro and
other projects in Bangladesh (such as BRAC), the average number of visits
to the clinic for treatment of illness by an insured individual   (when
additional payment for the visit is negligible and the distance to the
clinic is not a barrier) is three times in a year. On this basis, the
100,000 people served by the Kendro should receive medical treatment
300,000 times instead of 55,000 times. This quantitative comparison
is not wholly appropriate, because this says nothing about the quality
of the service and it should not be viewed as an advocacy for quantitative target setting. But these figures suggest the dimension of   the
needs as it relates to the level of the current efforts.

It appears that the present approach to curative services cannot
make them adequately accessible to the large number of villagers   in
the area. This amounts to a once-a-week fixed location clinic per union
(when the plan is fully implemented) supplemented by once-a-month home
visits by paramedics. A subcenter with a clinic in each union will provide for most of the population within a mile and a half radius, but
the clinic should be held daily rather than once a week and it needs to
be supplemented by assigning health workers readily available for
follow-up and other related services (such as preventive health care
and family planning).[1] The problem of making the services more generally accessible is under examination by the Kendro and is discussed
below.

Preventive Health Care

Preventive health care is provided in contacts with villagers at
the clinic and during home visits. The main emphasis, as noted earlier,
is on inoculation and vaccination. Adequate records of home visits and
people covered by preventive measures are not readily available.   A
generous estimate is that about 60,000 family visits are made in a year
(fifteen individual paramedics or teams making village rounds 200 days

---

[1]We are informed that there is always one paramedic on emergency
duty in each subcenter twenty-four hours a day, seven days-a-week, and
that a doctor is always on emergency call at the Kendro.

a year and visiting twenty families a day). This number of visits may be compared to the present target of the Kendro to visit each of the 20,000 families in the project area at least once a month, or 240,000 visits a year. In practice about fifty villages, in which reside most of the families enrolled in the insurance program and the family planning clients, receive more frequent and regular visits from the paramedics than the other villages.

BCG tuberculosis inoculation for the under-15 population and triple antigen for children have been initiated very recently (late 1976), but significant coverage is yet to be achieved. The Kendro estimates that 70 percent of the population in the project area have received primary smallpox vaccination either from the Kendro or from the public health service that also provides smallpox vaccination.

The actual impact on disease prevention and general health conditions is impossible to gauge without gathering pertinent data at two different times. Similarly, without at least two surveys of a population sample at a reasonable interval, no definite assessment of the nutrition situation can be made.

However, the Kendro personnel believe that incidence of diarrhea and scabies was significantly less visible in the villages served intensively by the Kendro than in other rural areas of Bangladesh. No quantitative measures were available, but the difference was substantial enough to convince the members of a joint review team of doctors examining the rural health service in the country.

To what extent improvement in the treatment of these two most common diseases is attributable to the efforts of the Kendro is not at all clear. Although the paramedics offer advice about sanitation, hygiene, and pure water during village visits, total time and effort devoted to this task is small. It is not accompanied by a systematic program to improve the supply of pure water or propagate the use of sanitary latrines. Therefore it is not likely that the basic conditions causing diarrea and skin infection have changed much. The explanation of the Kendro workers is that the people have learned how to deal with these diseases themselves from their contacts with the clinics and the paramedics. For instance, the traditional handling of diarrea patients was to deprive them of fluid and food, a stricture that only caused further aggravation, especially when the patients also suffered from malnutrition. The villagers found that treating simple diarrhea cases in just the opposite way was effective, and they probably began to treat and care for many cases themselves; hence the reduction in the visible incidences of diarrhea. When the people can handle a disease themselves, it is no longer a problem to be brought to the attention of outsiders. Similarly, the efficacy of soap and water and simple cleanliness practices in treating and preventing skin infection probably also impressed the villagers.

The Kendro workers also report a greater interest than before in growing leaf vegetables, legumes, fruits, and poultry, as a result of the demonstration in the Kendro and the distribution of seeds and seedlings.

Data, however, are not available on the extent of increase in such cultivation or any consequent change in dietary habits.

As in the case of curative services, the question that exercises the minds of the Kendro directors is this: Even if the target of visiting each family once a month by a paramedic is achieved and the subcentre clinics are located within walking distance of each village, will these gains suffice in providing adequate preventive health care for the people of the area?

Accurate data are not available on mortality, morbidity, and malnutrition of the total population, nor of special groups such as children and mothers. Furthermore the factors affecting these conditions, such as supply of pure water, use of latrines, distribution of the calorie and protein content of the diet among the population, are not fully known. Nevertheless no one will deny that large measures of improvement are needed on all these counts. The Kendro workers agree that the required improvements will not be possible with the present level and quality of contacts between the Kendro workers and the area population and the present strategy of service delivery. The potential alternatives and strategy issues that are being explored by the Kendro are discussed elsewhere in this report.

Family Planning Services

As stated earlier, approximately 12 percent of fertile couples in the project area were protected by contraceptive or permanent birth control measures at the end of 1976. Vital statistics of the villages served by the project do not exist, and the Kendro has made no systematic effort to collect such statistics. It is therefore not possible to judge accurately how many births have been prevented by the Kendro's efforts and what the impact has been on the population growth rate, if one takes into account the results of health care efforts as well as those of family planning.

The importance of the Kendro efforts in family planning, however, lies as much in the quantitative coverage of the population with birth control measures as in any future innovative approaches to the delivery of the family planning service. The important features of the Kendro family planning program, as noted in passing elsewhere, are manifestly as follows:

a. The use of specially selected and trained female paramedics for various surgical procedures such as tubectomy, menstrual regulation, and abortion, usually performed elsewhere by male medical doctors.

b. Application of a unified approach to health care and family planning that also permits one system of delivery and contact for the total range of family planning services--clinical and surgical services, selection of candidates for different contraceptive methods, advising on appropriate family planning methods in individual circumstances, follow-up for side effects,

use of new methods such as long-lasting injections requiring
careful preselection and follow-up, and related health services affecting family planning practices (such as, child-care,
care of pregnant and lactating mothers, health and nutrition
measures preparatory to birth control action.)

c. An institutional structure (yet at an early stage of develop-
    ment) that would permit participation of the beneficiary pop-
    ulation in the management of the health and family planning
    program, keep costs at an affordable level and help mobilize
    local resources, and increase the long range effectiveness
    and viability of the family planning program by making it
    an integral part of a broader rural development effort in the
    area.

These features have a direct bearing on the current debates about the
effectiveness of the national family planning program. The lessons of the
Kendro for the national program are discussed later.

Education and Training

A functional education program for rural residents and efforts to
improve the relevance and effectiveness of primary level education for
rural children and youth are still at an early exploratory stage and,
therefore, the question of an impact of these efforts has not arisen.

The women's vocational training efforts have been continuing for about
three years, but so far they have benefited directly less than fifty women.
The small number of women affected by the program, in spite of the relatively intensive effort involved and the fact that many who have acquired
the skills have failed to cut themselves loose from the apron strings of
the Kendro, indicates that a viable approach to providing women with usable
earning skills is yet to be found.[1] We come back to this question in the
concluding section of this report.

Well-deserved claim of achievement can be made in the training of the
paramedics. The training effort has not only supplied the necessary workers for carrying out the health care and family planning program of the

---

[1]On this point the Project Director's comment is as follows:

We accept your criticisms of our vocational training programme,
but the fault is not entirely ours. Over the past few years, many
voluntary agencies have started jute handicrafts groups, and the
market is somewhat saturated by now. We are therefore changing to
an emphasis on carpentry, bamboo and fishing nets, and hope that
next year, 1385 [of the Bengali calendar], 150 women will undergo
a one-year training at GK [the Kendro] and the subcentres. Moreover, we are organising "mother's clubs"--cooperatives within which
women will organise their production when back in the villages. Once
established, these groups will extend FP and agricultural innovations
to their villages as well as manufacture craft products.

Kendro, but it has also demonstrated a new and potentially   effective
alternative model for health and family planning that may be economically more affordable and more effective than the existing national
approach. The lessons of the project for staff training and personnel
utilization for the national health and family planning programs   are
discussed later.

Institutional Structure

Up to late 1976, it appears that the project has been preoccupied
with establishing a geographical base and devising a   technically
feasible form of delivering essential services in the   area of   basic
health care and family planning.

It is not that the leaders of the project have remained oblivious
to such issues as participation of the beneficiary population in the
management of the project and eventual local self-management without
the dominant role's being taken by an "outside" voluntary organization.
They are also interested in developing an institutional model that can
be replicated and will benefit from the experience and lessons of the
project, and incorporate the health and family planning activities into
an institutional framework for a multifaceted local rural   development
program. However, these questions have not yet received systematic and
sustained attention.

As noted in the next section, the project has paid some attention
to the problem of financial self-sufficiency.   There is a deliberate
effort to become gradually independent of foreign philanthropic assistance, to mobilize local and national resources, and to make the beneficiaries pay as large a share of the costs as possible, the insurance program (discussed in the next section) and the fees for the services rendered are intended utlimately to meet all of the recurring
costs of the health care and family planning activities. At present
with a very incomplete insurance program, close to 50 percent of the
recurring cost of the health care service is met by the insurance and
service fees.

The introduction of the insurance program has required the opening
of dialogue between the project people and individual village communities. Further expansion of the insurance program and greater acceptability of the program will undoubtedly require a more systematic communication with the beneficiary communities.

The importance of involvement of the beneficiary population in the
project and the fact that various elements of rural transformation are
intimately related to each other were brought home forcefully by the
tragic murder of a promising young male paramedic by vested interest
groups in a village.   A coalition of local landowners, moneylenders,
and quack doctors saw a threat to their exploitative priveleges   in
the Kendro activities which might mobilize the poor majority of the village
in their self-help efforts. The situation came to a head when the Kendro
obtained government permission to establish a subcenter on some abandoned

properties that had been illegally occupied by the influential families in the village.   This incident was a message to the project   leaders that even such a seemingly innocent activity as providing health care to the needy affected vested interests in the village, that making effective health care and family planning services available to the rural people was linked to a larger process of social transformation,   and that there would be no substitute for organizing the beneficiary population for self-help and a larger voice in their own affairs.

Heightened awareness of the need for a new institutional structure is reflected in the emphasis on plans for (a) creating a new tier of village-based auxiliaries to function under the supervision of the paramedics and other supervisory workers, (b) making the services more accessible to the villages through the subcenters and the village-based auxiliaries, (c) permitting systematic community involvement in planning and management of project activities through village and subcenter representative committees, and (d) establishing links with other local development programs through the representative committees.

CHAPTER 5

FINANCES AND COSTS

Resources and Budgets

Total financial resources available to the project and the major
items of capital and recurrent expenditures are shown in tables A, B,
and C.

Between July 1973 and April 1976, the total financial receipts of
the project amounted to about Tk 5.5 million,[1] of which approximately
Tk 4.8 million was a donation from external philanthropic bodies. Less
than Tk 100,000 came from local donations. The remaining amount was
derived from service charges and other receipts from the project activities (Table A). The major external donors were Oxfam-UK, Oxfam-Canada,
NOVIB of Holland, Canadian International Development Agency (CIDA), and
Terre des Hommes,a Catholic relief agency. Smaller grants were made by
the Ford Foundation, UNICEF, and Unitary Services of Canada.

A major part of the project resources during its initial years was
spent on capital items. The total capital expenditures during three years
up to April, 1976 was Tk 2.9 million, or about 53 percent of the total
available financial resources. Purchase of thirty-five acres of land
where the Kendro and its agricultural projects are sited cost about Tk
523,000. Construction of clinic and emergency hospitalization facilities,
offices, and dormitories, cost Tk 1.8 million. Advance payments and
security deposits towards construction undertaken in the following financial
year amounted to Tk 457,000. Furniture, equipment and assistance for subcenter facilities amounted to less than Tk 100,000 (Table B).

The above figures do not fully account for the total capital assets of
the project, which include ten acres of land received as donation from a
local landowner and on which the original facilities of the Kendro stand.
Other donated capital items are a well-equipped mobile clinic installed
in a motorized van, an ambulance car, and two other motor vehicles.

The yearly recurring budgets of the project for the three years until
April, 1976 were Tk 285,000, Tk 324,000 and Tk 359,000 respectively. The
most important recurring item is the staff salaries and wages which
accounted for 56, 43 and 51 percent of the total recurring expenditures
in the same three years. Other relatively large expenditure items are
fuel and vehicle maintenance, food service (although a large part of this

---

[1]US$1 = Approximately Tk 15 in December 1976.

cost is recovered from the staff), and drugs. It should be noted that the drug
costs shown in the table do not represent the full value of the drugs used in
the project, because many of the drugs are supplied to the project at a discount
or bulk-purchase price by UNICEF, and a substantial amount of drugs is received
free of cost from various sources, as are the contraceptives. As Table A shows,
direct costs for various program activities other than the personnel costs are
small.

Health Insurance Scheme

A health insurance program has been introduced in the project with the goal
of covering all or most of the recurring costs of the health and family planning
activities of the project. Under the insurance scheme, a monthly fee of Tk 2.00
per rural household entitles all members of the household to outpatient treatment in weekly clinics, emergency treatment in the Kendro or subcenter clinics
at any time, inoculations, and family planning service. Emergency hospitalization is also provided at a fixed low charge (Tk 5 admission and Tk 1 per day
without food which is supplied by the patient's family). Uninsured patients
are charged Tk 2.50 per visit to the clinic, and charges based on actual costs
are made to them for emergency care or hospitalization. For family planning
supplies and clinical and surgical services small charges are made to all clients.

In principle the insurance scheme is supposed to be introduced in a village
when at least 50 percent of the village families enroll as members. In practice,
it has not been possible to follow this principle. In mid-1975, for   example,
3,308 families from seventy-eight villages were listed as members of the insurance
program. This number represented less than 15 percent of the total families in
the project area and under 30 percent of the total families in the same villages
where the members live. In April 1974 the number of insured families was 2,279,
and in late 1976 the estimated number was 3,500 families. These numbers, however, include families who have not paid their monthly dues regularly and are in
arrears for several months. (Families delinquent in paying dues cannot claim any
service from the project unless all dues are cleared.) The number of families
with membership in good standing and dues paid up was estimated to be only about
1,000 in late 1976.

As Table C shows, the receipts from the insurance charges have been only
about one-half of the receipts from other health-related charges, such as clinic
fees, in-patient charges, and pathology fees.

The director of the project wrote in a report about the project:

The most crucial and time-consuming task in connection with
the insurance scheme is selling it to the villagers. Where the
scheme has been introduced, several weeks of house-to-house visits by teams of volunteers were necessary to explain the scheme
and convince the village folk of its advantages.[1]

----

[1]Zafrullah Chowdhury, "The Mother and Child in Bangladesh--A View from the
People's Health Centre," Assignment Children, UNICEF No. 33, Jan.-March 1976.

It is an equally difficult task to keep families within the scheme after they
enroll in it.

The task continues to convince villagers why they should keep paying   a
monthly fee, particularly when they are not even sick and not receiving   any
medical service from the project. However, the messages of the project workers to the villagers will carry conviction only if the services are available
and accessible to the villagers when and where they are needed. The shortcomings of the present pattern of services and some remedial measures under
consideration have been noted earlier. It is clear that the insurance program can expand significantly and make a substantial contribution to financial self-sufficiency of the health and family planning components of the project only if the measures taken assure greater accessibility of the services.

The current (noncapital) costs of the project for the three years reported are proportionately lower than the government expenditures for health and
family planning. Assuming all 100,000 population of the project area as the
beneficiaries of the project, per capita annual cost was Tk 2.8 in 1973-74,
Tk 3.4 in 1974-75, and Tk 3.6 in 1975-76. The total per capita government
health and family planning expenditure in 1975-76 was Tk 10 of which Tk 7
could be considered as recurring expenditure.[1]

It should be noted that the per capita project costs shown above covered
other project activities besides health and family planning, but costs for
these other activities were very small. The quality and quantity of services
offered to the population were far from even, the families living near   the
Kendro and the clinic sites enjoying the bulk of the benefit. On the other
hand, about 70 percent of all government recurrent health expenditures (excluding family planning and malaria control costs which are shown in the development budget) is spent on hospitals located in towns, which have less
than 10 percent of the population of the country,[2] rather than on preventive
and domiciliary health care for the rural population.

---

[1]"The total budget estimates for 1975-76 for the Ministry of Health,
Population Control and Family Planning, on both the revenue and development accounts, amount to Tk.746 million. Of that total one-third is recorded as recurrent (revenue) expenditure and two-thirds development.
However, almost half the development total goes to the population   and
malaria control programmes, which might more appropriately be considered
as recurrent expenditures." Oscar Gish, "The Development of Health Services in Bangladesh," Institute of Development Studies, University of Sussex, February 1976, p. 18.

[2]Oscar Gish, ibid., p. 23-24.

TABLE A

Recurring Expenditures of Savar Project
(July 1, 1973 to April 14, 1976)

Items	Year ending 30 June 1974	1 July 1974 to 14 April 1975	(Taka) Year ending 14 April 1976
Salaries	145 928.70	139 040.80)	
Wages	537.75	96.56)	
Support of Volunteers	12 001.54	9 269.66)	181 699.00
Staff Food Service	28 918.19	41 908.94)	
Fuel	12 824.80	17 606.30)	
Vehicle Maintenance	5 704.34	9 979.37)	20 281.00
Conveyance	2 063.74	2 011.22)	
Carriage and Cartage	2 510.29	----	
Drugs	24 284.74	38 768.06	120 473.00
Family Planning Supplies	2 905.08	3 768.55	N.A.
Agricultural Materials	8 520.54	35 960.27	N.A.
Education & Training Supplies	550.24	320.00	N.A.
Building & Equipment Maintenance	553.70	474.40	7 621.00
Utilities	9 740.88	3 699.85	6 403.00
Stationery & Printing	6 026.17	7 713.51	21 170.00
Postage & Telegrams	1 074.89	1 632.04	1 064.00
Telephone	2 510.29	1 342.05	N.A.
Books and Magazines	140.40	5.00	N.A.
Loan & Advances to Staff	15 800.00	2 000.00	N.A.
Sundry	2 504.90	8 009.80	N.A.
TOTAL	285 101.18	323 603.38	358 711.00*

*Excluding cost of vaccines and contraceptives.

Source: Gonoshasthya Kendro data.

TABLE B

Capital Expenditures of Savar Project
(1 July 1973 to 14 April 1976)

(Taka)

Items	Year ending 30 June 1974	1 July 1974 to 14 April 1975	Year ending 14 April 1976 (provisional)
Land	54 646.00	468 839.28	
Construction	730 046.57	282 355.48	809 261.29
Temporary Buildings	10 000.00		
Equipment	743.95	11 482.00	2 114.00
Furniture	2 990.25	3 368.50	2 184.75
Support for Subcentre Construction		724.80	41 688.00
Advance and Security Deposit		17 644.00	439 217.00
TOTAL	798 426.77	784 414.06	1 294 465.04

Source: Gonoshasthya Kendro data.

TABLE C

Total Financial Receipts of Savar Project
(1 July 1973 to 14 April 1976)

(Taka)

Items	Year ending 30 June 1974	1 July 1974 to 14 April 1975	Year ending 14 April 1976 (provisional)
Opening balance	200 375.86	215 439.54	861 889.83
External donation	927 196.27	1 556 950.04)	1 000 000.00
Local donation	38 571.00	28 268.10)	
Health insurance	29 981.00	28 937.25)	112 067.00
Clinic charges	40 134.47	44 512.65)	
Pathology charges	4 722.00	3 624.00	7 346.00
Hospital charges	6 124.50	12 582.30	22 341.00
Family planning charges	652.58	1 489.37	10 440.00
Other receipts	60 070.05	80 367.70	200 000.00
TOTAL	1 307 827.73	1 972 170.95	2 214 000.00

Source: Gonoshasthya Kendro data.

CHAPTER 6

CONCLUSIONS AND LESSONS

What do the experiences of the Savar Project signify about the key issues that have originally prompted this and other case studies? By key issues   we refer particularly to the integration of program efforts, community involvement, the educational processes, outreach to the poorest and most disadvantaged,   and the role of the voluntary organizations and their small-scale programs. We turn next to these questions and the lessons that the Savar Project holds for programs designed to improve the standard and quality of life of rural families.

Integration

In contrast to the national pattern, the project has integrated curative medical service, preventive health care, and family planning.   Even with its limited geographic   and population coverage the project provides ample justification for a combined effort against the fragmented approach of the national health and family planning programs. It obviously would not make   sense   for the Savar Project to recruit, train, and post three separate groups   of workers, three administrative and supervisory hierarchies, and three sets of physical facilities for treatment of diseases, prevention of diseases, and   family planning services. The integrated approach is manifestly the right solution, not only in terms of costs to the project and to the community,   but also in the efficient use of both the management personnel and the   field   level   workers. Equally important are the creation of rapport between the project workers and the beneficiary population, and an effective handling of the various needs which may fall between the stools in a three-way separation of responsibilities.

Legitimate questions arise about how far integration can go and what organizational and operational form the integrated approach should take.   There are other problems besides health and family planning, the solutions of which are important by themselves for improving rural welfare, but which also   affect in crucial ways the performance of the health and family planning services. How many of these other vital problem areas can be tackled by the same organization which has chosen to engage itself in one cluster of activities?   What are the alternatives?

Obviously the Savar Project cannot supplant the local government structure or assume responsibilities for all aspects of rural development in the project area. What it can do is to coordinate its own activities with those of other agencies, both governmental and private, that may be active in different aspects

of rural development. It can offer support and reinforcement to all these activities and seek the same for its own efforts; it can also take initiative in areas
of urgent need, especially when no one else is doing anything about these needs.

However, the local government structure is particularly weak in the project
area, and its role in development activities is very limited. Other private and
voluntary programs focusing on rural welfare are nonexistent in the project area.
There are no institutional mechanisms in the thana for overall development planning and implementation. There is therefore a great incentive in the Kendro to
venture forth into new and different development activities. So far, however,
these activities in agriculture, vocational training, education, and rural
technology have been only of an exploratory nature.

The establishment of the health and family planning program--developing a
viable service delivery approach; mobilizing resources; recruiting, training,
and supervising personnel; running the daily operations; and expanding territorial and population coverage--have kept the project leadership fully occupied.
Additional activities about which the project leaders have little direct experience and technical knowledge--as they do in health and family planning--would
certainly put a prohibitively heavy burden on management capacity, unless they
were to attract some new top-level workers with special background in the new
fields and to develop new leadership from the ranks.

As it stands now, the project is attempting to consolidate its gains in
health and family planning by exploring new measures to improve accessibility
and coverage of the services, achieving greater financial self-sufficiency,
and increasing meaningful community involvement. In the areas of agriculture,
education, and vocational training the future direction and pace of development
are still to be worked out. Perhaps more rapid progress has to await the implementation of the new measures in health and family planning before other development activities, emanating from it, can be effectively launched.

Community Participation

It is clear that the communities of the beneficiary population have played
more the role of passive recipients of services than of active participants in
the project. There are two distinguishable identities of the project: those
who reside in the Kendro, for the most part not native to the local villages,
who are sophisticated educated people not commonly residents of rural areas;
and the beneficiary villagers who queue up at the clinic or listen deferentially
to the paramedic visiting the village.[1] Communication between the project people
and the rural people has been on an individual or family basis rather than as a
dialogue with and within communities and groups in the villages.[2] The project
goals, the delivery approach, and the priorities are essentially those of the
project management, although undoubtedly some feedback has affected the percep-

---

[1]According to the Project Director, most of the staff (particularly the
paramedics) come from the villages, though they may not be from Savar villages.

[2]The Project Director notes that there is a deliberate effort to use the
channels of individuals and families. Community organizations such as cooperatives (e.g., the Comilla cooperatives in Bangladesh) "is usually a shorthand
for further consolidation of the power of rural elite--something GK does not want
to be party to."

tion of the project personnel.   There has been little or no systematic effort
to educate and inform the people about project goals, priorities, and service
components or to seek the people's ideas and views on them.   In the management
structure of the project, there has been no formal community representation
either at the village level or at the project level. [The autonomous Board of
Trustees of the project consists of two representatives of the Bangladesh Medical Association and three eminent social workers. The Board of Governors, which
has executive responsibilities, comprises representatives of each of the major
categories of the project staff together with a representative of the Bangladesh Medical Association, the Red Cross, and the faculty and students of the
university located in the thana.]

   There are various dimensions of community participation: (a) organization
of services in the community, on a community basis, and making the services
widely and easily accessible; (b) contribution by the community to the operation and maintenance of the services; (c) participation of the community in
planning and management of the services within the community; (d) community
input in overall strategies, policies, and work-plan of the project transcending individual communities; (e) and the breakdown of factionalism and
interest conflicts in the community to achieve broad-based participation,
particularly of the disadvantaged groups.

   The project management is at present considering some definite steps, as
mentioned earlier, to make the services community-based, raise the level   of
contribution of the community members to the project through the insurance
scheme and in-kind donation of land and labor, and formalize community participation in planning and management of the village activities. Concrete measures are yet to be formulated on any other dimensions of community participation.

   There is an acute awareness in the project of factionalism and interest
conflicts in the villages and of the fact that a village is not really   one
communal entity. The interests of the larger landowners, moneylenders, petty
traders, and the quacks in the process of social and economic change are not
the same as those of the landless laborers, the minifarmers, the craftsmen,
and the destitute women. The perceptions of a "landed gentry" family and the
family of landless laborers are bound to be quite different about such matters
as the need and importance of family planning, the agency best fitted to offer
the service, the "outsiders" who come to help, and the commitments and "returns"
to which one might feel obligated by accepting the service.   The patron-client
relationship tying the poor in a permanent dependency on the rich, on the one
hand aligns the poor with factions among the influential families (often lock-
ed in power feuds among themselves), and, on the other hand, it stands in the
way of the poor's own collective self-help efforts.

   It is recognized in the project that the absence of a true community of
interests was at the root of the problem that led to the loss of life of   one
project worker and has been hindering the effective spread of the project   or
efficient functioning of the insurance scheme. A broad-based community participation, with more than token representation of the underprivileged majority
in any formal participatory mechanism, is seen as the best remedy for intra-
village conflicts affecting the project activities. But the operational steps
for implementing this idea are yet to be worked out and tested. This certainly
will not be an easy task--given the existence of entrenched vested interests
and the long tradition of rural exploitation.

Education

The Savar Project has demonstrated a method of training field workers for health and family planning services that is viable in terms of both need   and supply. It has also demonstrated that certain specialized tasks in health care and family planning that are usually performed only by people with high level professional qualifications can be handled adequately and beneficially by para-professional workers who can be trained cheaply and effectively.

The informal approach in training, relying heavily on a kind of apprent-iceship for developing the necessary skills and knowledge, appears to have work-ed well enough in the close-knit staff structure of the project. In order to use the training approach on a wider scale in a larger organization, it will be necessary, without sacrificing the main emphasis on supervised apprenticeship, to systematize training content and activities as well as make more methodical assessment of the learning achievements and competence level of the trainees.

The training procedure for the proposed village-base workers is still to be worked out. It will probably follow the same approach as for the paramedics with emphasis on supervised practice and apprenticeship; it will probably also require some quality-control measures for ensuring a certain level of competence, since the village auxiliaries will not be in continuous contact with physicians and experienced paramedics.

As noted earlier, the record of progress in adult functional education, basic education for children and youth, and vocational training has not been particularly noteworthy.

The concept of functional education is liable to be confused and misinter-preted. There is a persistent tendency to maintain a view of education that is represented by separate and independent programs and often equated with an adult literacy approach or the "kinds of things done in schools." While all these are clearly identifiable as "education" and clearly identifiable educational programs are undoubtedly needed, truly functional education must be seen as essential ele-ments and distinct activities of other development efforts.

In a program aimed at providing basic health care and family planning ser-vices, helping the poorest rural families improve their condition, raising women's economic status and social dignity, and creating local institutional structures, a vigorous and continuing educational effort is needed. Different kinds of necessary knowledge and information must be disseminated to various groups. The people must be encouraged to create and participate in the institution that carry out the de-velopment activities. Above all the people must be made aware of the roots   of their problems and approaches to tackling them. These are essential in functional education.

An educational approach needs to permeate all the activities of the program because all development activities can be educational in the truest and broadest sense. All the workers of the program must become educational workers as well. The educational dimensions of all program activities need to be identified and given recognition in the planning and implementational steps of the activities. The workers should be made aware of their educational role and encouraged to play that role.

An observer of the project comes out with the impression that the broad functional educational dimensions have not received full recognition--hence the casual approach to public health education, the lack of a systematic effort   to

promote environmental hygiene and sanitation, and the lack of emphasis--
until recently--on community dialogue on program approaches and activities. A major problem, of course, is that the health and family planning
components have yet to establish real community roots. Without roots in
the community, it is very difficult for a program to launch educational
efforts that address themselves directly to the various practical needs
of different rural groups. It is possible that, when the health and family
planning activities of the project become truly village-based, the project
workers become part of the community, and the community members become project workers (not only in health and family planning but also in hygiene,
nutrition, agricultural production, cottage industries, and social and
cultural aspects), a conducive environment will be created for initiating
and maintaining relevant educational efforts. As the project activities
become truly based in communities, the process of villager involvement in
planning, managing, and assisting these activities becomes itself the means
for "conscientization" and learning for all the village people.

Reaching the Poorest

There is no reason to believe that the medical services of the project, to the extent that they are physically accessible to the villagers,
discriminate against any particular socioeconomic group, since the cost
to the beneficiary is very small. However, a significant exception would
be the families or individuals in total destitution and those that are unable to come up even with the modest insurance charge or the clinic fee.
The proportion of families unable to take advantage of the project services because of extreme poverty is hard to estimate in the absence of
total coverage of individual villages by the project and the lack of pertinent socioeconomic data. But it may be as high as 25 percent in some
villages. In the present approach of Kendro-based services and partial
population coverage, there is no systematic way to deal with the destitute without making the project entirely a charitable service. However,
if the project services become village-based with subcentres, village
auxiliaries and village participation in management, it would be possible
to identify the destitute families and establish a procedure for dealing
with them without sacrificing the financial viability of the project. To
the extent that distance of the clinics limits access to services, as it
indeed does, the poorer families will continue to be affected more severely than the well-off for obvious reasons.

As for family planning, it is difficult to judge the discriminatory
effects of the services, because project service records do not reveal
socioeconomic background. Very little is known about the differences in
attitudes and perceptions about family planning of people in different
socioeconomic strata in the Savar area, or in other parts of rural Bangladesh. However, the insignificant service charges (including those for
clinical services) need not place an economic barrier even for families
living in extreme poverty.[1]

---

[1]We are informed that the project now (September 1977) records socioeconomic data about all the clients using a two-part registration form.

Project workers are amply aware that the most serious health problem is extreme poverty. It makes people easy victims of malnutrition, poor sanitation and hygiene, and communicable diseases. This realization is the main motivation behind the agricultural activities and vocational training for destitute women. However, the agricultural activities are merely demonstration plots at the Knedro and a limited distribution of seeds and saplings. The project management appears to be unsure about the role and function of the project in this area or to what extent the project can or should become involved in agricultural promotion. In short, it has not decided what the agricultural extension mechanism should be.

The women's vocational program, centered on handicrafts training, is handicapped by a number of factors. There is very little cash surplus in the rural economy to be spent on items other than food and other survival needs because most rural families are at a subsistence or sub-subsistence level and they are forced to meet their consumption needs as best as they can from their own production. The effective demand for nonagricultural consumption goods is met by the craftsmen and artisans already living in the villages and their earnings are often at a poverty level. Furthermore, there is considerable competition for the limited market in handicrafts in cities and abroad and it requires strong management and promotion efforts to enter that market. It must be conceded that a women's vocational program would provide sustenance or supplementary income to a very small number of rural families.

The most practical approach to help destitute families would be to assist them to engage in farming activities that are highly labor intensive and high yielding per unit of land (since these families would have very little land), such as vegetable and fruit growing, poultry and duck raising, and sericulture. These could be combined with selected processing and manufacturing when it is clear that a market exists or can be created. Probably the agricultural work in the project and vocational training could converge by focusing on the economic plight of the poorest families. The agricultural activities could concentrate on farming and related income-earning work that could be undertaken by families having access to only one acre or less land. There is also the possibility of instigating some group projects with leased plots, public land, or ponds and old river beds. The cooperation of other voluntary organizations in the country with more extensive experience in small-scale farming might well be sought. Opportunities should be found to make use of the government extension service personnel and resources and government projects in agriculture, such as the one existing in the area (Kashimpur). To the extent that the government is sympathetic and responsive, special collaborative projects might be undertaken jointly by the Kendro and one or more government agencies.

Lessons of the Savar Project

Transferability of Lessons

The Savar Project has demonstrated an eminently sensible approach to making basic health care and family planning service available to the rural people in a poor country. Undoubtedly individuals with goodwill and some leadership ability can initiate similar private projects to serve limited numbers of people in other areas of Bangladesh or in other developing countries. Indeed, such nongovernmental small-scale projects do exist elsewhere in Bangladesh and abroad. While these projects serve their clientele well (compared to government services), they are not the solution to the health crisis of the rural people in the

developing nations. Only a national and public effort, appropriately
organized and receptive to the help of private and voluntary organizations, can cope with the magnitude of the problem.

To what extent might the approach of the Savar Project be found
adoptable (or adaptable) by the national health and family planning
programs in Bangladesh? The essence of the Savar approach, it may
be recalled, is the integration of preventive, curative, and family
planning services; use of paraprofessionals for certain essential
tasks conventionally performed only by highly trained and paid professionals; sharing the management and the cost responsibility with
the beneficiary population; and a recognition of the interaction of
the health and family planning program with other aspects of rural development. The answer to the preceding question will depend on three
factors: (a) how the present problem of accessibility and coverage of
the Savar Project is solved; (b) how the entrenched interest groups
that would resist the adoption of a people-oriented health delivery
system are tackled; and (c) how genuine and stronggovernment commitment is to the spread of an effective people-oriented health delivery
system.

As noted earlier, despite the innovative approaches and the achievements of the Savar Project, it has fallen short of its goal of making its
services accessible to all the families in the project area.   Unless the
project succeeds in its present plan to extend the coverage and accessibility of its services, the case for accepting the project approach as a
model for the national program is considerably weakened, even though the
present project performance in service delivery may be far better   than
the national program. The raison d'etre for the project approach is making health care available to those who are deprived of it under   the
national program approach.

Two groups whose interests are directly threatened by the successful
spread of the project approach are, on the one hand, the quacks and practitioners of indigenous medicine and, on the other, the medical establishment of the country consisting of the professionally qualified physicians.
Comprehensive and effective coverage of an area by the project may put the
quacks and the indigenous healers out of business. unless they are brought
into the fold of the project and retrained to serve as paraprofessionals.
The opposition of this group can seriously undermine the spread and acceptance of the project in the villages; on the other hand, it can be
turned into a powerful ally and a source of much needed skilled manpower
willing to live and work in the village. The Savar Project has apparently
paid little attention to this question. It might well try using elements
of indigenous ayurvedic and hakimi medicine in developing the therapy repertoire of the paramedics and the village-based auxiliaries.

If there is a reorganization of the national health service along
the project line, the medical establishment stands to lose the privileges and advantages it enjoys from the present urban-based hospital-
centered health service with the monopolization of functions as in a
medieval trade guild. There is an elementary conflict between the effective spread of preventive health care and the personal interest of

the physician in a society where curative medicine is a commercial commodity. Yet, policymaking, planning, and management of the health service are controlled almost entirely by members of the medical establishment. The professional training and background of the physicians, their notion of standard and quality of medical service borrowed from industrialized countries, and their private self-interest make them as a group (of course there are notable exceptions) very unlikely champions of any basic change in the health delivery system. This, at least partially, explains the plan to establish separate government health facilities in Savar, instead of working out an arrangement with the Savar Project for adequate coverage of the population--when many other thanas in the country have no health facilities. It may explain the lack of positive response from the Ministry of Health to a proposal for trying out the Savar approach in collaboration with the government service in a neighboring thana.

The weakness of the health delivery system is used as the argument for the separate administration of the family planning program, so that the latter can be implemented with more efficiency and vigor than the health service. But can there be a strong family planning program in a rural area where the basic health service is weak or nonexistent? In any event, the separation has given rise to bureaucratic conflicts, rivalries, and lack of cooperation among the government personnel all along the hierarchy from the capital to the remote villages.

The resistance of the medical establishment to change and the problems of intragovernment conflicts can be overcome only if there is a strong and enduring commitment on the part of the government leaders and policymakers to an effective rural health care and family planning program. The commitment to change probably exists in a general way and at a rhetorical level, if the speeches and pronouncements of government leaders are any indication. However, the actual operational implications of this commitment into a program are by no means clear. Hence the anomaly between the rhetoric and the government plans and programs (see Appendix II). It is likely that the government leaders and policymakers are not well served by their advisors who mostly represent the medical establishment. The remedy is to balance the conventional wisdom of the medical establishment with the advice of individuals (with both medical and nonmedical background) who have demonstrated their independence of the establishment by giving it prominent roles in policy formulation and planning.

A Practical Strategy

The question that still remains to be answered is what practical steps can be taken to apply or benefit from the lessons of the small-scale programs in managing large-scale national programs. A practical approach is the one Gonoshasthya Kendro has proposed (but which has not so far elicited an endorsement by the government): a joint pilot project of the government and the voluntary organization in one or more specific locations to test and develop the modality of applying lessons of the small-scale private program to the national public program.

Once the viability of an approach is demonstrated in small-scale programs and some basic criteria of viability and feasibility (such as compatibility of objectives between the private program and a national program and the cost of structure) for a large-scale expansion appear likely to be met, a pilot phase can be initiated on the basis of close collaboration between the government and the voluntary organization in a limited area (preferably in a standard territorial unit of administration, such as a thana). The objective of such a venture would be two-fold: first, to test and develop the specific adaptations and modifications of the approach of the small program inevitably needed for a national and public program; and second, to work out the operational steps for moving beyond the pilot phase and to use the pilot phase for training and orientation of the government functionaries in anticipation of further expansion of the approach. The government obviously has to be enthusiastic about giving the pilot project and follow-up a fair trial and to reinforce policy with resource commitment. The voluntary organization, on its part, must be understanding of the problems of national programs and large bureaucracies and be willing to be flexible without sacrificing the essence of its own approach.

For external assistance agencies, including those which have originally assisted the voluntary programs, the joint pilot efforts offer the opportunity to support activities that are sufficiently well-defined, specific, and visible, yet which may have high multiplier effects and long-lasting impact beyond the limited confines of a small voluntary organization project.

Another activity that would help make the small programs more effective, as well as facilitate the transfer of lessons from these to national efforts, is the establishment of an arrangement with some commonality of focus so that the organizers of the small programs may jointly exchange ideas and lessons, analyze critically issues and approaches, review methods and techniques applied in solving operational problems, develop procedures of evaluation and maintenance of service and feedback data, and prepare common training materials. In addition, the organizations, together with government personnel and independent experts, may consider the lessons and implications of their projects for national programs and the best ways of transferring the lessons to larger programs. Since the small private programs tend to operate on shoestring budgets and are not inclined to spare resources for anything not directly within the scope of their own projects, the interorganizational effort would probably be easier to bring about with some external assistance if not with external prodding.

Important lessons from the Savar Project on specific aspects of program design and implementation relate to training field staff, encouraging integration, program financing, and enhancing community participation.

Preparation of field level workers

Recruiting, training, and utilizing field level workers who are affordable and skillful, and able to establish rapport and empathy with their rural clientele is a perennial problem in all rural programs involving health care and family planning. The Savar experience suggests a number of general principles for preparing and utilizing field level workers:

a. The high priority technical tasks to be performed by field workers have to be identified. These will include tasks that are really crucial to the attainment of the project goals and to meeting the needs of the people but are <u>not</u> now performed because of an insistence on professional standards or because professionally qualified people cannot be afforded by the nation and the communities concerned. Diagnosis and treatment of selected common disease symptoms, clinical services connected with family planning including tubectomy and vasectomy, selected pathological tests are examples of high priority tasks that are not made available to rural residents because they are ordinarily performed by inaccessible urban physicians.

b. The technical tasks have to be defined and broken down into essential concrete steps so that they may be taught easily to people with limited educational background. The definition and specificity of the tasks also help the field workers differentiate between what they can do and what they should not attempt. One important element in the training of the paramedical health worker is an ability to identify symptoms that he should not attempt to treat himself but should refer to a clinic or a physician.

c. The effective training approach for the field level workers is supervised practice and apprenticeship as opposed to highly structured classroom lectures and printed texts. The practical experience is not only the means of acquiring essential technical skills but also of understanding social dynamics, interpersonal relationship and the day-to-day logistics of a program--all equally as important as technical skills for a worker on the front line. The theoretical background, of course, can be filled in as and when appropriate.

d. Preparation of the field worker is not a one-shot affair. The field worker's efficiency and morale depend on the level of backstopping and support he has by way of technical guidance and supervision. He must be able to refer to the supervisor any problem he is not able to handle himself. In a sense, the field worker's training and preparation should never end.

e. An effective field worker, must be able to identify himself with the rural people, to understand the rural situation, and to commit himself enthusiastically to his mission. In the Savar Project people with a broad formal educational background but also possessing the right attitudes and interests have been able to acquire the skills for various technical tasks usually performed by trained physicians. High formal educational qualification, to the extent that it alienates individuals from the rural environment and creates a superiority complex among them, may actually be a disqualification for rural field workers. On similar grounds, female workers, even when their educational attainments are deficient and some inconveniences are faced regarding their mobility, will generally prove to be more effective when a large proportion of the program clientele is rural families, largely women, and children. In brief, the recruitment and screening procedures for field workers should give much greater weight to the candidate's understanding of and attitude toward rural life and rural people than to their educational qualifications.

f. The gap between the established professional standards and roles of the professional workers in the service agencies and the needs of the rural people is so wide that often the one tier of paraprofessional workers just below the professionals may not begin to bridge

it. It may take an additional tier of village-based auxiliaries
to bring the services to the villagers. In the Savar Project,
for instance, it has been found to be too costly and too inefficient a use of human resources to aim at an adequate coverage
of the population by the paramedics alone. The village-based
health auxiliary, a member of the village community who is supervised and guided by the paramedic, is seen as an essential link
in the chain that connects the project services and the people.

Approach to Integration

It is clear that various health-related elements of rural development
--in particular, preventive health care, including environmental sanitation
to prevent communicable diseases, curative services, family planning, nutritional advice and nutritional care of special groups such as infants and
mothers--belong to one package. The intimate interdependence among these
elements, the overlap and close links among the various activities, and the
need for efficient use of human resources at both the management level and
the field level make it economically sensible to put these elements within
one organizational structure. Another advantage as observed in Savar is
the opportunity the integrated approach offers to gain public confidence
and credibility when it responds appropriately to specific urgent needs
within the spectrum of health-related needs.

Beyond the package of health-related services, there is no standard
prescription of what other elements of rural development should be brought
under the fold of the same organization. They would depend on area needs,
what other agencies and organizations are doing, and what management capacity and material and human resources can be mobilized to launch the new
activities.

A voluntary organization is able to make its own decisions about which
elements of an overall rural development effort should be brought together
into the package of its programs and services. On the other hand, a government agency with its own organizational hierarchy extending both upward and
downward and functioning with rigidly defined jurisdictional limits does not
have the same freedom. Integrated approach in government programs is a
likely prospect, only if there is a great deal of genuine decentralization
of decisionmaking and if representative local government bodies are strong
enough to coordinate and guide the local units of the national government
agencies.

Financing the Rural Health Service

An important lesson of the Savar Project is that primary health care
and family planning services are economically affordable even in the poor
rural areas of Bangladesh. Accomplishment of this goal, however, would
require a major redeployment of public resources going into health and
related services from urban areas into rural areas.   These would include
such considerations as mobilizing resources from the beneficiary communities, sharing a part of the cost burden with the direct beneficiaries,
and taking steps to make efficient use of all health and family planning
manpower.

A theoretical model for rural health service operating costs based on the experience of the Savar Project and other similar projects in Bangladesh will show the magnitude of total operating costs for a comprehensive primary health service for a rural area with 100,000 people and an approach to meeting these costs.

Cost Model for Rural Health Service
(Per Capita Annual Recurring Costs)

Medicine   Taka

Tk 3.00 per prescription (average 3 prescriptions per year)   9.00

Manpower

	Taka
Doctor -- Tk 1,500 per month (one doctor per 40,000 people	0.45
Paramedic--Tk 400 per month (one per 4,000 people)	1.20
Village Auxiliary (part-time)	
Tk 50 per month, one per 500 people	1.20
Travel for paramedics and doctors--20% of salaries	0.33
Staff Training--20% of all salaries	0.57

                                                             3.75

                                        Total........ 12.75
                                                (US $0.84)

(This cost figure does not include the cost of contraceptives and clinical family planning services such as tubectomy and vasectomy but includes the costs for family planning staff assuming that the same staff provides both health care and family planning services. The staff training cost does not include the costs for formal professional training of a physician in the medical college.)

For an administrative unit of 100,000 population the annual recurring costs for the health service that offers complete primary health care and family planning services will be approximately Tk 1,275,000. An insurance scheme of the Savar type (premium of Tk 2.00 per household per month) would bring a revenue of Tk 480,000 per year from about 20,000 households in the area. A small service charge of Tk 1.00 per prescription for all clients will raise another Tk 300,000 per year (assuming an average of three prescriptions per head in a year). The total from the insurance fee and the service charge will therefore amount to Tk 780,000. It is unlikely that all the households will enroll in the insurance scheme. However, as noted before, roughly the same amount can be raised by imposing a reasonable fee for consultation and medicine on noninsured clients.

The balance of about Tk 500,000 can be met by diverting to the rural health service about 70 percent of the present noncapital expenditure of the government (i.e., Tk 5.00 out of a total of Tk 7.00 per capita)   on health and family planning. The government funds, of course, have to be used in a system that deploys the manpower along the line indicated   in the model.

The above theoretical model only indicates the rough magnitude of costs and resources for a rural health service and an approach to financing a primary health care system. Even relatively large margins of error in the estimate do not really affect the basic argument. The per capita cost figure does not include the costs of the whole administrative superstructure nor of the facilities and services above the thana which are needed to support the thana level operation. The assumption is that with a new order of priority in health care, about 30 percent,   or some such proportion, of the national recurring budget should be sufficient to maintain the superstructure.

It is obviously impractical to suggest that the government health and family planning funds should be immediately reallocated from   the town-based services and institutions to the rural areas and that a radical reorganization of the health and family planning services should be instituted at once. But it is very practical to have a clear view of the direction in which the national programs should move and to take determined first steps in that direction as soon as possible.

While closing down existing institutions and services by cutting their budgets may be painful and disruptive, it should be easier   to shift increasingly larger proportions of a growing government budget in each successive year to a reorganized rural health care system.   The government health and family planning budgets have grown substantially over the past five years and they are likely to continue to grow in future years. An urgent first step toward a new beginning would be critically to examine, reformulate, or halt and slow down as appropriate the new development projects in the area of health and family planning that may have already been approved but as yet are unimplemented or on the drawing board. To the extent that the present development plans fail to fit a new order of priority and a new strategy for national health care and family planning, they tie the hands of the government and upset the recurring budgets for many years in the future.

Since the cost of medicine may constitute as much as 70 percent of the operating cost of the rural health service, any measure that can be taken to reduce drug costs would make a major difference in the national health service costs. Production in the country of common drugs using a maximum amount of local ingredients, regulating the proliferation   of brands of the same generic drugs, pricing and marketing policies of the multinational drug manufacturers and similar other questions affecting the price and supply of common drugs merit close scrutiny by the government.

Enhancing Community Participation

The empty rhetoric expended on the subject of community participation can be translated into meaningful reality if specific forms of participation are seen as having a central role in achieving the goals of a development project. Equally important is development of goals that are conceived in a wider perspective of enhancing human capacities, human values, and the quality of human community life.

If the Savar Project in its initial phase had looked beyond meeting specific and highly visible needs in the health and family planning field and had paid more attention to working out a participatory process, probably some of the steps only now being explored could have been taken much earlier. The participatory process may sometimes impose a price in short term efficiency and speed, but in the long run it will pay off.

There is almost always a problem of the community entity. Who constitute the community and who represent it? How are the factionalism and interest conflicts in the village resolved and how are the poor, the weak, and the inarticulate, made partners in the collective community enterprise?

This situation calls for a balance between central direction on the one hand and the exercise of the community's responsibility and its authority on the other. The central management of a project has to intervene in behalf of the weak and the voiceless when community decisions threaten vital interests of the under-privileged groups. This intervention, however, should not be arbitrary, but in conformity with the overall goals and policies of the project, formulated and clarified with the participation of the beneficiary population.

THE JAMALPUR PROJECT

In the wake of severe flooding, crop damage, and famine conditions in late 1974, the vulnerable groups of rural people--landless farm laborers, families headed by destitute women, and children of these families--became the victims of starvation, malnutrition, and disease. (Widows represent 10.4 percent of all married women in the 10-49 age group according to 1961 census.)

UNICEF supported an agro-demonstration project to help destitute women in Jamalpur in Mymensingh district (120 miles northwest of Dacca) by employing women in "food-for-food" productive activities beginning in February 1975. The project involved the women in producing drought-resistant crops in sandy river-beds, and the women were paid in kind with wheat supplied by the World Food Program.

A total of 828 women was employed for a period of four months in agricultural work. They produced 195 maunds[1] of sorghum, 2 maunds of sunflower seeds, and 5 maunds of maize. The soybean crop was damaged by flood.

The yield could not justify the costs in a strict economic sense. But the significance of the project was that new varieties of crops were introduced in the area, a social breakthrough was achieved in employing women for agricultural work outside the home, and the destitute were provided sustenance not through handout but through productive work.

After the harvesting of the crop these women became participants in a functional education program launched with the help of Bangladesh Rural Advancement Committee (BRAC), a private voluntary organization located in Dacca. The women students were given a ration of wheat when they were attending classes.

A family planning and child care program was also started for the women, and in this effort Gonoshasthya Kendro's assistance was sought. The Kendro set up tubectomy and vasectomy services, using paramedics under physician's supervision. Motivation and location of clients were performed by the thana family planning staff and village dais (traditional birth attendants). In a period of six months (March-September 1975), 634 tubal ligations

---

[1]One maund is approximately 40 kilograms.

were performed (110 among women in the project and 534 among their neighbors and relatives). Oral pill distribution also was added to the project for the women and their relatives in October 1975. Along with the education program, a child care program (feeding a protein rich meal, nutrition education   for mothers, preventive health care) was started to take care of the children when their mothers were in the classroom. The UNICEF-supported education program continued until December 1975, when the teachers of the group organized themselves to continue the education program in the area and designed a new project with BRAC help.

A similar but expanded "food-for-food" program was launched in January 1976 with 18,000 mothers in twenty-seven sites (and an average of four children   per mother). By the end of June these groups worked on 222 acres of sand-covered land and produced

> 467 maunds of sorghum,
> 51 maunds of soybean,
> 293 maunds of local millet, and
> 17 maunds of groundnut.

UNICEF recruited and trained fifty-four young local boys as Project Agricultural Demonstrators (PAD). They are expected to be absorbed later into the Agricultural Department as Village Extension Agents.

During the monsoon (July-September) a tree plantation drive was undertaken. One hundred thousand fruit trees, 50,000 timber trees, and an uncounted number of quick-growing firewood trees had been planted and were being nursed by the women. The women also had been given papaya saplings and seeds for arahar, a nonlytheritic variety of high protein legume for home gardens.

In October an estimated 6,000 acres of land were brought under winter vegetable cultivation by the women. UNICEF supplied 8,500 seed kits containing seeds of spinach, beans, and tomatoes.

Family planning service provided by Gonoshasthya Kendro spread to five thanas in the subdivision. Clientele as of October 1976 (since January) were as follows:

Tubal ligation	203
Vasectomy	96
IUD	488
Oral pill	953
Foam	138
Menstrual regulation	11

1,889 (including non-project clients)

The Kendro staff provided clinical services in five centers under a physician-supervisor, while motivation, distribution of contraceptives, and follow-up were done by government staff.

Child care services, also assisted by Kendro, was provided in 34 locations for under-five children and mothers. Activities included feeding, using World Food Program commodities, and playgroups. Total beneficary children numbered

17,000 as of October 1976. In seven of these centers government Family
Welfare Visitors provided basic health services, including treatment of
diarrhea and fever, and immunization under the supervision of Kendro paramedics, who also helped train the FWVs (who already had eighteen months
of mother and child health care training). UNICEF provided drugs   and
equipment. Thirty-four local youths were trained and recruited by   the
government to operate these centers.

A functional education component was planned to be included, but did
not get off the ground for a variety of reasons, including slow progress
in negotiation with government agencies that were to take over the   support of the program from UNICEF. In late November, six women instructors
of functional education were being trained by BRAC with the aim of beginning a program in only three out of twenty-seven sites.

The project plans called for expanding the approach by using FWVS for
mother and child care, including treatment of common diseases through the
child care centers. Kendro was to assist in the effort. The Kendro   was
looking into the possibilities of reviving the traditional services   of
dais (TBAs) and upgrading them into village-based extension agents   for
health care, nutrition, and family planning Maternal and Child Health (MCH)
services. Sixty such TBAs were being trained by the Kendro for this   purpose in late 1976.

For the functional education component 600 female instructors   were
to be trained who would also become extension agents in the field   of
health, nutrition, family planning, and farming projects (with BRAC technical assistance). These women were to be paid a modest salary by   the
Agricultural Department. More females were planned to be recruited among
PAD's and child care center supervisors, as well as through FWVs and functional educational instructors all of whom are female. To what   extent
these plans would be implemented were not certain at the end of 1976.

The overall Jamalpur Project turned out to be unaffordably costly.The
1976 budget amounted to about US$3 million (about $0.5 million for   supplies, staff and logistics support provided by UNICEF, and 11,000 tons of
wheat supplied from the World Food Program costing about US$2.5 million)
for a program benefiting a total of about 18,000 women.

Because of the heavy costs, the scope of the project was not expected
to be enlarged, and its continuance at the current level was not at   all
certain. There were other factors, too, that contributed to the uncertainties: the logistical problems already encountered in supplying the   food
grain, disbursing cash, and organizing training and supervision that involved several government agencies at different levels; the difficulties   in
working out relationships with local officials and the relationships   between UN agencies (WFP, FAO, UNFPA, to mention a few); and the difficulty
in finding enough land for project purposes (although some khas, or public
land, is still available).

There were some signs that improvement in the situation of the destitute women would emerge from the project efforts. Small groups of project
women--partly because of the effect of functional education--were interested in setting up group economic enterprises. UNICEF helped the groups
which came up with economic propositions with small amounts of seed money.

A sum of Tk 370,000 ($24,670) was given in 1976 to small-scale economic projects benefiting 400 women. Another 200 women were being trained for sericulture work by Small and Cottage Industries Corporation. This combination of functional education, health care and family planning, and small-scale group economic projects initiated with small amounts of seed money is seen by some of the project workers as a more promising and economically viable approach than distributing wheat for farm work, the yields from which do not cover even a fraction of the wheat distribution costs. (Of course, the "food-for-food" project began more as a temporary relief effort than a development effort.) At the end of 1976, it was not certain whether this approach would be given a fair trial and an attempt would be made to build a durable local project not permanently dependent on UNICEF funds, either because the potentiality of the approach seemed not to be fully appreciated by all of the concerned parties or the difficulties along the way were seen as insurmountable.

In the Jamalpur Project the Kendro has become involved in a relatively broad range effort to improve the socioeconomic condition of the disadvantaged group of people. The Kendro's own contribution is limited to health, family planning, child care, and nutrition. It has the opportunity here to test and implement its own health care approach in a different setting and in close collaboration with government health and family planning services. There is also the opportunity to explore and strengthen the interaction between health and family planning efforts and other development activities. The prospect of using Jamalpur as a testing ground is somewhat uncertain. The uncertainty is not the fault of the Kendro or of its approach.

Post-script: We have been informed in September 1977 that the project activities of Jamalpur had been shifted to the Bhatsala union of the neighboring Sherpur thana. An "integrated health and rural development programme" had been initiated there under the auspices of the Kendro with fourteen trained and six trainee paramedics.

APPENDIX II

THE NATIONAL HEALTH AND
FAMILY PLANNING PROGRAMS

The Rural Health Service

The strategy for development of health services, as stated in the first Five Year Plan, is to shift the emphasis from curative to preventive health care--so as to bring a balance between the two and to develop a delivery system that provides comprehensive health care to the rural population.   In order to achieve these goals a rural health complex comprising rural health centers and 25-bed hospitals with satellite subcenters is to be established in each thana.   Referral services are to be provided to the rural health complex through the subdivisional and district hospitals and other teaching and specialized institutions.

The goal is to establish over a period of several years one rural health center and hospital in each of the 356 rural thanas (average population   of 200,000) and one subcenter in each of 3,698 rural unions (average population of 15,000).   In 1976, approximately fifty thana health centers were in operation and 200 others (including the conversion of old health centers) were at various stages of construction.   Little progress, however, had been made by this time in building the subcenter facilities.   The specified staffing pattern for the thana center is two physicians (including the Thana Health Administrator with overall public health responsibilities), two nurses,   one family health visitor, and ancillary workers.   The head of the subcenter is proposed to be a medical assistant (paraprofessional with three years' training), assisted by a lady health visitor, and a compounder-dresser.

The capital costs for a complete thana center with hospital are estimated to be Tk 5.4 million, and the recurring costs around Tk 300,000 (without the field staff and the maternity and child health staff, the latter being included in the family planning budget) at 1975 prices.   The design and staffing pattern for subcenters are still unsettled and unnecessarily high price tag for the thousands that will be needed in the country.

The preventive aspects of health care are implemented through a cadre of health workers formed by former smallpox vaccinators, sanitary   assistants, and malaria surveillance workers and now known collectively as Family Welfare Workers (FWW).   Each FWW will be in charge of a population of 4,000 and visit homes in his area for the purpose of immunization (vaccination against smallpox, cholera, typhoid, and tuberculosis), general health education, malaria and tuberculosis surveillance, and maintenance of family health cards (through which service data can be collected).

The medical assistant in charge of the subcenter (when and where it will exist), or an assistant health inspector in the union, supervise the FWWs. All of the thana health workers are supervised and guided by the Thana Health Administrator. By 1976 some 12,500 former field level employees of the Ministry of Health had been given short orientation courses and redesignated as FWWs. The target is 18,000 FWWs for the whole country.

The Family Planning Program

The responsibility for family planning lies in the Division of Population Control and Family Planning headed by a secretary of the government   and Member of the President's Advisory Council (Minister) for Population Control and Family Planning. A high level National Population Council with the president of the country as its chairman approves overall policies on family planning.

The implementing arm of the Division is the Directorate General of Population Control and Family Planning with personnel posted at the district, subdivision, thana, and union levels. The headquarters staff is distributed   into three directorates for (a) service delivery; (b) training, research, statistics, and evaluation; and (c) information, education, and motivation.

The field organization is as follows:

District:
District Population Control and Family Planning Officer	1
District Technical Officer (Medical Doctor)	1
Medical Officer (Female)	1
Supporting Staff	

Subdivision:
Subdivisional Population Control and Family Planning Officer	1

Thana:
Thana Population Control and Family Planning Officer	1
Thana Technical Officer (Medical Doctor)	1
Family Welfare Visitor (FWV in charge of MCH and FP clinic in Rural Health Centre)	1
Supporting Staff	

Union:
Family Planning Assistant (FPA, Male)	1
Family Welfare Assistant (FWA, Female)	1
Family Welfare Visitor (FWV) in charge of MCH and FP clinic in Health Subcentre	1 per 3 unions

This organizational structure was established in August 1975 and is gradually being filled in. By mid-1976, a total of 1,326 FPAs and 2,065 FWAs has been recruited, given a month's pre-service orientation, and posted in 116 thanas. The educational requirement of at least matriculation (Secondary School Certificate)   for

female FWAs and the Higher Secondary Certificate for male FPAs has slowed
down recruitment. Almost all the posts of technical officers (physicians)
were vacant in mid-1976 because it was not possible to attract doctors to
the family planning program. The doctors apparently do not like to be
posted outside the capital or they find the career prospects unattractive
in the family planning program.

The target of the family planning program is to reduce the population
growth rate of 2.8 percent in 1976 to 2.0 percent in 1980 and achieve zero
population growth by the year 1985. Such an accomplishment would mean a
population size of 121 million in the year 2,000. This target requires the
acceptance and continuous use of birth control measures by 3.8 million fertile women in 1980 (or 20 percent of the female population of 15-49 years
age group) compared to 1976 estimates of 0.8 million (4.7 percent of the
relevant age group) users.

The program is described as following a multisectoral and integrated
approach with emphasis on community involvement. The emphasis on an integrated approach is manifested, not as much in the total program as in
two special activities: (a) zero population growth experiment in twenty
unions in five districts where some additional funds have been made available to supplement regular development projects for health, mother and
child care, family planning as well as education and agricultural production with the hope that these would hasten the acceptance of a small family
norm; and (b) special projects to secure the cooperation and support of
other government ministries, such as information and broadcasting, education, rural development, agriculture, social welfare and health in the use
of their field level personnel for family planning motivation and information dissemination.

Community involvement is to be achieved by utilizing village leaders
in planning and implementing family planning programs, forming mothers'
clubs and enlisting the support of local groups and organizations for family planning.

With the separation of general health care from the family planning
program, it is considered necessary to have at least maternal and child
health activities combined with family planning services. The MCH facilities in the thana health centers and union subcenters are therefore to
be established and maintained from the family planning budget, and the
FWVs in the thana and the unions are to be in charge of these facilities.
Health service doctors, as well as private physicians, perform sterilization operations for a fixed fee for each case referred to them by the
family planning staff.

The national family planning program has received substantial external assistance. IDA and six other cofinancing partners--Australia,
CIDA (Canada), KFW (Federal Republic of Germany), NORAD (Norway), ODM
(United Kingdom), and SIDA (Sweden)--are financing a three year US$46
million project launched in 1976. It is designed to provide a number

of inputs to strengthen the national program: (a) expanding the training of
health and family planning manpower (constructing, furnishing and equipping
a college of nursing, eight schools for training FWVs, eight rural health complexes to be used for training medical personnel, four model family planning
clinics for training medical students); (b) supporting the services of 3,700
FWAs; (c) pilot schemes for using other ministries in family planning education
and motivation; and (d) building up research and evaluation activities.

Comments

Despite the rhetoric of integration, there is a three-way separation now
of curative services, preventive measures, and family planning, while maternal
and child health care (and nutrition, the main problem of mothers and children)
at the present time is nobody's concern by default.

In the rural areas the curative service is available in thana headquarters
if and when a health center exists, the staff has been appointed, and medicines
have been supplied. The doctor and his staff sit in the center and wait   for
people to come. Whether or not the people come depends on their past experience
and expectations about the availability of the doctor and medicine and if they
can afford the time and money to travel to the center. The doctor, who engages
in private practice, is available only certain hours of the day. The medical
staff of the center has no connection with the field activities of the Family
Welfare Workers.

The preventive activities--essentially not much more than vaccination for
smallpox, cholera and tuberculosis--are the responsibilities of the FWW.   He
is, however, not authorized to prescribe even aspirin pills and has no referral
role, having no functional connection with the medical staff of the center.

Family planning motivation, advice, distribution of supplies, and recruitment of candidates for terminal measures are the functions of the family planning workers--FPAs and FWAs. FWWs of the health service are also expected to
perform these family planning functions, but because of the separation of the
departmental jurisdictions, these duties are considered additional and secondary to the normal FWW duties, and they are seen as a temporary arrangement until family planning personnel are posted everywhere.

Maternal and child health care is the responsibility of the Family Planning
Division, but because very few trained personnel (FWVs) and facilities (clinics
in subcenters and thana centers) now exist in the family planning program little
is available by way of service.

The upshot of all of the above is that basic ambulatory care that could
deal with most of the common diseases of the rural people and establish credibility for government services is virtually unavailable to the rural people;
and the major share of the health funds, both capital and recurring, go to
health centers and hospitals attempting to serve directly a small fraction of
the rural population without playing a backstopping role for a program to meet
the total health needs of the rural areas.

The Thana Health Administrator--a medical doctor without any special orientation or training in planning and managing a rural public health system   and
without a clear definition of his authority and relationship with the family planning staff and the health center staff--serves essentially as a personnel manager
for the thana's FWWs. (The uncertainty in relationships arises from the fact

that the medical officer at the health center is of the same status as
the Administrator and the family planning personnel belong to a different
government department.)

The interdependence and interaction of the three types of activities
are ignored in the organizational structure for health and family planning. The opportunity has not been exploited for enhancing the acceptability of family planning, preventive health measures, and MCH and nutrition practices by responding to the rural people's deeply felt and widely
perceived need for the treatment of common (but often extremely distress-
ing in physical, emotional, and economic terms) diseases. The organizations
are structured for bureaucratic convenience and in order to conform to inappropriate borrowed standards and models of health care rather than for
responding to people's needs in the most efficient way.

Integration in the present family planning program apparently means
two things: (a) providing some additional funds for local development
programs in half a dozen experimental areas as an inducement for accepting birth control measures, and (b) giving other ministries of the government a family planning IEC (information, education, communication) role--
seeking the assistance of other ministries that have contacts with rural
people in getting the fertility control message across. The vertical separation of departmental hierarchies does not give way to any merger of
program activities and goals at any level.

The other side of the coin of integration is decentralization and
community participation. Both the health program and the family planning program represent a total top-down approach with all aspects of
the program fully and rigidly controlled at the national government
level. Community involvement in these programs essentially means getting the community's compliance to the predetermined goals and procedures
of the government rather than a true participation in planning, managing,
and implementing local programs.

A different approach to health care and family planning that takes
integration, decentralization, and community participation seriously is
conceivable, at least on an experimental basis. In this approach   the
health and the population control and family planning divisions   would
be seen primarily as backstopping agencies--providing technical assistance and resources to the thana institutional structures in the form of
technically qualified personnel, training materials, supplies, and
guidelines on policies and objectives. The organization and use of
these resources with the help of the network of existing and emerging
village institutions (cooperatives and other groups) and within the
framework of other development activities in the thana would be the
responsibility of the local government bodies in the thana and the union
(the thana and union councils, the thana training and development cent
and specially formed bodies as required). Obviously, this approach requires a departure from the present highly centralized structure of public administration and the creation of strong local governments of truly
representative nature. But this is what will be needed to make the ideas
of integration and community participation real. A beginning towards

gradual decentralization and strong local governments and local integration of development programs probably can be made with health and family planning services, if the will and the vision exist at the top policymaking and planning level. Projects like Savar can be used to test and develop the operational steps for moving in this direction.

There are many logistical and management problems that handicap both family planning and health care programs. Unavailability or irregular delivery of supplies, neglect of assigned duties, laxity in supervision, false reporting   and record-keeping, demands for payment of services and supplies which are supposed to be free, discriminatory treatment of the poor and uneducated rural residents are common problems, not only in the health and family planning programs but in other government services, too. The approach to a remedy for the general malaise of corruption and inefficiency again is establishing accountability of government agencies and personnel at the local level to local representative bodies who are directly affected by the actions and performance of the government agencies.

Sources

WHO/UNICEF Joint Study on Alternative Approaches to Meeting Basic Health Needs of Population in Developing Countries (20th Session, Geneva February 4-6, 1975), Annex III.

Oscar Gish. The Development of Health Services in Bangladesh, Institute of Development Studies, University of Sussex, February 1976.

Government of Bangladesh, Population Control and Family Planning Division, "An Outline of the National Population Policy of Bangladesh," Dacca, July 1976.

_____. "Review of the Program on the Outline of National Population Policy," Dacca, July 1976.

World Bank, Population Project in Bangladesh, Appraisal Report, Washington, D.C., February 1975 (restricted document).

3 The Lampang Health Development Project: Thailand's Fresh Approach to Rural Primary Health Care

Lampang Project Personnel

EDITOR'S NOTE

This case study of the Lampang Health Development Project in Thailand should be of special interest to officials of developing countries and external assistance agencies who are looking   for fresh approaches to providing primary health care services--both curative and preventive--to the great majority of rural people who have long been without them. They will find in this report not only a description of the Lampang Project and how it evolved during its first four years of operation, but also a mid-course assessment of its progress and impacts to date, a candid discussion of some problems it has encountered, and a provisional appraisal of its replicability. The practical lessons--both positive and negative--that emerge from this experience can have relevance and utility for many situations.

Unlike all other case studies in this series, which were conducted independently by ICED in partnership with qualified researchers in the countries concerned, the present report was prepared and written by staff members and advisors of the Lampang Project itself, on the basis of a design developed by Dr. Manzoor Ahmed of ICED's staff. In order to tie this case study into the context of the overall ICED project and also to provide an independent international perspective on the Lampang Project, the case study is introduced by a separate ICED commentary.

ICED is especially indebted to Dr. Somboon Vachrotai, Director-General of the Department of Health in Thailand's Ministry of Public Health, and also Director of the Lampang Health Development Project, who graciously accepted ICED's suggestion that this case study be undertaken, and who guided and supported it from start to finish.

ICED's thanks are similarly extended to the following people who jointly prepared and wrote the case study: Dr. Pien Chiowanich, Dr. Choomnoom Promkutkeo, and Dr. Chaichana Suvannvejh of the Lampang Health Development Project staff; Dr. Ronald G. Wilson and Mr. John A. Rogosch of the University of Hawaii School of Public Health, resident staff at the Lampang Project; Dr. Nicholas Wright, a project consultant from Rutgers School of Medicine, and Mrs. Termotis R. Wilson, who typed the original manuscript.

Although the American Public Health Association had no direct role in the study, it made a useful contribution by reviewing a draft of the report and by disseminating the finished document to numerous public health groups around the world that could make practical use of the findings.

The opinions and interpretations expressed in this report are solely the responsibility of ICED and the case study authors.

LESSONS FROM LAMPANG
an ICED Commentary*

The Lampang Health Development Project has been of special interest to ICED because it represents one of the earliest attempts by any developing country government to apply systematically and on a sizeable scale the basic concept and principles of the "primary health care approach," that has been popularized in recent years by WHO and UNICEF and was endorsed by the Alma Ata International Conference on Primary Health Care in 1978.

Most well informed public health experts seem to agree that this unconventional approach makes good sense and is probably the only feasible and affordable strategy for coping with the serious and long neglected health needs of the rural families making up the great majority of the developing world's total population. The big question today about this "primary health care" concept, however, is not whether it is sound in principle but how to put it into practice in the real world. Any serious effort to do so immediately raises a host of difficult questions to which there are as yet few experience-based answers. Many policymakers and planners, well disposed toward the general idea of a primary health care system, are still looking for practical guidance on such questions as these:

. How does one actually go about "integrating" the essential components of a primary health care system--such as curative medical services, environmental sanitation, family planning, nutrition for young children, pre- and post-natal care for mothers--especially when these fragmented services are already in the hands of different specialized bureaucracies that are anxious to preserve their autonomy and to keep "going-it-alone"?

. How does one recruit, train and deploy new cadres of para-professional health workers, competent to provide the above combination of services on a mass scale, close to where the people live, and willing to work in a rural environment at incomes far below those of urban-based medical doctors? Also, how does one persuade the old-line medical profession to accept and support this "heretical" notion of allowing paraprofessionals, and even less trained village health workers, to perform some of the tasks traditionally reserved to full-fledged physicians?

. Granted that mobilizing community resources and participation is essential to getting the primary health care job done, how can government agencies go about generating such broad-based

---

*This commentary was written by Philip H. Coombs, Director of the ICED project on Helping the Rural Poor, which includes the present case study.

community participation?

. How much is an effective rural primary health care system
actually going to cost? Where is the money coming from? And can
a poor country really afford it?

. What steps can be taken to insure that the poorest families
in any community participate and benefit equally in this new type
of health system?

The Lampang Project cannot be expected, of course, to provide
full and final answers to all these questions. But it can shed valuable
light on some of them--light that can be helpful not only to Thailand
but to other countries faced with similar rural health needs and
problems. The authors of the present case study have given us a
revealing picture--viewed from the inside--of how the Project evolved
from its initial planning phase in 1973 through its first four years of
operation to the end of 1978. Their account is both descriptive and
analytical. They expose some difficult problems encountered along
the way and indicate some of the efforts made to overcome them.
Particularly important, they give their own provisional assessment
(based on still incomplete evaluation evidence) of both the achievements and the shortcomings of the project at this stage. Further,
they present some tentative conclusions on the costs and feasibility
of replicating the main features of the Project elsewhere in Thailand.

This introduction, on behalf of ICED, views the Lampang
Project in an international perspective, through the eyes of an
outside observer and in the light of ICED's other case studies of
innovative rural programs in a variety of developing countries. Its
purpose is not to praise or criticize or to pass any overall judgement
on the Lampang Project. Rather, its purpose is to call the attention
of others who may be interested in developing rural primary health
care systems to some of the significant implications of the Lampang
experience that may have relevance for many countries. In particular, using Thailand as an example, it comments briefly on the
following issues: (1) the present state of health delivery systems
in developing countries; (2) some basic requirements for expanding
the coverage and utilization of a primary health care system; (3) the
costs involved in meeting these requirements; (4) the realistic
problems of building a community-base; and (5) the sticky problem
of replicating the promising features of "demonstration projects."

It should be emphasized that the comments below are intended
as a contribution to an on-going dialogue, not as an exposition of
revealed truths. If this introduction manages to arouse the curiosity
of readers to examine the whole case study for themselves and to
draw their own conclusions, it will have served its purpose.

THE LAMPANG SETTING AND THE PROJECT'S STRATEGY

Before turning to specific issues it is important to provide a brief sketch of the rural health situation in Thailand that the leaders of the Lampang Project set out to improve. As will be seen, it has many similarities to other developing countries.

Though it is common to speak of any nation's "health delivery system" as if it were a single, unified mechanism, the reality is that most low income agrarian countries have three quite distinct and separate health systems: (1) a rapidly evolving modern *urban health system* (private and government) patterned along Western lines; (2) a thinly-spread *government rural health system* that bears little resemblance to the urban one; and (3) a *private rural health system* composed largely of various types of indigenous health providers. This was the situation in Thailand when the planners of the Lampang Project first put pen to paper in 1973.

The *urban health system* was based on a network of nearly 100 government-supported modern hospitals and closely allied private clinics that spread out from Bangkok (the hub of the system) to all provincial capitals. The vast majority of the nation's medical doctors and nurses--most of them trained in Thailand's six univerity level medical schools--were attached to this system. For many years Thailand had worked hard to build this impressive urban health system and could be justly proud of it. But it presented two serious problems. First, it was so preoccupied with *curing* illnesses that it paid little attention to *preventing* them, or to promoting the basic essentials for good health that could curb the rapidly growing insatiable demand for curative care. Second, it preempted the lion's share of the national health budget and health resources (perhaps as much as 90 percent), yet served and benefitted only a small segment of the national population (probably no more than 10 to 15 percent).

The *government rural health system* took the leavings and was quite something else. In theory it was responsible for providing health services to the 85 percent of the population living in rural areas, but in fact its capacity for doing so was grossly inadequate-- as illustrated by the situation in Lampang Province when the Project began in 1974.

The provincial hospital in Lampang town--at the lowest echelon of the modern urban health system--had 300 beds, an outpatient department and a staff of 22 physicians and 58 nurses to serve, in principle, a population of over 600,000 people, largely rural.

Also in Lampang town--though not organically connected with the provincial hospital and under the jurisdiction of a different department in the national Ministry of Public Health--was a Public Health Office that headed up the rural health system. Structurally it was a three-tier system and in principle it included: (1) a "first-class health center" (later called a "district hospital") in each district,

with one doctor and a few beds for emergencies; (2) a smaller rural
"health center" in each *tambol* (subdistrict) that concentrated
largely on maternity cases and selected preventive health measures;
and (3) a network of village midwifery centers.

The system was much smaller in reality, however, than in
theory. Only one-quarter of the districts(3 out of 12) had a district
hospital and only two of these had an attending physician (the only
two in the whole rural health system below the provincial capital).
Only one-third of the subdistricts (26 out of 75) had a rural health
center, staffed by a sanitarian and midwife. Only 33 of the province's
538 villages could boast a midwifery center. Thus, at best, no more
than one out of every three or four rural families in the province could
be said to be "covered" by this rural health system, even theoretically.
But in fact a community survey in 1974 revealed that only 15 to 17
percent of the rural people in Lampang Province actually made use
of the system's facilities--presumably because the system did not offer
the kind and quality of services (especially curative services) the
people wanted.

The third health system mentioned earlier--the *private rural
health system*--also existed in Lampang. Its precise dimensions are
unknown, partly because it is scarcely visible to the naked eye of
Western-trained health statisticians and also because most "modern"
medical specialists tend to disparage its "unscientific and unsanitary practices." There is little doubt, however, that its various
"health providers"--including traditional midwives, herbalists,
injectionists, and magical and spirit doctors--were more numerous
and served far more rural people in Lampang Province than the
entire staff of the official health system. A great many rural people--
especially the poorest--placed great stock in them and in fact had no
real access to any other sort of health care service.

Faced with these hard facts, the Lampang Project planners set a
basic goal of overhauling and strengthening the official rural health
system so that five years hence it would be providing needed and
desired health care services--including curative as well as preventive
and promotive services--to at least two-thirds of the rural residents,
with special emphasis on the two most vulnerable groups: women in
their child-bearing years and preschool age children. To pursue
this goal they adopted a multi-pronged strategy aimed at the following
objectives:

(1)   The reorganization of the existing provincial (government)
      health system, including integration of curative, preven-
      tive, and promotive health services within and between
      the provincial hospital and the rural health care
      facilities.

(2)   The upgrading of existing government health workers and,
      especially important, the creation of a new cadre of
      clinically trained paraphysicians (*wechakorn*, in Thai)
      who would be competent to handle common illnesses and
      other basic health services at the subdistrict health

centers, within easy reach of the villages.

(3) The creation of a vital community base for the system, including in each village a local health committee and several trained volunteers who would provide a variety of health services to their neighbors, link their community closely to the system as a whole, and make possible a new process of "upward planning, downward support."

(4) Improvement of the efficiency of the whole system, primarily by improving its management through an internal, multi-directional system of information flows that would enable managers at all levels to monitor the system's performance and to make better-informed decisions.

With strong backing from the national Ministry of Public Health and with assistance from the U.S. Agency for International Development--channelled through two professional organizations, the American Public Health Association and the University of Hawaii's School of Public Health--the leaders of the Project endeavored over the next four years to implement this multi-pronged strategy. They learned as they went, tried to stay flexible, and seized various "targets of opportunity" that arose--such as the mobile vasectomy unit operated by the provincial hospital. Like "public health" pioneers everywhere, their philosophy and view of health was much broader than that of the curative centered, urban-oriented medical profession; hence one of their inevitable problems was to win the cooperation and practical participation of hospital-based physicians in building a stronger and more balanced rural health system.

REQUIREMENTS FOR EXPANDING THE REACH OF THE SYSTEM

A rural health system's progress must be judged by three different criteria: (1) the expansion of its geographic and population "coverage," i.e., the proportion of the population that theoretically has physical access to it; (2) improvements in the range, quality and cost factors of the health services it offers; and (3) the actual utilization of these services by its potential clientele.

The case study presents persuasive evidence--albeit quite incomplete and tentative at present--that the Lampang provincial rural health system has made significant progress, judged by all three of these criteria, during the Project's first four years of operation (see Tables 5, 6 and 7). It is important to recognize, however, that not all of this progress is attributable solely to the Project. Even before the Project had been conceived, the Royal Thai Government had committed itself to a nationwide expansion of rural health facilities and personnel, and this expansion, as implemented in Lampang Province, happily coincided with the Project's special efforts during the first four years of its operation. Thus, for example, between 1974 and the end of 1978 the number of district hospitals rose from three to five (each with its own doctor),

and the subdistrict health centers increased from 26 to 61. There
was a corresponding large increase in the usual complement of
government nurses, nurse aides, sanitarians, and midwives (see
Table 6). Had it not been for this sizeable expansion program,
funded outside the Project budget by the Government's "regular"
provincial health budget, there could not have been this dramatic
increase in the geographic/population "coverage" of the system.

On the other hand, had it not been for the innovative features
of the Project, this expansion would have followed the conventional
pattern and simply reproduced the old system on a larger scale,
with all its serious shortcomings. As it was, however, the Project--
according to preliminary evidence--seems to have contributed
significantly in terms of the second and third of the above three
criteria. It helped to broaden the scope and improve the quality
of the system's services, and to increase the utilization of its capacity.
The Project's greatest contribution in these respects, it would appear,
came from training and deploying the new cadre of paraphysicians
(*wechakorn*) who, for the first time, made it possible for the rural
health centers to provide substantial curative services (which the
villagers were most eager to have), as well as to strengthen their
preventive/promotive health services (including family planning).
Thus, for example, according to available service statistics on the
first district to be implemented (Hang Chat) under the Project,
the number and proportion of total estimated illness cases handled
by the health centers doubled between 1974 and 1977; the number
of supervised pregnancy cases more than doubled; and the number
of family planning "acceptors" served by these district facilities
nearly trebled. (See Tables 7, 8 and 11.) If the 1979 follow-up
baseline surveys reveal comparable trends throughout the whole
province, then it will be reasonable to conclude that the Project has
indeed made a sizeable contribution to increasing the supply,
quality, and utilization of the rural health system's services.

It should be noted, however, and this point is relevant to many
other situations, that it will never be possible to measure the
Project's specific contribution with any degree of quantitative
precision. This is because the changes that are occurring in the
rural health services in Lampang Province and in the health status
of its population are the result of a *combination* of causal factors--
of which the Project is only one--and their respective contributions
cannot be neatly disentangled and measured separately. Indeed,
it will be exceedingly difficult even to measure with any significant
degree of accuracy the combined impact of all these forces--this
because follow-up baseline surveys, despite their theoretical
attractiveness, have an exasperating habit of not being really
comparable to the original baseline surveys, and the "control areas"
against which changes in the "implementation areas" are to be
judged, have an equally exasperating habit of not remaining
"uncontaminated."

THE COST IMPLICATIONS

What can we learn from the Lampang Project at this stage about the costs of building a rural primary health care system that is adequate in size and quality to serve the needs of the majority of the population in any given rural area?

The attention of the Project evaluation staff, of course, is focused on the costs of the Project itself and on what it might cost to replicate its main features in other provinces of Thailand. But this is only a fraction of the total cost picture that government policy-makers and planners must take into account in assessing the feasibility of duplicating the "Lampang model" elsewhere. To be realistic they must look at the *whole* Lampang rural health system, not simply at the special components provided by the Project. Thus they must weigh the costs of *all* inputs and components, including the added capital investment in new facilities and the increased recurrent costs for additional personnel, supplies and so forth.

We can get a rough notion of the overall cost picture in Lampang Province by looking at what happened to the "regular" provincial health budget (excluding Project expenditures) between 1974/75 and 1977/78 (see Tables 12 and 13). It will be noted that total expenditures (including capital costs, which accounted for 45 percent of the total) more than trebled in this short period, largely reflecting the major expansion of facilities and personnel referred to earlier. The figures do not tell us where the capital expenditures went, but it is reasonable to assume that more than half went into doubling the capacity of the provincial hospital, and the rest into new district hospitals and subdistrict health centers. However, the breakdown of *operating* expenditures (shown in Table 13) as between the provincial hospital and the district health facilities and services is more revealing. Total operating costs for the entire provincial health program increased four-fold between 1974/75 and 1977/78-- a tremendous rise by any standard. What is equally significant, during the first three of these four years, the share of total opera-ting funds allocated to the district facilities (as distinct from the provincial hospital) rose from 28 percent to 53 percent of the total, reflecting a strong build up of the infrastructure of the rural health system.

This is exactly what one might expect when a government sets out seriously to expand the geographic and population coverage of a skimpy rural health system. It requires sizeable capital outlays to expand facilities and, much more important in the long run, a permanently higher annual operating budget to cover increased personnel, supplies and other recurrent costs of the expanded rural system. Added to the old cost structure are the additional costs of any new features, such as the training and support of paraphysicians and village health volunteers. To be sure, the efficiency of the whole system might also be improved simultaneously, but this would result mainly in more and better quality services rather than in any substantial reduction in the amount of money spent.

It should also be noted that by the time the Lampang rural health system achieves close to 100 percent coverage--some years hence--much more capital will have been invested and the operating costs will be much higher still. At the end of 1978, half the districts still had no hospital and 14 of the 75 subdistricts were still without a health center. Moreover, as pointed out in the case study, there is need to fill some important present gaps--for example, to add a vigorous child nutrition program in each village, to mount an extensive immunization program, to provide stronger support for the village volunteers, and to tune up the system in other respects. All this will cost more money.

The point we wish to make is not that a broad-scale rural primary health care system is too expensive to be afforded. On the contrary, it is undoubtedly the least expensive way to do the job and it probably *can* be afforded by any country willing to give it a high enough priority. The point we wish to underscore is that no one should have any illusions that a good rural health system can be bought "on the cheap." It is not simply a matter of adding one more stage at the bottom of the existing system by persuading each community to join the system and to bear the extra costs. It is a matter of greatly strengthening the entire infrastructure of the system *above* the community level so that it can properly support community self-help health activities and provide important health services that are beyond the capacity of individual villages.

WHAT DOES IT TAKE TO ACHIEVE "COMMUNITY PARTICIPATION"?

The Lampang Project planners believed--along with many others--that an effective and affordable rural primary health care system requires a strong community base. Thus they provided for replacing the conventional "top-down" approach to delivering health services with what could be termed a new system of "upward planning, downward support." This implied that each community would not only have its own volunteer health workers and local services but a health committee that would diagnose the community's health problems and needs, set its own priorities, make its own plans, mobilize its own resources for implementing these plans, and seek such outside assistance as would be necessary to supplement local resources and efforts. In turn, the obligation of the health system above the village level would be to respond to these locally defined plans and needs with appropriate support.

This seems a very rational and appealing concept. But as the Lampang experience confirms, it is a very difficult one to apply in real life--villages and villagers being what they are, government agencies and agents being what they are, and both being unaccustomed to such a partnership. The evidence in the case study tells us that this vital aspect of the Lampang strategy, though by no means a failure, has fallen disappointingly short of the initial hopes and expectations. But this should come as no surprise to anyone familiar with numerous other attempts to generate "community

participation" (not only in the health field). Almost invariably such
attempts have either failed outright or have required much greater
and more sustained effort than anticipated (particularly by the well
intentioned--but inadequately informed-- urban people who initially
design them).

The authors of the case study attribute the underperformance
of the village health committees and volunteers to several factors:
insufficient encouragement and support by the health center staff;
lack of a sufficiently clear definition of the functions of the local
committees and health communicators; the breakdown of the government logistical system for resupplying household medicines to the
health post volunteers; and the fact that some volunteers, pressed
for time by their regular work and other obligations, could not make
themselves available at hours most convenient to their "clients."
The authors also report that the village health volunteers have
requested more training, particularly on first aid and dealing with
emergencies, and a broader job description.

These explanations all ring true. But one wonders whether the
problem is not more deeply rooted, perhaps even in the planning
process itself and in some erroneous underlying assumptions. One
such assumption seems to have been that two weeks of compact,
pre-packaged initial training, followed by only one day a year
of "refresher training," would suffice to give the health post volunteers all they would require to carry out, largely on their own, the
crucial roles and responsibilities envisaged for them in the plan.
A correlary assumption was that it would be sufficient, in order to
keep the volunteers actively and effectively tied in with the "system,"
to be visited only once a month by a rural health center staff member,
who would review their daily log book and give them such advice,
assistance and supervision as they might require. A third apparent
assumption was that the village health committee (which is typically
only one of several such local committees inspired by various government agencies with different objectives and priorities in mind) would
embark more or less spontaneously on a new and undefined health
planning process and would give clear direction and active support
to the work of the volunteers.

In retrospect, these assumptions were clearly flawed. They
obviously expected too much of the villagers, particularly in light
of the relatively meagre support the provincial health system was
prepared to give them. We do not know the facts in this case,
but we do know that history teaches that community development
planners often get the cart before the horse. They decide on their
plan *in absentia* without first getting to know the villages and the
villagers in question well enough, and without seeking and listening
to their advice. Villagers, after all, have a great deal of practical
local wisdom, or they would not have survivied this long in the face
of so many adversities. They may be illiterate and they may seem
quite unsophisticated to the educated urbanite, but they are no fools.
If an outsider urges them to take on new time-consuming functions
and responsibilities to improve their own lot and it seems at the time

to make sense to them, they will usually be willing to give it a try, particularly if they are assured of receiving such outside support as they may require. But then if the outside support falters or proves inadequate, and if they are left on their own for long stretches without seeing or hearing from their new "partners," it is hardly surprising if their initial enthusiasm wanes and their own efforts slacken.

ICED has examined a few cases where voluntary organizations eventually achieved a fairly effective working relationship with community health workers. But in no case was it easy; it required a great deal of persistent and patient effort over many months, including weekly visitations to the villages and close supervision and continuous on-the-job training of the local health workers by professional members of the central health staff. It also requires establishing a real sense of mutual trust and respect and giving the local workers a sense of being a valued member of a professional team-- not simply a local errand boy. Obviously it is much more difficult for a large and necessarily bureaucratized government health service to act with the flexibility and spirit of a voluntary organization. But this does not alter the fact that these are basic requisites for getting an effective community-based health system going.

All of this is not to deny that the Lampang Project has made a good start toward establishing a strong and viable community base. Given all the constraints and difficult logistical problems, it seems to have done remarkably well. But it is still only a start, and to bring this effort to full fruition will clearly require a more intensive effort. We suspect that, among other things, it will require re-examination and revision of the initial assumptions implicit in the original plan; expanded provisions for continuous on-the-job training for village volunteers and committees, taking various forms; more frequent and helpful visitations to the villages by the wechakorn and other health center staff; a new effort to develop workable local planning methods with the help of village committees; and not least of all, a new concerted educational effort directed at the villagers at large (as distinct from spasmodic and relatively super-ficial "information" efforts) that will give them a fresh perspective and appreciation of their own life and environmental circumstances and lead them by their own logic and choice to adopt improved family and community health practices.

The purpose of the above remarks, however, is not to give unneeded advice to the Lampang Project. It is rather to call the attention of outside readers of this report to a very basic truth that has been once again confirmed by the Lampang experience: to develop strong community participation is not only an essential requirement for a viable primary health care system but it is also a much more complicated affair than is often assumed.

SOME OBSERVATIONS ON REPLICATION

Mindful that many "demonstration" projects in the past have proved economically impossible to replicate because insufficient attention was paid to costs by their designers, the planners of the

Lampang Project were determined from the outset to avoid this pitfall. They not only tried to be "cost conscious" in mapping their initial strategy but they also included provisions in the overall evaluation process for monitoring and analyzing the cost-effectiveness of various Project activities and system "tasks."

Calculating costs for this type of project, however, is difficult at best. One-time-only "developmental" costs must be differentiated from "normal" repeatable costs beyond the developmental stage; "joint costs" shared by two or more different activities must be allocated between them on some reasonable basis; projection of the costs of replicating various distinctive features of the demonstration project in a different context presents many sticky problems; and so forth.

Notwithstanding these complexities, however, the authors of the case study have made an heroic effort to estimate what it would cost to implement the main features of the Lampang Project in other provinces of Thailand. These features include especially: (1) the system reorganization, including the integration of medical and health care services within, and coordination between, the provincial hospital with the rural health facilities; (2) the wechakorn para-physicians at the subdistrict health centers; (3) the village health volunteers and the involvement of local communities, and the private sector; and (4) improving the management and efficiency of the whole system.

The authors emerged with what at first glance seems a surprisingly low estimate of replication costs: for an extra expenditure equivalent to only 11 percent of the external assistance funds used in the Project its main features could be reproduced elsewhere.

Three important considerations should be borne in mind with respect to this estimate of replication costs. First, the bulk of the external assistance funds were devoted to: (a) developing training methods and materials, which are now available for broader use at a fraction of their original cost, and (b) to evaluation and research activities that the authors assume will not need to be continued in other areas. Second, the 11 percent estimate does not include any of the very sizeable capital and associated operating costs that the Government must incur in other provinces to expand and strengthen the basic infrastructure of the system (without which the innovative Project features would have far less impact). As we saw earlier, these expansion costs in Lampang Province have considerably exceeded the budget of the Project itself, and substantial further government expenditures will be required before the Lampang rural health system its elf can be called "complete." Third, the above replication cost estimate also does not include provision for the additional elements that the authors feel are still needed in the Lampang area, such as a greatly strengthened child nutrition program, stronger support for the village committees and volunteers and further strengthening of the Department of Community Health in the provincial hospital.

In short, it is vitally important to view this 11 percent estimate in the context of the overall costs of the *whole* system in order to avoid the illusion that this is the only cost requirement for achieving a full-blown primary health care system. In reality it is but a small fraction of the total increased expenditures required.

Apart from these cost considerations, the Lampang case reveals some other interesting insights into the matter of replication. As it happens, the Government of Thailand, apparently satisfied that the Lampang Project was turning out well, did not even wait for cost estimates and other evaluation evidence to be completed before taking steps to replicate (in modified form) some of the main features of the Lampang Project. Specifically, the Government recently decided to incorporate two of the principal Lampang features in an ambitious new "20 Province Project" assisted by the World Bank. The plan calls for (1) training 1500 wechakorn-like nurse practitioners, employing the training methods and materials developed by the Lampang Project, and (2) training sufficient health volunteers over the next five years for all the villages covered by this large new project.

This strong vote of confidence in these innovative features of the Lampang Project before the Project has even run its full course and been finally evaluated is historically quite unique and testifies to the Government's stout determination to move with dispatch toward spreading primary health care throughout rural Thailand. On closer inspection, however, one is prompted to pose some gnawing questions, not to second-guess the Government's decisions but to illustrate the importance of viewing a primary health care system *as* a system.

First of all, the nurse practitioners under the "20 Province Project," though trained in the manner of the wechakorn, will apparently be used quite differently. They will all be assigned, not to the rural health centers, but to provincial and district hospitals where they will work under the immediate supervision of medical doctors. They will be engaged largely in clinical services and curative care, but not in any preventive/promotive activities in the villages. Thus, unlike the wechakorn, they will not become the mainstay of strengthened rural health centers close to the bulk of the people.

The wechakorn are apparently to be replaced in the health centers by midwives who are given only four months of special training in clinical services. While this is certainly useful, it appears to constitute a substantial watering down of the basic idea of the wechakorn as the key to strengthening the health centers, to bringing both curative and preventive/promotive services closer to the villages, and to reducing the unnecessary flow of common illness cases to the hospitals. Unless we have our facts wrong, this significant weakening of the Lampang Project strategy reflects the continuing strong influence of the hospital-centered medical philosophy as against the broader and more village-oriented primary health care philosophy.

It also raises a further question. How will the numerous village
health volunteers in the "20 Province Project" be given the strong
and steady support they require? Will the health center staff be
up to the task?   If not, where will the support come from? And if
adequate support is not forthcoming can the village health volunteers
be expected to keep up their morale and efforts and to make a substantial contribution on their own?

Our intent in posing these questions is not to challenge the
efficacy of Thailand's "20 Province Project" but, once again, to
underscore the importance of viewing any primary health care system
in its entirety, as a system, made up of interacting, mutually reinforcing components. In any such "system"--be it an agricultural
production system, a school, or a health system--if any important
component is missing or malfunctioning, or if its relationship to
other components is out of kilter, then the performance and
productivity of all the other components and of the whole system
will suffer. Therefore, there are important risks to be guarded
against in replicating only selected features of an innovative
demonstration project, seen in isolation. Unless these features are
carefully fitted into their new context they may turn out to be disappointing misfits.

THREE GENERAL CONCLUSIONS

These introductory comments have attempted to illustrate some
of the important principles and lessons that can be derived from the
experience of the Lampang Health Development Project of potential
value to others seeking to develop a wide-reaching and affordable
rural primary health care system. Three important general conclusions emerge from this discussion:

First, to build a workable and affordable primary health care
system that will serve the great majority of needy rural families is
a considerably more complicated, time-consuming and expensive
undertaking than is generally realized by those who have not actually
tried. Nevertheless it has to be done, because this is undoubtedly
the most effective and feasible way--probably the *only* way--to meet
the crucial and long-neglected basic health needs of rural people.
Whether it *will* be done is largely a question of each individual
country's political priorities, and of the willingness of both the
medical profession and the public health profession to cooperate
fully in the effort.

Second, securing the genuine and extensive participation--not
simply the token or half-hearted participation--of rural communities
at the base of such a system is especially complicated, yet absolutely
essential to its success. This invariably requires strong and steady
technical and other kinds of support and encouragement from a substantially strengthened and reorganized health infrastructure above
the village level.

Third, to plan and build and manage a primary health care system successfully, it is vitally important to keep viewing it *as* a system of highly interdependent and mutually supporting parts and to the surrounding social-economic-cultural milieu if the whole system is to function effectively. Regardless of how well any particular innovative feature may work in the context of a demonstration project, it cannot be expected to work equally well if plucked out separately and transplanted from the demonstration "system" to a quite different context--unless great care is taken to adapt it properly to all the other components of the receiving system.

These few general conclusions by no means exhaust all the important lessons that can be drawn from the Lampang experience. We suggest to our readers that as they examine the case study they try to discover on their own what the Lampang Project has to teach us all about such other important matters as: (1) improving the management and efficiency of a primary health care system; (2) the realistic problems of integrating a medically-dominated urban hospital system with a rural system seriously deficient in curative services; (3) the importance of evaluation, but also the serious limitations of expensive, sophisticated methodologies for measuring *quantitative* changes and impacts, which may in the end not answer some of the most important *qualitative* operational questions of prime concern to policymakers; (4) the most appropriate--and the least appropriate --kinds of help that external assistance agencies can render in this field, and the best ways of rendering it; and (5) perhaps most important of all, practical ways to insure that the poorest segment of rural communities enjoy equal access to and equal benefits from a primary health care system.

No one project, of course, can be expected to shed more than partial light on any of these basic issues. But because such relatively large and systematic, government run projects of rural primary health care are still few and far between, we must be especially grateful for such light as the Lampang Project affords, and to the authors of the case study who have given us the opportunity to see the light.

CHAPTER 1

PROJECT BACKGROUND

ORIGIN AND DEVELOPMENT OF PROJECT

Health leaders in Thailand have long recognized the need to strengthen the government health care delivery system and extend basic health services to cover the majority of the Thai population, 85 percent of which resides in under-served rural areas. During the 1960s, the rural population grew at over 3 percent a year and suffered primarily from easily-diagnosed and easily-treated conditions, such as communicable and infectious diseases common in Southeast Asia, diseases of pregnancy and childbirth, malnutrition, gastrointestinal problems, skin infections, and accidents. Scarcely 25 percent of the rural population had convenient access to government health facilities; and even where such facilities were available they were often not utilized. Only 15-17 percent of the rural population would seek health care from government facilities and personnel. Only 2-3 percent of the national budget was allocated for health services, and the limited numbers of trained medical and health personnel gravitated to Bangkok and other urban centers.

In the ten years before the conceptualization and development of the Lampang Health Development Project, the Ministry of Public Health implemented two pilot projects aimed at strengthening the rural health services delivery system and extending basic health services that would be available, accessible, affordable, and acceptable to the rural population. The experience gained in these projects--the Pitsanuloke Project and the Saraphi Project--had a direct influence in planning the Lampang Project.

The first of these was implemented by the Ministry of Health in 1964-68 in Pitsanuloke Province (population about 500,000) to strengthen rural health services through the construction of rural health centers, recruitment of additional health personnel, and retraining of all existing rural health personnel. Subdistrict (having a population of about 5,000) health workers were selected by local people to work on a voluntary basis, but they were eventually trained and hired as sanitarians to help staff the subdistrict level health centers. The important approaches of this effort were (1) strengthening rural health services facilitated by integration of health and medical services at the peripheral service units, (2) extending rural health services by recruiting villagers to be new health

workers, (3) establishing a revised record-keeping and reporting
system based on family folders, and (4) establishing a patient
referral system between the local health centers and the provincial
hospital. Regular supervision and a patient referral system were
attempted, but could not be maintained. The project was considered
a partial success, but it lacked adequate evaluation for detailed
analysis and planning purposes.

The Ministry of Public Health implemented the Saraphi Project
in Chiengmai Province in 1968-71 with a view to developing a model
for rural health services that would emphasize Maternal and Child
Health, Family Planning, Nutrition, and Communicable Disease
Control services and promote the active participation of the community and village health volunteers and health communicators. A
central district health center, five subdistrict health centers, and
six midwifery centers were constructed and staffed by newly-
recruited government health workers. The highlight of the project,
however, was the recruitment and training of health post volunteers
in three subdistricts and health communicators in another two subdistricts. Child Nutrition Centers were established through
community participation; village health posts were established and
staffed by village health post volunteers; well-child clinics were
strengthened in all service units; and a patient referral system
was attempted between the village health post and the government
health centers. The experience gained, although not adequately
evaluated, suggested that village health post volunteers and health
communicators could (1) effectively promote village level health
services, (2) strengthen the referral of patients to appropriate
facilities, and (3) encourage community participation in operating
the child nutrition centers.

Although these two earlier projects had ended their status as
"projects," a number of the innovations they fostered were subsequently applied in modified form in other areas by the Ministry of Health
and by the planners of the Lampang Project.   In particular, the
basic ideas for selecting and training local health post volunteers
and health communicators were borrowed by the Lampang Project
from the Saraphi Project.

In 1970, a national survey on the utilization of health services
in Thailand revealed that less than 20 percent of rural villagers,
when ill, utilized government rural health centers. Subsequent
analyses of the national health services revealed that the major
problems centered on the following: inadequate health service
coverage, inadequate health service manpower production and distribution, inadequate health data, poor coordination between public
and private health sectors, lack of communication between suppliers
and consumers, lack of community organization, inadequate health
service infrastructure, and poor administrative and management
practices resulting in fragmentation of services, duplication of effort,

and inefficient use of severely limited resources. Ministry of Public Health leaders were determined to find ways and means of solving these problems so as to bring basic health services within easy reach of a majority of the rural population.

In 1971 the U.S. Agency for International Development (US AID) had contracted with the American Public Health Association (APHA) to develop and evaluate new approaches for integrated rural health care delivery systems for improved health, population, and nutrition services in the developing world. The US AID-APHA proposal called for "long-term (up to eight years) pilot, experimental work to be carried out in four representative less-developed country locations...with a large population base (500,000 or more) in such a manner that general conclusions on accessibility, acceptability, and affordability can be drawn."

In 1972, the APHA approached the Royal Thai Government and the University of Hawaii to elicit their interest in collaborating on a "DEIDS" (Development and Evaluation of an Integrated Health Delivery System) project for Thailand. In 1973, a joint team of US AID, APHA, and University of Hawaii School of Public Health (UHSPH) representatives reached agreement in principle with the Thai Ministry of Public Health to plan a "DEIDS" project for Thailand, and the APHA and UHSPH recruited a health professional from Hawaii to work with the Ministry for six months to help plan the project. The plan for the DEIDS/Thailand Project was completed by late 1973 and was submitted, approved, and funded in 1974. Significantly, the Project Proposal stated that "after careful consideration with AID, it was decided that the planning/monitoring/evaluation system for the project should be expanded, beyond the original goal of measuring how many people are reached, to include planning and programming questions, and longer-run questions of cost-effectiveness and replicability." The Proposal also emphasized that "unless flexibility is possible during Phase III (implementation) activities, an acceptable low-cost system will be difficult to develop. Since the design of a high-coverage delivery system is unproven in Thailand, it must start with a reasonable hypothesis and let the program evolve from there through constant evaluation of services structure, utilization and cost."

The "DEIDS/Thailand Project" was inaugurated in September 1974, with the Royal Thai Government (RTG) and the APHA signing the "Project Agreement" for development and evaluation of a health delivery system in Lampang Province; and in December 1974, the University of Hawaii signed a subcontract with the American Public Health Association to provide technical assistance to the RTG in support of the DEIDS/Thailand Project. The administrative and collaborative structure of the Project provided for "central funding" from US AID (under the US AID-APHA/DEIDS Contract), a Project Agreement between APHA and the RTG to provide financial assistance, and a subcontract between the APHA and the UHSPH to provide technical assistance. The Project, approved by the Cabinet of the Royal Thai Government, has since been administered by the Ministry of Public Health and implemented by the Ministry's Department of Health and the Lampang Provincial Health Office. The Government's role in planning the Project and its steadfast commitment to the goal and objectives of the Project have been noteworthy.

The northern province of Lampang, with a 1974 population of over 600,000, was selected by the Ministry of Public Health to be the site for the "DEIDS/Thailand Project," now best known as the "Lampang Health Development Project." The selection called for: (1) a population over 500,000 (2) fair communications to and within the province, (3) a noninsurgency area, (4) moderate economic status, and (5) endorsement by provincial officials.

Figure 1 traces the evolution in Thailand of the key concepts and basic elements of an integrated rural primary health care system that were utlimately incorporated in the Lampang Health Development Project.

PHILOSOPHY AND RATIONALE

Given the limitations of budget, trained health manpower, health facilities and other resources needed for implementing and maintaining a viable and effective health delivery system, planners of the Lampang Project sought ways to expand health services that would be the most cost-effective. They recognized that it would be far too expensive to build adequate facilities and train enough physicians, even if they were willing to reside and work in rural areas. Therefore, project planners decided to retrain existing categories of health workers (nurses, midwives, and sanitarians) to provide a limited range of relevant and competent curative services as intermediate clinical care providers or as community health paraphysicians called *wechakorn*. * The limited number of available physicians could readily supervise the corps of wechakorn physician-extenders, and thereby significantly extend clinical care services to the subdistrict (population about 5,000) level. For more sophisticated clinical care by physicians, a patient referral system was planned to link all service facilities.

The planners were convinced that an *integrated* system that provided a combination of curative, disease prevention, and health promotion services--with special emphasis on nutrition, family planning, and maternal and child health services--would be more cost-effective than fragmented single-purpose services. They also believed that integrated services would be more comprehensive, convenient, and acceptable to the consumers. Hence, the Lampang Project aimed at the integration of previously separate health services and the reorganization of health system infrastructure. It was expected that by strengthening management practices and operating the health system through informed decisionmaking, based on a streamlined health information system, improved performance, efficiency, and effectiveness could be achieved.

Wechakorn, Thai for physician extender or paraphysician, is a term coined by Lampang Project leaders, derived from *wecha,* meaning medicine or medical care, and *korn,* meaning provider or practitioner.

FIGURE 1: DEVELOPMENT OF CONCEPTS AND BASIC ELEMENTS FOR PRIMARY HEALTH CARE AND INTEGRATED RURAL HEALTH SERVICES IN THAILAND (1964–1986)

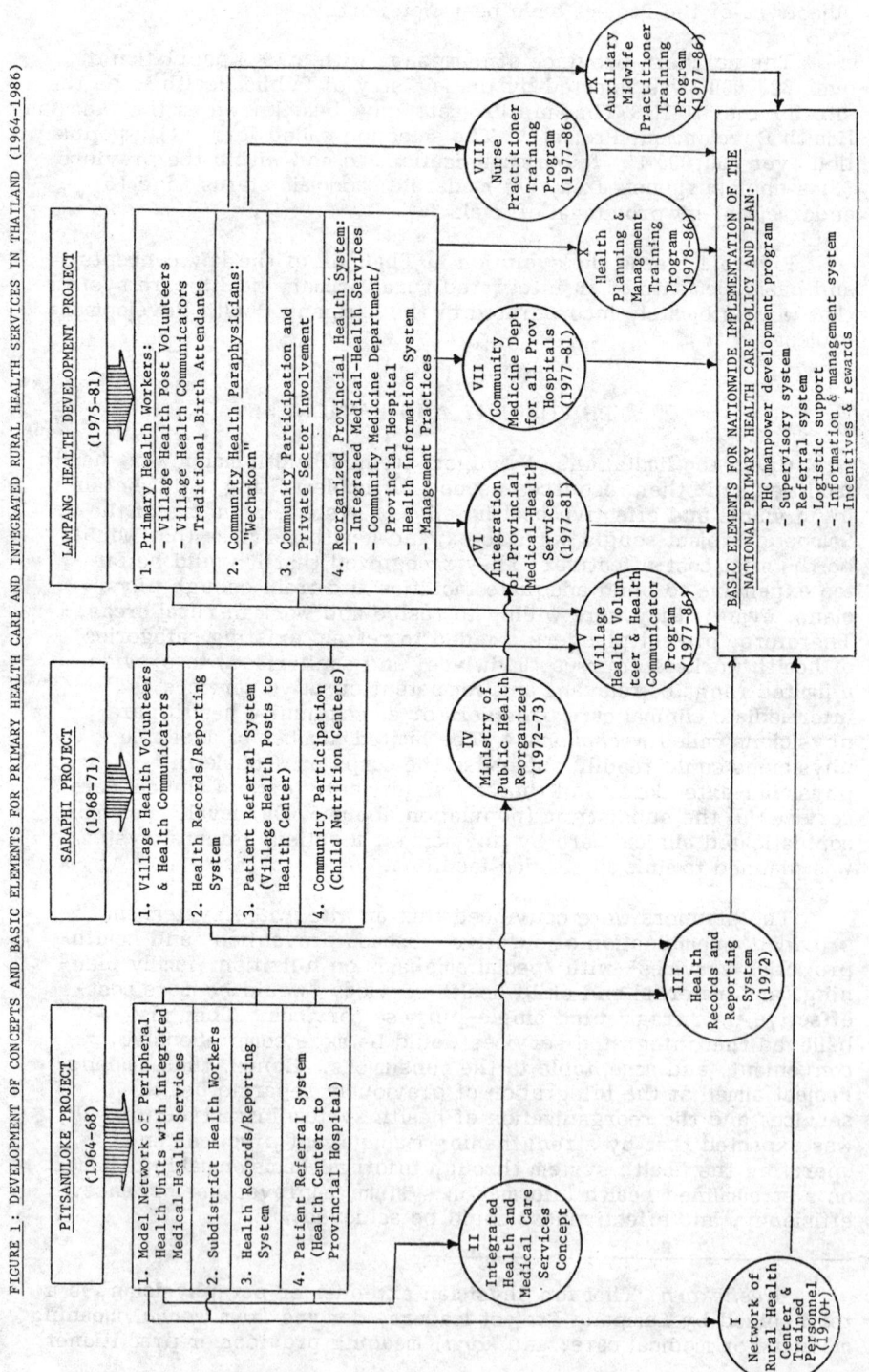

The central strategy of the Project coincided with the concepts inherent in the "primary health care" approach advocated by the World Health Organization. The mobilization of all available private sector and community resources would vastly increase the coverage of the coordinated government-private health care providers. Community organization and community participation in an expanded health system would be essential. The concept of village health volunteers and health communicators, present in earlier projects, required further testing but seemed promising. It was felt that village health volunteers could be supervised and guided by the wechakorn and other health workers at the nearby health center, and that the wechakorn would provide the first referral point for village volunteers. It was recognized that most rural deliveries are performed by traditional birth attendants. Thus, rather than attempt to change this pattern, plans were made to train the traditional birth attendants in more sanitary practices and to recognize conditions requiring more skilled attention.

GOAL AND OBJECTIVES

The ultimate *goal* of the Lampang Project is to improve the health status of the population of Lampang Province. The more specific *objectives* for reaching this goal are:

1. to expand health care coverage to at least two-thirds of the rural population, especially women in their child-bearing years and preschool age children, with an emphasis on family planning, nutrition, and maternal and child health services;

2. to establish a model integrated provincial health service delivery system which extends integrated curative-preventive-promotive health services to every subdistrict health center, and to establish preventive-promotive health services in every village through trained village health volunteers; and

3. to establish a provincial health care system that is cost-effective, meaning "lower-cost" per service unit, the key features of which can be replicated nationwide within the limitations of Royal Thai Government resources.

To achieve these objectives the planners envisaged a vertically integrated, multi-tier health care delivery system, illustrated diagramatically in Figure 2. The system as a whole was designed to expand both curative and preventive/promotive services in proportions appropriate to the health needs of the local population. It was also designed to make optimum use of scarce highly-trained health manpower and sophisticated facilities and equipment through

FIGURE 2: DISTRIBUTION OF EFFORT
BY LEVEL AND TYPE OF SERVICE

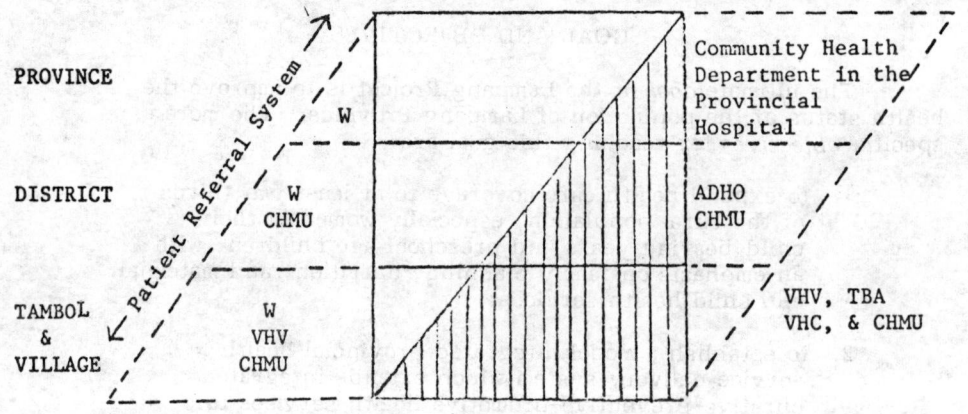

```
                              C U R A T I V E

                                                    Community Health
PROVINCE                                            Department in the
                           W                        Provincial
                                                    Hospital

DISTRICT                   W                        ADHO
                           CHMU                     CHMU

TAMBOL                     W                         VHV, TBA
  &                        VHV                       VHC, & CHMU
VILLAGE                    CHMU
```

      W   = Wechakorn (Paraphysician)
    VHV   = Village Health Volunteer
    VHC   = Village Health Communicator
    TBA   = Traditional Birth Attendant
   ADHO   = Assistant District Health Officer
   CHMU   = Community Health Dept. Mobile Unit

an appropriate division of labor among the different tiers.

The bottom tier, comprising the subdistrict (tambol) health center team and affiliated village level volunteer health workers, would devote about three-quarters of their total effort to preventive/promotional work and the remaining quarter to handling simpler curative cases (referring more difficult cases to higher levels). The district hospital at the middle level and the provincial hospital at the top would devote the bulk of their effort (about three-quarters) to more sophisticated curative services and in addition would provide important supervisory and support services to both the curative and preventive/promotive work at the bottom tier.

The specific strategies of the project and the various staff and institutional arrangements it provided to insure the effective functioning of the system depicted in Figure 2 will be examined below. First, however, it will be useful to examine the health system as it existed prior to the project and also the demographic features and health status of the rural population.

NATIONAL HEALTH CARE STRUCTURE

The Ministry of Public Health is the major health service provider in Thailand, overseeing a widespread network of hospitals and rural health centers reaching out to all 71 provinces, to over half of the 570 districts of the country, to about 60 percent of the subdistricts, and to almost 10 percent of the villages. The Ministry in Bangkok is organized as follows (see Figure 3):

1. The Office of the Under Secretary of State for Public Health coordinates the work of five ministry departments and directly administers the provincial health care system.

2. The Department of Medical Services is responsible for specific hospitals in the Bangkok area and for special-function hospitals (including psychiatric care) in other parts of the country.

3. The Department of Health, with eight technical divisions, provides a variety of support for ministry programs relating to the environment and population.

4. The Department of Communicable Disease Control coordinates all immunization and disease control programs.

5. The Department of Medical Sciences is responsible for laboratory research and services.

6. The Office of Food and Drug Control is the national unit responsible for control of food and drug production and distribution.

Besides these service functions, the Ministry also trains a large number of health workers to staff its network of health facilities.

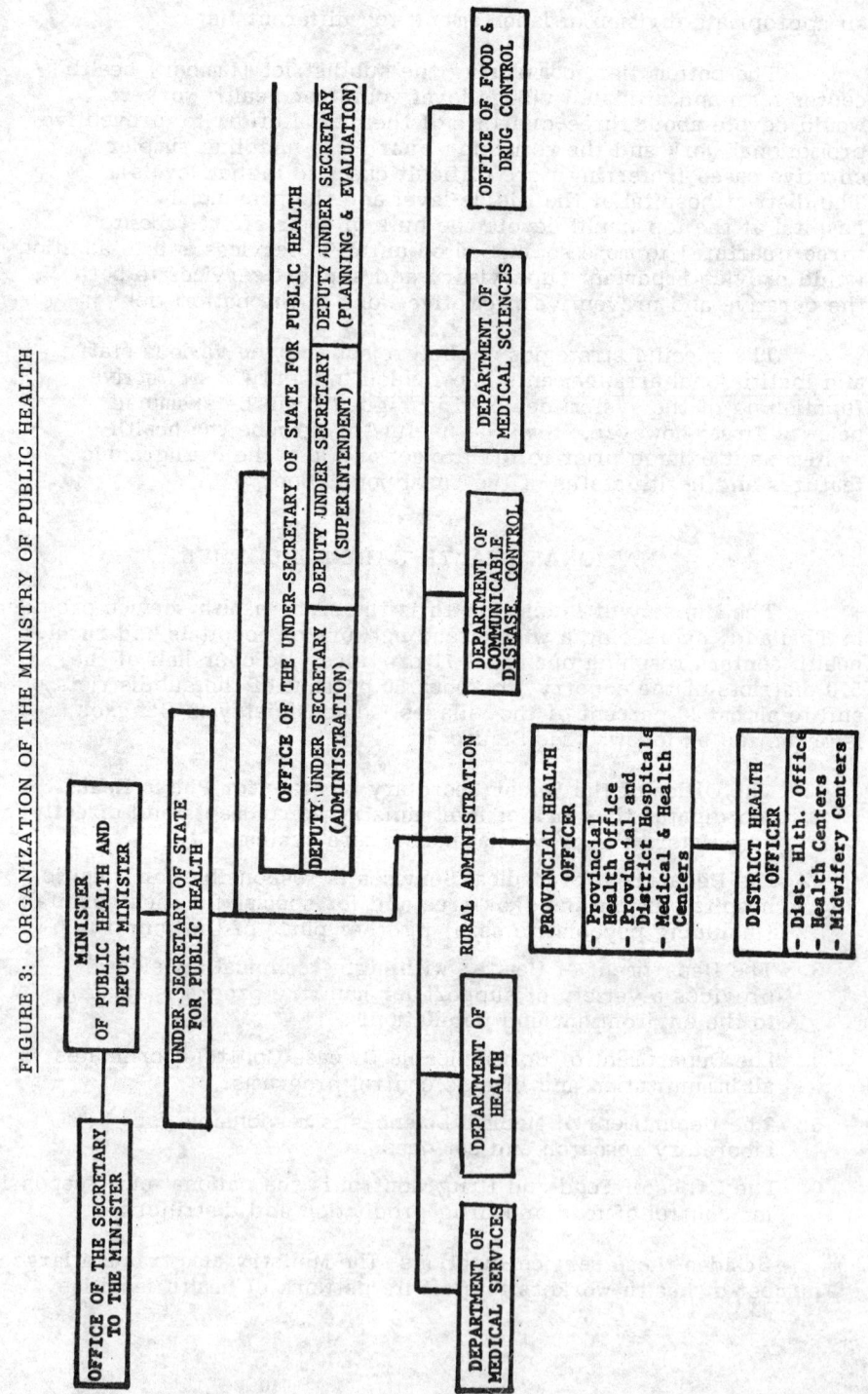

FIGURE 3: ORGANIZATION OF THE MINISTRY OF PUBLIC HEALTH

FIGURE 4: NETWORK AND ADMINISTRATIVE RELATIONSHIP
BETWEEN MINISTRY OF PUBLIC HEALTH AND
MINISTRY OF INTERIOR, THAILAND (1978)

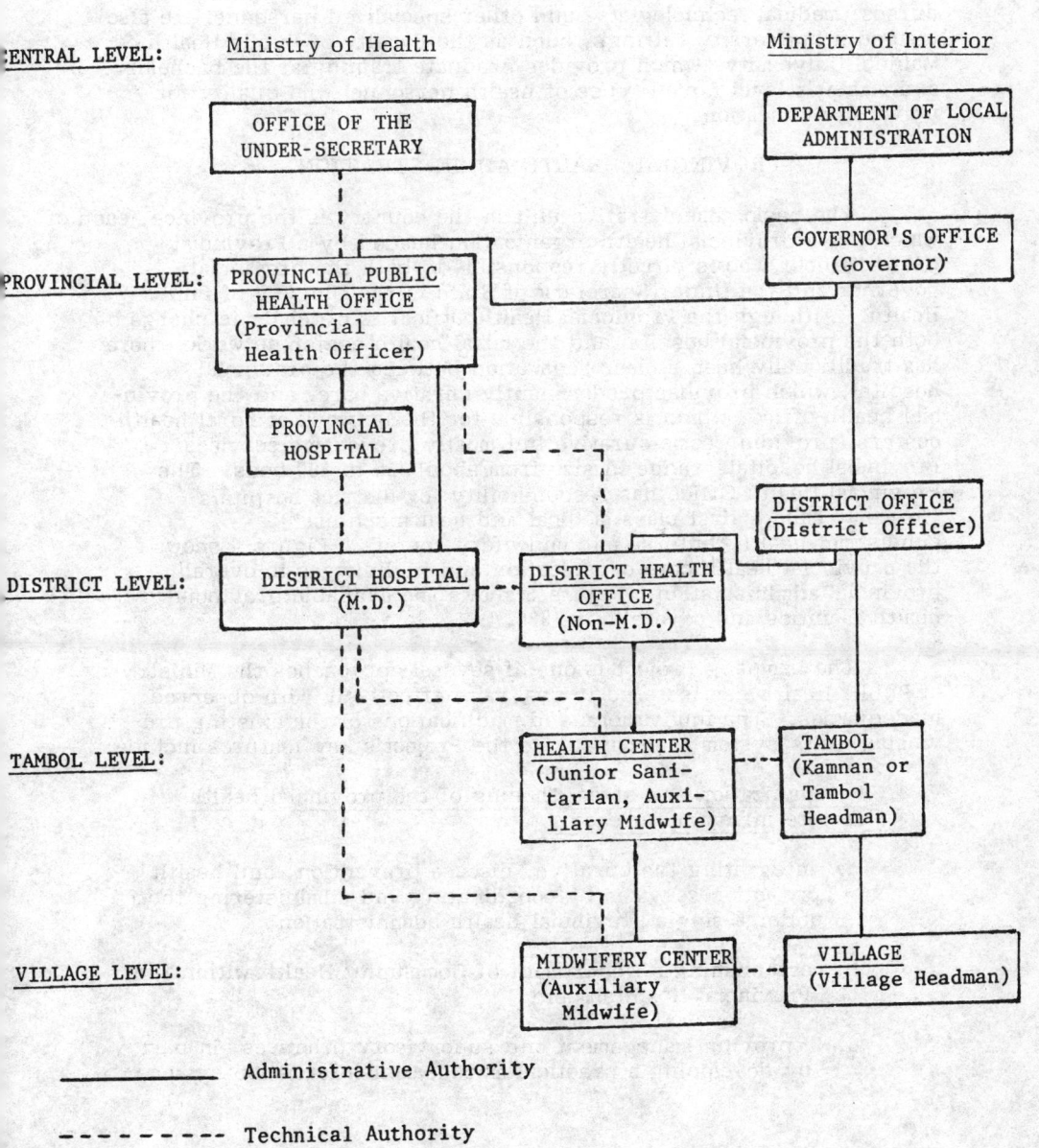

Administrative Authority

- - - - - - - - -   Technical Authority

It provides preservice training for nurses, midwives, male sanitarian health workers, nurse aides, and a variety of other auxiliary personnel. It also offers a wide array of refresher courses and other types of continuing education to its personnel.

Other more specialized and highly trained health personnel are produced outside of the Ministry. Physicians are trained in six medical schools, three of which are located in Bangkok. A large number of nurses, medical technologists, and other specialized personnel are also trained in university settings, such as the Faculty of Public Health of Mahidol University, which provides graduate training at the bachelor and master's level for all types of health personnel who qualify for university education.

PROVINCIAL HEALTH ADMINISTRATION

The basic administrative unit in the country is the province, each of which has a provincial health organization headed by a Provincial Health Officer who is directly responsible to both the provincial governor and the Under Secretary of State in the Ministry of Public Health. Although the Provincial Health Officer is officially in charge of both the provincial hospital and the rural health center network, there has traditionally been a clear separation between the provincial hospital, which provides predominantly curative care, and the provincial health office, which is responsible for the network of rural health centers, providing some curative but mostly preventive services. Provincial hospitals range in size from about 150 to 600 beds. The Provincial Health Office has responsibility for district hospitals (formerly called "first class medical and health centers"), subdistrict health centers, and midwifery centers. Figure 4 shows the provincial health care organization and its linkages to overall provincial administration. Figure 5 shows the available provincial health facilities and coverage in 1976.

The Lampang Project is one of several approaches the Ministry of Public Health has fostered to deal more effectively with observed inadequacies. The innovations and modifications of the existing provincial health system that constitute the Project's key features include:

1. Reorganization and strengthening of the provincial health service infrastructure by:

    a. integrating the curative, disease prevention, and health promotion services by coordinating and administering them under a single provincial health administration;

    b. establishing a Department of Community Health within the Provincial Hospital; and

    c. improving management and supervisory practices, in part by developing a practical management information system.

FIGURE 5: CURRENT MINISTRY OF PUBLIC HEALTH FACILITIES
AT THE PROVINCIAL LEVEL 1976 [a]

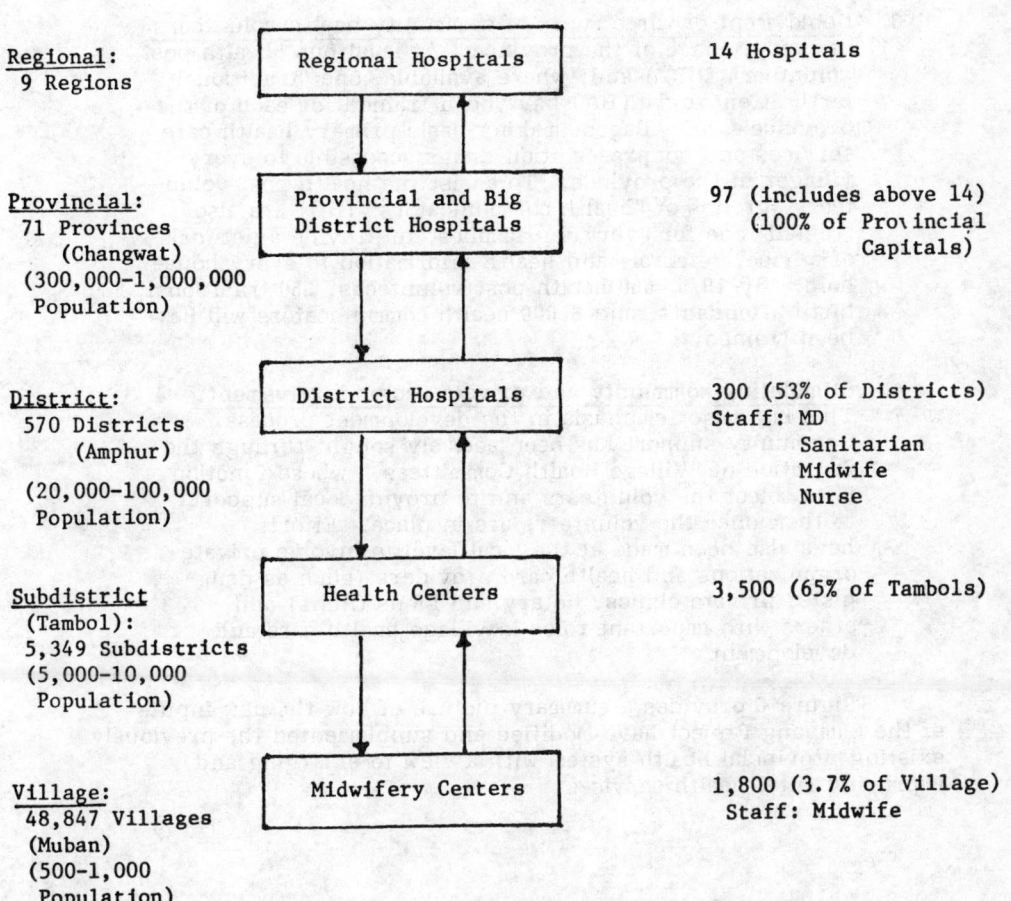

Regional:
9 Regions

Regional Hospitals   14 Hospitals

Provincial:
71 Provinces
(Changwat)
(300,000-1,000,000
Population)

Provincial and Big
District Hospitals

97 (includes above 14)
(100% of Provincial
Capitals)

District:
570 Districts
(Amphur)

(20,000-100,000
Population)

District Hospitals

300 (53% of Districts)
Staff: MD
Sanitarian
Midwife
Nurse

Subdistrict
(Tambol):
5,349 Subdistricts
(5,000-10,000
Population)

Health Centers

3,500 (65% of Tambols)

Village:
48,847 Villages
(Muban)
(500-1,000
Population)

Midwifery Centers

1,800 (3.7% of Village)
Staff: Midwife

[a] Source: MOPH Planning Division, 1976

2. Development of community health paraphysicians (wechakorn) to overcome the lack of skilled curative services available at the periphery. Ninety-two wechakorn, recruited from among nurses, midwives, sanitarians, and nurse aides have been trained for one year in the provincial and district hospitals, after which the majority return to assignments in subdistrict health centers.

3. Deployment of three types of community health volunteers in every village of the province. At least one "health post volunteer" (HPV) and, where available, one "traditional birth attendant" (TBA) have been trained for each of the province's 545 villages, making basic primary health care services and nonprescription drugs accessible to every villager in the province. To assist the health post volunteers, groups of "health communicators" (HC) are also trained, one for every ten families, to provide a network of advice, referral, and health information to every household. By 1979, 650 health post volunteers, 350 traditional birth attendants, and 6,000 health communicators will have been trained.

4. Stimulating community and private sector involvement. This is a major emphasis in the development process. Community support has been actively sought through the formation of "Village Health Committees," whose function is to select the volunteers and to provide local support to them once the volunteers are in place. Efforts have also been made at the local level to involve private organizations and health care providers (such as druggists, private clinics, Rotary and Lions Clubs) and others with important roles in village health care and development.

Figure 6 provides a summary picture of how the new inputs of the Lampang Project have modified and supplemented the previously existing provincial health system with a view to enlarging and improving rural health services.

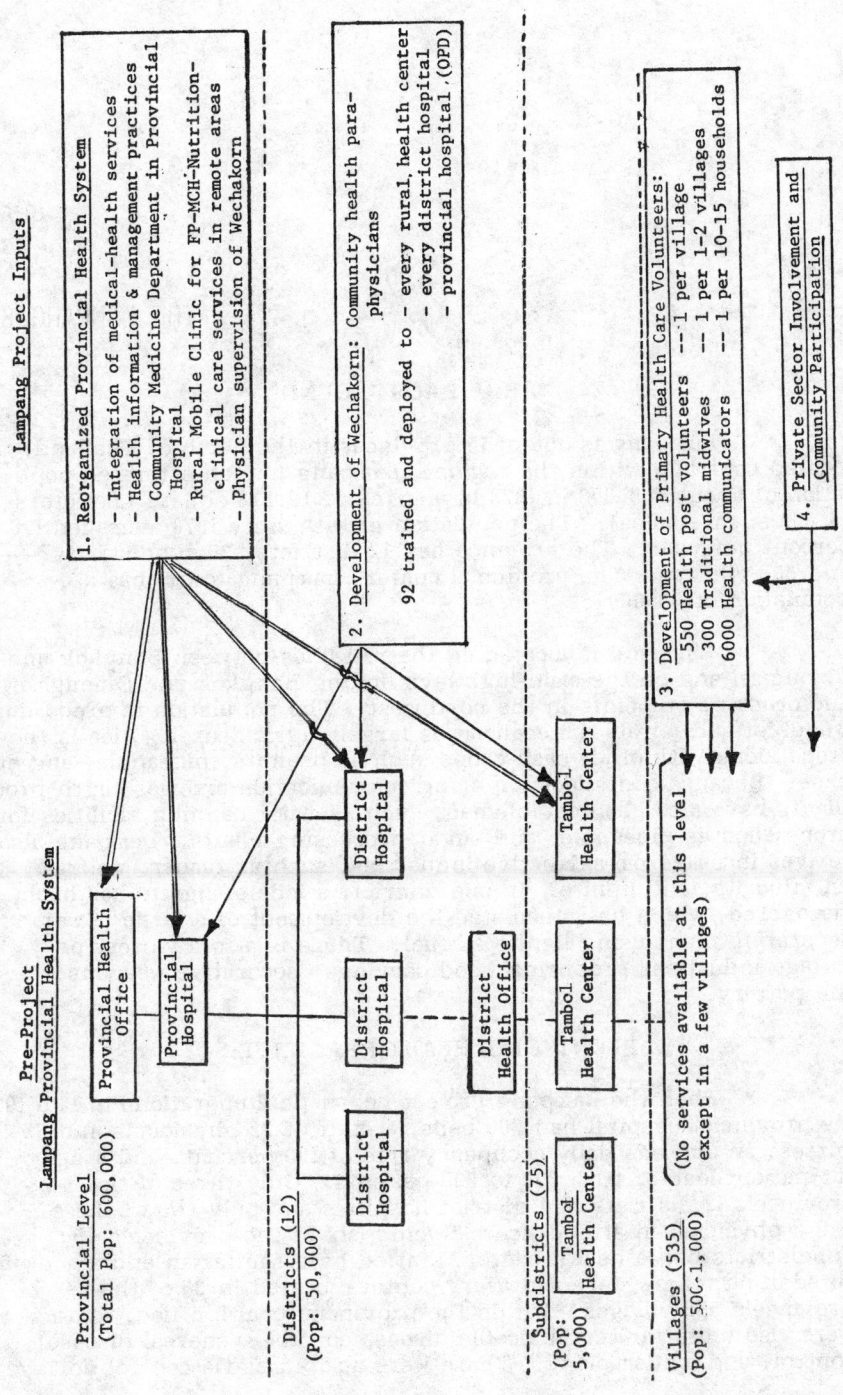

FIGURE 6: LAMPANG PROVINCIAL HEALTH SYSTEM AND THE INPUTS OF THE LAMPANG HEALTH DEVELOPMENT PROJECT

Lampang Project Inputs

1. Reorganized Provincial Health System
   - Integration of medical-health services
   - Health information & management practices
   - Community Medicine Department in Provincial Hospital
   - Rural Mobile Clinic for FP-MCH-Nutrition-clinical care services in remote areas
   - Physician supervision of Wechakorn

2. Development of Wechakorn: Community health para-physicians

   92 trained and deployed to - every rural health center
   - every district hospital
   - provincial hospital (OPD)

3. Development of Primary Health Care Volunteers:
   550 Health post volunteers -- 1 per village
   300 Traditional midwives -- 1 per 1-2 villages
   6000 Health communicators -- 1 per 10-15 households

4. Private Sector Involvement and Community Participation

Pre-Project
Lampang Provincial Health System

Provincial Level
(Total Pop: 600,000)

Provincial Health Office

Provincial Hospital

Districts (12)
(Pop: 50,000)

District Hospital

District Hospital

District Hospital

District Health Office

Subdistricts (75)
(Pop: 5,000)

Tambol Health Center

Tambol Health Center

Tambol Health Center

Tambol Health Center

Villages (535)
(Pop: 500-1,000)

(No services available at this level except in a few villages)

CHAPTER 2

THE LAMPANG SETTING

AREA BACKGROUND

Lampang is one of 16 provinces in the north of Thailand, located centrally within the region. Lampang had an estimated population of about 660,000 in 1978 in an area of 12,518 square kilometers (4,890 square miles). The population growth since 1970 averaged 1.8 percent per year. The province has 12 districts, 75 subdistricts, and 538 villages. The provincial center Lampang town, has a population of 50,000.

Lampang is located on the rail lines between Bangkok and Chiengmai and on the main highways linking Bangkok and Chiengmai and other major points in the northwest. The population is predominantly Buddhist and rural; the economy is largely agricultural. Rice is the main crop, along with other cash crops such as peanuts, pineapple, and sugar cane. Because of its location along communication arteries, agro-processing plants have also been established, such as major canning facilities for crops such as pineapple, and sugar processing plants. Lampang also derives income from extractive industries, such as timber, wolfram, tin, fluorite, and lignite. In one district, a lode of lignite has been discovered, which has stimulated the development of a large power generating plant using lignite as fuel. There is also a variety of cottage industries producing wood carvings, decorative weapons, and pottery.

PROVINCIAL HEALTH FACILITIES

When the Lampang Project began field operations in late 1974 the provincial hospital had 300 beds, a staff of 22 physicians and 58 nurses, an average daily occupancy rate of 100 percent, and a daily out-patient load of from 300 to 500 patients. Only three of the province's 12 districts had district hospitals and only two of these had a physician in attendance. Twenty-six of the province's 75 subdistricts had a health center, staffed by a sanitarian and a midwife. In addition, there were midwifery centers located in 33 of the province's 538 villages. Within the provincial health office, there were also units for communicable disease control, venereal disease control, and epidemiology. There were also a malaria control unit, a regional sanitarian center, a leprosy control center, and a regional midwifery school also located in the health service complex.   In addition to government-sector health services, there were at least 20 private medical clinics in Lampang town (staffed mostly by hospital physicians in nonofficial hours), and two private hospitals of 25-50 beds each. In the rural areas,there were a variety of indigenous practitioners, such as herbalists, injectionists, traditional birth attendants, magical and spirit doctors.

The services provided by each type of government health facility mentioned above can be summarized as follows:

1. *Provincial Hospital:* Basically curative health services are available with the primary specialties and a few sub-specialties represented. Patients requiring more sophisticated care are referred to the teaching hospitals in Chiengmai or Bangkok. Male and female sterilization, as well as IUDs, birth control pills, and Depoprovera injections are available in the hospital's family planning unit.

2. *District Hospital:* Clinical care is provided for most acute illnesses, trauma episodes and minor surgery, along with short-term, acute in-patient care. It also provides the full range of maternal and child health and family planning services, including vasectomy (in one district hospital), IUD insertion, pills, and Depoprovera injection.

3. *Subdistrict Health Center:* Provides first aid and emergency treatment for minor illness and injury, pre- and post-natal care, deliveries, child and school health, nutrition center services, family planning services including pill and condom distribution, sanitation and environmental health (privies and clean water supply).

4. *Midwifery Center:* Offers pre- and post-natal care, deliveries, family planning services, including pill and condom distribution.

During the ensuing four years the provincial and district level hospital facilities were substantially augmented, not as a direct result of the Lampang Project but as part of the government's nationwide effort to enlarge rural health facilities. By 1978, there were five district hospitals, all with doctors and wechakorn assigned, and one more scheduled for completion in 1979.

HEALTH STATUS OF THE POPULATION

The community health survey conducted in 1975 established a baseline against which many of the objectives of the Lampang Health Development Project (LHDP) will be measured. It also provides a

picture of health status in the first experimental area brought into
the LDHP (Hang Chat--E1) and its two control areas (C1 and C2).
One of the control areas (Mae Tah--C1) is in Lampang Province, the
other, C2, is in an adjoining province and will not be considered
further here (see following Figure 7). About 20 percent of households, or 1,500, in E1 were sampled. The comprable figure for C1
was 10 percent or 1,100. The data to follow characterize some 100,000
people, or about 15 percent of the estimated 1975 population in
Lampang Province.

   Households in the two sampled areas were predominantly
rural and mostly engaged in agriculture. Only 20-25 percent were
considered poor.* Almost half the households had access to a
water-seal latrine. Most families obtained their drinking water from
shallow wells, half of them within their own compounds. Only 10
percent took further steps to boil or filter their drinking water.

1.   Illnesses and Choice of Remedial Services:

   In the two weeks before the survey, 9 percent of the
   sampled population claimed to have been ill. The most
   common symptoms were diarrhea, shortness of breath,
   painful or cloudy urination, stomachache, fever,
   headache, cough, and vomiting, in that order.
   Fifty-five percent of illnesses did not last over
   6 days.

   As shown in Table 1, fifty to sixty percent purchased
   medicine directly and only 27 percent went to
   government health facilities for diagnosis and treatment.

   While much illness is self-limited, prolonged self-
   treatment or reliance on traditional healers may at times
   lead to more serious disease and disability by delaying
   the application of more appropriate medical care. Although
   government health services may be utilized more in area
   E1, as compared to the 1970 national survey results, the
   absolute figure remains low. The finding that relatively
   few individuals sought care in the more expensive private
   sector suggests that the population in area E1 has less
   access to this sector (confirmed by local observers), but
   also, as compared to the national sample, is less able to
   afford such care when ill.

---

   *This statistic is based on subjective judgments by the in-
dividual interviewers, taking into account the quality of the family's
housing, its possessions such as farm animals, and the amount of
arable land it owned or tilled. Fragmentary evidence from other
surveys suggest, however, that the percentage of seriously poor
families in the rural sector of Lampang Province may be substantially
higher than 20-25 percent.

FIGURE 7: GEOGRAPHICAL PHASING OF PROJECT IMPLEMENTATION

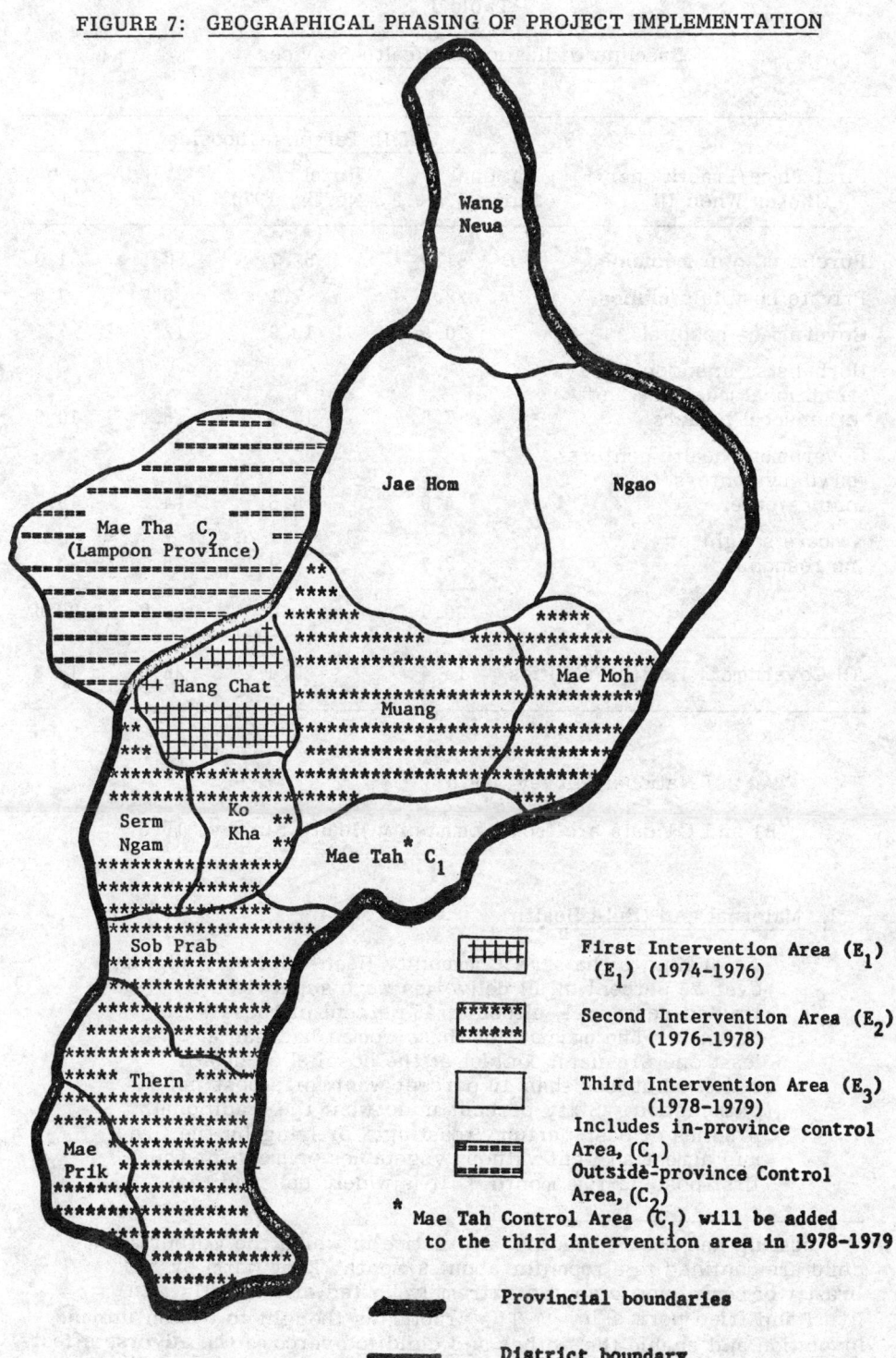

Table 1

Baseline Utilization of Health Services

First Place/Practitioner Chosen When Ill	% of Ill Persons Choosing			
	National Survey, 1970	Rural[a] North, 1970	E_1[b]	C_1[b]
Purchased own medicine	51.4	52.7	50.5	61.0
Private hospitals/clinics	22.7	7.1	8.7	7.3
Government hospital	10.5	13.9	12.7	7.1
Herbalists, injectionists, traditional midwives and other local healers	7.8	17.4	8.8	10.9
Government health centers/ miwifery centers/ clinics/other	4.9	6.5	14.2	10.7
No care sought or no response	2.7	2.4	5.1	3.0
	100.0	100.0	100.0	100.0
All Government Health Facilities	15.4	20.4	26.9	17.8

[a]Part of National Survey, 1970

[b]E1 and C1 data are from Community Health Survey, 1975.

2. Maternal and Child Health:

According to the same Community Health Survey, slightly
over 75 percent of all deliveries were supervised by
trained personnel, although 45 percent of these were
at home. The majority of these women had had at
least one pre-natal contact at the hospital or health
center, but less than 10 percent went for a post-natal
examination. Sixty percent underwent the traditional
practice of post-partum "roasting," or lying by the fire,
and almost all went without vegetables or meat for the
first post-partum month.* It is widely believed that

*Roasting has been a traditional practice in which the mother and
child are confined to a room for about a month, kept warm by a
brazier of coals, and given an extremely limited diet--mostly rice-
gruel and fried pork skin.   The practice is thought to hasten uterine
involution and enable the mother and child to overcome the adverse effects
of delivery.

the post-partum mother should refrain from eating a variety
of (frequently nutritious) foods in the belief that the practice
will protect the health of suckling infants. Salted baked rice
and pork skin are the main foods permitted. While there is
difference of opinion about some foods, some restrictions of
food is the usual practice even among younger mothers.

Analysis of the pregnancy history data revealed a 1974 infant
mortality rate of 53.6 (per 1,000 live births) in area E1,
and 74.2 in area C1. Although the official national rate from
reported deaths is 25 per thousand live births, independent
estimates from the Survey of Population Change, believed
to be more accurate, suggests a rate between 75-80. Nutritional surveillance information for children under 6 indicates
that 13-15 percent may be second or third degree malnourished
against a Thai weight-for-age standard. These findings in
E1   are   supported by independent data from other districts
in Lampang Province.

3.   Fertility and Family Planning:

It is clear that fertility in Lampang has been falling rapidly
since the late 1960s, well ahead of the rest of Thailand.
Contiguous provinces, probably in response to vigorous
family planning efforts, have shown an even more rapid fertility decline. All sources indicate crude birth rates in the
vicinity of 20 per 1,000 population and confirm that population
age structure and changing marital patterns do not explain the
decline in both E1 and C1. The national rate is currently
estimated at 32.

Over 50 percent of eligible married women were currently using
a method, most often the pill, in E1 and C1 in 1975. It is
important to note the likely role of family planning in bringing
married women in contact with government health services.
As shown in Table 2, a much larger proportion of women used
services than did children under 6, although both rates are
relatively high.

Since it seems likely that other maternal and child health
services are promoted through the strong interest in family
planning, integration of these services can further
activate and extend the benefits to children.

The Project design is basically a quasi-experimental pre-test/
post-test type, with two control areas. In the Lampang operational
area, there are three sequentially-phased experimental areas designated
E1, E2, and E3 for implementation, corresponding to the districts listed
below. E1 is a single district, E2 comprises seven districts, and E3
has four districts. Mae Tah is one control district (C1) within Lampang
Province (which will be the last district for implementation of Project

Table 2

Proportion of Women (Age 15-44 years) and Children (age
under 6 years) Using Government Health
Services in Areas E1 and C1

Target Population	E1	C1
Married women 15-44	54.6%	53.8%
Children under 6	31.1%	31.1%

Source: 1974 Community Health Survey, LHDP.

interventions), and another control district (C2) is in Lampoon Province
adjacent to Lampang. The preceding map (Figure 7) shows the phased
intervention areas and the two control areas.

Geographical Phasing of Project Implementation

Project implementation was planned in three stages: the first stage
(October 1974 to October 1976) covered one district (E1), Hang Chat;
stage two (October 1976-78) covered the seven districts of the southern
part of the province (E2)--Muang, Mae Moh, Ko Kha, Serm Ngam, Sob
Prab, Mae Prik, Thern; and the third phase will extend the project
to all remaining districts (E3) -- Wang Nua, Jae Hom, Ngao, and Mae
Tah (C1). E1 contains about 7 percent of the province's population,
and E2 and E3 contain about 60 percent and 33 percent, respectively.

CHAPTER 3

ORGANIZATION, PERSONNEL,

AND MANAGEMENT

PROJECT ORGANIZATION

To describe the Lampang Project organization is a complex task because project personnel include existing staff members from the provincial health organization, professionals assigned from other units within the Ministry of Public Health and other government agencies, as well as other technical and administrative staff hired specifically for the Project. Project field operations -- delivery of services, training, supervision, management -- are carried out by resident provincial health staff. Those who have come to the Project from the outside act as planners and stimulators, helping to introduce and evaluate the new approaches that are the heart of the Lampang Project. In the final analysis, it is the provincial health organization that must deliver health services to the population of Lampang. The Lampang Project aims to make this process more pervasive, more efficient, more integrated, more community-oriented, and more affordable.

One activity which is not normally a responsibility of the provincial health organization (and one for which it is not equipped) is project evaluation. Evaluation activities--surveys, data processing and analysis, etc.--are carried out by special evaluation staff with necessary coordinating support from the province. Project evaluation staff assist the provincial health staff in strengthening its own information and analysis systems.

The Lampang Project has been organized into a number of components to assist in Project implementation at the provincial level, and to coordinate support from the central ministry in Bangkok. Figure 8 outlines the general Project organization and staff. The Project Director is the Director-General of the Department of Health, one of the five departments within the Ministry. The Project Director takes responsibility for coordinating all support with the various agencies both inside and outside the Ministry of Public Health, and he has established a Project office within the Department of Health. In Lampang Province,

FIGURE 8: LAMPANG PROJECT ORGANIZATION
AND KEY PERSONNEL

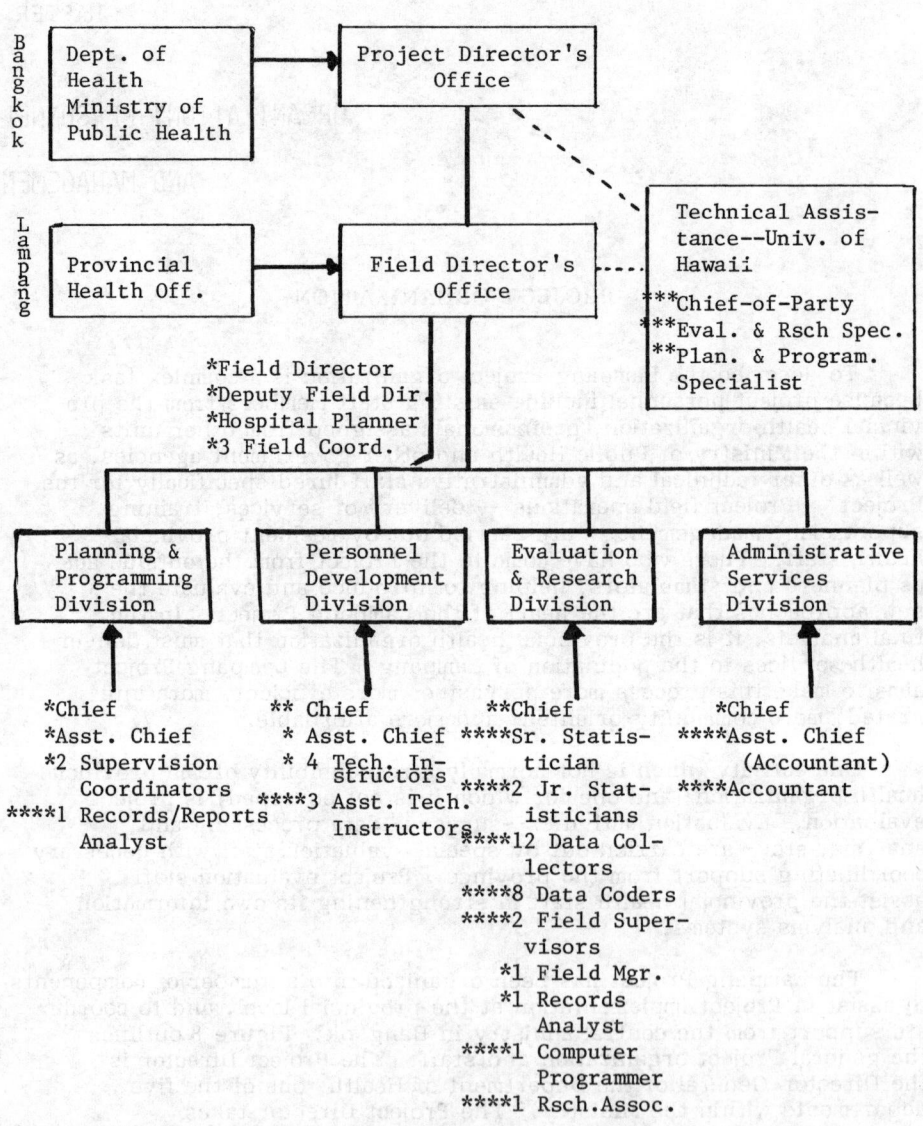

*   Regular MOPH and Lampang Provincial Health Personnel
**   Special assignment personnel from RTG agencies (including
        MOPH) and institutions.
***   U. S. Personnel (Univ. of Hawaii)
****   Hired from private sector.

the Project Field Director oversees Project operations at the provincial level, and all Project division chiefs report to him. Because the heart of Project operations is improved coverage and delivery of health services within the province, it was recognized from the outset that the Field Director must also be a senior provincial health official. Consequently, the Project Field Director has been the Provincial Health Officer from the outset.

Under the Field Director are four Project Divisions: the Planning and Programming Division, the Personnel Development Division, the Evaluation and Research Division, and the Administrative Services Division.

The Planning and Programming Division has responsibility for assisting the provincial health staff in planning and implementing the various modifications and innovative approaches in the Project. The small staff of five professionals have assisted health staff at all levels of the province in selecting the paraphysician wechakorn, in organizing the village committees, in selecting village health volunteers, in stimulating participation from private sector groups, and in organizing programs of special emphasis, such as nutrition surveillance and services and expanded family planning services. In short, the Planning and Programming Division has been responsible for assistance in planning all activities related to service delivery.

The Personnel Development Division, with a staff of training specialists, has responsibility for planning and implementing all training and orientation required to implement the various project approaches. This includes the design and development of the wechakorn paraphysician curriculum, organizing the training schedule in cooperation with the provincial hospital and other health facilities, and preparing all related training materials. It also includes developing a two-week training curriculum and field training programs for the health post volunteers and traditional midwives, and the two-day training sessions for the health communicators. In addition, the division organizes orientation programs for the various service and supervisory personnel at the provincial level; it also implements a training-for-trainers program for those provincial staff who carry the burden of field training. The Personnel Development Division prepares all teaching materials and aids needed for each of the training programs, and draws on a wide range of experience available at other training institutions for assistance.

The Evaluation and Research Division has responsibility for monitoring Project progress and for measuring its impact on service delivery and on the health status of the target population. Because the demands of the evaluation process are unique and outside the normal range of provincial health service activity (and will not be continued at the end of the Project), the Evaluation Division has carried out its activities with its own personnel. Given its wide range of activities, the Evaluation Division has the largest staff of all Project divisions.

The Division of Administrative Services was set up to administer financial and administrative services. It prepares the Project budget, oversees Project expenditures, controls fiscal and administrative procedures, and prepares all required financial reports.

In addition to the Project divisions, a technical assistance staff of three faculty members of the University of Hawaii School of Public Health work as integral members of the Project staff, providing technical consultation in the areas of planning and management, manpower development, evaluation and research. They also assist in coordinating activities with international agencies. The American Public Health Association monitors and manages the project in behalf of the U. S. Agency for International Development.

In addition to the Project staff and UHSPH technical assistance staff resident in Lampang, division chiefs may draw on outside consultants for special technical needs when required. The Evaluation and Research Division and the Personnel Development Division in particular have used outside consultants in carrying out their operations. Most of these consultants have come from institutions within Thailand. Occasionally, consultants from abroad have also been invited.

ORGANIZATIONAL CHANGE AND INTEGRATION

Although the Ministry of Public Health has nominally brought together the hospital and rural health services under one administrative unit (the Provincial Health Office), an effective system of cooperation and coordination at the provincial level has not yet been fully developed.

The Lampang Project has sought to establish a closer alignment between the curative hospital services and the preventive/promotive services of the rural health facilities. This process is considered essential, since the hospital is viewed as the nucleus for medical and health care in the province, providing leadership in training and technical support, as well as service delivery. As part of the design for reorganization, a Department of Community Health--Thailand's first department of this type in a provincial hospital--was established to provide a link between the hospital and rural health centers.

The Community Health Department's Mobile Health Clinic Program provides an interesting example of how the activities of the provincial hospital and rural health care infrastructure have become integrated under the Lampang Project. This particular activity grew out of a nationwide mobile vasectomy program organized by the Ministry of Public Health's National Family Planning Project to meet an evident large demand among rural males for vasectomies. Responsibility for operating a mobile unit in Lampang Province was accepted by the new Community Health Department of the provincial hospital.

Initially the Lampang mobile clinic sessions were confined to vasectomies, but as a result of heavy villager response and requests for other types of services they were expanded to provide out-patient curative care, immunizations, nutrition education and food supplements. The mobile clinic usually goes to two locations a month (generally a rural health center, but occasionally a district hospital that lacks vasectomy services) and spends two days at each location. One week in advance a health education team goes into the scheduled area and works with the health post volunteers and health communicators to inform the villagers of the forthcoming clinic and to motivate them to attend. (A number of HPVs have set a good example by being among the first to seek a vasectomy.)

The mobile clinic staff generally includes one or two surgeons from the provincial hospital, assisted by a small team of surgical nurses or wechakorn. This team works hand-in-hand with the local health center team during the clinic sessions, thus providing them useful on-the-job training. These mobile clinic sessions have had a positive effect in attracting large numbers of villagers to the local health centers, in stimulating and training local health care activities, and in greatly increasing the number of vasectomies. In the first year of operation the mobile clinics performed more than one thousand vasectomies and over three thousand immunizations, and treated nearly seven thousand out-patients.

The training and supervision of the wechakorn paraphysicians has also served to improve the links between the hospital and the rural health centers. Most of the one-year training period is spent in the provincial hospital, first in the didactic classroom phase, and then in the clinical preceptorship rotations. During the training period, the wechakorn trainees develop a strong relationship with their physician-instructors. Not all physicians in the provincial hospital accept the idea or the added burden of training nonphysicians in a broad range of clinical care. However, recognition of the need for, and utility of, the new paraphysician is increasing because of the clear contributions made by the nurse-wechakorn who are assigned to the provincial hospital.

Introducing the wechakorn into the provincial hospital, the district hospitals, and the rural health centers has broadened and strengthened the pattern of health care at each of these facilities. In the provincial hospital, nurse wechakorn are utilized in screening patients in the Out-patient Department, relieving the burden placed on the few physicians normally responsible for these services. Wechakorn also assist in the provision of routine care in the wards, and in providing night call services. In the district hospital, one wechakorn is assigned to assist the physician. Seventy to seventy-five percent of the wechakorn, however, return to health centers at the subdistrict level, where there is no physician available.

IMPORTANT ROLE OF THE WECHAKORN

The deployment of wechakorn to subdistrict health centers seems to have brought the most dramatic change in health care at the subdistrict level. Rural villagers previously utilized the subdistrict health center minimally, knowing that a full range of clinical services could be found only at the district or provincial hospital. With the deployment of the wechakorn to the subdistrict level, care for illness and other health-related needs, including expanded family planning services, is now available near the village.

Wechakorn paraphysician candidates are selected from existing health services personnel--nurses, midwives, sanitarians, and nurses aides-- and given an intensive year of competency-based training that equips them to deal with most common health problems, as well as to recognize those more complex conditions requiring the attention of a physician. Although wechakorn continue to maintain their former responsibilities after they complete training and return to their assignments, the one year of competency-based training broadens and strengthens their role and responsibilities at their respective facilities. Their training enables them to diagnose and treat a wide range of the common health problems and illnesses found in the rural areas, utilizing antibiotics and other modern treatments. Their preventive and promotive service activities, formerly their main work, have also been expanded with training in insertion of IUDs and injection of Depoprovera, and in organization of community-based nutrition surveillance and service programs.

Another responsibility that has been added to the role of the wechakorn and other subdistrict health center workers is supervision and technical support for the community health volunteers. At least one health post volunteer is trained for each village to provide primary health care to his fellow villagers. For each HPV, there are approximately ten health communicators in a village. There is one traditional birth attendant in approximately ever two villages. The training and deployment of these three types of community health volunteers is one of the Project's major thrusts in strengthening health care coverage in the rural areas and in enabling the villagers to help themselves.

The important task of maintaining the morale and motivation of the volunteers and of providing adequate technical and logistical support belongs to the subdistrict health center staff--the midwife, the sani-tarian, and the wechakorn. In an average subdistrict, the health center has responsibility for 5 to 10 health post volunteers, 50 to 100 health communicators, and about 5 traditional midwives. Each health post volunteer should be visited, at a minimum, once a month to gather information on the volunteer's activities, to assist in solving any problems that may have come up, and to facilitate the resupply of household drugs. Although village volunteers are a promising path to improved health care at the village level and facilitate better use of scarce health manpower resources, their required supervision and support adds new burdens to health workers at higher levels.

The primary health care network of village volunteers is, on the one hand, an extension of the government health care system, but on the other hand is a community-based, private sector system organized to blend as smoothly as possible with the values, traditions, and life-style of rural villagers. There are important reasons for this approach. Not only is the government currently unable to bring health services to every village (and cannot do so in the near future), but it appears that it is not absolutely necessary for the government to reach every one of the villages. Recognizing that villagers in Thailand have a long history of reliance on their own ingenuity and resources without outside assis-tance, it seems reasonable that, given some stimulation, direction, training, simple medical supplies, and reassurance, villagers can build on native self-reliance in meeting their primary health needs.

COMMUNITY SUPPORT AND COORDINATING BODIES

To establish and maintain such a network of village health care requires a foundation of community support and participation and the sympathetic cooperation of governmental and other organizations at all levels. Thus, in the early planning stages, Project staff proposed that several types of committees be formed, or, if already existing, be oriented to generate support at all key levels. These included: (1) Village Health Committee, (2) Subdistrict Councils, (3) District Advisory Committees, and (4) a Provincial Coordinating Committee.

The Village Health Committee is potentially one of the most important of the community groups. In each village, the former health committee, originally established to improve sanitation and water supply, has been reorganized or a new committee formed. Usually the village committee includes the village headman and other influential members of the village. The first step in the community social preparation process is establishing the committees as a means to provide initial orientation about the objectives and approaches of the Project, to learn of the community's health concerns, and to elicit their support and active participation. Subdistrict health center workers, in cooperation with Project staff, visited every village to organize the committees.

Once the committees were established, their first task was to identify and select the village health volunteers for their area. In the very early stages of the Project a sociometric survey method was used to identify the volunteers, but, though effective, it was found to be too time-consuming and costly for large-scale use. When given a specific task, such as volunteer selection, the village committees were eager and cooperative. However, once the volunteers were trained and returned to the village, the further role of the com-mittee's continuing role has not been well-defined. Committee members in more recently intervened areas have been trained as health communicators, thus obviating the selection of a separate group of villagers to carry out this function. This provides committee members with a clearer role and draws more directly on their special influence in the community.

Subdistrict Councils are a normal coordinating group established by the government for the purpose of local administration. A Subdistrict Council is made up of heads of government units at the subdistrict level, as well as influential citizens from the communities. Subdistrict Councils are oriented by the Project and have been instrumental in coordinating support from other government sectors.

District Advisory Committees, normally made up of the local district officer and all heads of government units, are crucial to the acceptance and effective operation of the Project in each district. Since all health workers fall under the authority of the district officer, his clearance is required before the Project can move into any given area. Under his leadership and support the District Advisory Committee serves as an important mechanism for securing cooperation for the Project from all relevant government units. For example, the district officer and district facilities have been involved in training village health volunteers and in providing assistance to specific activities such as nutrition by other key government units, including agriculture, community development, and education.

The Provincial Coordinating Committee, headed by the governor and composed of all the heads of provincial government agencies (including the Provincial Chief Medical Officer) and district officers, has been a mechanism to inform all government units of the Project's goals and activities as well as to seek advice in dealing with any problems involved in the new approaches. Both governors assigned to Lampang during the Project's period of operations have been strongly supportive, and the Coordinating Committee has been a means for the governor to express and extend his support.

Community Volunteers: The clearest expression of community support is the participation of village volunteers themselves. They receive minimal compensation and yet contribute their time and space in their households to serve their neighbors. The contribution must be both recognized and nourished by the government health services.

Experience in the Project has indicated that the key elements in maintaining the volunteer contribution are regular supervision and encouragement by local government health workers and timely maintenance of the health post volunteers' household drug supply. Where these two elements have lapsed, volunteer morale and performance have declined.

Local Practitioners: Finally, in the interest of mobilizing all available health resources, the Project has sought to involve private sector groups and individuals to the greatest extent possible. Traditional birth attendants have been utilized in every village where they are active.   A number of the health post volunteers have previously been herbal practitioners, injectionists, or malaria volunteers. Many druggists--both in the village and urban areas--not only sell medicine but also provide advice on diagnosis

and treatment to their customers. The Project has secured the cooperation of many of the druggists in monthly reporting to the Provincial
Health Office on certain specific illnesses they have observed and also
the level of their drug sales. In return, the Project has provided short
training sessions for the druggists in appropriate prescription of the
medicines they sell.

Private Organizations: Recently, a Thai private sector organization, Community-Based Family Planning Services (CBFPS), has established
a network of village volunteers who primarily distribute contraceptives
(oral pills and condoms), but who now also provide antiparasite medications
and some primary health care services. CBFPS has paid particular
attention to developing an effective management system, based on a
paid district coordinator who works closely with the local district
health officer, and a simple, rapid feedback reporting system. Their
success in management has prompted the Project to invite CBFPS to
implement its approach in one district of Lampang Province and to
compare its results with the Project-implemented areas.

MANAGEMENT, INFORMATION AND SUPERVISION

As the Lampang Project began operations, it had to grapple with
and seek to overcome the problems of inadequate management practices
and a cumbersome information system within the provincial health
organization. From the provincial to the district level, and from
the district level to the subdistrict health center level, supportive
supervision--routine visits for problem-solving, on-the-job training,
and feedback on performance--were infrequent and inadequate. Moreover,
the provincial information system--including more than forty individual
reports and records--was an unnecessary burden at all facility levels
and generated a huge amount of data which, even if up-to-date and
accurate, seldom reached decision points in a timely or useable form.
As a result, reliable information on performance of facilities and
personnel was seldom available for management decision-making at
various points and levels. Moreover, the flow of information had
been generally in one direction only, with little feedback to the units
generating and needing the information.

Old and New Management Problems

As will be seen, the Project staff initiated a variety of measures
to remedy these existing management and information deficiencies.
It must also be noted, however, that several features of the
Project created new management burdens and information needs.
For example, creation of a new tier of health workers--the village
health volunteers--added a new management burden to the subdistrict
health center staff. Health center workers must now provide supervisory and logistical support and gather information on a cadre who
were not formerly under their responsibility.

Further, at the subdistrict level, the addition of wechakorn
paraphysicians introduced new demands for technical supervision and

management. Midwives and sanitarians at the health center level were normally supervised and supported by senior sanitarians and midwives from the district and provincial levels. But the wechakorn, with their new clinical skills, clearly required a different type of technical support than formerly provided. Specifically, they needed technical guidance and continuing education from skilled clinical practitioners such as the doctor at the district health center, from physicians who trained them in the provincial hospital, or--at a minimum--from an experienced and skilled wechakorn.

The health center normally stocked a limited range of drugs, medical supplies and equipment, but to practise their new clinical skills, the wechakorn required a broader range of drugs, medical supplies, and equipment. This placed new demands on the district and provincial logistics system. The wechakorn's expanded role in clinical care also required improvements in the medical referral system from the subdistrict health center to the district hospital, and from the district hospital to the provincial hospital.

Each subdistrict health center staff had to assume the new responsibility of overseeing the activities of six to eight health post volunteers, two to three traditional midwives, and 50-80 health communicators in the area. A number of subdistricts, however, do not have health centers and hence health centers in an adjacent subdistrict must assume responsibility for two subdistricts. In order to make the work more manageable, two or three health center workers divide responsibility for supervision geographically, so that each may visit regularly only two or three volunteers. Health staff are expected to visit the volunteers at least once a month, when they review the health post volunteer's log book and fill out a volunteer performance summary extracted from the daily log book.

The logistical mechanism for supplying the health post volunteers with household drugs had to be changed during the course of the Project. Initially, health post volunteers were given a suppl y of the drugs from the health center which they could sell at a slight profit, using the returns to purchase resupplies. The local health worker was assigned the task of collecting the money and coordinating orders for resupplies through the Provincial Health Office, which in turn ordered supplies from the Government Pharmaceutical Organization. After the first year, it became apparent that the government drug supply network was less effective than expected; health workers found it inconvenient to collect the funds and deliver the drugs, particularly when volunteers often did not have money available to repay the initial credit. At the same time, health workers did not always visit volunteers with sufficient frequency, because of seasonal communication difficulties or other more pressing activities. The resulting lack of medical supplies was deterimental to the HPV's local credibility, morale and performance.

To improve the supply network, the Project established an agreement with one of the major pharmaceutical suppliers in Lampang to

order the household drugs directly from the Government Pharmaceutical
Organization and take responsibility for resupplying the volunteers
through local drug outlets at the subdistrict level. This arrangement
has relieved the subdistrict health workers of the burden of money
collection and supply but has imposed an inconvenience on the health
post volunteer. He must now come to the subdistrict to pick up his
drug resupply. Since transactions are on a strictly cash basis, this can
be an obstacle to regular resupplies being purchased.

   With experience managerial solutions have continued to evolve.
Most recently, the Project added a district coordinator to assist the
District Health Officer. One of his major responsibilities will be
to support village health volunteers.

   Support for wechakorn in the district and provincial hospitals
has presented only minimal problems since the wechakorn work in
close proximity to their physician supervisors and can consult with
them and receive in-service training regularly. However, for
wechakorn located in the more distant subdistrict health centers,
technical support is a crucial need and often a difficulty. In
districts that have physicians at the district hospital, clinical
conferences are held when the health center workers come to the
district for the monthly staff meeting. It has been less feasible
for the district hospital physicians to travel around to the subdistrict health centers to provide on-the-job supervision and
instruction, in part because of demands on them at the district
hospital and also because the district hospital has no officially-
defined role in supervising subdistrict health center activities.
Another mechanism for providing technical supervision to the
health center wechakorn has been the organization of provincial
hospital clinical conferences each month by doctors who formerly
trained the wechakorn. These have been useful in the early stages
when the number of wechakorn was small, but as their number increased
these conferences became less feasible. There is a clear need--and
an expressed request from the wechakorn themselves--for individualized,
extended technical supervision at their work sites, but this need has not
yet been adequately met on a regular basis. A number of former
wechakorn instructors--hospital staff from the Community Health Department in the provincial hospital and Project trainers--have made sporadic
but useful follow-up visits to health center wechakorn. A more
regularized supervision system is under consideration, perhaps using
a senior, skilled wechakorn.

   Supplies and equipment needed by the wechakorn at their health
centers was a problem for the first group of wechakorn because, as
former midwives and sanitarians, they had not been authorized to
order antibiotics, for example, or to insert IUDs. Although there had
been an orientation for provincial senior staff concerning the role of
wechakorn, when the first group completed its training there was
still some confusion about what they were authorized to do. For
example, a few provincial staff members questioned supplying the
wechakorn at the health centers with a new lines of drugs and equipment.

This problem has, for the most part, been resolved as a result of continued discussion and clear demonstration of their own competence by
the wechakorn.

Streamlining the Information System:

In order to facilitate the management process and the monitoring
of Project progress, the Project and provincial staffs have worked
together in an attempt to streamline and lighten the burden of the
existing information system and to make it more useful and effective.

Since village health volunteers were not previously part of the
provincial health care system, a new system of reporting on their
activities had to be established. Given the fact that volunteers are
not government employees, only minimal demands for reporting could
be made on them. The solution adopted was for each health post
volunteer to be trained to keep a daily log of service contacts, which
includes information on the contact's name, age, sex, reason for the
contact, treatment prescribed, and payment for any drugs dispensed.

The health worker from the local subdistrict health center visits
the volunteer each month and abstracts data from the daily log for use
in a monthly volunteer activity reporting sheet, which is then compiled
for each district. The monthly district report summarizes the total
number of services contacts for illness care, total family planning
acceptors and contacts, the number of family planning supplies
distributed, and the amount of money collected for drug sales.
The volunteer reports are then sent to the Provincial Health Office
(and to the Lampang Project Evaluation and Research Division) for
routine monitoring. The Evaluation and Research Division periodically analyzes and summarizes volunteer performance and distributes
a report to the Provincial Health Office and related Project divisions.
Information on the activities of the traditional midwives and village
health communicators is not routinely gathered.

The Lampang Project has made efforts to streamline the routine
reporting system by deleting items that are of marginal use, but there
has been considerable resistance to these attempts both in the provincial health office and at the Ministry level. The Programming and
Planning Division, along with the Evaluation and Research Division,
has routinely reviewed the monthly reports coming in from the
various rural health facilities, and has extracted data that are
relevant to routine monitoring. These data, which summarize
performance of the various health facilities by category of activity
(e.g., family planning, maternal child health, nutrition, and illness
care) are distributed to Project and provincial health decision makers.
The burden of reporting on peripheral health staff has, therefore, not
been reduced substantially, but specific information items from these
reports have been selected to make relevant information easily
accessible to Project and provincial staff for management purposes.

In addition to information from routine reporting mechanisms,
the Evaluation and Research Division, as part of its overall project

assessment and evaluation function, has carried out a number of surveys
which provide baseline information on health status and health service
utilization. These data have been useful in identifying the level of
health status and health service problems, in pinpointing their
location, and in identifying where program emphasis should be
placed. For example, one important result of baseline surveys was the
recognition that the nutrition problem in Lampang Province is more
serious than had been assumed. The Community Health & Nutrition
Survey detected high levels of malnutrition and also identified the areas
of greatest prevalence.

Figure 9 provides a summary diagram of the information sources
and flows described above.

FIGURE 9: HEALTH INFORMATION SOURCES AND CHANNELS OF FLOW

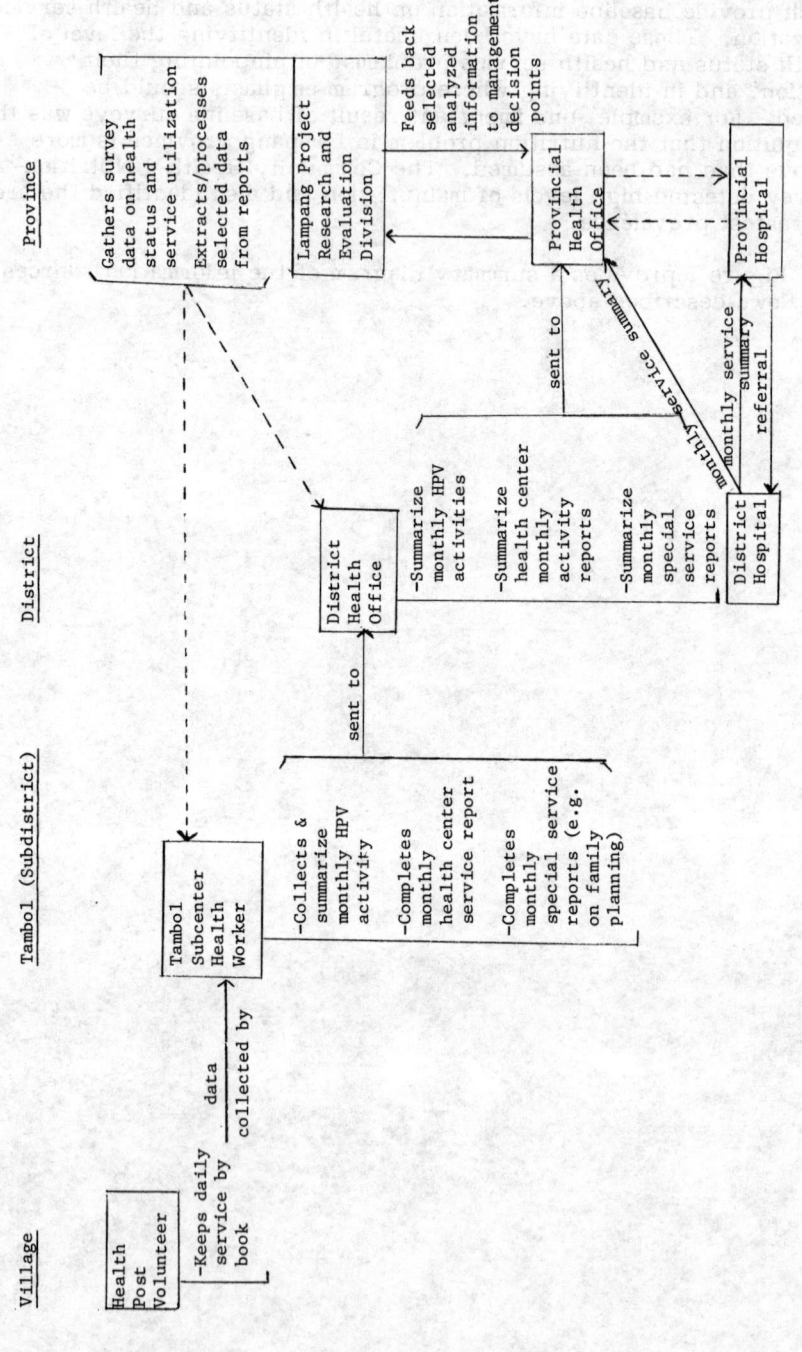

CHAPTER 4

TRAINING OF HEALTH PERSONNEL

AND INFORMATION DISSEMINATION

Under the overall planning and supervision of the Project Personnel Development Division, pre-service, in-service, and refresher training have been provided for a variety of Government health personnel and local health volunteers as summarized in Table 3.

Table 3

Summary of Lampang Project Training Activities

Training Category	Length of Training	Number Trained as of August 1978	Estimated Number yet to be Trained	Total Trained at End of Project
Wechakorn	1 year	96	30[a]	126
Health Post Volunteers	2 weeks	572[b]	100	672
Health Communicators	2 days	4,846	1,000	5,846
Traditional Midwives	2 weeks	244	100	342
Trainers	2 weeks	133	---	133
Administrators & Supervisors	1 week (half days)	72	---	72
Service Personnel	1 week	195	75	270

a   The fourth group of 30 began training in 1978 and will finish in May, 1979.

b   Includes 50 volunteers trained by Community-Based Family Planning Services in Ngao District.

WECHAKORN TRAINING

A major effort has been devoted to training the wechakorn because of their strategic importance to the entire Project. Their basic role is: (a) to greatly expand the availability of both curative and preventive/promotive health services in rural areas; (b) to reduce the burden on medical doctors in the district and provisional hospitals of handling simpler cases so that they can concentrate on more serious and complicated ones; and (c) to be the principal link between the village health volunteers and committees and the higher echelons of the expanded health care system.

As noted earlier, the wechakorn candidates have already had a certain amount of training and experience in the health field, usually as sanitarians, nurses, nurse-aides or midwives. The wechakorn's training is designed to equip him/her to take a strong leadership role among the health center team, and to establish a relationship with the village health volunteers that is crucial to providing effective health care coverage in the area. After completion of the one-year training course, the wechakorn is able to:

1. provide medical care for patients suffering from common illness and injuries by using available resources under the physician's overall responsibility;

2. recognize cases that are beyond his capability, refer patients, and consult physicians as necessary;

3. supervise the health center team members;

4. administer the health subcenter or assist in clinical and administrative work in the district hospital; and,

5. promote and guide community health development programs.

The training approach used for wechakorn is problem-oriented and the methods are competency-based. The methods of training wechakorn were adapted from the MEDEX model, which originated in the United States during the late 1960s.* The short one-year duration requires that theoretical and classroom material be minimized and practical clinical experience be maximized. Emphasis is on "learning by doing"; hence,

---

*MEDEX is a "physician extender" training program, inaugurated at the University of Washington in the 1960s to retrain medical corpsmen for physician-supervised practice in the United States. The program was later developed in several other universities, including the University of Hawaii, which introduced the program internationally for the first time in Micronesia (Trust Territory of the Pacific Islands) during the early 1970s. The term "medex" refers to the individual physician extender, and is derived from the French words *une extension de medecin,* extension of the doctor.

the training course is divided into two major phases: the didactic, or classroom, phase, which lasts 16 weeks, and the preceptorship, or practical clinical phase, which lasts 36 weeks. The didactic phase is broken up into a series of discrete units, employing problem-oriented modules. Each module is a self-contained learning unit, which includes a pre-test and post-test for each learning objective and the substantive materials the trainees must learn before successfully completing that module. The various modules are the basis of the classroom sessions and may require from a day to several weeks to complete. Since the physicians in the provincial hospital have the major role in training wechakorn, they were invited to participate in preparing the modules and other training materials. With initial assistance from the Health Manpower Development (MEDEX) Staff of the University of Hawaii, Provincial Hospital and Project staff worked together to write and refine the modules and the other materials for the training curriculum. The current content of training and time required for wechakorn is as follows:

1. Core Skills:

    1.1 History taking and medical terminology   30 hours

    1.2 Physical examination, anatomy and physiology 60 hours

    1.3 Laboratory examination   30 hours

    1.4 Use of formulary   6 hours

    1.5 Introduction to comprehensive health care 6 hours

    1.6 How to use protocol   6 hours

2. General Clinics:

    2.1 Skin problems   30 hours

    2.2 Ear, Eye, Nose and Throat problems   30 hours

    2.3 Chest problems   30 hours

    2.4 Abdominal problems   30 hours

    2.5 Genito-Urinary/Kidney, Ureter, Bladder problems   30 hours

    2.6 Diarrhea/Vomiting/Dehydration   12 hours

    2.7 General problems   30 hours

3. Emergencies   84 hours

4. Maternal and Child Health

    4.1 Maternal and Child Care

    4.2 Family Planning

5. Community Health and Field Supervision

    5.1 Nutritional problems   30 hours

5.2 Prevention   30 hours

5.3 Vital statistics   18 hours

5.4 Community Health Education   18 hours

5.5 Supervision   12 hours

Twenty-nine weeks of the 36-week preceptorship are spent in the provincial hospital, rotating among the various departments, both in-patient and out-patient, as well as on night duty. Working under close supervision of physicians in the departments, wechakorn learn to take histories, examine patients, diagnose problems, and prescribe the proper treatment. Protocols guide the learning process for the wechakorn by providing simplified decision chains which systematically present the steps in dealing with a patient presenting a given problem (or set of problems), in order to arrive at a diagnosis and prescribe proper treatment, or to know when to refer the patient to a physician if necessary.

In addition to the 29 weeks of hospital rotations, wechakorn spend four weeks working on community health development at the rural health center level, one week on community health resource planning, and another two weeks on electives in the hospital. At the end of the training program, each wechakorn trainee is given a written and practical test, and faculty members from various medical schools throughout Thailand are invited to act as the examiners. During the practical examination each wecha- korn is given a series of patients to examine, diagnose, and prescribe treatment, and their findings and actions are judged by the panel of medical school faculty.

Some difficulty was anticipated, and encountered, in jointly training individuals with different backgrounds and educational levels. This was partially overcome by special refresher sessions to bring everyone to a standard level. At the end of training, there were no significant differences among the final test scores of the various trainee categories.

Over half of the wechakorn are women--midwives, nurses, and nurse aids. Table 4 summarizes the backgrounds and final assignments of the first three groups of wechakorn trained.

Table 4

Wechakorn Background and Final Assignment
(As of December 1978)

| | | Wechakorn Location after Training | | | |
Background	Number Trained	Rural Health Center	District Hospital	Provincial Hospital	Other
Nurse	14	--	2	10	2
Midwife	51	49	2	--	--
Sanitarian	25	24	1	--	--
Nurse Aide	4	2	--	--	--
Other	2	--	--	--	--
Total	96[a]	75	5	10	4

[a]92 wechakorn are in Lampang Provincial assignments. Two
nurses aides and two Border Policemen were sent for
training by special request. The fourth, and last,
group of 30 wechakorn are currently in training,
scheduled for completion in May, 1979.

TRAINING OF HEALTH POST VOLUNTEERS

The health post volunteer is the focal point of primary health care in each village. One volunteer is chosen in each village, or more than one in large villages that are widely dispersed. The people normally selected as health post volunteers are generally mature (over 30), established members of the community, who are most often farmers or small shopkeepers. They are unlikely to migrate out to seek better paying jobs; hence the problem of attrition has been minimal and where it has occurred, has been covered by retraining programs. Although the volunteers are usually expected to be able, at a minimum, to read and write, this requirement is flexible.

The rural volunteer is trained to:

1. provide simple first aid and illness care to his fellow villagers, using nonprescription household drugs provided by the government;

2. refer more complicated cases to the local health facilities;

3. support community nutrition surveillance and nutrition service programs;

4. advise villagers about family planning and distribute pills and condoms;

5. inform mothers and children about services provided by local health facilities;

6. distribute (in a few areas) drugs for malaria, tuberculosis, and leprosy patients living in the village;

7. support and supervise the health communicators in the village; and

8. coordinate government activities with local villagers.

The training course for groups of 25 to 30 health post volunteers lasts ten working days, or two weeks. Through a series of lectures, discussions, and practical activities, trainees are given instruction in the recognition and care of minor diseases; in recognizing which types of people should be referred to other health facilities for care; in recording births, deaths, and migration; in making the daily log; and in supervision and community motivation. Training is usually arranged at some facility close to the volunteer's home, normally at a village temple, school, or government facility.

Training is carried out by health workers and other government officials in the area where the volunteer is located, assisted by provincial and project training staff. The materials used are prepared by the Lampang Project training staff in the Personnel Development Division, and at the end of training each volunteer is given a Health Post Volunteer manual which can be kept in his/her home for easy reference.

The health post volunteer is provided with an initial supply of household drugs on credit, at a discount. He/she sells the drugs at a slight profit, then pays back the cost of the consignment to purchase a new supply. Thus the health post volunteers gain a small amount of income from their work, but it is usually quite nominal ($5-10/month only).* In addition, they and their families are provided free medical care at the health center and provincial hospital. By the end of 1978, 572 of the targetted total of 670 had been trained.

At least once a month, the wechakorn or another health center worker visits the volunteer to help solve any problems, to provide technical and logistics support, and to gather information from the daily logbook for inclusion in the Tambol health center's monthly report. One day of on-the-job refresher training is provided each year for health post volunteers, the village committee, and other local health personnel so that problems can be dealt with jointly.

TRAINING OF HEALTH COMMUNICATORS

Health communicators are the second type of village volunteer developed by the Lampang Project. One health communicator is chosen for about 10-15 households, making a total of about 10-15 communicators for each village. Their role is to promote the services of the local health post volunteer and the subdistrict health center. They also receive and disseminate health information among the households assigned to them, under the overall supervision of the health post volunteer.

The health communicator candidates are selected by the village committee and sent in groups of 50-75 to a training center near their home. Their two days of instruction includes:

Introduction to Lampang Project	1/2 hour
Functions of the Communicator	1/2 hour
Nutrition	1 hour
Maternal and Child Health	1 hour
Family Planning	1 hour
Observation of the occurrences of common communicable diseases	1 hour

*20 Bahts = US$1

Local health service system	1 hour
Household medicine	1 hour
Human relations	1 hour
Receiving and disseminating health information in a village	1 hour
Sanitation	1 hour
Child Nutrition Center	1 hour
Cooperation with the Ministry of Interior	1 hour

Teaching is done through small group discussions and lectures, supplemented with handouts, posters, models, and slides. As of mid-1978, 4,846 communicators had already trained and about 800-1,000 were still to be trained before the completion of the project.

The health communicators are generally younger than the health post volunteers and thus tend to be more transient in their services. However, because of lack of clarity of their contribution, the impact of their attrition or service performance has not been observed.

TRAINING OF TRADITIONAL MIDWIVES

Traditional birth attendants, or "granny" midwives--almost all women--still deliver a majority of the children born in rural areas and attend to pre- and post-natal care. Because they are usually older and closely involved in family affairs, they have great influence in the village. Traditional midwives are selected in every village where one is present if they are not over 60 years of age. In some areas that are well served by government health facilities, the number of traditional midwives has been decreasing, with the result that only one midwife could be identified and recruited to serve two villages. The traditional midwives are trained in groups of about 25 at the Lampang Regional Midwifery School for a period of two weeks. During the course of the training, which is carried out by Project and Midwifery School staff, the trainees learned to:

1. give advice to mothers and children in using health services from local facilities;

2. detect abnormal pregnancies and refer them to health centers

or to the district or provincial hospital;

    3. do normal deliveries using aseptic techniques;

    4. advise mothers and children about good nutrition;

    5. give minor medical care using household medicines;

    6. distribute pills and condoms and encourage villagers to practice family planning; and,

    7. report births to the health post volunteer or village headman.

The content of the two-week curriculum includes:

Introduction to participants	1/2 hour
Pre-test (question and answer method)	1/2 hour
Introduction to Lampang Project	1 hour
Sanitation and personal hygiene	1 hour
Mother and child health	25 hours
Family planning	4 hours
Household medicines	1 hour
Recording of births	1 hour
Integrated health service in the district and role of the Traditional Birth Attendants	2 hours
Sterile technique	3 hours
Nutrition for mothers and children	3 hours
Patient referral system	1 hour
Introduction to Child Nutrition Center	1 hour
Post-test (question and answer method)	1 hour
Observation at antenatal clinic, well baby clinic and obstetric ward at Lampang Hospital	9 hours

    Since the traditional midwives are usually illiterate, the midwifery school training has been adapted to their special needs. The general content is presented in an informal setting by demonstrations and observations, and by lectures making use of role playing, models, pictures, movies and slides. The trainers are all local women who speak the local dialect.

    Traditional midwives are entitled to free medical care at the local health center, district, and provincial hospital. They are normally supervised by the government midwives in the subdistrict health centers and receive refresher training once a year. Two hundred and forty-four traditional midwives had been trained by the Project as of mid-1978, with about 100 more still to be trained by the end of the Project.

TRAINING OF ADMINISTRATORS AND SUPERVISORS

All administrators and supervisors from the Provincial Health Office and the provincial hospital, including physicians, chief nurses, dentists, pharmacists, district health officers and supervisors of the Provincial Health Office received one week of orientation training to:

-- understand the Project goals and approaches;

-- orient them to the operation of integrated health services and how it will affect them;

-- orient them to the importance of their own roles and of others on the health team.

The training is completed in five half-day sessions to reduce the time that senior staff must be away from their responsibilities. Follow-up on-the-job training for one day is also provided twice each year.

TRAINING OF SERVICE PERSONNEL

All staff who provide services at the provincial hospital and district hospitals, health centers, and midwifery centers are given one week of training to orient them to the Project's goal and methods and to demonstrate how the project approaches will affect them in their individual jobs. Most of the people who receive the training are nurses, laboratory technicians, dental hygienists, junior health workers, midwives, and practical nurses. On-the-job training is provided in addition to routine supervision.

Training of Trainers

A two-week training program was organized for all provincial health staff who assist in training village health volunteers and in orienting service personnel. Trainer trainees learn classroom teaching methods, curriculum and lesson plan preparation, use of teaching and audio-visual aids, and organization of training programs. The course is held at a teacher training college in a nearby province and is run by the college staff and project staff. The content of the training is as follows:

-- Orientation

-- Principles of Teaching

-- Psychology in Rural Health Development

-- Sociology and Human Relations

-- Public Speaking

-- Technology of Teaching

-- Good Community Teacher

-- Role of Mass Communication in Public Health Work

-- Teamwork of Group Process

-- Organization of Training Programs

-- Practice for Teaching

-- Evaluation for Training Programs

At the end of 1978 there had not yet been a systematic evaluation of the adequacy or effectiveness of the various training programs described above.

PROJECT ADVISORY COMMITTEES AND THEIR FUNCTIONS

In order to orient and publicize the approaches and methodologies of the Lampang Project and to gain support in problem solving and resource assistance, several advisory committees have been established within the Ministry of Public Health and in other sectors of the government. Although the committees have generally not played a major role in project operations, they have provided an occasional forum for keeping people informed and enlisting support.

The first of these committees is the Lampang Project Policy Committee, composed of high-level government policy-makers and planners from a variety of relevant ministries and agencies. The Policy Committee, chaired by the Under Secretary of State for Public Health, reviews project progress and current constraints about twice yearly, and provides advice and assistance in facilitating project operations. Members of the Policy Committee include representatives of the National Economic and Social Development Board, Department of Technical Economic Cooperation, Civil Service Commission, Bureau of the Budget, Ministry of Interior, Ministry of Public Health, Bureau of State Universities, and various faculties of medicine and public health.

Another high-level advisory committee is the Lampang Project Executive Committee, composed of representatives from various departments and divisions within the Ministry of Public Health. This committee, chaired by the Project Director (Director General, Department of Health), provides technical advice and support to Project staff in resolving issues that can be handled within the Ministry of Public Health. It is also a mechanism for keeping various units within the Ministry informed of project progress.

As noted earlier, at the provincial level the Provincial Coordinating Committee, chaired by the Governor of Lampang Province and including the heads of all government departments in the province as well as all district officers, coordinates support at the provincial level and is a vehicle for keeping all provincial units posted on the progress of the project. Similarly, in each district a District Advisory Committee, chaired by the District Officer and participated in by heads of all district government units, performs advisory and coordinating functions at that level.

All of these committees serve to publicize Lampang Project activities to the widest possible audience. Another major vehicle for reporting the project's progress, and for gaining advice and recommendations from a wide variety of interested parties, is the Project's Annual Review. Annual Reviews have been held each year since 1975, serving as a forum for presenting project progress to date, discussing problems encountered, seeking effective solutions, and for productive discussions in dealing with salient issues. The Annual Review is attended by representatives from most government and nongovernment agencies with an interest in health and rural development, including agencies represented in the Project Policy Committee and Executive Committee, and other government and international agencies.

Another important vehicle for project information dissemination is the exchange visits that have occurred since the beginning of the project and which continue with increasing frequency. A number of project staff have been requested as consultants to other projects and programs within and outside of Thailand. Project staff have assisted the government of Korea and the government of Pakistan in their efforts to build basic health care programs similar to the Lampang Project. A number of project staff have attended international and domestic workshops, seminars, and meetings to make presentations related to the project. The Lampang Project is now receiving several hundred visitors each year from nearly every continent, and representing a wide variety of government, nongovernment, and international agencies. The large number of visitors have been a useful mechanism for generating interest and support for the Project around the world.

CHAPTER 5

EXPANSION

AND INITIAL IMPACT

Before the project became operational in 1974, the population of Lampang Province was considerably more deprived of government health services than in Thailand as a whole. As Table 5 indicates, a much smaller percentage of Lampang's districts and subdistricts had health centers, and the ratio of available doctors, nurses and hospital beds to the population was much lower than the national average.

EXPANSION OF THE HEALTH SYSTEM

By 1978 the picture had changed dramatically. Health service facilities and personnel in Lampang Province had expanded greatly, as shown in Figure 10 and Table 6, with still further expansion scheduled for 1979. The provincial hospital (not included in Table 6) was in process of doubling its bed capacity and becoming a regional hospital; it had a new Community Health Department to backstop health personnel and facilities at lower levels; and it was operating a new multipurpose mobile clinic in remote rural areas. The number of district hospitals had risen from three to five (with a sixth one scheduled for 1979), each with its own medical doctor. But the most striking increases were in the number of subdistrict health centers (from 26 in 1974 to 61 in 1978) and of various categories of government health workers at the district and subdistrict levels, along with large new cadres of village level health volunteers.

Much of this expansion was the result of intensified efforts by the Ministry of Public Health that were separate from the Lampang Project plan, but the Project itself also contributed substantially, especially in training wechakorns for the subdistrict centers and numerous village volunteers.

The net effect of all these expansion efforts was to boost considerably the "theoretical" geographic and population coverage of government health services in Lampang Province. The real test would be, however, the extent to which this increased capacity would be utilized by the potential clients and the impact it would have on the health status of the Lampang population.

FIGURE 10: MAP OF LAMPANG PROVINCE SHOWING
DISTRIBUTION OF HEALTH SERVICE UNITS (1978)

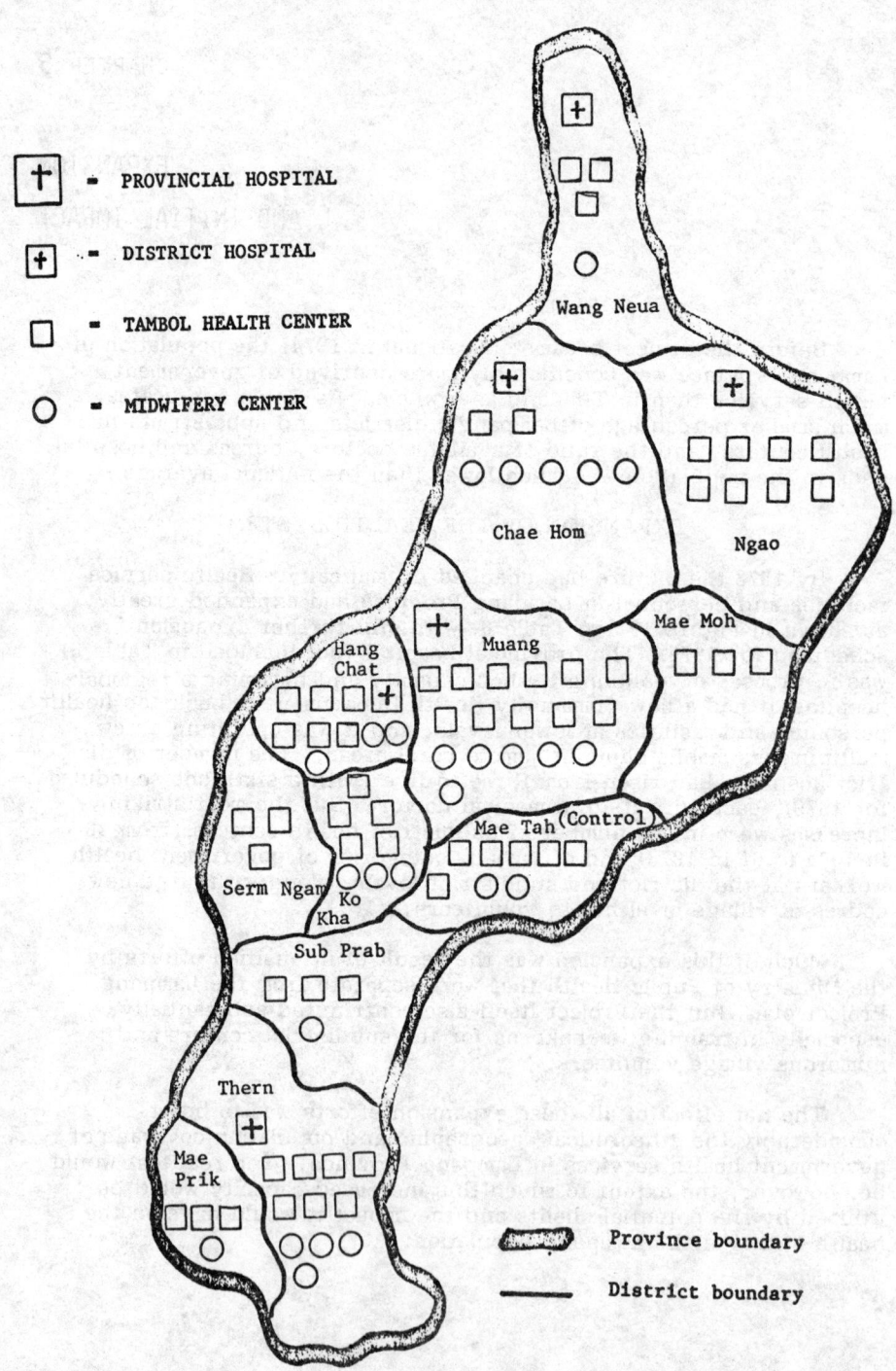

Table 5

Geographic and Population Coverage by Government
Health Facilities and Service Personnel in
Thailand and in Lampang Province,
1973

Health Facilities and Personnel	Thailand (1973)	Lampang (1973)
Health Centers		
Districts covered	45%	33%
Subdistricts covered	57%	35%
Villages covered	4%	6%
Hospital Beds	91/100,000	48/100,000
Personnel		
Physicians	9/100,000	3/100,000
Nurses	20/100,000	9/100,000
Midwives	9/100,000	10/100,000
Sanitarians	7/100,000	5/100,000

Table 6

Growth of Government Rural Health Service Facilities and Personnel
in Lampang Province [a]
1974 to 1979

Year	Number of			Number of Service Units			Number of Government Personnel					Personnel added by Project Implementation			
	Districts	Subdistricts	Villages	District Hospitals	Health Centers	Midwifery Centers	MD	N	NA	MW	S	W	HPV	VHC	TBA
1974	11	75	538	3	26	33	2	3	--	58	30	--	--	--	--
1978	12[d]	75	538	5	61	26[b]	5	7	17	78	44	47	572	4846	244
1979[c] (est.)	12	75	538	6	65	n.a.	6	n.a.	n.a.	n.a.	n.a.	75	672	5846	342

[a] Does not include provincial hospital.

[b] A number of midwifery centers have been upgraded to health centers.

[c] Completion of Project installations.

[d] A subdistrict converted to a full district in 1976, making a total of 12.

MD = physician   N = Nurse   NA = Nurse Aide   MW = Midwife   S = Sanitarian
W = wechakorn   HPV = Health Post Volunteer   VHC = Village Health Communicator
TBA = Traditional Birth Attendant
n.a. = No estimate available

It would be premature at this stage to attempt any final
judgment on Project impacts since the evaluation studies are
scheduled over a period of seven years whereas Project implementation
is only in its fourth year. It is possible, nevertheless, to reach
some tentative judgments, based on preliminary data available on
certain areas and on numerous observations by well-informed
observers. This preliminary evidence sheds useful light on:
(1) the performance of village level health volunteers; (2) trends
in general illness care services; (3) infant delivery services;
(4) nutritional services; and (5) family planning.

To place this preliminary evidence in proper perspective it
should be recalled that the basic evaluation design for the Lampang
Project is geared to the phased implementation of integrated primary
health care by areas (E1, E2 and E3), with two control areas, C1
in Lampang Province and C2, an adjacent district in Lampang
Province. The principal means of measuring subsequent changes
in health services and status, in addition to regularly reported
Ministry of Public Health service statistics and other independently-
collected selected data bearing on Lampang, are: (1) baseline
and follow-up cross-sectional community health and nutrition
surveys, (2) separate and periodic analyses of administration,
tasks, and costs, and (3) special studies. Follow-up surveys to
the initial baseline community surveys (conducted in 1974) will be
initiated in 1979 and should provide considerably more information
on the matters discussed below.

PERFORMANCE OF VILLAGE HEALTH VOLUNTEERS

Once the *health post volunteers* were trained and on the job,
a pattern that emerged quickly was a surge in service contacts
(primarily distribution of medicines and oral contraceptive pills),
followed soon, however, by a sharp decline, and then by a slowly
rising trend. The pattern shown in Figure 11 for Hang Chat
District (E1) and Muang District (E2) is typical.

This marked decline was undoubtedly associated with problems
encountered in keeping the health post volunteers resupplied and in
maintaining high morale through routine supervision; but most
continued to function nevertheless, even if at a lower level than at
first. Where supervision has been regular, performance has been
good. Some health post volunteers, living in villages near rural
health centers, have been bypassed by the villagers. Other health
post volunteers who work away from their houses for most of the
day may not be available to provide optimum service.

Despite these initial problems, it is estimated that in their
first year of deployment, health post volunteers in different
villages in E1 provided services ranging from 13 to 38 percent
of all villagers seeking care--a clear gain.

Follow-up studies of health post volunteers indicate their
interest in more first aid training and higher monetary incentives.

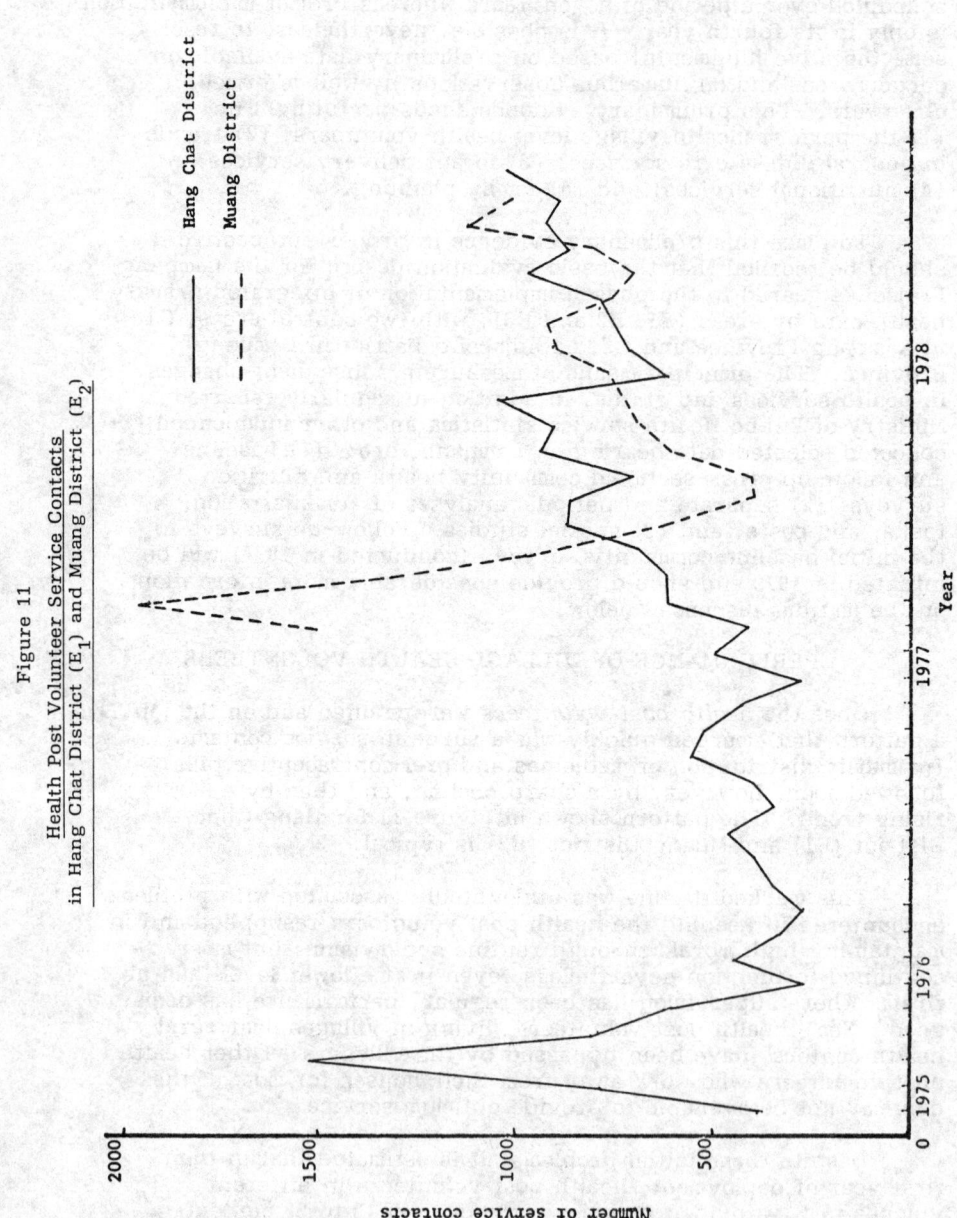

Figure 11

Health Post Volunteer Service Contacts
in Hang Chat District (E_1) and Muang District (E_2)

Although data are not routinely collected on the activities of
health communicators it appears that, apart from being usefully
mobilized in support of the field activities (especially the mobile
clinics) of the Community Health Department, they have been
relatively inactive. Undoubtedly one main reason has been the
uncertainty over their role and lack of clear direction from the
Village Health Committees. It seems evident that the communicators
cannot be counted upon in the future to report vital events, but they
may be helpful in invigorating child nutritional activities.

The *village health committees,* once having selected the
local health post volunteers and health communicators, also tended
to become inactive--though some have voiced the desire for more
curative services in their village. Again this inactivity apparently
reflects a lack of clarity about the specific functions of the committees and also, perhaps, the historical passivity of villagers
in their relationship to government agencies.

The trained *traditional birth attendants* have clearly been
active with respect to pregnancy (and its prevention), delivery, and
post-partum care. Beyond carrying out these activities at a higher
level than before, however, under the supervision of the wechakorn
and/or government midwife, they seem to have been relatively
inactive in other matters. As with the health communicators,
the TBAs have not been helpful in the reporting of vital events.

TRENDS IN GENERAL ILLNESS CARE SERVICES

Table 7 presents estimates for 1974 through 1977 of the
actual distribution of general illness care services, by level and
location, for Hang Chat District (E1) compared to control area
Mae Tak (C1). The "targets" in the left-hand column of Table 7
represent the estimated proportion of total patient visits that
should--appropriately and desirably--be handled at the different
levels of the extended health care system. The clear emphasis
is on extending care to the village--or near the village--while
simultaneously extending the capacity of the whole system to
provide integrated basic health services, including illness care
for the approximately 2 illnesses per person annually reported
in the Community Health Survey.

The other columns in Table 7 contain reported data and
estimates of what has actually happened from 1974 through 1977.
These reported data, it should be noted, are considered incomplete
in certain instances, and some of the estimates are necessarily
only rough approximations. Nevertheless they suggest a number
of significant changes that are taking place--at least in part as
a consequence of the Project.

The overall target of channelling 65 percent of all illness
cases through the government's extended health care system

Table 7

General Illness Care Services to E_1 and C_1 Populations by Location of Service 1974-1977

Location of Service	Targets (1979) Visits	(%)	Visits and Percent Distribution 1974 Visits	(%)	1975 Visits	(%)	1976 Visits	(%)	1977 Visits	(%)
A R E Provincial Hospital	4,230	5	6,177	7	3,846[e]	4	6,827	8	6,148	6
District & Subdistrict Health Centers	21,149	25	15,968	19	13,011[d]	15	22,168	26	34,672[f]	40
A HPV	29,607	35	[a]	--	10,103	12	4,872[c]	6	8,387	10
Sub-Total	54,986	65	22,137	26	26,950	31	33,867	40	49,207	56
Others, including Traditional Healers	29,608	35	--	74	--	69	--	60	--	44
E_1 Estimated Total Episodes[b]	84,594	100	84,594	100	85,578	100	86,562	100	87,544	100
A R E Provincial Hospital					7,403	7	9,263	8	10,159	9
Distict & Subdistrict Health Centers					7,130	6	10,020	9	11,892	10
A HPV (None in place, 1975-77)					0	0	0	0	0	0
Sub-Total					14,533	13	19,283	17	22,051	19
Others, including Traditional healers					--	--	--	--	--	--
C_1 Estimated Total Episodes[b]					115,132	100	115,716	100	116,300	100

Source: All data are from Provincial Service Statistics.
(See next page for footnotes)

Footnotes to Table 7

[a]No HPVs were in place in 1974.

[b]Based on the Community Health Survey, an average of two significant illnesses per person each year were assumed to require attention. The Project target is to attend to 65% of these illnesses with a concentration of care at the village or near village level.

[c]It was observed that HPV activity subsided after the first 6 months, but then increased slowly (see Fig. 12).

[d]It seems possible that use of the health centers fell in 1975 because many of their key personnel were in training to become wechakorn.

[e]This figure seems too low, perhaps representing an undercount or failure to register addresses at hospital visits, or an artifact of project data for the last 5 months of 1975 to a full year.

[f]The newly-built District Hospital was only open for 9 months in 1977.

(the remainder being handled by various types of private practitioners) seems well on its way to achievement. According to Table 7,
the estimated percentage climbed steadily from 26 percent in 1974 to
56 percent in 1977, and it is expected to reach or surpass the target
by 1978/79. The pattern of distribution of cases by level and location, however, deviates considerably from the targeted pattern, for
a number of apparent reasons.

The provisional hospital visits by Hang Chat (E1) people held
relatively steady from 1974 through 1976, except for a temporary
sharp dip in 1975 (which appears to be a statistical aberration in
the reporting system). However, the significant decline from 1976
to 1977 (from 8 to 6 percent of the total cases handled) suggests the
possible beginning of a trend toward limiting provincial hospital
visits to more serious cases, with the district hospitals and subdistrict health centers absorbing a growing share of the less serious
cases. This possibility is reinforced by the dramatic rise in the
proportion of total visits handled by the health centers in Hang Chat
(E1), from 19 percent in 1974 to 40 percent in 1977 (substantially
above the target level). There seems little doubt that the presence
of the newly trained wechakorn contributed greatly to this sharp
upward trend.* By contrast, the health post volunteers have
clearly undershot their target by a wide margin, suggesting that
further steps are needed to strengthen the role and activities of
the HPVs and other volunteers at the village level.

The record of illness care services in control area C1 (where
the Project is not yet operational) differs sharply from E1. The
estimated total volume and percentage of cases handled by the
(unextended) government health care services increased somewhat
(from 13 percent in 1975 to 19 percent in 1977), but far less than the
increase in E1. The proportion of cases involving the provincial
hospital increased each year rather than declining. The proportion
going to the health centers also increased (from 6 percent in 1975
to 10 percent in 1977), but far less than in E1.

Though further evidence and evaluation are still required,
one can reasonably draw three tentative conclusions at this stage:
first, the recently extended health system in E1 is already delivering
substantially more illness care services to the people of the area than
earlier; second, the newly strengthened health care centers are
siphoning off a sharply increased proportion of the "easier" cases,
thereby freeing up the provincial hospital to concentrate on more
difficult cases; and third, additional efforts are still required to
increase the performance and effectiveness of the village level volunteers.

_____

*Given the nearness of Hang Chat to the Lampang Municipal
Area and the projected expansion of provincial hospital capacity,
it may be difficult to keep this desirable trend from reversing in
future years.

INFANT DELIVERY SERVICES

The available statistics presented in Table 8 suggest that the overall target of having 95 percent of deliveries supervised by trained health personnel was reached by 1977 in Hang Chat (E1), but that the relative distribution of supervised births did not follow the sub-targets. While there is instability in some of the numbers, and the estimated births may be incorrect, it appears that the provincial hospital's share of deliveries is still unduly high and may not be decreasing significantly. The presence of the wechakorn seems to have increased dramatically the proportion of deliveries supervised by them or the trained auxiliary midwives at home or at the health centers in 1977. The trained TBAs seem slowly to be losing ground, confirming a trend that has been observed over the past several years.

As mentioned earlier, the expansion of the provincial hospital and also the training needs of the Lampang Midwifery School may make it difficult to restrict access to the provincial hospital to only those women referred there with pre-natal complications.

NUTRITION

The emphasis of the Lampang Project in addressing the health needs of preschool age children has already been mentioned. Nutritional status in this vulnerable population group is of special concern, especially in view of the high incidence of serious malnutrition revealed by the baseline surveys in E1 and E2 and by subsequent surveillance reports. (See Table 9.)

Clearly 10 to 15 percent of preschool children in E1 and E2 are moderately to severely malnourished, and another 30 to 40 percent are mildly undernourished. This finding came as a surprise to health policymakers who, judged by the Cost and Task Analysis conducted by the Project, had not recognized the prevalence of serious undernourishment. In E1 only 4 percent of the total budget was spent on nutritional activities in 1975-76. The coverage of preschool children by the Child Nutrition Centers in Hang Chat (E1) is estimated at no more than 5 percent, and many who attend these centers may not actually need special nutrition care.

Having identified a group of severely malnourished children, an effort was made to have HPVs and wechakorn follow these cases and supply regular supplemental food. The results of the first six month followup are shown in Table 10. Since much of the weighing was done by less trained HPVs, some misclassification was expected. While information is incomplete, it appears that less than half, and possibly as few as one-quarter of the children, improved over the period. It should be emphasized that although some improvement was seen, many such children still remained malnourished.

Table 8

Deliveries to Hang Chat Women (E_1) by Location

of Supervising Personnel, 1974-77

Location of Supervising Personnel	Target Distri- bution (%)	Deliveries							
		1974		1975		1976		1977	
		No.	(%)	No.	(%)	No	(%)	No	(%)
Provincial Hospital	-- 25	263	26	296	32	297	33	267	30
Health Centers[a]	-- 35	166	18	196	21	176	19	394[e]	44
TBA (trained)	-- 35	n.a.	39[b]	331	36[c]	239	26	204	23
Subtotal	95	n.a.(Est) 83		823	90	712	79	865	97
Other	5	n.a.(Est. 17)		91	10[d]	191	21[d]	27	3
TOTAL[f]	100	924	100	914	100	903	100	892	100

[a]Supervision by the trained midwife at the health center or at home.

[b]Based on the proportion of Hang Chat women with 1974 births supervised by TBAs, revealed by the Community Health Survey (1975).

[c]Home births supervised by TBAs trained by the Lampang Project (estimated 75% of total number in villages). Figures for last 5 months of 1975 projected to whole year may be too high.

[d]Calculated by exclusion. Thought to be too low in 1975 and too high for 1976.

[e]Delivery totals for 10 months projected to 12 months.

[f]Total births based on estimated total populations of 42,000 to 43,000 from 1974-77, with estimated fall in birth rates from 22.0-20.5 per 1,000 over the same period.

Table 9

Nutritional Status of Pre-School Children in Hang Chat (E_1)

District and Portions of Muang District (E_2)

Nutritional Status Classification[a]	E_1[c]	Percent E_2[d]	E_2[c]
Normal	56	45	47
Primary undernutrition	31	44	37
Secondary undernutrition	11	10	12
Tertiary undernutrition	2	1	3

[a]Gomez weight-for-age against Thai standard.

[c]Surveillance data, N (children) = 4,000

[d]Community Health Survey, sample of all six E_2 districts, N (children) = 1,500.

Table 10

Followup of Sample of Seriously Malnourished
Children in Hang Chat (E_1) 1977-1978

Children Identified as 3° undernourished by Nutritional Surveillance[a]		Number	Percent
Misclassified[b]		6	8
Died before followup		3	4
Improved[b]			
to 2° status	5	20	25
to 1° status	3		
Unspecified	12		
Unchanged		32	42
Unknown[c]		16	21
TOTAL		77	100

[a]Nutrition surveillance in 1977 estimated that 2% of Hang Chat children under 6 were severely (third degree) malnourished.

[b]A minimum estimate.

[c]It is known that some of these 16 children improved while others were misclassified. The exact numbers are unknown, however.

A few children died and the largest single group were those whose
status was unchanged. The notes of the followup workers make it
clear that many HPVs were not fully cooperative and some wechakorn
were unable to take an active role. Half the children who received
supplements received them at home, the balance coming to the health
center. In only two of seven health centers was staff performance
considered satisfactory. Where food supplements were delivered or
collected, the child was much more likely to improve.

These results must be judged disappointing. Since the
improvement of child nutrition is a priority of the Project, new
approaches may need to be devised to stimulate the villages to
recognize the problem (perhaps through the dramatic recovery of
a severely malnourished child in the village) and to activate the
HPVs (perhaps by means of an incentive in selling supplemental
food). Ultimately, food supplements should be locally made,
pointing to a possible role for the private sector. Finally, the
role of health education to train mothers how to prepare local
foods properly, and to decrease the role of superstition, needs
expansion through HPVs and HCs, and to be reinforced by re-
stimulated wechakorn. There may well be a role for a trial of
mothers' clubs in some villages to carry out continuous surveillance
and to promote better nutritional practices.

FAMILY PLANNING

The baseline Community Health and Nutrition Survey in E1
and C1 indicated very high levels of current family planning practice
before Project interventions were introduced. With a current contraceptive prevalence rate at 50 percent and above, a rapid further
large increase in acceptance could hardly be expected.

Followup data on current family planning practice will not be
collected until the Community Health and Nutrition Survey is
repeated at the end of the Project in 1980. However, family planning
service statistics do provide some evidence of how Project activities
may be affecting family planning acceptance. Table 11 summarizes
new family planning acceptor data for the period of Project operations
in E1 and C1 areas.

The growth of family planning acceptance from 1974 to 1977
is clearly greater in area E1 than area C1. The sharp increases in
1976 are for pill acceptors and women receiving DMPA injections
at health centers rather than at the provincial hospital. The
placement of the wechakorn has much to do with the increased
acceptance in area E1 and its timing. The striking increase in
number of sterilizations in the district facilities of area E1 in
1977 represents the activities of the mobile vasectomy clinic
of the Community Health Department. This mobile clinic has
amply demonstrated that rural men with low income and limited
educational background are interested in vasectomy. The response
has been vigorous and 1978 will show further gains in the acceptance
of this method.

Table 11

New Family Planning Practice Acceptors
in E_1 and C_1, 1974-1977

Service Location	Method	1974 E_1	1974 C_1	1975 E_1	1975 C_1	1976 E_1	1976 C_1	1977 E_1	1977 C_1
Provincial Hospital	Sterilization M/F	75	n.a.	76	71	69	76	37	69
	IUD	127	"	78	142	66	179	70	125
	Injection	--	"	1	--	2	--	4	3
	Pill	24	"	33	65	62	71	32	78
	TOTAL	226	"	188	279	149	321	143	275
District Hospitals and Health Centers	Sterilization M/F	1	"	--	--	--	--	187	--
	IUD	1	"	--	--	--	--	10	--
	Injection	--	"	41	--	207	--	251	--
	Pill	476	"	574	819	799	791	801	816
	TOTAL	478	"	615	819	1,006	791	1,339	816
TOTAL - Hospital + District		704	"	803	1,098	1,205	1,212	1,482	1,191

[a]Data for Hang Chat District Hospital are for 9 months, the period the facility was newly opened.

If the provincial hospital data are separated from the total new acceptors, the contrasting pattern of acceptance at the district level is striking. Whereas in E1 there was a 49 percent increase in new acceptors between 1975 and 1976, and a 33 percent increase from 1976 to 1977, there was a slight decrease in C1 over the same period. There was also a small decrease in provincial hospital new acceptors who came from Hang Chat. Although conclusions must be tentative, the sharp increase in new acceptances in E1 seems to correspond with the introduction of wechakorn and community health volunteers. Furthermore, the proportion of new acceptors traveling to the provincial hospital for services has decreased in Project operational areas, but has not decreased in the control area. This strongly suggests that the expanded availability of family planning services at the district level and below have attracted more new acceptors, reducing the need to use the provincial hospital.

Once the mobile clinic began operations in October 1977, there was a surprisingly vigorous response in most of the areas where the service was introduced. In the first year of the mobile clinic (Oct. 1977-Sept. 1978) over 1,000 men received vasectomies. Interestingly, a majority of these were poor farmers, with four or less years of education and with three or less children. The initial impact of this clinic on the pattern of family planning acceptance can be seen in Table 11. It should be noted that in the same period the mobile clinics also provided over 3,600 immunizations (mostly cholera and typhoid) and services to more than 6,500 outpatients (two-thirds of them women).

CHAPTER 6

COSTS, RESOURCES AND
REPLICATION REQUIREMENTS

A frequent criticism of special demonstration projects is that
they may produce excellent results and impact, but frequently employ
methods that the implementing government cannot afford to replicate
and institutionalize in other parts of the country. For this reason,
as the Lampang Project began, emphasis was placed on analyzing what
additional resources would be required for the government to
incorporate the Project's key features into the health structures of
other provinces. At this point in the project, a comprehensive
analysis of costs and outputs is not complete. However, some
interim information and findings are presented below that point
to encouraging, even if tentative, conclusions.

REGULAR PROVINCIAL HEALTH SYSTEM COSTS

Table 12 summarizes the actual and projected expenditures of
the provincial health care system for the four years the Lampang
Project has been in operation. The figures conform to the standard
government accounting categories and do *not* include external
assistance (dealt with separately below).

During the period of Project implementation there have been
heavy capital outlays--amounting to 45 percent of the total budget
over four years--for the expansion of the provincial hospital and
construction of several new rural health facilities. These high
capital outlays are unique to Lampang and only a few other provinces
where the provincial hospital is being expanded and upgraded to
regional status. A substantial portion of the sizeable increase in
operating costs is also associated with this expansion of facilities,
reflecting the additional personnel and supplies required to operate
them. This general expansion of capacity, it should be emphasized,
was not part of the Lampang Project plan as such, but the Project
aims to intensify the utilization and efficiency of the entire provincial health system, including the new capacity.

In order to get a better picture of actual provincial service
costs, Table 13 presents operational costs only, by service locations
(i.e. provincial hospital and district and subdistrict health
facilities). It can be seen that the bulk of provincial health service

Table 12

Annual Provincial Health Budgets
by Functional Categories
(in U.S. dollars)

| Year | Capital Costs | Operational Costs | | | | |
		Personnel[a]	Expendable Supplies	Other[b]	Total operational Costs	Annual Total
1974-75	$ 531,538	$ 425,252	$ 359,730	$ 111,460	$ 896,442	$ 1,467,980
1975-76	822,070	622,731	502,442	111,548	1,236,721	2,058,791
1976-77	2,038,713	658,329	1,545,136	336,598	2,140,062	4,178,775
1977-78	2,285,971	1,040,971	1,321,119	480,778	2,851,664	5,137,635
4 year Total	$ 5,718,292	$2,756,079	$3,728,427	$1,040,384	$7,124,889	$12,843,181
Yearly Average	$1,429,573	$ 689,020	$ 932,107	$ 260,096	$1,781,222	$ 3,210,795

Sources: Lampang Project Planning and Programming Division for 1974-76;
Provincial Health Plan for 1976-78.

[a]Personnel costs include salaries, wages and overtime.

[b]Other costs include travel, per diem, and allowances, matching funds, central funds, and miscellaneous.

costs are associated with the provincial hospital, and that rural health facilities operate on small budgets. This is explained in part by the fact that the most highly-trained and highly-paid personnel are concentrated in the provincial hospital, and the types of services available there are more sophisticated and hence, more expensive. It also reflects the lower priority traditionally given to rural health services. However, the Government's current effort to change this situation is evidenced by the three-fold increase in the operating budget for district health services in 1976-77.

Note: US$1 = 20 Thai Bhats

Table 13

Annual Operational Costs by Geographic Location[a]

| Year | Provincial Hospital | District Health Facilities[b] | | | Total |
		E1 District	C1 District	Other 9 Districts	
1974-75	$ 642,399	$ 24,601[c]	$ 19,681[b]	$ 209,761	$ 896,442
1975-76	889,244	31,589[d]	31,589[d]	284,299	1,236,721
1976-77	1,015,109	93,746	93,746	937,461	2,140,062
1977-78	--	--	--	--	2,851,664

[a]Segregation of individual district costs from the aggregate provincial
health budget was done as part of the Project's Cost Analysis Study,
but data are only available for the baseline year 1974-75. However,
since provincial hospital costs and total provincial health costs are
known for subsequent years, average district health service costs
can be estimated for 1975-78 by dividing the total operational budget
for provincial rural health activities by the number of districts (11)
in the province. This is admittedly a rough average since the size
and available facilities in the eleven districts are uneven.

[b]Includes both district hospitals and subdistrict health centers.

[c]E1 and C1 district costs obtained from Cost Analysis Baseline Survey.

[d]E1 and C1 figures derived by dividing total district health budget
by the number of districts (11).

PROJECTED COSTS OF REPLICATION

To ascertain what additional costs beyond the normal provincial
health resources might be required to implement the key features of
the Lampang Project in other areas, a first required step is to review
the level of outside contributions. Table 14 summarizes annual
external assistance to the Project over the past four years. The
total $2.8 million (provided by US AID via the American Public
Health Association and the University of Hawaii) is equivalent to
an addition of approximately 22 percent to the total provincial
health budget (including capital outlays) over the four year period,
or about 39 percent in terms of the total operational budget.

The required budgetary increments for duplicating the main
features of the Lampang Project in other provinces, however, would
be considerably less. This is because a large portion of the research

Table 14

Annual Non-RTG Donor Contributions to Lampang Project
1974-75 Through 1977-78

Source	1974-75	1975-76	1976-77	1977-78	Total
APHA	$366,599	$366,599	$627,000	$627,000	$1,987,148
UHSPH Technical Assistance	114,526	189,589	256,219	260,210	820,544

APHA   = American Public Health Association

UHSPH   = University of Hawaii School of Public Health

and development, training, demonstration, evaluation and technical assistance costs that were essential to the Lampang Project and were supported mainly by external funds, would not have to be repeated in full. For example, almost all of the special evaluation activities directed at measuring the Project's various impacts would not have to be continued elsewhere. Similarly, the sizeable initial investment in designing training programs and developing training methods and materials for the wechakorn and other new categories of personnel would not have to be repeated since the end products of this investment are now available and can be readily used in other provinces at relatively little cost.

By examining carefully the various cost categories in the Project budget and estimating the proportion of each that could be considered necessary for replication, we have reached the conclusion that only 11 percent of the externally supported costs shown in Table 14--or roughly an average of $300,000 spread over four years-- would be required as additional inputs to implement the key features of the Lampang Project in other provinces. For a province the size of Lampang, and at price levels prevailing over the past four years, this would amount to an average annual budget increment of $75,000. Taking as an illustration Lampang's aggregate provincial health budget over the past four years, this would average out to 2.5 percent per year of the cumulative total budget (including capital outlays), or 4.2 percent of the cumulative operational budget.

While the actual percentages applicable to other provinces would vary somewhat according to the size of their geographic area and population, and the size of their existing health system and budget, the above illustrative figures drawn from Lampang Province provide

a useful indicator of the order of magnitude of the costs of replicating the main features of the Project in other provinces.

A more detailed and perhaps more accurate picture of the
probable costs of replication can be seen from a different angle,
by examining the costs of developing and implementing specific
major project components (albeit on the basis of rough cost
data). The largest component is the cost of training the various
personnel categories. In 1976, the estimated "normal" (i.e.
post starting-up) costs of training each of the Project's innovative
health worker categories were:

Health Post Volunteer	=	$124/person
Health Communicator	=	$ 17/person
Traditional Midwife	=	$112/person
Wechakorn	=	$2,000/person

These early estimates of training costs for village volunteers
are probably higher than present costs because the subsequent
training program for trainers prepared subdistrict health workers
to assume volunteer training responsibilities, thereby reducing the
higher-cost inputs of the Project Personnel Development Division
staff.

Training the first group of wechakorn was expensive, with
an estimated average cost of over $6,000 per trainee. However,
these included heavy initial investments in developing the training,
purchasing training equipment and supplies, and extensive technical
consultant costs for those assisting in developing the program.
Thereafter, wechakorn training costs benefited from economies of
scale, leading to an average trainee cost that has stabilized at
about $2,000.

If the training costs in a single district are compiled, and
the other inputs needed to implement integrated health services are
added, some measure of required additional resource inputs can be
estimated. For example, in Hang Chat, the first operational
district, implementation costs that were incurred in addition to the
normal government budget are presented in Table 15. Since all
implementation was done in a two-year period in Hang Chat, training
costs are divided between two years. When comparing the total inputs
related to Project implementation with the average annual district
health budget of about $28,000, the supplementary inputs seem very
large. But the major portion of the added costs are for training,
which would not normally be borne by the district itself. Furthermore, training costs are an initial investment, which, being largely
nonrepetitive, are much smaller when prorated over the life span of
service contributed by health workers.

The estimated replication costs presented above are necessarily
rough and subject to refinement as additional facts and analysis become
available. They suggest, however, that the costs of reproducing the

Table 15

Two Year Project Inputs in Hang Chat District
(1974-1976)

Cost Category	Two-Year Costs*	Average Cost/Year
HPV Training	$ 9,300	$ 4,650
(a) 75 x $124/trainee = $9,300		
Communicator Training (b) 652 x $17/trainee = $11,084	11,084	5,542
Traditional Midwife Training (c) 44 x $117/trainee = $ 5,148	5,184	2,574
Wechakorn Training (d) 7 x $2,000/trainee = $14,000	14,000	7,000
Total Training Costs (Sum of above (a+b+c+d)	$39,532	$19,766
Supervision ($5/day x 4 days/month)	4,160	2,080
Supplies/Materials ($250 x 7 centers)	3,500	1,750
Total Additional Inputs	$47,192	$23,596
Estimated Average Government District Health Budget	$56,190	$28,095

*Excludes initial starting-up costs.

main features of the Lampang Project throughout Thailand in coming
years should be well within the financial capabilities of the government.

It is recognized, of course, that additional resources would
permit more rapid replication. For example, in the World Bank-
financed Population Project, now underway in 20 additional
provinces of Thailand, a number of Lampang Project-like features
have been incorporated. With a total budget of approximately
$68 million ($34 million in loan and grant assistance), about 50 percent
is being devoted to capital construction of all types, and the remaining
50 percent to training, evaluation, and other operational costs. The
Ministry of Public Health thus understands that rapid replication
activities require some additional support, but in fact, much of what
has been developed and evaluated in Lampang can be replicated more
cheaply. Per diem rates for trainees are being reduced, wechakorn-
like training is being shortened, and a variety of other steps have
been taken in the project to trim costs.

CHAPTER 7

CONCLUSIONS AND LESSONS

In the fourth year of the Lampang Project, with interventions well underway but with evaluation activities incomplete, where does the Project stand with regard to achievement of its major objectives? What has been learned? What experience has been translated into Ministry policy and plans for primary health care and integrated health services?

Any appraisal at this time must necessarily be incomplete and tentative, based on only a baseline survey, fragmentary longitudinal data of uneven quality extracted from routine provincial records, and on the qualitative, but knowledgeable, reports of many experienced observers.

A further important caveat to bear in mind is that the Lampang Project is not writing on a clean slate, nor is it a total health system unto itself. On the contrary, it seeks to modify, redirect, expand, and make more efficient and effective an existing health system, based on a conventional Western model, that was failing to bring appropriate primary health care services to the great majority of rural families. Moreover, it was introduced at a time when the Ministry of Public Health was already committed to a major expansion of the existing health system's capacity, especially to serve more rural people. Without the Project, however, the system would have been expanded substantially in its old image, thus perpetuating its old imbalances, fragmentation and inefficiencies.

Thus the major goal of the Lampang Health Development Project has been to improve the health status of the population of Lampang by pursuing the following *specific* implementation objectives:

1. To expand health care coverage to at least two-thirds of the rural women in child-bearing years and preschool children.

2. To establish an integrated model of provincial health service delivery extending to the subdistrict level and linked to a village health volunteer network established in every village.

3. To establish an integrated health care system that is "low cost" (i.e. more cost-effective), the key features of which

are within the resources of the RTG to replicate
nationally if found effective.

Evaluation objectives include: the measurement of consumer
accessibility to and acceptance of services in the experimental and
control areas; an assessment of the performance of health personnel
and the efficiency (through improved mangement) of the health
delivery system; measurement of the impact of services on the health
status of the population over time (as compared to specific targets);
and lastly, an assessment of the financial, social and administrative
feasibility of replicating the key features introduced by the Project.

A series of questions bearing on the Project's objectives will
serve as a useful frame for this preliminary appraisal:

A. *To what extent can integration of illness care, disease
    prevention, and health promotion services, as well as
    government and private health sector services, actually
    be attained?*

The Lampang experience suggests that more integration can
be achieved, despite the historical separation of "medical care" and
"public health" services. The administrative reorganization by the
Ministry of Public Health in 1974-75, placing all provincial hospital
and health services under a Provincial Health Officer, helped to
expedite the integration goals of the Project. But even more important
perhaps in reorienting attitudes, are the manpower development and
role changes instituted by the Project. While wechakorn training is
necessarily mostly clinical in orientation--to relieve the heavy demand
for illness care at the hospitals as well as to bring clinical services
closer to the villagers--community health skills are also emphasized.
The wechakorn typically comes from a rural health center, where
the preventive/promotive orientation is relatively strong, and he
returns after clinical care and community health training with a
renewed commitment to the preventive/promotive services stressed
by the Project--maternal and child health, family planning, and
nutrition.

In an underserved rural population oriented to episodic medical
crises, the risk is that preventive services will be submerged by the
demand for curative care. This risk is clearly lowest for family
planning, which, because of the high demand and continuing interest
at highest government levels, has been well-integrated in the
provincial health services for some time. The risk may be highest for
nutrition, which is not widely recognized by the people as an important
problem and is confounded, much as family planning once was, by a
maze of traditional myths.

A major contribution of the Project to integrated health services
is the organization of the Community Health Department at the Provincial Hospital. While this department is not yet permanently established,
there is every indication that it will be soon. Hospital physicians
rotating from other departments, go out with the mobile unit into the
rural areas to provide curative and preventive services and supervise

the work of the rural health centers. This rotating activity will expand in the future. At the central level the Community Health Department provides a focus for preventive services at the hospital, and it has absorbed a number of preventive functions and staff from the Provincial Health Office.

"Integration" of the private sector in an overall government-coordinated health care system will be more difficult. Private pharmacists in the towns have been cooperative in resupplying medicines to the HPV, but they were approached only when the government system was unable to provide needed supplies in a timely manner. The private Community-Based Family Planning Services, which since 1975 has been very successful in organizing private family planning services in many parts of Thailand, agreed to organize an experimental district (Ngao) within the Lampang Project area. Its program is being expanded on a pilot basis in Lampang to include provision of simple medicines, health education, and perhaps community nutritional surveillance.

So far as is known, traditional health practitioners (indigenous healers, herbalists, injectionists, etc.) as well as small merchants selling household medicines in the villages, have for the most part gone along with--or at least tolerated--the program, while traditional midwives have actively joined it.

    B.   *Can at least two-thirds of the target population be reached with expanded and integrated health services?*

The answer is almost certainly "yes," although complete documentary evidence is not available at this writing. Already a large proportion of eligible women (slightly over 50 percent in the baseline Community Health Survey) are being reached with family planning services. There is also evidence, at least in area E1, that almost all deliveries are now attended by trained personnel. Prenatal and postnatal services, however, appear to be weak, and this weakness suggests the need for improved supervision and followup. A higher level of complete pregnancy care can be achieved only if the wechakorn can galvanize the interests of the villagers and the service efforts of the village-based TBAs and the health center based auxiliary midwives.

The same is true for immunizations, but here the problem is compounded by the special requirements of bringing appropriate biological materials to the village in viable condition. There may need to be special immunization campaigns in Lampang, especially oriented to Diphtheria-Pertussis-Tetanus Toxoid (DPT) and bacille Calmette Guérin (BCG) for preschool children, and tetanus for the general population (with particular emphasis on women in their child-bearing years). The need to continue giving smallpox vaccinations is highly doubtful. Coverage will be very difficult to measure unless mothers are supplied with cards for themselves and their babies. Cross-sectional surveys can only establish (more reliable for smallpox and BCG) the proportion of children (but not the specific children) immunized at least once over a reference time period.

Nutritional surveillance and follow-up case work is also a great
challenge. Nutrition services have been under-financed (primarily
because nutrition is not recognized by the province as a major problem), and services that are available seem not to reach children
most in need. As described earlier, the Project has documented that
between 10-15 percent of preschool children in areas E1 and E2 are
moderately to severely undernourished. What remains to be done is
to systematically identify these children (already accomplished in
some areas) and to establish an effective system of follow-up. Health
education at the village level will need to emphasize better selection,
preparation, and (within family) distribution of available foods.

As noted earlier, the project aims to reach 65 percent of the
total Lampang population with basic health services. In an earlier
section of this report it was seen that total coverage is increasing,
and although the proportion of care provided by rural health centers
appears to be increasing on target, the relative contribution of the
HPVs is below expectations. The proportion of care provided by the
provincial hospital has not increased significantly, at least for E1
residents, which is a positive sign.

Throughout the implementation period, the number of rural
health centers and district hospitals (formerly first class health
centers) has been increasing rapidly. Staffing of the district hospitals has also been strengthened; all have full-time physicians,
a significant step forward over the incomplete staffing of the early
1970s. The Lampang Provincial Hospital has acquired regional status
and is in the process of doubling its bed capacity. All these developments will improve overall population coverage and a more appropriate
distribution of cases between levels of the system. It will be
increasingly difficult to differentiate from other forces the contribution
of the Project in promoting overall coverage, but the expansion of
rural coverage, coupled with the growing availability of wechakorn,
can be expected to shift the pattern of primary care toward the
periphery of the health system. However, care within the village
may weaken and be by-passed unless more support, regular supervision, and continuing education are provided for the HPVs and
TBAs.

C. *Can underutilization of existing government peripheral
health facilities be overcome?*

The emerging answer is optimistic. There is little question
that the wechakorn have made an extraordinary difference in increasing utilization of rural health facilities, although it is not clear that
their activities will reduce or even hold constant the demand for more
expensive health care at the provincial hospital. Hospital planners
are clearly assuming that there will be more demand.

Wechakorn themselves may be overwhelmed with curative care
and find little time for preventive/promotive activities, unless the
village health volunteers become more active and are better supported.
To date, the potential role for planning by the village health committee

seems unrealized. It should be kept in mind, however, that villagers are often distracted by the requests of many other governmental programs to set up various development-oriented committees. Health may not appear to be the most attractive or important of these. More-over, given years of political passivity and the influence of rural Thai culture, villagers are unlikely to make demands or perhaps even requests of the local bureaucracy. The current situation is charac-terized more by "downward support" than "upward planning."

    D. *Can the health status of the population--fertility, mortality, morbidity--be measurably improved by integrated and expanded health services?*

It has been shown that fertility has been declining in Lampang for some time, and baseline surveys indicate that 50 percent of eligible women in areas E1, C1, and C2 were practising family planning when the Project began. Given the apparent trend and its tempo, it may be difficult to attribute further change to the Project (though evidence presented in Chapter 5 suggests a positive contribution). It should be mentioned that the Project may in any event contribute to greater efficiency in fertility control. The distribution of pills by active HPVs may be expected to improve continuation, and the Mobile Unit's successful efforts to promote vasectomy will release women from the need to take hormones over a long period of time. For many couples, sterilization, especially vasectomy, is the most appropriate and desired method, and the Project has made improvements by offering a high quality service, supported in many ways by village volunteers.

As for morbidity and mortality, the answer will rest on trends to be measured in future Community Health Surveys. Because of the inclusion of two control areas, one of them, contiguous, but remote and unlikely to be contaminated by Project effects, the Project is protected against falsely concluding that there has been a change attributable to its activities. Clearly, mortality is declining in Thailand, and this may be assumed to be so in Lampang as well. Morbidity is more elastic in nature and thus harder to measure, but following the definition used in the baseline Community Health Survey, one might reasonably expect a parallel decline in disabling illness. Attribution of such declines to the Project could be overshadowed by the significant expansion of general health services in Lampang since 1974. One anticipates posi-tive effects on morbidity and mortality from Project activities, but they may be difficult to measure and even more difficult to associate clearly with specific Project inputs.

    E. *To what extent can management and efficiency of health services be improved?*

Changing management practices is a sensitive matter, more easily accomplished at lower levels if the system supports lower-level decision-making. The addition of assistant district health officers may improve supervision and support at the rural health centers, much as the wechakorn should both stimulate and respond to the HPVs.

Many management decisions, even within the project, continue to be
based mainly on experience and intuition. This is often effective,
but tends to underutilize information collected for management purposes.
The Project's efforts to collect data and to focus selected information
on management decisions, have been impressive thus far, but may need
further strengthening. The Ministry of Public Health is currently
conducting a series of rural health services management workshops
for provincial personnel throughout the nation.

One basis for measuring efficiency has been laid in the Cost and
Task Analyses in the hospital and health centers. It is clear that,
in the rural health centers at least, there was customarily a significant
amount of "idle" time. If staff capabilities are strengthened and the
demand for services by villagers increases, it seems likely that the slack
time will be reduced. The evidence presented in Chapter 5 suggests
that this is already happening.

F. *Is it possible to replicate the Project's key features in other
     areas, given normally available resources?*

The key features to be considered here are the reorganized
hospital/rural health service infrastructure, the wechakorn paraphysician, the village health volunteers, the involvement of the
community and the private sector, and an improved management system.

Starting with the view of the provincial hospital as the nucleus
of health services at the center of an inter-related network of health
centers and peripheral services reaching into the villages, the Department of Community Medicine was established to promote the hospital's
community health role. The idea of reaching outside the hospital's
compound to support and coordinate a variety of curative outpatient
and preventive services in the larger community is not easily accepted
by physicians trained under the Western medical model. Many feel
their extensive training is wasted in dealing with the usually mild and
often self-limited complaints of rural people. Trained to take care of
rare, "interesting cases," they are not eager to move outside the
hospital, even temporarily. The Department of Community Medicine
in Lampang has grown slowly, gradually winning acceptance in the
hospital and at the rural health centers. Soon its small staff will be
increased by three wechakorn, greatly increasing its capacity to
provide preventive/promotive services at the hospital and curative
care and supervision in the rural areas. The usefulness and replicability of such a department is evident, but although the Ministry of
Public Health plans to establish them in all provincial hospitals, final
decisions on their structure, role, and activities have not yet been
made.

The Ministry of Public Health, in advance of definitive evaluation
of the Lampang experience, has elected to train sufficient village
health volunteers (HPVs and HCs) for 20 provinces in the Five Year
Plan which began in 1977. The MOPH plans to use the Lampang Project
training materials and job descriptions. In addition, the Ministry will

train 1,400 nurse practitioners for the same 20 provinces. Unlike the
wechakorn, all trainees will be nurses. This designation will avoid the
problem of Civil Service recognition of a new class of health worker.
The nurse practitioners, however, will be assigned only to the provincial and district hospitals--not to the more rural health centers where
there is a greater demand and need for illness care. Training will
emphasize clinical skills, rather than disease prevention and health
promotion for the village level. A plan is also underway to give four
months of clinical training to midwives. These workers would return
to the rural health centers to provide much more limited curative
services and support for the village volunteers than is provided by
wechakorn.

        The supervisory implications of the Ministry's plans for "para-
physician" training will require great attention and effort. While
there will be few problems with the nurse practitioner, who almost
always will work with a resident physician, the issue remains of how
to tie the village volunteers to the specially trained midwife and how
to provide logistical support and supervision to both from the district
and provincial hospital. The Lampang Project experience suggests
how difficult this may be to achieve, especially in the absence of
wechakorn or their equivalent in every subdistrict health center.

        Replication of the management system begins with careful orienta-
tion and training of provincial and district level health staff. It
means the use of carefully honed information for decision-making
and implies two way communication. It means the efficient referral of
patients to the most appropriate level of health care. Current plans
to further strengthen planning and evaluation activities at the
provincial levels will certainly be helpful.

        Finally, although the data related to costs of the Lampang Project
are preliminary in nature, it seems that replication of the major
features are well within the government's financial capabilities. Most
of the Lampang Project's outside resources are nonrepetitive, having
been applied to development of training methodologies and materials,
and to evaluation and research. As the Ministry of Public Health
implements similar features in other areas of the country, the
costs should drop substantially as economies of scale apply.

        Figure 1, shown at the beginning of this paper, summarizes the
evolution of integrated rural health care in Thailand, and the Ministry
of Public Health's directions for the near future. It seems clear that
plans for future implementation have incorporated features similar to
those in Lampang, as well as the experience and lessons learned there.
The completion of the Project evaluation and documentation process
promises to provide further information and lessons that will be of use
to the Ministry in implementing expanded rural health care. Consequently, the Lampang Project seems very likely to achieve its goal of
serving the mainstream of Royal Thai Government health policy formulation, health planning, and programming.

4 CBFPS in Thailand: A Community-Based Approach to Family Planning

S. Burintratikul
M.C. Samaniego

EDITOR'S NOTE

The Community-Based Family Planning Service (CBFPS) in Thailand views family planning as only one of a combination of basic requirements for improving rural family life. Hence its unconventional approach has been to integrate family planning efforts whenever possible with other family improvement efforts, such as primary health care services. At the time of this case study, CBFPS was preparing to launch an ambitious multi-pronged community development program with family planning services as the springboard.

CBFPS is also unique in another respect. As its name implies, community-based volunteer workers are the mainstay of its organization and service approach--a fundamental strategy that has now been adopted by the Thai Government for the whole country. Thus this case study demonstrates the special role a private organization can play not only in contributing to the realization of national family planning goals but in helping to pioneer a more integrated and community-based approach to rural development that the government as well as voluntary agencies can employ.

The principal investigators and authors of this report were S. Burintratikul and M.C.Samaniego of the Management Services Division of the Bangkok branch of the SGV-Na Thalang and Co., a multinational auditing, accounting and consulting firm. Mr. Samaniego, a senior member of the Bangkok office of the firm, had been keenly interested for some time in CBFPS and readily agreed, when approached by ICED, to lend a hand in preparing the case study --not as a commercial assignment but as a public service.

The introductory chapter was written by Manzoor Ahmed of ICED's staff who worked with the authors in designing the study and accompanied them on preliminary field visits.

The study would not have been possible but for the unstinting cooperation of Mr. Mechai Viravaidya, the dynamic and innovative leader of CBFPS, and the generous help of numerous CBFPS staff members and volunteer distributors. Full responsibility for the content of the report, however, including all evaluative judgments, rests solely with the authors and ICED.

INTRODUCTION*

The purpose of this introductory commentary is to provide a view of the CBFPS experience from the vantage point of ICED's comparative perspective and its concerns in relation to the overall project of which this case study is a part. This introduction gives an overview of CBFPS performance, highlights some of the important points brought out in the report, and underscores the significant practical lessons of the CBFPS experience.

Bringing information and supplies of contraceptives within easy reach of the people was the aim of the community-based distribution projects supported in a number of countries since 1973 by the International Planned Parenthood Federation (IPPF).

Mechai Viravaidya, then the Secretary-General of the Planned Parenthood Association of Thailand (PPAT), decided in 1973 to take advantage of IPPF assistance and conceived the idea of an experimental project for community-based family planning services in parts of Thailand and neighboring Laos across the Mekong River. For various reasons, all of the PPAT leaders did not endorse the project and Mechai found himself in disagreement with them on other issues and resigned from PPAT. IPPF, however, decided to back the project and the Community-Based Family Planning Services (CBFPS) under Mechai's direction came into being in 1974 as an independent entity with nominal links with the PPAT, the local IPPF affiliate.

In quantitative terms, the achievements of CBFPS over a period of three years (1974-1977) are impressive by any standard. The project extended by the end of 1977 to 113 districts and 12,000 villages (out of a total of about 600 districts and 45,000 villages in the country) serving 10.1 million people or 23 percent of the national popluation. About 7,600 individuals--shopkeepers, farmers, teachers, and housewives by profession--distributed pills and other contraceptives and provided information about family planning practices to people in their own villages. Almost 200,000 eligible individuals have become acceptors of family planning measures as a esult of CBFPS efforts. CBFPS records show that in 1976, (the most recent year for which complete figures for both CBFPS and the national program are available) over 10 percent of the total acceptors in the country were recruited by CBFPS.

The economics of the CBFPS efforts is not fully clear to us because of overlapping categories of income and expenditure data (see Chapter 5 of the report). On the whole, it appears that CBFPS average annual expenditures for the past three years (1975-77) have been on the order of US$500,000. By comparison, the direct government expenditure (from the national budget and foreign assistance sources) during the second plan period (1972-76) was 565 million baht or over US$5.6 million per year. This government outlay did not include the personnel salaries and physical facilities which are

_____

*This introduction was prepared by Manzoor Ahmed of the ICED staff.

covered by the health service budget.* Any precise unit cost comparison would be difficult to arrive at (though an attempt is made in
this report), but it would be reasonable to conclude that CBPFS has
reached some 10 percent of total acceptors in the country at substantially less than 10 percent of the national expenditures for family
planning. According to CBFPS sample surveys, in the CBFPS districts
between 1974 and 1976 pregnancy rates declined by 40 percent,
compared to an average 20 percent in neighboring districts served
only by the government program.

The striking achievement of CBPFS is that it has overcome the
familiar barriers of geographical access to family planning information and contraceptive supplies by making these available in the
village community itself. Another distinguishing feature is that
CBFPS is a non-government private sector effort of sizeable dimensions that mobilizes private resources, including manpower and mangement talents, but functions in cooperation with the government within
the framework of the national family planning program. A third significant characteristic is its attention to long-range cost feasibility
of family planning services, including in particular its effort to
make community level distribution and communication activities at
least partially self-financing. Finally, another interesting feature
of CBPFS is its trial attempts to combine family planning services
with elements of health care and its current vision of building an
integrated community development approach around the nucleus of
family planning service in each community.

Proving out the Idea of Community-Based Service

The idea of drawing on individuals from communities for assistance in delivering family planning services to the respective
communities was not an invention of CBPFS. It, however, made the idea
widely known and acceptable in Thaailand through its relatively large
and aggressive program. Practical confirmation of an idea is always
harder than formulating the idea itself. The contribution of CBFPS,
therefore, cannot be underestimated because the idea was not novel.

The principle of using community members as auxiliaries was
already receiving favorable attention from the Department of Health
and such institutions as the Faculty of Public Health in Mahidol
University, when CBFPS began to function. In the northern province of
Lampang, for instance, the Department of Health has been conducting
since 1975 an experimental project to deliver basic health care based
on the use of village health post volunteers and village health
communicators. The Lampang project itself was the outgrowth of earlier
experiments in the northern region of Thailand. The volunteers and
communicators in this project serve their own villages and
are supervised by paramedical workers of the Department of
Health based in local health centers. The Public Health Faculty of
Mahidol University also has been experimenting since 1975 in the Po-thang

---

*See American Public Health Association, International Health
Program, Report of the Second Evaluation of the National Family
Planning Program in Thailand, July 1977, p. 19.

district 85 miles north of Bangkok, with village volunteers who exclusively
provide family planning services (information, distribution of   contraceptives, and referral to clinics) in their own villages.

CBFPS achievements, however, have clearly contributed to making the
use of the village-level auxiliary in health care and family planning   an
accepted national policy. The rapid expansion of the CBFPS project and its
effective results demonstrated not only the feasibility of using voluntary
auxiliaries in the villages but also the value of this approach in   overcoming geographical and social barriers. The distributor in the   village,
while bringing contraceptives practically to the doorstep of the villagers,
minimizes the typical communication gap resulting from the cultural   and
social "distance" between an "outside" government employee and the   villagers.

Government acceptance of the community-based approach is   reflected
in a major new initiative.Under a large family planning project   supported
by a consortia of external donors led by the World Bank, the community-based
service approach is to be instituted in 20 provinces during the years 1978-
80. The approach, which is expected eventually to spread nationwide,   is
based on the use of village health-post volunteers and village health communicators who, backed up by paramedical workers, will deal with   primary
health care needs including family planning services in their   respective
villages. CBFPS is expected to be associated with this national project,at
least in some of the districts, particularly in recruiting and training village level auxiliaries and instituting a supervision and monitoring system
for the village level activities.

Role of Voluntary Organizations

CBFPS has demonstrated that a non-government voluntary organization
can play an important role in facilitating a national program for   family
planning services.   This support has been provided by complementing   the
clinic-based family planning activities of the government health service by
providing village-level services, thus reducing the burden of the   health
personnel in the field; and by mobilizing manpower and resources from   the
private sector which otherwise would remain untapped for the national   program.

The existence and accomplishments of CBFPS, on the other hand, have
been possible because of the support, sympathy and cooperation   it   has
received from various quarters in the government. Its inception was technically under the auspices of the National Family Planning Committee of   the
government and its program and the external assistance it received has been
subject to government approval. The Director of the National Family Planning Program (who is also the Director General of the Department of Health)
has been a staunch and consistent friend of CBFPS. At the operational level,
the provincial and district medical officers have been assigned an advisory
and guidance role for their respective areas and arrangements have   been
worked out for referral of CBFPS' clients to district and provincial   hospitals (as well as health centers) for clinical services and any   complications arising out of contraceptive use. It is unlikely that the CBFPS activities could have expanded as much and as rapidly as they have   without
the backing and sympathy of at least some officials in influential positions.

The CBFPS leadership, particularly its founder and director, Mechai, has consistently cultivated the support and friendship of government agencies. One of the key parameters of CBFPS' accomplishments is Mechai's ability to secure the required sympathy, advocacy, and cooperation from individuals and units of the government. The program has been projected as an integral part of the national family planning program and its goals have been proclaimed to be at one with the national goals. Mechai's revealing advice regarding the approach to aligning the bureaucracy on the side of a voluntary organization is: Do your best to prove your effectiveness and efficiency and give credit to the bureaucracy for whatever achievements you have made.

Although the commonality of purposes and a relationship of mutual support and cooperation have made it possible for CBFPS to come into being and to flourish, it would be wrong to assume that there is no diversity of views in the government about the CBFPS role or that there is no possibility of conflict. There is a point of view, though not the dominant one, in official circles that would concede a pioneering or trail-blazing role for private organizations and would rely on them for trying out new strategies or program approaches, but would not entrust such organizations with what is seen as government functions. A major, nationwide role for CBFPS or any other private organization in the family planning program would be considered inappropriate by the advocates of this point of view. The CBFPS role in the future in the face of government adoption of the community-based approach, therefore, remains an open question.

A direct conflict between the Department of Health family planning services and CBFPS village-based activities has not yet arisen, mainly because government experimental activities with village-based workers so far have been in non-CBFPS districts. The World Bank-supported project is also not expected to overlap with CBFPS districts, at least in the immediate future. The Fourth National Family Planning Program (1977-81) has, however, stipulated that all provinces, districts, and sub-districts will be covered by the village distribution program by the end of 1981. Unless this plan is modified in the course of its implementation overlapping and duplication will transpire. Obviously it would be an unjustifiable duplication to place both government auxiliaries and CBFPS distributors in the same villages with the same or overlapping functions.

The rationale for bestowing a major role on a private organization like CBFPS in the national family planning effort could be one or a combination of the following:

-- The private organization experiments with new approaches and strategies which is sometimes difficult for a government organization with all its bureaucratic and institutional constraints.

-- The private organization performs the same tasks as the government organization more efficiently and effectively.

-- The private organization mobilizes resources and manpower that are difficult for a government organization to do.

-- The private organization relieves the burden of the government organization and personnel and complements and supports the government efforts.

-- The private organization follows an integrated approach by combining family planning activities with other development activities and self-help actions on the part of communities aimed at improving the quality of their life which again is sometimes difficult for government organizations with their rigid jurisdictional divisions and bureaucratic style of operation.

To what extent do these reasons apply to CBFPS? We have seen that CBFPS has played a major role in demonstrating the feasibility of the community-based service approach in family planning and in gaining its acceptance as national policy. Having performed this role, has CBFPS now outgrown its usefulness? The answer probably is in the affirmative if CB-FPS has to justify its existence solely on the basis of its past role in popularizing the community-based service approach. Because, the role has been played effectively and the lesson has been learned. A prominent future position of CBFPS in the national program, therefore, has to be justified on other grounds.

It appears, as noted earlier, that CBFPS performance compares favorably with government programs in respect of both the efficiency of resource use and effectiveness in gaining acceptors and reducing pregnancy. However, the comparison has been between the CBFPS approach and the conventional clinic-based government approach. The present performance record may not hold good if the government organization can successfully adopt the community-based approach. How successfully the bureaucratic structure of a government organization can adapt itself to the needs of a community-based approach remains an open question despite the apparent determination of the government to pursue this approach. Perhaps CBFPS can play a role in reorienting and assisting the government organization to make the necessary transition. Indeed, cooperation of this nature between the CBFPS and the Lampang Health Project as well as the World Bank-assisted family planning project of the government is being contemplated.

On the other hand, there appears to be room for improving the efficiency of operation of the present CBFPS program itself. This writer, from field visits in several districts and discussions with distributors and central office personnel, gathered the impression that there have been sloppy record-keeping by village distributors, delayed and irregular reporting to the central office, time lag in consolidation and analysis of field data, and insufficient emphasis on continuation and retention (as opposed to recruiting new acceptors). These factors cast some doubt about the accuracy of CBFPS statistics, but more importantly, they militate against setting and enforcing performance standards, and weakens the motivation for reducing dropouts and maintaining sustained achievements. It is obviously not possible to be too demanding on the volunteer distributors about record-keeping, but this is something that the paid district supervisors of CBFPS can attend to by taking a little time to go over the records with the distributors during their periodic visits and complete them as necessary.

The village distributors generally have gone through one initial and brief orientation session. Since then, there has not been an opportunity for formal orientation or refresher sessions, though there is a plan for retraining within 6-8 months. There also appears to be insufficient communication with the village distributors in the form of printed materials, bulletins, illustrative materials, etc. These forms of contact are needed not only to equip the distributors with new information and ideas but also to create and maintain an _esprit de corps_ in the CBFPS family.

Since efficiency of operation is a trump card that CBFPS holds, it must be vigilant to maintain this advantage.

CBFPS depends for its existence on external financial and commodity support. Most of the funds that are collected locally are in fact the sale proceeds of the pills and condoms supplied by outside donors. It should be noted, however, that free supplies only pile up costs directly or indirectly unless ways are found to convert the supplies into cash to cover a part of the operating expenditures. This CBFPS has done successfully. It has also achieved a certain degree of success in selling condoms among the urban population and other promotional products such as T-shirts and scarves. The sale of promotional products has not only brought income to the organization but also has helped to "desensitize" the public about family planning as an open topic for discussion.

Quite possibly some of the external assistance would have been available to the national program in any event, either as assistance to the government program or to other private organizations, but there seems little doubt that the project's innovative approach and the energy and devotion of its leadership have attracted a quantity of external support in addition to what would otherwise have been available. CBFPS has also attracted into the national family planning program a certain amount of management and technical talent from the private sector and has harnessed the enthusiasm and idealism of a number of competent young people. These talents and energy constitute a net contribution of CBFPS to the national effort.

At present, in a sense, CBFPS relieves the burden of the government health workers and supplements the clinic-based activities of the government by taking on the task of supplying family planning information and contraceptives in the villages. When the government adopts the community-based service approach for primary health care including family planning through health-post volunteers and neighborhood-level communicators, can the CBFPS still play a complementary and supporting role? There is no straightforward answer to this question. It is conceivable that the distribution of contraceptives and the attendant activities will remain in the hands of CBFPS while other primary health care functions are performed by the volunteers tied to the government health service. This separation of responsibilities may be justified on the ground that family planning service requires continuous, regular, and sustained contact with each "eligible" individual in the village in greater measure than primary health care services. The weakness of this "disintegrated" approach may be overcome by ensuring close cooperation and connection between the family planning and primary health care workers in the form of mutual referrals and joint discussion of strategies, plans, and performance. Another possibility is to entrust CBFPS with responsibility for managing the voluntary part of the primary health care program of the government--recruiting, training, and supervising the volunteers and maintaining contacts between them and the clinics and health centers. After all, CBFPS has accumulated valuable experience in utilizing community members as volunteers and, as a voluntary body itself, is probably better situated to deal with a voluntary operation than a government organization. These two alternatives do not exhaust the possibilities regarding CBFPS roles in relation to the government program. What answer is found acceptable and feasible will depend on the attitude and expectation of the government regarding private voluntary bodies and on what CBFPS leadership sees to be the appropriate role for the organization.

The question of a transition from an exclusive family planning focus to a community development approach that promises to open new frontiers for CBFPS occupies the minds of its leaders. This significant possibility is discussed in the following section.

The Integrated Approach—New Frontier for CBFPS

CBFPS began in 1974 with the limited aim of opening distribution points for contraceptives in each community. This perhaps was a reflection of the prevalence of the single-purpose approach and the fact that external assistance from IPPF was available for experiments with "community-based distribution." The pragmatic and open-minded leaders of CBFPS were not, however, oblivious to the ultimate goal of increasing the total welfare of families for which family planning is one of many necessary elements. They were also not inattentive to the possibility of enhancing the acceptance of family planning when basic social and economic needs of families are addressed. The CBFPS management was fully receptive to the rhetoric of the "integrated approach" and were willing to seize any opportunity that arose to try such an approach.

The opportunity to combine family planning services with aspects of health care came with the Integrated Family Planning and Parasite Control Program (FPPC) assisted by the Japanese Organization for International Cooperation in Family Planning (JOICFP) and again with the Integrated Family Planning, Health and Hygiene Program (FPHH) assisted by the United States Agency for International Development.

The FPPC project, launched in mid-1976, was operational in five districts by the end of 1977. The project, because of a high percentage of parasite infestation among the Thai population and the relatively simple diagnosis and therapy process, helped to create a positive image of CBFPS and to make its message acceptable to the people.

The FPHH project, initiated in 1976 with the collaboration of the Faculty of Public Health of Mahidol University, expanded to 40 districts by the end of 1977. Under this project, a select list of household drugs were added to the stock of contraceptives placed with each CBFPS distributor and the distributors were given a brief orientation on health and hygiene problems in rural communities and families.

These two sub-projects, while broadening somewhat the functions of CBFPS and its community distribution network, still remain rather narrowly focused on family planning and very limited aspects of health care. They, however, mark an advancement from the single-purpose approach and help the case for integrated community-based service that has only recently been accepted as a national policy and is still to be implemented on a large scale. Undoubtedly, the two CBFPS experiments continue to generate valuable experiences in the functioning of a community-based primary health care and family planning program.

An ambitious and qualitatively different approach from previous efforts is anticipated in an assistance proposal submitted in late 1977 to the Netherlands Organization for International Development Cooperation (see Annex V). Under this proposal for a pilot project, it is envisaged that in the northern province of Chiengrai a number of key services crucial to the welfare of rural families would be integrated with the family planning services. The distributor in each community is expected to be the nucleus of a self-help group consisting of the acceptors in the community. It is anticipated that CBFPS will assist the groups in creating and enjoying the benefits of the following common services and facilities:

-- Comprehensive family planning services

-- Low cost primary health care with the distributors trained as
   dispensers of common household drugs

-- Improved marketing opportunity for farm produce with CBFPS
   assisting in village-to-market transportation

-- Cheaper farm inputs through direct and bulk purchase

-- Low cost farm animal and equipment rental service

-- Low interest loans

-- Technical advice on agriculture and home industries

The key to the effectiveness of this effort would lie in preparing the
distributors to play their new and difficult multipurpose development   agent
role. If CBFPS achieves even modest results in using the base of a   family
planning program in a community to launch a broader integrated community development program, CBFPS will have charted a new direction for itself and will
have found a new significant role not only in the national family planning efforts but in the total rural development program of the country. In anticipation of the new broader role and functions of the organization, CBFPS has taken
formal steps to convert itself into The Population and Community Development
Association of Thailand.

Question of Self-Sufficiency

It is unrealistic to expect that CBFPS, as it is organized now, would
be financially self-sufficient in any true sense in the foreseeable future. When
CBFPS leaders speak about self-sufficiency, they really mean covering the operational costs of the program activities from the sale proceeds of donated contraceptive pills and condoms; CBFPS would still be dependent on external assistance
for donated commodities. The practice of charging a subsidized price for pills
and condoms (in line with the government policy at the time), however, has provided a flexible source of revenue to the organization.   It has also been
relatively helpful in improving the accuracy of distribution records   and in
cutting waste of supplies by clients. The small fee (of 5 to 9 bahts--25 to 45
U.S. cents--per monthly cycle of pills) has not been known to cause a financial
hardship to the clients.

In 1977 close to 60 percent of CBFPS operational costs were raised   by
the sale of contraceptives. In October, 1976, however, the government   had
reversed its earlier policy and began to distribute pills without charge through
the health service. Service statistics for 1977 seem to indicate some   adverse
effect of the government free pill policy on the performance of CBFPS.   The
eventual impact of the free pills on CBFPS, however, may not be serious or   even
significant as long as the present clinic and health-center-based approach   of
the government continues. While in the vicinity of a government health center
the client is likely to opt for the free pills from the government, in villages
beyond the radius of 5 kilometres of the center, as most villages are, it   would
be probably more economical in time and effort for the client to pay the small
fee to the neighborhood CBFPS distributor. A real conflict may arise when   the
government expands its program of health post volunteers and takes away the special advantage of the CBFPS agent. But then, as we noted earlier, the   conflict

would be a broader one than just the pricing of the pills.

Regardless of the effect the official pricing policy for contraceptives may have on CBFPS, the policy has become controversial in other ways. A team with Thai and American experts evaluating the National Family Planning Program recommended a reconsideration of the policy on several grounds including the following:

-- The reported upsurge in acceptors since the announcement of the free pill policy may be at least partly the result of wastage and misuse of pills as well as poor record-keeping as no financial accounts are now involved.

-- Surveys indicate that over 95 percent of the families do not find the small fees charged previously as any hardship.

-- The free pill policy has taken away the source of a readily available cash income to the health centers that could be used for their essential health and medical supplies.

-- The family planning program cannot remain permanently and totally dependent on foreign assistance and the people must learn to contribute to their own development.*

Whatever policy is pursued by the government on pricing contraceptives, CBFPS may still be able to charge small fees to its customers and make its village level activities at least partially self-financing if it can make a creditable showing in its new integrated development venture, thereby making the small payments a worthy investment for the customers of CBFPS services.

SIGNIFICANT LESSONS FROM THE CBFPS EXPERIENCE

The report discusses in the concluding chapter the lessons of the CBFPS experience for those who are concerned nationally or internationally with a community-based approach in family planning and similar basic services for rural families. In this section, we will reemphasize some of the points made in the report and point to others which seem significant to us.

It has to be kept in mind that the context of the CBFPS program is special in a number of ways. It has been commented upon by many knowledgeable observers that the sociocultural situation in Thailand probably · makes it relatively free from the inhibitions about family planning that afflict many other developing countries. The economic role of women outside home and the tolerance towards family planning by Buddhist religion are cited as factors conducive to the acceptance of family planning in Thailand, although the relative importance of these factors in comparison with other Asian countries is a debatable topic.

---

*APHA, op. cit., pp. 29-30.

CBFPS undoubtedly has been fortunate in being guided by a charistmatic, devoted, and exceptionally ingenious leader. The origin, growth, and the special character of CBFPS cannot be imagined in isolation from the contribution and dedication of its leader.

It is not commonplace in developing countries for the national government to be fully committed to an integrated health care and family planning program and to be actually shaping the national program along this line. As we noted earlier, the acceptance of an integrated approach by the government and its receptivity to a community-based service approach created an unusually favorable atmosphere for the CBFPS program to be initiated and expanded rapidly.

Recognizing these favorable circumstances for CBFPS and recognizing that each situation is unique in many ways, it is still useful to consider the lessons from the CBFPS experience for designers and managers of community-based services for rural families. These lessons are, of course, not to be applied uncritically in other situations but are to be used in deepening one's understanding of crucial concerns in planning, implementing, and improving other programs.

1. Many advantages of utilizing community members as auxiliaries in providing family planning, basic health care, and other basic services in rural communities are quite evident. Such an approach breaks the barriers of geography and "social distance" to reaching the rural people, can make the beneficiary population participants in the running of the programs, can help shape the programs to fit the specific conditions, and can mobilize untapped local resources.

2. It is quite feasible and practical to find ordinary people in the community without any special qualification, talent, or expertise and to put them to work in programs that are vital to the welfare and development of the community. These ordinary lay people, when placed within an appropriate organizational structure and given appropriate back-up support, can make extremely valuable contributions to the programs and make them much more effective than possible only with "outside" professional and paraprofessional personnel.

3. CBFPS experience shows that the beneficiary population would make financial contributions in the form of charges for services and commodities if these are within their means and they value the benefits offered by the program. These payments obviously are a source of revenue for the program and a step towards eventual self-sufficiency. The accounting and record-keeping required because of the payments impose a discipline in respect of standards of performance and the use of resources in the program. The beneficiaries probably value the service or commodity more when they pay for it. The spirit of self-help and self-reliance is fostered when people make a contribution rather than receive a handout. Obviously, situations and cases of extreme poverty have to be taken into consideration and payments that impose a genuine hardship on the intended beneficiary of a program cannot be helpful to the program.

4. Voluntary organizations can play a very important role in achieving national goals in respect of providing basic services to rural families. We have noted earlier the various roles that voluntary organizations can play. What roles such organizations can perform and how effectively these are performed depend very much on the mutual expectations and relationships established between the government and the voluntary organizations. The government can facilitate

the functioning of voluntary organizations by specifying in the national programs certain tasks and roles which voluntary organizations are specially capable of undertaking because of their voluntary nature and freedom from bureaucratic strangleholds. On the other hand, the voluntary organizations have to define their own role in relation to the scope and objectives of the national programs, maintain a dialogue with the government regarding their potential role and contribution, and provide appropriate inputs in shaping government policies and programs in conformity with the needs of the communities.

5. It is clear that the designing and implementation of a new strategy and program approach make a high demand on leadership   and management capabilities. Only an exceptional program will be fortunate to have a truly charismatic leader as its head. But no innovative program can hope to succeed and make the desired impact without the benefit of some out-of-the-ordinary leadership and management talents.   An innovative program, particularly one requiring mass participation   and community support, calls upon its leadership to engage in such   varied and complex tasks as maintaining relationships with diverse   elements including the government agencies and external assistance organizations, influencing and educating public opinion, attracting idealistic   and talented workers and inspiring them to continue in the program in   the face of many frustrations, creating and maintaining confidence   about the program among donors and supporters, and getting new ideas and approaches understood and accepted by various concerned parties. The most difficult and important of the leadership tasks is to find a way   to institutionalize the innovative approach so that it can   continue to function and can be replicated without the exceptional leadership   and management talents required at the initial stage. The main lesson is that it is unrealistic to expect an innovative program to succeed without the guidance of some top level leadership and management talents.

6. Although the CBFPS is not an experimental project to prove the comparative merits of a single-purpose and an integrated   service approach, the evolution of CBFPS into a multipurpose integrated program probably holds a significant lesson. A genuine community-based   approach, it appears, cannot continue to function on the basis of a narrow, rigid, imposed-from-outside program scope and objectives.   A program that subscribes to the values and ethics of a   community-based service has to subordinate its immediate and narrow objective--be   it the acceptance of contraceptives, or the treatment of parasites,   or vaccination against preventable diseases--to the ultimate needs and interests of the community people. These needs and interests of community as perceived by the community can be the only basis for an authentic community-based service program. The particular interest of an outside agency like the CBFPS can evoke a response from the community if it is a genuine need, but it has to fit into the total pattern of crucial   concerns and priorities of the community. This is where the integrated approach comes into play.

CHAPTER 2

THE CONTEXT OF CBFPS

GENERAL BACKGROUND

Thailand (formerly Siam) had one of the highest population growth rates in the world in the early seventies. It is located at the very heart of mainland Southeast Asia, with Burma on the west and north, Laos on the upper east, Democratic Kamphuchea on the lower east, and Malaysia on the extreme south. It has a land area of 198,000 square miles and is divided into four regions, Central, Northeast, North, and South. Bangkok is the capital city and center of all major activities in the country.

The Central Region (including the east) is drained by the Chao Phya River and is the geographical and economic heart of the kingdom with its extensive network of water supply and rich fertile areas. The region is Thailand's "rice bowl" and perhaps that of all Asia.

The Northeastern Region is characterized by a large and high sandstone plateau sloping gently down towards the Mekhong River and Laos. Despite having a large land area equal to one third of the country, irrigation is difficult here and agricultural production is low. However, this region contains rich deposits of rock salts and potash.

The North is a region of mountains and valleys that comprise one quarter of the nation. The mountains running north and south through the region are densely forested; the river valleys cutting through them are narrow but fertile.

The South is a long sliver of land extending from central Thailand down the Malay peninsula. The land area is mainly covered by rain forest and bordered by several beaches. The rubber industry is the main agricultural activity in the region.

Table I presents Thailand's estimated population by region at the end of 1977.

SOCIOECONOMIC FEATURES

Thailand is a developing country whose economy is based primarily on agriculture. Nearly 80 percent of the labor force is engaged in primary production. No particular culture has ever exerted a predominant influence over Thai social development. Historically, it is the only nation in the region that has not been colonized.

Table 1

Thailand's Estimated Population by Region
1977

Region	Population
Central*	13,667,000
Northeast	15,574,000
North	9,354,000
South	5,444,000
Total	44,039,000

*Including Bangkok and the East.

Source: National Economic and Social Development Board.

Economic Structure and Development

Agriculture, which has traditionally made the most significant contribution to Thailand's economic growth in terms of income, employment,
and export earnings, is expected to retain this major role in the future.
However, other sectors, notably industry, are also increasing   in   the
achievement of a more balanced economy. The ratio of agricultural output to gross domestic product declined from 34.0 percent in 1965 to an
expected 28.45 percent in 1977.

The major crops produced by the agricultural sector are rice, rubber,
maize, sugar, jute and kenaf, and cassava. The industry sector is made   up
chiefly of light consumer   goods industries, wood and cement products,   pe-
troleum refining, various kinds of electronic goods, and automobile assembly.

The First National Economic Development Plan was launched by the
Royal Thai Government in 1961 to accelerate the rate of economic growth.
Significant achievements were effected in building up various economic infrastructures indispensable for long term economic development. In the
Third Plan (1972-1976), policies on population and employment were for the
first time included in the national economic plan. The Fourth National
Economic and Social Development Plan (1977-1981), which is currently being
implemented, has gone a step further by setting as one of its development
objectives the reduction of population growth and improvement of manpower
quality. This step reflects the fact that recognition is being given to
the population problem, and that serious efforts are being taken by the
government to cope with it. Table 2 represents basic economic data of
Thailand.

Education

Thailand has more than 30,000 elementary schools, over 400 secondary
schools with about 200,000 students, and over 3,000 private schools   with
more than 800,000 students. There are nine state universities, numerous
teachers' training colleges, over 100 government-supported vocational and
technical schools and colleges that offer training in agriculture and

Table 2

Basic Economic Data---Thailand
1977

LAND AREA (Sq. Km.)	514,000
POPULATION (in Millions)	44
Growth Rate (1976)	2.5%
TOTAL LABOR FORCE (in Millions)	19.7
Employed	18.6
Unemployed	1.1
LITERACY RATE	82%
GNP (at Current Prices in Million US$)	18,174
Per Capita GNP Current (US$)	350
GDP Growth (1977-1976)	10.1%
SECTORAL SHARE TO GDP/NDP (estimated)	
Agriculture, Fishery and Forestry	28.46%
Industry	21.19%
Construction	5.90%
Others	44.44%

Source: National Economic and Social Development Board.

specialized industries. In addition, there are private schools and colleges
providing training in secretarial and commercial fields. Government ministries,
including those of industry, interior, and agriculture, also conduct short intensive training courses for out-of-school children and adults, especially in
the provinces. Currently, the compulsory education program covers six years of
schooling, provided free by the government. The literacy rate of the population
is estimated to be 82 percent.

Population education, in principle, is now incorporated into Thailand's
formal educational system. The Ministry of Education (MOE) started introducing
poulation education at the high school level in 1975. However, implementation
of this decision has had very limited coverage because of the shortage of qualified teachers. In July 1976, MOE established a Population Education Unit to
undertake both formal and nonformal population education. Commencing in 1978,
implementation of a comprehensive population education plan will be carried out
by developing qualified teachers as well as by gradually introducing courses of
population studies at all educational levels from primary through high school.
Preparations have also been made to develop population education materials for
out-of-school adults in the villages. This nonformal education will be undertaken by posting a series of periodical wall newspapers on population themes
in village reading centers.

Cultural Traits

The Thai people are in general self-dependent and individualistic, nonaggressive and nonextremist, polite and respectful of seniority. Even though there is no caste system in Thai society, a virtual class structure based on political power, social connection, economic standing, and family background exists especially among the elite in Bangkok and other urban areas. Thai culture, though fused with other cultures, has its own individuality. Continuing external influences, from Malays in the south, and the Lao and Burmese in the north, have led to distinctive regional dialects, foods, traditions, and beliefs.

Buddhism is the national religion and more than 90 percent of the population are Buddhist. The Buddhist temple has normally been the center of all important village activities. It follows that the influence of Buddhism upon the Thai way of life and mode of thought is thus predominant and profound. One important point, however, is that as far as family planning is concerned, Buddhism is not opposed to birth control. An old Buddhist proverb even says, "Too many births cause suffering." There is therefore no conflict between religious beliefs and family planning concepts and practices.

POLITICAL AND GOVERNMENT STRUCTURE

Thailand has a constitutional monarchy with the Prime Minister as the head of state. The King, however, provides guidance and advice. A highly centralized system of territorial administration prevails and is organized into Changwads (provinces), Amphoes (districts), Tambol (sub-districts), and Mubans (villages).

Attempts at democratic government have been short-lived, whereas authoritarian ruling bodies have remained in power in most of the life span of Thai political history. The Thai political system is characterized by an uninstitutionalized pattern of change that has traditionally been brought about by the ruling class. In all political change, however, the bureaucracy has remained as the backbone in the implementation of all government policy; it has thus become predominantly powerful in the Thai society.

The strength of the bureaucracy has, in a sense, been reinforced by the political apathy of the majority of Thai people. Apart from the urban, well-educated population, the rural Thai have remained politically passive, usually accepting government decrees, whatever they may be, and conforming to them. Although the efficiency and effectiveness of the bureaucracy are debatable, its role in the national economic and social development is indispensable, and cooperation with the bureaucracy is virtually a matter of necessity.

DEMOGRAPHIC FEATURES AND THEIR REPERCUSSIONS

Like many other developing countries, Thailand has faced the problem of an accelerating population growth and decline in mortality, primarily as a result of improved health standards and services. Based on the population census in 1970, the annual growth rate at about 3 percent, was one of the highest in the world.

The rapid growth rate has given rise to an unbalanced composition of the population structure. Inevitably, young people have come to overwhelm the whole population. According to the same 1970 census, only 52 percent of the population were 15-64 years of age, or of the working age. The rest, considered for the most part as dependents, were those below 15 (45%) and those 65 or older (3%). There were 93 dependents for every 100 persons of working age. Table 3 gives relevant basic demographic data of Thailand. Table 4 presents the projected population of Thailand.

Table 3

Basic Demographic Data - Thailand

	Year	Data
Density (per km.^{2})	1977	80
Population (in millions)	1977	44
Birth Rate per 1,000 population	1977	34.5
Death Rate per 1,000 population	1977	9
Rate of natural increase (%)	1976	2.5
Infant mortality rate per 1,000 live births	1970	85
Maternal mortality rate per 1,000 live births	1970	4
Eligible women of reproductive age practising contraception (%)	1976	over 30
Cumulative family planning acceptors in national program (in millions)	1972-76	2.5
New family planning acceptors (in millions)	1976	0.6
Urban population as percentage of total population (%)	1974	16
Age structure (%)	1970	
0-14 years		45
15-64 years		52
16+ years		3
Total fertility rate	1970-74	4.8

Source: World Bank, <u>Thailand Population Project Appraisal Mission Working Papers,</u> July 1977.

Table 4

Projected Population of Thailand
(In Thousands)

Projections	1970	1980	1990	2000
Constant Fertility[1]	36,181	50,955	73,595	107,971
Medium Rate[2]	36,181	50,527	69,420	89,624
Thai Target Rate [3]	36,181	47,731	57,004	65,729

[1]The total fertility rate remains constant.

[2]The total fertility rate declines at a moderate rate.

[3]There is a decline in the total fertility rate resulting in the achievement of a 2.0 percent growth rate by the end of 1981, a net reproduction rate of 1.0 by 1990.

Source: World Bank, Thailand Population Project Appraisal Mission Working Papers, a preliminary report, July 1977.

It is apparent that the need to reduce the fertility rate further is imperative and fully justified on the basis of population size alone. It is most likely that the quality of life will be impaired by an inability to provide adequate services for such a large population considering the present state of Thailand's socioeconomic development. Aside from creating an immense demand on food, employment, health services, and education, a movement of the population from the villages to the towns will further aggravate present urban problems. All-out efforts are therefore needed in attempting to reduce   the population growth rate significantly.

THE ROLE OF GOVERNMENT IN FAMILY
PLANNING SERVICES

Throughout the first half of this century, the Royal Thai Government (RTG) had continually upheld a policy encouraging large families and a high rate of population growth. It was not until 1958, when a World Bank Economic Mission first pointed out the implications of rapid population growth   in Thailand's development efforts, that the RTG started to review its existing population policy. A number of unrelated studies and seminars on population by several government departments were subsequently undertaken during   the period 1959-1967. These included the establishment of the Institute of Population Studies at Chulalongkorn University and the Institute for Population and Social Research at Mahidol University in 1966. However, no   corcrete population policy was announced by the RTG. Despite the lukewarm support of

the RTG for family planning, the Ministry of Public Health (MOPH) commenced a pilot
project in 1964 and started providing family planning services in 1968 as part of
its Family Health Project.

In 1970, the RTG declared a National Population Policy, and the National
Population Policy Committee (NPPC) was established for planning and coordinating
policies on family planning. To strengthen the role of family planning services,
the MOPH was made responsible for implementing this newly approved policy, and the
Family Health Project was retitled the National Family Planning Program (NFPP). In
1974, the National Family Planning Coordinating Committee (NFPCC) was set up to replace NPPC and it has been functioning since then. The NFPCC's functions encompass
the supervision and coordination of family planning programs and population activities of various agencies, as well as external aids thereof.

National Family Planning Program (NFPP)

The NFPP represents the first organized endeavor by the RTG to tackle population problems. In the First Five-Year Plan for the NFPP (1972-1976), a national
demographic target was established for the first time that aimed at a reduction of
the population growth rate from 3 percent to 2.5 percent, and an expansion of family planning services through several approaches. Among these were the utilization of paramedics in delivering clinical contraceptives; the expansion of
inservice training for physicians, nurses, and auxiliary midwives; the accelerated
development of special maternity hospitals as institutions for family planning; and
the provision of postpartum family planning services. By the end of the plan period,
the program was well established and had exceeded its acceptor targets.[1] (Table 4A)
The results of the 1975 World Fertility Survey indicated that 33 percent of women of
reproductive age for the whole kingdom and 27 percent for the rural areas were
practising some form of contraception, the rate of which is among the highest in the
world. As noted above this resulted in a drop in the rate of population growth from
a peak of 3 percent in 1970 to around 2.5 percent by 1976. Despite this decline,how-
ever the Thai population in the year 2000 is expected to double the 1970 figures.

Realizing a hugely unmet potential demand for family services, the Second
Five-Year Plan for the NFPP (1977-1981) attempts to reduce further the rate of
population growth from 2.5 percent in 1976 to 2.1 percent by 1981. This effort
calls for a broadening as well as a strengthening of the services provided by the
existing program. Under this Second Plan, implementation plans have been drawn up
that include the expansion and improvement of the delivery of family planning services, particularly in those areas having high birth rates; the broadening of categories of personnel qualified to disseminate family planning information and

---

[1]World Bank, Thailand Population Project Appraisal Mission Working Papers,
July 1977, pp. 6-7. These World Bank papers also summarize the accomplishments
made under the First Plan for the NFPP (1972-1976) as follows: a. recruitment of
2.5 million acceptors; b. increase of number of MOPH family planning service delivery
points from 270 in 1970 to 5,400 in 1976; c. training of 20,000 paramedical and
medical personnel; d. improvement on data collection system; and e. small scale
implementation of IEC activities in support of family planning.

Table 4A

National Family Planning Program
Targets and Acceptors, by Method
1972-1976

Year	PILL Target	Acceptors	IUD Target	Acceptors	STERILIZATION Target	Acceptors	ALL METHODS* Target	Acceptor
1972	235,000	327,582	90,000	90,128	25,000	32,668	350,000	456,694
1973	280,000	268,674	90,000	93,449	30,000	49,606	400,000	422,176
1974	280,000	305,244	90,000	89,739	35,000	80,482	405,000	494,479
1975	280,000	345,117	90,000	75,163	40,000	90,184	410,000	535,023
1976	280,000	344,779	90,000	76,259	40,000	104,449	410,000	592,478
TOTAL	1,355,000	1,591,396	450,000	424,738	170,000	357,389	1,975,000	2,500,850

*The totals also include acceptors using methods other than those listed.

Source: Ministry of Public Health

services; the expansion and intensification of Information, Education, and Communications (IEC) activities; the expansion and improvement of evaluation and research
activities; and the development of cooperation and coordination with other agencies
for implementation of special projects. The acceptor targets set for achieving the
foregoing demographic objective are presented in Table 5.

Table 5

National Family Planning Program
New Acceptor Target By Method and Year, 1971-1981

Year	METHOD PILLS	IUD	STERILIZATION	INJECTIBLES	TOTAL
1977	350,000	95,000	90,000	40,000	575,000
1978	350,000	100,000	95,000	42,000	587,000
1979	360,000	105,000	100,000	44,000	609,000
1980	370,000	106,500	100,000	45,000	621,500
1981	385,000	106,500	100,000	45,000	636,500
Total	1,815,000	513,000	485,000	216,000	3,029,000

Source: Ministry of Public Health

To recruit these additional 3 million or more acceptors, family planning
services will have to be vertically and horizontally intensified. Apart from an
increase of health delivery facilities at all administrative levels (district,

subdistrict, and village), the services will also be provided through the lower
levels of these delivery points. Under the Second Plan, village volunteers will
provide condoms and resupply pills, and auxiliary midwives will provide injectible contraceptives and IUD services at health centers and midwifery centers.
Higher levels of medical staff are expected to concentrate more on permanent
methods of contraception: doctors will perform sterilizations at district hospitals, and mobile teams of doctors and nurses will perform vasectomies at points
where doctors are not regularly available. Table 6 presents the existing and
required numbers of health facilities in Thailand.

Table 6

Existing and Required Numbers
of Health Facilities

| | Number of Health Facilities | | |
	Hospitals[1]	Health Centers[2]	Midwifery-Centers[3]
Existing	360	3,720	1,455
Required	603	4,957	3,720
Planned by end of Program (1981)	464	4,208	2,675
Existing as % of Required	60%	75%	39%
Planned as % of Required	77%	85%	72%

[1]Staff--doctor, nurse, auxiliary midwife, and sanitarian.

[2]Staff--auxiliary midwife, and sanitarian.

[3]Staff--auxiliary midwife.

Source: Ministry of Public Health.

World Bank's Project[1]

The World Bank was invited by the RTG in November 1974 to review Thailand's
demographic situation and the NFPP, with a view to assisting the government in preparing the Fourth National Economic and Social Development Plan (1977-1981) and
providing a basis for external assistance for population activities during the
Fourth Plan. Based on its 1975 Sector Report, the World Bank commented favorably
on the NFPP and made two important recommendations. The program should place top
priority (1) on the extension and improvement of the delivery system for family
planning services to meet the existing demand; and (2) on the expansion and improvement of family planning IEC to strengthen the long-term demand for family planning
services.

[1]This subsection was condensed from World Bank, Thailand Population Project
Appraisal Mission Working Papers, July 1977.

Late in 1976, an appraisal mission was sent by the World Bank, followed by a post-appraisal mission in early March 1977, to evaluate the project proposal prepared by MOPH for the Bank's financing and the co-financing of several other governments. The Thailand Population Project undertaken by these two missions sought to assist the RTG in achieving the demographic target set for the Second Five-Year Plan for the NFPP (1977-1981) by recruiting some 3 million additional acceptors, thus adding some 1.6 million continuing users by the end of the Plan. A related objective is to reduce both maternal and infant mortality rates by about 20 percent. Since there appears to be a long-run relationship between low infant and child mortality and low fertility, it may be expected that in due time these improvements will influence families to have fewer children.

This three-year (1978-1980) project consists of two sets of components: "national" and "provincial." The "national" component is designed primarily to train additional paramedical personnel required for the period, to ensure the availability of family planning services, to expand and strengthen IEC as well as research and evaluation activities, and to strengthen the headquarters staff of NFPP. These project activities will be undertaken to meet limited needs in 52 selected provinces. The "provincial" component is designed by contrast to accelerate the expansion of family planning and rural health services in 20 selected provinces characterized by low-to-moderate family planning acceptance, high population densities, and poor health facility coverage.

In general the project will support the strengthening and extension of family planning services throughout Thailand by (a) increasing the supply of nurses, auxiliary midwives, and practical nurses/midwives, who are the key personnel in providing family planning services; (b) intensifying the NFPP throughout Thailand, with special attention to certain provinces; and (c) increasing the demand for family planning services through an expanded IEC program, particularly in the rural areas.

The proposed project's estimated cost is US$66.3 million, of which US$20.7 million or 31 percent is foreign exchange. It will be financed by (a) an IBRD loan of about US$25 to 30 million; (b) loans or grants from various co-financing partners which are expected to be at an equivalent of about US$10 to 27 million; and (c) an RTG contribution expected to total an equivalent of about US$17 to 24 million.

THE ROLE OF PUBLIC AND PRIVATE
AGENCIES IN FAMILY PLANNING SERVICES

A number of public and private organizations have actively participated in providing family planning services and undertaking various IEC activities in support of family planning. Several ministries interested in family planning integrate information on family planning into their ongoing adult education and extension activities, especially those oriented towards women. Private agencies, on the other hand, typically develop their definite and distinct family planning programs for provision of services as well as motivational activities.

As mentioned earlier, the Ministry of Education has already started its implementation of both formal and nonformal population education since 1976. The Labor Department of the Ministry of Interior, through its Labor Training Center, has been holding several courses annually on population for industrial workers. The Department of Community Development of the same ministry holds various courses in health and family planning at the village level. The MOPH in cooperation with the Department of Accelerated Rural Development, the Department of Public Welfare, and the Border Patrol Police (all of the Ministry of Interior), undertakes several special projects in an effort to improve the accessibility and availability of family planning services in remote and sensitive areas. The Ministry of Agriculture's extension program, especially through special women's clubs, provides for education on family planning, nutrition, and other aspects of basic health.

The private organizations that are active in providing family planning services are the Community-Based Family Planning Services and the McCormick Hospital in Chieng Mai Province. The McCormick Hospital, situated in North Thailand, has been pioneering an experiment on the use of injectible contraceptives among rural Thai women. Its endeavor to demonstrate the safety of this method of contraception is world-widely recognized. Until the end of 1976, its ten-year attempt already had provided three-month injection services to over half a million Thai females. The Community-Based Family Planning Services (CBFPS) through its village distribution network provides contraceptives to the rural population by using the non-clinical approach. In addition to providing family planning services,   family planning informational materials are produced and distributed through its village distributors. Audiovisual presentations are also utilized in promoting family planning concepts and practice.

The Planned Parenthood Association of Thailand (PPAT) is the voluntary organization whose activities are oriented primarily towards family planning IEC. The PPAT has been working closely with various branches of the Ministry of Interior, especially in workers' population education and occupational training programs for youth. Several family planning motivational programs have also been developed for industrial workers, slum dwellers, and some minority groups. Although with lesser emphasis, distribution of contraceptives and vasectomy services through mobile educational and medical teams have also been provided by the PPAT.

In general cooperation between the public (MOPH) and private (CBFPS and others) sectors involved in family planning has been very close, and this has resulted in increasingly effective implementation of the family planning activities in the country.

CHAPTER 3

HISTORY AND DEVELOPMENT OF CBFPS

The history and development of CBFPS have been marked by two important features. One is the cooperation that has obtained between CBFPS and the Ministry of Public Health (MOPH), which is in charge of the national family planning efforts. The government has officially acknowledged this coalition of interests, and it may perhaps be said that it has given CBFPS the necessary flexibility in actions and policies to forge ahead in a measure of zeal and confidence. The other important feature is the person of Mechai Veravaidya, founder of CBFPS, through whose farsigtedness the cooperation has been achieved. In fact, the history of CBFPS is in effect a chronology of Mechai's effort to achieve what he has believed to be important for Thailand as a whole. CBFPS's history begins with Mechai's return to Thailand from his studies in Australia in 1965.

MECHAI

Mechai[1] has been described as aggressive, hard-working, intelligent, engaging, and irresistible. Returning from Melbourne in 1965, he joined the National Economic and Social Development Board (NESDB) as an economist. He became the Chief of the Development Evaluation Division of NESDB within a few years. It was during this association with NESDB that he was able to see how the productive efforts of farmers are adversely affected by the high population growth rate. Desirous of contributing his efforts to Thailand's development, he turned his thoughts to the solution of the population problem.

Two alternative solutions presented themselves: one was to increase productivity; the other, to slow down population growth. He chose the latter because it appeared to be more manageable. Alone he could not contribute much in solving the chronic problem of low productivity, but he could do something to support family planning activities. Mechai realized at this point that implementation of most government activity of this kind had historically been ineffective. One of the reasons for limited effectiveness was that existing development projects undertaken by the government almost invariably brought about too abrupt, sometimes painful, changes to the villagers. Not only were the changes mentally disturbing to the villagers, but they provided no proof of material success as well. More importantly, the projects all too often utilized predominantly top-down and one-sided approaches, and they attached too little importance to participation on the part of the rural people themselves. This last point, according to Mechai, accounted for the failure of most development projects designed to reach the village level.

Mechai therefore came to the conclusion that he would have to modify the thrust of existing development practices if he wanted his family planning

---

[1]It is normal practice, and not considered impolite, in Thailand to call people by their first names.

efforts to succeed. He would have to reach the grassroots level and assist the
village people to help themselves. At this stage, however, this was merely a
concept that had to be converted into an action plan.   This was no easy task.

INITIAL MOVES TOWARD FAMILY PLANNING

The first and foremost step in the action plan was to put across the idea
of family planning to the public. Mechai fully utilized his resourcefulness in
this attempt. Apart from writing a host of articles in local magazines stressing
the need for family planning in Thailand, he, together with his colleagues, also
made use of every available opportunity in public gatherings (as an interviewer,
writer, and panelist) to raise family planning issues.   Reactions to the family
planning ideas were varied, but the efforts were satisfactory in that there were
favorable responses from both private and public sectors.

In 1970, family planning was adopted by the Royal Thai Government (RTG)
as a national policy, and a National Population Policy Committee was   formed.
In the initial stage, implementation of family planning efforts was carried on
solely by the Ministry of Public Health (MOPH).   However, the   efforts and
responses were somewhat limited when compared with the magnitude of the   task
ahead. There was a limited number of health service centers in remote   areas.
There existed certain obstructive governmental measures against family planning
which had resulted from a "pronatalist" population policy of the RTG for   more
than half a century. There were such legal strictures as the prohibition   of
advertising contraceptives through mass media, high import duties on contraceptives and contraceptive raw materials, and government "child-rearing" subsidies
given to government officials (extra 50 baht/child/month), to name but a few.

The next move for Mechai was to associate himself directly with existing family planning establishments. He joined the Planned Parenthood Association of Thailand (PPAT) in 1971 as a part-time consultant. PPAT had been   a
direct affiliate of the International Planned Parenthood Federation (IPPF)[1]
since 1966 and had been operated as a family planning voluntary organization in
close cooperation with the MOPH. In 1973, Mechai became the Honorary Secretary-
General as well as Executive Director of PPAT. During his work with PPAT   his
personal connections with international agencies engaged in family planning services were successfully established.

ESTABLISHMENT OF CBFPS

By the early 1970s the limited effectiveness of clinic-based family planning programs undertaken in developing countries became evident. Ineffectiveness
was due basically to the shortage of qualified personnel who could distribute oral
contraceptives. At an IPPF International Conference in London in July 1973,   representatives from IPPF affiliates all over the world discussed alternative ways
and means of solving this problem. Particular attention was given to the community-
based distribution approach as an alternative to the existing clinic-based distribution system. The representatives were requested to conduct   feasibility   studies

---

[1]The International Planned Parenthood Federation is a nonprofit, international
organization founded in 1952 to cope with the population problem of the world through
a promotion of family planning associations in various countries, whereby family planning services can be provided to the national populations. The Planned Parenthood
Association in a country is the only affiliate and is financed by IPPF. By 1974,
IPPF had more than 90 affiliates all over the world.

in their respective countries to serve as practical tests and confirmation of the effectiveness of the concept. Late in 1973, the Community-Based Distribution (CBD) Department was established by the IPPF Management and Planning Committee to carry out the community-based distribution system, which relied primarily on the idea of social marketing of contraceptives and, in doing so, of utilizing indigenous community resources. Mechai, as a representative from PPAT from its inception, took an active part in this development and CBFPS became more than a mere idea.

Preliminary Work on Community-Based Distribution

Mechai's first experiment with the community-based distribution approach was conducted from July to November of 1973 in connection with his work for PPAT. Through the active help of indigenous volunteers, including village leaders, traditional itinerant entertainers, and other selected individuals, small-scale experiments were conducted, the results of which were encouraging in that the communities under test seemed to respond satisfactorily to improved availability of family planning services. This experiment was financed by the transfer of a grant of about US$1,000 from IPPF. In December 1973, IPPF approved the transfer of US$10,000 to Thailand for preliminary work on a CBD program and further testing of the concept.[1] However, despite the preliminary experiment and IPPF funding approval, the project would have to be sanctioned by the Board of Directors of PPAT in order to validate its status and implementation. Mechai's persuasiveness brought about the required approval.

With these funds, Mechai conducted a feasibility study project in the northeastern and eastern parts of Thailand and in Laos from December 1973 to February 1974 to determine further the viability and practicability of the community-based approach of contraceptive distribution. Concurrently, he also launched a pretesting of the project at the village level in a number of villages in Banglamoong District, 142 kms. east of Bangkok. In the course of this grassroots experiment, the project was opposed by MOPH, which took the position that oral contraceptives were dangerous drugs and that the village volunteers might be inadequately trained. According to the law, only doctors could prescribe and distribute oral contraceptives.[2] The matter was discussed with MOPH, and the training of distributors was up-graded to cover health and hygiene purposes, although the main thrust of the effort was still primarily on family planning services. To ensure effective coordination and smooth operation by the village distributors, district level officers were contacted and clarifications were made of the project's objectives and its contribution to the community's welfare prior to actual

---

[1] Late in February 1974, an additional grant of US$10,000 was also made to cover this initial experiment.

[2] It should be noted however that MOPH previously had permitted the distribution of oral contraceptives by nondoctors, namely, trained midwives, and medical practitioners, in 1970. Almost fourfold increase of oral contraceptive use was accomplished within one year. This important decision made by the Thai MOPH was noted by IPPF as one of the practical confirmations for IPPF's policy of the nonclinic system of contraceptive distribution.

operations of the project. With the excellent cooperation of Dr. Khom Pongkhan, the Medical Officer at the First Class Health Center and one of the most influential figures in the Banglamoong District, training of 70 village distributors for family planning services was successfully completed by the middle of February 1974. In this same period, another successful pretesting was also conducted at one predominantly (85%) Moslem district in an attempt to train and gradually increase new distributors moving from village to village. Great care was taken in supervising and observing the performance of village distributors in the pretested areas. Lessons learned from the supervision of village distributors, the handling of false rumors about family planning, and other detailed observations of the locale were significant inputs into the planning for subsequent operations.

A complete project feasibility proposal for implementing community-based contraceptive distribution in Thailand was finally submitted to the Community-Based Distribution Advisory Board in New York on 28 February 1974. At this meeting, approval of a further $15,000 was made by the Secretary-General to ensure continuation of the project's operations pending the official funding approval of the IPPF Management and Planning Committee.

In the meantime, during March and April of 1974, an opportunity arose to provide family planning services through existing government personnel. The Teachers' Council Medical Center in Bangkok, where school teachers from all over the country annually assembled for their refresher courses, was selected as the first target. A program, later entitled Public Institution Program, was accordingly designed to train and motivate teachers to widen the family planning client base as well as to increase the number of volunteer distributors. Within this two-month period, a family planning motivation course was completed by some 46,000 teachers. More than 3,000 of them were trained to become volunteer teacher distributors. Concurrent to this program, the Mail Order Service, which later became part of the Private Sector Program, was also initiated on a small-scale basis to supply contraceptives to rural school teachers.

In the second half of April 1974, the IPPF Management and Planning Committee approved a funding of $200,000 out of the total 1974 targeted project expenditure of $299,000. The remaining sum was intended to be financed by local fund-raising efforts. The major thrust of the project was primarily the Village Program covering 24 districts in Thailand, while the Public Institution Program and the Private Sector Program played supportive roles.

Formal Setting-Up of CBFPS

Even with the approved fund from IPPF, the community-based project was still being opposed by certain people within PPAT, of which Mechai was then the Honorary Secretary-General and Executive Director. These opposing parties, for their own reasons, brought the matter before the National Family Planning Coordinating Committee (NFPCC), the highest ranking government body which coordinated all family planning efforts in the country. The purpose was to use NFPCC as a vehicle to disapprove the project and thus block its nation-wide implementation. Mechai anticipated this move and arranged to be present in the NFPCC meeting to explain to the Committee the project's rationale. After his explanations and a subsequent favorable vote of 9 to 0,[1] the project received the full authorization of NFPCC for implementation on 20 May 1974. However it had to be under the

[1]No vote was against, but there were two abstentions.

close supervision of an Advisory Committee comprising physicians, bankers, and specialists in rural development. Mechai assumed the role of Project Director.

Considering the unfavorable atmosphere within PPAT, Mechai worked to establish a separate entity to implement this pilot project.   The Community-Based Family Planning Services(CBFPS) was accordingly set   up by Mechai with a view to providing necessary managerial flexibility   and also insulating the important routine work of PPAT from any possibility of backlash in the case of failure of the new project.

Rationale and Objectives of CBFPS

The rationale of the CBFPS project, as stated in the original project proposal, was basically an attempt to introduce a community-based approach in promoting and providing family planning services at grassroots level by utilizing indigenous personnel and channels of communication and distribution, and as an extension of and supplement to the existing scarce and overburdened rural health services in Thailand. The project was seen to be potentially able to accommodate family planning demand well beyond that reached by existing governmental and commercial endeavors.

The primary objectives of the project, as defined by Mechai   at that time, were initially confined to family planning services:

1) To test the possibility of markedly expanding access to and information about contraceptive methods.

2) To create new and increased demand for family planning in the village level, and thus increase the number of couples practicing family planning and decrease in the pregnancy rate.

3) To become financially self-sufficient within four years.

The underlying hypothesis was that the following factors would render the project effective in accomplishing the above objectives:

1) Systematic utilization of community personnel and resources through careful identification, selection, training, motivation, and supervision.

2) Geographical convenience of information, communication, and availability of contraceptives within the community.

3) Cultural acceptability of seeking and receiving advice from a resident member of one's own community.

4) Reduction in the time and cost of acquiring contraceptives through the existing services.

5) Greater appreciation of the value of contraceptives by acquiring them at bearable cost, and hence increased usage than by receiving them free-of-charge.

6) Sale of contraceptives at reduced prices simply to cover the project's operating costs.

Organization and Administration

Mechai had already started renting an office for the CBFPS project in February 1974 while the feasibility study was still being undertaken. By the end of May, the number of project personnel had reached 24. This number included the project evaluation staff, local supervisors at the district level, and the office personnel. The then existing structure is shown below.

Organization Structure
of CBFPS
(May 1974)

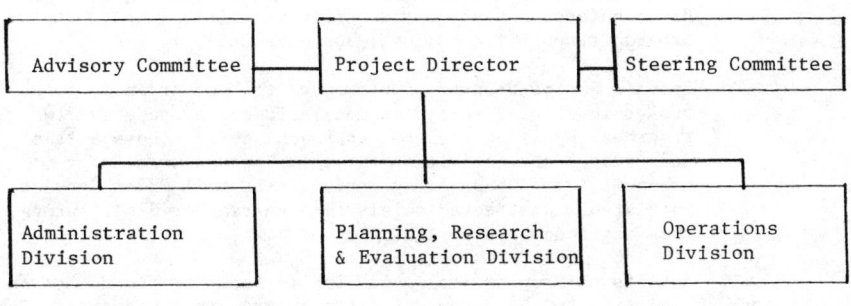

Source: CBFPS, Summary Report of Activities during the First Five Months (January-May 1974), June 1976.

Research, Monitoring, and Evaluation Methodology

Research and monitoring activities at this preliminary stage were conducted primarily by the project's staff with close cooperation from several institutions. These included MOPH, National Economic and Social Development Board, National Statistical Office, Army Survey Department, and Mahidol University, a local medical educational institution. Accomplished local statisticians were retained as consultants in the preparation of sample surveys, statistics, and data processing.

Although systematic design and data processing were undertaken, the village distributors were still the primary data sources. Difficulties were encountered in this area of data collection because of the weak performance of certain volunteer distributors in keeping records. Closer supervision of local coordinators stationed in the districts was undertaken to improve the situation.

Results of Program Operations during
Pre-operating Period (January-May 1974)

The project implementation during the period prior to the establishment of CBFPS was planned to embrace primarily three program approaches:

1) Village Program (VP)--implemented through selection and
    training of village distributors (one distributor for
    200 to 1,000 population); district supervisors (one for
    40,000 to 100,000 population) who supervised distributors
    in early development of acceptors, supply delivery, and
    record keeping; and through medical supervision of district
    medical officers. Only two districts were covered in this
    period.

2) Public Institution Program (PIP)--implemented through existing
    government organizations which had a certain medical infrastruc-
    ture to provide family planning services for their members by
    targeting their members as acceptors and training them as
    distributors. Only the teachers were participants in this
    program through the National Teachers Council.

3) Private Sector Program--implemented through organizations,
    professions, or disciplines not included in the above two
    programs, by using the same approach as PIP. No specific
    and independent activities for this program were under-
    taken in the pre-operating period. The Mail Order Service,
    initiated and effected solely through teacher distributors, was
    thus regarded as a part of PIP.

The results of program implementation in terms of the number of
acceptors in relation to the number of distributors are presented in Table
7.

Table 7

Solicitation of Acceptors
(February-May 1974)

	Village Program			Public Institution Program		
	No. of Accts.	No. of Dists.	Accts. Dists.	No. of Accts.	No. of Dists.	Accts. Dists.
February	196	70	3	–	–	–
March	481	70	7	73	–	–
April	628	70	9	297	800	*
May	835	70	12	597	3,243	*

*negligible

Note: The figures presented are cumulative.

Source: DBFPS, Summary Report of Activities during the First Five Months
         (January-May 1974), June 1974.

SIGNIFICANT PROGRESS IN THE DEVELOPMENT OF CBFPS
DURING THE FOUR YEAR OPERATIONS (1974-1977)

Since the establishment of CBFPS in May 1974, a number of changes have taken place to achieve a more effective and efficient implementation of the project. Significant strides were made in strengthening existing program operations, extending program area coverages, broadening program operations towards a more development-oriented approach, systematizing research and evaluation methodology, streamlining project's organizational and administrative policies and procedures, and, most important of all, attempting to achieve a certain degree of self-sufficiency. Most of the changes were brought about by the farsightedness of Mechai and his key personnel. Another significant development in the four-year existence of CBFPS was the growing strong commitment of the staff to the organization's objectives. In Mechai's words, "It is perhaps because of our feeling of impermanence."

Primary Objectives of CBFPS

After a few years of operations, the primary objectives of the project were expanded to encompass a broader scope than that initially stated in the original project proposal. The following reflect, as stated by Mechai, a more aptly-phrased set of objectives for CBFPS than the original objectives mentioned above:

1) To provide a subsidized marketing; Information, Education and Communications (IEC); and distribution system as a base from which participation in the national family planning program can effectively be made.

2) To ensure that the activities of family planning services are perceived as a self-help program, and provide the basis for integrating other services necessary for effecting a broader development orientation at the village level.

3) To develop CBFPS as a training center whereby communication and exchange of ideas, experience, and attitude towards demography in general and family planning services in particular, and community development concepts can be fruitfully made among interested international as well as local organizations.

Expansion of Program Operations and Area Coverages

As mentioned earlier, the three programs (Village Program, Public Institution Program, and Private Sector Program) were initiated during the pre-operating period (January-May 1974). Subsequent developments brought about more horizontally as well as vertically intensified program operations. However, the Village Program consistently remained the basic thrust of CBFPS throughout this four-year period.

Village Program. The program area coverage gradually increased from 23 districts in 1974 to 113 districts by the end of 1977.[1] This embraced

---

[1] For administrative purposes, Thailand is divided into 72 provinces (Changwat); each province has an average of 8 districts (Amphoe); each district has an average of 9 subdistricts (Tambol);and each subdistrict has an average of 9 villages (Muban).

12,011 villages containing 10.1 million population or approximately 23 percent of the total population.[1] The 1462 village distributors who distributed the pills to 11,474 acceptors in 1974 was increased to 7,588 distributors and 160,000 pill acceptors in 1977. The number of pill acceptors per distributor thus rose tremendously from 8 to 53. Horizontally, the program was thus intensified and expanded.

The program was extended to include parasite control services under its umbrella in the middle of 1976. This involved providing pills and providing free examination of acceptors for parasites. This Family Planning and Parasite Control Program was launched in conjunction with MOPH, Mahidol University, the Teachers Council Medical Center, and the Bangkok Metropolitan Administration. The distinctive feature of this integrated program is its broad coverage which encompasses both rural and urban areas. It therefore brought together the approaches utilized by the Village Program and Public Institution Program whenever applicable, as well as its own peculiar operations. Although it was still at an experimental stage, 13,683 rural acceptors and 9,822 urban acceptors were solicited by the end of 1977.

Furthermore, the Integrated Family Planning, Health and Hygiene Program was implemented in conjunction with MOPH and Mahidol University in the middle of 1977. By the end of 1977, 40 districts had been covered by this program, and 12,180 acceptors were solicited.

It should be noted too that several aspects of the program operations were greatly streamlined during this four-year implementation period. Criteria for selection of districts, procedures for preliminary survey, development, training, supervision, and retraining were fully experimented and developed. Relationships with several government departments were further established and strengthened to ensure full cooperation and coordination.

Public Institution Program. In addition to the Teacher Program launched through the Teachers Council Medical Center in 1974, several other institutional programs were also undertaken. The Industrial Family Planning Service Project targeting industrial workers, the Integrated Family Planning and Malaria Pilot Program, the Family Planning Services for Low-Income Government Housing Residents, and the Family Planning Services for Members of Cooperatives of Thailand were put into effect and contemplated for further implementation in conjunction with a number of authorities concerned. Despite its concentration on the Bangkok metropolis, the program was able to solicit 26,000 pill acceptors by the end of 1977, or an average increase of 35 percent per annum over 1974.

Private Sector Program. Throughout its implementation, the program has placed its emphasis on the promotion of the use of condoms, and the distribution of promotional items to promulgate the family planning concept. To render the program effective, several types of services were originated including the Mail Order Service, the Family Planning Supermarkets at provincial bus terminals, the Retail Condom Distribution, and the Distribution of Promotional Commodities stamped with family planning catchwords.

---

[1] By the end of 1977, the total population was estimated to have reached 44 million.

Specifically, the Family Planning Supermarkets also acted as referral points for IUD and sterilization services. A Sterilization Service Center, operated in conjunction with the Ramathibodi Hospital and the Patpong Medical Clinic, was also set up to provide further medical treatments as well as family planning consultations to interested individuals.

Development of Monitoring, Research, and Evaluation Methodology

A Planning (later called Monitoring), Research, and Evaluation Division was established at the project's inception in May 1974. A permanent team of researchers was recruited to carry out the monitoring and research functions.

The Monitoring Unit was responsible for data collection, coding, tabulation, analysis, and reporting of program activities, as well as periodic field spot-checks of distributors' records. Detailed monthly and quarterly reports were prepared and categorized by program and by geographical area. Incorporated in these reports were data on the number and category of pill customers, the number of pill cycles distributed by brand, the number of condom pieces ·distributed, the number of referrals by reason, cash received, and stock level. The primary data were collected by village distributors and collected monthly by field supervisors. The Studies and Research Unit was charged with all surveys and studies of program impact and effectiveness, including specifically such activities as questionnaire design, field interviews, editing and analysis of data, and preparation of the final report. It conducted three independent surveys on a continuous, year-round basis as follows:

1) Household Impact and Effectiveness Survey: to determine the effect of family planning services launched on the practices and behavior of the population of the sample village. This survey was carried out in the last quarter of 1974, followed by follow-up surveys in early 1976 and 1977. However, because of delay in processing and translation of survey results, only the findings and conclusions of the first survey have been completed and published.

   However, in order to help evaluate the impact and effectiveness of the CBFPS's Village Program, a preliminary comparison of findings from the three surveys has been prepared for management purposes. In a nutshell, it was found out that a 40 percent decrease of pregnancy rate in the operational districts was brought about after two years of operations (1974-1976). Aside from a 30 percent increase in the number of couples practising family planning, more families also had future plans for family planning. In addition, 71.1 percent of children less than two years of age were born out of planned, rather than unplanned, pregnancies. Annex III presents condensed comparative findings of the First, Second, and Third Impact and Effectiveness Surveys conducted in 1974, 1976, and 1977.

2) Customer Survey: to determine the characteristics and changes in attitudes, knowledge, and practice of family planning over time among family planning acceptors. Two sample surveys were conducted by November 1975 and November 1976. Only the re-

sults of the first survey have been made available.

Based on the preliminary findings (Annex II), it was found that 42 percent of the customers were between 25 and 34 years old, and about 70 percent had completed four years of education. The majority (80%) were gainfully employed and engaged in agriculture. Although most of the customers knew more than one method of family planning, taking pills was preferred to other methods by 75 percent of them. About 98 percent of those who were taking pills referred to CBFPS distributors as their source of contraceptives, and the majority were satisfied with the convenience of obtaining pills from this source.

3) Distributor Behavior Survey: to determine the knowledge, behavior, and performance of a sample of village distributors. The first round and second round of this survey were undertaken in December 1975 and December 1976, respectively. Only the survey results of the first round have been completed and published.

The preliminary findings of this first survey (Annex V) indicate that the majority (62%) of the distributors were male and aged 35 and above. Almost all of them (99%) had full-time occupations, the majority of which were equally dispersed between rice farmers (38%) and shopkeepers (39%). Based on CBFPS distribution records, male shopkeeper-distributors aged 35-39 years had recruited the largest number of acceptors.

It is apparent that only the Village Program was covered by these systematic surveys. Certain small-scale researches and studies were also undertaken by this unit; for example, Survey on Condom Retail Distribution, and Attitude Survey of Participants in the Teachers Program.

By late 1977, however, the research and studies function was discontinued and transferred to the Faculty of Public Health, Mahidol University. This decision was made by CBFPS's management in the light of the US AID requirement that research and evaluation work, especially on Family Planning, Health and Hygiene Program, be done by an independent agency. Only the Monitoring Unit was left to be responsible for the preparation of internal report requirements, analysis of performance results, as well as the conduct of special minor surveys for internal uses.

Organizational and Administrative Development

Until 1977, CBFPS had been run almost independently of PPAT and maintained merely a nominal relationship that was without any legal status. It was finally registered in October 1977, under the umbrella of "Population and Community Development Association", whose legal charter appears in Annex VI. As a basis for self-sufficiency in the long run, the Population and Community Development Co., Ltd. was also established in 1977.

The organizational structure of CBFPS has experienced several minor changes as more programs have been implemented. In late 1977, the project managerial organization[1] was eventually divided into three main divisions; namely, Operations Division I, Operations Division II, and Finance and Administration Division, each of which was headed by a Division Head. A Deputy Director and these Division Heads reported directly to the Project Director. One regional office[2] was also set up in Chiengrai, a northern province, to facilitate superivision over intensified operations in the area.

Table 8 shows the growth in the number of project staff during its four year-operations.

Table 8

Number of Project Staff
(1974-1977)

Location	1977	1976	1975	1974
CBFPS (Bangkok)	90	89	69	41
Provinces	71	70	52	24
Total	161	159	121	65

Source: CBFPS's files.

Endeavor Towards Self-sufficiency

Along the course of its development, the CBFPS relied mainly on IPPF funding and donated contraceptives for its program implementation. Its dependence upon IPPF cash grants had decreased, however, from 89 percent in 1974 to only 38 percent at the end of 1977, although all the contraceptives used in the program were donated by IPPF.

New external sources of funds were also developed to finance additional programs of the project., The United States Agency for International Development (US AID) provided necessary finance for the Family Planning, Health and Hygiene Program (FPHH) for the period of 1977 to 1980. The Japanese Organization for International Cooperation in Family Planning (JOICFP) was solicited to finance the Integrated Program on Family Planning and Parasite Control (FPPC) from 1976 to 1981. Several other international organizations and foundations (namely, the Population Council,

---

[1]More of the organization and management aspect will be discussed in the next section.

[2]A plan to establish the second regional office for the Northeast at Mahasarakam Province is under way.

Rockefeller Foundation, and Church World Service) also made certain contributions to assist in the project implementation.

Critical Determinants of the Development of CBFPS

The development of CBFPS has been marked by certain key factors that have contributed to its current measure of success. The first and most important of all is the role of Mechai, the Project Director. Throughout its course of development, CBFPS has undertaken most of its activities through the initiation, continuous support, and farsightedness of Mechai. Furthermore, he is currently indispensable in soliciting foreign as well as local financial support and cooperation. He is also responsible for maintaining the original flexibility that responds at the proper time to new organizational requirements.

However, it is not too farfetched to foresee the possibility that this strength may eventually become the organization's weakness in the event that Mechai can no longer continue or devote enough time to CBFPS. Mechai, however, is confident that he will be able to find a solution to this problem when the time comes. He has in effect started the training of understudies.

As has been noted above, CBFPS is basically dependent upon grants and donated contraceptives. In fact, the project's survival is determined by the continuity of this support. A declining trend of foreign support has already been apparent in the case of IPPF that will cease to provide funds and contraceptives to the project by the end of 1982. Obviously, should this trend continue with other programs or be advocated by other donor organizations, the CBFPS project may well be jeopardized in the long run because of its built-in nonprofit-seeking constraint.

Another potential danger to the existence of CBFPS lies in the measure of support given to it by the RTG. Apart from the fact that its current operations are successfully run in good cooperation and coordination with MOPH, it must be remembered that the government did not initiate this program. The Second Five-Year National Family Planning Program (1977-1981) has already stipulated that a community-based health care and family planning program of the government will be implemented throughout Thailand by the end of the Plan. Unless clear distinction and delineation is made in regard to this potential operational overlap, the CBFPS project may be put in a difficult position. The possibility of avoiding this unfavorable circumstance will depend upon the attitude of the government towards the actual contribution of the private agencies in providing family planning services to rural Thailand and upon CBFPS's effort to convince the government of the importance of its role.

CHAPTER 4

CURRENT FEATURES OF CBFPS OPERATIONS

The current operations and activities of the project reflect not only the influence of its original concepts and strategies, but also a conceptual extension into more development-oriented approaches.   To a certain extent, certain aspects of health care have been integrated into existing family planning programs, although family planning services still remain the focal point of all project activities.

BASIC THRUST OF EXISTING PROGRAM OPERATIONS

CBFPS, under its current program structure, regards as its top priority the provision of family planning services directly to the village people.   The critical elements in the thrust of CBFPS are therefore the <u>family planning services</u>[1] and the <u>rural service clientele</u>.   The implication is that all activities at the village level will have to be spearheaded by family planning efforts.

Other supportive elements of the project include the promotion and the provision of family planning services to urban residents working in industrial organizations or professions, and urban dwellers in general.   The programs designed for these urban targets have made significant contributions to the local fund-raising efforts as well as to the expansion of family planning client base.

Briefly, the primary target of the Village Program today is the administrative unit of the district which is also the central analytical unit   for program evaluation.   Implementation of VP is carried out primarily by selected villagers who are trained to become village distributors. A government district health officer or a medical officer, who is appointed as district advisor, coordinates the activities by performing certain administrative duties and providing medical supervision and clinical referral services for the distributors and acceptors.

The Public Institution Program, on the other hand, is designed to reach the professional or occupational sector of the population **through** existing government and industrial organizations that have large memberships and some medical infrastructures.   Although distributors are established as resupplying agents in the selected organizations, PIP hinges heavily on CBFPS's efforts instead of the distributors' in motivating and educating family planning service clientele.

---

[1]The family planning services here refer to all activities performed to solicit acceptors who practice some forms of contraception, including IEC (Information, Education, and Communications) elements undertaken by the project in support of family planning.

The Private Sector Program is intended to cover the population sector that falls outside the first two programs. The primary objectives are to promote the family planning concept and to improve contraceptive practices   of this untapped sector of the potential market. The family planning services provided by this program range from the sale of contraceptives   and   promotional items to clinical referral services for sterilization and IUD insertion.

The services of the Integrated Family Planning and Parasite Control Program are provided for the rural areas where the Village Program is well established. For the urban areas, the program introduces parasite control information and medication and population education in schools, slum areas, and industrial organization.   The main objective of the program is thus to disseminate knowledge, to provide consultations and medication services in regard to parasite control through the utilization of the project's existing rural and urban distribution networks.

The Integrated Family Planning, Health and Hygiene Program is   an integrated program that aims to provide basic health and hygiene   services in conjunction with family planning services to the rural communities.   It attempts to utilize the well-established program design and implementation of CBFPS in broadening the types of services currently rendered.

A more detailed description of these programs follows.

THE VILLAGE PROGRAM

Implementation of VP has been carried out continuously in   several regions of Thailand since its inception in 1974. By the end of 1977,   the total number of districts covered by VP reached 113, the majority of which were in the north and northeast, as shown in Table 9.

Table 9

Number of Districts Covered by
Village Program

Region	No. of Districts	Year/Accumulated No. of Districts under CBFPS			
		1977	1976	1975	1974
Central	88	25	18	8	4
East	45	7	4	4	4
Northeast	173	33	20	18	8
North	136	37	18	11	5
South	102	11	7	7	2
Total	594	113	67	48	23

Source: Tabulated from CBFPS, Summary Report of Activities 1977, January 1978.

With the work of 7,588 village distributors, 12,011 villages containing a population of 10,163,793 were provided with family planning services after four   years
of VP operations (Table 10). Figure I presents the administrative and distribution structure of the program.

Table 10

Number of Villages and Size of Population
Served by Village Program

| Year | District | Number of | | Distributor |
		Village	Population	
1974	23	2,586	2,029,834	1,462
1975	25	3,049	2,460,087	1,857
1976	19	2,030	1,857,911	1,230
1977	46	4,346	3,815,961	3,039
Total	113	12,011	10,163,793	7,588

Source: CBFPS, Summary Report of Activities 1977, January 1978.

Selection of Areas for Operations

        The district for CBFPS operation is selected either at the request of local
officials, ranging from district health officer to provincial governor, or independently determined by CBFPS's staff. The criteria applied in determining whether the
proposed district(s) should be selected for VP implementation comprise basically the
MOPH ranking of family planning practices, cost effectiveness, and other qualitative
considerations.

        MOPH Ranking of Family Planning Practices. In its annual review   of   the
National Family Planning Program, MOPH publishes a detailed ranking of provinces according to the number of families practising family planning as well as family planning methods used. If a proposed district is ranked low or shows a great potential
for family planning acceptance, it is likely to be chosen for VP   implementation.
This potential cannot, however, be determined independently from the remaining criteria.

        Cost Effectiveness. As a matter of procedure, the following data have to be
obtained, estimated, or taken into account:

    -- Total population residing outside the metropolitan area, its
        distribution as well as its per capita income.

    -- Fifteen percent (15%) of the total rural population is estimated
        to be eligible women of reproductive age (15-45).

    -- Thirty percent (30%) of these eligible women is assumed to practise
        family planning by one method or another.

FIG. 1

CBFPS VILLAGE PROGRAM

ADMINISTRATIVE AND DISTRIBUTION STRUCTURE

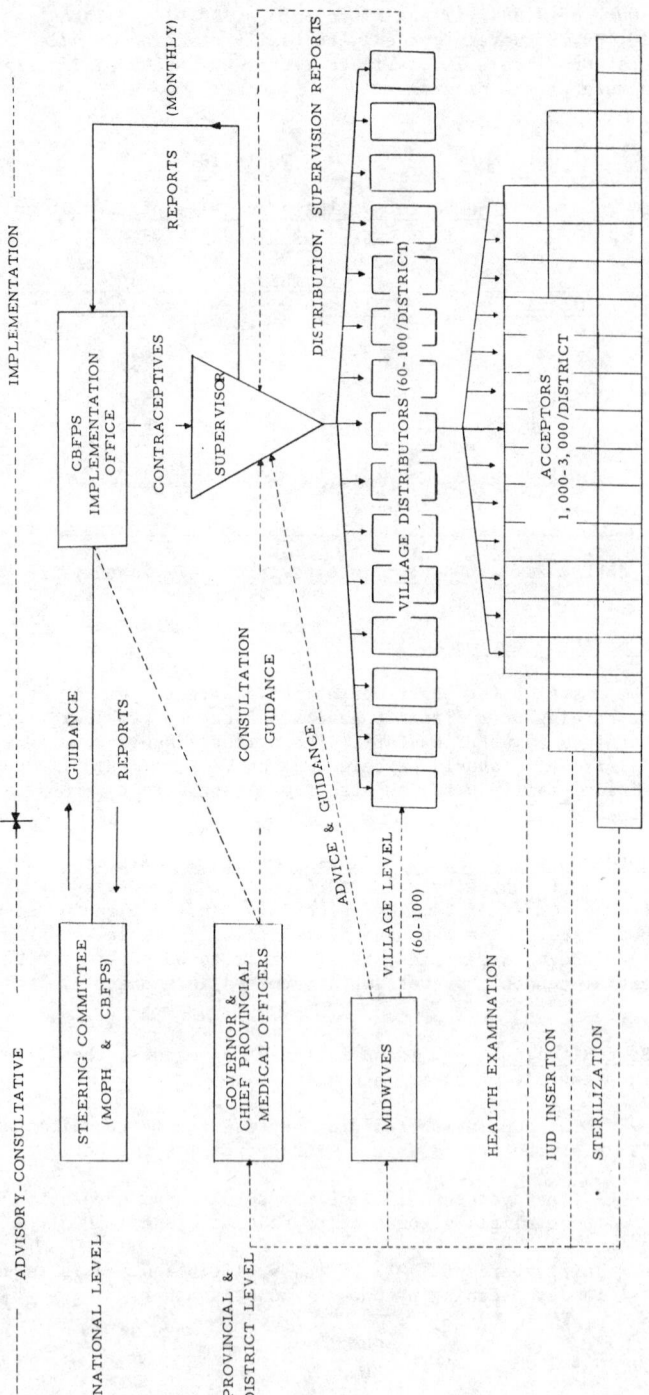

Source: CBFPS.

-- Sixty percent (60%) of eligible women practising family planning is estimated to take oral contraceptives.

-- Fifteen to twenty percent (15-20%) of potential oral contraceptive users is set as CBFP's targeted acceptors.

-- Two hundred percent (200%) of contraceptives used by the targeted acceptors is estimated to be the total contraceptive requirement of the district, since 100% of contraceptives will be placed with the District Health Officer as stock supply.

-- An estimated proportion of volume of each brand of contraceptives to be sold, along with its price,is then computed. The total sales of all brands becomes the local income estimated for the district.

-- All distribution costs are calculated for program operations in the district.

Comparison of estimated local income and targeted distribution costs constitutes a quantitative basis for determining the cost effectiveness of program operations in the proposed district.

Other Qualitative considerations. Other factors will likewise be given due consideration in the selection of areas for operations; such as whether the district is a sensitive area where Communist terrorism is predominant; or whether it has already been under, or will be penetrated by, other MOPH's family planning programs.

After a number of districts have been carefully identified for VP operations, they will have to be approved by a steering committee, comprising representatives from MOPH and CBFPS. If it is approved, the MOPH undersecretary will send a transmittal letter to all provincial health officers concerned requesting cooperation with CBFPS program implementation. CBFPS will also present another letter informing the provincial governors of the program operations to ensure good coordination and full cooperation from all local government officials concerned. A formal contact made with local officials thus utilizes existing bureaucratic channels to solicit due recognition of the program.

Program Implementation for Selected Districts

At this implementation stage, there still exist several preceding steps prior to the actual launching of program operations in a particular selected district. These embrace preliminary contact, development, training,motivation, distribution, supervision and retraining, and monitoring.

Preliminary Contact. This initial step is intended to establish preliminary contacts in person with local officials and make classifications as to the program's objectives and how it will benefit the community. These local officials include the governor, provincial health officer, other MOPH provincial officers, district chief officer, and district health officer. Particularly, CBFPS's staff has to attend a monthly meeting of subdistrict chiefs and village heads and introduce the program to these community leaders. During this period, an advertisement for recruitment of District Supervisor[1] is also placed. Normally, it takes three to five days to complete this first step.

Development. The activities undertaken in this step include: recruitment of the district supervisor; selection of appropriate distributors through personal interviews and observation of distributors' residences; collection of all relevant statistics about the district; preparation of training schedules and other administrative requirements; and coordination with local officials concerned for the planned training session.

A village distributor[2] is selected from a village of 500-1,500 population whereas a district supervisor is employed to supervise and attend to the needs and functions of the distributors in each district containing an average population of 70,000.

Training. The training program is designed specifically for selected distributors. This one-day training session also brings together several key local government officers with a view to making clear the government's recognition of the CBFPS program. These normally include the Provincial Health Officer, Chief District Officer, Medical Officer at the district hospital, District Health Officer, Auxiliary Midwives, and Sanitarians of various Government Health Centers within the district. The training inputs, which are given through lectures by the CBFPS's key staff and Medical Officer, encompass the basic human reproduction system, family planning methods and their misconceptions, simple screening checklist, contra-indicators, remedy and record-keeping, and motivation for family planning services.

In addition to lectures which are delivered in very simple terms, the other media utilized for training purposes are film showing and easy-reading

---

[1]A district supervisor is a permanent, salaried staff member of CBFPS. His qualifications include ten years of schooling, being the owner of a motorcycle, being a district resident, being well-informed on all subdistrict locations, and having a guarantor. His salary ranges from $40 to $65 per month.

[2]A village distributor must possess the following qualifications: (1) Have leadership qualities, be trustworthy, be well-known in the village; (2) Have a working career and reside in the village; (3) Have one of the following careers: shopkeeper or grocer, subdistrict medical practitioner, traditional practitioner; traditional midwife, schoolteacher; (4) Be interested in and willing to work for the community; (5) Be a male or female, 25 to 40 years of age; (6) Reside in the center of the village area to facilitate contacts with the clientele; (7) Be literate; (8) Have no bad financial record; and (9) Be able to treat the matters of others confidentially.

messages, pictures, and articles posted and exhibited in the auditorium.   At
the end of the training session, distributors bring home 18 cycles of   pills
and two dozen condoms on consignment, a plastic record-keeping binder   with
family planning materials[1] and referral forms, and a colorful aluminum depot
sign. An equivalent volume of consignment stock is also placed with the District Health Officer, who will be responsible for stock control and, in some
cases, cash collection. The training budget normally does not exceed $760 for
each particular district. Annex IV shows a training program schedule at Banmee District.

        Motivation. The distributors are responsible for carrying out the mo-
tivational activities within their respective villages. Aside from putting up
depot signs inviting buyers of contraceptives at his house, a distributor also
seeks the cooperation of school teachers to teach family planning songs   to
school children. He also uses the word-of-mouth approach in recruiting close
friends as acceptors before extending his efforts to other people in the village. Attempt is also made by distributors to ensure that false rumors   are
countered with correct conceptions. Follow-up of acceptors is another major
responsibility of the distributor.

        Distribution. Distribution activities begin simultaneously with   the
distributor's motivational activities within the village. The distributor is
provided with a simple checklist and guidelines to enable him to observe   if
prospective users have indications of any recent illness, varicose veins, and
yellow eyes. In case of uncertainty, the prospective user is requested   to
visit the local midwife for physical examination, and if necessary, to be   referred to the government doctor in town who is responsible for medical   supervision. As part of his motivational activities, the distributor is   supposed
to enhance the confidence of users who have experienced some early use   dis-
comforts.

        Two brands of pills are distributed by the distributor; namely,Norinyl,
and Eugynon for U.S. $.25 and $.45 per cycle, respectively. Condoms are   also
sold for US$.45 per dozen. Five cents from each cycle of pills or from   each
dozen of condoms sold is earned by the distributor. The distributor who refers
users for IUD insertion or sterilization to the local doctor is given a   prize
of two free cycles of pills and the Government Health Center is awarded US$.50
for each case of clinical contraception service.

        Apart from the distribution responsibility, the distributor has to main-
tain certain records, such as the name and address of buyer, the number   of
cycles corresponding to the month of use, and the number of repeat users   and
dropouts for each month.

        Supervision and Retraining. At the actual launching of the distribution
step, three levels of supervision activities immediately follow. At least once
a month, a district supervisor is required to visit, resupply stock, collect income from distributors, assemble records, and help the distributor with   any
questions or difficulties which may have arisen during the previous month. Some

_____

[1]Specifically, the family planning materials include (apart from CBFPS's
history, development and operations) MOPH's leaflets on marriage guidance, prevention of pregnancy, IUD, vasectomy, and CBFPS's guidebook on record-keeping
and report preparation.

of these questions may be referred further to the local doctor. At the second level of supervision, a field visit is made every three to six months[1] by a CBFPS central field operations staff who has a number of districts (six on the average) under his control. During the period of about five days, the field staff is responsible for making random checks on the activities of the district supervisor and the village distributors. The findings are directly reported to the operations division manager in Bangkok for further discussions and improvements.

The third level of supervision refers to administrative supervision which is the responsibility of the District Health Officer. These supervision activities basically include issuance of contraceptive stock; observation of the district supervisor's performance; providing general consultations; and in certain cases control over collection of income from distribution[2], especially in certain remote areas.

Retraining of the village distributors is supposed to be conducted six to eight months after the first training. This one-day training session's objectives are primarily to keep the distributors informed of the progress of VP operations and activities, to provide an in-depth training on family planning concepts and practices, as well as to encourage fruitful discussions among them on problems met and ways and means to resolve them. At the end of this training, a certification from MOPH is conferred on each distributor. The training budget for this activity is approximately $400 per district.

In addition to the training and education aimed at the distributors, the program also disseminates family planning information directly to the village clientele. This is regarded as the external motivational inputs provided by CBFPS, but only in the second twelve months of distribution. The first twelve months of motivation and distribution to the village clientele is left entirely to the responsibility of the village distributor. These external motivational inputs include the following: film showing, prizes for lucky acceptors, village posters, participation of family planning activities in the local temple festivals, and the distribution of promotional items, such as T-Shirts, posters, stickers and booklets. Figure II shows the graphic presentation of overall steps in the program design.

Cash Outlay for Opening a New District

Table 11 presents the estimated cash outlay needed for developing a new district for VP operations. These data, however, exclude the cost of consignment stock of contraceptives and condoms.

----

[1]Ideally, it should be made once every month. This however cannot be done because of a shortage of field operations staff. Currently, there are 19 field operations officers, that is, 4 unit heads and 15 officers to oversee 113 operational districts, or an average of 6 districts per officer.

[2]To avoid any possibility of fraud, a district supervisor is required to hand in the collected cash during the regional meeting of district supervisors, which is held every 20 days for each particular region, instead of passing the amount to the District Health Officer.

Table 11

Estimated Cash Outlay for
Opening a New District

Activities	Estimated Outlay/District
Site Survey	US$ 125.
Development	390.
Training	760.
Supervision	100.
Retraining	400.
CBFPS's Motivation	700.
TOTAL	US$2,475.

Source: CBFPS.

SUPPLEMENTARY PROGRAMS

The other programs, aside from the Village Program which is regarded as the mainstay of CBFPS, are considered supplementary.

Public Institution Program (PIP)

The current operations undertaken under PIP comprise the activities implemented in several organizations including the Teachers Council Medical Center, the industrial organizations, Communicable Disease Control Department, the military establishments, the National Housing Authority, and the taxi cooperatives.

The stages in launching PIP in these organizations involve basically the same process as that of VP. The only distinctive feature of PIP is that the external motivational inputs are provided by CBFPS directly to the potential acceptors from the beginning of distribution activities. The distributors from several organizations are trained altogether by CBFPS's staff.

PIP has been launched in connection with the Teachers Council Medical Center since 1974 and directed at the school teachers from all over the country who come to Bangkok for their summer refresher courses. They are targeted as acceptors and distributors. The motivational activities have already been conducted for 210,000 school teachers and 3,600 of them were selected to be village distributors.

The family planning program for industrial organizations has been implemented in close cooperation with the Labor Department since 1975. After three years of operations, 243 factory employees from 243 industrial organizations were trained to be distributors for family planning services.

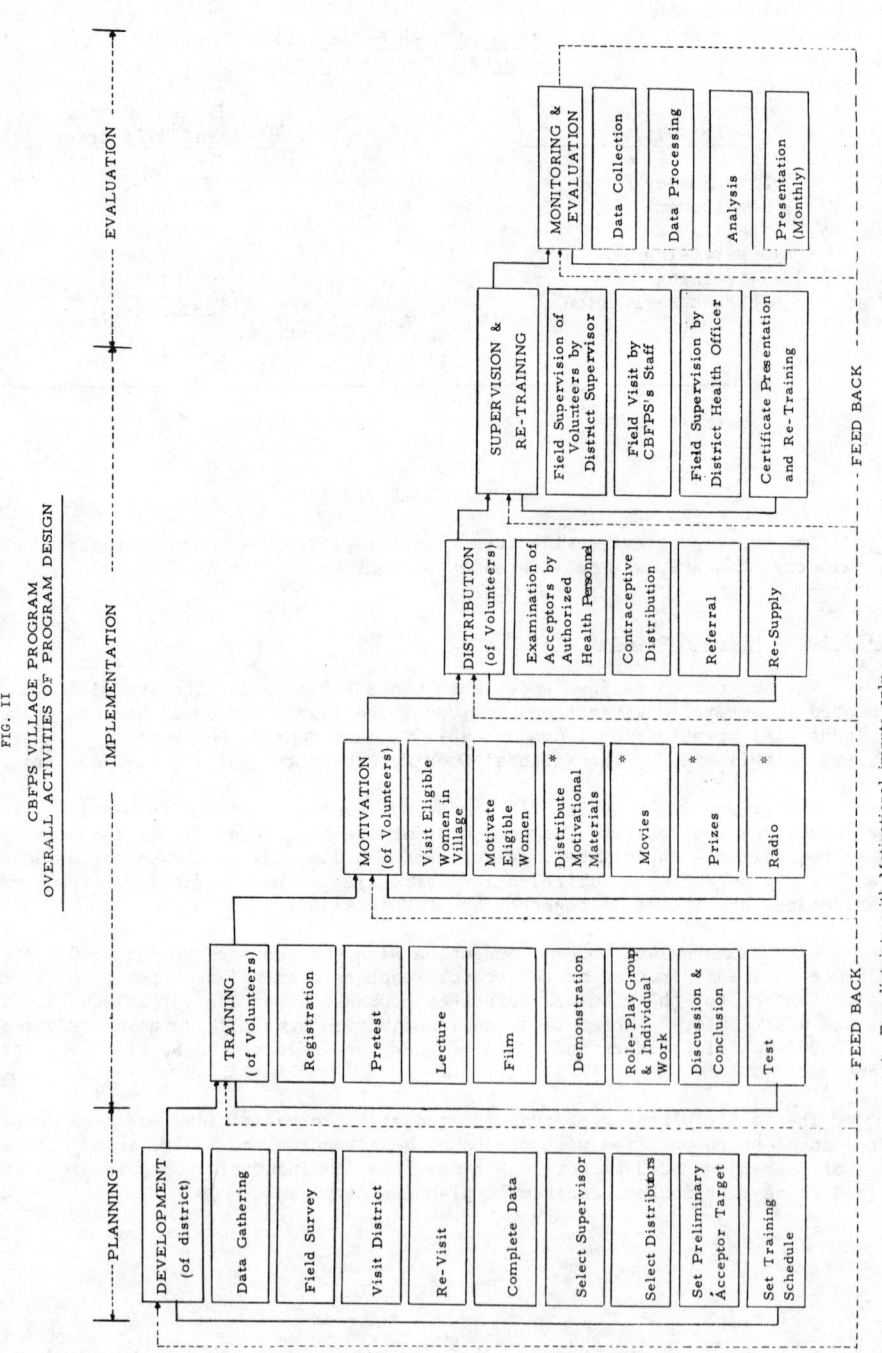

FIG. II
CBFPS VILLAGE PROGRAM
OVERALL ACTIVITIES OF PROGRAM DESIGN

Source: CBFPS

* For districts with Motivational imputs only

Integration of family planning services with the malaria control program was initiated in 1976. This was done in cooperation with the Communicable Disease Control Department, MOPH. The implementation of these integrated services was carried out, however, through the malaria agents and malaria provincial heads. CBFPS took part by training these personnel on contraceptive distribution. This program is still being implemented, but on a trial basis.

Through arrangements with some military establishments, CBFPS has already started its program operations in certain military communities since 1976. Some of these military personnel were trained to be motivators and to disseminate family planning information and practices in certain remote areas of 36 provinces. The family planning services in these areas are rendered by other government units. This program is being studied for further expansion.

An attempt has also been made to motivate, give consultations, and provide services on family planning to residents in the government low income housing projects. By the end of 1977, 197 building units have been covered by the project through cooperation with the National Housing Authority.

Through several leagues of taxi-driver cooperatives, a number of taxi-driver families have been motivated to become acceptors and recruited as distributors. By the end of 1977 about 100 family distributors (spouses) have undergone the training program of CBFPS.

Private Sector Program

With its emphasis on distribution of condoms and family planning promotional items, the current Private Sector Program operations cover four distinct activities; the Mail Order Service; the Family Planning Supermarkets and Sterilization Services; the Retail Condom Distribution; and the Distribution of Promotional Commodities. The main objectives of this program are to improve people's attitude towards the condom and to increase male participation in family planning.

The Mail Order Service was started in December 1974 for condom distribution. This service is intended to provide convenience and to increase condom usage among different people. The mail order system encloses a sample condom, very easy to mail. By the end of 1977, approximately 800,000 have been distributed, but the responses have been insignificant.

In 1976, three Family Planning Supermarkets were set up at three major provincial bus terminals in the Bangkok Metropolis. Approximately 500,000 passengers pass through these terminals every day. The main purposes of establishing these supermarkets are to disseminate family planning information, to sell promotional items, and to act as referral points for interested persons who want to obtain IUD or sterilization service. A Sterilization Service Center and the Patpong Medical Clinic provide IUD and sterilization services as well as family planning consultations.

The Retail Condom Distribution can be regarded as the only sales-oriented activity of the project. Donated condoms are repackaged locally to give a better product appearance and to increase its marketability in the local condom market. It is sold under the brand name Mechai. A sales force team is charged solely with the sales of condoms through retail dealers all over the country. Despite a product constraint, where quality is beyond control, the condoms distributed obtain a reasonable degree of market acceptance. Currently, the average sales volume reaches 14,400 dozen per month. These direct sales in the local condom market have significantly contributed to the local fund-raising efforts of CBFPS.

Distribution of promotional items was initiated in 1974. These inexpensive commodities comprise T-Shirts, underpants, socks, pens, safety period circles, and handkerchiefs. Family planning information and slogans are printed on the products to help spread family planning ideas and to desensitize family planning practice. Significant income is also generated from this selling effort.

Integrated Family Planning and Parasite Control Program (FPPC)

The primary objectives of the Integrated Family Planning and Parasite Control Program (FPPC) are to disseminate knowledge and information and to provide services on parasite control to village people through the existing village distribution network and to urban residents in several private and public institutions. The program was initiated in the middle of 1976 in response to the results of a survey of Department of Communicable Diseases Control, MOPH, showing that approximately 60 percent of Thailand's population were infested with parasites. Implementation of this program has been made by CBFPS in conjunction with MOPH, Mahidol University, the Teachers Council Medical Center, and the Bangkok Metropolitan Administration. Funding of FPPC has been granted by JOICFP (Japanese Organization for International Cooperation in Family Planning).

The two main components of this program are the rural and urban activities. Program implementation in the rural areas is carried out through family planning village distributors and headmasters who act as motivators. Stool examinations and drugs for parasite treatment are provided by CBFPS with the cooperation of MOPH. The urban program is directed towards schools, factories, slums, and other institutions. The program activities encompass the introduction of parasite control information and medication as well as population education.

By the end of 1977, five districts were covered by this pilot integrated program. Stool examinations were conducted for 13,683 people, and 10,020 of them were treated with drugs. For urban residents, stool examinations of 9,822 students in 108 schools were made. Drug treatment was given to approximately 64 percent of the total infested cases. Implementation of the program also covered 43 factories. Launching of the program in slum areas is still in the survey and study stage.

Integrated Family Planning, Health and Hygiene Program (FPHH)

The Integrated Family Planning, Health and Hygiene Program (FPHH) was started in the middle of 1977 by attempting primarily to improve the health and hygiene condition of the rural communities through integration with family

planning activities. Household drugs are added in the contraceptive distribution of the Village Program. Training of village distributors under FPHH
is conducted in a two-day session by adding one full day session on health
and hygiene topics in addition to the orientation on family planning knowledge and practice.

In addition to provision of family services, FPHH also set the
following program objectives:

1) To test the relative cost effectiveness of alternative delivery
systems:

a. with and without free introductory supplies of
contraceptives;

b. with and without the addition of health.

2) To compare the quasi-commercial self-sufficiency of the
above variations.

3) To obtain data outputs on contraceptive acceptors, period
prevalence, and pregnancy rates.

FPHH is partially funded by the United States Agency for International Development (US AID) and has been launched since June, 1977, in
conjunction with MOPH and the Faculty of Public Health, Mahidol University, covering a period of 4 years.

It is expected that at the end of the program, 120,000 continuing
family planning acceptors will have been recruited. At the end of 1977,
or after the first seven-month operations, FPHH was undertaken in 40
districts[1] in all regions of Thailand, and 12,180 acceptors have been
recruited. Implementation of this program has currently been made in a
number of districts by providing family planning services (priced contraceptives and condoms) and health service, and by providing the same combined services but with a two-month free introductory supply of pills and
condoms. It is planned to cover 40 additional districts by the end of
May 1978.

ATTEMPTS TOWARD A BROADER DEVELOPMENT PROGRAM

Attempts have been made by CBFPS to move towards a more development-
oriented program in order to improve rural family lives. In October 1977,
a project proposal on "Integrated Self-Help Village Development: A Fertility-Related Approach to Community Development" was submitted to the
Netherlands Organization for International Development Cooperation to seek

---

[1]Twenty districts were provided with priced contraceptives and
condoms as implemented in CBFPS's Village Program. The other 20 districts
were launched through the same village distribution network but with two-
month free introductory supply of pills and condoms.

partial funding of the project. Annex V presents certain major features of the proposed project.

The approach utilized in this proposed project lies basically in the integration of a number of additional services to the existing family planning services provided in various districts of Chiengrai province, North Thailand. This province was chosen because it contained most of the northern operational districts, the most successful region in terms of family planning services. Crucial to the approach is the village distributor who is regarded as the key change agent at the village level. Through him, a series of other services such as low-cost primary health care, nutrition, improved marketing opportunities for farm produce, cheaper raw materials, seeds, fertilizer and others, and low-interest rate loans; can be added.

PROJECT MANAGEMENT AND ORGANIZATION

Management of CBFPS project operations reflects a combination of functional and project orientation in planning, implementation, and control of all program activities. As shown in Figure III, the Project Director together with the Deputy Director and three other Division Heads functionally supervise the overall project operations. These key personnel normally meet, though not on a very formal basis, to discuss matters in regard to policies, planning, as well as control of ongoing program activities. Their gatherings virtually represent the role of a management committee in a business concern.

Management of each respective program, however, is carried out on a somewhat independent basis. Primary emphasis is given to the Village Program and the Integrated Family Planning, Health and Hygiene Program, which are basically designed to serve the rural areas. The Operations Division I (OD-I) is responsible for the implementation of these two programs. The Operations Division II (OD-II) oversees the performance of all remaining programs: the Public Institution Program, the Private Sector Program, and the Integrated Family Planning and Parasite Control Program. Because of the wide coverage of the Village Program, the operations under the OD-I are further divided on a regional basis with each Operations Unit responsible for each particular region. However, under the OD-II, control is done primarily on a program basis, except for the Operations Unit VII and VIII whose responsibilities lie in the implementation of rural FPPC and urban FPPC, respectively.

The two operating divisions are served by the Finance and Administrative Division (FAD) on matters concerning accounting, administation, inventory, feedback information on program operations, and other special services like the preparation of materials for family planning, graphic presentation, and family planning exhibition. A number of reports have also been regularly prepared by the FAD, as follows:

Monthly Reports

Report on Family Planning Services Provided Classified by Program
Report on Preliminary Data Classified by Region
Summary Report of Village Program Activities Classified by Region
Report on Condom Distribution Classified by Market Region

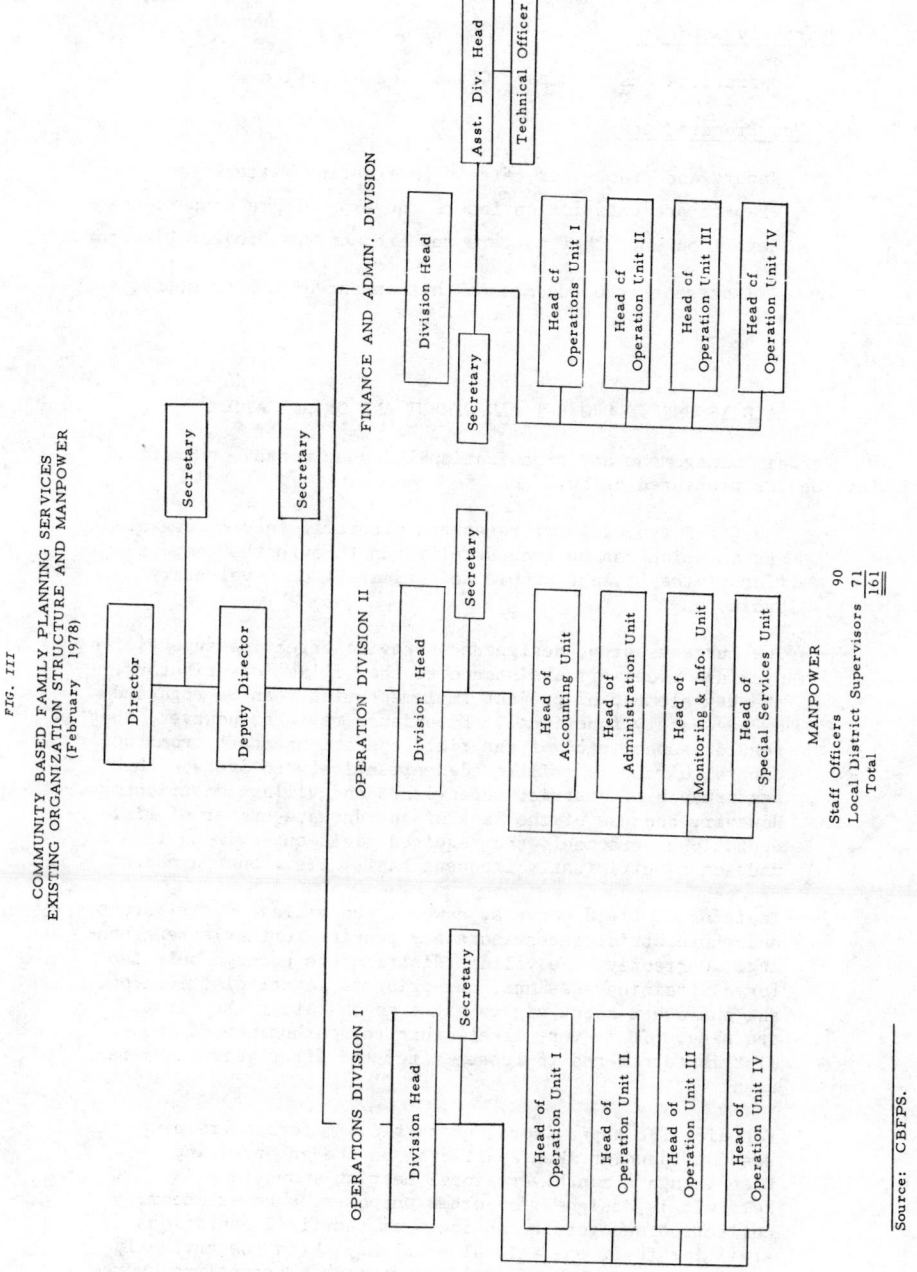

FIG. III
COMMUNITY BASED FAMILY PLANNING SERVICES
EXISTING ORGANIZATION STRUCTURE AND MANPOWER
(February 1978)

Source: CBFPS.

Quarterly Report

>   Operations Status Report Classified by Region

Ad Hoc Preparations

>   Report and graphs for certain interesting matters
>   Graphic presentation on income and expenditure comparison
>   Report on any other matters required by the Project Director.

Annex VI presents the educational attainment of CBFPS's supervisory staff.

MAIN ISSUES IN PROJECT MANAGEMENT AND ORGANIZATION

Certain management and organizational issues worthy of critical examination are presented below:

-- The CBFPS typically represents a nonprofit service organization which can be successfully run through the cooperation of the village people and primarily on a voluntary basis.

-- The current setup, designed to provide effective supervision over and necessary assistance to the village distributors, the key element of project implementation, can be regarded as adequately functional. Experience reveals, however, that regular supervision of the field operations staff from the central office is still needed effectively to oversee the performance of district supervisors and village distributors. However, because of the lack of an adequate number of field operations personnel, the required field supervision is not made on a sufficiently frequent basis; i.e., once a month.

-- Training of field workers, namely, the village distributors and the district supervisors may require further strengthening. Currently, the village distributors undergo only two formal training sessions, one prior to actual distribution, and the other about six to eight months after the first training. It is very likely that the enthusiasm of the distributors tends to lessen after the first year of operations.

   For district supervisors, no particular formal training session is undertaken apart from on-the-job training. Even though a monthly regional meeting among them is held, it is designed for other purposes, such as income collection and getting advice from the field operations staff for their operational problems. With the currently insufficient number of field operations personnel to oversee the district supervisors' performance, more training effort is needed to ensure effectiveness and efficiency of supervision.

-- Recruitment of District Health Officers, aside from numerous contacts made through existing bureaucratic channels, as part of the field staff reflects a well-planned strategy in solicitation of effective and permanent cooperation from local government officers. An incentive of 2.5 cents per cycle of pill and 15 cents per dozen of condoms sold is also given to these local officers to motivate them for better performance.

-- Since CBFPS is run as a private, nonprofit organization whose continued existence heavily relies upon foreign grants and donations without sufficient internally-generated funds, there may be a feeling of having inadequate job security among the CBFPS's staff. To mitigate this potential problem which could affect staff morale, the Population and Community Development Co., Ltd., was established and the present key personnel are listed on the Board psychologically to ensure that organizational continuity can be maintained in the long run.

-- In the middle of 1977, a study team was commissioned by IPPF to appraise the evaluation procedures of CBFPS, whose summary of findings is presented below:

> The data on acceptors recorded by distributors were not sufficiently reliable for drawing valid conclusions. However, they might well be indicative of trends, though inaccurate in absolute terms, for project evaluation.

> Long delays in processing the survey results were apparent, and therefore inadequately valuable to management for policy and strategy development.

> The applicability of the findings in the Household Impact and Effectiveness Survey were limited to the regions surveyed. They are not representative of other regions not covered by the Survey, primarily because of differences in the original sample frame and subsequent changes in the sample actually used.

> Difficulties were encountered in drawing comparisons between nonproject control districts and project districts, because of the relative influence of the government's family planning program. As such, reliable and valid conclusions could not be derived.

> Major reservations were made regarding the feasibility of obtaining required data based on the designed questionnaires.

-- In addition to the above findings and conclusions, recent field investigations also point out the following:

> Records on acceptors were loosely and not properly kept by village distributors. Difficulties in record-keeping were recognized, however, because of insufficient knowledge of distributors, inability to use judgment in recording variant data, burdensome requirements of forms, and so forth.

Records on dropouts were completely ignored by the
village distributors.

A number of users classified as having "discontinued"
were not actually permanent dropouts since they might
resume family planning practice in later months.

Also among the dropouts were some who simply changed the
source of family planning services, from the distributors
to the government health center or commercial drugstores,
often because of certain side effects encountered in taking
the pills bought from the distributors.

-- In an attempt to enhance the staff's knowledge and to promote
   management development, an in-house training program on "Principles of Management" was conducted for all unit and division
   heads. Key management staff were also sent to attend some
   other training seminars on an individual basis.

-- To strengthen internal communications and create mutual understanding of the overall organization's progress, the staff
   meeting is regularly held with a view to imparting the
   CBFPS's performance and connections established with external
   organizations, as well as to discussing internal problems
   within the organization.

-- The remuneration scale of CBFPS was surveyed by the Management
   Audit Department of IPPF London[1], and it was concluded that on
   the average it offered approximately 12 percent lower than the
   remuneration for comparable positions by other private enterprises. Annex VII presents a salary structure of CBFPS staff.

-- One of the most distinctive features of CBFPS is its organizational flexibility. Along the course of its four years'
   development, a number of organizational reshuffles have been
   made to update the existing structure and to attend to the
   growing complexity of the organizational requirement.

-- To further prop up its international image, CBFPS plans
   to set up a training center to be used as a means for the
   exchange of ideas, experiences, and lessons learned in the
   field of demography in general and family planning services
   in particular. Necessary facilities for the envisaged training center are being prepared.

---

[1]IPPF, Management Audit Report on CBFPS, London, February–April, 1977.

CHAPTER 5

FINANCIAL RESOURCES
AND PERFORMANCE OF CBFPS

CBFPS has been supported by funds and commodities donated by international organizations supporting family planning. One major policy it has
followed is to ensure accountability for all donated funds and commodities
by thorough auditing to assure donors that resources are used properly.

SOURCES OF FUNDS AND COMMODITIES

As mentioned previously, CBFPS operations have been financed in two
particular ways; that is, grants (in cash), and donation of family planning
devices, including contraceptives and condoms. These donated family planning
devices are resold to family planning customers at one-half to one-third of
market prices, and are thus converted into cash for financing the operations.
Table 12 shows CBFPS's foreign sources of funding during 1974 to 1977 and the
committed funds from donors for the year 1978.

Table 12

CBFPS's Sources of Funds
(1974-1978)

Donor	1978	1977	1976	1975	1974
IPPF	$170,172	$174,527	$260,000	$275,000	$235,000.
JOICFP[1]	88,302	35,000	37,425	----	-----
USAID[2]	118,720	181,120	----	-----	-----
TOTAL	$377,194	$390,647	$297,425	$275,000	$235,000.

[1]The total fund of $72,425 was granted for the period of June 1976 to December 1977.

[2]The total fund of $299,840 was granted for the fiscal year of June 1977 to May 1978.

Source: CBFPS's Accounting Unit.

It is apparent that IPPF has remained the principal donor of funds
since CBFPS's inception in 1974. However, because of its trend towards self-
sustenance, which will be discussed shortly, CBFPS will no longer be provided
with grants from IPPF from 1979 to 1982. Only family planning devices will be
donated to CBFPS. Thanks to Mechai's farsightedness on this foreseeable

shortfall of funds in the previous years, JOICFP (The Japanese Organization for International Cooperation in Family Planning) and US AID (the United States Agency for International Development) were successfully approached to provide additional funding for CBFPS in 1976 and 1977.

Funding from JOICFP has been secured primarily for the Integrated Family Planning and Parasite Control Program (FPPC), started in June 1976. Late in 1977, through Mechai's persuasive effort, JOICFP agreed to extend the funding period from four to six consecutive years. The financial support from this source has favorably shown an upward trend.

US AID's financial assistance has been directed towards the Integrated Family Planning, Health and Hygiene Program (FPHH), in which CBFPS acts as an executing agency under the close supervision of MOPH of Thailand. Apart from grants, contraceptives, condoms and health supply kits will be supplied to CBFPS through MOPH. Funding of this program commenced in June 1977 and will continue for a total period of four years. US AID has so far expressed a strokg support for CBFPS.

Table 13 presents CBFPS's sources of family planning commodities for the year 1974 to 1977. In addition to these commodities, CBFPS has also received a number of other kits and equipment in support of its motivational activities, such as audio-visual aids, motorcycles, motor vehicles, and so forth.

Table 13

CBFPS's Sources Contraceptives and Condoms
(1975-1977)*

| Source | 1977 | | 1975 | |
	Contraceptives (Cycle)	Condoms (Dozen)	Contraceptives (Cycle)	Condoms (Dozen)
IPPF	249,933	--	3,398,752	1,317,504
JOICFP	--	2,000	--	--
US AID**	1,700,000	84,000	--	--
MOPH	--	--	28,800	300,000
TOTAL	1,949,933	86,000	3,427,552	1,617,50

*Nil for 1976

**Through MOPH.

Source: CBFPS

FINANCIAL PERFORMANCE AND FINANCIAL POSITION

Because of the absence of consolidated financial statements of CBFPS and a complete financial picture of FPPC and FPHH, the financial analysis gives particular emphasis to CBFPS's performance achieved under IPPF's funds.

Table 14 shows CBFPS's efforts in generating local income, primarily
through the sale of donated contraceptive supplies. As can be seen, reliance
on grants from IPPF had shown a declining trend from 89 percent in 1974 to 38
percent in 1977. More than 85 percent of the local income was derived from
the sale of donated condoms and contraceptives, whereas less than 15 percent
was accounted for by the sale of family planning promotional commodities (fund
raising program). Despite this favorable trend towards quasi-selfsufficiency,[1]
comparison between the actual and budgeted local income of CBFPS's programs
reveals an unfavorable performance (Table 15).

Table 14

Percentage Share of Local Income
to Total Funds Received (IPPF Grants)
(1974-1977)

Source	1977 Amount	%	1976 Amount	%	1975 Amount	%	1974 Amount	%
IPPF Grants	$199,507	38	$260,000	47	$275,000	72	$235,000	89
Local Income Through Commodity Sale	328,674	62	298,391	53	105,126	28	30,500	11
TOTAL	$528,181	100	$558,391	100	$380,126	100	$265,500	100

Source: CBFPS.

Table 15

Comparison of Actual and Budgeted Local Income
By Program, 1976-1977* (IPPF Funds)

Program	1977 Budgeted	Actual	Variance	1976 Budgeted	Actual	Variance
Village Program	$212,874	$179,903	(32,971)	$130,528	$139,220	$ 8,692
Public Institution Program	43,247	27,456	(15,791)	52,852	27,813	(25,039)
Private Sector Program	201,450	105,416	(96,034)	166,240	99,275	(66,965)
Fund Raising Program**	65,000	15,898	(49,102)	60,000	32,083	(27,291)
TOTAL	$522,571	$328,674	(193,897)	$409,620	$298,391	(110,603)

*Data for 1974 and 1975 were not available
**Sale of promotional items initiated by CBFPS.

Source: CBFPS.

[1]The situation in which internally generated funds derived from donated
family planning products fully cover all project expenditures.

The expenditure structure of IPPF funded programs consists primarily of five main components: operations, administration, research and evaluation, fund raising, and fixed assets, as shown in Table 16. It is not surprising that expenditures for operations had gained an increasingly higher proportion in the overall structure, since new districts of the Village Program were consecutively opened in the past. This can also be anticipated to be the trend in the foreseeable future.

Table 16

Expenditure Structure of
IPPF Funded Program Activities
(1975-1977)

Category	1977		1976		1975	
	Amount	%	Amount	%	Amount	%
Operations	$310,629	63	$328,094	59	$232,419	55
Administration	91,964	19	114,566	20	100,074	24
Research & Evaluation	52,172	10	82,014	15	55,026	13
Fund Raising*	28,637	6	27,818	5	26,913	6
Fixed Assets	11,469	2	7,562	1	9,053	2
TOTAL	$494,871	100	$560,054	100	$423,485	100

*Comprising product and selling costs.

Source: CBFPS.

Comparison of actual and budgeted expenditures of these IPPF funded activities (Table 17) displays a satisfactory performance on an overall basis in the two recent years. Particularly, actual expenditure for operations was appreciably favorable in each of the years.

On the program basis, it is clear that similar favorable results were also obtained, as shown in Table 18.

In overall terms as may be seen from Table 19, CBFPS achieved a favorable operational performance for IPPF-funded activities in 1977. The performance in 1976 also saw a net surplus, despite an operating deficit which was due primarily to gains from other income. Table 20 presents comparative financial positions of CBFPS in regard to IPPF-funded activities.

Table 17

Comparison of Actual and Budgeted Expenditure
of IPPF Funded Activities (1976-1977)

	IN US $					
	1977			1976		
Category	Budgeted	Actual	Variance	Budgeted	Actual	Variance
Operations	$432,185	$310,629	121,556	$393,756	$328,094	65,662
Administration	121,625	91,964	29,661	109,810	114,566	(4,756)
Research & Evaluation	107,068	52,172	54,896	112,475	82,014	30,461
Fund Raising	50,000	28,637	21,363	50,000	27,818	22,182
Fixed Assets	11,200	11,469	(269)	4,000	7,562	(3,562)
TOTALS	$722,078	$494,871	227,207	$670,041	$560,054	109,987

Source: CBFPS.

Table 18

Comparison of Actual and Budgeted Expenditure
of IPPF Funded Activities--By Program (1976-1977)

	1977			1976		
Program	Budgeted	Actual	Variance	Budgeted	Actual	Variance
Village Program	$181,420	$120,211	61,209	$182,615	$142,263	40,352
Public Institution Program	31,916	11,521	20,404	30,362	25,585	4,777
Private Sector Program	70,000	69,222	778	55,350	47,190	8,160
Fund Raising Program	50,000	28,637	21,363	50,000	27,818	22,182

Source: CBFPS

Table 19

Community-Based Family Planning Services
Statement of Income and Retained Earnings
(IPPF Funds)

| | | IN US $ | |
	1977	1976	1975
INCOME			
IPPF Grant	174,527.00	260,000.00	275,000.00
Local Income			
--Contraceptive	320,318.49	272,355.32	80,968.86
--Fund Raising	17,176.48	34,387.45	27,546.40
	512,021.97	566,742.77	383,515.36
Less Discounts and			
Returns Inwards	8,821.46	8,351.94	3,388.98
Total Revenue	503,200.51	558,390.83	380,126.38
EXPENDITURE			
Administration	91,964.00	114,565.84	100,074.25
Operation I (1)	195,195.95	237,992.08	223,585.63 (3)
Operation II (2)	144,069.82	117,921.21	---
Research Evaluation	52,171.71	82,014.11	55,025.84
Fixed Assets	11,469.45	7,561.50	9,052.80
Total Expenditures	494,870.93	560,054.74	387,738.52
SURPLUS (DEFICIT) FROM			
OPERATIONS	8,899.94	(1,037.82)	(4,205.48)
OTHER INCOME (CHARGES)			
Gain (Loss) on			
Foreign Exchange	3,065.44	4,550.00	4,242.50
Other Income	--	1,575.00	2,400.41
NET SURPLUS (DEFICIT)	11,965.38	5,087.18	2,437.43

Note (1)   In-charge of Village and Public Institution Programs.
     (2)   In-charge of Private Sector and Fund Raising Programs.
     (3)   There was only one operations department in 1975

Table 20

Community-Based Family Planning Services
Balance Sheet as at December (IPPF Funds)

	IN	US	$
ASSETS	1977	1976	1975
CURRENT ASSETS			
Cash on hand and at bank	76,340.89	22,174.49	6,166.08
Advances	4,492.72	2,290.47	857.50
Other receivables			
cheque return	--	--	787.65
Office rent deposit	1,600.00	--	--
Debtors	38,849.20	45,729.89	23,309.00
Accrued income from IPPF	--	--	47,822.50
TOTAL ASSETS	121,282.81	70,194.85	78,942.73
LIABILITIES AND FUNDS			
CURRENT LIABILITIES			
Bank overdraft	--	--	8,719.95
Accrued expenses	74,335.82	14,831.85	39,976.95
Deferred income	--	20,350.00	--
TOTAL	74,335.82	35,181.85	48,696.90
FUNDS			
As at January 1	34,981.61	29,925.82	27,808.40
Net surplus (deficit)	11,965.38	5,087.18	2,437.43
Total Liabilities			
and Funds	121,282.81	70,194.85	78,942.73

COST EFFECTIVENESS

        In addition to the analysis of actual versus budgeted expenditures, the
cost effectiveness of the project may be roughly determined by examination   of
certain unit costs;   that is, cost per distributor, and cost per acceptor. The
actual cost per district opened in 1976 was $1,215. With an average of 100 vil-
lage volunteers trained per district, the average cost per distributor was
$12.15. This is equivalent to merely about 50 percent of the estimated cash
outlay for opening an operational district($2,475).

The cost per acceptor attained by CBFPS amounted on the average to $2 in 1976 and 1977, as shown in Table 21. The unit cost achieved by MOPH[1] was approximately $8 which was four times higher than CBFPS's.

Table 21

Cost per Acceptor
(1976-1977)

Year	Operations Cost	Increase in No. of Acceptors	Cost/ Acceptor
1976	$142,263	65,498	$2.17
1977	120,211	57,190	$2.10

Source: CBFPS

TOWARD SELF-SUFFICIENCY

Using IPPF funded operations as a model for determining CBFPS's self-sufficiency, it may be concluded that the project is moving towards a quasi-self-sufficiency position, rather than a fully self-sufficient state. As shown in Table 22, even with donated contraceptives and condoms, CBFPS could finance only 66 percent of its expenditure in 1977. Nevertheless, the change from 1976 to 1977 was appreciable. Apparently the trend looks favorable to CBFPS's long-term existence. At any rate, the attained degree of quasi-self-sufficiency indicates a need for further funding to CBFPS. Moreover, the project will still have to acquire free or donated family planning devices as a means of generating income for financing its program operations. This also points out that CBFPS cannot attain full financial self-sufficiency under its existing earning structure.

Table 22

Degree of Self-Sufficiency Attained by CBFPS
(1976-1977)

	IN US $	
	1977	1976
Actual income from all programs	328,674	298,391
Actual expenditure required	494,871	560,054
Quasi-self-sufficiency (income/expenditure)	66%	53%

Source: CBFPS

[1]This was an average figure in 1971. No exact statistics were presently available. According to some MOPH officers interviewed, the figure   should have already reached $10.

CHAPTER 6

IMPACT AND OUTLOOK

The rapid growth of CBFPS operations within the last four years, from 23 operational districts in 1974 to 113 districts three years later and covering almost one-fourth of the total population, is by itself an indication of a positive contribution to the resolution of Thailand's population problem. The extent to which the services provided have exerted significant influence over the actual birth rate of the population, and the acceptors' attitude toward family planning as well as other relevant aspects will further determine the real impact   and effectiveness of the project. Since the mainstay of CBFPS is the Village Program, the primary emphasis is thus given particularly to this program, although the effect of the other supplementary programs is also pointed out.

OVERALL IMPACT AND EFFECTIVENESS

Implementation of CBFPS's programs has been carried out within the context of the National Family Planning Program (NFPP) of MOPH. Various aspects of the NFPP have been fruitfully contributed by the CBFPS's efforts in an attempt to improve the rural family lives.

1) On an overall basis, CBFPS has steadily increased its share in recruiting new family planning acceptors for the NFPP since its inception in 1974.

Table 23

Number of New Acceptors* Recruited by MOPH
and Non-MOPH Agencies (1974-1976)

	1976		1975		1974	
	Number	%	Number	%	Number	%
MOPH	504,439	80.5	433,165	81.0	411,897	83.3
CBFPS	65,498	10.4	43,123	8.1	22,689	4.6
Others	57,302	9.1	58,735	10.9	59,893	12.1
TOTAL	627,239	100.0	535,023	100.0	494,479	100.0

*Acceptors of IUD, pill, sterilization, and injectible methods.

Source: MOPH, Review on the NFPP, August 1977; and CBFPS's files.

From a mere 4.6 percent of total new acceptors in 1974, CBFPS was able to double its percentage share two years later and contributed more than the combined contribution of all other private and voluntary amortization.[1]   However, if we consider only the number of pill acceptors, the share had   even reached 17.4 percent in 1976 (Table 24). It should also be noted that   this impact of CBFPS's efforts reached both rural and urban populations, whereas MOPH had concentrated primarily on rural communities.

Table 24

Number of New Pill Acceptors   Recruited
By CBFPS and Non-CBFPS Agencies

	1976		1975		1974	
	Number	%	Number	%	Number	%
Non-CBFPS	311,209	82.6	301,994	87.5	282,555	92.6
CBFPS	65,498	17.4	43,123	12.5	22,689	7.4
Total	376,707	100.0	345,117	100.0	305,244	100.0

Source: MOPH, Review on the NFPP, August, 1977; and CBFPS's files.

2) The CBFPS's community-based distribution network helps extend the arms of MOPH in distributing family planning services to reach the grassroots acceptors. Since the NFPP is based on a high degree of integration of family planning with basic health services, the family planning services have been provided to villagers through MOPH's rural health network and facilities. However, the fact that existing midwifery centers in 1977 covered merely 39 percent of the total requirement of the village level should point out the important contribution of CBFPS in meeting the family planning demand in the under-served villages. Through its village distributors, CBFPS has also partially helped improve the utilization of MOPH's existing rural health facilities by referring villagers to them.

---

[1] The other non-MOPH agencies engaged in family planning are PPAT (Planned Parenthood Association of Thailand) which concentrates mainly on IEC (Information, Education, Communications) activities, the McCormick Hospital which specializes in contraceptive injectibles, as well as other voluntary organizations.

3) The CBFPS's Village Program has achieved   significant results in
reducing the pregnancy rate. The preliminary research results[1]
revealed that the pregnancy rate in the operational districts dropped by 40 percent compared with the rate prior to program implementation. A breakdown by region is shown below.

Region	Drop of Pregnancy Rate (%)
North	42.7
Northeast	45.6
Central	46.3
South	24.4
Overall	40.2

4) CBFPS has also been successful in recruiting new acceptors in the
most difficult regions of Thailand. Apart from the overall   increase in the number of acceptors among the operational districts
by 30 percent,[2] it is noticeable that the high rates of increase
in the South where large families were prevalent and in the Northeast where majority of the people were poor were also effected, as
shown below:

Region	% Increase in No. of Acceptors
North	10.8
Northeast	58.3
Central	16.4
South	61.3
Overall	29.8

5) Among the sources of family planning services in the villages,
CBFPS's distributors captured a significant share from the government units and the other private sources, although the government units still had a major share. The percentage shares of
these sources shown here were determined by CBFPS sample surveys
in 1974, 1975, and 1976.

Source of Family Planning Services	Percentage Share		
	1st Rnd	2nd Rnd	3rd Rnd
Government unit	79.4	49.4	57.5
Village Distributor (CBFPS)	--	26.7	25.1
Other private sources	20.6	17.9	12.9
Not require family planning services	--	6.0	4.5
Total	100.0	100.0	100.0

---

[1]CBFPS, the Impact and Effectiveness Survey: Data Comparison of Round 1,
2, and 3, (1974, 1975, and 1976), a preliminary report.

[2]Ibid.

The 1.6 and 5 percent decreases of the village distributor and the other private sources, respectively, were due primarily to the free contraceptives distributed by MOPH through its rural health network.

6) Despite an impressive growth rate in the cumulative number of pill acceptors, as shown below, there were also a large number of dropouts.

| | | (%) | | Programs | |
| | | | | Public | |
Year End	Total	Increase	Village	Institution	Private
1974	22,689	--	11,474	11,027	188
1975	65,812	190	47,262	17,810	740
1976	131,310	100	105,017	24,134	2,159
1977	188,500	44	160,000	26,000	2,500

A number of reasons for discontinuity were disclosed by village distributors:

a. Switching to another source of family planning services.

b. Change of family planning method from oral contraceptive to sterilization, or IUD, or injectible.

c. Being pregnant because wanting more children or forgetting to take pills.

d. Husband not residing for time being.

e. Being over reproductive age.

f. Having serious, negative side-effect after taking pills.

g. Having heard false rumors about family planning; for instance, "family planning was a Communist plan to curb the size of Thai population.

Exact statistics on the number of dropouts as well as their associated reasons have not yet been available.

7) CBFPS's programs can be regarded as adequate in reaching the poor. The areas covered extend to all regions of Thailand. Based on a survey,[1] about 70 percent of the population covered were farmers. Approximately 10 to 14 percent were

---

[1]CBFPS, Impact and Effectiveness Survey, First Round, 1974.

laborers and only fewer than 5 percent were business people or government employees. Only 10 percent of the population covered possessed
their own land, but lived in poorly constructed homes with only one
bedroom. The family planning services provided by CBFPS are therefore oriented towards the poor people of Thailand.

8) Utilization of IEC activities to enhance the impact and effectiveness
of the community-based program has been adequately made   by CBFPS.
These include distribution of family planning materials;   production
of wall newspapers for posting by distributors; and using audio-visual
vans to show entertainment films during which the local   distributors
and family planning services are introduced. Particular mention should
be made of a host of gimmicks used to convey messages as well as to desensitize and popularize the family planning practices among the village audience. Among them are the use of monks to bless the contraceptives to show their religious support; the condom-blowing contest;
teaching children to sing the family planning song by schoolteachers;
and renting water buffaloes for ploughing at a cheaper price for those
who practice family planning.

Nevertheless, specific targets for IEC activities have not yet been
established by CBFPS in determining (a) how many among the potential
and existing users need reinforcing messages to reassure them that
practising contraception is acceptable and safe; (b) who need to be
informed about the different methods of contraception available to
them and the pros and cons of each; and (c) who need to be educated
about the benefits of birth control to them, their children, and
their community. These activities should be aimed primarily to improving continuation rates and shifting acceptors to more reliable
and more permanent methods. Most importantly, in the longer term,
the approach should be directed at the change of values, social
norms, and practices associated with childbearing, family size,
role of women, and family life. The existing practices of CBFPS
are oriented towards a broad client base rather than any specific
categories of potential and current users.

9) CBFPS has made a significant contribution to the promotion of condoms
and vasectomies among the male acceptors in Thailand. This has been
carried out primarily through the Private Sector Program and Public
Institution Program. There is a great deal of IEC elements in this
endeavor (that is, distribution of free condoms, sale of promotional
items, and various displays of family planning products). The retail
sale of condoms also can be regarded as successful in widening the
acceptor base. Through the use of the brand name "Mechai," the sales
currently reach an average volume of 14,400 dozens of condoms per
month from being virtually nonexistent four years ago. This accomplishment has taken place, in spite of the constraint of condoms
whose quality is beyond CBFPS's control--a fact that has reportedly
created problems for the retail sales. Although exact statistics
on demand for condoms are not available, the impact of "Mechai" (a
synonym of condom in Thai language) has been felt among all sectors
of the population and should conceivably help boost the condom

industry demand.[1]

With respect to male sterilization, CBFPS's Sterilization Center and Patpong Clinic already had undertaken more than 500 cases of vasectomy by the end of 1977. A plan to cooperate with the Sterilization Association, a newly established voluntary organization specializing in vasectomy and tubal ligation for a more extensive work on this permanent contraception method has been underway.

Particular mention should also be made on an independently conducted intensive family campaign at Mahasarakam Province in Northeast Thailand between February and June 1977. The campaign was undertaken to test the possibility of utilizing existing village distributors in motivating villagers for a more permanent method, with a one-month heavy motivational inputs from CBFPS. At the end of the campaign, 717 vasectomies were solicited, exceeding the target of 600. The survey results reveal that the CBFPS village volunteers, and other motivational sources such as film showing, traditional itinerant entertainers, and others had been equally significant sources of motivation for vasectomized clients (54% and 46%, respectively). Moreover, almost one half (45%) of vasectomized customers were those who had never practised family planning before.

10) One distinctive feature that creates a negative aspect for CBFPS is its being a private organization which distributes family planning services through the sale of contraceptives. Being a private entity that implements a socially-oriented project and assumes the role of the government in providing family planning services, CBFPS is looked upon with some skepticism by several parties.[2], especially in the bureaucracy. The doubts lie primarily in its rationale for existence, coupled with its income generated from the sale of donated contraceptives. The fact that it does not have prominent social dignitaries as figureheads in its organization as do other nonprofit institutions in Thailand only aggravates the situation and further convinces skeptics that CBFPS may exist for certain individuals' private interests rather than for the society. Nevertheless, these are mostly hidden criticisms.[3] Mechai counters these negative issues by saying that only time will prove the rationale of CBFPS and by pointing out that its financial records are always open for inspection.

---

[1]It is only in recent years, when the name 'Mechai' has been widespread among people of all ages, that advertisements of certain top-brand condoms have been seen in Thai daily newspapers and on television.

[2]This information was gathered from personal interviews with a number of disinterested external parties.

[3]Except for defamatory articles in the newspaper by PPAT's staff.

OUTLOOK OF CBFPS

Future Plans and Aspirations

        Mechai, Director of CBFPS, has delineated the future plans for the next
five years as follows:

-- For 1978-1979, CBFPS will give more emphasis to solidification of activities
    in certain districts which have already been successful with family planning
    services. This will receive priority over the expansion of area coverage or
    opening up of new districts. The rationale is that CBFPS aspires to move a
    step further into a broader development process by integrating some other ser-
    vices with the existing family planning services, like low cost primary health
    care, nutrition, improved marketing opportunities for farm produce and in-
    creased income per unit of produce sold. The project proposal on Integrated
    Self-Help Village Development submitted to the Netherlands Organization for
    International Development Corporation exemplifies the approach.

-- For the remaining three years (1980-1981), the plan will reemphasize the ex-
    pansion of operational districts of the Village Program by attempting to open
    up 100 new districts per year. As for the Public Institution Program,   the
    extension of services will be made further through utilization of mobile
    industrial services.and mobile school services. Particularly, the Integrated
    Family Planning and Parasite Control Program will be expanded to cover
    primarily schools in urban rural areas. Schools with a good financial
    status will be first targeted in order to utilize this surplus income to
    finance activities in poorer institutions. Small sterilization clinic cen-
    ters will also be established by CBFPS to promote a more permanent method
    of contraception. CBFPS will finally release itself from the Private Sector
    Program, particularly, the retail condom distribution activities by sub-
    contracting the Population and Community Development Co., Ltd., to carry out
    the task.

        Recognizing the financial constraints of the project, Mechai aspires
to have direct participation and cooperation of the government. CBFPS will
still have to rely upon donor organizations in the form of free family planning devices for years to come. The current situation has, however, already
indicated a declining trend of foreign grants, as also admitted by MOPH.[1]
Looking ahead to long-term family planning in Thailand, Mechai expects locally
donated funds to support the activities, mainly from the government. He hopes
therefore that through the government budget, CBFPS can operate its programs
for the country primarily on the grounds that it is more efficient and cost
effective. Even though this is conceptually sound, he also admits that it may
take years before the government will accept the concept.

---

[1]MOPH, Review on the National Family Planning Program, August 1977, p. 4.

Outlook of the Project

    The future well-being of the CBFPS project as a whole will almost
certainly be governed by three important determinants or questions.

    The Enigma of Government Support. Under the Fourth National Family
Planning Program (1977-1981), the government (through MOPH) plans, among
other things, to implement the village distribution program for family
planning, health, and hygiene services in rural Thailand. This program
will be carried out through the village communicators and the village distributors, also known as health-post volunteers, whose number will reach
246,400 and cover all provinces, districts, and subdistricts by the end
of the Fourth Plan. These village personnel will be selected among the
community residents by villagers in close cooperation with the health officers. Each village communicator will be chosen for every cluster of 8-
15 households. Only one distributor will, however, be operating in a
village.

    The role of village communicators is primarily to perform IEC
activities within their designated clusters. They also impart necessary
information and provide proper coordination to the health officers and
the village distributors. The distributors' role encompasses all functions of the communicators, but is extended to provision of family planning, health, and hygiene services. These include primarily health care,
distribution of household drugs, and distribution of contraceptives and
condoms. All services are free-of-charge.

    This MOPH program will almost certainly pose a direct competition
to the CBFPS Village Program. Although a pilot experiment in 20 provinces
was deliberately conducted in separate areas not encroaching on the CBFPS's
operational districts in 1977, it may be expected that overlapping will
necessarily take place in 1981 when the MOPH program is fully implemented,
unless, of course, the current policy is changed. This program will directly affect the CBFPS's village distribution activities. Even though the
effect of this operational duplication cannot yet be clearly seen, distribution of free contraceptives through the government rural health centers has already exerted a strong influence over CBFPS's efforts in contraceptive distribution. Table 25 below shows the effect of the government's donation of free contraceptives, which commenced in October 1976,
on CBFPS's contraceptive distribution in the Northeast where the effect
was most felt. However, the effect did not take place until December 1976.
This unfavorable consequence was due primarily to the poverty of the people
in that region. Effect on the other regions was comparatively insignificant because of the limited coverage of health centers.

    However, the free distribution still continues and gets even more
intensified and widespread   through several other public and voluntary
organizations. It is anticipated that the remaining regions will be greatly
affected within the next few years.

    The outlook of CBFPS will therefore be significantly affected by
the extent to which the government commits its support to the project's
Village Program.

Table 25

Effect of Government Free Pills On CBFPS's
Village Program (Northeast)
July 1976 - June 1977

Monthly/Yearly	Cumulative Acceptor	Increase (Decrease)	Pill Distributed (Cycle)	Increase (Decrease)
1976				
July	21,248		9,754	
August	22,726	1,478	10,173	419
September	23,368	642	10,201	29
October	23,962	594	10,515	313
November	24,247	285	11,669	1,154
December	24,559	312	10,449	(1,220)
1977				
January	24,889	330	9,723	(726)
February	25,147	258	8,937	(753)
March	25,333	186	10,110	1,173
April	25,698	365	8,887	(1,223)
May	26,237	539	9,034	147
June	26,771	534	7,671	(1,363)

Source: CBFPS.

The Continuing Role of Mechai. It cannot be overstressed that the success
of CBFPS hinges heavily on Mechai's personality and outstanding versatility. By
his continuous representation in several international conferences, Mechai has
successfully utilized his capability in attracting foreign donor organizations
to provide financial support for family planning activities in Thailand. His
farsightedness has also contributed to a continuity of funding for the project.
Even though some other key personnel in the organization have been instrumental
in the project implementation stage, Mechai has always assumed the role of program initiator in converting creative ideas and concepts into impressive program
proposals for implementation. With his far-reaching contacts with a host of international figures and organizations, he will have to spearhead the project in
developing new programs and soliciting grants accordingly at least in the foreseeable future.

Presently, there seems to be no single CBFPS staff person who can fully
assume Mechai's indispensable role. The management succession problem will continue to exist under the current organizational setup. The only possible solution is to institutionalize management practices that are presently carried out
by Mechai. Aside from developing an understudy, the name "CBFPS" should be
promoted more extensively than the word "Mechai," and personnel should be
oriented more towards the organization. Personality should bow to structure.

With less direct involvement on Mechai's part, a potential risk may
conceivably develop in the future. The possibility is that the whole organization may develop into a less enthusiastic, less energetic, and less efficient
entity than it is today if it loses the personal encouragement and instigation

of Mechai. Nevertheless, this simply points up the necessity of having a good organization plan and strategy for the future under the guidance and leadership of a director, whoever he may be, if CBFPS wishes to survive in the long run.

Continued Procurement of Free Contraceptive Devices. As earlier pinpointed, CBFPS is not financially self-sufficient,despite the donated contraceptives and condoms. It will have to continue to acquire these devices free-of-charge in order to utilize them to generate income for financing the program operations. From this perspective, it may be anticipated that the CBFPS project will not be able to reach, under the present program operational structure, the stage of complete self-sufficiency in which revenue from the sale of its own products, without donations, will be sufficient to support the overall program operations.

The prospect of the CBFPS project, contemplated from this particular angle, dwells primarily upon its ability to seek alternative program operational structures in which locally generated income can be sufficiently earned to cover its operational expenditures as well as to finance its continued growth.

CHAPTER 7

CONCLUSIONS AND LESSONS

Upon reaching the current stage of development, the CBFPS project has undoubtedly brought about a significant and profound impact on the family planning
practices in rural as well as urban Thailand. Not only have its present achievements served as another practical confirmation of the concept of nonclinic, community-based family planning service distribution, the project has provided   an
impressive start from which institutional development efforts in the grassroots
sector of the population can be firmly established for greater effectiveness. The
experience and lessons learned from this experiment should therefore help provide
conceptual as well as practical bases for determining its replicability in   other
areas and parts of the world.

CONCLUSIONS BASED ON CURRENT ATTAINMENTS

It is unfair to evaluate the overall success of the project at this early
stage (3 years and 8 months after its inception). The conclusions drawn below
were arrived at primarily from a review of CBFPS's current achievements, and they
take into account its future potential in attempting to improve rural family life.

1) The project is successful in its endeavor to provide easy and conven-
    ient access to and information about contraceptive methods through
    local mass participation. For the first time family planning services
    have been available within the village communities through a non-
    government distribution network, reducing time and cost of acquiring
    the services. Also proven is the concept that family planning ser-
    vices can be appropriately provided by a "man-on-the spot," whether
    he is farmer, storekeeper, or teacher, without causing hazards to
    the acceptors.

2) The village-based distribution network of family planning services
    helps to transcend and overcome the cultural barriers existing in
    different localities, and thus to provide a basis for enhancing the
    acceptability of change in a community. The key agents of change
    are well-established in the locality where demand is felt.

3) Despite the key role of village volunteers in distributing contra-
    ceptives, the project also requires a significant amount of super-
    vision to ensure performance effectiveness of all field personnel
    concerned. Since the social marketing aspect of the community-
    based distribution is essential to the effort towards self-
    sustenance, the sales collection system for a wide program coverage
    has to be well planned as well as sufficiently flexible to cope with
    any anomalies that may transpire. The system for the resupplying of

stock at the village level also has to be functional in providing adequate and timely logistical support to the distributors. Put in another way, apart from the proper supervision
over the performance of the field workers, effective systems
must be set up to prop up the "marketing" element of the
approach.

4)   The project is effective in reaching the rural and urban poor.
With its systematic doorstep coverage, the project is flexible
and far-reaching in its distribution of contraceptives.   The
price is only one-half to one-third of the market prices   for
those who can afford it, and it is free for those who cannot.
Nevertheless, because of financial constraints, the project
has to effect a balance between the saleable and the promotional
commodities in order to ensure its operational feasibility in
the long run. It should also be borne in mind that acquiring
contraceptives at a price creates greater appreciation of their
value than if they were obtained free-of-charge, hence a
greater likelihood of more widespread family planning practice.
In other words, it is not enough merely to supply contraceptives to reach the intended clientele;   there must be assurance
that they will be used by acceptors.

5)   Effectiveness in soliciting acceptance of family planning by
the rural community calls for adequate motivational activities
as well as awareness of the destructive effect of adverse
rumors. The word-of-mouth approach utilized by a distributor
and the work of a visiting team that saturates the targeted
community are barely adequate. Tactfulness and a carefully
planned effort to understand false rumors and to counter them
has been proven by CBFPS to be essential in gaining acceptance
from the intended clientele.

6)   The CBFPS project is commendable in its ability to seize and
utilize the available opportunity. Because of a limited
acceptance of condoms in the rural areas, the project directs
its distribution efforts to the more educated urban communities with a view to desensitizing the family planning practice
and generating income for financing the operations. Achievement has been effective in broadening the base of condom
users, promoting the project among the urban population,
and enhancing the possibility of attaining a degree of
self-sufficiency.

LESSONS LEARNED FROM THE PROJECT

The experience and lessons learned from the CBFPS experiment
described below may well serve as a basis, wherever applicable, for
implementation of family planning programs in other countries.

1)   The successful development of a project depends heavily
upon a strong and dynamic leader. In a project of this nature where the
ability to attract funds is as important as the ability successfully to
implement it, the project requires farsightedness and originality on the
part of the leader. Since the termination of outside support is normally
predictable, the leader will have to project ahead the likely programs to

be initiated and drawn up for further funding to continue the project's existence. In the case of CBFPS where permanent sources of funds are not available,
competing for survival is of paramount importance.

2) Another significant aspect of a project of this type is the necessity
of cooperation between the public and private sectors. It is apparent that the
government represents the only establishment at the grassroots level. Because
of this fact a project that is run by a private agency must seek the close cooperation of the government for its very survival. Similarly, a project should by
all means clarify its objectives and maintain a low profile as far as relations
with the government departments are concerned. No attempt should be made to
threaten competition with the bureaucracy. Instead, due credit should be attributed to the government programs to prove the project's sincere support.
Actually, utilization of local government bodies means cost savings and can be
effective, so long as proper supervision is given and adequate incentives are
available.

3) The success of a project is determined primarily by the effectiveness of community-based activities. CBFPS exemplifes this truth very well.
It has been proved that with proper assistance the villagers can effectively
help themselves. The key element to their effectiveness lies basically in the
identification, screening, and selection of the village volunteers who will act
as the prime change agents and motivators of new concepts and ideas. Continuity
of services can also be provided in the rural communities through the village
distributors.

4) Planning and monitoring activities represent significant ingredients
to project effectiveness. Extensive coverage of operations and the regional
differences of the participating people in the project entails these important
functions. Planning is needed in every phase of project implementation, from
the preliminary survey to the actual distribution of services. It is also
essential to assure cost effectiveness in opening a new district as well as
the ability to provide services for intended acceptors. Monitoring also helps
provide feedback of the operational performance to management to develop proper
policy and strategy. Most importantly, the project must be flexible and resi-
lient, able to account for the operational disparities and to resolve them
appropriately.

5) To carry out the tasks effectively, a successful project needs
sense of commitment among its staff. Even though this depends heavily upon
the ability of the project leader, the willingness of the staff to contribute
enthusiastically to the project's success is vital. The project must be identified as their own, rather than pictured as a set of tasks imposed from without.
With the survival of the project hinging upon external funds and donations,
CBFPS staff feel a strong responsibility to exert their best efforts in working
for the project's success.

6) To be successful, it is also imperative that a project maintain
good public relations generally. Although CBFPS chooses to be controversial
in putting across the family planning ideas to the public, it has been able
to solicit cooperation from most agencies it approaches. Animosity or hostility should be kept to a strategic minimum. Any problem of misunderstand-
ing should be solved in a direct and understanding manner. CBFPS has been
quite successful in learning these somewhat difficult truths.

7) The use of family planning strategy in introducing self-supporting development programs can be very effective. This is so primarily because family planning is simple; it requires low capital investment and running costs on the part of the project proponent; it calls for minimum or bearable cost on the part of the clientele, but gives tangible advantages to them in a relatively short time without demanding profound changes in their way of life. Through the family planning village distributors, many other fruitful messages and services indispensable to the community can be further conveyed and provided to the village people. Since the distributors are actually the villagers' own neighbors, the cultural acceptability of new ideas will be greatly improved.

8) The manning of volunteer workers is crucial to the success of such a project. It is important that the contributions of these people are recognized by all parties involved. The CBFPS experience indicates that the volunteers want to gain the respect of their community by working primarily for the project rather than for more tangible benefits. They feel proud to be consulted by their neighbors. Nevertheless, continuous supervision over their performances should also be maintained and conducted by well-informed local personnel.

9) Wholly aside from aiming at recruiting family planning service acceptors in the short run, the primary purpose of educating the rural people on more profound matters such as child-bearing, women's role in the family, and family life in general should also be kept in mind. The key to success in this area lies in continuity of communication and, indeed of, education itself.

ANNEX   I

SUMMARY OF COMPARATIVE FINDINGS
OF IMPACT AND EFFECTIVENESS SURVEYS
FIRST TO THIRD ROUND*
(1974,   1976,   1977)

Introduction

To determine the impact and effectiveness of the CBFPS's Village Program
which has been implemented primarily through the village distributors, the following hypotheses were postulated as criteria:

1. The pregnancy rate at the time of interview must decline.

2. The existing number of women practising birth control must increase.

3. The number of women wishing to practise birth control in the future
   must increase.

4. The number of children born during the period of these surveys
   (0-2 years of age) must decrease.

5. The children born during the period of these surveys must result
   from planned pregnancies.

6. The attitude towards birth control must improve.

7. The ideal number of children must decrease.

8. The spacing of each birth must be longer (more years).

9. The number of villagers having heard or knowing of the work
   of village distributors must increase.

10. The number of villagers seeking services from village distributors
    must increase.

Comparative Data

The characteristics of the survey sample of 2,000 females included being
married, between 15-44 years of age, and widely dispersed in all regions of Thailand based on the population density of each region. About 45 percent of the
females in the sample were 20-29 years old and about 70 percent were farmers
with 4-year schooling.

---

*Translated from CBFPS's preliminary report which was presented in Thai.

Comparative Findings

The comparative findings are shown in tabular form below.

Table 1

Percentage of Pregnant Women at Time of Interview
and Percentage Reduction in Pregnancy Rate

| | Operational Districts | | | Reduction of Pregnancy Rate | |
	1st Round	2nd Round	3rd Round	1st Round - 3rd Round	
Overall	13.7%	12.3	8.2%	40.2%	
North	8.4	5.5	4.9	42.7	
Northeast	15.0	15.2	8.3	45.6	
Central	13.4	13.2	7.2	46.3	
South	17.2	11.6	13.0	24.4	

Table 2

Percentage of Women Practising Birth Control
and Percentage Increase

| | Operation Districts | | | Percentage Increase | |
	1st Round	2nd Round	3rd Round	1st Round - 3rd Round	
Overall	34.6%	40.9%	44.9%	29.8%	
North	61.2	64.1	67.6	10.8	
Northeast	24.0	29.3	38.0	58.3	
Central	40.3	46.5	46.9	16.4	
South	18.6	31.4	30.0		

Table 3

Percentage of Women Wishing to Practice
Birth Control in the Future

| Region | Operational Districts | | |
	1st Round	2nd Round	3rd Round
Overall	66.7%	76.4%	74.1%
North	82.0	87.9	84.1
Northeast	64.3	72.6	77.0
Central	67.9	79.0	76.2
South	52.8	58.0	55.4

Table 4

Percentage of Couples Having Planned Pregnancies
during 1st Round and 3rd Round

Region	3rd Round	
	Planned	Unplanned
Overall	71.1%	28.9%
North	85.3	14.7
Northeast	72.0	38.0
Central	68.5	31.5
South	65.2	34.8

Table 5

Percentage of Women Agreeing to Birth Control
and Percentage Increase

Region	Operational Districts			Percentage Increase (Decrease)
	1st Round	2nd Round	3rd Round	1st Round - 3rd Round
Overall	91.3%	93.8%	97.1%	6.4%
North	98.9	100.0	98.4	(0.5)
Northeast	95.9	94.2	99.0	3.2
Central	85.7	92.9	96.2	12.3
South	83.1	95.5	93.8	12.9

Table 6

Ideal Number of Children
(Mode Average)

Region	Operational Districts	
	2nd Round	3rd Round
Overall	2	2
North	2	2
Northeast	4	4
Central	4	3
South	2	2

Table 7

Number of Years of Spacing Each Birth
(Mode Average)

Region	Operational Districts	
	2nd Round	3rd Round
Overall	over 4 yrs.	over 4 yrs.
North	3	over 4
Northeast	over 4	over 4
Central	over 4	3
South	over 4	over 4

Table 8

Percentages of Females Having Heard of
the Village Program

Region	Operational Districts	
	2nd Round	3rd Round
Overall	49.5%	78.5%
North	69.1	95.6
Northeast	56.0	94.5
Central	35.2	59.3
South	40.7	64.4

Table 9

Sources of Services of Females
Practising Birth Control

Sources	Operational Districts		
	1st Round	2nd Round	3rd Round
Village Distributor	- %	26.7%	25.1%
Government Unit*	79.4	49.4	57.5
Other Private Sources	20.6	17.9	12.9
Not Require Family Planning Devices	-	6.0	4.5
Total	100.0	100.0	100.0

*Free contraceptives have been distributed since October 1976.

THE FIRST CUSTOMER SURVEY:
PRELIMINARY FINDINGS

The total sample of CBFPS customers taken in ten districts opened in 1974 was carried out in the last quarter in 1975.   The sample size was 750 customers of which 700 were interviewed and 687 questionnaires were valid and   classified.

Age

Eighteen percent of CBFPS customers were aged between 15 and 24, while 42 percent were aged between 25 and 34. Customers aged between 35 and 44 accounted for 35 percent of pill users. Only 4 percent of all users were aged between   45 and 49 and less than 1 percent were older than 50.

Education

Seventy percent of the customers had completed four years of education while 14 percent had between one and three years and 13 percent had no education at all. Husbands, however, had slightly higher educational attainment than their wives.

Employment

Most of the pill customers were gainfully employed, the major occupation being agriculture which accounted for 80 percent of all occupations. Only 4 percent of the customers were not gainfully employed or not paid for their work. Nine percent worked as hired labor and 5 percent were shopkeepers. It was noticeable that in two water districts the proportion of customers who were employed workers was higher than in the other eight districts. The pattern of employment was similar for the husbands of clients, with 80 percent of all husbands employed in agriculture.

During the time of interview, 7 percent of the women were pregnant. Fifty-four percent of the women had between three and six children, 32 percent had two children, 12 percent had upward of seven but less than   ten while 3 percent did not have any children at the time of the survey.

Nineteen percent said they wanted additional children, 62 percent wanted only one more and 28 percent wanted two more while 8 percent wanted three more. The remainder did not specify how many more children they wanted.

Knowledge, Attitude and Practise

The majority of customers knew more than one method of family planning. All customers knew about oral contraceptives while almost all knew of the IUD. Ninety-three percent and 85 percent knew of female and male sterilization respectively while 70 percent knew of the condom.

The survey revealed that 75 percent of the present pill acceptors said that taking the pill was their most popular choice of contraceptive method while 12 percent preferred female sterilization, 5 percent preferred injectables, 2 percent preferred male sterilization and just over 1 percent preferred the IUD. It was noticeable that only 0.7 percent preferred condoms, while 2 percent said they were not sure which they liked best.

Source of Contraceptives

Twenty-four percent of the women interviewed were not using contraceptives at the time of the survey. Of the remaining 76 percent or 532 customers, 98 percent said they were getting their oral contraceptives from CBFPS distributors. Of these 14 percent said they were also occasionally getting pills from the government health centers, 5 percent, other sources which indicated that they were switching their source of supply from time to time.

In matching names of the customers and the record-keeping books of distributors, it was confirmed that 98 percent of all customers interviewed had actually received pills from CBFPS distributors, despite the fact that their names were on the list.

Ninety-two percent of customers received their oral contraceptives exclusively from one distributor while 8 percent received oral contraceptives from more than one distributor. In three districts, the survey revealed that customers moved from distributor to distributor more than in other areas, in particular the districts of Kok Samrong and Bang Nam Priew and Ban Phaew in which 20, 15, and 10 percent respectively alternated from one distributor to another whenever convenient.

Customer Satisfaction

Fifty-seven percent of the customers said they collected their pills from the house or depot of the distributor, 34 percent from the shops or stores operated by the distributor while 4 percent said the distributor delivered contraceptives to their houses.

Forty-five percent of customers said they collected their contraceptives only in the evening while 25 percent said there was no particular time. Twenty-six percent collected their pills at different times ranging from early morning, late morning to early afternoon. Only 5.5 percent said that they collected their pills at night. The survey also showed how customers purchased their pills. Seventy-seven percent said they walked to collect their pills from the distributor, 10 percent said they went by boat--this was confined to the two water districts of Ban Phaew and Bang Nam Priew.

Seventy-two percent of pill customers said they spent less than 15 minutes in travelling time while 17 percent spent between 15 and 25 minutes and 6 percent between half an hour in purchasing pills.

Eight customers said they were not satisfied with the contraceptive service. Half of this number was in the district of Yasothorn where the customers said that their distributor was selling at a price higher than the health center (5 baht or 25 US cents). Two cases were reported in the district of Sri Chiengmai where customers complained that the distributor did not have sufficient time to provide them with adequate information and service and one customer said that the distributor did not have pills at the time of request.

On the availability of contraceptives, 94 percent of all customers said that they were able to purchase pills each time they made a visit to the distributor, the rest said that at times the distributor did not have sufficient stock or the distributor was not available at the time of visit.

Knowledge of CBFPS Distribution Program

All pill customers had good knowledge of CBFPS activities. Sixty percent said they had heard of the program for the first time directly from the distributor. Twenty-five percent from friends and neighbors, 4 percent from relatives, while 3 percent said they knew from nurses, 2.6 percent from the depot sign and 2 percent from the village headmen. Ninety-nine percent of the customers said they were satisfied that a community representative was providing oral contraceptives with the following reasons being given: the majority (78 percent) said it was very convenient since no transporation was necessary. Thirty-seven percent said that it was quick and convenient in terms of ease in getting oral contraceptives. Twenty percent said that the distributor was extremely friendly, while 5 percent said that the credit system made available by some distributors was a major reason in preferring community distributors.

Only five customers said they were not satisfied that a lay community person was the distributor of oral contraceptives, saying such things as only drug stores should dispense pills,there was no physical examination, the pills provided by distributors caused side effects, the pills should be given out free, and fear of the pills not being the genuine contraceptives.

COMMUNITY-BASED FAMILY PLANNING SERVICES
THE FIRST DISTRIBUTOR SURVEY: PRELIMINARY FINDINGS

The survey was carried out during October-November in ten of the 24 districts launched by the CBFPS in the final quarter of 1974. The sample size was 450 of which 93 percent were interviewed.

Sex

Sixty-two percent of the distributors were male and 38 percent were female.

Age

Seventy-six percent of male distributors were aged 35 and above while 70 percent of the female distributors were younger than 35 years of age.

Occupation

All but 1 percent of distributors had a full-time occupation or profession, of which 38 percent were rice farmers, 39 percent shop-keepers, 7 percent crop-farmers, 3 percent were teachers. The others included postmen, village headmen, silk weavers, traditional midwives or traditional medicine men. This last group accounted for 4 percent of the total. The others represented vegetable growers, hired workers and livestock farmers. Only 1 percent of the distributors did not have a full-time occupation. Seventy-one percent of the distributors also had a secondary occupation: one-fifth of the distributors said their secondary occupation was shopowner, 12 percent said they were farmers and 9 percent hired workers. The other 6 percent were market garden-ers and 2 percent raised livestock.

Record-keeping of Pill Customers

Most distributors said they had no difficulties in keeping records of acceptors while 8 percent said they experienced the following differ-ences:

1. Not enough time (4.3%)

2. Did not fully understand the form (1.59%)

3. Unable to get complete information on acceptors (0.91%)

4. Cannot read or write, could not identify the types of pills to be recorded or could read but could not write (1.1%)

Twenty-two percent of the distributors said they did not keep records themselves but somebody in the household helped in record-keeping of acceptors. This is broken down as follows:

-- 10 percent said their spouse helped
-- 6 percent said sons or daughters helped
-- 3 percent said relatives helped and, 0.2 percent said the neighbors
-- 3 percent said the supervisors helped during their regular monthly trips.

Contraceptives

Eighty-three percent of the distributors said that they were satisfied that the present price being charged by the program was the correct and acceptable price, while 15 percent said it was too expensive and two percent said it was too cheap. Less than one percent expressed no opinion.

Sixty-six percent of the distributors said that villagers did not want colored condoms; 18 percent said there was demand and 16 percent were not sure.

On the question of injectible contraceptives, 46 percent of the distributors said that villagers did not want them while 42 percent said villagers wanted injectibles. Twelve percent were not sure. As for spermicides, 70 percent of the distributors said there was no requirement by the people while 27 percent did not know what spermicides were and three percent said there was some demand.

Seventy-four percent of the distributors said that they have enough contraceptives stock each month, 26 percent said some months they did not have enough contraceptives which was due to the following reasons:

1. Did not receive sufficient supply from the supervisor (9%).
2. There were generally more customers than anticipated (8%).
3. Unexpected increase of customers in a specific month and stock ran out (5%).
4. Other reasons were as follows:
   a. Not able to contact supervisor (2%).
   b. Slow delivery of pills (2%).
   c. Distributor was not home when supervisor visited (1%).
   d. Lost stock of contraceptives (.23%).

Methods of collection of proceeds from sales by supervisors according to the distributors were as follows:

1. The supervisor came and collected from the distributors each month (81%).

2. Supervisor came and collected occasionally but not every month (10%).

3. Distributors took the money to the supervisor in town every month (4%).

4. Distributors occasionally went to town and gave the money to the supervisor (2%).

5. Other methods accounted for 2% including handing the money to the doctors at the local health centers.

Unfavorable Elements or Comments which Distributors Heard from the Villagers

Eight percent of the distributors interviewed said they had at one time or another heard villagers say the following unfavorable things about CBFPS distribution system:

1. The quality of the pills was dubious, they did not dissolve when eaten and it was possible to be crippled by the pills.

2. Approximately 2.3 percent had heard villagers say that they did not like the program because there was no physical examination. Some said that it was an unnecessary burden for other people to work as distributors, some said they did not like some persons who became distributors.

3. Did not have sufficient faith in the ability of the distributor (0.9%).

4. It is a foreign imperialist plot to destroy Thailand (0.68%).

5. Against religion (0.23%).

6. Against Thai culture (0.23%).

7. A government health worker had said that "if you buy from the government health centre the money goes to the State, if you buy from the distributor it goes to an individual."

Performance

CBFPS distribution records showed that male shopkeeper-distributors aged between 35-39 years had recruited the largest number of acceptors.

Attitude Towards Abortion

Fifty-eight percent of the distributors interviewed said they did not agree with abortion being available in the event of contraceptive failure, while 42 percent said they agreed. The same proportion said that they were against abortion as a method when a family had enough children, while 42 percent believed it should be regarded as an additional method.

ANNEX IV

TRAINING PROGRAM SCHEDULE AT DISTRICT AUDITORIUM
BANMEE DISTRICT, LOPBURI PROVINCE
July 31, 1976

TIME	ACTIVITY
8.00 a.m.	Registration of distributors and materials distribution
8:45 a.m.	Opening remarks by Chief District Officer
9:00 a.m.	Lecture on 'Population Problems and Family Planning' by CBFPS's Village Program Operations Division Head
9:45 a.m.	Address on 'Objectives and History of CBFPS' by Mechai Viravaidya, CBFPS's Director
10:15 a.m.	Break
10.30 a.m.	Film showing on 'Physiology and Family Planning'
11.00 a.m.	Lecture on 'Contraception Methods and their Misconceptions' by Medical Officer of the District Hospital
12.00 p.m.	Lunch and distribution of contraceptives and condoms
13.00 p.m.	Explanations on record-keeping and operational procedures on price, delivery, and procurement of contraceptives by CBFPS's staff
14.05 p.m.	Lecture on 'How to Motivate and Solicit Acceptors' by Mechai Viravaidya
14.45 p.m.	Break
15.00 p.m.	Open discussions and problem answering by Mechai Viravaidya and Medical Officer
15.45 p.m.	Closing remarks by Chief District Officer

ANNEX V

A PROJECT PROPOSAL OF THE
COMMUNITY-BASED FAMILY PLANNING SERVICES

INTEGRATED SELF-HELP VILLAGE DEVELOPMENT:
A FERTILITY-RELATED APPROACH
TO
COMMUNITY DEVELOPMENT

SUBMITTED TO

NETHERLANDS ORGANIZATION
FOR INTERNATIONAL DEVELOPMENT COOPERATION

OCTOBER 1977

Objective of the Project

        The operating objective of this rural development project is
to train existing and successful village family planning volunteer workers
to be key agents of change in a self-help, integrated development process:
the terminal objective is to reduce fertility and improve livelihood opportunities for village families and communities.

        The effective practice of family planning of a community will be
used as a starting point to launch a broad, integrated, village level development program. The greater the degree of participation and success of a
community's fertility management, the greater the availability of livelihood
and development opportunities, services and facilities. These will include:

1. Comprehensive Family Planning Services
2. Low Cost Primary Health Care
3. Nutrition
4. Improved Marketing Opportunities for Farm Produce and
    Increased Income Per Unit of Produce Sold
5. Cheaper Raw Materials, Seeds, Fertilizer and Other Goods
    Direct From Factory
6. Low Cost Farm Animal and Farm Equipment Rental Service
7. Low Interest Rate Loan (Group Non-Pregnancy Farm Loans)
    With Special Rebates Ranging from Reduced Interest
    Rates for Borrowers for a Pregnancy-Free Year
    to Amortization of Loan Capital Through Recruitment
    of New Members

8. Barefoot Teacher Service
9. Technical Advice in Agriculture and Home Industries

The project is aimed at small village farmers, their families and communities.

It is envisaged that successful communities will be given assistance to create agricultural, marketing, credit and health cooperatives, and to act as demonstration areas for other villages.

PROGRAM IMPLEMENTATION

Location and Choice

The proposed site for the project is Chieng Rai, Thailand's northernmost province, with a population of 1,300,000 and land area of 20,069 square kilometers, of which 64 percent are mountains. It is one of the largest provinces yet isolated from the rest of the country. Transportation cost and profiteering have made services expensive to the villagers. Chieng Rai is in the center of the golden triangle of opium growing, with hill tribes and refugees fleeing in from neighboring Laos.

In 991 villages of the province, through its field office there, the CBFPS has trained village-based family planning volunteer workers who are supplying some basic family planning services and information to the people. It is a continuous, nonseasonal activity and through supervision and re-supply by full-time staff, the volunteer workers are part of a wider organizational framework. Approximately 89 percent of the people in Cheing Rai are engaged in agriculture with 73 percent owning their own small piece of land. Average rainfall is 2,260 millimeters per year--the lowest in the country. Twenty-five percent of the families have income of less than US$3,000 per year.

These volunteer workers have learned and have performed their tasks remarkably well, enabling Chieng Rai Province to become the leading province in Thailand in oral contraceptive users resulting in a decline of pregnancy by 41 percent in two years. This performance in family planning is likely to be a mark of their ability to handle other opportunities in community development. Experience to date confirms the wisdom of delegating action to village leaders whose performance has been careful, enthusiastic and imaginative. Many have gained prestige in their own communities through their family planning work and have become a key agent of change at the village level. Their advice in the field of family planning has been seen to work, so both what they have to offer and the wider program that supports them, are credible to the community.

This project proposal represents an addition of an economic and social component to the existing family planning program. No other similar activities or programs are being carried out in the province of Chieng Rai or anywhere else in Thailand.

On average there are 58 villages per district. Children under the age of 15 account for 53 percent of the population.

Strategy

Existing CBFPS volunteer workers and agents of change will be given special training to inform and provide a range of services to their villages. Support activities will later be provided by project staff and other specialists in training interested farmers and to release the flow of a series of services into the villages. The range and volume of these services will depend on the three program models which range from light input to comprehensive input.

SERVICES

The range of services, opportunities, and facilities available to farmers are as follows:

1. Comprehensive
2. Moderate
3. Light

Model I -- Comprehensive Input

All nine services will be available to villages which are selected for this model. A group of fifty-three villages in the district of Vieng Papao has been identified and village agents and interested community representatives will be given special training first to participate in all (or as many as possible) available development activities and be eligible to partake of all the services and benefits. Very close attention on a daily basis will be paid to this area through the placement of a full-time professional staff member. The district of Vieng Papao is one of the least developed districts with little influence from the outside major centers.

Model II -- Moderate Input

Only village agents in 150 villages from all of the other 17 districts will be instructed to participate in a limited number of development inputs and will be eligible for only a selected range of benefits. They will comprise the ten closest villages to the local CBFPS district supervisors' home. They will be given the main responsibility of coordinating the activities. Additional guidance and supervision will be provided by the project manager and other staff to be stationed at the CBFPS field office in the capital district of Chieng Rai Province.

Model III -- Light Input

A more limited level of opportunity will be provided to villages which fall under this category. Any of the 991 villages in the entire province can avail itself of the services but the people must use more of their own initiative once the program is made known to the people.

EVALUATION

During the first year, prior to program launch, a random sample base line survey will be conducted to record certain socioeconomic data as well as attitudes and demand of people to enable the measurement of the impact and effectiveness of the program over specific periods of time and to facilitate program adjustment. This survey will be repeated on an annual basis. The information gathered in these surveys will be utilized in conjunction with data collected in earlier CBFPS surveys and other on-going monitored service statistics within the project.

At the end of the first year, successful villages initially eligible for only Model II and Model III inputs will become eligible for Model I comprehensive input based on achievement in fertility management and development progress. At the same time, villages which had been selected for the comprehensive input in the first year would have many of the available services curtailed if they register little achievement.

INTEGRATION SCHEDULE AND MIX

Integration of various development activities of the program will occur at two levels, namely

1. Vertical integration within each broad development discipline
   or sector; and

2. Horizontal integration of one discipline or sector into another.

The first step is vertical integration in the sector of health, with sequential (horizontal) integration into other sectors such as agriculture, industry, finance, and education. While horizontal integration takes place, further vertical integration can also occur in other sectors simultaneously.

Initially the most successful volunteer workers from villages with the highest family planning practice rates will be brought together for additional training to become primary health care workers to provide household drugs for basic illness and anthelmintics (for intestinal parasites) for their villagers. Each agent will receive an incentive on the volume of all goods and products distributed.

In the event that the first step results in an increase in family planning practice rate and improvement of level of health, the second element is introduced--horizontal integration into the discipline of agriculture, by launching the "Better Market Program," or improved marketing opportunities, whereby families that control fertility and participate in the health scheme can get approximately 30 percent more for some of their agricultural produce by depositing them at the house of the distributor. A project truck will take these products to pre-arranged market where a higher price can be obtained without deduction for profit by middlemen. A margin will be deducted for transporation to be later used to pay for the school-health care of the village. They can also buy consumer and investment goods more cheaply, again arranged by CBFPS and delivered by truck. Farmers who initially fall under Model II will have their produce handled by the local CBFPS supervisor, while Model III villages will have to come to the field office themselves if they wish to have better marketing opportunities.

The type of produce can expand as the program grows. Families and villages that have participated and demonstrated success will be eligible for a wide variety of resources needed for farming including cheap high-yielding seeds, quality livestock, fertilizer and pesticide purchases on credit, low rental farm machinery and implements, inward and outward marketing service and other credit facilities to build up the social and economic structure of their communities. A small margin for services rendered will be deducted by the project to help meet operating costs of program expansion and cover losses.

TRAINING IN AGRICULTURAL AND FOOD PRODUCTION
INPUT FOR THE INTENSIVE MODEL (MODEL I)

Seeds and Saplings

1. Rice
2. Vegetables
3. Fruits
4. Feed Grains
5. Mushrooms
6. Maize
7. Oil Seeds
8. Tobacco
9. Cotton
10. Sericulture

Farm Animals

1. Pigs
2. Chickens
3. Fishes
4. Buffaloes

ANNEX VI

COMMUNITY-BASED FAMILY SERVICES EDUCATIONAL
ATTAINMENT OF SUPERVISORY STAFF

NAME	Educational Attainment	Position Title
1. Mr. Tavatchai Tritongyoo	B.A. (Economics)	Deputy Director
2. Mr. Praveen Payapvipapong	M.P.H. (Public Health)	Division Head --Operations Div. I
3. Mr. Tanothai Sookdhis	B.A. (Economics)	Division Head --Operations Div. II
4. Miss Somchit Tipprapa	M.S. (Statistics)	Division Head --Finance & Admin. Div.
5. Mr. Asa Kanchanahoti	B.A. (Sociology)	Asst. Div. Head --Operations Div. II
6. Mr. Vilas Lohitkul	B.Sc. (Sanitation)	Unit Head --Operations Unit I
7. Mr. Prachai Tungriyanont	B.Sc. (Sanitation)	Unit Head --Operations Unit II
8. Mr. Sophon Siriwong	B.Sc. (Sanitation)	Unit Head --Operations Unit III
9. Mr. Somchai Phukphuancharoen	B.Sc. (Sanitation)	Unit Head --Operations Unit IV
10. Miss Siriyong Ruewiwat	M.S. (Economic Development)	Unit Head --Operations Unit V
11. Mrs. Saranrat Chaipotpanich	B.A. (Economics)	Unit Head --Operations Unit VI
12. Mr. Vilas Techo	B.Sc. (Public Health)	Unit Head --Operations Unit VII, VIII
13. Miss Sumal Jangsiricharoen	B.A. (Accounting)	Unit Head --Accounting Unit
14. Mr. Chusak Jongsamak	LL.B.	Unit Head --Administration Unit
15. Miss Rajitta Na Pattalung	M.A. (Population Studies)	Unit Head --Monitoring & Information Unit
16. Mrs. Pornthip Theriault	M.A. (Instructional Media)	Unit Head --Special Services Unit

ANNEX VII

AVERAGE SALARY SCALES (GROSS PAYS)
OF CBFPS'S STAFF*
(April 1977)

Position	Monthly Gross Pay (US$)
Copy typist	132
Personal secretary	306
Junior clerk	139
Senior clerk	179
Unit head	323
Division head	609
District supervisor	50
Field operations staff (supervision)	169

These average salaries were found to be about 12 percent below those paid by outside private sources. Although it is difficult to find the salary scales of comparable government positions, comparison of certain individual positions may give a crude comparative picture. For instance, a Field Operations Staff is normally a fresh public health graduate who will receive a monthly gross pay of $87.5 should he/she decide to work for the government. For a Unit Head or a Field Operations Staff with approximately 4-year experience, the most he can get from the government with the same working years is $127.5. It can therefore be said that CBFPS offers significantly higher salaries than those paid by the bureaucracy.

---

*This survey was carried out by IPPF Management Audit Department during February-April 1977. The remaining description was however made by the case writer.

5 Social Work and Research Centre: An Integrated Team Approach in India

Pratima Kale
Philip H. Coombs

EDITOR'S NOTE

The Social Work and Research Centre (SWRC), based in the State of Rajasthan, India, is an indigenous and highly unconventional non-governmental organization devoted to helping the rural poor toward a better life. During its first five years the SWRC initiated a series of actions in a semi-desert rural area with a population of some 80,000 people, dealing with water development, agriculture, health, nutrition, family planning, maternal and child care, literacy, formal schooling, rural industry, and special programs to improve the earnings and status of women. These activities have become increasingly integrated with one another and increasingly rooted in the village communities.

The SWRC is integrated also in a different sense: its own activities, by conscious design, have become productively linked with those of various government and private agencies operating in the same area--an unusual feat for a nongovernmental agency and one that enhances its prospects of having a salutory influence on larger-scale public programs.

Along with its evident successes, SWRC--like all other innovative organizations working on rural development--has had its share of difficulties, misfires, and disappointments. But its leaders have made a point of facing up to these candidly and learning from them. Thus these negative lessons, along with the many positive ones coming out of SWRC's first five years of experience, can be useful to others similarly concerned with improving the lot of the rural poor.

The principal investigator of this study and the author of the preliminary draft of this case study was Dr. Pratima Kale, a member of ICED's staff whose long familiarity with rural India and background in sociology and nonformal education qualified her well for this assignment. Because of her departure from ICED to accept a challenging new position, the final version of the report was prepared by the Editor of this volume.

Although the study constitutes an independent and impartial appraisal of SWRC, for which the authors and ICED assume full responsibility, it would not have been possible without the willing and generous cooperation of the Centre's founding Director, Bunker Roy, its Joint Director, Aruna Roy, and other members of SWRC's "team". In addition to their abundant help to Dr. Kale during her

INDIA
ADMINISTRATIVE
DIVISIONS 1971

*visits to Tilonia and the surrounding project area, they carefully
reviewed her preliminary draft report and provided much useful
additional information and a few factual corrections where warranted.
To their credit they did not in a single instance suggest toning down
or qualifying any of the more critical comments. On the contrary,
they pointed out some blemishes not noted in the original text and
suggested that these be added in the interest of accuracy. They
were also kind enough to say that while they hoped the study would
prove useful to others it was already proving useful to SWRC.*

THE BACKGROUND AND AN OVERVIEW

The Social Work and Research Centre (SWRC) is an indigenous
voluntary organization that got its start in 1972 in a backward rural
subdivision of Ajmer District in Rajasthan State in India. During its
first five years of operation--up to mid-1977, the cut-off point of the
present study--this innovative organization initiated a wide assortment
of rural development efforts involving water development and irrigation,
agriculture, community health, rural industry, and both nonformal and
formal education. These programs have become increasingly integrated
and village-based, and they have established a network of cooperative
linkaes with various governmental and nongovenmental organizations.
The Director, Joint Director, and a team of young university graduates
have been putting into practice their basic concept of "professional-
ization of rural development" and have devised a number of effective
means for strengthening this process. The Centre has explored strategies for getting villagers directly involved in program activities and
managed to reach some of the poorest sections of communities in a
focused manner.

Although the SWRC is still a relatively small organization, the
available evidence suggests that its activities have already had a
beneficial impact on the lives of more than one-quarter of the 80,000
people in the Silora Block of Ajmer District. In addition, SWRC has
established active satellite centers in the Jawaja Block in Rajasthan
and in three other northern Indian states--Punjaab, Haryana, and
Himachal Pradesh.

AIMS AND METHODS OF THE STUDY

With all these characteristics, the Social Work and Research
Centre offers a very pertinent and interesting case study for ICED's
international project described in the Preface. Its experiences to
date contain a variety of significant innovations and practical
lessons--both positive and negative--that could be instructive to
planners and program managers in other developing countries and
elsewhere in India. The basic purpose of this case study, therefore,
is to bring some of these lessons to light and make them available
to all who might wish to know about them. Its further purpose is to
provide an outsider's perspective and commentary that the SWRC itself
might find useful as it seeks to broaden and strengthen its own
activities.

In particular the study attempts to derive significant operational lessons--both positive and negative--from the SWRC's experiences
that can shed useful light on five key questions of wide concern today

among policymakers and program planners and managers in many developing countries who are searching for practical ways to improve the quality of family life among the rural poor.

1) How to achieve more effective <u>integration</u> at the local level among various family improvement activities, and better coordination among the various organizations associated with them.

2) How to achieve extensive community participation in the planning, operation, and economic support of such activities in a spirit of self-reliant community cooperation.

3) How to incorporate relevant and cost-effective educational components in these activities to meet the basic learning needs of both their "operators" and their "consumers".

4) How to take fuller advantage of the flexibility of voluntary organizations to complement the rural development efforts of government and to test out innovative approaches that can generate useful guidance for larger-scale government programs.

5) How external assistance organizations, both public and private, can be most helpful to developing country efforts in these directions.

With these objectives in view, the study examines critically the main elements and dimensions of SWRC's program in the context of its rural setting in Rajasthan, including its institutional objectives and evolution, organizational structure and management, program activities and their educational components, staff recruitment and training, costs and finance, and the impacts that SWRC appears to be having on the lives of rural people.

The analysis is based largely on documentation, data, and impressions gathered during two visits to SWRC in Tilonia in November 1976 and June 1977, supplemented by additional information provided by the Director and Joint Director to fill gaps in a preliminary draft of this report they were asked to review. During the above visits extensive informal discussions were held with the managers and various team members of the SWRC, including village workers; program activities and staff meetings were observed on the campus at Tilonia and in villages; records, files, and documents, including earlier progress reports and impact studies, were reviewed and analyzed. Because of time constraints and other practical problems it was not feasible to collect additional fresh village data systematically.

The study, in brief, represents an impartial effort to interpret and assess the SWRC program to date on the basis of observations, discussions, and the analysis of existing records, including both qualitative and quantitative evidence. It is an attempt to understand the specific situations of the SWRC through the perspectives of the participants and to relate those specific details and observations to some broader issues in rural development that confront many developing countries.

THE SWRC'S UNORTHODOX BEGINNINGS

The Social Work and Research Centre entered the field of rural development through an unusual door and in a somewhat controversial manner. Bunker Roy, its founder-director, initiated his experiment in integrated rural development in the Silora Block of Ajmer District in 1972, with a ground water survey.[1]

As a voluntary organization the Centre departed sharply from the traditional ideologies, style, and strategies of the many voluntary organizations involved in India's rural development whose roots trace back to the independence movement, the social reform movement, the Gandhian movement, and various religious and semi-religious movements of the late 19th and early 20th centuries. Rural social change had been one of the dominant themes in these earlier movements; therefore their programs typically stressed social education, basic education, formal schooling, literacy, and women's education (though some eventually expanded into such areas as agricultural extension, cottage industry, and construction of rural roads and facilities). The founders of the SWRC were similarly interested in rural social change as an ultimate goal, but they believed that economic change was a prerequisite to social change and also the best initial means to mobilize rural people to improve their own lot. Hence they gave primary emphasis at the outset to programs designed to yield direct economic benefits.

The new Centre, despite its name, also deviated from the "social work tradition" in India, which had acquired an urban, middle class, academic stance. The adherents to this tradition had often addressed themselves to the human problems of urban slums, but they had not generally immersed themselves in the world of rural poverty. Similarly, the kinds of research contemplated by the founders of the new Centre deviated from the concepts and traditions of research popular among academic social and physical scientists. The SWRC's research was to be a much more pragmatic, "dirty hands" type of research, tied directly to action.

It is hardly surprising, therefore, that many experienced people long associated with one or another of the above traditions viewed with considerably skepticism the new Centre's unorthodox entry into rural development with a team of geophysicists and geologists.

The approach that the SWRC's founders proposed to take also differed drastically from the conventional approach to rural development by specialized governmental and international agencies. This customary approach was a

---

[1]Bunker Roy, a young university graduate with an M.A. in English literature, an urban middle class family background, and an exclusive schooling experience in Delhi and Dehra Dun, became convinced of the need for a fresh approach to rural development by exposure to the terrible Bihar Fa ine in 1966-67 and by working as a volunteer on a water development program in Ajmer District with a group of mission-aries from 1967 to 1971. These experiences convinced him that a coordinated multipronged approach to rural development involving a large measure of self-help by the rural people was essential to any real progress. With this in mind, he gathered a small group of young university graduates to establish the Social Work & Research Centre

piecemeal one, involving a series of narrowly focused, single-purpose
"sectoral" programs, operated independently and from the top down by
various specialized ministries or their even more specialized subdivisions, frequently aided by their specialized counterparts in various
external assistance agencies. The SWRC, by contrast, proposed to pursue
a quite opposite strategy that sought to integrate these fragmented specialized programs and to build and operate them, not from the top down
but from the bottom up.

Moreover, the new Centre did not fit the conventional concept of a
"development project" to which most ministries and external assistance
agencies have become wedded. The Centre's founders defined their general
objectives and guiding principles, but they had not designed the sort of
"project plan" that would pass muster, for example, with the World Bank
or the UNDP or major bilateral aid agencies. In other words, they had no
neat and tidy plan, encompassed by a clear-cut time schedule, that defined in detail the proposed program activities, organizational and administrative arrangements, projected staff, physical inputs, financial requirements, and quantitative targets, and that included built-in evaluation provisions beginning with an initial battery of "baseline surveys" against
which to measure future progress.[1]

What Bunker Roy and his colleagues had in mind was not a "development
project" of the usual type, but a highly unconventional and flexible experiment that could engender a new kind of rural development "movement."

The SWRC's Objectives

The innovativeness and unconventionality of the new SWRC were manifest
in the following themes that emerged strongly and repeatedly in the early
statements of its objectives and principles--themes that were to give shape
to the Centre's eventual style, infrastructure, and pattern of program activities.[2]

Theme 1:   Joint Effort of the Professional and the Farmer in a Move
           Toward Professionalization of Rural Development.

One of the main functions of SWRC, it was asserted, was "to
bridge the gap between the farmer and the professional" and to "establish communication" between the two. The Centre aimed at generating

---

[1]In retrospect, it seems most unlikely that the new Centre would ever
have gotten off the ground if its young founders had followed conventional "project preparation procedures" and had deferred the launching of SWRC
until enough funds were available to insure its survival for the first few
years. Moreover, had the new enterprise been strait-jacketed by a pre-
tailored "project plan" it could not have evolved in the flexible and ad hoc
way it did.

[2]Quotations from The Profile of a Concept in Practice, SWRC, October 1976

"employment among [urban] specialists by bringing them closer to the
problems and life styles of the rural areas." It was to be the Centre's responsibility to "give them facilities, equipment,   and the
conditions [to enable them] to contribute their best."

        In addition to attracting individual professionals,   the
SWRC aimed at involving technical colleges and other institutions "to
carry out specific projects in rural areas where their skill and experience in intermediate technology [could] be of great help."

        In the initial stages, the SWRC was to be committed to pro-
viding "three basic technical services in rural areas: water
development, medical, and educational." The local farmer   was   not
seen merely as a recipient of such technical services, however,   but
as a participant in development along with the professional. This was
symbolized in SWRC's institutional emblem depicting the rural farmer
joining hands with the urban professional. In all these symbols and
plans, the Centre was visualized as a tool for bringing the   modern
sector in close contact with the farmer and his rural family life, and
for enabling rural people to give the urban specialists a better understanding of rural life and development from a human angle--a   process,
it was believed, that would also require some "unlearning"   by   the
urban specialists.

Theme 2:   Emphasis on Economic Change.

        The founder-members strongly argued, as noted earlier,   that
it was only through economic benefits that any social change   could
gradually take place, and therefore it was SWRC's major goal to "bring
about social change through economic change." This clearly   meant
that the Centre was to "lay emphasis on providing economic benefits in
a direct or indirect form" and it was through such tangible   results
that the SWRC hoped to "develop faith and confidence in the minds   of
rural people."

Theme 3:   Inter-Institutional Cooperation.

        It was stressed at the outset that it was essential for SWRC
to "establish a good working relationship with the State Government in
all programmes, to cooperate and seek State Government help in all matters and get their approval before implementing any programme...." It
was not the purpose of SWRC to compete with the services being provided
by government but to supplement and reinforce them. In addition to involving the state government, the SWRC was to seek "help of other rural
based institutions working toward the same objectives." The Centre was
thus seen as an institutional partner among many others and was "not to
embark on any development activity in isolation."

Theme 4:   Integration, Economy, and Replicability.

        The Centre was to "emphasize an integrated approach to rural
development" with a view to providing different services "from   one
centre--one campus" to the rural community. A strong effort was to be

made to "give an economically self-supporting base" to the Centre; i.e., "to
generate enough income by giving the services on a 'no profit-no loss' basis."
In short, the aim was "to provide a simple, cheap and effective technical and
socio-economic service" that could be replicated in other areas.

THE RURAL SETTING

The founders of SWRC could hardly be accused of stacking the cards in
favor of easy success for their experiment. Indeed, if it could be made to
work under the rugged conditions in the Silora Block of Ajmer District it
could probably work anywhere.

Rajasthan, situated in northwestern India between the Indo-Gangetic
plains and the Deccan Plateau, is one of India's largest, driest, and poorest states. Its 25 million population in 1971 had a per capita income of
Rs 575 (about US$67) against a nationwide average of Rs 645. Its literacy
rate was barely 19 percent (less than 14 percent in rural areas) compared
to 30 percent for all India. Its health expenditures in recent years averaged Rs 16 per capita compared to a national average of Rs 28. Rajasthan
ranked lowest of all Indian states in family planning in 1973, with 6 percent "acceptors" against 15 percent for the country at large.

Rajasthan's backward economic and social status—notwithstanding its
rich cultural heritage—is rooted in its inhospitable ecological conditions,
the low state of its agricultural and other technologies, and the low productivity of its labor force—90 percent of which is engaged in agriculture
and related activities.

Most of Rajasthan's total land area of 342,274 sq. kilometers (132,152
sq. miles) is arid or semi-arid. Only 17 percent of its limited arable land
was irrigated in 1970 (compared to 74 percent in neighboring Punjab State and
22.8 percent for all India), and 62 percent of its villages were classified
as having "inadequate water supply."

Silora Block, one of eight administrative subdivisions of Ajmer District
where SWRC is based and conducts the major share of its activities, mirrors
these same statewide conditions. Most of the land is parched much of the time.
The average annual rainfall is only 45.72 mm. (about 18 inches), with recorded
fluctuations in recent years from a low of 9 inches in 1965 to a record-break-
ing high of more than 40 inches in 1976. Its two rivers are dry outside the
rainy season. Only 19 percent of the cultivated land (comprising just over
half the total land area of 117,000 hectares) is irrigated by tanks and wells.
Recent SWRC surveys showed that 2,758 irrigation wells were in use while 2,535
others were out of use because of the inadequate supply or poor chemical quality of the water.

The main rabi (i.e., rainy season) crops in Silora are wheat, barley,
and gram; the principal kharif(dry season) crops are bajra, maize, and jowar.
Low yields are the norm and crop failures a perennial hazard.

Silora (see map) has only one town (Kishangarh); most of its 80,000
people live in 110 villages, ranging in size from 30 households (about 200
individuals) to more than 500 households (over 3,000 individuals).   The
average nuclear family has six members; the typical extended family exceeds
ten members. Tilonia, the village in which SWRC's "campus" is located, had

Figure 1.

SILORA BLOCK
AJMER DISTRICT
RAJASTHAN

at latest count a population of 1,630 and 263 households.

Agriculture, animal husbandry, and related activities are the main source of employment and means of survival for the great bulk of Silora's population--landowners and landless alike. The land ownership pattern is very unequal. In Tilonia, for example, 74 families have less than 1 hectare; 77 hold from 1 to 2-1/2 hectares, 73 have from 2-1/2 to 5, and only 29 families possess more than 5 hectares. Many of the larger owners are absentee landlords. The landless and near-landless depend heavily   on part-time work on other people's land to eke out a bare existence.   A marginal number of workers are employed, or partially employed, in secondary occupations such as stone quarrying, construction, and indigenous crafts.

An important sociological feature of the villages, which presented serious difficulties for the new SWRC, is that they are not really communities in the full sense; they are aggregations of separate   caste communities. Though the proportions vary, the social structure of   most villages includes representation of four main upper castes and an assortment of lower castes, all associated historically with a hierarchy of functions, occupations, and levels of prestige. The upper castes include the Rajputs (the traditional warriors, including "royal" families, now mainly involved in agriculture); the Jats (cultivators); the Brahmins (traditionally the teachers and intellectual class); and the Gujars (the traders and businessmen). The lower castes include the Harijans ("untouchables") and other "scheduled castes," particularly the Regers and Chamars, historically associated with tanning and leatherwork, weaving, cloth printing, and other "inferior" occupations.[1]

A rough sketch map of the physical lay-out of any village clearly demarcates these socioeconomic divisions. The upper caste households generally have "pucca" houses surrounded by stone walls and are physically segregated from the lower caste neighborhoods whose households are typified by "katcha"houses and mud walls.

Although the upper castes enjoy higher status, prestige, and influence and tend to dominate the trades, services, education, and village affairs, membership in a high caste these days does not always mean high income and better living conditions.

This fragmentation of villages into separate caste groups, arranged more or less in a pecking order of prestige and power, makes for the lack of strong and cohesive village-wide institutions and planning and decision-making processes that can serve as instrumentalities of local development. Encouraging the growth of such local organizations, SWRC soon discovered, was at least as difficult a challenge as encouraging the growth of better

---

[1]"Scheduled castes" are so called because they are listed on a government schedule of historically disadvantaged groups that, under national policy since Independence, are to be accorded special access to employment, education, and other public services in order to eradicate inequalities of the traditional caste system.

crops and the general improvement of health, nutrition, and education, yet
it was a necessary prelude to such general improvement in the conditions
of village life.   As an early SWRC report observed, "One of the   main
reasons for many sound economically viable projects failing to yield   the
expected results is the lack of good reliable grass roots organization...."

SWRC'S ORGANIZATIONAL SET-UP

A Western-trained management expert would be hard put to fit   the
SWRC into any of the textbook   organizational models,   yet he would undoubtedly be impressed (and a bit mystified) to   discover that   SWRC's
seemingly loose management system has produced   more action   and results
relative to its size than many rural development   organizations patterned
after the textbook models.

Part of the explanation is to be found in SWRC's integrated three-tier
team approach that combines dynamic central leadership with a wide   diffusion of responsibility and initiative among various team members, from the
campus-based "specialists" right down to the local village workers.   The
physical arrangements and close community-like atmosphere of SWRC's central
"campus" that constantly brings key team members into close proximity   and
informal contact are undoubtedly a further part of the explanation.

The campus is a former TB sanitorium on the outskirts of Tilonia, leased
to the Centre at a nominal rate by the state government of Rajasthan.   This
forty-five acre site with its arable land, a complex of facilities,   and public transport connections with the towns of Kishangarh   (headquarters of
Silora Block) and Ajmer to the southwest   and with Jaipur to the northwest,
provides a very convenient "hub" for SWRC's wide-ranging activities.

In the initial institution-building phase, SWRC's program activities
were largely concentrated on the campus, but with the increased   emphasis
on "outreach," starting in 1975, the locus of program activities has shifted progressively to individual villages, with the campus playing a coordinating and backstopping role. This trend applies not only to the expanded program activities within the Silora Block but also to the spin-off activities of SWRC in the Jawaja Block in Rajasthan and in the northern states
of Haryana, Punjab, and Himachal Pradesh.

SWRC is officially registered as a charitable society under a colonial
act of 1860 and as such has a governing board responsible for its basic policies. Its primary leadership, however, is provided by Bunker and Aruna Roy
who, as a couple, work as the Director and Joint Director under a small, supportive governing board.[1] The Director, who spends much time "on the road,"

---

[1]Members of the   Governing Body include: President (recently resigned),
Professor Ravi J. Matthai, Indian Institute of Management, Vastrapur, Ahmedabad;
Vice-President, Dr. K. D. Gangrade, Principal, Delhi School of Social Work;
Shri Virendra Prakash, Chief, Projects Apparaisal Division, Planning Commission,
Government of India, New Delhi; Shri S. R. Das, Headmaster, Lawrence School,
Sanawar, Simla Hills, H.P.; Shri P. S. Dwivedi, Lecturer, St. Stephen's
College, Delhi; Shri Sanjit Roy, Director, SWRC.

is the chief entrepreneur, liaison with outside organizations, recruiter, fund raiser, and articulator of SWRC's principles, objectives,   and achievements. The Joint Director is the able and orderly "inside" administrator, coordinator, and stimulator who keeps a close eye and firm guiding hand on day-to-day operations, including human relations, logistics, and financial affairs. It is an effective division of labor that matches the leaders' complementary talents.

The three-tier team operating in the Silora Block as of mid-1977 included fourteen "specialists" (with university or technical degrees), who have immediate responsibility for particular program activities; twenty-six local "professionals," such as auxiliary nurse midwives (ANMs), agricultural assistants, craft teachers, pharmaceutical compounders, balwadi (pre-school) teachers, and experimental primary teachers; and fifty-four "field workers," including such "paraprofessionals" as village health workers (VHWs), dais (traditional birth attendants), and "helpers" in various program activities, plus an assortment of custodial and other support personnel. The total team numbered ninety-five members in the Silora Block in 1977. In addition, another forty-five members were attached to three SWRC outposts in other areas.

The "specialists" are almost all from other parts of India, whereas the "professionals" and "paraprofessionals" are largely local. The team members are not strictly "volunteers"; they are all on SWRC's payroll. The top "specialists" receive salaries in line with or somewhat above   corresponding government scales; the wages of the "professionals" and field workers are commensurate with those prevailing in the local market. Not surprisingly, there is a substantial turnover among the "specialists," who are generally   fresh graduates that view a limited stint with SWRC as a challenging and valuable experience and as a useful prelude to a "regular" career post befitting their particular educational background and professional training. A few of the key specialists, however, have remained from the start and provide important continuity.

The accent of SWRC has been on youth. The "specialists" range in age from 22 to 28 (except for the Director and Joint Director who, five years after the program was established, had reached the ripe old age of 31 and 30, respectively!). Most of the local "professionals" and "paraprofessionals" are equally young--except for the dais who are mostly in their 40s or early 50s.

No two-dimensional organization chart could possibly give an adequate picture of the internal relations and dynamics of SWRC. However, the simplified diagram in Figure 1 may provide at least a useful sketch of its internal structure.

INCOME AND EXPENDITURES

From the outset the SWRC has had to piece together its annual budget and program pattern largely from grants received from a variety of private and government agencies.   Since most of these grants have been tied to specific projects and purposes of special interest to the donors, this has left the SWRC with very limited "uncommitted" funds with which to cover general organizational and administrative costs, or to expand ongoing programs, or to initiate new ones in line with its own priorities.

Figure 1.   THE ORGANIZATIONAL SET-UP

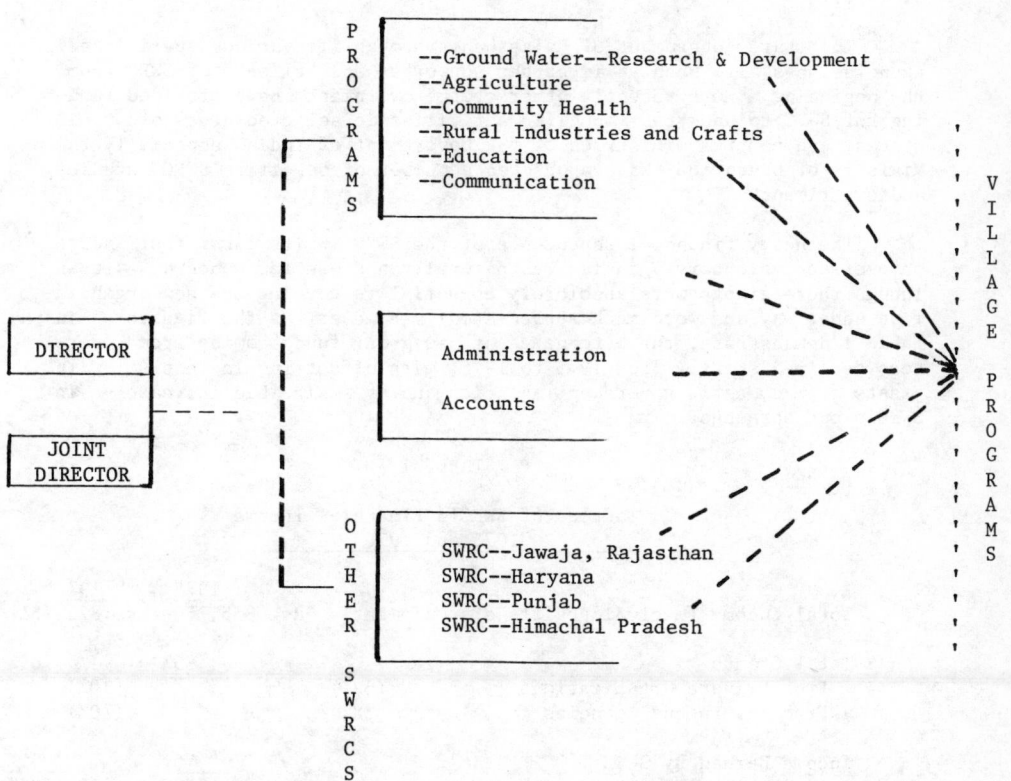

Oxfam-UK has been a consistent and generous supporter of the SWRC and has been mindful of its need for some flexible "general" funds.   Other important private contributors have included Oxfam-Canada, Catholic Relief Service, and Christian Aid, whose grants have been mainly for specific pur-poses, including items of needed equipment. (Not included in SWRC's annual income statements are numerous important gifts of equipment from   private organizations that had an estimated value exceeding Rs 500,000 by the   end of 1976.)

The state government of Rajasthan, through its various specialized agencies, has also been an important supporter and "client" of SWRC from the beginning. More recently other state governments have provided fund-ing for SWRC to undertake specific activities in selected areas of their states, and central ministries of the Government of India--especially the Ministry of Education--have sponsored a number of specific SWRC studies and experiments.

The heavy financial dependence of the SWRC in its first four years on overseas voluntary agencies was naturally a cause for concern   (even though these grants were absolutely essential to getting the new organiza-tion under way and were much appreciated). However, as the figures   in Table 1 demonstrate, the percentage of new grant funds coming from over-seas declined sharply from 1975 to 1976, with offsetting increases   in grants from domestic government agencies and by a sizeable increase   in SWRC's own earnings.

TABLE 1

Sources of SWRC's Financial Income
1975 and 1976

		1975	1976
Total Income (excluding gifts of equipment)		Rs 855,750*	Rs 821,781
Total Grants		85%	69%
From Private Organizations	(62%)		(30%)
From Government Agencies	(38%)		(70%)
Income Earned by SWRC		15%	31%
		100%	100%

*Some of the 1975 grant funds were carried over to 1976, making possible an increase in total expenditures from Rs 760,278 in 1975 to Rs 890,393 in 1976.

Along with this shift in the sources of income there was also a sizeable shift in the SWRC's pattern of expenditures between 1975 and 1976 as shown in Table 2. Overall expenditures rose from Rs 760,278 to Rs 890,393, but the pro-portions shifted substantially, reflecting (1) a decline in the percentage go-ing to overall management, (2) a sharp rise in the share going to projects outside Silora, (3) a sharp decline in the Ground Water Development and Research Program within Silora, and lesser reductions in the share devoted to

the Community Health and Education programs in Silora. The reasons for these
shifts will become apparent when these various programs are discussed in
later chapters.

TABLE 2

Recent Shifts in the Pattern of SWRC
Program Expenditures

		1975		1976
Total Expenditures	Rs	760,278	Rs	890,393
Overall Management Costs		17%		15%
Program Costs		83%		85%
Breakdown by Programs:				
a) Ground Water Development and Research		27.3%		4%
b) Agriculture		10.4%		10%
c) Community Health		21.0%		15%
d) Education and Crafts		19.3%		18%
e) Rural Industries		----		16%
f) SWRC--Jawaja	15.8%		13%	
g) SWRC--Haryana	6.3%		15%	
h) SWRC--Punjab	0.5%	22.0%	9%	37%
		100.0%		100%

Finally, the sharp rise in the proportion of overall income represented
by Income Earned by SWRC (from 15 percent in 1975 to 31 percent in 1976) was
also accompanied by significant shifts in the amount coming from various programs (see Table 3). The Craft and Rural Industries Programs in Silora had
become the big earners, replacing the Ground Water Development and Research
Program in this role. The Health Program and the Education Programs, the two
biggest spenders, represented the lowest earners. (This is not to suggest
that they were less important or desirable but simply that SWRC was still
farthest away in these areas from becoming self-financing.)

TABLE 3

Breakdown of SWRC Earnings by Program

	1975	1976
Ground Water Program	52%	9%
Crafts and Rural Industries	16%	47%
Community Health	12%	9%
Agriculture	10%	11%
Miscellaneous	10%	24%
	100%	100%

TWO PHASES OF SWRC'S DEVELOPMENT

  An analytical review of the SWRC's development from its inception in 1972
to the cut-off point of the present study in mid-1977 reveals a distinct turning point in 1975. Chapter 2 reviews what we shall call "the initial phase of
development," roughly up to mid-1975. The following four chapters (3 through
6) deal with what might be termed, "the beginning of a new phase" in which the
SWRC began building on the foundations laid down in the initial phase and also
began branching out to further geographical areas. For convenience, these
four chapters deal respectively with Community Health, Water Development, Rural
 Industries, and Education. It should be borne in mind, however, that there
were growing linkages and increasing integration among the activities in these
four areas.

CHAPTER 2

THE SWRC'S
INITIAL PHASE OF DEVELOPMENT

During the first three years the new organization was feeling its way, formulating and reformulating specific objectives and action plans, testing its strategy, and initiating operations in its three priority program areas: water development, health, and education. This period was also marked by suspicion and resistance from the rural communities in and around Tilonia,and by a mixture of interest, curiosity, skepticism, and controversy on the part of outside observers.

WATER DEVELOPMENT: THE OPENING WEDGE

Water, as noted earlier, was the critical bottleneck to agricultural development in the Silora Block and hence to improving the income and living conditions of the people. Credit was a related bottleneck, for in order to develop potential irrigation supplies farmers needed credit. But under the regulations of the credit agencies any application for credit had to be supported by a detailed and competent ground water survey of the area that demonstrated promising water potentialities. The new Centre's first concerted effort, therefore, was aimed directly at breaking these bottlenecks. In the words of a 1975 SWRC follow-up report, "The need for this service was seen as one of the most crucial ones in the area and the Centre's work was initiated with a ground water survey of the Silora Block." This project soon received "support, recognition, and approval of the Government of Rajasthan."

The technical group began by conducting a preliminary survey of the ground water potential of some 51 villages in the Silora Block of Ajmer District--a project the Rural Electrification Corporation was willing to support in preparation for the eventual electrification of the whole Block. This was soon followed by another much more detailed ground water survey for the Agricultural Refinance Corporation (ARC), covering all 110 villages in the Block. This comprehensive survey examined the ground water potential, soil and water quality, potentialities for agricultural extension programs, and possibilities of extending institutional credit to farmers. In 1975-76, after scrutinizing SWRC's report, the Union Bank of India with the approval of the Reserve Bank of India, sanctioned a sum of Rs 35 lakhs for the development of minor irrigation in the Silora Block, mainly for small and marginal farmers.

Meantime the SWRC made an effort to follow up on its water surveys by obtaining equipment and tools (including a mobile drilling rig, drilling accessories, two compressors, two tractors, and three jeeps) with which to provide direct customer services to individual farmers and organizations for improving their water supply. In 1974-75 SWRC helped about a hundred farmers with surveys of their lands for locating water spots and with drilling services. Similar services were provided to organizations in Udaipur and Chittorgarh Districts. The customers were charged fees for the services on a "no profit—no loss" basis, with charges adjusted to their ability to pay.

The water development team also initiated a new research program in search of practical methods to solve the critical water balance problem of the area, which had increasingly troubled these young professionals. More water was being taken out from the open wells in many areas than the amount percolating into the ground as recharge, thus lowering the water table. They soon discovered that many of the irrigation-cum-percolation tanks were constructed in such a way that the water could not seep into the ground. Through experimentation they determined that the percolation tanks could be revitalized by perforating the rocky bed beneath them to soft layers below with the help of the drilling rig. This method was evaluated and endorsed by the Rajasthan Ground Water Department (that provided the funds for this research program) and by experts from the University of Rourkee, the UNDP, UNICEF, and the International Commission on Irrigation and Drainage. This opened up an important new activity.

AGRICULTURAL EXTENSION

Another logical follow-up to the initial water development and research program was to get started on an agricultural extension program aimed at assisting farmers to apply new technologies and raise their productivity. The SWRC felt, however, that rather than to start right off with trained agricultural experts (who might assume they had all the answers) it would be better to begin with less trained people who were sympathetic to the farmers and their problems and willing to listen and to learn. Thus the new Agricultural Section of SWRC was initiated by two young men, one a history graduate with a strong interest in agriculture; the other a gardener's son. These young men joined hands with the water development specialists and started working on questions of irrigation and agricultural production and on establishing a direct dialogue with farmers.

The government of Rajasthan gave formal approval for cultivating the land on SWRC's campus for research and demonstration purposes in November 1974, and this gave a boost to SWRC's new agricultural program. New varieties of wheat were sown on demonstration plots along with additional crops such as maize, bajra, jowar, jeera, sunflower, dhania, grams, sesame, groundnut, mustard, and hybrid grass. A small program for distribution of seeds, fertilizers, pesticides, fruit plants, and saplings right to the doorstep of the farmers (a service they had never before experienced) was gradually added to the demonstration program.

As part of the extension services the Agricultural Section also set up a special training program for marginal farmers in advance of the rabi and kharif seasons. These training sessions were attended by some fifty to a hundred farmers, with visiting state government agricultural experts serving as resource persons. Once Tilonia became recognized as a training center of sorts, the district agricultural officer started using the research and demonstration plots for popularizing the new varieties of seeds and fertilizer application.

BREAKING INTO THE HEALTH FIELD

By the middle of 1973, SWRC's original team of geophysicists, geologists, agricultural extension workers, a geographer, and an economist was strengthened by the addition of a medical social worker, a doctor, a pharmaceutical compounder, and several local field workers. While the technical specialists' team attempted to deal with the water and agricultural extension problems, the female medical social worker, trained at the Tata Institute of Social Sciences in Bombay, struggled with the social and human aspects of the local community of Tilonia and other nearby villages to explore possibilities for social services, including medical and educational programs, and to prepare the ground for the villagers' acceptance of more approaches in the field of health.

As some of the "old-timers" remember it now, these urban-educated graduates had a somewhat "simplistic and romantic notion of villages and the villagers" which had to be modified through extensive contacts with the community that was strongly resistant and hostile toward the newcomers. The young folks' occupancy of the abandoned TB sanitarium was viewed with suspicion by the villagers, who wondered why they were there. The modern, unmarried social worker walking around the dusty roads of Tilonia, who could communicate in the beginning only in Hindi and not in the local Marwari dialect, was watched with particular curiosity. Her companionship with young men on the campus became a topic for spicy gossip among the villagers. Her promotional efforts in preventive health care and education seemed to be unappealing to villagers, who made it clear that if the group really wanted to do something useful they could provide immediate relief from pain--which meant curative services.

To meet the villagers' demand and to use this as an entry point to the community's recognition and trust, a dispensary was established on the SWRC campus. It soon began to give tangible results and attracted a growing flow of patients from Tilonia and other nearby villages. In the following two years, from 1973 to 1975, 60,000 patients were treated at the dispensary and two "eye camps" were held for patients from twenty-three villages with eye problems.

In spite of this apparent success, the Western system of medicine continued to be in competition with the traditional and more familiar local system. As the medical social worker put it, "The knowledge that the populace lacked faith in modern medication; were frightened of doctors and hospitals, associating them only with death; and had easy access to vaids, fakirs, and Babas, placed before us a maze that was both interesting and difficult." The old wives' tales were hard to combat: "Localized pain is branded and bled; typhoid remains untreated due to a belief that medicines prevent the disease from leaving the body;disinfected wells are believed to cause sterility and impotency; and the cutting of the umbilical cord by the midwife is equated with murder."

To pave the way beyond the curative treatment at the dispensary and to broaden SWRC's community contacts, the medical social worker conducted a survey of the surrounding community with help from some local educated youth. "This in fact proved to be the crucial aspect since it provided a clear insight into the community, its social fabric, its stratification, power controls, leadership patterns, economic levels and caste factions, thus helping us build a very firm base and allowing us to tap the enormous amount of local resources available within the villages."[1]

It was still premature to bring preventive health services directly to the villages (though that had been the initial hope). The villagers were not yet ready to get into the health business themselves,   but their burgeoning demand for curative medical services prompted SWRC to establish in February 1975 a subdispensary in Chota Naraina in the northern section of Silora Block.

A SHAKY START ON EDUCATION

Education--the third element of the originally intended   integrated package--was initially interpreted by SWRC as literacy. Overcoming the widespread illiteracy in the area seemed as great a challenge as overcoming   the shortage of water.

The preliminary work on literacy began in June 1973 when a   "100% literacy" program was launched for the village of Tilonia in   collaboration with the Ajmer Adult Literacy Association, the Inspectorate of Schools,   and the Silora Block Development Office. Fourteen literacy classes   were organized for different groups of boys and girls, men and women. Teachers   from the local primary and middle schools, field workers associated with SWRC, and other volunteers were recruited to conduct the classes. They were given freedom to plan their own class schedules; records of attendance were maintained; the Adult Education Association carefully supervised the program and provided examiners to evaluate the results.

Soon the kinds of difficulties and disappointments experienced by many conventional literacy campaigns throughout the developing world began   to appear. The villagers' attendance, especially among the Jats, continued to fall sharply; the teaching materials proved uninspiring; most teachers seemed to lack initiative, interest, and ingenuity in dealing with more mature, out-of-school learners; and many of them left as soon as the school year ended in May.

One notable exception that proved the rule was Sudama,   the   local priest's son who worked with other SWRC programs. He made a special   effort to establish close relations with members of his literacy class and   achieved impressive results. The Third Report on the Adult Literacy Programme in the Village Tilonia (May-June 1974) made note of this exceptional success   case: "In view of the excellent service he (Sudama) rendered to the programme, the Secretary, Adult Education Association, gave him [a] hundred percent raise in his allowance." The same report, however, described serious difficulties in the program elsewhere, which finally led to closing down the fourteen literacy classes. It was clear that a different educational strategy was   needed, one that also addressed other important learning needs and that   did   not equate "adult education" simply with "literacy."

---

[1] A Dossier on Basic Education, SWRC, undated.

Other modest forays were made into the general field of education in 1974. A balwadi (preschool) was created at the campus for the children of women attending the craft center. Preliminary efforts were made to initiate an experimental program in nonformal education under a sponsorship grant from the Centre for Educational Technology, Ministry of Education, Government of India. The Directorate of Adult Education in the same ministry sponsored a survey of existing institutional and other potential educational resources in the area and the extent of their utilization.

INITIAL ATTENTION TO RURAL INDUSTRY AND CREDIT

Although rural industry had not been one of the initial priority target areas of the SWRC, it soon became one. A study of socioeconomic conditions in seventeen villages in the Silora Block was conducted by the SWRC group in February-March 1974, with funding from the Rajasthan Khadi and Village Industries Board located in Jaipur. This study highlighted the need for new programs for the poorer sections of rural artisans, craftsmen, and women in the area. A new women's program was soon established to give local women an opportunity to use their traditional Rajasthani skills to make clothing and other craft items for sale in the cities as well as for local use.

During that year it was felt by all the members of the SWRC that until institutional credit was organized for the rural poor the integrated approach to development would be seriously inhibited. This belief encouraged the SWRC to initiate discussions for the opening of a rural branch of a bank. After much effort and much resistance on all fronts the bank was established (on the SWRC campus) and the first few loans were made to craftsmen under the rural industries program. By the middle of 1975, ten loan applications had been processed for local tanners under the Differential Interest Rate (DIR) Scheme for poor farmers and artisans.

REACTIONS OF OUTSIDERS

While key people in some state and local government agencies and Oxfam were consistently supportive of SWRC, and some central government agencies were beginning to move in with a helping hand, the image of SWRC in different rural development circles, both domestic and international, was a mixed one. The program was watched by different observers with great interest and curiosity, but many of their questions remained unanswered in the early stages of SWRC's development.

The notion of starting a voluntary rural development program with some water surveys and with an emphasis on economic change still seemed strange to many who had grown up in the "social welfare" tradition. The idea of recruiting unemployed urban graduates to work with the rural people struck some as an example of technocracy run by amateurs, and others as one more of those Utopian notions that was bound to fail. Even if SWRC could manage to get a few specialists to rural Rajasthan, it was argued, the elitist orientations they brought with them could hardly survive the challenges of rural resistance. Those familiar with SWRC's ground water research and technical advice to farmers argued that these

services were useful only for the big farmers who could afford them and
that SWRC's economic development approach did   not reflect a "people's
approach" or a concern for the poorer sections of the rural communities.
The emphasis on institutional cooperation with government agencies seemed
to be rather unusual in the light of experience shared by many   voluntary
agencies and was criticized by some as an attempt to maintain the status
quo. Those who favored careful experimentation and systematic evaluation
of "pilot projects" as against hasty and speedy expansion of experimental
programs questioned the wisdom of starting additional SWRC centers   in
other areas before the Silora experiment had "proved itself."   While all
these arguments were not necessarily presented in a united front,   they
could be heard during those days in different circles and different parts
of the country.

However, there were enthusiastic advocates and supporters   as well
as doubters and critics. The founders of the SWRC had gathered   an initial group of sympathizers, and as word spread and more and more visitors
came to observe, the group became steadily larger. All this interest and
attention surrounded SWRC with a lively and wholesome atmosphere of controversy.

A COMMENTARY ON SWRC'S INITIAL PERIOD

The first thing that impresses an objective outside observer   is
that the SWRC not only survived its first three formative years as a going concern--no mean accomplishment in itself--but laid useful foundations
for the future, developed a momentum, and learned some important lessons
that were fed back into the operation with all deliberate speed.   A few,
though not all, of the initially stated objectives had begun to be realized, but major challenges clearly remained open for more forceful   and
imaginative attack in the next phase. The following accomplishments and
disappointments seem especially noteworthy.

A Human Resource Base: By mid-1975 SWRC's founders were well   on
the way to proving their contention that able and well-educated   young
urban "specialists" could be attracted into rural service, could   learn
from the rural people and adapt to their different environment and way of
life, and by working in partnership with them could make a useful contribution to improving their lives. A number of such urban young   people--
with specialties ranging from medicine, social work, economics, geology,
geophysics, and agriculture to the humanities--had joined the new Centre,
had worked hard and shown initiative, and had begun to make a difference.
This core team had begun to flesh out with the addition of a few   local
"professionals" and "field workers," though many more such additions would
be needed. The management side of this human resources base was   significantly strengthened in 1975 when Aruna Roy resigned her prestigious post
in the Indian Administrative Service, for which she had been especially
trained, and became the Joint Director of SWRC.

Program Development: Two of the three priority programs--in health
and in water development and research--had moved ahead rapidly and already
scored impressive accomplishments. This could not be said, however,   of
the other priority area, education, where the "100% literacy campaign" had

misfired rather badly and where initiatives on other fronts were as yet little more than probings. A promising fourth program area--rural industries-- had been identified and was beginning to be opened up, with a sharp focus on helping women and members of the poorest lower castes.

Inter-Institutional Cooperation: A widening network of institutional relations was getting established and spreading out in various directions-- including ties with government agencies ranging from the block and district to the state and national levels, with both domestic and overseas voluntary agencies, and even with international organizations. These ties found expression not only in moral and financial support for SWRC but in valuable operational cooperation in the field and a productive dialogue with all sorts of interested and interesting people. Many observers from this institutional network had visited the Tilonia campus and shared their reactions--both critical and enthusiastic--with SWRC members. All these contacts, whether formal or informal, helped maintain a two-way flow of communication and a lively dialogue with the outside world. The urban-reared specialists on the campus who were in close daily communication with one another and parties to this external dialogue could hardly feel isolated in the village of Tilonia.

Partnership with the Villagers: One of the most serious gaps that still remained at the end of the initial phase was the lack of a strong outreach dimension to SWRC's programs. Relatively little progress had yet been made in forming active partnerships with villagers for helping them to develop their own self-improvement programs.

Up to now, in the institution-building stage, the bulk of program activities, other than the water surveys and village surveys, had been concentrated at the campus. Literally thousands of villagers had come there for medical care; groups of small farmers had come to see agricultural demonstrations; women had come for craft training and production, bringing their young children along for day care in the balwadi. This was certainly all to the good. It meant rendering useful services that people wanted badly enough to come and get them. It was a way to get to know and win the confidence of villagers and to overcome their suspicions and resistance.

But it was still not the same thing as the partnership between the urban experts and the rural people or the mobilization of community resources for economic and social change that SWRC had set out to achieve. And SWRC's managers were acutely aware that there is a thin but important line for any new rural institution between becoming a facilitating and backstopping instrumentality of an authentic bottom-up, self-help movement and remaining a separate self-contained institution that risks making rural people dependent rather than self-reliant.

The SWRC team could hardly be faulted for not having moved the center of gravity from the campus to the villages in so short a time. They had meant to and they still intended to, but the political, psychological and sociological obstacles proved to be considerably more complex than had been anticipated. This remained, therefore, a major item of unfinished business to be tackled in the next phase.

Guidelines for the Next Phase: There were valuable lessons to be culled from these first three years of operational experience, and these were not lost on the SWRC team.

They could take comfort in the fact that the initial thrust into   the water problem had evidently been wisely aimed, well-executed, and was likely to pay important future dividends.   But if these dividends were to be shared   by the smallest and poorest subsistence farm families, ways would have to be found to put together a "package" of complementary inputs and other essentials   to help the poor get moving.   This would require among other things a broader   and less conventional approach to agricultural extension.

The dispensary had proved to be effective in attracting a rural clientele and providing services they very much wanted, but it was still a form of   service to the community rather than a partnership with the community.   Moreover, unless a strong locally-based preventive health movement were established   that attacked the root causes of ill-health, it would never be possible to catch   up with the need and demand for clinic-based curative services.   By the same token, unless a strong, community-based program were established for eradicating   the causes of ill-health and for spreading the practice of rational family planning and responsible parenthood, sickness and disease would continue to plague every village and continue to be exacerbated by excessive population growth.

The failure of the literacy program proved once more that a fresher, more innovative, much more functional approach was needed, not simply to   literacy but to all the basic learning needs of villagers, young and old.   This fresh approach needed to link education effectively with other development activities, to build it around clients' needs, to make it more relevant, interesting,   and useful to them, and to make education an integral part of a package of develop- ment activities, not an isolated activity on its own or simply an end in itself.

Members of the SWRC team were keenly aware of these various strengths and weaknesses and of the priority tasks that lay ahead as they took stock of their accumulated experience in the first months of 1975.   The next four chapters ex- amine what they did about it.

THE COMMUNITY HEALTH PROGRAM

The key themes that marked the beginnings of a second stage in SWRC's development, beginning in early 1975, were: (1) a stronger emphasis on "outreach" and on directly involving villagers in the programs; (2) a more integrated approach to building programs around clients' needs and to linking SWRC activities with those of other institutions and services; (3) a more selective and focused attempt to reach the poorer sections of communities with programs for economic and social benefits; and (4) stronger efforts to incorporate appropriate educational components in various programs to meet the crucial training and learning needs associated with them.

The Community Health Program exemplified these themes as it began to move out from the dispensaries and directly into the villages. It was a slow and difficult process, but it made significant headway between 1975 and 1977.

BRINGING HEALTH CARE TO THE VILLAGES

SWRC's dispensary at Tilonia and its subdispensary at Chota Naraina had added a much needed supplement to the existing health care system in Silora Block.[1] However, this hospital- and clinic-centered health care system had three major deficiencies. First, it required villagers to come to the health center for services, which for many involved not only a difficult if not impossible journey but a frightening confrontation with the "modern" world of science and technology. Second, the almost exclusive focus of the system on curative medicine meant that preventive health measures, including health education, were getting at best a very low priority. Third, the practical costs of using this system were often prohibitive for the

---

[1]This system included: a government hospital in Kishangarh (19 km. southwest of Tilonia); a larger and better equipped hospital in the district town of Ajmer; a Primary Health Care Centre in Rupangar, north of Tilonia; a government Ayurvedic hospital; a government dispensary and family planning center in Harmara (3 km. north of Tilonia). The district health office operated a few specialized programs dealing, for example, with malaria eradication and vaccinations, and was serving five villages directly through government health workers. A number of private practitioners operated in the areas, mainly in and around the towns of Kishangarh and Ajmer.

poorest families, even when the services were nominally "free" or heavily subsidized.

The New Community-based Health Strategy

By the spring of 1975, having won the trust of many villagers through its popular dispensary services and having learned much more about the inner workings of villages through the investigations of its medical social worker, SWRC was ready to embark on a broader health care strategy designed eventually "to provide basic health care services <u>at</u> <u>the</u> <u>doorstep</u> in every village in Silora Block."

This new strategy, devised by the resident campus doctor, the medical social worker, and a newly arrived lady doctor, adapted the Chinese concept of the "barefoot doctor" to the conditions of rural Rajasthan. Its stated long term objectives were:

-- to make basic health care available in every village;

-- to utilize all available skilled, semi-skilled, and unskilled resource personnel within the community;

-- to disseminate the skills to the lowest possible levels to gradually make the village a self-sufficient unit of health;

-- to work towards increased education and awareness among villagers since these are the sustaining factors in development;

-- to provide the necessary guidance and supervision through the use of qualified professionals;

-- to incorporate health into the farmer's way of life rather than abstract it and treat it as a separate entity.[1]

Underlying the new strategy was the concept of an integrated "health team" with a new division of labor between the team members at the local level and the more highly trained members above the village level.   In practice, during the developmental period, this new SWRC health team usually included a medical doctor, a medical social worker, two to three auxiliary nurse midwives (ANMs), a compounder, two to three field assistants trained in health, and an expanding number of village level health workers (VHWs).

---

[1]<u>Community Health Programmes</u>, SWRC, December 1976.

A procedure was devised for inviting individual villages to participate in the system by their own choice, with the clear understanding that in so doing they would have to accept certain community-wide responsibilities for making it work and for insuring that the benefits were available to all subgroups in the village, including the poorest and most disadvantaged. When the scheme was first tried out in June 1975 the villages took considerable convincing, but as word spread, more and more villages expressed interest in having their own health service.

The procedure generally begins with a dialogue between health team members from the Tilonia campus and the Gram Sabha—the local village organization—that leads eventually to a broad-based village decision to participate, the selection of their own VHW, and a somewhat formal contract with SWRC. Following is a brief eye-witness account of how the procedure worked in the village of Kathoda on a cold November evening in 1976. By then the central health team was beginning to make contact with villages beyond a 10 km. radius from Tilonia.

Kathoda is a small village of about thirty-five households, 25 kms. northeast of Tilonia and distant from any pucca road or bus service. Only a jeep can make its way through to the village and only the local people can find their way in the open sandy desert land with no roads or signs. Its residents had heard only vaguely about the work of SWRC, but Sudama, one of the health assistants from Tilonia, had paved the way for an initial meeting by contacting a few of the village elders in advance.

After a bumpy jeep ride for about two hours, the health team arrived that cold evening in November in Kathoda at about 8 p.m. because that was the only convenient time to find the villagers in their homes. The local group of prominent Rajputs and Jats and a few others began to gather together in the moonlight outside the big compound wall of a pucca house of a Rajput family. The health team made it firmly clear that the meeting would not begin until they got representatives of all different sections of the village including the Harijans, Malis, Chamars, and others. Messages were sent in all directions and men began to arrive one by one. It took about two hours to gather a group of about twenty to twenty-two men, giving the team a clear sense of endless time that was always at hand in the village surroundings.

Sudama, who was experienced by this time in conducting such meetings, told the group briefly about SWRC and its health program. The first objective of the meeting was achieved when the group agreed that there were no medical facilities in the village or nearby, and that it would be very helpful for the village to have its own health program. The team also explained that each household in the village would have to contribute funds for the health scheme each month and the amount could be collectively determined that evening during the meeting. The amount collected each month would be utilized for the local health worker's salary, which would be paid through the Centre. A committee of seven or eight members was appointed to be responsible for collecting money and for supervising and assisting the village health worker. The team also explained that each patient receiving medication from the health worker would have to pay 25 percent of the actual costs of medicines, and Rs 2 for each injection given by the SWRC team members as against Rs 11 generally charged by private physicians in the nearby towns.

The role of the village health worker was then explained. He was expected to do health work in the mornings and evenings in addition to his daily routines and farm work. He would visit all households in Kathoda once a week irrespective of caste or family income and take care of simple medication for   common diseases. More difficult cases would be taken over to the dispensary in Tilonia or to the government hospital in Ajmer or Kishangarh. The health worker was to be trained for two weeks at the Centre and, following this training, he would be expected to visit the Centre every Sunday. The central health team would visit the village every two weeks when the health worker would arrange to set up   a camp at the village for the doctor's visit. The Centre would try to help   the health worker get a loan to buy a bicycle and the villagers would also help him with his transportation to and from the Centre.

After a fairly open and candid discussion of pros and cons, the   local group decided to collect 25 paise from each household each month, and   selected the 17 year-old Lakhpat Singh from the local Rajput family, who had   completed eight years of schooling, to be the village health worker. The young   man's father agreed to this and Lakhpat Singh was greeted by the crowd as the   new "doctor sahib" of the village.

The meeting, which lasted nearly two hours, was one of many such   village gatherings, but was seen by the doctor as a relatively easy one to handle, characterized by a quick decisionmaking process.

With this meeting, the village of Kathoda was incorporated into   SWRC's community health program. Meeting the requirements of the job in terms of age, sex, schooling, and village residence, Lakhpat Singh became a member of   the health team.

The pivotal role of the new local health workers can be clearly seen from the following job description:

1) The VHW is expected to visit each home at least once a week and to note down names of patients with health problems and symptoms; to give simple, appropriate treatment on the spot and to refer difficult cases to the SWRC dispensary or to the government hospital.   The VHW is generally expected to accompany the patients in such cases and to follow up with regular treatment at home according to doctor's advice.

2) He can dispense the following drugs on his own: aspirin, supra sulfa, sulpha gaunidine, iron, B complex, Diavol, cough mixture, carminative mixture, dehydration mixture, Vitamin A & D capsules, eye drops, ear drops, nose drops, dressing materials for first aid. Other drugs can be administered only with the doctor's prescription.

3) He maintains records of births, deaths, and diseases. The charts and figures are submitted to the SWRC health team each month. He also conducts simple health surveys in his community.

4) He attends the VHW's meetings at the Centre in Tilonia every Sunday. At this time he gets his registers, records, and receipt books checked by the health team. He gives a weekly report of his health

work; discusses his problems with the group and
collects medicine for the following week.

5) He collects the villagers' contributions each month
   and deposits the amount with the SWRC health team
   before collecting his own salary.

6) He conducts one or more meetings each month with
   villagers to discuss various problems of sanitation,
   hygiene, diseases, nutrition, food, etc. He shares
   his new knowledge with the villagers and brings their
   problems to the Sunday meetings for discussion and help.
   For the village meetings he is expected to use and also
   prepare charts, posters, filmstrips, and other visual
   materials.

7) He works with the health team on immunization of each
   child against smallpox, DPT, and maintains immunization
   records. He maintains height/weight charts for children
   under 5 and organized special clinics for children of
   that age group.

8) He is expected to work with men while the local dai
   works with women to motivate couples for family planning. He maintains records of eligible couples.

9) He is alert to symptoms of TB and refers new cases to
   the doctor for laboratory tests and x-rays. He works
   with the positive cases of TB for their follow-up and
   educates the families to take proper care of TB
   patients.

10) He works on prevention and treatment of malaria,
    including sanitation and hygiene.

11) He works with the SWRC field assistant to keep the
    well water disinfected with the use of bleaching
    powder as a preventive measure.

12) He organizes regular health clinics in the village
    in cooperation with the SWRC health team and arranges
    to get patients together for the doctor's visit.

13) He maintains lists of patients with eye problems including
    blindness, and maintains lists of patients who need to be
    operated on. The eye problems are occasionally handled
    through eye camps.

The initial two-week training at the campus, which is organized
twice a year, is aimed at preparing the novice for the performance of
the above jobs. The training is practical and attempts to give   the
basic knowledge of the human body, common diseases and associated symptoms and simple treatment, first aid, deficiency diseases,   drugs,
hygiene, sanitation, family planning. The training is also   intended

to develop essential skills to maintain records, identify symptoms, give
treatment, offer first aid, organize and educate community groups,   and
prepare educational materials.

As a rule, with a view to involving the government personnel   in
the training program, the district T.B. officer, the district health officer, the gynaecologist, and the eye specialist from the nearby hospital
are usually invited in order to combine theory with observation   and
practice. The VHW is given a cyclostyled copy of a booklet for   reference which gives him all the essential information as he works by   himself in his village.

Continuing on-the-job training and the referral system are built
into this program, which brings the VHW in close contact with the   central health team every week. His performance is closely supervised and
he constantly receives professional guidance. The doctor visits   his
village once every two weeks and he can refer difficult cases to   the
dispensary any time of any day according to needs. The Sunday meetings
also provide a mechanism for replenishing medicines and supplies   that
the workers bring to their respective villages.

The salary range of the VHWs is Rs 50-90 per month (approximately
US$5.80 to 10.50). The worker's performance is assessed   each   month
against four goals: basic illness care, preventive measures, community
contact, and collection of health data in the village. As his performance improves, he is moved up the graded salary structure.

The Supportive Role of the Local Dais

Although the VHW program covers many areas of curative and preventive health care, the male workers in the village subculture   cannot
directly deal with women's problems of pregnancy, childbirth, pre- and
postnatal care and family planning. A maternity center was established at SWRC in May 1975, but was not sufficient to deal with the problems
on the larger scale. The auxiliary nurse midwives from SWRC had   tried
to deal with some of the women's problems through visits and   personal
contacts with women and with dais who had been working in those villages
as traditional birth attendants. Some of the dais, particularly the one
from Tilonia, had brought a few patients to the maternity center   for
complicated deliveries and many of them were familiar with SWRC's   work.
However, something more was needed, and bringing the dais directly onto
the health team seemed a promising solution.

With this in mind, an attempt was made in early 1977 to organize a
two-week training program for traditional dais, but it did not work out.
The SWRC staff found that the dais (virtually all illiterate   and unaccustomed to "schooling") were apparently unable to grasp what   the
staff was trying to get across (possibly in too didactic a fashion). It
was decided instead to give these twelve middle-aged dais some in-service
training with practical demonstrations in the field and to get them to
come to Tilonia each Saturday for reinforcement training on such   important specifics beyond their customary ken as methods of prenatal   care,
hygienic deliveries, and infant and maternal nutrition. This   approach
worked out much better than the more formal training program and   was
further strengthened when SWRC created an illustrated booklet for   the
guidance of dais.

Following the VHW program pattern, the dais are expected to attend meetings with the health team every Saturday where they give weekly reports on pregnancies, deliveries, infant diseases, deaths, and related problems in their respective villages. Through their oral reports they help the ANMs maintain village records on these items. They collect folic acid and iron pills for free distribution during the following week among pregnant women and lactating mothers, and compare notes with the health team and with one another. Each dai is equipped with a kit which includes essential tools, medicines, and supplies. While dais can handle normal deliveries in the patients' homes, they are expected to diagnose possible complications and bring difficult cases to the maternity center at SWRC for professional help. All these services are offered by dais for a monthly salary of Rs 40 each (approximately US$4.65). Although the health workers have made some demands for a raise in their salary, dais seem to be quite pleased with the regular income combined with the professionals' recognition of their traditional jobs.

A COMMENTARY

It is obviously too soon to attempt a full scale appraisal of the SWRC's new village-based health program. It is nevertheless possible to present indicative evidence of the achievements thus far, to point out some of the problems encountered, and to draw a few tentative conclusions.

The Contribution of the Dispensaries

The main SWRC dispensary at Tilonia and the newer subdispensary at Chota Naraina have unquestionably made a substantial addition to the curative services available to the rural people in Silora Block, particularly those within 10 km. of Tilonia. From 1973 to mid-1977 the dispensaries treated close to 100,000 patients (including repeat visits by many) at no cost for medical services and only 25 percent of the cost for medicines dispensed. Although there has been no systematic follow-up study, it seems reasonable to assume that this large volume of treatments has had a significant and salutory impact on the health of numerous people in the area. In a country where private spending accounts for approximately 75 percent of total expenditures on health, and government expenditures for only 25 percent, this quasi-public health service has clearly made an important contribution, especially to many poorer families that would otherwise go without modern medical care.

Perhaps equally important, the dispensaries have done much to acquaint villagers with the work and true motives of SWRC, to win their confidence, and thus to pave the way for developing a community-based program that would bring basic health care services to their own doorstep and initiate important preventive health measures.

The Village Health Worker Scheme

This innovative scheme is especially important as a test case of the practical possibilities, problems, and potentialities of developing community-based primary health care systems in poor rural areas. All things considered, it may be said that the experiment got off to an encouraging start in its first two years, notwithstanding inevitable difficulties. Starting from scratch in 1975, the new VHW system by 1977 was actively functioning and yielding discernible benefits in more than a dozen villages with a combined population of about 20,000. This in   itself is a remarkable achievement considering the small size of the Tilonia health team, the many practical problems that had to be overcome, and the sizeable workload involved in training, supervising, and backstopping the new "barefoot doctors."

The scattered evidence available indicates that, on the whole, these young local health workers have applied themselves seriously and responsibly to their new duties and have performed remarkably well.   Typically, according to their weekly reports, they have averaged four to five individual family visits per day, or better than 100 community-wide house calls per month. The intensity of the service, of course, has varied with the village size, and also with the enthusiasm of the individual VHW and his available time from other responsibilities. The reports also show   that they have treated many simple cases of disease or minor injuries on the spot and referred more complicated ones either to an SWRC dispensary or to a more convenient government health facility.

The VHWs have also organized local group meetings to provide   nonformal education on good health practices, emphasizing preventive measures and using various audio-visual aids, including some they created   themselves. In addition the VHWs have organized their villages for scheduled service visits by health specialists (dealing, for example, with malaria eradication, vaccinations, eye diseases, and water purification) and   for the biweekly visits of SWRC health professionals from Tilonia.

Although no systematic check has been made on the attitudes of villagers toward the program, the general response seems to have been almost uniformly favorable. To cite but one example, the Gram Sabha   of Tyond village sent a letter to SWRC in June 1977 expressing the general   satisfaction of the local people with their VHW's home visits, treatments, and referrals (and also recommending that his salary be increased!).

The SWRC health team at Tilonia has devised a system for regularly evaluating each VHW's performance and for holding monthly evaluation sessions to review the situation and assess results. A recent evaluation report had this to say about some of the VHWs: "(Madanlal Sharma   from Tyond) is able to treat minor illnesses effectively. ... He has worked out a referral system (with the Chota Naraina dispensary) and sends   slips along with patients." The report goes on to say, "He is an   effective motivator. Three women from his village came forward for tubectomies during the family planning camp." The report complains about Ram Karan Jat's irregular work because of his school work and examination. However,   it notes "a marked improvement" in the performance of the health worker   from Junda. As his clients go to the Primary Health Centre at Rupangarh for curative services, he "lays more stress on preventive care." Kailash   Sharma from Gelota has "worked out a very good referral system. ... We have had a fairly good response for family planning from this village."   "(In Mandavaria) the 'under fives' have been inoculated against D.P.T. Malaria eradication work is going on with the help of the National Malaria Eradication Programme workers. The wells have been disinfected." "All   the children over 3 months in Tilonia and a majority of children from neighboring villages have been inoculated."

It would be wrong to leave the impression, however, that the new VHW scheme has developed smoothly without a hitch. Two problems in particular have been a cause for concern.

First, some of the local councils (Gram Sabhas) have not held up their end of the bargain adequately; they have shifted the burden of collecting monthly health fees to the VHW,and fee collections have frequently run well below 100 percent (due in part, no doubt, to the extreme poverty of some families). This has jeopardized the self-financing principle and forced the SWRC to absorb some of the cost of VHWs in its own hard-pressed budget.

The second problem has been the high dropout rate among potential and active VHWs. There have been eight dropouts from the first twenty VHWs trained (up to early 1977). Of the second batch of twenty potential VHWs identified after a careful selection process stretching over nine months, only five ultimately showed up for training, and two of these dropped out after a few months of active service (to accept employment with the Dairy Development Corporation).

This problem may perhaps be explained in part by the heavy workload and low financial compensation associated with this presumably "part-time" activity. But a more basic explanation seems to be the scarcity of literate and competent young men in these villages with at least eight years of schooling who are not already otherwise engaged, and the understandable preference of such young men for a better paying full-time job with a more promising future--if one comes along.

This type of "manpower" problem can readily arise in any community-based rural development activity whose success depends heavily on competent and energetic local workers, particularly if they are required to be young men with at least a full primary schooling. Though it is by no means an unsolvable problem that rules out the feasibility of community-based programs, its solution will clearly require an ingenious exploration of alternative possibilities.

The Maternity Program

This recently inaugurated program using ANMs and dais reached about a dozen villages in its first year, but SWRC members are quick to emphasize that the goal of reaching the entire affected population of women and children in Silora Block is still far off.

One of its priority goals is to prevent tetanus and anaemia among pregnant women, lactating mothers, and infants. All 250 women in Tilonia attending the special prenatal clinic, SWRC reports, have been protected against tetanus and anaemia, "but not without terrific resistance for a variety of what appear to be illogical reasons"--one being that "the traditional dai is yet to be fully convinced of the need to give folic acid and iron pills; it appears to go against local beliefs."

Nevertheless, there is no doubt that the traditional dais have by and large begun to use improved, more hygienic techniques in delivering babies,   and they are identifying complicated pregnancy cases and referring them to the   maternity center for delivery. They are also motivating women for family   planning and tubectomies, especially those with four or five children   Those SWRC-trained dais who earlier refused to conduct deliveries for lower-caste   women have all testified that the Tilonia dai has been helpful in changing these attitudes and eliminating the caste barriers in their work ethic.

The fact that the dais are illiterate has not impeded   their   effectiveness. They understand their own local culture,   are respected by the   community for the services they render and,   unlike most outsiders,   can   deal effectively with conservative grandmothers   and   mothers-in-law   even   in delicate matters such as family planning.   And being older   and   settled   in their way of life, they do not   present   the   kind of "manpower" problem   associated with the young male VHWs.

The Demand for Health Services

One of the most convincing signs that SWRC's   health program   is   making headway is the spreading demand for local health services by villages that do not yet have VHWs,   and the increasing awareness of health problems and of the desirability of preventive actions being generated by the nonformal   educational efforts of the VHWs in their own villages.   Two villages in the Jaipur District, over the line from Silora Block,   have already   joined SWRC's progran and have their own VHWs.

Information Needs

The health workers, dais, and ANMs have been collecting, somewhat sporadically, a growing accumulation of local data pertaining   to births,   deaths, malnutrition, infant weights and sizes, inoculations, family planning   candidates and acceptors, and so forth.   To a limited extent some of this information has been used for planning   health care activities in individual villages.   Three villages, for example, have been selected for a concentrated nutritional effort for children under five as a result of local surveys of nutritional status.

On the whole, however, such data have not been systematically   collected or analyzed for management and evaluation purposes because of a lack of available talent and because SWRC has been understandably reluctant to burden   its busy program "operators" with additional reporting chores at the expense   of their regular activities.   The time is fast approaching, however, when it will become important for SWRC, both for internal management and external relations purposes, to use some of these early baseline data and additional data yet to be collected to identify with greater specificity the various impacts of the program on local health conditions.   It will also be important for SWRC to obtain a more detailed picture of the costs associated with various   functions and activities in order to be able to assess results in relation to the   costs of achieving them, and to compare the costs of SWRC's   approach to health care with alternative approaches.

Integration with Other Health Services

It is important to note that SWRC has not attempted to provide a   complete health care system on its own.   Given its limited resources, this   would

have been impossible, and in any event probably unwise. A well-functioning
rural health system requires a well-balanced, well-staffed and equipped,and
well-integrated infrastructure running from each village (where the bulk of
the services are rendered) to referral, training, supervisory and logistical facilities above the village level. There must be a clear division of
labor and functions, good communication, and mutual respect and trust among
the various actors at each level.

The SWRC was well advised to direct its own limited resources   and
energies toward the goal of evolving such a comprehensive and integrated system, not by "going it alone" but by integrating its efforts with the existing government and private health services and facilities in the area. Thus,
for example, government health specialists have participated in   training
SWRC's village health workers; the government has provided medical supplies
to SWRC; the VHWs have freely referred difficult local cases not only   to
SWRC's dispensaries but to other health centers as well, and have cooperated
in organizing their villages to receive preventive health services (vaccinations, anti-malaria measures, etc.) from visiting government specialists.

In short, SWRC has dovetailed its health services with   the existing
health system in the area, as reflected in the map of that system shown   in
Fig. 2. In so doing, SWRC has made two clearly significant   contributions.
First, its popular and busy dispensaries have supplemented other   existing
facilities and expanded a much needed service in the area.   Second, and
perhaps much more important in the long run, its modest-sized VHW   program
has introduced an innovative and potentially highly important new   dimension to the existing system by providing it with the beginnings of a   genuine community base. If the government health authorities are sufficiently
impressed with the utility and viability of this demonstration, it   could
well lead to a major transformation of the old system to the considerable
benefit of all concerned.

Costs of the Health Program

How close has SWRC come thus far to its goal of providing   effective
primary health care services to all villagers, regardless of status,   at
costs low enough to be borne largely by the villagers themselves?   What are
the separate costs of the various specific activities and inputs that   enter
into the overall health program? And how do the costs of SWRC's community-
based health approach compare to what the costs of rendering equivalent services would be through the more conventional type of "top-down" health delivery system used by most governments?

Unfortunately, these important questions cannot be answered with   any
degree of confidence on the basis of the financial data available at the time
of this case study. SWRC's accounting system is well designed to serve   the
needs of auditors and donor agencies, but it does not readily lend   itself
to the kinds of cost analysis needed for management purposes or for answering
the types of questions posed above. Moreover, the costs reflected in SWRC's
financial accounts substantially understate some of the real costs   involved,
such as the cost of certain medicines provided to SWRC by government without
charge or below cost, gifts of equipment and the like by private donors, the
full rental value of the campus site, and not least of all, the costs   of
treating patients who are referred by SWRC's village health workers to health
facilities other than SWRC's own dispensaries. Finally, it was not feasible
for ICED to secure comparative figures on the costs of government health ser-

DISTRIBUTION OF HEALTH SERVICES

SILORA BLOCK
AJMER DISTRICT
RAJASTHAN

BHILAVAT
NOSAL

BHADOON

PANER JAJOTA

KATHODA

RUPNAGAR JUNDA
TYOND PAANWU

CHOTA

KARKERI

SURSURA

SALEMABAD

NAYAGAON GELOTA

RELAVATA HARMARA
KAHNIAWAS

KUCHIL

BHOJIAWAS TILONIA
PHALODA S.W.R.C.

CHUNDRI
BANDRSINDRI

MADANGANJ

Govt. Hospital
Govt. Allopathic Dispensary
Govt. Ayurvedic Dispensary
S.W.R.C. Dispensary
S.W.R.C. Village Level
Health Worker

SILORA BARANA

BALAPURA

scale

2 1 0 2 4 6
miles

vices in the area in order to estimate what it might cost government to render equivalent services to those now being provided by SWRC.

It will be very worthwhile, some time within the next two years, for the government or some other funding source to underwrite a special cost analysis study that could provide reliable answers to the above questions, which bear importantly on the economic viability and replicability of SWRC's approach to basic rural health care.

Meanwhile, the following data available to the present study shed partial light on these questions and tempt one to speculate a bit.

According to financial data provided by the SWRC, total expenditures on the Community Health Program in 1976 were Rs. 113,525 (excluding any contribution to general administration and overhead), or 15 percent of total SWRC program expenditures. The largest items were salaries (53 percent) and medicines (17 percent). Total income received by SWRC from patients' payments for medicines and from community health fees equalled only 10 percent of these total health expenditures, requiring the SWRC to bear the remaining 90 percent.

If one assumes that a total of 20,000 people were served by SWRC's health program (probably a conservative estimate when one combines those included in VHW villages and those in non-VHW villages treated by SWRC dispensaries), the average per capita cost would be in the range of Rs. 5 to 7. These figures do not include, of course, as noted earlier, any subsidized costs to SWRC on medical supplies obtained from the government or the cost of medical services to villagers referred either by VHWs or by SWRC dispensaries for treatment at other health facilities.

The above data in combination with other information suggest the following tentative conclusions and speculations:

First, SWRC is still a long way from achieving a largely self-supporting rural health care system. To make it even 50 percent self-supporting would clearly require very substantial increases in the present levels of community contributions and individual patient fees.

Second, the apparent per capita cost of SWRC's health program appear to be quite modest in terms of the variety and convenience of health services being provided. In other words, the return on the investment is probably unusually high.

Third, it is questionable, however, whether the per capita cost can be held down to the 1976 level if and as SWRC's Community Health Program undergoes sizeable expansion in the future. (According to the Director, "One can easily expect the figures [on the number of people served] to increase by 5 times in the next 5 years".) For one thing, SWRC's small health team at Tilonia is already carrying a very heavy work load and probably needs to be supplemented even to sustain this present load.[1] In addition, it may become

---

[1] The Tilonia-based health team that runs the dispensary and also handles the VHWs includes: one doctor (a lady), one medical social worker (a lady), two assistant nurse midwives, and one compounder (pharmacist). The Chota Naraina Dispensary has two ANMs, two field assistants and one compounder.

necessary to increase the salaries of VHWs in order to recruit and hold a sufficient number, unless some workable alternative is found. It may also be necessary, especially in the larger villages, to divide the present heavy workload among two or more VHWs or to share it with some new categories of local workers (such as volunteer "community mothers' assistants," for example, who could take over the work of weighing infants and giving nutritional education and support). The "economies of scale," it would appear, have probably already been largely exhausted; hence from here on personnel costs may well increase as a percentage of rising overall unit costs.

This is not to suggest, it should be emphasized, that the program should not be expanded or that the investment in better health services would not be very worthwhile even at somewhat higher per capita costs. It is merely to caution that adequate rural health services cannot be bought "on the cheap."

Fourth, it seems unlikely that the government could replicate SWRC's integrated community-based health approach at as low a per capita cost as SWRC can achieve (which, again is not to deny the desirability of the government's adopting such a strategy). It would be unrealistic to expect the general run of government employees, however devoted and conscientious they may be, to put in the long and irregular hours and to undergo the extensive personal inconveniences and sacrifices that typify SWRC's health staff. This is quite apart from the practical question of whether and how the unique spirit of the VHW system could be replicated within the framework of a fully governmental program.

Finally, it is clear that a well-functioning community-based rural health care system is bound to have higher per capita costs than the conventional hospital and clinic-based system. As already noted, for a community-based system to function effectively it requires not only a strong institutional and human resource base in each community but a strong infrastructure above the village level to provide essential training, supervisory and referral services, and logistical support. Such an infrastructure in many situations will need to be stronger than the existing structure. There is good reason to expect, however that the increased expenditures required to institute and operate a broadscale, community-based rural primary health care system would be offset by a far more than proportionate improvement in the resulting health services and family health status.

The above speculations, however, should not be taken as gospel. There is urgent need, we suggest, for a thorough cost analysis not only of SWRC's health program but of the entire health system in Silora Block in order to assess the costs and feasibility of extending a well-functioning community-based primary health care system to all villages in the area. Such a cost study in this sample area could be useful throughout rural India.

CHAPTER 4

THE WATER DEVELOPMENT
AND AGRICULTURAL PROGRAMS

The ground water development and research activities that the SWRC had undertaken in its initial phase of development had four distinct though related objectives in view: first, to assess the water potential of the area for agricultural purposes; second, to lay the basis for a rural electrification program; third, to develop a technical solution to the water percolation problem that plagued many local water tanks; and fourth, to assist individual farmers to develop and improve their own water supplies.

The initial surveys and research efforts of the initial phase began to pay off in government decisions and actions during the second phase and led to an extension of the previous efforts elsewhere in Silora Block and in other states.

As a result of the SWRC's earlier water survey of fifty-one villages for the Rural Electrification Corporation, the state government of Rajasthan approved a plan in 1975-76 for the electrification of the entire Silora Block by 1978, making it the first block in the state that would achieve full electrification.

Soon after this initial survey for electrification planning purposes, the state government of Rajasthan commissioned the SWRC to conduct a more detailed survey of the entire Silora Block, this time from the point of view of locating specific areas with enough potential water supply for increasing agricultural development. This more extensive and intensive survey carried into the second phase of the SWRC's development. It covered for each subarea the geology, existing and potential ground water supplies, the range of water levels in existing wells, soil and water quality, and the potentials for agricultural extension.

On the basis of this survey and on specific instructions from the Agricultural Refinance Corporation (ARC), the block was then divided into four ecological zones and the SWRC team was asked to recommend specific development strategies for each zone. The team recommended that Zones A, B, & C could be taken up for a program of constructing new dug wells and tube wells and deepening existing wells by boring or blasting. It also recommended certain fertilizer applications, according to water conditions, and chemical treatment where necessary to make the water more suitable for drinking. Zone 4 in the southern part of the block, however, where the water potential was poorest, was recommended only for the extension of existing wells and for application of the drilling techniques developed through SWRC's research for improving the percolation and recharge rates of tanks and ponds.

The latter techniques had won the approval of both national and international water experts and were getting a positive response from   farmers. The SWRC in its second phase was therefore given financial support by   the Government of India to apply the technique in a drought prone area   in another part of Ajmer District.

On the basis of its work with water surveys in Silora Block, the SWRC was requested to undertake similar work in other areas. For example,   the Seva Mandir a voluntary organization, asked for a water survey of thirty-five villages in the Udaipur District of Rajasthan in conjunction with a general development plan for the area. This resulted in surveying sixty new   well sites for tribal families.

Meanwhile SWRC also stepped up its research and advisory and   drilling services for individual farmers, industries, and institutions on a no-cost no-profit basis. By 1977 some 150 wells had been drilled.

It should be noted that these extensive activities relating to   water supply were handled by a relatively small SWRC team--generally   including a geologist, geophysicist, cartographer, and a small number of assistants--supplemented, from time to time, however, by qualified specialists borrowed from government agencies or other organizations.

In principle, most such survey and research work normally falls within the province of government, especially since government participation   is usually essential to mobilizing the large development investments needed   to follow up such surveys with positive action. As a practical matter, however, the government's capacity to conduct such surveys and research is so limited and strained that many areas go unattended for years. Thus the availability of SWRC's expertise to supplement the work of government was welcomed by government and farmers alike and undoubtedly set the stage for earlier and more rapid agricultural development in the Silora area and certain other   areas than would otherwise have been possible.

EXPANSION OF AGRICULTURAL EXTENSION

In the second phase the rather meager agricultural extension efforts of SWRC's initial phase were expanded somewhat, but they still remained relatively modest in scope. The agricultural team in this later period generally consisted of one or two agricultural graduates and two local assistants.   By working closely with the state government's agricultural services, however, and by tying in with the water development team and the community health program, the effectiveness of their efforts was multiplied.

The major effort of the agricultural program centered on demonstration and training activities at the SWRC campus. In cooperation with the   District Agricultural Officer and the Block Development Officer, demonstration plots were sown with new varieties of wheat, vegetables, and other crops; experiments were conducted with kharif and rabi crops with the needs of small farmers in mind; and extension education camps were conducted for   farmers from surrounding villages (generally with fifty to a hundred participants). A start was also made on an outreach program, centering on the distribution of seeds and other inputs. By 1977 the outreach program included nineteen villages.

Interestingly, the VHWs came to play a useful role in this agricultural outreach effort. Being young farmers themselves, they provided an important communication link between the farmers of their village and the campus. When they came for their regular Sunday meetings with the health specialists, they also brought questions for the agricultural specialist as well as orders from their neighbors for new seeds, fertilizer, and pesticides and carted home these inputs for local distribution. SWRC purchased the supplies at whole- sale from the government, sold them at cost, and the local health worker earn- ed one rupee per bag as his delivery commission.

The health workers were not passive messenger boys in this liaison arrangement. They made complaints when seeds were faulty, asked for soybeans to experiment with, and in general made it clear that they and the farmers they represented were informed consumers who knew what they wanted, and not newcomers to agricultural innovation.

TACKLING THE PROBLEMS OF MARGINAL FARMERS

It is generally the larger and more prosperous farmers, who have cash reserves and a good credit rating and who can afford to take reasonable risks, that benefit most from water development schemes and from new technologies disseminated by agricultural extension services. The marginal farmers, who usually far outnumber the more prosperous ones, have to scratch hard for the sheer survival of their families and are generally bypassed by the benefits of new development schemes and agricultural support services. In fact there are numerous instances where their position has actually been worsened by new development schemes and the introduction of new technologies, such as high-yielding varieties of rice and wheat.

This universal problem in the developing world had been much on the mind of the SWRC team from the outset, but it had been difficult to find a good handle to take hold of to do something really substantial about it. A promising opening came in early 1975 when an SWRC proposal to conduct a socio-economic feasibility study for development of small and marginal farmers and agricultural laborers in the Jawaja Block of Ajmer District in Rajasthan was approved for funding by the Indian Ministry of Agriculture under the Drought Prone Area Program. By May 1975 a small subcenter of SWRC was established in Jawaja (currently headed by an economist who joined SWRC-Tilonia in its early stage and thus had acquired a familiarity with problems of poverty in a dry rural area). At about the same time SWRC was commissioned by the Agricultur- al Refinance Corporation Scheme to conduct a detailed water survey in part of Jawaja Block.

The ecological and socioeconomic conditions of the Jawaja Block are fully as severe as those in Silora. Only half the land is arable, the other half being largely barren. The average annual rainfall is low; only one-quarter of the cultivated land is irrigated by pumps or tanks, and an excep- tionally dry year can have a disastrous impact on thousands of families. The most vulnerable are those with little or no land, and they are the majority. More than half the farm families have less than one acre--not enough to meet their own minimum food requirements, much less to yield a surplus for the market. The highest per capita income is Rs. 314 in Pakharia in the De- luara Circle; the lowest is Rs. 30 in the poorest circle of villagers in Barakhera. Most of the villages have a high level of debt to money-lenders and a very low record of institutional borrowing at lower interest rates.

The SWRC feasibility study brought these miserable conditions into clear perspective, analyzed the natural resources of the area, and identified potential measures for tapping available resources and generating additional income for marginal farmers. One of the key conclusions was that "it may not be optimal to attack the problems of poverty [in this area] by trying to raise the income from agriculture." It was felt that, given the land and water conditions, programs to promote animal husbandry would be more effective, coupled   with efforts to promote job and income creating small rural industries.   Thus the report (in April 1977) proposed package programs for pasture development, animal husbandry, veterinary services, the introduction of new technologies   such as improved breeds of sheep, cattle, and goats, artificial insemination,   and improved fodder varieties, as well as marketing facilities for animals and animal products. Supplementary measures were also proposed to encourage   small-scale industries and crafts and to improve community health and education.

At the cut-off date of this case study the SWRC team in Jawaja,encouraged by the favorable reception its feasibility report received, were engaged   in spelling out detailed plans for implementing this proposed package-approach   to improving the conditions and prospects of marginal farmers and landless   families. It remains to be seen, of course, how much solid support will be forthcoming and how feasible the plan actually proves to be, but at least it appears to hold greater promise than the conventional agricultural extension approach.

As the Jawaja feasibility study was coming to a head, a new specialist, trained in agriculture, agricultural engineering and management, joined SWRC-Tilonia and began work on a similar plan for attacking the problems of marginal farmers in Silora. This has since been submitted for funding to the   Indian government's program of "Peoples'Action for Development."

In rough outline, this Silora plan is geared to a government program for distributing land (generally rather poor land) to landless laborers,   Harijans, and other scheduled castes, and proposes a package of measures for improving the productivity of this land. The package includes such measures as leveling   and reclaiming the land; tapping available ground water supplies; introducing high-yielding varieties of seeds, fertilizer, and insecticides (where appropriate); crop rotation; provision of low interest loans; and strengthening the marketing system. The educational activities include short term training of farmers   at the Agricultural University in Udaipur, farmer training camps for rabi   and kharif crops, and the involvement of students from the Agricultural University in working with the farmers through summer jobs. The project would identify 200 marginal farmers each year and work with them intensively for five years with a package plan on an experimental basis.

A COMMENTARY

The Water Development and Research Program clearly did much to get   the SWRC off to a strong start. Its results were respected by technicians in   and outside government; it represented something tangible and functional that farmers and others could appreciate; it was directly addressed to what   everyone knew was a crucial problem for the area's development; it led rather   quickly to follow-up actions by government electrification, water development   and credit agencies; and it was an effective means for educating SWRC itself   about the basic conditions of the area and its people.

Standing alone, however, the water program could probably have had only a limited impact on the social and economic development of the whole area, parti-

cularly for the poorest section of the population. It had to be followed up
with complementary actions pertaining to agriculture and ultimately with   a
well-designed "package program," specifically tailored to the needs and circumstances of marginal farmers and the landless.   This became increasingly
apparent to SWRC, which at the present writing is just beginning to cut its
teeth on this more comprehensive approach to the small subsistence   farmer.
This approach will undoubtedly involve a good deal of "learning by doing,"
improvisation, trial by error, persistence, patience, and indomitable opti-
mism.

     This challenge of how to help the small and indigent farmers is not
unique to Rajasthan, however. It confronts all of India and practically all
other developing countries. It has lately been commanding   the attention of
major international and bilateral assistance agencies, and no one claims to
have the answers. The experiences of the SWRC in the next few years, therefore, should prove of interest--and perhaps of significant help--to   many
others who are seeking solutions to the same basic problem.

     It is already clear from SWRC's experiences to date, if it was not al-
ready clear from the experiences of many others, that conventional agricultural extension techniques that concentrate on "selling" farmers "new technologies" are by no means a sufficient answer, especially for the small and
poor farmer. These techniques at their best can only be one useful part of
a broader combination of measures needed to transform the lives of the poorest of the rural poor.

CHAPTER 5

THE RURAL INDUSTRIES PROGRAM

It will be recalled that the three initial priority areas envisaged by the founders of SWRC were water development, health, and education.   Soon after the Centre got into operation, however, and as evidence of its flexible and pragmatic approach, a fourth priority activity emerged--namely, the revitalization of traditional crafts and rural industries. This proved to be a practical way to generate new employment and income   (albeit on   only a modest scale at first) and to focus on improving the lot of specific disadvantaged groups, including especially their female members.

The socioeconomic survey, conducted by SWRC under the sponsorship of the Khadi and Village Industries Board in 1974, called sharp attention   to the problems of economic survival among traditional craftsmen and   artisans. The weavers, the leather workers, the block printers, including many women, had learned their traditional caste occupations and crafts from   childhood. But because of unfavorable market conditions, lack of funds and raw   materials, and in some cases in order to escape the low status and stigma attached to these caste occupations, many had given up their occupations either to go to towns and cities for new jobs, or to work in their villages as   agricultural laborers or construction workers.

As these circumstances came into clearer focus, SWRC decided to   initiate some special efforts to keep these traditional crafts alive   in the hope of fostering increased employment and income in the lower-caste groups traditionally associated with them.

THE WOMEN'S CRAFT PROGRAM

The women's program, started in January 1974, was initially a social education program that also explored possibilities for adding   economic incentives through crafts and tailoring. The village postman in Tilonia, who turned out to have a diploma in tailoring, became involved in the tailoring and craft classes that were held in Tilonia in the evenings and that   also included social education and literacy lessons. Similar centers were later established in the villages of Phaloda and Buharu. The Phaloda center   was eventually shifted to Chundri, and a new center was established at Harmara.

During its second and third years the craft program in Tilonia turned into a daytime production center, while the social education and   literacy aspects continued to function in the evenings. The Chamar women who   had earlier worked as unskilled laborers on construction sites or had looked for

occasional famine relief work were attracted to this program while the upper
caste Jat, Rajput, or Gujar women stayed away. The Chamar women found this
new work less strenuous and more interesting, and the economic as well   as
social benefits seemed to be quite attractive.

By early 1977 about 200 women were enrolled in the Tilonia   program,
though only a minority of these attended regularly. On the typical day about
sixty women came to the center to produce clothing, craft items, and   block
printed textiles. They were paid on a piecework basis and their daily earnings generally ranged from 3 to 8 rupees, or up to Rs. 180 (about US$20) in a
month--a quite significant sum for disadvantaged women in these circumstances.

The group included all ages, from teenage girls to grandmothers. It was
not uncommon to find three generations of the same family participating in the
production program. The teenagers generally had a little schooling and   were
eager and quick to learn new skills to prepare themselves for homemaking   and
to earn some cash income. Most were already married but still living   with
their mothers until the time came for moving in with their husbands' families.

More often than not, well-intentioned craft programs of this sort   have
soon foundered for lack of an effective marketing mechanism. The local demand
is soon saturated and there is no workable link to distant urban markets   and
export markets. SWRC sought to avoid this fate by taking a number of steps to
break into such markets as those of Delhi and Bombay. In October 1975 an   exhibition of Tilonia crafts was held at the Triveni Kala Sangam in Delhi,   and
another was held in May 1977 at an art gallery in Bombay. Contacts were made
with the Handicrafts and Handlooms Export Corporation, the All India   Handi-
crafters Board, the Central Cottage Industries Emporium, the Khadi and Village
Industries Board, and a British agency located in the U.K. In addition,   a
number of small buyers and city shops became interested. A female free-lancer
became associated with SWRC and began to build links between the crafts center
and the city markets on a commission basis. Another female consultant   from
Delhi offered her services to SWRC to develop new designs likely to attract
city buyers.

Some of the more enterprising women wanted to strike off on their   own
(though still using SWRC's marketing services), but to do so they required some
working capital to purchase raw materials and equipment (e.g., a sewing   machine). SWRC arranged to get loans of Rs. 500 each for eighteen such women.The
loans were provided by the new Tilonia Branch of the Union Bank of India   (located on the SWRC campus) under the DIR (Differential Interest Rate) Scheme especially designed to assist small farmers and artisans and illiterate   women
entrepreneurs. The loans were to be repaid in regular installments   deducted
from the women's earnings, while SWRC paid the interest in their behalf.

To make it easier for women to spend their days at the production center
SWRC established a balwadi   preschool) and later an infant creche where their
children would be cared for and given a nutritious meal. In addition,   the
health dispensary, right next door, undertook to provide maternal and child care
services, including immunization for the children and family planning and nutritional education for the mothers. The production program also developed   a
stronger social education dimension. As the illiterate village women began to
see the practical economic benefits of the program and to confront the   intricacies of bank loans and marketing, they developed a greater interest in literacy
and social education.

In contrast to the Tilonia center the craft centers at Buharu and Chundri attracted a high proportion of higher caste women (though   from relatively poor families) and have continued to function more as social education and craft training classes than as actual production centers.

Yet another variant is represented by the new crafts and   social education center established in Harmara in January 1977. It has attracted women from the Reger caste who inherited unique skills of embroidering on leather. At the center they soon began to branch out   into embroidering on cotton and woolen fabrics. This center will   probably develop a strong production orientation similar to Tilonia's.

THE LEATHER WORKS PROGRAM

Many of the villages in the SWFC area include members of   the Chamar or Reger lower castes that have traditionally been involved   in tanning and leather work. Although many have given up their   caste occupation, others continue to spend up to half the year catering   to the local demand for leather products and the rest of their time   seeking construction work and other unskilled employment.

In spite of its tradition of colorful and decorative   leather items with embroidery, this area of Rajasthan has not developed   a system of effectively utilizing the hides of dead animals   in   the locality. The tanners generally obtain the raw hides from Nasirabad in Ajmer District or at wholesale rates from Kanpur in Uttar Pradesh. As an alternative they often buy processed leather, which proves to be too expensive. The Khadi and Village Industries Board is equipped to offer some help in these matters, but few Chamars and Regers have been aware of these services.

Exploring possibilities of solving some of these problems, the SWRC gathered a group of leather workers from nearby communities   and hired their services for making leather goods which were presented at the crafts exhibition in Delhi in October 1975. It was soon realized, however, that although the leather items looked attractive and   could be sold fairly easily, the leather was not processed properly and was prone to develop bacterial infection and mould. To find an answer   to this problem, the SWRC team contacted the Central Leather Research Institute in Rajkot in Gujarat State, which was known to have evolved an effective method of curing and tanning leather in a less expensive and time-consuming fashion.

With a view to bringing this modern technique to the   Rajasthan villages, a representative of the Leather Research Institute was   invited to SWRC. The chemical engineer at SWRC organized a demonstration-cum-training camp for local tanners in Harmara in collaboration   with the researcher from the Leather Research Institute. About forty   tanners from Harmara, Relavata, and Buharu attended the two-week camp   in September 1976. They were impressed with the new technology and accepted it with enthusiasm. They also came to appreciate the economic advantages of improving the quality of locally available hides through proper methods of handling dead animals and of sharing community pits for tanning and processing as against individual pits.

To follow up on this initial effort, SWRC arranged to get bank loans of Rs. 2,000 each for seven Regers who volunteered to join a new scheme. As part of this scheme, SWRC undertook to obtain the chemicals and other raw materials from the manufacturers and hand them over to the tanners at actual costs. The tanners now use the new technique for processing the leather   and   also make leather goods for which they get paid by the center   Portions of their earnings are used to repay the bank loans,and the leather goods are sold along with the women's craft items in the urban markets.   Five of the Regers participating in this scheme work on the campus where their work is supervised   by the SWRC team, and they also get help on new designs and patterns.   The other two Regers prefer to work in their own villages and visit the campus   according to their convenience.

As this small-scale experiment began to give results, a project   proposal was prepared to set up a tannery and footwear unit in Harmara,   3 km. northwest of Tilonia.   The proposal has been approved for funding by a   well known industrial house, Mahindra and Mahindra, in Bombay.   The Regers   collected a community contribution of Rs. 1,000 and secured the land in Harmara for the set-up.   The project will get into operation when it has met all official requirements and a functional set-up with a building, equipment, and   tools has been established.

The plan visualizes a cooperative management of the tannery   and footwear unit and includes provisions for   in-service training of local people in technology, supervision, stock-keeping, marketing, institutional credit, collaboration with outside agencies, administration, and management.   In   the early stages, many of these elements will be closely supervised and   managed by the SWRC team, but the center hopes to hand it over to local people   over a period of about ten years.

Regers from other villages have shown considerable interest in the new method of tanning.   The SWRC is planning to conduct similar   demonstration-cum-training camps in the scientific methods of tanning in far-flung   villages like Relavata, Jajota, and Bandrsindri   because they have a large   percentage of Reger population.   This time the training camps will be organized by the SWRC without outside technical help, using instead some of the   previously trained local tanners as instructors.

It is interesting to note how SWRC's health program and   communications section tied in with the new rural industries program.   The women   in the Reger community in Harmara had already joined the crafts center in their village.   The health team moved in soon after the initial contact with Regers, only to realize that the community had a fairly large number of   positive cases of T.B.   The health team arranged for their treatment and undertook to educate the families in prevention and treatment of T.B.   The Communication Unit of SWRC made film-strips on the tanning technique during the   initial training camp and on prevention and treatment of T.B.   These film-strips were then used in connection with the community education and training activities.

PROGRAMS FOR OTHER ARTISANS

Similar programs have been organized or are being worked out for other artisans in the block.   The "Own Your Own Loom Scheme" has been devised   for the weavers who are otherwise employed by the Banias in their   handloom factories.   With loans from the bank under the DIR scheme or from the Rajasthan Handloom Project Development Board, some nine weavers have resigned from their factories and set up their own looms. Similar arrangements have been worked out with the traditional Balais, the weavers who work on pit looms.

Block printing has been a well-known folk art in Rajasthan, and the town of Kishangarh and the village Rupanagar are especially   well known for their special block prints and designs. These two communities were approached by SWRC but rejected the center's assistance. Contacts were then made with another printers' community in the town of Bagru near Jaipur. The SWRC worked with these printers in designing special print patterns in black and beige, or red and beige color combinations. This particular type of cloth with these prints   has become quite popular and is beginning to be known as the "Tilonia fabric."

AN EFFORT TO HELP OUT-OF-SCHOOL YOUTH

In response to a proposal submitted to the Ministry of Education to set up a work center program for rural artisans in the villages   around Tilonia, approval was granted in March 1977 for a training component for traditional skills like weaving, cloth block printing, and leather   work. The work center has succeeded in attracting quite a number of   trainees, especially young women belonging to scheduled castes. In the first   half of 1977 the program managed to train about fifty local people in different trades. The products made by the trainees are marketed by the SWRC.

The integrated aspect of this work program may be seen   as a distinct innovation: the cloth produced by the weavers is printed in   the printing unit and then made into garments in the tailoring section   and subsequently marketed.

After the trainees have been sufficiently trained, the SWRC   takes responsibility for setting them on their own feet by arranging loans for them from the Union Bank of India.

Workers Cooperatives: The SWRC is on the verge of forming   two cooperative societies for the persons who get trained through the work center program. One will be a women's cooperative for weaving, printing, and garment making. The other will be for leather workers: a rural tannery unit and production unit. Previous cooperatives in this part of the country had not been successful, largely because of shortages of   materials and poor management. However, the SWRC believes that cooperatives are the best way of organizing the people and bringing them together to get tangible results. Thus the SWRC will be keeping a paternal eye on these two new cooperatives to insure that they get off to a sound start. Once the members get the hang of it, the SWRC will withdraw from the society.

A COMMENTARY

There is nothing new about voluntary agencies or governments attempting to create employment and income opportunities for disadvantaged   rural
people by providing training in cottage industries, various crafts, or   more
modern skills. The record of success for such efforts, however, has generally been disappointing, if not downright dismal. The usual reasons are, first,
that the main focus is often mainly on training to give people new skills, but
with too little attention to the measures required to help them apply   their
new skills once they have acquired them; and second, that even if the training
leads to actual production, there is no effective and economically viable marketing system for disposing of the output at profitable prices.

What is interesting and different about the SWRC's initiatives in this
field is, first, that they focused on already existing traditional skills and
products rather than on introducing "modern" and unfamiliar skills and   products (in short, they tried to exploit the existing strengths of the area);
second, they recognized that "training" and the possession of skills is   not
enough as these are but components of a total production and marketing "system"
that must also include a flow of essential raw materials, credit, and other inputs, and above all the means of disposing of "products" on an assured   and
profitable basis; and third, that people cannot be narrowly viewed like machines,
simply as "producers," because to be good producers they require complementary
"social" development supports such as basic education, assistance in caring for
their children, and improvement in health and other basic requisites for improving the quality of life.

It remains to be seen how successful these various initiatives in small-
scale rural industrial development will prove to be in creating new employment
and income for the poorest sector. Realistically, one should allow for   some
failures along with the successes. But, come what may, even at this early
stage the SWRC's initiatives in this field have helped to verify the initial
premise on which the SWRC was founded--namely, that social change must   be
sparked by economic change, and this requires opening access to new opportunities for economic advancement on the part of those confined to the poorest
economic status.

Significant also is the fact that these "production oriented" activities
contributed the most of any programs toward making the SWRC a self-supporting
enterprise. SWRC's total expenditure in 1976 on the rural industries   and
social education and crafts programs combined was Rs. 170,049, of which 75.5
percent went for raw materials, only 6.5 percent for salaries, and 18 percent
for miscellaneous administrative costs. Against these expenditures, the programs returned revenues to the SWRC totaling Rs. 120,408--equivalent to   70
percent of total expenditures. As "marketing agent" for the various   craft
projects, the SWRC earned a 10 percent margin--not quite sufficient to defray
its own overhead and administrative costs involved, yet a major contribution
to them. SWRC officials believe that market conditions will not tolerate a
higher margin; hence they are now endeavoring to achieve economies in these
overhead and administrative costs.

Meanwhile, as limited as the scale of these "production" programs is,
a significant number of the poorest people in the area have already begun to
improve their economic position, and their prospects for further improvement
seem encouraging.

Here again it is worth noting that the SWRC did not "go it alone" in the rural industries program. It played a critical entrepreneurial, catalytic, and coordinating role, but such success as there has been thus far is attributable in no small measure to the way SWRC has drawn upon existing government services and other institutions and individual experts to provide new technologies, help in training, improved product designs, credit supplies, and marketing outlets. It is also noteworthy that the SWRC's health team and communications specialist also contributed to the effort.

CHAPTER 6

THE EDUCATION PROGRAM

SWRC's Education Program is quite separate from the training and educational components that have been built into the health, agriculture,   and
rural industries programs by the "noneducators" responsible for these "sectoral" programs with occasional help on visual aids (mainly film   strips)
from the SWRC communication specialist.

The Education Program has concentrated on separate   "educational"
projects moulded in the image of formal schooling and of traditional interest to ministries of education. Its initial projects followed highly conventional patterns (adult literacy classes, social education classes for women,
and a balwadi for preschool children), but its subsequent projects   became
more innovative, in part because of the encouragement and support   of   innovatively-minded government education officials in Rajasthan and Delhi   who
saw SWRC's project area as a promising laboratory for trying out fresh ideas.

A FRESH START ON LITERACY

Some time after the early collapse of the "100 percent literacy" campaign, a less ambitious but perhaps more realistic approach to   literacy
training began to emerge--more by accident than design.   The tailoring
instructor at the Tilonia crafts production center and the village health
workers in Panwa and Kakniawas found a growing interest in literacy among
their women "clients" and decided to set up their own modest literacy programs to cater to this demand.

Significantly, these "classes" are not held in schools, but in   the
front yards of houses, behind the mud walls, in the most natural surroundings
of the village--the buffalo in one corner, a few men relaxing or dozing in
another corner after the day's work, and children of all ages walking   in
and out. Sitting together in the center, a cluster of women of all generations strive to master the magic letters, words, and number symbols. There
is very little added to this settting in the way of audio-visual aids   or
instructional materials, and the teaching methods are crude. But the   new
element in the situation is conspicuous motivation. As the learners   with
their slates compete to show the visitors how they can write their   own
names and numbers up to 100, it becomes evident that literacy has come   to
have greater meaning for the women "producers" at the Tilonia craft center
since they started earning money, taking bank loans, and becoming exposed
to marketing mechanisms, prices, quality standards, and new designs. Letters and numbers now have a functional utility and practical value   for
these women and are seen as a doorway to a more modern way of life.   A
similar phenomenon has been taking place among other women who had experienced at first hand the benefits of participating in a "modern" maternal
and child care and community health program.

As more villagers whose lives are changing begin to ask for literacy
training, a grant may be forthcoming from the Ministry of Education   to
support an expansion of SWRC's fresh start on literacy.

SERVICES TO WORKING MOTHERS AND THEIR CHILDREN

During the second phase of SWRC's development, two more balwadis were
established in the villages of Bhojiawas and Tyond, and a new creche   was
added to the balwadi/craft center complex on the Tilonia campus. Interestingly, these child care centers led the way toward integrating the isolated
education program with other SWRC programs. With the cooperation of   the
health program, the balwadi and creche children all receive a nutritious
daily meal, regular health checkups, and immunizations. And by linking the
day care centers to the craft production program the working mothers   can
have their young children well cared for while they are earning income.
Thus, through these program linkages, both the children and mothers benefit.

A BROADER APPROACH TO SOCIAL EDUCATION FOR WOMEN

The original social education class for women at the Tilonia   campus
turned into a crafts production center in the daytime (fitting the   strong
interests and practical needs of the poorer women), with the social   education remaining available through evening classes for those who wished   to
participate. It was still, however, a separate and relatively conventional
type of program with the ever-present stress on literacy. Meanwhile   new
crafts and social education classes were created in two other villages, one
of which also began to evolve into a crafts production center.

More recently SWRC has embarked on a quite different and probably more
promising approach to social education. With the support of the Department
of Social Welfare of the Ministry of Education and Social Welfare, SWRC in
April 1977 organized an experimental 21-day "training camp" in social education for forty women in Harmara in which staff members from other   SWRC
programs participated as resource persons. It covered discussions on a
wide variety of topics directly tied to improving rural family life, such
as health, nutrition, growing food, child care, hygiene and sanitation,
family planning, cottage industry, self-employment cooperatives, appropriate
technology, and schools. This trial venture, representing another   step
toward integrating the Education Program with other programs and with   the
basic needs of the villagers, won a sufficiently warm response to encourage
SWRC to schedule similar social education camps in four other villages during 1977-78.

A BOLD EFFORT TO TRANSFORM PRIMARY EDUCATION

A study conducted by the SWRC Education Section in 1974, in collaboration with the National Centre for Educational Research and Training (NCERT)
in the national Ministry of Education, examined the reasons for poor attendance and high dropout rates in the local primary schools. The findings indicated that the children of primary school age in poor rural families had
a number of household and farm duties that made it difficult for them to
spare time for schooling; that the school curriculum did not relate   sufficiently to the children's rural life and special needs, nor prepare them for

urban jobs; and that most of the teachers did not belong to the villages
in which they taught and hence they had little communication with   the
parents and the rest of the community.

In an effort to find practical solutions to these and related problems, a three-year experimental action research program was devised.
Its basic objective was to test out a fresh approach to primary education that would serve the basic learning needs, interests, and   life
styles of all village children in the area from age six to eleven, including previous dropouts. With funding and technical assistance from
NCERT, the experiment was launched in June 1975 in three village schools
(in Tilonia, Buharu, and Phaloda) that were turned over by the Rajasthan
authorities for SWRC to manage (a quite unusual trust).

The experiment, now in its third year, includes several strikingly
unconventional features that were bound to draw fire from some of the
parents and more traditional educationists but by the same token to win
the applause of forward-looking educators.

First, the regular teachers in the experimental schools were   re-
assigned to other areas (in the belief that they would find it difficult
to adapt to new ways). To replace them, six young local secondary school
graduates with no previous teacher training were recruited: two farmers,
two priests, an unemployed youth, and a widow. They were given   relatively brief initial training at the SWRC campus, followed by weekly
workshops throughout the school year with the SWRC staff and various
visiting experts. During these workshops there were free and open discussion of problems encountered in the classroom, critical evaluation of
how the program was going, and introduction of useful supplementary ideas
and information. Different members of the SWRC staff, plus education
officials from Rajasthan and Delhi as well as staff members of the Regional
College of Education in Ajmer, participated in the initial training and in
later workshops and school visits. The spirit was one of guidance, assistance, encouragement, and teamwork, not of "supervision" in the old sense.

Second, the school time schedule was adapted to the convenience of
the learners; the younger ones and others who were free could attend the
morning shift (8 a.m. to noon), while those with daytime duties   could
come in the evening from 7 p.m. to 10 p.m. (This was especially important for previous dropouts, most of whom had acquired substantial   daytime obligations.)

Third, although the basic learning objectives of the official syllabus
were retained--especially language skills and numeracy--substantial changes
were made in the curriculum and in educational methods with a view to providing the children with more relevant, interesting, and useful learning
experiences relating to their own social, economic, and ecological environment and to such matters as agriculture, animal husbandry, crafts,   and
rural industry. Each school--viewed as a "learning center"--had its own
garden and animals, and the village itself was occasionally used as a
"classroom." Special teaching materials and learning aids were developed,
and the old "rote memory" examinations were changed. Traditional didactic
methods were replaced by the "project method," group discussion, observation
tours, and other more open and flexible pedagogical methods.

Provision was made at the outset for continuing self-evaluation and for periodic checks on student participation and progress (with the technical help of the Regional College of Education). By the end of the second year (1976-77) the proportion of six- to eleven-year-old children in the three villages attending either the experimental schools or regular schools had risen substantially and the rate of dropouts had declined, although 100 percent participation was still a good way off. At that point an evaluation was conducted by the Regional College of Education of the comparative scholastic achievement of children in the three experimental schools and their counterparts in two traditional government schools in the area. Significantly, the results, summarized in Table 4, showed somewhat higher average mean scores for the experimental school children in three out of four skill areas, including reading comprehension and arithmetic.

TABLE 4

Comparative Mean Achievement Scores of Children
in Three Experimental Schools and Two Regular Schools

Name of School	Arith-metic	Reading Compre-hension	Listening Comprehension Poem	Story	Environ-mental Studies
Class IV					
Experimental Schools	20.75	51.25	49.00	78.50	33.00
Panchayat Samiti School					
Harmara	19.75	39.83	38.83	81.67	28.88
Government School, Tilonia	22.94	39.50	23.21	50.42	28.35
Class V					
Experimental Schools	14.33	72.44	57.67	95.11	48.33
Panchayat Samiti School					
Harmara	7.95	67.04	38.10	112.71	26.57
Government School, Tilonia	7.28	50.21	44.42	106.28	30.08

Source: SWRC, August 1977.

The community response to the experiment varied from "poor" or "skeptical" to "positive" and "encouraging." While the block-level government officials were cooperative, the responses from the Panchayat (the village council) and its head, the Sarpanch, were less favorable in Tilonia and Buharu. This reaction was explained by the SWRC team as a conflict between the power structure and the parents because the project emphasized approaching parents directly rather than through the Panchayat. The response was more positive among the lower castes and among dropouts than among the upper castes such as the Jats and Gujars, but in general the response was more encouraging toward the end of the first year. The villagers from Phaloda, for example, offered free labor for digging wells for the school. Some children from Tilonia, however, were shifted by their parents to the   regular school to avoid further participation in the experiment.

The experimental schools also encountered some "housekeeping"   difficulties. The kitchen garden program ran into problems of watering   plants when the schools were closed and of getting other routine chores done.   It was also difficult to coordinate the school schedule with dairy work, and the animal husbandry program encountered both labor and cost problems.

All in all, however, the experiment in the first two years seems   to have gone encouragingly well, with one year still to run. The big   question remains as to what would happen then.

AN INVENTORY OF LOCAL EDUCATIONAL RESOURCES

With the encouragement and assistance of the Directorate of Nonformal Education in the Ministry of Education in Delhi, SWRC's education staff undertook in 1975 an unusual inventory of potential educational resources   in the Silora area, including a rating of how much they were actually   being used.

The concept of education employed in this survey was far broader than conventional schooling or its nonformal equivalent. The investigators   had in view all kinds of local basic learning needs, including not only   "the three-Rs" but needs that cut across such fields as health, nutrition,   environment, agriculture, household improvement, occupational skill training, and cultural activities.

Considerable effort was devoted to developing a meaningful   typology for classifying various types of "educational resources"--institutional and noninstitutional, human, physical, and financial--and also a methodology for rating their utilization.

The final report, issued in March 1977, identified an astonishing variety of potential educational resources in the area, including   numerous institutions (e.g., schools, Panchayat Samatis,Gram Panchayats, village cooperatives, youth clubs, Mahila Mandals, and Jati Sudhar Samatis);   numerous local residents with special talents and skills; and a wide range of facilities, materials, equipment, aids, and situations that could be harnessed for educational purposes.[1] The report also found, however, that most of   these resources were either entirely unused or were grossly underused for   educational purposes--including the schools and teachers themselves. (The   fact that 90 percent of the teachers were not residents of the villages in which they taught was seen as a major obstacle to their playing a larger educational role in the community.)

---

[1]Others who may be interested in conducting such an inventory will find the SWRC report useful: Study of the Unused and Underutilized Educational Resources of Silora Block, Ajmer District, Rajasthan (India); SWRC, March 1977.

The researchers concluded that this underutilization was not for lack of interest or goodwill--"it was amply evident that this was available in plenty." Rather, they cited two other main reasons. The first was the "self-centered nature" of the limited membership of various local institutions: "No sincere effort could be noticed on their part to reach out to the community nor to involve the latter in their area of operation." The second was the "paucity of agencies, programmes and people actively and creatively engaged in the task of organizing the tapping [of] the potential local resources for use in educational programmes." Although the report makes no direct reference to SWRC in this connection, it would appear that undertaking this entrepreneurial role could be a challenging and useful function for SWRC's Education Section in the years ahead.

COMMENTARY

Ironically, the educational activities of SWRC, taken as a whole, reflect two very different and somewhat conflicting views of education.

The first is the traditional "educator's view" that equates education with schooling (or its nonformal equivalent) and sees it as a separate "sector" with its own distinct programs and identity. This in essence is the view underlying SWRC's Education Program. The second is the "rural development view"   that equates education much more broadly with learning, regardless of how or where the learning occurs, and that sees education as an indispensible ingredient of every development activity whose success requires changes in human behavior based on new understanding, knowledge, and skills, and on altered attitudes. This view is reflected in the educational components of SWRC's health, agri- culture, and rural industry programs reviewed in previous chapters.

The experience of SWRC's Education Program, especially in its early years confirms once again that separate rural education projects moulded in the image of formal schooling run a high risk of becoming divorced from the real human needs, interests, and motivations of the intended clientele, from other develop- ment activities, and hence from the mainstream of rural development in the par- ticular area.

The failure of the "100 percent literacy" program is a particularly illum- inating case in point, but the lessons it teaches apply also to rural adult education generally. The villagers did not reject literacy; what they rejected was the kind of literacy they were being offered--which seemed to have little meaning for their day-to-day life--and the way this literacy was being taught. Their patience and motivation soon ran thin when they discovered that mastering literacy was going to be much more difficult and time-consuming than they had supposed. Their intuitive cost-benefit calculus told them that the practical payoff was not worth the time and energy they would have to divert from other activities.

The problem was not simply that the reading materials were uninteresting and the teaching for the most part uninspiring. An equally important cause of their disenchantment was that rural adults who have not experienced substantial formal schooling are ill-at-ease and even resentful at being taught like children

in a classroom setting. Moreover, they have great difficulty absorbing abstract symbols, ideas, and information unless they are directly and clearly
related to the realities of their daily life and to their immediate concerns.
In brief, the failure of the literacy program to demonstrate its relevance
and to inspire sustained interest and motivation on the part of the learners
proved its undoing.

It clearly takes a powerful motivation--such as the craft production
women in their new outdoor literacy classes are now displaying--to overcome
these psychological obstacles. It is significant that these women   are
making progress even though the available learning materials are grossly inadequate and their teacher is untrained. Undoubtedly they would   progress
faster if these deficiencies were remedied, but without the strong motivation to start with, such pedagogical improvements would probably be in vain.

The increasing steps being taken to link the Education Program   with
other SWRC programs--as, for example, through the participation of health
and agricultural staff members in the new social education camps for women,
in training the experimental school teachers, and in the elementary schools
themselves--can do much to increase the relevance and interest of these education activities for local people and to bring the Education Program into
the mainstream of SWRC's overall rural development effort. One suspects,
however, that there is still a long way to go in this direction, particularly in terms of removing the didactic teaching methods and other trappings
of formal schooling from all out-of-school educational activities, and in
terms of fitting the content to the expressed interests, needs, and motivation of each particular clientele.

In the area of formal education itself, SWRC's bold experiment in re-
forming rural elementary schooling clearly has important implications, not
only for the Silora area but for other parts of India and other developing
countries. The important issue, however, is whether the experiment will be
sustained long enough to take permanent root and, if so, how its useful
lessons can be spread to other schools within and well beyond the project
area. Without a strong and determined effort along these lines this promising experiment could easily suffer the fate of so many "pilot projects" that
have disappeared without a trace soon after the special funds and enthusiasm
have run out.

A similar question is what if any follow-up there will be to SWRC's
unique inventory of underutilized educational resources in the Silora area.
Will it turn out to have been simply an interesting research exercise that
gets shelved and forgotten? Or will it be seized upon as an operational
springboard for a new SWRC effort to help organize these available resources
to serve a great variety of basic learning needs in the area? If it is the
latter, as one hopes, this could drastically reorient SWRC's Education Program, set it on a highly innovative course, and bring about a synthesis of
the two divided worlds of education reflected in SWRC's previous activities.

CHAPTER 7

CONCLUSIONS AND LESSONS

The Social Work and Research Centre's first five years provide a fascinating story of an experiment in rural development at the grass roots level--a story packed with human drama, diverse initiatives, a mixture of successes, disappointments, and suspense, and some useful lessons about integration, community participation,   educational strategy, and future possibilities for voluntary organizations.

It would be premature to attempt a definitive evaluation of SWRC at this time because its story is still unfolding and the full conse-quences of its actions to date are not yet discernible.   This final chapter therefore presents only an interim assessment of SWRC's   pro-gress toward its objectives and draws attention to a number of pertinent lessons suggested by its experiences to date.

AN INTERIM ASSESSMENT

We noted earlier in this report that an outside observer is at first bewildered by the motley assortment of program activities initiated   by SWRC and the wide diversity of clienteles they seek to serve. Moving back over the five-year period through this maze of program directions, however, and taking a second look at the framework of objectives and guiding prin-ciples originally set forth by SWRC's founders, one begins to see   more clearly that this framework has in fact given shape and coherence to what might otherwise appear to be a potpourri of miscellaneous activities.   As a general rule, whatever works within this framework stays on, while   ill-fitting activities are weeded out.

The Record of Progress Toward SWRC's Initial Objectives

One useful way to assess SWRC's progress is to check its actual actions against the following list of its initial objectives:

(1) Objective: *To create a rural institutional base for providing technical services to the 80,000 rural people living in the Silora Project area.*

Action: The SWRC "campus" at Tilonia has become well estab-lished as an operational base and is a beehive of activity.

(2) Objective: *To give initial priority to water development, health, and education.*

Action: SWRC has launched substantial program activities in these three fields and in addition has initiated activities in agriculture, crafts production, and rural industry.

(3) Objective: *To work in close partnership with the local people, assisting them to improve their conditions through community-based self-help actions.*

Action: Winning the trust of the local people and stimulating their participation in community-based self-improvement programs proved to be a slower and more difficult process than anticipated. However, some encouraging though limited breakthroughs have been made (particularly in health, agriculture, and rural industry) that bode well for the future.

(4) Objective: *To "professionalize rural development" by combining the talents and energies of young urban specialists (university graduates) with those of local "professionals" and "paraprofessionals" (to be trained by SWRC) in a three-tier team.*

Action: A "professional subculture" has been created, centering at the SWRC campus, that effectively meshes the efforts of urban specialists and local professionals and field workers in a spirit of democratic partnership and serious professionalism. There is need, however, to broaden and strengthen the local membership on the lower tiers of the team structure.

(5) Objective: *To give initial emphasis to activities that can yield economic benefits for the people in order to win their confidence and to create a favorable climate for social change.*

Action: The water, agriculture, crafts production, and rural industry programs are directly aimed at generating economic benefits for various subgroups and in varying degrees have already begun to yield such benefits. Ironically, the health program (traditionally classified under social rather than economic development) appears to have led the way in winning the trust and patronage of the villagers. The education program on the other hand, though one of the largest "spenders," has been relatively slow in producing demonstrable economic or social benefits.

(6) Objective: *To integrate SWRC's various development programs in order to make them mutually reinforcing and more cost-effective.*

Action: In the initial phase there was relatively little integration among SWRC's several programs. Steady progress has since been made, however, with the health program in the vanguard, the rural industry, and agriculture programs following close behind, and the education program taking up the rear.

(7) Objective: *To coordinate SWRC's activities with government agencies and other rural institutions having similar development objectives.*

Action: SWRC has made striking headway in this respect: it has established effective working relationships with a variety of state and national government agencies and a number of nongovernment institutions, with mutually beneficial results.

(8) Objective: *To make a special effort to reach and assist the poorest and most disadvantaged people.*

Action:   SWRC has an increasingly good and unusual record here. It has insured that the benefits of the health program reach the poorest members of communities; it has made focused efforts to improve the economic status of destitute women, economically depressed low-caste artisans, and out-of-school youths; and its planned "package program" for marginal farmers and landless laborers, if successful, will be a further important step in this direction.

(9) Objective: *To become substantially self-supporting by providing services on a "no profit-no loss" basis.*

Action:   Although SWRC's positive efforts and progress here have been impressive ("earned income" rose to 31 percent of the total budget by 1976), they are still far short of their goal. The indications are that sizeable further progress will be very difficult, mainly because of the sheer inability of many poor families to pay for such services as health and education.

(10) Objective: *To create new SWRCs in other parts of rural India as soon as feasible.*

Action:   Despite the expanding workload in the Silora area, SWRC has managed to establish operational beachheads in additional areas of Rajasthan and in three other Indian states.

We can draw the general conclusion from the foregoing facts that SWRC has adhered quite faithfully to its original objectives and has made discernible progress on each one--though significantly more on some than others. What is perhaps' most important for the future is that SWRC has learned many practical lessons from experience and has developed a strong momentum that can carry the program forward at an accelerating rate during the next five years--providing it has ample resources and continuing effective leadership.

Tangible Achievements

A second useful approach to assessing SWRC's performance is for one to examine its record of "tangible achievements" in terms of how   many individuals and families its various programs have served (bearing   in mind that it is a relatively small organization operating with   limited resources in a limited geographic area).

A tally of these achievements up to mid-1977 is shown in Table 5, which was prepared at ICED's request by SWRC's management on the basis of program records. The table also includes projections of   further achievements foreseen by SWRC's management over the next five   years. It will be noted that the expected future achievements considerably exceed the previous ones, reflecting the confidence in the momentum, know-how, and expanded capabilities that SWRC has now developed.

TABLE 5

Tangible Achievements of SWRC
(to July 1977)

Technical Socioeconomic Service	Those who have already benefited	Those likely to benefit in the next 5 years
1. Ground Water Development Drilling open wells/tube wells for farmers, industrial sites, educational institutions.	150	Approximately 600; another drilling unit is being commissioned in SWRC Haryana in Khori Mohindergarh District where the demand is heavy.
2. Ground Water Survey--for locating water for new wells for farmers, industrial sites, voluntary organizations, schools and others	60 well sites in Udaipur District; 125 marginal farmers in Ajmer District; 10 industrial sites for RIMDC	The Ground Water Survey for the ARC (Agricultural Refinance Corp.) has been completed for 110 villages in Silora Block and 198 villages in Jawaja Block: Rs. 35 lakhs as a result have been sanctioned for minor irrigation in Silora Block. It is expected more than 1000 farmers will benefit in 5 years.
3. Agricultural Extension		
1. Custom ploughing services	530	In the next 5 years it is
2. Seeds distributed to	280	expected that more than 10,000
3. Fertilizers	30	farmers will benefit from the new
4. Pesticides	35	schemes to be implemented soon.
5. Reforestation	180	
6. Demonstration plots	30	
4. Medical and Health		The response from the community
1. Patients treated from 1973 at 2 dispensaries	100,000(+)	to the medical services has been encouraging. One can easily
2. Preventive and curative services through 9 barefoot doctors reaching population of	20,000	expect the figures to increase by five times in the next 5 years. Another similar program
3. Maternity cases	130	is being duplicated with UNICEF
4. Eye camps (2)	100	help in SWRC Haryana.
5. TB cases screened	102	
6. Family planning	20	
5. Education		
1. Establishment of 3 experimental primary schools in 3 villages	300 children including previous 100-150 dropouts	It is hoped the government will multiply this approach and in the next 5 years it will cover more than 1500.
2. Nonformal education classes in 6 villages	150	More centers are to be opened in the other SWRCs and in due course over 1000 men and women should be covered.
6. Social Education Three craft centers where women are being trained to sew with a view to arranging loans for them to own their own machines.	400	More than 2,000 women.

TABLE 5 (continued)

Technical Socioeconomic Service	Those who have already benefited	Those likely to benefit in the next 5 years
7. Rural Industries		With the establishment of a work center through the Ministry of Education and with the state government (RIMDC) interested in helping the backward classes, one can expect in the next 5 years more than 500 families benefiting from this scheme.
1. Weaving: number of families benefited from outlet provided by SWRC	10 families	
2. Cloth printing	2 families	
3. Handicrafts: women making small items on contractual basis	106	
4. Leather tanning	37 families	
8. Preschool Education: Nutrition		In SWRC Haryana more than 20 villages are to benefit from this scheme with support from the state government and UNICEF.
1. Establishment of balwadis in villages	150	
2. Nutrition program-- feeding scheduled caste pregnant women and children	150	
9. Training		
1. Marginal farmers in rabi and kharif camp in Silora Block	100	
2. Training schoolboys, teachers and SWRC staff how to make and use puppets/filmstrip kit	150	
3. Nonformal education teachers	12	
4. Primary school education teachers	6	
5. Leather tanners (families)	30	
10. Self-Employment Scheme		
A survey has just been completed for Government of Punjab for identifying potential youth for self-employment	400	
11. Low-Cost Housing		
1. Construction of low-cost Panchayat Ghar for village of Khori--first of its kind in the country.	Whole village	
2. Demonstration of low-cost housing for Harijans; houses are being put in Khori for Harijan families.	100 families	

Source: Prepared by SWRC for ICED.

The statistics of achievements shown in Table 5 do not, of course, provide an accurate measure of the actual impact of these various activities   on   the lives of the participants. They do not reveal, for example, whether the   100 farmers who participated in the rabi and kharif training camps actually raised their productivity and income as a consequence. However, depending   on   the nature of the particular activity, these figures provide at least presumptive evidence of significant impacts and benefits already achieved or in the offing.

It seems reasonable to assume, for example, that the 150 wells drilled by SWRC are helping to raise the productivity of the farmers who paid for the ser- vice on a "no-profit-no loss" basis.It also seems reasonable to suppose that the health of many of the 100,000 villagers (including repeaters) who have visited SWRC's dispensaries and of many of the 20,000 served by the village health work- ers and dais are better off today than would have been the case in the   absence of SWRC's health program. There are also definite indications that a number of indigent women in the craft production program are now actually earning   some much-needed cash, and that the low-caste families engaged in weaving,   tanning, and leather work--granting their number is small--are beginning to get a   new lease on life. In the absence of adequate data, however, the magnitude of these various benefits can only be guessed at.

It should also be recognized that the main benefits of some of SWRC's past and present activities still lie in the future. For example, the benefits that will ultimately accrue to the young people participating in the   experimental elementary schools will come later. Similarly, the benefits of the earlier water surveys will depend on how these are followed up by government investments   in irrigation, agriculture, and rural electrification. At the moment the prospects here seemed promising.

To sum up this interim assessment, it may be said with assurance that, not- withstanding numerous practical difficulties, SWRC has on the whole gotten off to a strong start in its first five years. It has adhered closely to its   original objectives and strategies and gone a good distance toward demonstrating   the validity of their underlying assumptions. It has managed to put in motion a wide variety of development activities that have already directly touched an impressive number of local residents, including some of the poorest. And although   it   is impossible at this stage to measure with any precision the specific economic and social benefits that have accrued or are likely to accrue in the future from these activities, there can be little doubt that a sizeable number of individuals   and families, including some of the poorest, have already benefited appreciably.

This is not to say that all of SWRC's activities have been equally effective or that all has gone well. SWRC has had its share of miscalculations, misfires, and disappointments. But allowing for its unconventional nature and the ambitious mission it set for itself, SWRC's overall record of performance thus far is   im- pressive and encouraging.

The main purpose of this case study, however, is not to commend or criticize SWRC's overall record but to discover specific lessons--both positive and   nega- tive--from SWRC's various experiences that might be helpful to others in   the future and perhaps also to SWRC itself. Some of these lessons have already been brought out in the concluding commentaries of earlier chapters. In the remainder of this chapter we will refer back to some of these and suggest additional ones.

LESSONS ON INTEGRATION

SWRC's experience helps to demystify and clarify the ambiguous term "integration" as it is popularly used today in connection with rural development. First of all, it demonstrates that integration has various meanings (all of them legitimate) and can take a variety of useful forms. Second, it emphasizes that integration is a relative matter, not an all- or-none phenomenon, and that it usually progresses step by step and cannot be expected to spring full blown from a carefully conceived "integrated plan" on paper. Third, it sheds useful light on some of   the common obstacles and essential conditions for moving toward greater integration.

Four Varieties of Integration

SWRC's experience illustrates at least four different type-cases of integration that have their counterparts in many other situations.

(1) Integration of the essential components of a particular program. Any organized development activity or program, viewed as a dynamic "system" or "subsystem," clearly requires the right combination of components   to function effectively. If any critical one is missing, or is poorly coordinated with the others, the whole activity suffers and may even fail.

This could well have happened to SWRC's craft training program for women, but fortunately did not. Originally the craft training   was included within a social education framework. The women participants, however, were simply not interested in learning craft skills but rather in actually producing craft items for sale. To do this, however, they required not only the skills, but also the necessary raw materials and equipment and access to profitable market outlets beyond their own village. To develop urban markets, however, they needed to develop attractive new designs and to adhere to high quality standards. And to set up their own small production enterprise they also needed some initial credit to purchase materials and their own equipment (such as a sewing machine or loom).

SWRC came to recognize the importance of these essential "system" components and made provisions for them, albeit rudimentary ones. Once they were all in place and properly integrated, the women began earning some much-needed cash--and SWRC began recovering most of its costs for this program.

The rural industry program for traditional tanners and leather workers followed a somewhat similar course. In this case the workers already possessed the skills, but they could not employ them profitably without improved technologies, more efficient management, a supply of credit on reasonable terms, and access to broader markets. SWRC took the necessary steps to provide these missing components.

The health program began with an initial core component--the dispensary --then added other related components, including nutrition, maternal   and child care, family planning, immunization and other elements, making for a much more comprehensive health service covering both curative and preventive

measures. It also moved some of these services right down to the village level
where they would be directly and easily accessible to the whole community. The
net result is that SWRC's community health program as it now stands is   considerably more integrated than most government rural health services, which are
organizationally fragmented along specialied lines and often do not reach many
villages.

In somewhat similar fahion, SWRC's water program became progressively
broader and more integrated. It began simply with water surveys,   then
added well-drilling services, then agricultural extension services, and now
it is about to embark on a more comprehensive and integrated "package program"
for marginal farmers. Like the health program, it stands in contrast to most
government water and agricultural services, which are also fragmented organizationally along specialized lines and therefore do not constitute a comprehensive and integrated agricultural production support system.

(2) Integration between separate programs. SWRC's water, health, and
educational programs initially struck out independently in their own separate
directions as if they belonged to different organizations. Gradually,   however they found more and more fruitful ways to link up with each other.

Health and nutrition services became integrated with the balwadi
program. When the village industry program encountered a serious TB problem
in certain villages, the health team moved in to correct it. On their regular
Sunday visits to the SWRC campus the village health workers took on an additional role as "bottom-up" extension and supply agents for the farmers   of
their villages.

After "going it alone" for a considerable time the education program
began calling upon the expertise of other programs by inviting their personnel
to participate in training the experimental school teachers and later   the
village women attending the new social education training camp. They   even
served as visiting "teachers" in the elementary schools.

The communications specialist had no separate program of his own;
he busied himself helping to strengthen the training and educational components of the health, agriculture, and rural industry programs by preparing
useful visual aids and training their staffs to prepare their own.

There is room for further useful linkages between various SWRC
programs, but now that the habit has been established it seems likely
that interprogram integration will continue to grow.

(3) Vertical integration between the villages and outside support
services. SWRC's experience with developing a community-based health system
underscores the importance of integrating the activities of the village level
health personnel with specialized personnel, facilities, and support services
outside the individual village. If the village health workers and dais are to
maintain credibility and effectiveness in their own community they must enjoy
the continuing close support and supervision of more highly trained health
workers; they must be able to get answers when they need them and to make
prompt referrals of difficult cases to others better qualifed to deal with

them; they must be assured of the timely replenishment of their medical
supplies; and they must keep learning and growing professionally. They
are the front line troops of a broad-gauged, community-based health system; but for the system to work effectively it must be closely   inte-
grated--not simply from the top down but from the bottom up.

When the "package program" for marginal farmers gets under way, a
similar kind of vertical integration from the village level upward will
be essential (in addition to horizontal integration of the various components within the package).

(4) Integration of efforts among complementary organizations. SWRC
abounds with examples of this type of integration, which is one of   its
unique accomplishments as a voluntary organization. The water surveys, as
already noted, were linked from the outset with various government agencies
concerned with water development, rural electrification, and raising   the
productivity of small farmers. The government agricultural agency   provided SWRC with input supplies for demonstration purposes and distribution
to small farmers, and sent agricultural specialists to participate   in
SWRC's farmer training program. SWRC's health program is closely   linked
in a variety of ways with the state government and private health services.
The most innovative activities of the education program--in particular, the
experimental primary schools and the survey of underutilized local educational resources--resulted from close linkages with innovative officers in
the national and state ministries of education.

Basic Requisites for Improving Integration

The four types of integration cited above--integration *within* programs,
between programs, between *levels,* and between *organizations*--do not   exhaust the possibilities, but perhaps they can help dispel some of the   prevailing confusion about the practical meaning of integration.

SWRC's experience also sheds some useful light on another frequently
asked question: What are the necessary conditions for achieving greater
integration?

The *obstacles* to integration are all too familiar. They are commonly
found in the narrow training and vision of specialists and in their natural
impulse to concentrate single-mindedly on their own particular "targets."
They are also found in the powerful tendency of specialized organizations
to "go it alone" and to guard their jurisdictional turf against intrusion
by others. Further inhibitions stem from the highly centralized   and
hierarchical nature of most large organizations involved in rural development. Where integration matters most is at the local level, but to achieve
it requires considerable decentralization of detailed planning and decision-
making and substantial latitude on the part of lower echelon agents of these
large specialized organizations to work across agency lines and with the
local people in devising the best solutions for meeting local needs.

SWRC, it must be said, was blessed from the outset with important
immunities and advantages not easily replicated in older and larger organizations. First of all, its highest echelon was at the block level,

close enough to the scene of action so that its top managers could have a
clear view of the local realities. Moreover, they had a strong disposition to diffuse responsibility among the various team members and to give
them wide latitude. Second, as a new organization with a young and relatively inexperienced staff, SWRC was not only committed in principle to an
integrated approach but it could also move more easily toward applying the
principle because its members did not have to "unlearn" things or uproot
old habits and attitudes that ran strongly counter to the whole idea of
integration.

Undoubtedly the greatest advantage of all, however, resided in the
close community and dynamic "professional subculture" that developed on
the Tilonia campus. Specialists tied to different programs lived   together, traveled together, traded ideas and observations daily, and learned
a great deal from each other and from exchanges with the numerous visitors
who came through. Out of this process they all evolved a broader and more
unified view of rural development and of how their respective specialties
fitted in to the larger whole and related to each other. They also acquired
an increasingly better understanding of the development potentialities and
limitations of the project area and of the practical needs, circumstances,
and outlook of the local people.

Even with all these special advantages, however, SWRC's movement toward
greater integration, in all its different meanings and forms, has been   a
relatively slow and intricate process. Its experiences in this respect suggest the following pertinent lessons that may be of interest to others.

First, there clearly is no one formula or model for achieving greater
integration; it takes many different forms and requires a variety of strategies. It is to no small extent a matter of seizing favorable opportunities as they arise.

Second, integration must begin in the minds of the specialists   who
plan, manage, and operate development programs. Before much can happen
they must first acquire a broader and more unified vision of rural development that transcends their own specialty. Only then can they really appreciate the advantages of integration for enhancing the effectiveness of their
own specialized efforts, or begin to recognize an attractive opportunity for
better integration when they see one.

Third, close physical proximity and frequent informal dialogue among
different specialists working in the same area with the same clienteles
are an especially effective means of creating favorable conditions for
achieving greater integration of what would otherwise be fragmented effort.

Finally, even in the best of circumstances, improved integration of
various rural development efforts can only be achieved by a step-by-step
process. It also requires goodwill, ingenuity, patience, and persistence
on the part of all concerned.

LESSONS ON COMMUNITY PARTICIPATION

The new SWRC team members arrived in Tilonia in 1972-73 imbued with what they now confess was a somewhat "simplistic and romantic notion of villages and villagers." They soon found themselves surrounded by suspicion, hostility, and resentment on the part of the very people they had come to help. "Community participation" could be strongly felt, but it appeared in negative forms of resistance and rejection. Since then the situation has improved considerably. But SWRC reminds those who tend to have simplistic dreams about community involvement in rural development that its own dreams of five years ago still are a long way from being fully realized.

Helpful Steps in Winning the Confidence of Villages

There are good historical reasons, of course, why villagers in many parts of the developing world are skeptical and suspicious of strangers bearing gifts and seeking to intervene in their lives. They have had many bad experiences with outsiders over the years; they have learned to look out for themselves; and they are not about to abandon the customs, beliefs, and practices that have held their families and clans together in adversity for many generations in favor of unfamiliar and untried innovations urged upon them by urban strangers who clearly know less than they do about the realities of rural life.

The situation in the Silora Block is especially difficult in these respects because of the dire poverty of so many people, the static and seemingly hopeless state of the local economy, the divided and stratified character of the social structure, and the lack of established community-wide organizations open to participation by all. Most villages in this area are not really communities in the full sense; they are loose federations of separate caste groups, tied to traditional occupations and arranged in a pecking order of prestige and power. Members of higher castes generally control the "power structure" and are the decisionmakers and managers of village affairs. They are also the ones likely to benefit most from any new services or opportunities that arrive from the outside--such as agriculture extension, irrigation, credit, health, or schools. Those at the bottom of the social-economic order, who are entrapped in extreme poverty with no apparent way out, are largely bypassed by such rural development services and accept their deprivations fatalistically as they struggle to survive another day.

The first major task of the new SWRC, therefore, was to achieve a better understanding of the people and the villages, to win their trust and cooperation, and to size up the development potentialities of the area. The health dispensary was an important early step in this direction because it responded in a practical way to what the local people-- of all castes and economic levels--saw as a basic need. They were, and still are, more interested in curing immediate physical ailments than in preventing future ones. The dispensary was also a useful place to get better acquainted with some of the villagers. The surveys later conducted by the medical social worker threw valuable light on the sociology, politics, and inner-workings of the villages themselves. The water surveys placed in clearer perspective the ecological characteristics and economic potentialities of the area. All these early steps laid useful foundations for building community participation.

The recruitment of several villagers to join the SWRC "team" as agricultural assistants, health assistants, and in other "professional" roles, was especially helpful in building a bridge of understanding and trust--albeit a fragile one--between the new organization and its adopted "clients."   The bridge grew stronger as village health workers and dais were added to   the team.

Not until the health and rural industries programs began penetrating some of the villages and establishing a local base, however, could it be said that SWRC was finally beginning to win substantial "community involvement" in the sense that local people began playing an active role in planning,   operating, and supporting SWRC's programs. Up to then the programs had been largely concentrated on the campus and were doing things _for_ the people,   not   _with_ the people.

LESSONS ON EDUCATION

SWRC's educational experiences are particularly instructive because they exemplify in microcosm some important universal confusions regarding   appropriate educational components for integrated rural development.   These confusions stem primarily from the widely held conventional view that   equates education with schooling; nonformal education with adult education; and adult education with literacy classes. This anachronistic view also perceives   of education as a separate sector (comparable to health, agriculture, and   rural industry), with its own distinct set of activities.

It was this view that evidently prompted the founders of SWRC to designate education as one of SWRC's three initial priority sectors and that   explains why the Education Program, started off with "100 percent literacy" classes and the social education classes for women (which also stressed literacy). These activities were not tailored to the expressed needs and interests of the rural people in the Silora area; they reflected the standard educator's preconception of what unschooled rural adults most need to learn, and they were essentially carbon copies of conventional educational models that had   been tried many times before with questionable success elsewhere in India and   in other countries.

The point is that this narrow, isolated, institution-bound view of education is quite inadequate for meeting the diverse and constantly evolving basic learning needs of various subgroups in any poor rural area. It is also basically inconsistent with the whole idea of an integrated and community-based approach to rural development.

By its very nature rural development requires extensive changes in   the attitudes and behavior of the rural people themselves--changes in their methods of work, in their dietary and health practices, in family and community relationships, and in a host of other respects. The fundamental role of education --viewed broadly as _learning_ and not simply as schooling or its nonformal shadow --is to provide rural people with new insights into their own life and environment and with new knowledge and skills that will encourage and enable them to accept and adopt these various changes when they can see for themselves   that it is in their own best interest to do so.

Viewed in this broader and more functional and dynamic way, education can be seen not simply as one more development sector but as an essential nutrient for all kinds of development activities. While there is definitely a place for certain separately organized educational activities (such as elementary schools), much of the required learning must be built right into the various development activities themselves.

This in fact is what happened more or less spontaneously with SWRC's health, agricultural, and rural industry programs, quite outside the designated Education Program. It was clear that, if the village health workers and dais were to perform their new functions effectively, they would have to be "trained," not just in a one-shot "training program" but continuously on the job. If the villagers in turn were to adopt new health, sanitary, and nutritional practices, they too would need to learn new things, and it was up to the village health workers and dais to teach them in the course of their daily rounds. The same applies to the marginal farmers, the tanners and leatherworkers, and the women craft producers. If they were to improve their lot, they would obviously have to learn new things and end up doing things differently. Fortunately, the teams responsible for these programs were not inhibited by the educator's usual assumption that the best way to learn all these necessary things was through a structured "class" conducted by a "teacher" in a classroom setting. They innovated, improvised, and adapted as they went along. When the first attempt to train the illiterate dais in a classroom failed (because it did not fit their learning style), it was quickly abandoned in favor of a much more informal approach, and it worked. The regular weekend discussion meetings with the dais and village health workers are undoubtedly a more effective approach to training and upgrading them than a more formal training "course" because they tie the learning directly to their practical day-to-day experiences. The demonstration and explanation of new technologies to the traditional leather tanners in a highly informal open-air situation in their own village were undoubtedly far more appropriate as pedagogical methods than collecting them in a classroom to be talked at.

A few other interesting features of SWRC's assorted educational activities are worth noting. First, these activities did not conform to any preconceived overall educational plan; they were largely pragmatic responses to various perceived needs and opportunities that surfaced along the way. This was undoubtedly a very good thing, so long as the "perceived needs" fitted the felt needs of the learners themselves and not simply the preconceptions of the designers of the activity. No educational master plan constructed before the event could possibly have anticipated all of the important learning needs that arose as SWRC's program unfolded, and this observation will continue to be valid in the future.

Second, all of these various educational activities were "nonformal," with the notable exception of the experimental elementary school project. This fact points up the ubiquitous role of nonformal education in rural development and the relatively limited role of formal education.

Third, each of these educational activities was addressed to the special needs (whether real or fancied) of a particular subgroup--illiterate adults, destitute women, preschool or school-age children, marginal farmers, tanners and leather workers, and so forth. This adaptation to needs is as it should and must be, for no single educational program, "curriculum" or "delivery system" could possibly meet all of the diverse learning   needs of these different subgroups.

Although it was not feasible for the study to include a refined   evaluation of each educational activity, it was plainly evident that some   were succeeding better than others. On the whole it seemed apparent that   the cost-effectiveness of the versatile educational components integrated   with the various operational programs were more cost-effective in meeting   their objectives than the separate nonformal education programs for adults   under SWRC's Education Program. On the other hand, the experimental primary school project could turn out to be very cost-effective, especially if it is   continued for several more years and if special steps are taken to spread   its proven techniques to many other schools.

The following lessons for educational strategy and planning in the   context of integrated rural development are suggested by the foregoing considerations and by evidence presented elsewhere in this report.

(1) It is essential in such a situation to employ a broad concept of education that equates it with learning, that embraces the full gamut of rural clienteles and their learning needs, that also embraces the full spectrum of different available methods and modes of education, and that avoids the error of treating education as a separate sector of development.

(2) Schools can be very effective instrumentalities for meeting certain of the essential learning needs of rural children and   youths, provided their methods, content, and structure are realistically adapted to these needs and to the convenience and living environment of the learners. Schools should not be expected, however, to meet all of the essential needs of these young people, but only such   basic studies as the "three-Rs" and elementary science for which schools are especially appropriate.

(3) The bulk of organized educational provisions for meeting   the important functional learning needs of various subgroups in   rural communities must necessarily be "nonformal" in nature. But this   term covers an extremely wide range of learning objectives, content,   and possibly educational arrangements and methods.

(4) Planning of such activities should begin with an identification of the important learning needs and motivating interests of the particular group of learners, not simply as an outsider sees them but as   the learners themselves see them. Once these learning needs are clarified, and only then, the most promising and feasible methods for meeting them, compatible with the convenience and learning styles of the clientele, should be selected from among the possible alternatives.   In short, planners of nonformal educational activities should begin with   the learners and their needs and not with some preconceived institutional "solution" before the needs have even been determined.

(5) Conventional adult literacy classes aimed at abolishing literacy in poor rural areas have a high probability of failure. A much more promising approach is to direct literacy efforts at selected individuals   and subgroups in the community who have a specific and substantial functional

need for literacy in their daily life and who are likely to be highly motivated and able to make good use of these new skills. Even then, the conventional classroom style of teaching literacy to children by rote memory and in abstract form should be avoided in favor of a more "natural" approach in which literacy is learned functionally in conjunction with other matters of substantial interest and use to the learners.

(6) Whatever arrangements are chosen to meet particular learning needs, they should be sufficiently low-cost to be affordable, and replicable on a larger scale. This is one good reason for making creative use of all types of potential educational resources available in the area. An equally important reason is that using these familiar local resources will often be more effective than using unfamiliar outside resources.

NEW HORIZONS FOR VOLUNTARY ORGANIZATIONS

Traditionally, most voluntary organizations operating in rural areas have kept their distance, often for good reasons, from government agencies or other organizations and pursued their own purposes independently. SWRC is a striking exception to this general rule. Its experience demonstrates that where government policies are reasonably enlightened and official attitudes toward voluntary organizations are hospitable, there are sizeable possibilities for fruitful cooperation.

In a relatively short time SWRC has developed a wide network of symbiotic relations with various government agencies and other organizations. These have taken three main forms. First, in a number of instances SWRC has filled important gaps beyond the present reach of government services and, in reverse, government agencies have filled gaps in SWRC's capabilities, for example by providing needed supplies and expertise. Second, SWRC has used its flexibility and special talents to pave the way for large-scale government investments beyond its own capacity, as in the case of the water surveys. Third, SWRC has provided a favorable laboratory for research and for testing out innovations of strong interest to government officials, but which a flexible nonprofit private agency is in a better position than government to undertake.

All this suggests the possibility--at least in countries where the conditions are favorable--of a much wider and more influential trail-blazing role for voluntary organizations, working in tandem with interested government agencies. Voluntary organizations like SWRC are especially well-suited to trying out fresh approaches to socially complex problems and integrating fragmented sectoral programs.

SWRC's experience also points up some important problems, limitations, and vulnerabilities of voluntary agencies--especially in connection with staff, leadership, and finances--that must be borne in mind, particularly by sympathetic officials of both public and private funding agencies who recognize and would like to strengthen the special potentialities of voluntary organizations.

SWRC's staff recruitment strategy has taken good advantage of the size-able pool of "educated unemployed" in the cities, recognizing full well that this strategy would inevitably entail a relatively high staff turnover.   A fair amount of such turnover is certainly advantageous for this type   of operation, because it insures a steady infusion of fresh ideas, energy,   and enthusiasm. But a sufficient degree of staff continuity is also essential in maintaining organizational and program stability, direction, and momentum. Fortunately, SWRC seems to have struck a workable balance thus far between turnover and continuity, but it always faces the risk of having this balance upset.

Creative leadership, with good managerial ability that attracts good people and gets the best from them, is the key limiting factor for any organization like SWRC. The capacity of such leadership sets the limits on the load the organization can effectively sustain in any one area, and on the number   of areas to which it can extend its usefulness. SWRC has been singularly fortun-ate in its leadership, but significant further expansion will demand a greater breadth and depth in its leadership supply and structure.

Securing sufficient finances on which to base stable plans and commitments is the constant worry of top leaders of organizations such as SWRC and   often forces a serious diversion of their time from important program affairs.   The problem is further complicated by the need of such organizations for sufficient "general funds," as distinct from specific "project funds," to cover   organiza-tional costs (often not provided for in project grants or contracts)   and   to provide room for maneuverability in taking program initiatives on   their   own. Unfortunately, such general support funds are far harder to come by than speci-fic project funds. SWRC has sought to solve this problem by becoming as self-supporting as possible through "selling" its services on a "no profit-no loss" basis.   By normal standards it has so far done remarkably well. It has also reduced its heavy (and always risky) dependence on foreign philanthropic sources. But SWRC may well be approaching the outer limits of its ability to recoup the costs of important services such as health, education, and assistance to margin-al farmers.   Ironically, the more it succeeds in reaching and helping the poor-est families, the greater its difficulty will be in becoming self-supporting.

There is an important message here for all public and private funding agencies that have proclaimed a special commitment to helping the poorest of the rural poor and that have also expressed great faith in the capacity   of voluntary organizations to play important roles in this regard. If the decision-makers of such organizations are really serious, they must find ways not merely to provide money for "projects" that fit their own particular interests and objectives but to provide additional "flexible" funds to enable any demonstrably competent voluntary organization to cover its general administrative costs and to maintain its freedom to exercise control over its own program. Unless they adopt this more "generous" policy, the interested funding agencies may unwittingly be helping destroy the very independence, vitality, and flexibility that make the voluntary agency a peculiarly useful instrument of social and economic development.

6 BRAC: Building Human Infrastructures to Serve the Rural Poor

Manzoor Ahmed

EDITOR'S NOTE

    Any development practitioner looking for fresh ideas and practical lessons concerning integrated, community-based programs for meeting the basic needs of poor rural families will find this report on the Bangladesh Rural Advancement Committee (BRAC) of considerable interest.

    BRAC is a strictly home grown, locally staffed and managed program, born as an emergency relief measure in the turmoil of a great national struggle for independence. It has since evolved--and is still evolving--into a unique multifaceted rural development program whose experience to date offer a variety of positive lessons for others along with some equally important negative ones that the leaders of BRAC are quick to point out without a trace of defensiveness. BRAC's managers have maintained from the outset an experimental attitude and flexibility of mind and a demonstrated readiness to convert past weaknesses into future strengths. Through this open-minded process of trial and error and learning-by-doing, the BRAC program has grown steadily in strength and in its dimensions and effectiveness.

    What this report presents--to borrow the language of the cinema-- are some revealing snapshots of BRAC as of early 1977, with a series of selective flashbacks to significant episodes in its earlier career. The report also undertakes to assess the significance of these past and current experiences, the impacts that BRAC has had thus far on the lives of villagers and villages in the area it serves, and the new directions expected to emerge in subsequent months and years. The concluding section places in perspective a number of lessons from BRAC's experience that would seem to be of particular interest and value to development practitioners elsewhere in Bangladesh and in other developing countries.

    The principal author of this report was Manzoor Ahmed, deputy director of the ICED project on Helping the Rural Poor. He and his fellow investigators made extensive use of available quantitative data and documented information such as earlier project plans and proposals, service records, periodic reports, and the results of limited previous evaluation efforts. These were supplemented by a sample household survey conducted in 10 villages in the so-called Sulla Project area to collect basic reference data on the socioeconomic

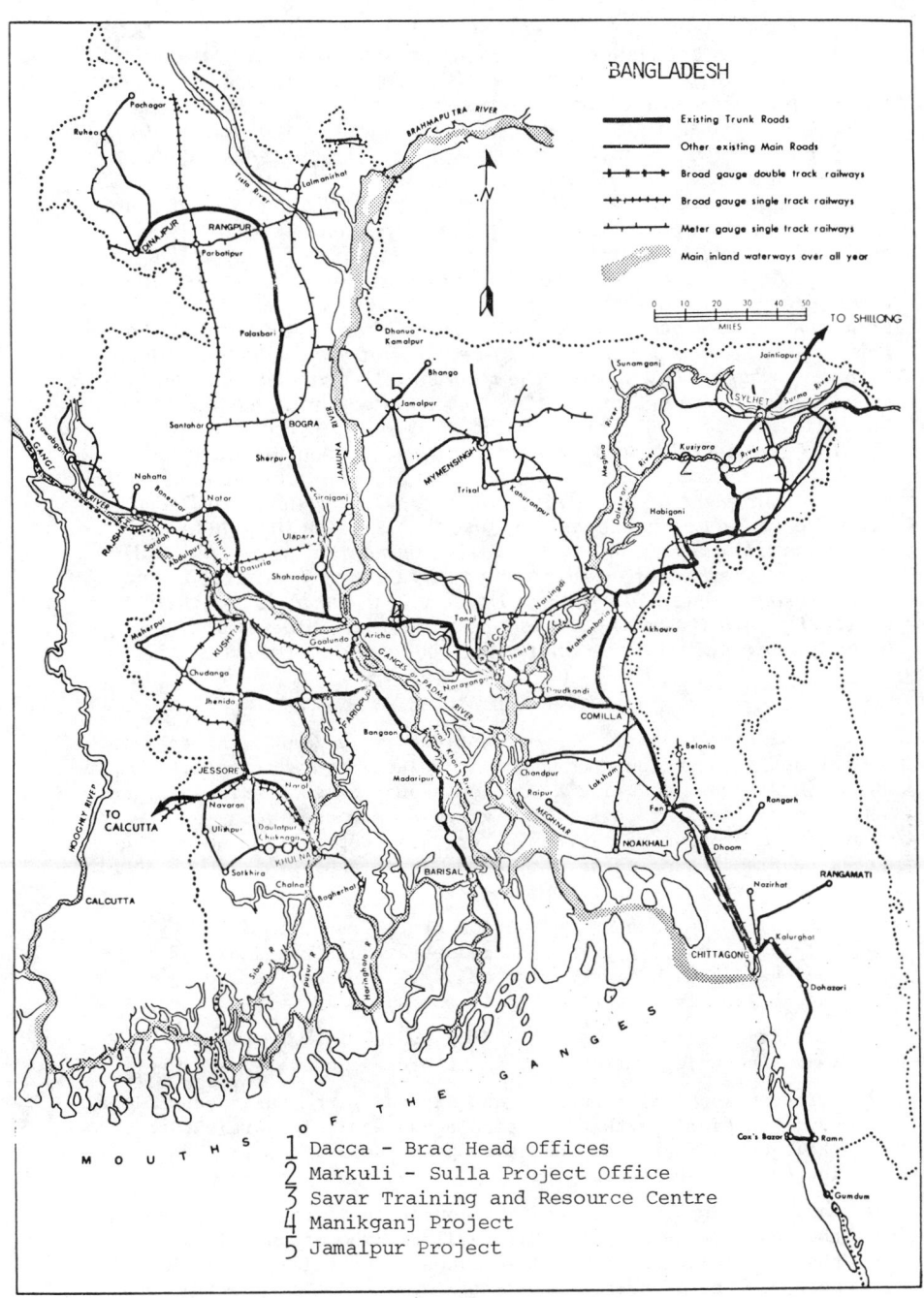

1° Dacca - Brac Head Offices
2 Markuli - Sulla Project Office
3 Savar Training and Resource Centre
4 Manikganj Project
5 Jamalpur Project

circumstances of families, the extent of their participation in BRAC activities, their knowledge of the program, and their own assessments of what BRAC has done, or could do in the future, to improve their own lives. In addition the investigators visited all the project sites, joined the daily cycle of activities of some of the field workers, and spent many hours interrogating workers and project leaders in the field and at the headquarters.

Although full responsibility for the content, interpretations and findings of this report resides with the author and ICED, it is appropriate here to express ICED's appreciation to all our colleagues in Bangladesh who contributed so importantly to this study. They include :   Dr. Mohammed Ashraf Ali of the Institute of Education and Research at Dacca University for conducting the household sample survey and writing up sections of the preliminary draft report; to Saleh Chowdhury, a journalist with professional training in social work, for helping in the sample survey and sharing his insights into rural life; to Dr. Mohammed Selim, Director of the Institute of Education and Research and more recently Educational Advisor to the Ministry of Education, for his sage advice, encouragement, and interest in the study; and to UNICEF officials in Dacca, particularly Carl Schonmeyer and Joseph Acar, for their help with both logistical support and substantive comments. Above all ICED is indebted to the Executive Director of BRAC, Mr. F. H. Abed, and his numerous co-workers both in Dacca and in the field for their generosity with time and patience in meeting all requests of the investigators and for their unstinting cooperation with the study.

THE BACKGROUND AND AN OVERVIEW

The Bangladesh Rural Advancement Committee (BRAC), an indigenous voluntary organization, functions in selected rural areas of Bangladesh. It attempts to bring a limited amount of external assistance and the idealistic impulses of a group of educated young people to bear on the problem of extreme poverty and deprivation among the rural people in Bangladesh. It has designed a program with a combination of activities that aims at:

a) improving the economic situation of the rural families by helping them adopt more productive farming practices and increase earning from nonagricultural sources, including income-supplement activities of women;

b) providing basic preventive and curative health care and family planning services at an affordable cost;

c) building local institutions and expanding the basic educational opportunities, so that the people can actively participate in their own affairs and the development activities can become increasingly self-managed;

d) making an impact on the living condition of the poorest and the most disadvantaged rural families, who often fail to become the beneficiaries of rural services not specially geared to the needs of the poorest.

The significance of the BRAC program and the reason for ICED's interest in examining it lie in the broadness of BRAC's vision that,

nonetheless, focuses on the basic needs of the deprived rural
families and recognizes the value of an integrated approach to
meeting these needs.

Background and Setting

The program began in 1972 in a cluster of villages in the Sulla,
Derai, and Baniyachang thanas (sub-districts) of Sylhet district in
the aftermath of the war of liberation as a relief effort for those
war victims whose homes, cattle, and boats for fishing and transportation had been destroyed and whose fields had lain fallow for a
year. Being on the international boundary between Bangladesh and
the Indian states of Meghalaya and Assam and having a 60 percent
Hindu population, the project area of about 200 villages (120,000
people in 160 square miles of territory) suffered more than its
share during the war. With the assistance of OXFAM of England and
Canada, BRAC provided construction materials to rebuild the houses,
timber to build boats, and other assistance to help the people re-
settle in the villages. BRAC soon discovered that the villagers,
back from refugee camps to their homes, while no more dependent on
charity for their daily ration of food, were in a state of destitution not very different from that in the refugee shelters. It was
clear that sustained development efforts, not mere temporary relief
measures, were needed to have any tangible impact on the living
condition of the people in the area.

The Sulla area is unique in some ways but similar in others to
the rest of the Bangladesh countryside. Topographically the area
falls in the depressed haor (semi-permanent lake) region, which
means that most of the area is submerged for six to eight months in
a year. The total cultivable land in the project area is about 64,000
acres, of which 60,000 acres are suitable for only one deep-water
rice crop in the winter. For over six months in the year, the area
takes on the appearance of a sea--a watery expanse extending to the
horizon in all directions with little scattered islands sheltering
people and animals in thick clusters of huts made of bamboo and
corrugated iron sheets.

The topography of the area sets a limit to its agricultural
prospects and increases its isolation from the urban centers and the
rest of the country. On the other hand, fishing is an important
occupation in the area. It is the primary means of livelihood for
20 percent of the families and a secondary occupation for most of
the rest.

The density of population in the area is close to 700 per square
mile--less than one-half of the national average only because much of
the land area is not habitable. With over a quarter of the families
having no farm land, and about 20 percent possessing farms over one
acre in area, most of the landholdings are below the one acre level.
Even when farming and fishing are combined, a practice that is followed by most of the families, the primitive technology and the low
level of productivity in both activities assure at best a precarious
living. Both farming and fishing are susceptible to the vagaries of
nature--the unpredictable late autumn floods and hailstorms occasionally wipe out the one rice crop (boro) primarily grown in the
area; irregular floods also affect the fish harvests adversely.

The ecological features of the area are somewhat forbidding as
far as economic development is concerned--probably more so than the
typical rural area of the rest of the country. However, in terms of
the level of poverty, the dependence on primary production activities
based on primitive technologies, the high rate of population growth,
the low level of education, the inadequacy of government institutions
and public services, and the basic cultural patterns and values, the
area is not significantly different from other rural areas in the
country and is subject to the same challenges, problems, and prospects of development as the rest of Bangladesh.

Major Program Elements

The 200-odd villages of the project area, chosen because of
relief needs and geographical contiguity rather than administrative
convenience, cover the whole of Sulla thana, three unions of Derai
thana, and two unions of Baniachang thana. Spending a little over
Tk 4 million (about US$207,000) in the course of three years to the
end of 1975 (excluding the initial relief expenditures), BRAC
appears to have served directly at least one-half of the area
population with one or more of its program activities. BRAC has faced
and attempted to solve with varying effectiveness many pronlems that
other rural programs, large and small, public or private, will have
to face and resolve in the future.

-- BRAC has apparently identified a cluster of basic needs of the
   rural people that are amenable to deliberate collective efforts,
   if they are supported by a sufficient input of technical and
   financial resources. It has fashioned a program to utilize these
   resources for a direct assault on the problem of satisfying the
   basic needs.

-- BRAC has recruited for its staff a group of young men and women,
   most of whom are university graduates. While the knowledge,
   skills, and educational background of such people can be an
   asset to a development program, the high educational qualifications can also alienate them from the rural people, and their
   values and temperament may make them unsuitable for rural work.
   BRAC has attempted to capitalize on the idealistic impulses of
   the young, to instill in them the spirit and values of the
   organization, to give them the necessary understanding of the
   issues and intricacies of implementing a multipurpose rural
   development project, and to develop their ability to relate to
   and communicate with the rural people.

-- The field staff of BRAC is complemented by local young men and
   women from rural families who are recruited, trained and utilized
   for various roles in the implementation of the program.

-- The program has apparently managed to work with the village power
   structure; it has gained their tolerant acceptance if not actual
   support of a program which helps the underprivileged in the
   village but eventually and potentially threatens to upset the
   existing power structure.

-- The program functions within the context of services and
   activities of the government departments concerned with
   rural areas, however inadequate these services may be. One
   of BRAC's tasks is to work out a compatible relationship
   between itself and the government agencies and programs at

both the local and national levels and to secure the cooperation of the government agencies whenever necessary and possible.

-- In order to increase farm productivity, create new employment, and improve the nutritional balance, the program has introduced some new farm practices, facilitated the supply of essential inputs, and helped in procuring and maintaining farming and irrigation equipment. All of these, though on a limited basis, have apparently been done without using a large complement of specialized agricultural extension staff.

-- The program in addition to providing health, family planning, and functional education services to women, has attempted to bring women into the mainstream of economic and development efforts by using local women personnel in some of the program activities, by offering special skill training to women, and by encouraging the formation of women's cooperative economic enterprises.

-- One component of the program is the attempt to encourage village youths to undertake collectively community service activities as well as cultural, sports, and recreational activities to enliven the overall community atmosphere. Selected youths are also given training to help in the management of cooperatives.

-- The health and family planning component of the program is founded on the concept of a low-cost basic preventive and curative service delivered by community-based auxilliaries and backstopped by paramedics and qualified physicians and clinical services. A health insurance plan is a significant feature of this effort.

-- BRAC has invested considerable effort and resources in an experiment to raise the effectiveness and efficiency of its adult education program. BRAC's early efforts were troubled by the typical problems of most well-intentioned traditional literacy programs, such as difficulty in sustaining learner interest and motivation, teaching techniques that smack of infantile pedagogy, inappropriate content materials, and lack of followup materials. With the technical support of World Education, Inc. of U.S.A. and World Literacy of Canada BRAC has developed methods and materials for a functional education program that promises to produce better results and to be more relevant to the total development efforts carried out by BRAC.

-- One of BRAC's main objectives is to build local institutions
   and organizations that will permit the development efforts to
   be carried out with the active involvement of the rural people
   and will lead the way to greater self-management of these efforts by the local people. To this end, BRAC has put a heavy
   emphasis on building community centers and forming cooperative
   societies of different types.

All of these elements of the BRAC program, as noted earlier, have by
no means achieved a high level of effectiveness; the performance   varies
between communities in the project area. The important point is that all
of these elements are seen as the necessary constituents of a program for
improving the quality of life of rural families.

Since the initial development phase of Sulla (called Sulla Project,
Phase II) came to a conclusion at the end of 1975, BRAC has initiated   a
third phase of the Sulla Project, extended its development activities   in
rural locations in other districts, and reoriented and reorganized its program activities in both Sulla and other locations on the basis of the experiences acquired from the early Sulla efforts. The basic program objectives of BRAC, however, have remained unchanged; the redirected   program
activities are designed to achieve the same basic goals more effectively.

Goals of the Study

The purpose of this case study is to carry out an analysis of various
necessary operations and tasks that have been undertaken in designing, managing, and implementing the program. In this process, evaluative judgement
including assessment of various components of the program is made to   the
extent permitted by available information.

Certain operations are common to all programs aiming at the improvement of rural living conditions: diagnosing the local situation   with
respect to the development needs, potentialities, and obstacles; designing
a strategy of actions and building an organizational structure; recruiting,
training, and utilizing the staff; selecting learning contents and preparing and supplying learning materials; developing and applying appropriate
learning methods; securing the involvement of the clientele and building
or strengthening local participatory institutions; establishing working relationships with the government agencies at the different levels and   with
the local power structures; and mobilizing resources of various types from
local and external sources. All these are tasks that have to be tackled at
a certain level of effectiveness by all programs of rural development.   An
analysis of BRAC experience, it is hoped, will shed light on the procedures,
methods, techniques, and steps adopted as well as on the obstacles and the
favorable circumstances encountered in carrying out the vital tasks of program implementation in one case. The BRAC experience also provides   an
opportunity for examining not only the practical application and meaning of
the concepts of integrated rural development, but also the participation and
involvement of the clientele in self-sustaining and self-managed development
programs--concepts that are emphasized by BRAC and other programs focusing
on the disadvantaged segment of the rural population.

The case study has attempted to match the implementation steps taken with the results achieved, not only in terms of the stated and predetermined goals, but also of the unanticipated byproducts and costs incurred in terms of money as well as human and material resources. The assessment of the results as far as possible is necessary for analyzing and understanding the process of implementation. The negative aspects of the program can be as instructive as the positive achievements as far as the case study is concerned.

A further aim of this case study—in combination with similar other case studies undertaken by ICED—is to make a contribution to building an inductive-empirical base for extracting useful lessons and formulating general principles, operational guidelines, and evaluative criteria for conceptualizing, designing, implementing, managing, and evaluating other programs that will improve the situation of the rural poor.

An Overview of BRAC

By the end of 1976 BRAC grew to be a multifaceted development program of considerable size employing over 180 full-time staff members with an   annual operating budget of about Tk 5 million. The BRAC activities, with general guidance and support from the Dacca central office, spread to several rural locations with at least 300,000 potential beneficiaries in three districts. In addition, BRAC contributed to the national rural development effort by publishing a monthly rural newspaper that circulated throughout the country, by establishing a training program that provided training to rural development workers of other organizations in the country, and by developing and producing functional education and health education materials that could be used by other programs. The total program is organized as a number of sub-projects (though usually referred to as "projects" in BRAC parlance), each of which is briefly described below.

The Sulla Project.

Sulla is the oldest and best known of BRAC projects. It is in Sulla that BRAC began its relief activities and then initiated the rural development program that came to be called Sulla Project, Phase II. This phase of the Sulla Project began in November 1972 and lasted until December 1975 when Sulla Phase III   was launched.

The activities carried out during Phase II included construction of gono-kendro (community center) in the project villages, a functional education program, agricultural development, promotion of cooperative societies, fisheries development, vocational training for women, and a health care and family planning program.

For the implementation of the above activities, a fairly elaborate field organization with full-time staff personnel was built up. The project area was divided into 11 sectors, each with an Area Manager and a field camp where 4 to 5 field-level development workers, known as Field Motivators, resided and functioned under the guidance of the Area Manager. The 11 field camps were supervised by 2 zonal program coordinators. A Field Coordinator had the overall responsibility for directing the project. The health care and family planning program was implemented by 30 paramedics, divided among the field camps   and supervised by 4 medical doctors.

Phase III plans (January 1976 to December 1978) still emphasized health care and family planning as a major project component. Functional education was to be reoriented to stress its roles of "consciousness-raising" and helping specific interest groups more directly in being organized for collective self-improvement activities. There was to be, on the whole, an emphasis on helping functional groups of landless laborers, women, young people, and fishermen in improving their situation through collective efforts instead of conducting separate sectoral activities.

During the first year of the third phase, women Field Motivators and paramedics were recruited and trained for the first time, a step that was expected to be the beginning of a new trend. Otherwise the field organization remained essentially the same as during the second phase.

Manikgang Project.

This project located in the Manikganj thana, 40 miles west of Dacca, was initiated in April 1976 after BRAC became familiar with the area   and its population by conducting a rural works project in the thana.   The Manikganj project embodies the lessons of experience in Sulla and reflects the emerging program approach of BRAC.

The health and family planning component remains a major sectoral activity in this project. All other development activities, however, are not planned to be sectorally separated but rather designed according   to the specific preference and capacity of functional interest groups,   such as landless laborers, women, youth, rural artisans, and managed mainly through the collective efforts of these groups rather than by BRAC's own personnel. Functional education is to be used as the main vehicle of organizing the functional groups and developing their capacity to engage in self-help activities. Rural youth, especially the educated ones uncertain about their vocation and purpose in life, are regarded as an important resource to be tapped for becoming "agents of change" and local organizers of the collective activities. BRAC plans include provisions for training, technical assistance, and limited financial assistance to the local youth organizations.

Jamalpur Project.

This project in 30 villages near Jamalpur town in Mymensingh district had its origin in an involvement of BRAC in conducting a functional education program for destitute rural women who were participants in a UNICEF-sponsored food-for-work project. At the conclusion of the UNICEF project, the rural women and the local instructors of functional education earlier trained by BRAC were eager to continue the education and development effort, if only they could receive some guidance and assistance. BRAC assisted the group of 15 women instructors/development workers in preparing an operational plan and found for them a source of financial assistance to implement the plan. Launched in early 1976, the plan included the following: functional education centers and groups for women in each of the villages;   a family planning program, including child health and maternal care; improvement of preventive health measures and hygiene in the villages; joint savings and cooperative economic projects for women (including horticulture,

poultry raising, and use of fallow land); and formation of women's organizations for self-help efforts. This project for underprivileged rural   women
is directed and managed entirely by BRAC workers, who are all   local women
originally recruited as functional education instructors for the UNICEF project.

The Materials Development Unit.

Dissatisfied with conventional adult literacy methods and   materials,
BRAC found the need for developing a more effective approach   to functional
education and creating relevant educational materials for this purpose. As
a part of this effort to design a   new   functional education program   (for
which BRAC received technical assistance from World Education, Inc., a technical assistance agency based in New York), a materials development unit was
established at BRAC headquarters in Dacca in 1974.   The staff of the   unit
was intimately involved in developing the new educational methodology, identifying the relevant lesson content, preparing and field-testing   the   trial
materials, and preparing the successive sets of functional education materials. The unit, with a full-time staff of four writers, evaluators,   and
illustrators, is engaged on a continuous basis in assessing and modifying
the old materials and designing, field-testing, and producing new materials.

Training and Resource Centre (TARC).

As BRAC began to build a sizeable field organization with full-time
personnel and initiated a functional education program that required special training for instructors and supervisory staff, the need arose for a
systematic staff training arrangement. With the assistance of a consultant provided by the Ford Foundation and banking on its own training needs
for field personnel, BRAC developed a series of short training courses or
"modules" on topics considered important in improving the skills and competence of the staff. These topics include communication, organizational
analysis and needs assessment, program planning, group dynamics, leadership, "consciousness-raising," and functional education methodology. The
training center--based partially in the Dacca office and partially in Savar,
20 miles northwest of Dacca, where the facilities for the center, including
residential accommodation, were under construction--employed six full-time
trainers in late 1976. The center, besides meeting BRAC's own needs, also
conducted training courses for rural development and functional education
workers on commission from other voluntary organizations in Bangladesh.

Gonokendro.

Recognizing the scarcity of relevant reading materials for   rural
readers, BRAC began to publish in 1973 a monthly tabloid of 8 to   12
printed pages with development-related information,   articles,   and news
items. Although the journal was seen originally as a means of providing
reading materials to neoliterates emerging from the functional education
courses, it turned into a more general interest rural journal   (without
the gradation of vocabulary and careful selection of the texts required
for neoliterates), especially after UNICEF offered to underwrite the cost
of distributing 60,000 copies every month to rural primary school teachers.

The Research and Evaluation Project.

Soon after the beginning of its development phase, BRAC saw a need for a system of orderly collection and analysis of base-line information about the project area and population and of service data. It saw   a need for a general assessment of the changes or lack of changes resulting from BRAC activities. Aided by a grant from the Ford Foundation, a small research and evaluation unit was set up which at the end of 1976 had five full-time research assistants and statisticians. The plans for   research and evaluation included the following: base-line sample surveys of pro- ject areas for selected socioeconomic indicators; assessment of the impact of specific sectoral activities, such as health and family planning;   and an in-depth economic-anthropological study of selected villages, in order to evaluate the overall socioeconomic impact of the project activities on the village communities. Assistance of researchers from local   research institutions were available for designing and conducting the surveys. The services of an anthropological researcher from the Marga Institute in Sri Lanka was available for designing the village studies and training   the research workers for this purpose.

Rural Works Program.

The works program, by means of which rural agricultural laborers are paid wages in cash or in food grains during the "slack" farming season for work in useful community works projects, has become a regular annual BRAC activity. BRAC used the works program to build physical infrastructures to improve the agricultural potential of the Sulla and Manikganj project areas, to provide a means of sustenance to vulnerable groups in the pro- ject area at a time of food shortage and unemployment, and to involve lo- cal people in planning and implementing development schemes in their   own localities. In Manikganj, the works program was the means for BRAC   to get acquainted with the area and its population, to establish BRAC's   own credibility and reputation among the local people, and to identify promis- ing members of local youth groups and involve them in BRAC development activities.

During the 1975-76 dry season 30 works projects, including embank- ments, irrigation canals, drainage canals, roads, and fishery and irri- gation ponds, were completed in Sulla and Manikganj. The projects pro- vided 87,000 man-days of employment and cost a total of Tk 545,000.

Various facets of these program components and how they relate to each other in shaping the total rural development thrust of BRAC   are examined in the following sections of this report.

CHAPTER 2

FUNCTIONAL EDUCATION

A Conventional Beginning

Widespread illiteracy among the rural people was seen by the organizers of BRAC as a major contributing factor to rural underdevelopment and poverty. Spread of literacy was considered necessary for communicating new knowledge and ideas to the people and for creating among them an awareness of their situation and of ways of changing this situation.

A strong literacy drive was therefore launched early in the project as a major element of its rural development strategy. With a goal of eliminating almost 90 percent illiteracy in the Sulla Project area within a period of three years, 255 literacy centers were opened in 220 villages in 1973, and 300 local men and women were trained and employed as teachers.

It was a conventional literacy campaign, concentrating on the skills of reading and writing, with traditional pedagogic techniques in a classroom environment. Some efforts were made to include rural topics in the lessons. There was a great surge of enthusiasm initially and 5,000 villagers enrolled in the courses.

But interest waned quickly and the dropout rate shot up. Some centers closed down because learnerd did not show up, and others took as long as twelve months to complete the six-month course because of high absenteeism. Only 5 percent of those enrolled completed the course.

A combination of factors contributed to the failure of this educational effort. An unusually high level of flood in 1973 not only damaged many of the centers and made them unusable but also caused extra economic hardship to the people of the area. BRAC launched the campaign on the assumption that there was a high level of demand for literacy and all that was needed was to provide the opportunity to attend literacy classes. Very little attention was given to appropriate teaching techniques for adults, and the lessons were prepared on the basis of preconceived notions of what was good for the learners. The most serious problem was that the learners soon discovered that the acquisition of literacy skills required considerable effort and time; yet these skills and the reading lessons bore little relevance to the immediate and burning problems of their life. Customers for the literacy courses, therefore, declined sharply.

The Functional Approach

Having reached the conclusion that mere teaching of alphabet and arithmetic was not enough to hold the interest of the learners and of no direct benefit to the rural learners, BRAC began searching for a new approach. It was felt that new methodology and materials had to be developed that would be perceived as useful and relevant by the learners in their daily life. In this

task BRAC enlisted the assistance of consultants from World Education,
Inc. to develop, test, and implement on a pilot basis an adult functional
literacy education program designed (a) to maintain learners' interest
and participation in the educational program, (b) to enable learners to
read with understanding and write legibly simple texts likely to be of
use to them, and (c) to modify learners' attitudes and behavior toward
family planning, nutrition, health and agricultural practices.

The main steps followed in implementing the new functional education
program were assessment of learners' needs and interests, development of
learning materials and methods, training supervisors and instructors, and
implementation of a pilot phase in order to test and revise materials and
methods.

The assessment of learning needs was based on a canvassing of the
villagers' views on their main concerns and problems about which they needed new knowledge and information. This was supplemented by the BRAC field
workers' knowledge and understanding of the general rural condition.   A
survey was carried out in 19 villages in the Sulla Project area to collect
general information about village socioeconomic situations and to determine
the villagers' perception of their learning needs. Consequently, several
major content topics for the functional education program were identified:
(a) soil and use of fertilizers, (b) high yielding rice cultivation, (c)
animal husbandry and poultry, (d) fisheries and pisciculture, (e) cooperatives, (f) nutrition, (g) hygiene and public health, (h) family planning--
male orientation, (i) family planning--female orientation, (j) child care,
and (k) cottage industries.

In early 1974, a materials development unit, consisting of an education and training adviser, one illustrator, three writers, and a typist,
was set up in BRAC's head office in Dacca. The first round of materials
--large charts with drawings, "generative words," and short suggestive sen-
tences--was the product of brainstorming among the materials development
unit staff centering on the themes identified as the main concerns of the
rural people. A consultant from World Education with experience in materials development for functional adult education programs served as a resource person for the unit.

Methodology and Materials

The preparation of materials was, of course, contingent upon a methodology for the use of the materials. The World Education consultants introduced to the materials development unit and other senior BRAC personnel the
functional education methods developed for World Education-assisted programs
in Thailand, Turkey, Indonesia, and other countries. The main elements of
this methodology were:

   (a)   identification of key concepts relating to the learner
         group's major problems and potential ways of dealing with
         these problems;

   (b)   preparation of lessons (pictures, words, sentences, reading
         and writing exercises, arithmetic exercises) centered   on
         the selected key concepts;

(c)   group discussion of the key concepts (aided by relevant
      pictures and drawings), encouragement of active par-
      ticipation by group members, presentation of practical
      experiences, and comparison of conflicting ideas and al-
      ternative action possibilities;

(d)   introduction to relevant words, sentences, and arithmetic
      exercises following the discussion as a means of recording
      and expressing ideas, increasing knowledge, and gaining ac-
      cess to useful information; and

(e)   recognition of the instructor, not as a traditional teacher,
      but as a facilitator of group discussion and group learning.

      (Credit for farm production, for instance, may be a theme
      that would be the basis for an extended discussion of the
      learners' situation in relation to farm credit and would
      also supply the key words and sentences for one or more
      lessons. The identification of the main themes and the
      generative words derived from the themes is done through
      the needs assessment exercise mentioned above.)

In conformity with this methodological approach, the BRAC staff
developed a basic functional education course for the rural learners
of Sulla comprising 80 lessons--56 of which were regarded as   core
materials for both male and female learners and 24 as variations designed to fulfill the special needs of either the male or the female
learners. Sets of posters with the illustrations, words, and sentences
for the lessons bound in the form of a flip-chart were prepared for use
with each learning group. The same lessons and exercise sheets were
printed in handy book-size pages and bound in a looseleaf book for each
learner.

The materials were tested with 1,175 learners in 59 learning groups
in Sulla when the first cycle of the functional education course   was
launched in May 1974. On the basis of a review of the first cycle experience, the materials unit decided to reduce the number of lessons in the
six-month course (two or three sessions per week) from 80 to 70 and the
number of differentiated lessons for men and women was reduced to 14 from
the original 24. Many illustrations were revised to improve their capacity
to communicate messages and generate group discussion. The written content
of some of the lessons was also changed.

The revision and modification of the lessons and adaptation of them
to the needs of new learner groups in different geographical areas are a
continuous responsibility of the materials unit. Its members spend much
of their time in the field observing the actual use of the materials, testing new materials, and gathering ideas for improving the lessons. A current
round of revision of the materials (late 1976 and early 1977) is discussed
later in this chapter.

Training Instructors and Supervisors

Orientation and training were necessary for both supervisors and instructors in the program in order to familiarize them with appropriate use of the materials and methods and, probably more importantly, to change their conventional perception of the role of the instructor in a learning group. The members of the materials unit and other BRAC personnel designated to become trainers of field personnel, together with the assistance of a World Education consultant, worked out the orientation and training content and method for the supervisors and the instructors.

The Field Motivators, who have overall responsibility for initiating and supervising all village level activities of BRAC, were also to be the supervisors of the functional education activities. The instructors for the learning groups were to e young men and women with some post-primary formal education background, chosen on a part-time basis from the same villages as of the learners.

The first cycle of functional education courses, however, was launched in May 1974 without going through the supervisory training phase. The cycle began directly with the recruitment and training of 61 instructors in the project area. The importance of a thorough understanding of the concept and process of functional education by all supervisory personnel of BRAC and the need for continuous support and guidance to the instructors were soon realized, and training sessions for all BRAC personnel with supervisory responsibilities were arranged before the second cycle of courses.

The World Education consultant who had earlier assisted in designing the functional education program returned in September 1974 and organized a five-day training session in Dacca for 11 area managers, members of the materials development unit, and other core personnel of BRAC who would subsequently have training and other responsibilities in the functional education program. Immediately following this session, a five-day course for the Field Motivators was held at the Sulla Project site at Markuli. The training was conducted by the Area Managers and the World Education consultant attended as a resource person.

In addition to the initial training of instructors, short workshops, follow-up meetings, and refresher courses were organized for the instructors by the Area Managers and Field Motivators, and they, in turn, attended review meetings organized by the training and materials development staff at the head office.

The training sessions, passing through initial trials and errors, have evolved into a common pattern (known as the BRAC Functional Education Training Module), though variations for specific groups are possible and even encouraged. The session normally lasts for five full days. The specific objectives of the training are: (a) to help participants shed their inhibitions in group situations and understand the dynamics of an effective group as well as the worth of individual members in the group, (b) to eliminate the traditional notions of "experts" and "teachers" and to demonstrate that everyone in a group can enrich the group's

learning experience, (c) to familiarize the participants with the materials
and methods of the course and their role as facilitators of group interaction, and (d) to let the participants engage in practice and demonstration of the methods to be used later with the learners.

The major activities of the training sessions include the following:
identification and discussion of the participants' own expectations about
the training session and its outcome; brainstorming about anticipated problems in functional education groups and the participants' own misgivings
and doubts about the approach; discussion of the familiar methods of teaching literacy and numeracy; simulation games and role-playing to sharpen understanding of the learners' and instructors' roles as well as the general
rural situation; discussion of the specific steps in the functional education lessons; demonstration lessons by the trainer and the participants who
volunteer; discussion and demonstration of effective group procedures; and
critical analysis of the participants' experience in the training session
at various stages along the way and of the entire experience at the end.
When feasible some of the demonstration lessons are conducted with actual
illiterate learners. An instructor's guide that outlines the objectives
and steps for each of the 70 functional education lessons has been prepared in 1974. It serves as a useful training aid as well as a handy reference for instructors in the field.

Reading Materials

With the aim of providing relevant and informative reading materials
to rural readers, BRAC began publishing the monthly journal, Gonokendro
(The People's Forum) in April 1973. Written and edited by a full-time
staff of two, the tabloid-size eight-page paper (later increased to 12
pages) started with an initial print run of 2,000 copies. The circula-
tion shot up to 30,000 copies when UNICEF agreed to buy and distribute
copies to 30,000 rural primary school teachers as a supplementary reading material for themselves and their students. UNICEF later decided to
distribute 60,000 copies to cover most rural primary schools in the country.
Besides the primary school teachers, the general distribution in the rural
areas was less than 1,000 copies in mid-1976, even though BRAC tried to promote subscription among the functional education participants.

A content analysis of one volume of Gonokendro (12 issues from April
1975 to March 1976) showed that the materials in the journal were on agriculture (rice, jute, horticulture, wheat, fishery, cattle, and poultry);
health and nutrition; family planning; women's socioeconomic situation;
cooperatives and the rural economy; primary education; and general information (10 to 20 percent of the space). Each issue also contained some liter-
ary and entertainment pieces covering about 10 percent of the columns. The
lead articles in the 12 issues were headed as follows: "Deep water rice,"
"Population Education in Bangladesh," "Main causes of malnutrition," "Cattle
Wealth of Bangladesh," "Our fishery resources," "Preparation for winter farming," "Cultivating improved varieties in the Boro season," "Population growth
has to stop," "Food for work," "Foreign market for jute has to be protected,
"Ups and downs in jute farming."

Although the paper is well-written in an attractive racy language
and is well edited and covers topics likely to be of interest and use
to rural readers, it requires a level of language proficiency significantly beyond the level of an average neoliterate. It is well suited
to primary school teachers and others who have language skills expected
at least of primary school completers. This is the group it serves now
--not, by any means, an unimportant service. But it does not fill the
alarming vacuum that now exists in neoliterate reading materials   with
systematically chosen texts of graded levels of complexity.

The Results

As noted earlier, with 35 male and 26 female instructors, the first
cycle of courses was opened for 734 men and 441 women from over 50 villages in the Sulla Project area. Another 85 villagers joined the learning groups after the formal beginning, making a total enrollment of 1,260.
The new participatory learning process and the emphasis on familiar problems of rural life aroused a high level of enthusiasm;   regular attendance and retention showed marked improvement in comparison to the earlier
literacy efforts. A total of 520 learners (41 percent) completed all 80
lessons, and another substantial number completed more than half of the
course. A second cycle of courses was offered in June 1975 in 53 centers
with 1,338 learners, of whom 616 or 46 percent, completed the lessons.

What is the significance of these results? For one thing, a much
larger number of rural people compared to that of the previous literacy
efforts considered it worthwhile to devote the time and energy to completing the lessons. Moreover, the attention and effort given to preparing the materials, developing the methodology, and training   the
instructors, as well as the participatory learning process employed in
the program must have made a qualitative difference in the learning
outcome that could not be indicated merely by the completion rate.

The important question, however, is: What is the achievement of
the participants in the educational program in terms of (a) literacy
and numeracy skills, (b) new knowledge and information useful in improving rural living conditions, (c) critical awareness of the situation in
which the participants find themselves, and (d) use of the newly acquired
knowledge and awareness to change the situation?

BRAC has not undertaken any systematic evaluation to provide a definitive answer to this question. BRAC workers, however, through their
continuous contact with the rural people in the project area, including
the participants in the educational program, have formed their own views
about the results of the educational efforts and have accordingly influenced the subsequent course of the educational program. ICED investigators, on the basis of extensive discussion with workers in the field
and at headquarters and visits with the rural participants of the program, have reached the following conclusions:

1. Most of those who finish the course do not achieve a level of skill sufficient to write an informative letter to a friend or a relative or   to read a newspaper column. They also do not achieve a level of self-sufficiency in literacy skills that would permit them to improve their skill level on their own if reading materials for neoliterates were available. A small proportion, no more than a quarter (estimated generously) of those who complete the course, achieves a level sufficient to continue to improve their skills if they have relevant reading materials for neoliterates and the opportunity to use   frequently their skills in their daily life. In the absence of both, most   of these people are likely to relapse into illiteracy. For a rural resident in a Sulla village, it would take extraordinary individual motivation and determination to continue to make use of his newly acquired literacy skills and to improve them.

2. To the extent that the lessons cover information and knowledge useful to improvement of rural living conditions and an understanding of   the dynamics of the rural socioeconomic situation, and to the extent that the skills of the instructors and their supervisors are sufficiently put to use (these skills vary in the groups), there is a greater knowledge and understanding among the participants about various rural problems and their   own situation than in a comparable group of nonparticipant rural residents. (To be any more precise about the level of knowledge and understanding of the learners would call for a somewhat elaborate evaluation effort beyond   the scope of this study.)

3. There is, however, no clear evidence that the knowledge and awareness gained from the functional education program have been put to effective use. The level of participation in the various BRAC development activities, either as beneficiaries or as contributors of the functional education group members, is not significantly different from that of nonmembers. Nor does the "standard of living" of the group members as a group appear to be different from that of the nonmembers. It is evident that the BRAC program organizers, at least initially, have not viewed the participation in functional education as a precondition or an essential element of participation in other development activities. Nor has the functional education program led to such initiatives and self-help efforts among the participants as to cause them to be marked apart as the focus of special development efforts either by BRAC or other agencies.

Implications of the Early Experience

The functional education experience in Sulla reconfirms what has been found repeatedly in literacy efforts: that in a nonliterate environment and a primitive rural economy with most people engaged in subsistence activities, literacy is not a practical necessity, and it is extremely difficult to maintain motivation and interest in literacy efforts, even when these efforts form a part of a broader functional education program. In fact, in these programs the literacy components tend to dominate the program and distract attention from   other important goals of the program, such as that of creating a critical awareness of the learners' situation and the dissemination of useful knowledge.

The rural people are generally interested in literacy, as their initial response to any kind of literacy effort shows, because they see in it a visible and tangible objective to attain skills which the privileged ones possess

and also a promise of change in their own condition. A rude awakening
soon follows when mastering the skills proves to be hard work and the
promise of change turns out to be elusive. Interest wanes and the dropout rate mounts. A functional education program deemphasizing literacy
and stressing the intangible "conscientization"[1] objective   probably
would not evoke the same kind of initial enthusiasm among the people;
but if the program were well-conceived and well-managed, the interest
in it would be likely to increase cumulatively and should be more enduring than in a traditional literacy program.

     The Sulla experience also indicates that just initiating a number
of development activities, including educational programs, in the same
area and under the same organizational auspices will not lead spontaneously to an integrated development effort with the educational programs
supporting and reinforcing the total development effort. The educational program has to be directly and deliberately geared to satisfying the
needs of knowledge, skills, understanding, and group efforts for various
development activities--especially if popular support and initiatives are
called for in these development activities.   An independent functional
education program with a heavy emphasis on the mechanics of literacy does
not satisfy these needs effectively.

     The implications of the Sulla experience have led the BRAC leader-
ship to two somewhat conflicting responses: (a) a revision of   the
functional education materials laying a greater stress on the mechanics
of literacy and arithmetic, and (b) a greater emphasis on the "conscientization" role not only in the educational effort but in the total
development approach of BRAC.

     The primary aim of the revision of the materials, undertaken   by
the Materials Development Unit, seems to be improvement of the achievement level in literacy skills of those who complete the course.   The
number of lessons is to be raised from 70 to 100, apparently because a
larger number of lessons is considered necessary for achieving a functionally useful level of proficiency in reading and writing.   Every
eleventh lesson in the course is to be a review lesson focusing on the
mechanics of literacy and arithmetic such as the vowel signs and   the
arithmetic functions. The sequence of the lessons is to be based   on
the level of complexity of the mechanics. Some modification of content
in the light of experience and a more logical clustering of lessons by
major themes are also to be done in the course of the revision. Changes
of the "generative words" and specific content items are also intended
to make the materials usable widely in different parts of the country.
Expansion of BRAC activities in various locations and the increasing
interest by voluntary organizations as well as government agencies in

----

[1]Raising the level of consciousness about one's own condition
through a dialogical process--a concept advocated and popularized by
the Brazilian educationist Paulo Freire.

the BRAC functional educational materials have made it necessary to produce a general package of materials.

While the effort continues to improve the literacy achievements of the functional education program and to prepare a general educational   package that can be used in different situations by different organizations   (with varying levels of interconnection between the educational program and   other development efforts, or even without any well-defined link), the leaders of BRAC have embarked on new activities that deemphasize literacy as a component of functional education, assert the centrality of "conscientization" in education as well as in the total development approach of BRAC, and   attempt to make the educational activities supportive of other   project   activities in direct and specific ways.

For example, the plan for the future of Sulla   Phase III   provides that "functional education classes will be organized for disadvantaged homogeneous groups such as the landless, the women, the sharecroppers, fishermen, etc., in order to organize them for action programmes to realize their creative potential."[1] (Writer's emphasis.) In addition, a general conscientization program of the villagers will be undertaken through a series of village workshops engaging the villagers "in a critical analysis of socio-economic structures and major contradictions, community problems and formulation of action plans for social change."[2]

In Jamalpur, a functional education program for destitute women, begun as an ad hoc activity with the support of UNICEF as a part of the Food-for-Work program, has evolved into a BRAC development project with "functional education" as one ingredient. The total project anticipated organizing poor women from 28 villages for achieving a series of interrelated objectives relating to population control, cooperative economic projects, health and nutrition, agricultural production, women's own organizations, and raising village women's consciousness. Education is not seen as a separate and independent activity.

In the Manikganj project, initiated in 1976, functional education is seen as the means for forming village level organizations for carrying out development activities, setting program priorities, and ensuring   popular participation in the activities. The proposal for the project states:

> The functional education programme will be the initial
> and main thrust of BRAC's work in Manikganj.   BRAC's
> functional education programme is a problem posing method-
> ology in which literacy and numeracy revolves around a pro-
> blem perceived by the people but codified to focus attention
> and stimulate discussion. It offers open-ended questions
> with answers resulting from a concerted effort to analyse
> the situation and find alternatives. This is done by bring-
> ing the learners together in a group with the teachers acting

---

[1]BRAC. Sulla Project, Phase III, Dacca, 1976, pp. 4-5, (mimeo).

[2]Ibid.

as the facilitator. The teacher and learner become actors
in a process of mutual communication. Together they try to
identify problems and seek solutions. No distinction   is
made between those who know and those who do not. All participants come together in their search for and desire   to
change their situation and better their lives. Through this
process, the individual is able to describe what he sees and
feels, to evaluate its relative importance, to make comparisons with other situations and to formulate concrete   responses. Once he is able to locate the different areas of his
problems he will then see the need to come together in such
groups as youth organisations, mothers' clubs, cooperatives,
etc. to deal with various problems of credit, health, family
planning, nutrition, education, agriculture, etc. Thus the
BRAC programmes aimed at nurturing such village-level insti-
tutitions will grow out of the very desire of the people for
concerted action.

As the learners themselves establish the programme priorities, BRAC's programmes will be developed to respond to these
needs. The people will be able to identify the programmes as
their own and be prepared to participate actively.[1]

Although the functional education program of BRAC was designed
with World Education assistance, it had been strongly influenced from
the very beginning by Paulo Freire's ideas. The Freirean language
and terminologies have become more pronounced in the recent project
plans. In the Sulla Project, the methodology of Freire had been
attempted by using generative words and themes, by presenting "coded"
pictures, and by applying a process of group dialogue. However, the
essence of Freire's approach--conscientization leading to liberating
actions to transform the situation of the oppressed learners had remained unrealized. The way was blocked by the habits and attitudes
of the traditional literacy programs, as reflected in the dominance
of the new program by literacy, and the view that functional education is an independent activity. There had also been the inherent
difficulties of implementing a totally new program based on a radically different approach. The more recent project plans attempt to
make the educational activities truly functional in the sense of education that enables rural people to engage in collective and individual actions that respond to their survival needs and help improve
the quality of their lives.

The concept of functionality of education reflected in the new
project plans are yet to be fully developed, tested, and implemented,
as these plans mark the beginning of a new phase of BRAC (as of 1976).
The implications of the departures in the functional education program

---

[1] BRAC, Manikganj Project, p. 16-17 (mimeo).

in terms of methodology, content, field personnel, and the organization and
management of BRAC field activities are yet to be fully worked out, although
the general trends and directions are evident from project plans.

Reconciling Literacy and Functionality

On the whole, the BRAC program managers appear to be minimizing and un-
derrating the divergent rationale and philosophies of (a) the approach underlying a functional education course with a predetermined lesson   sequence
that imposes a literacy bias and criterion of learning achievement on all
rural learners and an all-purpose readymade educational package to be used
by various organizations in various situations; and (b) a truly functional
program that is shaped and controlled by each learning group's priorities
and perception of the crucial problems and is characterized by a "conscientization" effort that directly leads to actions for changing the existing
situation. The latter approach would call for:

(a)   Instructors or learning group facilitators who are not just
      tutors of literacy skills but are individuals with a   high
      level of sophistication and a highly developed critical aware-
      ness about the dynamics of the rural situation who can help
      organize not just the educational activity but also the action
      programs that accompany or follow the educational efforts. The
      instructor has to become also the field worker for the develop-
      ment activities to be launched collectively by the learning
      group.

(b)   Generation of learning materials by the learning groups them-
      selves, based on the specific situations they face and the
      action programs they choose to undertake. A central materials
      development unit can prepare resource materials and prototypes
      to be drawn upon by the groups and can provide guidance and
      techniques to the groups and the instructors for creating at
      least a significant proportion of their own learning materials.
      The instructor/field worker has to have training in improvising
      relevant learning materials and in assisting the learning groups
      to create their own learning tools and content--another task for
      the materials development unit.

(c)   Planning, implementing, and managing the BRAC activities at all
      levels, particularly at the field level, in a way that recog-
      nizes the central importance of "conscientization" of the parti-
      cipants and shuns the temptation to impose solutions or manipulate
      compliance of participants in the name of efficiency or any other
      pretext.

(d)   Adequate provisions for acquiring functionally useful levels of
      literacy skills and supplying relevant reading materials for those
      who are interested. While literacy should not dominate the func-
      tional education program and should not be a major criterion for
      judging the performance of the program or of the learners, literacy
      need not be relegated into an inconsequential position in the pro-
      gram. Just as the literate "do-gooders" should not impose liter-
      acy on others at the slightest pretext, neither should they withhold
      it arbitrarily. Literacy will probably maintain its attraction for

the rural people, and only by allowing everyone a crack at it
(or more than one crack) is it possible to know who has the
motivation and the determination. As the momentum of development quickens, the customers for literacy will grow too.   It
is, however, evident that those who survive a basic   cycle
need further assistance in bringing their skills up to   functionally usable levels. They also need relevant reading materials and help in availing themselves of opportunities to   use
their new skills. Improving the general learning environment
and expanding the scope of literacy use can be an element   in
the various development activities undertaken in the village.

(e) Pragmatic strategies and tactics to overcome the inevitable ob-
     stacles put up by the local power structure that has a vested
     interest in maintaining the status quo or seizing control of
     the development activities. While resistance may arise to an
     educational program seen as a pure literacy effort, an authen-
     tic "conscientization" effort is bound to face much more vehement
     and sinister opposition. In each situation the BRAC workers and
     the local participants have to make a realistic assessment   of
     the several obstacles, issues, and activities that give rise to
     possible confrontation. They must be ready to take advantage of
     all progressive elements and forces in the locality as well   as
     in the national political scene. BRAC is obliged to weigh care-
     fully against potential outcome of its effort the possible dan-
     gers of exposing the deprived rural residents to even greater
     deprivation and even oppression by initiating an educational
     effort. Its assessment should be shared fully with the parti-
     cipant groups.

The degree of effectiveness BRAC will achieve in its functional education efforts will depend on how successfully BRAC tackles these questions.
Insofar as functional education is intimately linked with the whole development approach of BRAC, the realization of the overall development objectives
of BRAC also will depend heavily on how well these issues are handled.

CHAPTER 3

HEALTH AND
FAMILY PLANNING

The Health Situation

The health problems in the Sulla Project area are similar to those found throughout rural Bangladesh. Caused by the absence of basic hygiene and sanitation provisions and frequently complicated by malnutrition, preventable and communicable diseases abound. Adequate information about the prevalence and incidence of diseases in the area is not available.   The service statistics of BRAC and the observations of its health workers indicate that diarrhea and gastro-intestinal diseases, internal parasites, and respiratory infections account for about 60 percent of the total morbidity in the area. Infection of the skin and of ears, eyes, and throat amounts to another 15 percent of the diseases. If common cold and general bodily aches and pains, described as rheumatism, are added to the above list, it would cover over 80 percent of the diseases for which the people of Sulla sought treatment from BRAC paramedics (see Table 3.1).

Undernutrition and malnutrition are particularly noticeable prior to the harvesting of the boro, the only rice crop in much of the area. Specific nutritional deficiencies in the form of night blindness and stomatitis are frequent. Tuberculosis is prevalent, although its intensity is   not known. Incidence of malaria has gone down recently and smallpox, a scourge in the past, seems to have been eliminated as a result of an internationally assisted government eradication campaign against malaria and smallpox.

Mortality rate for the area, on the basis of a 1975 sample survey, is estimated to be around 15 per 1,000 population with a heavy concentration among infants, children under five, and pregnant mothers. The survey has shown that two-thirds of all deaths in the project area occurred among children up to the age of 4 years. The rate was 186 per 1,000 for infants (from birth to age 1). It fell sharply to 23 per 1,000 for children (1-4 years). From age-groups 15-19 to 45-49 the death rate was more or   less constant around 1 per 1,000, and it rose gradually for older people over 50.[1] The population growth rate for the area is estimated by BRAC at 2.5 percent. Both the crude birth rate and the crude death rate in the project area, according to the sample survey, is slightly lower than the national rate (40 and 15 respectively compared to 47 and 17).[2]

---

[1]BRAC, Base-line Survey of Sulla (October-November 1975), Dacca, 1976.

[2]However, the infant mortality rate was found to be higher than in another thana with good demographic records. Matlab Demographic studies (May 1967-April 1968) indicated an infant mortality rate of 125 compared to 186 in Sulla in 1975. (BRAC, Base-line Survey of Sulla (October-November 1975), Dacca, 1976, pp. 4-5.)

Table 3.1

Incidence of Diseases Treated by Paramedics in Sulla
July-September 1976

Disease Symptoms	Number of Cases	Percentage
Diarrhea	982	10.4
Dysentery (chronic and acute)	1 727	18.2
Worms	1 043	11.0
Hyperacidity	285	3.0
Common cold	992	10.5
Acute bronchitis	423	4.4
Pneumonia	263	2.8
Ear, eye, throat condition	630	6.6
Skin infection	763	8.0
Rheumatism	787	8.3
Others	1 590	16.8
TOTAL	9 485	100.0

Source: BRAC Service Records.

Services Other Than BRAC

The stipulated pattern for government personnel for health care in a thana is one health administrator (physician), a medical officer and other staff for a 25-bed hospital, two or three health inspectors, and a family welfare worker for vaccination and preventive care per 5,000 people. The family planning staff is supposed to include a thana Family Planning Officer, a number of Lady Family Planning Visitors for maternal and child health care as well as some clinical services such as IUD insertion, and three family planning workers per union (one male and two female). In 1976, the government personnel and facilities in the area did not conform to this standard. In the project area, encompassing one thana and parts of two other thanas, there were two physicians serving as Thana Health Administrators and 15 other health workers for two thanas. The family planning personnel included, besides the two thana officers, 14 field workers. The thana health center existed only in one thana, Derai. It had offices for the health officials, a dispensary and outdoor clinic (open about two hours a day, six days a week), a 25-bed indoor treatment facility, and a seldom used operation theatre.

The government health personnel are known to remain confined to the thana center waiting for the people to come to them and providing such curative services as inadequate and irregular supplies of medicine permit. Frequent complaints about the absence of the doctor, the nonavailability of medicine, and the considerable distance that most of the thana residents have to cover to come to the center discourage effective use of the center. Visits to villages by the health workers are made mainly for vaccination drives against smallpox and cholera. The family planning program, which has recently undergone a major reorganization at the national level and the impact of which is still to be felt in all the rural areas, has remained ineffective in both motivational work and in recruiting acceptors.

The private practitioners of western medicine in the area include 11 doctors (2 regular medical graduates, 3 LMFs, and 6 national doctors).[1] All of these doctors are located in four bazars (trading centers) in the area. A number of "village doctors" (compounders or pharmacist's assistants, and practitioners of indigenous medicine) are also mostly located in the bazars. All health workers, government and private, are men.

BRAC Health Care and Family Planning Approach

True to its character as a relief program in its initial phase, the early BRAC activities in the health area consisted of fielding four medical teams in 1972 to provide daily outpatient services in four camps. When

---

[1] LMF (Licentiate of the Medical Faculty) doctors, licensed by the State to practise medicine, have four years' training after 10 years of general schooling, compared to five years' training after 12 years of schooling for MBBS. The LMF program was discontinued under pressure from the medical establishment to "raise the standards of the medical profession."

National doctors are trained in a private medical school, not recognized by the government as equivalent to the state medical colleges.

a cholera epidemic became a real threat and beyond the capabilities of
the small medical teams to handle, the doctors also trained a group of
villagers in the techniques of taking care of cholera and severe diarrhea cases. In addition a child feeding program was undertaken with
UNICEF assistance. Up to 15,000 children of poor families in the area
were given a ration of corn-soya milk as a supplement to their diet to
avert the dangers of serious malnutrition.

As the BRAC activities began to evolve into a development program
from a relief operation, the need arose for converting the ad hoc medical relief effort into a program of medical care, public health,   and
family planning that would become an integral part of the total   rural
development effort of BRAC.

The disease pattern in the villages, encompassing a preponderance
of communicable and preventable diseases, and the health manpower situation in the rural areas dictated a solution that had been found effective
in a number of other developing countries. It was to raise a cadre of
paraprofessional health workers from the rural residents themselves (paramedics) to treat the common diseases and conduct preventive and health
education activities. It was decided that the common clinical facilities
and technical medical personnel would provide backup support to both the
health care services and the family planning services. The main objectives of the health care and family planning program, as these were seen
at the time of initiating this program in mid-1973, were:

a. to train a cadre of paramedics to treat 18-20 common illnesses,

b. to make available inoculation and vaccination against the common
    preventable diseases,

c. to motivate and educate villagers to take preventive sanitation
    and public health measures, and

d. to form a cadre of female family planning workers to serve as
    distributors of contraceptives and recruiters   of   acceptors
    with the paramedics' guidance and supervision.

Organization of the Services

The paramedic is in a central position in the delivery of health
care in BRAC. Each paramedic, responsible for 4,000 to 5,000   people
in five to eight villages, visits the villages once a week or as nearly
so as possible, treats the specified common health problems, discusses
and provides advice on sanitation and hygiene measures, and looks after
the health problems of mothers and children brought to his attention by
the family planning organizer in the village.

The health and family planning activities are organizationally
linked with other BRAC activities through the camp, the base unit for
all activities in a cluster of villages. The paramedics are also based

in the camps (one or two for each camp), where they conduct a daily clinic
for an hour in addition to the village rounds and maintain liaison with
other BRAC personnel and activities. The Area Manager, head of the camp,
and the Field Motivators, who initiate and guide the village activities,
also have general supervisory responsibilities for the health and family
planning activities in the villages.   Existing groups for functional
education, cooperatives, and women's activities are used in most motivational and educational work relating to preventive health measures, sanitation, nutrition, and family planning. In this effort, the Area Managers
and the Field Motivators work as a team with the paramedics.   Educating
the public about the health insurance scheme (see below) and mobilizing
support in its favor again require a team effort by all BRAC field personnel.

Technical supervision of the paramedics is the responsibility of the
three physicians based in three health centers in the project area   (a
ratio of one physician to 40,000 people--the present overall ratio in rural
Bangladesh). The physicians provide initial and refresher training to the
paramedics, look after the patients referred to them by paramedics and the
family planning organizers, and supervise the paramedics' work by frequent
field visits. The main task of the physicians is to provide technical support and supervision to the paramedics and to take care of the referral
cases. They do not deal with patients directly except in exceptional emergencies. The centers where the doctors are based are modest facilities
where simple surgical procedures, common pathological tests, and such family
planning services as IUD insertion, tubal ligation, and vasectomy can be performed.

The village level family planning functions (i.e., making direct contacts with child-bearing age women, informing them of the contraceptive
alternatives, distributing supplies, maintaining records of acceptors, advising about side effects, recruiting candidates for terminal methods, and
so forth) are the responsibility of the Lady Family Planning Organizer
(LFPO). She serves a village (about 100 families) and is a native of the
village. She makes referrals to paramedics and the physicians as necessary.
She looks, however, to the Field Motivators and the Area Manager for guidance and active help in educational and motivational work, specially   in
dealing with existing community groups or when special community assemblies
are arranged for this purpose.

The health care and family planning components of the second phase of
the Sulla Project (1973-76) have functioned on the basis of the   organizational structure described above. This structure aims at bringing the basic
health care and family planning services to the people's doorstep,   meeting
the most urgent need, hitherto unmet, of simple domiciliary care, utilizing
the available health manpower efficiently, emphasizing preventive measures
and basic health care in place of expensive hospitals and sophisticated curative services, and integrating health care and family planning with other
aspects of rural development.

Experience in the Sulla area with this organizational approach, however, has pointed out some practical problems and has led BRAC to explore

certain modifications of this approach in the third phase of the Sulla and in new projects in other locations.[1]

First, it was found that there was a preponderance of adult males being treated by the paramedics, even though disease pattern and specific mortality rates indicated that child-bearing women and children under five were most in need of medical services. For example, the age and sex distribution of patients treated by paramedics in the Markuli area during a one-month period (from August 10 to September 10, 1974) was as follows:

Age in Years	No. of Male Patients	Percentage of Male Patients	No. of Female Patients	Percentage of Female Patients
0-5	111	13.5	96	11.6
6-15	109	13.3	50	6.1
Over 15	319	38.8	139	16.9
TOTAL	539	65.6	285	34.6

Women were apparently reluctant to come themselves or bring their children to paramedics, who were young men and mostly unmarried. The treatment of pediatric and obstetric-gynecological problems requires a personal rapport with the mother that is not easy for young men to establish in a Bengali village.

Second, despite the weekly village visit of the paramedics, the degree of contact between the paramedics and the villagers and the accessibility to medical service were found to be insufficient. A villager often had to wait up to a period of one week or travel some distance to one of the camp clinics before he could get help on any urgent medical problem.

Finally, the paramedics were found to be spending most of their time in the village providing curative services and very little time teaching preventive care and health education. Moreover, the once-a-week visit to the village for a few hours did not create a rapport and mutual trust between the paramedics and the villagers that is essential for the acceptance of new ideas and information.

The changes initiated in organization and staffing to overcome the problems encountered in Sulla were three-fold: (a) formation of a cadre of auxiliary women health workers who under the supervision of paramedics would establish a continuous presence of the health program in each village--each being based in her own village and each serving no more than 100 families on a narrower and more specific range of health problems than those treated by paramedcis (see below the discussion about personnel); (b) employment of women paramedics and a significant increase in their numbers (see the chapter on women's programs); and (c) emphasis on

---

[1] BRAC, The BRAC Health Care, Preventive Medicine and Family Planning Program, Dacca, n.d.

public health education, preventive measures, and nutrition education through
a systematic community-centered effort, particularly through women's groups
such as mothers' clubs (see the chapter on women's programs).

In addition, it was seen as an important objective to develop the organizational structure and the service delivery system in a manner that   would
make the health program increasingly self-sufficient in financial and management terms. The health insurance scheme designed to achieve this goal is discussed below in the section on financing.

Health Personnel

Categories and Functions

Three categories of personnel form the health and family planning staff
of BRAC. They are (a) the newly introduced (in 1976) village-based auxiliaries, known variously as the Peoples' Healer (Shasthya shevika) or locally
as the Daktarnee (the lady doctor) and the older category of Lady Family Planning Organizers (LFPO), (b) the paramedics, and (c) the qualified physicians.
Women auxiliaries are seen by BRAC as the most effective means of reaching
rural families; consequently, BRAC has no current plan to use men as village
health auxiliaries.

As noted above, the village-based auxiliary or the peoples' healer is
the response to the need for maintaining a continuous contact of the health
program with each village and for ensuring greater accessibility of the services to the village people. Her tasks, therefore, are three-fold: (a) providing specific treatments for selected common and uncomplicated disease
symptoms such as diarrhea, dysentery, scabies, headache and fever, and intestinal worms (the list may vary somewhat depending on the village needs);
(b) providing specific advice and information to mothers about nutrition,
child care, vaccination, and family planning; and (c) distributing oral contraceptives. This list is not intended to be rigid or restrictive. The
healer may be given more limited responsibilities (for example, when an LFPO
is functioning in the same village) or additional tasks depending on   the
ability to learn and performance of the healer and the need of the village.
The additional tasks that the healer may take over are vaccination and inoculation and midwifery.

The functions of the LFPO have been mentioned already. With the healers
placed in each village, the role of the LFPO needs reassessment. The logical
solution would appear to be to combine the LFPO and healer functions and to
retrain the interested and competent LFPOs for the healer's job. BRAC, however, is not certain about the proper course to follow. Apparently, women of
relatively high level of education and social status are interested in becoming healers, whereas the LFPO's position is seen somehow related to the tasks
of traditional birth attendants or dais, ranked relatively low in the social
status hierarchy. Having two separate groups of village level workers for the
health and family planning services offers the advantage of aligning the support of some influential village women for the health activities, but it has
the disadvantage of affecting adversely the social esteem and credibility of
the LFPO and of separating the interrelated health and family planning activities. The solution ultimately accepted will depend on trials, underway

currently (1976) in selected villages, with different patterns: newly recruited healers performing both health care and family planning tasks, LFPOs converted into healers carrying out their old and new functions, and division of duties between LFPOs and healers in the same villages.

The responsibilities of paramedics have been discussed in the previous section. With the posting of healers in each village, the paramedic continues with his usual weekly village visit, but now visits homes identified by the healer as having health problems and follows up previously treated cases. He devotes more time to health education and preventive care by attending meetings of village groups, such as mothers' clubs, functional educational groups, and primary schools. With a potential decrease in the paramedic's work load, and in view of the seriousness of another problem in the villages, the idea of training paramedics for treating and preventing common diseases of cattle and fowl is being examined in BRAC. It is not known whether the treatment of cattle and people by the same person will be found acceptable by the people. Presumably, the cattle will have no objection to this arrangement!

The functions of the physicians--anyone with MBBS, LMF, and National Certificate, and all three types are represented in BRAC staff--have been described above. As a BRAC document states,

> The classic role of the physician as that of a
> healer is being redefined in BRAC. We view   him
> first and foremost as a teacher, then a   planner
> and lastly one directly involved in curing.[1]

With an increasingly important role of the village-based healer as the front line worker of the health and family planning program, her training and ultimate technical backstopping and supervision of her performance are the responsibility of the physician posted in the health center serving a particular area.

Recruitment and Training

The criteria for recruitment as a people's healer are that (a) she is a female member of the community, preferably over twenty years of age, (b) she is acceptable to the community, and (c) she is enthusiastic about her new responsibilities and willing to move freely about the village. She may be illiterate if she meets the other criteria.

The training of the healer is carried out in one of the villages and conducted by physicians or paramedics supervised by physicians. The main methodology is demonstration and practice of the tasks--identifying the disease symptoms, mixing and applying medicine, communicating with clients, handling money, and so forth--repeating these as many times as necessary to ensure mastery of the tasks. For the benefit of illiterate healers, the drugs are premixed with individual dosages separated or marked and each drug color-coded for easy identification. The initial training of healers lasts up to four weeks in two to three hours of daily sessions. Refresher sessions are held as needed.

---

[1]BRAC, The BRAC Health Care... Ibid., p. 12.

Since LFPOs do not handle medicine, a less rigorous training method has been followed in their case. The one week training for them includes discussion and demonstration about the need for family planning, the relationship of family planning to nutrition and child care, means of contacting child-bearing couples, and the recording of data. The training is conducted by the paramedics and the Field Motivators.

To qualify as a paramedic in the BRAC health program, the candidate must (1) have at least matriculation certificate (10 years of formal education), but relaxable in the case of female candidates; (2) be well motivated and willing to travel from village to village; and (3) be acceptable to the village communities to be served by him. Until mid-1976 all paramedics in BRAC were men; since then a group of 15 women have been placed in training to become paramedics.

The training of paramedics is conducted by the BRAC physicians and is held in the project area, except for one week's special training at the Cholera Research Laboratory in Dacca on diarrheal treatment methods developed at the laboratory. It is a fairly rigid well-structured training course that lasts for six months and includes two months of classroom sessions on theoretical aspects and four months of supervised practice.

A training manual for the paramedics has been prepared that lists the distinguishing symptoms, danger signs to be watched, and specific treatments for the following common diseases:

1. Diarrhea
2. Dysentery (acute, bacillary)
3. Dysentery (chronic, amoebic)
4. Enteric fever (typhoid)
5. Common cold and influenza
6. Pneumonia
7. Sore throat
8. Bronchitis
9. Scabies
10. Boils
11. Burns
12. Ringworm
13. Roundworms and threadworms
14. Anaemia
15. Fever
16. Headache
17. Rheumatism
18. Stomach ulcer
19. Malnutrition and vitamin deficiencies (including night blindness and stomatitis)
20. Women's conditions (including pregnancy and post delivery problems)

In addition, the procedure and dosages for immunizations (DPT, tetanus toxoid, smallpox, BCG and TABC) are described in the manual.

The training also emphasizes the basic philosophy and mottoes of the program, the supervisory and management responsibilities of para- medics, communication with village people, and the importance of preven- tion.

The quality that is given the highest importance in the recruit- ment of a physician is his enthusiasm for the BRAC program and   its objectives and his willingness to learn from his own experience. There is no formal training program in BRAC for a physician. His profession- al training does not prepare him for the role he is expected to play as a teacher, planner, and provider of technical backstopping in a compre- hensive rural health care system. However, for the professional   and intellectual rejuvenation of the physician and as a kind of   special incentive, there is provision for short study tours in other developing countries to observe the rural health problems or innovative projects and for attending short advanced public health education and manage- ment courses.

Services Provided

In the Sulla Project area in 1975 curative and preventive services were provided by 31 paramedics. As noted earlier, they provided treat- ment for the common ailments and referred complicated cases (about   5 percent of the patients) to the physicians.

The number of cases treated by the paramedics and physicians   in 1975 was about 50,000, mostly among the members of the insurance scheme (see below). With 13,500 members in the insurance scheme in 1975, and each member requiring treatment on an average of three times a year, the number of noninsured patients was very small.

Although anyone in the project area could take advantage of the cur- ative service by paying the cost of medicine (an average of 2.50 taka) and a modest service fee of Tk 0.50 per consultation, even these charges were apparently high for many families. The insurance scheme was intended to overcome this problem by distributing the cost burden evenly in the popula- tion. However, as mentioned earlier, the reluctance of women to be treate by male paramedics and the inadequate provision of service in the absence of a village-based health worker prevented the spread of the insurance scheme. Therefore, on a regular basis, the benefits of the curative ser- vices were enjoyed mostly by a small proportion (about 12 percent) of the area population. As a part of the plan to expand the benefits, the vil- lage-based people's healer scheme was initiated in 1976, and training of female paramedics was begun. At the end of the year, 30 people's healers (Shasthya shevika) were working in 30 villages, mostly with insured groups and 15 female paramedics were in training.

One specific preventive measure widely available was primary small- pox vaccination for all children. DPT and BCG injections for children as well as tetanus toxoid for pregnant mothers were to be made   selectively available in 1976 and were planned to be made generally available subse- quently.

Besides general advice by paramedics on prevention and hygiene during contacts with the villagers, group efforts on health education were carried out through mothers' clubs as well as functional education groups, primary schools, and cooperative society meetings. The most systematic of these efforts were the mothers' clubs, 73 of which were started under BRAC auspices and were functioning in the project area in 1976. The mothers' clubs activities are described in the chapter on women's programs.

Family planning services were offered through 87 Lady Family Planning Organizers in the project area in 1976. The services included contact with eligible couples and explanation of the methods, means, and importance of family planning; distribution of oral pills, condoms, and EMKO foam; followup of side effects; and referral to clinics for insertion of IUD or terminal methods.

The family planning program started in January 1974 and reached a peak of 2,105 acceptors in May 1975. Since then, the number of acceptors seems to have reached a plateau and has remained around 2,000 in 1976. In December 1975, 1,892 women were on pills, 38 had IUDs inserted, and 40 men had undergone vasectomy.[1] Tubectomy was not made available until 1976 because, as the BRAC leadership put it, the husbands in male-dominated societies avoided the much simpler procedure of vasectomy and prevailed upon their wives to undergo tubal ligation. The plan was to have a sufficient number of vasectomy clients first and then to offer both vasectomy and tubal ligation. As it turned out, the campaign for vasectomy did not have a great success, and the denial of tubal ligation probably imposed more hardship on women willing to take a terminal measure than the pain they were spared. Tubectomy, therefore, began to be available in 1976.

The services of LFPOs were available in 1976 to 87 villages, or less than half of the 200 villages in the project area. The current acceptance ratio, if computed on the basis of the total eligible couples in villages actually served (estimated to be about 10,000) rather than of the eligible couples in the whole project area (about 20,000) is approximately 20 percent--compared to a national estimate of about 5 percent.[2]

While 20 percent acceptance rate is relatively high, what precisely this means in terms of impact on population growth rate was not clear. Some benchmark data for 1975 were collected by BRAC, but no comparative demographic data for a later check were available. In any event, the program was not extensive enough or had not been in existence long enough to provide any definitive conclusion regarding its impact. The rate of continuation among contraceptive acceptors after 12 monthly cycles of pill distribution was reported to be 62.6 percent after 12 monthly cycles and 54.9 percent after 18 cycles of distribution.[3]   Physical side   effects   of   pills   were   reported   to

---

[1]BRAC, Sulla Project Report on Phase II, pp. 24-25. Service statistics for December 1976 showed 2,082 continuing pill acceptors, and a total of 74 IUD acceptors and 59 vasectomies in Sulla by December 31, 1976.

[2]According to the BRAC oral pill follow-up survey of February-March, 1976, the estimate of acceptance rate is 21.1 percent of the eligible married women in the villages covered by family planning services.

[3]BRAC, Oral Pill Follow-up Survey: Family Planning in the Context of Integrated Rural Development, Dacca, March 1977, Table 13.

be the single most important reason for discontinuation. (See Tables
3.2 and 3.3.)

Financing the Health Program

A primary health care service designed to meet the basic health
care needs of the people on a permanent basis cannot remain dependent
forever on philanthropic support of voluntary organizations.   It is
BRAC's belief that its low-cost health delivery approach will make it
possible to have a self-sufficient community health service financed
by the community's own resources with some supplementation from   the
national government or other outside sources.

The group health insurance scheme is designed to mobilize community resources for the health program and to keep the cost burden   for
the rural families at an acceptable level. The main features of   the
scheme, as it operated in Sulla till 1976, are as follows:

a.   A group consisting of at least 75 percent of the population
     of a village with a minimum of 175 people can enter the
     scheme.

b.   The annual premium of 4 kilograms of paddy (unhusked rice)
     per person is payable in advance (collected after the
     main harvest).

c.   The insured families must accept and cooperate in BRAC's
     preventive health program (particularly, inoculation and
     vaccination).

d.   BRAC provides weekly paramedical curative health service
     to the group, including referrals to doctors when neces-
     sary, without further cost.

(With the introduction of shasthya shevikas, curative care is
available on a continuous basis in each village. The preventive
measures such as vaccination and mother and child care through the
mothers' clubs are, in principle, available to all project   area
people, irrespective of participation in the insurance scheme.)

The insurance scheme was launched in May 1975 and a drive was
organized by the paramedics and the Field Motivators to enroll members and form village committees for the collection of the annual
in-kind premium. BRAC estimates are that throughout the project
40 to 50 percent of the families were prepared to join the scheme,
but only 10 percent of the villages could muster 75 percent coverage to qualify for group insurance. By early 1976, only 37 groups
covering 13,500 people had joined the scheme.[1]

---

[1]BRAC, Sulla Project Report on Phase II, p. 22.

Table 3.2

Stated Primary Reasons for Discontinuation
of Contraceptive Use

Reasons	Number	Percentage
Physical side-effects	247	30.8
Desire for another child	156	19.4
Accidental pregnancy	130	16.2
Not needed for unspecified reasons	91	11.4
Other reasons	36	10.7
Husband's objection	37	4.6
Fear of method	28	3.5
Forgetfulness	27	3.4
N =	802	100.0

Source: BRAC, Oral Pill Follow-up Survey: Family Planning in the Context
of Integrated Rural Development, Table 15.

Table 3.3

Physical Symptoms Mentioned Most Frequently for
Discontinuing Contraceptives

Symptoms	Most Important Reason (Percentage)	Second Most Important Reason (Percentage)
Dizziness	27.2	24.9
Excessive Bleeding	21.8	5.8
Headaches	13.0	15.9
Irregular Bleeding	7.9	4.8
Vomiting	7.5	11.6
Colic	3.8	3.7
Disability, neurosis	3.4	13.2
Lack of appetite, dyspepsia	1.7	3.2
Fatigue	1.7	5.3
Difficulty in breast feeding	1.2	2.1
Bleeding between periods	0.8	2.6
Weight gain or loss	0.8	0.5
Other breast problems	0.4	0.0
Skin diseases	0.4	0.0
Others	8.4	6.4
	100.0	100.0

Source: BRAC, Oral Pill Follow-up Survey: Family Planning in the Context of Integrated Rural Development, Table 16.

At a time of relatively low paddy rice (late 1976) the annual per
person premium of 4 kilograms of paddy valued at Tk 6.00   covered
roughly 50 percent of the drug costs on the basis of 3.3 consultations
per person per year at an average drug cost of Tk 3.50 per consultation.
The trends in cost of production and the international prices   suggest
that rice prices will stabilize at a higher level of around Tk 100.00
per maund (40 kgs.). The current premium rate of 4 kgs. would therefore
cover about 80 percent of the drug costs--if the drug costs also remain
stable.

Recurring costs other than for medicine are estimated to be no more
than two-thirds of the drug costs on the basis of the cost structure proposed by BRAC for the third phase of the Sulla Project. Following broadly the BRAC cost projections for the Sulla Project, the following   per
capita annual recurring costs are derived:

		Taka
Medicine		12.00
Other supplies (contraceptives, clinical		
supplies, vaccinations, etc.)		2.00
Personnel		
Doctor (Tk 1500 per month/30,000 people)	0.60	
Paramedics (Tk 750 per month/4,000		
people)	2.50	
Shasthya Shevika/LFPO		
(Tk 150 p.m./1,000 people)	1.80	
		4.90
Travel (20% of doctor & paramedic salaries)		0.62
Training (10% of all salaries)		0.49
	TOTAL.......	20.01

BRAC leaders believe that it would be feasible gradually and sufficiently to increase the insurance premium during Phase III (1976-78)
to cover all of the medicine and supply costs. The personnel costs have
to be met from other sources. BRAC's proposal for Phase III states that
the salaries of paramedics and the shasthya shevikas will be "required
to be borne by the Village Development Committee who will receive grants
from the Cooperative Society. The cost of administration and doctors'
salaries will require funding from outside sources."[1] Whether the Village Development Committee can pay the salaries of the health worker will,
of course, depend on how successful, economically and otherwise, the cooperative societies are.

Recordkeeping and Evaluation

A reluctance to devote any substantial effort to maintaining more
than the most rudimentary service data and other project statistics is
clearly detectable in BRAC. As stated in a project document, "Paper is

---

[1] Ibid., p. 10.

not only expensive, it creates an army of clerks when we want an army of health workers."

The paramedic maintains a notebook in which he enters the date and the village visited every working day and records the patient's name, age, sex, symptoms, diagnosis, treatment, and money collected for medicine. These records are reviewed monthly by the physician.

The LFPO used to maintain two notebooks, one for listing the target couples and the other for acceptor information. These have been replaced by a card to be maintained by the LFPO for each married woman between 15 and 45. The cards are used to record name and age of husband and wife, number and ages of children, type of contraception accepted, period when used, and reason (if any) for discontinuation. The cards are used for referral service in the clinic.

The shevika is required only to record the number of patients seen and whether they are adults or children.

If the data recorded by the paramedics and LFPOs were consolidated and analyzed, they would provide the basic quantitative indication of curative medical services provided and the acceptance and retention rates for family planning. These, however, would not provide any accurate indication of the impact of the health efforts in terms of morbidity, mortality, and overall health situation of the population; nor would there be an indication of the effects on birth rate and population growth rate or of the differential characteristics of acceptors, dropouts, and non-acceptors in the family planning program.

Recording of births, deaths, morbidity, nutrition status, and socioeconomic characteristics of patients and family planning patients on a continuing basis is regarded by BRAC as "a very expensive and time consuming process"[1] and not an appropriate task for the health workers. The necessary evaluative data about the health and family planning activities as well as other aspects of the BRAC project are planned to be collected by a sample survey of the population every three to four years. Such a sample survey of 1600 households was conducted for the first time in Sulla in late 1975. A follow-up survey of oral pill acceptors was undertaken in February-March 1976. Both of these, being the first surveys, provided useful benchmark data (but no comparative data for assessing the impact of the program).

Outlook for the Future

Whether the BRAC health and family planning program will survive and grow as a viable approach to meeting the health and family planning needs of the rural people in Bangladesh and whether it will influence significantly the national programs will depend, first, on the results of the efforts under way to extend the accessibility and

---

[1]The BRAC Health Care.... op. cit., p. 15

coverage of the services to the total project area population and, second, on how successfully a management structure evolves that is compatible with local management of the program (without the guiding hand of BRAC) and with the overall organization and management of development and local government in the area.

Greater Access.

As noted already, access to and coverage of the services are affected by cultural factors (the women's reluctance to face men paramedics), physical factors (once-a-week presence of the paramedic for a few hours), and the nature of the service (dominance of an "outpatient" type curative service and the lack of dialogue, social interaction, and a seeking of advice and reassurance that is possible only with the presence of a health worker in a village). Attempts to remove these barriers to quantitative and qualitative improvement of the program are being made by the introduction of the village-based auxiliaries (healers) and the recruitment of new female paramedics. The outcome of these recent moves in both quantitative and qualitative terms are yet to be seen.

Visible Impact.

The extension and intensification of service coverage should begin to be reflected in the health and demographic status of the area population in the near future. BRAC apparently has not paid sufficient attention to assessing the impact of its services on such indicators as the rates of morbidity, mortality, and births. It appears to be particularly modest about its effect on the high mortality rate. One of its reports states: "A fall in death rate may be noted but is not anticipated. Food production, flooding, and social stability will probably have greater effects on mortality rates than the health care or preventive medicine program."[1]

Obviously, a high mortality rate is not the main problem; it is but an indicator of the health status of the population. An improvement in the general health status should reduce mortality rate, especially when certain segments of the population are found to be particularly vulnerable and are contributing disproportionately to the total mortality rate. A concentrated attack on the health hazards of infants, children under five, and mothers who fall victims to communicable diseases and preventable but fatal infections such as tetanus is quite feasible and compatible with BRAC's health care approach and is likely to curtail both the specific and overall rate of mortality significantly.

Improving Records.

BRAC's reluctance to have the health workers spend much time on collecting and recording statistics is understandable. On the other hand, the fairly intensive coverage of rural families envisaged by its service delivery approach (having a ratio of no more than 150 families to one village-based auxiliary) should permit the maintenance of a set of selected data about the health situation in the area without imposing too

---

[1]The BRAC Health Care..., p. 16.

402   MEETING THE BASIC NEEDS OF THE RURAL POOR

heavy a tax on the worker's time. The information recorded may include
births, deaths, incidence of selected disease symptoms, children's nutritional status (using a simple QUAC stick or other appropriate measurement), contraceptive acceptance, and continuation of contraceptive   use.
The periodic sampling of the population still would be useful for assessment of the impact of overall BRAC efforts and may be supplementary   to
the regular recording of information. The advantages of consolidation of
the selected data--say, on a monthly basis for each paramedic's area and
on a quarterly basis for the project area--are many: (a) it would provide a ready check on the health situation of the area; (b) it would
help determine appropriate emphasis on specific therapies, preventive
measures, and educational actions for each locality at a particular
time; (c) it would encourage the workers to maintain systematic contact with their clients and remain fully informed about the health situation in the area; and (d) it could be a tool for creating an awareness in
the communities about their health and population situation and about the
results or lack of results of their collective efforts.

Coopting Indigenous Medicine.

    BRAC has taken an initiative to coopt the practitioners of the
various forms of nonallopathic medicine (ayuverdic, unani, and homeo-
pathic) into the comprehensive health care system for a rural area.
The advantages of this move are seen to be three-fold:

    First, the potential power of these practitioners of medicine to
resist the spread of the BRAC approach and to create misgivings about
it among the rural population will be neutralized. Second, to the extent the therapies and health measures of the indigenous and non-allo-
pathic medicinal practices are relatively effective, cheap, and compatible with popular beliefs, these practices may be included with beneficial results in the repertoire of treatments of the paramedics   and
the shasthya shevikas. Finally, these practitioners of medicine--being
a group of people living in the rural areas and catering in their own
way to the health needs of the rural population could be put to good
use as paramedics within the primary health care system and could be
prevented from being the purveyors of poor medical service at a high
cost to the patients.

    The success of this move will depend on whether a commonly agreed
list of therapies and health measures can be prepared, whether the local
"doctors" can be brought into a specially designed paramedic   training
program, and whether these "doctors" perceive the move to be in   their
long-range interest. Identifying elements of nonallopathic medicine
that can be incorporated into the curative and preventive practices   of
the basic health care system of the country calls for a substantial research and investigation effort. The prospect of government assistance
and collaboration of other agencies in the country concerned about rural
health could be explored by BRAC.

Improving Family Planning.

    As for family planning, the tasks before BRAC are to extend the
coverage of the services to all the project area villages (instead of

less than half the villages as in 1976) and to push the curve of the acceptor
rate upward beyond the plateau that the curve seems to have reached. An optimal acceptor rate among the couples of childbearing age at the present stage
is about one-third of the total (leaving out those who are already   pregnant
and those in a state of post partum amenorrhea).[1] However,   identifying and
reaching the appropriate clients in this group and maintaining their acceptor
status would require a more precise and differentiated approach than a general
"shot-gun" approach to the provision of family planning service, which   actually may do more harm than good by interfering with the natural fertility
reducing effects of the biological factors.

The potential of traditional and nonwestern methods of restricting births
appears to have been ignored in BRAC family planning efforts. There has   been
almost an exclusive reliance on just one birth control technology--the   pill
(other than the terminal measures of vasectomy or tubectomy).   While this
dependence on one method may have been justified and may have to continue--
given the fact that this is culturally an alien technology and produces,   at
least for some, adverse physiological side effects--the other indigenous   and
"non-technological" methods such as rhythm, abstinence, late marriage, breast-
feeding (in order to extend lactational amenorrhea), azl (coitus interruptus)
warrant a fair trial. The offering of wise and appropriate counsel to potential candidates about methods other than the standard prescription of   pills
would require a personal, well-motivated, non-stereotyped approach.

Another issue that has to be resolved is the overlap between the functions
of the Lady Family Planning Organizer and the shasthya shevika.   The   logic
and rationale behind the integrated health care approach of BRAC calls for   a
merger of these two positions in the village. If indeed there is a social stigma attached to those in family planning services, there is all the more reason
to combine the positions of the LFPO and the shevika in order to assure a greater social acceptance for those in family planning services. Such a move,   of
course, should be accompanied by an educational effort to remove the roots of
the prejudice. The trial under way with different combinations of roles and
functions of the village-based worker will probably suggest the best course of
action in this respect.

Organizational Issues.

A number of organizational and management issues has to be tackled during
the third phase of the Sulla Project (and in the course of initiating BRAC-spon-
sored health programs in other locations). How can the health care system continue to function when the BRAC umbrella and resources are removed?   What kind
of organizational structure will ensure that the needs of the people will   be

---

[1]The period of temporary sterility after a live birth. This period is
estimated to be 17 months in Bangladesh for a woman who breastfeeds her child.
Use of contraceptive pills ends the state of amenorrhea and   increases   the
probability of conception if the woman is negligent about   taking the   pills
regularly or if she drops out. See Lincoln C. Chen, et al, Recent Fertility
Trends in Bangladesh: Speculation on the Role of Biological Factors and Socioeconomic Change, Dacca, The Ford Foundation, December 1976.

adequately served, that the necessary resources will be available, that the workers will be paid, and that they will perform their duties? How can the group insurance scheme be kept alive and prevent the paramedics and the shevikas from being individual private entrepreneurs? How can the beneficiary population participate in the management of the program and keep it compatible with their overall development needs and priorities?

The approach that is favored by BRAC and expected to be worked out in detail and gradually implemented over the next two or three years is the transfer of the management responsibilities to a representative body at the thana level with subsidiary bodies at the union (a unit of 10-20 villages) level. The committees at the thana and the union levels, formed with a representation of the different categories of workers in the program and the beneficiary population (and with the representation of BRAC management at the initial stage), will be made responsible for making appropriate arrangements and taking the necessary steps for:

-- collecting the group insurance premium

-- seeking and receiving supplementary resources needed for operating the program

-- organizing training and supervision of the workers and maintaining the standard of their performance

-- paying the workers

-- procuring, storing, and distributing the supplies

-- maintaining appropriate liaison with other development activities and agencies within the area and outside

Supplementation of the locally generated resources of the program may come from the Thana Development Committee or a central federation of the village cooperative societies that is expected to emerge from the BRAC development efforts in the area. Another possible source is a government subvention to the program for performing functions of the national health and family planning services. The extent of supplementation available from the Thana Development Committee, or, for that matter, the mobilization of local resources possible through a general acceptance of the health program and widespread enrollment in the group insurance scheme, will depend on the overall development achievement of the total range of BRAC project activities in the area and the climate of hope and confidence created by these activities.

It is BRAC's expectation that the thana and union committees for health will be affiliated or partially overlap with representative bodies (e.g., the Thana Development Committee) which will emerge in order to oversee, manage, and keep alive the overall development program for the area initiated by BRAC.

It is evident that if the BRAC health and family planning program develops along the line envisaged and becomes capable of offering comprehensive health care service to the area population, an accommodation has

to be reached with the government health and family planning activities in
the area.   There are three possible alternatives.   The government could
provide financial assistance to the program, ensure that the entire area
population is served, and see that specific government health and family
planning objectives are fulfilled.   In this case, the government personnel and facilities from the area could either be withdrawn or turned over
to the management of the local program.   This alternative should not be
seen as the abdication of government responsibility for health care and
the transfer of government functions to a private organization.   If the
BRAC goals are fulfilled and local representative organizations emerge to
take over the management of health and other development services,   the
health care program would become the program of the local communities
(rather than of BRAC).   The government public health service would provide
technical and financial support to locally managed programs instead of running the local program itself.   Ideally, this is the direction in which all
government development agencies should move if fostering self-reliant communities and mobilizing local resources are considered important goals.   A
second possibility is the continuation of the status quo whereby both   the
government health service and the BRAC project would attempt to serve inadequately the health needs of the local population without consolidating their
efforts and resources and without the emergence of local organizations assuming greater management responsibilities for the local program. Under   this
alternative, BRAC would play a useful role in filling at least a part of the
gap in local health care as long as the government service remains weak and
out-of-reach of most of the rural people. Obviously, the full potential of
a community-based primary health care system with appropriate backstopping
from the national government and support from other extra-community sources
will not be realized under this option. The least desirable alternative is
that two rival structures of facilities, personnel, and services would attempt to expand themselves without any effort to cooperate and complement
each other wasting national resources, creating confusion and distrust among
the people, and leaving the basic health needs of the people badly served.

CHAPTER 4

AGRICULTURAL DEVELOPMENT

In the Sulla Project area, almost all of the cultivable land (60,000 acres out of a total of 64,000 acres) is one crop rice land suitable   for boro rice farmed during the dry season (November-April) after the flood water recedes. The farm land remains inundated the rest of the year.

An ICED sample survey revealed the predominance of agriculture in the economic life of the area. Over 53 percent of the households relied for their livelihood exclusively on farming their own land; about 20   percent of the landless families depended on farm labor as the main source of in- come. For over 10 percent of the households fishing was the primary source of family earnings. The same survey also showed that the pressure on the limited farm land was high: 54 percent of the families had farms less than one acre in size; 17 percent had farms of between 1 and 3 acres; and   only 3 percent of the families had over 3 acres of farm land. Twenty-six percent of the families owned no farm land. According to BRAC's independent esti- mates, landless and near landless families would constitute at least one- third of the households in the project area.

The agricultural needs of the area, defined by the ecological limita- tions, are as follows: (a) to make the best use of the limited cultivable land during the short farming season by increasing the productivity of rice on land with sufficient moisture and producing on the rest of the   land other crops requiring less moisture in order to increase total agricultural income and to improve the nutritional balance, (b) to make a special effort to help farmers with small landholdings use high yielding seeds and fertili- zers, and (c) to help the landless and the near landless make intensive use of plots attached to the homestead to meet at least partially their basic food and nutrition needs and also to help them make collective use of com- munal or state land whenever available.

The government assistance for agricultural development, in principle, consists of agricultural extension service, provisions for agricultural in- puts, and support of farmers' cooperatives. The extension field staff in the thana is headed by the Thana Agricultural Officer, TAO (usually with a university degree in agriculture). The TAO supervises the Union Agricul- tural Assistants, each of whom is responsible for rendering technical ad- vice to farmers in about 20 villages with up to 10 thousand farmers. The inputs supplied by the government at subsidized price include low-lift pumps, fertilizer, pesticides, and seeds. It is the government policy under its Integrated Rural Development Program (IRDP) to encourage the formation of primary cooperative societies of farmers at the village level and a central federation of cooperatives at the thana level which then can be the main channel for providing credit, inputs, and extension ad- vice as well as the means for attaining economies of scale in various farming activities.

In practice, the government infrastructure for agricultural development has not functioned at any reasonable degree of effectiveness for various reasons. The principal reasons include: inadequate training, supervision, technical backstopping, and incentives for the extension staff;
limited supply of inputs and credit insufficient to meet the total needs;
village social structure and land tenure that allows the benefit of cooperatives and government inputs to be enjoyed by relatively larger landowners; and inefficiency of the overall administrative structure that causes
frequent breakdown in the logistics of supply, supervision, and maintenance
of services. The net result is that the government agricultural services
reach too few with too little too ineffectively. The IRDP with its goal of
creating village level cooperatives with broad-based membership appears to
offer some prospect for invigorating the agricultural services and increasing the efficiency of the scarce inputs. Other national level efforts are
underway to improve the extension service and the supply of inputs, but the
results of these efforts are yet to be felt in the project area. BRAC   in
its third phase program in Sulla is attempting to supplement and support the
IRDP efforts in the project area to expand the structure of cooperatives and
increase its effectiveness. (see discussion in ch. 7.)

The main features of BRAC agricultural activities in Sulla during the
second phase were agricultural support blocks, camp demonstration plots, introduction of new vegetable crops, support to landless groups, and assistance
in flood protection and irrigation.

Components of the Agricultural Program

Agricultural Support Blocks

The agricultural support blocks were intended to enable BRAC to concentrate its limited resources and personnel on a limited area of land   and   a
small number of farmers to produce a demonstration effect in respect of   improved practices in rice cultivation.   During each planting season   20-30
agricultural support blocks, each with an average of 50 acres of land,   were
organized by BRAC workers in the eleven camp areas for cultivation of   high
yielding varieties of boro rice with equipment and inputs within the means of
local farmers. Five to six hundred farmers in the support blocks received the
following types of support:

-- Block farmers were brought together into regular meetings early
   before the onset of the agricultural season and during the season in order to plan and implement the agricultural plan for each
   block.

-- Farmers were assisted in planning the input needs, arranging finances,
   and procurement. Most farmers were able to arrange the supplies with
   their own resources.

-- Farmers were advised about preparing compost pits and the use of
   organic fertilizer.

-- Some of the farmers received credit from BRAC for fertilizer and
   seeds.

-- High yielding rice seeds were supplied by BRAC at cost. New
   short-duration high yielding varieties were introduced   by
   BRAC, particularly for land vulnerable to early flooding.

The responsibility for the extension work with the support block
farmers lay primarily with the Field Motivators who were supervised by
the Area Manager for each camp. Information about the increase   in
yield resulting from the block support activities was not collected by
BRAC. BRAC, however, claimed that "support block farmers in most cases
were able to show substantial improvement in yield."[1] The farmers themselves perceived the activities to be sufficiently beneficial to continue
their participation in the blocks during successive years.

Camp Demonstration Plots

Each of the eleven BRAC camps in the Sulla Project area set up its
own demonstration plots, and the BRAC personnel residing in the camps
contributed the labor to grow various crops in these plots. An average
of two acres was leased from local farmers for rice or wheat demonstration, and an additional half acre was used for different varieties   of
vegetables and legumes. The plots were the means for practical farming
experience for the BRAC workers, demonstration of methods and results,
and a way of establishing credibility for BRAC extension service. As
reported in a BRAC report:

> ...[At first] the sight of university graduates ploughing
> and transplanting brought laughter and sarcasm from villagers.
> The seriousness and persistence of BRAC workers soon changed
> their attitude to one of respect.   When the plants stood out
> as some of the best that they had seen grown in the area, the
> cultivators started asking for advice and requesting BRAC work-
> ers to visit their fields.[2]

New Vegetables

Prior to BRAC activities in the project area, vegetable growing was
almost unknown in the area, and vegetables were regarded as an inferior
type of food. BRAC launched a vegetable growing campaign in order   to
make better use of land unsuitable for rice and to supply the nutritional needs of the population. In cooperation with the Mennonite Central
Committee (an American voluntary organization active in improving   the
productivity of small farmers in Bangladesh), vegetable seeds were imported and distributed each year to 10,000 families and primary   and
secondary schools in the project area. Vegetables new in the area such
as carrots, broccoli, and Chinese cabbage were grown successfully alongside those already grown in the area such as tomatoes, cauliflower,   and

---

[1]BRAC, Sulla Project Report on Phase II, pp. 12.

[2]BRAC, Sulla Project Report on Phase II, pp. 12-13.

radishes. Up to 800 acres of land were put under vegetable cultivation in
the area per year.

Seeds were given free the first year, but in subsequent years they were
sold. Instructions on seedbed preparation, transplantation, and care of plants
were provided by BRAC field motivators, and growers' plots were repeatedly visited by them at the initial stage. Horticulture exhibitions were organized in
each camp, and prizes were given to the best growers. Although seeds were not
distributed free after the first year, no problem was encountered   in selling
the seeds.

BRAC also encouraged the growing of fruit trees in the area. After the
unusually high floods of 1974 when all the papaya trees in the area were destroyed, BRAC transported thousands of papaya saplings, as well as seedlings
and saplings of coconut, banana, mango, and guava, and distributed them   at
cost to villagers.

Support to Groups of Landless

BRAC organized groups of landless laborers for cultivation of fallow land
leased from local landlords or of state-owned land. Only about 600 acres of
such land was available for lease, and all together 300 landless farm laborers
in groups of 25 on an average benefited from this effort. The land available
for this purpose was not readily cultivable; it required leveling and clearing, and the supply of water had to be arranged and water channels laid out.
BRAC workers advised the groups on preparing the land and making a farm plan
for optimal use of the land, supplied credit for purchasing the necessary inputs, and provided the services of low-lift irrigation pumps and power tillers,
the cost of which was recovered after the harvest. The program increased the
income of the beneficiary families substantially, but the size of the program
was limited by the high pressure on cultivable land in the area.

Assistance for Irrigation and Flood Protection

Agriculture in the project area suffers from too much water during most
of the year and too little of it in relatively higher land during the   dry
season. BRAC procured 19 low-lift diesel pumps of 2-cusec capacity to irri-
gate boro land without sufficient residual flood water. The pumps   were
leased to groups of farmers in the support blocks and among the landless
groups.

BRAC charged a rental of Tk 225 per acre for the pumps and took care of
the fuel, maintenance, and operation of the pumps. The average area irrigated
by each pump was 52 acres. This compares favorably with the average of about
20 acres in the government (Agricultural Development Corporation) program for
extensive use of low-lift pumps to increase cropping intensity. The government in its program subsidized the cost of pump use, charging about Tk 1,000
as rent for each pump for a season (irrespective of acreage covered) with
fuel and operation costs paid by the farmers. BRAC, on the other hand, realizing over Tk 10,000 for each pump per season, more than covered the capital
and operating costs of the pumps. This was possible because BRAC saw to it
that a sufficient amount of land was included in the irrigation plan of the
group renting the pump and that a breakdown would not occur ruining the crop

and the farmers' investment in time and money. Besides ensuring the supply
of fuel, spare parts, and proper operation of the pumps through its   own
well-trained operators, BRAC also had a small maintenance shop for the over-
haul and repair of the pumps and other equipment such as 10 power tillers
and two outboard motors for the small boats used by the staff during the
floods. (The power tillers were rented to farmers without draught animals
and the groups of landless farmers.)

Building flood protection embankments, as well as drainage and irrigation channels, were undertaken during the dry season of 1974-75 and 1975-
76 as a "food-for-work" program under which workers received their wages in
wheat supplied for this purpose by Oxfam of Canada and U.K. Additional protection embankments and water channels were also excavated during the same
years by voluntary efforts of the local people organized by BRAC workers.
It is reported by BRAC that:

> During the early floods of April 1974, when the neighbouring
> areas suffered total destruction of their crop, the BRAC area
> only suffered a 40 percent crop loss due to the successful effort
> of the BRAC workers in mobilizing and activising entire villages
> for building dams and embankments day and night to fight the
> rising water.[1]

The Third Phase Plans

The third phase plans for Sulla (implementation of which began in
1976) call for continuation of the agricultural work begun earlier and
propose some new elements: a rice seed multiplication project,   new
initiatives in animal husbandry, and increased emphasis on supporting
agricultural opportunities for groups of landless and women from poor
families.

With the spread of high yielding rice varieties, the supply of good
quality seeds becomes a critical bottleneck. Government seed farms currently meet only a fraction of the total demand of the country, and it is
difficult for farmers to arrange procurement from the limited government
supply without direct BRAC intervention. The small farmers themselves
find it difficult to put aside seed grains and to control the quality of
seed production without some assistance. The BRAC project is intended
to train and support some model farmers to undertake seed multiplication
on a commercial basis. Best quality first generation seeds are to be
procured by BRAC and supplied to the farmers who will be provided a price
guarantee and whose fields will be supervised by a qualified agronomist
to ensure quality control. BRAC will arrange proper storage of the seeds
in specially constructed ferro-concrete bins in the humid climatic condition of the area. It is expected that the production, storage, and sale
of high quality rice seeds will eventually be taken over by the central
body of the local cooperatives or the Thana Development Committee   and
will become a source of income for the central body.

Preparation of land in the Sulla area, as in the rest of the country, is almost entirely dependent on cattle draught power. Feeding the
cattle is a serious problem during the six months of flooding when the
cattle remain confined to the pens. During the dry winter months the
situation improves, but as more fallow land comes under cultivation the

---

[1]BRAC, Sulla Project Report on Phase II, p. 14.

the competition between grazing and farming land becomes more intense. The paucity of veterinary care is another problem that means wastage from   ill health and premature death of cattle. BRAC plans to introduce high yielding fodder crops such as Guinea grass and alfalfa, begin extension work on locally suitable silage methods, and start a basic veterinary service by training the paramedic in the diagnosis, treatment, and prevention of the common cattle diseases (as well as the diseases of poultry and ducks).

A special effort is to be made during the third phase to form cooperative groups of landless farm laborers and destitute women and to make use of all available land on lease either from the state or from local landowners. BRAC will support these groups initially until the first harvest, while the land is levelled, irrigation facilities built and the first crop planted. It will also make credits available on the basis of production plans of   the groups by arrangement with a commercial bank. In addition, BRAC workers will provide continuous extension support to these groups.

Fishery Development

BRAC estimates that 20 percent of the households in the Sulla Project area depends on fishery as a major source of income.

The natural water bodies of the area are owned mostly by the state, and the fishing rights in these waters for a specified period are leased to cooperatives of local fishermen. Since collective fishing requires high capital inputs in nets, boats, and royalty payments to the government as well as in storing, transporting, and marketing the highly perishable commodity, the cooperatives are financed and controlled largely by nonfishermen moneylenders who provide credits at usurious rates and serve as middlemen for marketing. As a result fishermen as a class are one of the most exploited and poorest groups in the area.

BRAC supported a number of fishermen's cooperative societies by providing them boats and nylon twines for fishing nets. Altogether 15 medium-sized fishing boats and 10,000 pounds of twine were distributed. But, by BRAC's own admission, this had only "peripheral impact." It is estimated that an average cooperative society of 150 members requires a working capital of Tk 100,000 to 120,000 to fish in a water area leased for two years. The fishermen can reap the full benefit of their labor and extricate themselves from the vicious cycle of exploitation, if they can procure this capital on reasonable terms and arrange for marketing their catch without depending on the moneylenders and the middlemen employed by the moneylenders.

In the third phase of Sulla, BRAC proposes to meet the full credit requirements of a number of societies under financial arrangements with commercial banks similar to those planned for landless groups. BRAC also plans to assist in organizing a fishermen's cooperative marketing society and training a number of fishermen for marketing activities.

In order to help youth and women's groups in the fishermen's communities, BRAC also organized, during the second phase, the digging of six large ponds under the "food-for-work" program which were used for pond-fishery. The   ponds were stocked with quick-growing Nilotica fingerlings imported by UNICEF   from Thailand. A number of the youth group members were sent to Jamalpur for training in Nilotica culture.

Concluding Points

While the impact of the fishery program during the second phase of the Sulla Project was, by BRAC's own account, marginal in improving the well-being of the fishermen, the achievements of the agricultural program were also not very clear. Once again the reason for the lack of a clear picture of the results is BRAC's reluctance or inability to devote the necessary effort (and workers' time) to a collection of elementary benchmark data and a collection and recording of information about the services provided   and the results achieved. Basic information about the initial condition of the farmers in the support blocks and the changes in their condition   brought about by BRAC services could have been collected without substantial expense of time and money, and it would have identified and made clear the benefits derived from the effort.

What is now known is that the total beneficiaries of the two main   and intensive efforts--the support blocks and group farming by landless laborers --were relatively small in number. In any one season a maximum of 600 farm-ers and 300 landless laborers were involved in the two activities out of   a total of over 15,000 heads of farmers' and landless laborers' families   in the area. About 40 Field Motivators spent most of their time during   the farming season with the farmers' and laborers' groups (a ratio of one motiva-tor to 25 farmers). This is a relatively high extension worker-to-farmer ratio by any standard with its consequent cost implications.

To the extent that credit, supply of inputs, and logistics (and not just the knowledge gap) were the impediments to increased agricultural productivity in the area, the support blocks and the camp demonstration plots were unlikely to have much spillover effect on other farmers in the area. Obviously,   the scarcity of rentable land, subsistence support when the land is prepared   and planted, and credit for inputs were the main obstacles for the landless labor-ers' groups. Supply and logistics apparently were also major problems for the support block farmers as is clearly indicated by the BRAC emphasis on procure-ment of seeds and fertilizers and the operation and maintenance of power pumps and tillers.

Under these circumstances, the approach to serving the total farming pop-ulation and to improving the overall agricultural situation would be to estab-lish and strengthen the institutions that serve the supply and logistical needs, such as the cooperatives, the government distribution mechanism of seeds and fertilizers, and the supply and maintenance of the irrigation pumps   and tillers (again the responsibility of the government Agricultural Development Corporation). BRAC put great stress on the formation of cooperatives--this be-ing the central institutional strategy of the BRAC development approach (see the chapter on institutional structures). However, the support block opera-tion does not appear to have been linked directly with the formation   and strengthening of the cooperatives or, for that matter, with other BRAC compo-nents, such as functional education and the health program. All of these run parallel to each other with only incidental overlap of clienteles rather than in a strategic concentration of multifaceted program efforts on the same com-munities. Nor were there attempts to work with the Agricultural Development Corporation for better utilization of irrigation pumps and tillers in the area or for improved distribution of seeds and fertilizers. Of course, in this case the willingness to cooperate and work together must be mutual, and the government agencies often are not overly eager to admit that they

need the help of a private organization. On the problem of seeds, BRAC has its
own project for the third phase.

The agricultural extension work of BRAC carried out by the Field Motivators appears to be based on standard technical prescriptions and generally accepted notions about the improvement of rice and vegetable cultivation rather
than on specific technical analysis and recommendations derivative of   such
analysis. The Field Motivators had neither special training in agriculture, nor
the technical advice and services of an agronomist or a soil tester.   On   the
other hand, if the obstacles to agricultural improvement were more institutional
than technological, specialized technical knowledge of the field workers   and
the backstopping of an agronomist would be less important. The problem would be
to use effectively already known and applicable techniques. However, the services of an agronomist would be required in the third phase for the seed multiplication project. It should be possible to utilize him in a broader role   of
providing technical support to the extension team.

In view of the high pressure on land and the large number of very small
landholders depending on farming for their livelihood, it would be very important to explore the question of optimal economic use of the small farms   and
the limits and possibilities of changes in cropping pattern and cropping intensity. This is also an important question for the landless groups who manage to
lease some land.

BRAC made a special effort to improve the lot of the landless laborers by
organizing group farming projects, and it plans to continue this effort during
the third phase with both the landless laborers and destitute women. As noted
already, these efforts are handicapped by the limitation of land available for
renting out and by the financial and technical support needed to put the groups
to work on land which is often of marginal quality. Despite all the efforts,
the return realized by each individual member of the group may be too small to
make an appreciable difference in his standard of living--partly because   of
BRAC's understandable desire of not leaving out any of the landless families
in a village project. It therefore becomes important to look for a broader
range of income earning opportunities for the landless families, such as a
combination of rural public works, nonfarm activities, farm laborers' work,
horticultural and animal husbandry activities around the home, group farming
projects, and group economic projects in agricultural processing.   Ideally,
the planning, managing, and participation in the group farming projects should
be organized within the framework of a broader approach to improving the earning and employment opportunities of the poorest rural families. The institutional vehicles of functional education groups, cooperatives, and membership
in health insurance schemes can be used then to reinforce the economic improvement efforts, to give a sense of cohesion and purpose to the participants, and
to facilitate a larger role of the participants in the management of these
efforts.

There are indications that BRAC is attempting to apply the lessons of the
experiences in Sulla in its new projects, particularly in Manikganj. The Manikganj Project put a heavy emphasis on the institutional structure in the villages
--organizing youth's and women's organizations and cooperative societies,   and
planning and implementing various development activities, including agricultural
activities, through the groups in an integrated manner. We return to this question in the chapter on institutional structures.

The third phase efforts in fishery development--to the extent that capital funds are available and participation is made broad-based--should have a greater impact on the condition of the fishermen than the second phase activities.

No attention has been paid so far to the long range fishery prospects, nor to the possibilities of technological improvements in raising both yield and employment in fishery activities in the area. This would probably require a regional approach extending beyond the project area, also resources and expertise difficult to muster without government support. In any case government support would be needed for any long-range fishery development in the area, because the government is the owner of the fishing grounds and the ultimate authority for imposing and enforcing regulations in such matters as fishing seasons, selective catching, terms of fishing rights. These questions deserve attention as they affect the welfare of a sizeable proportion of the population in the project area.

Activities that have been designed by BRAC to contribute to the improvement of social and economic status of women fall into two categories:

(a)   integrating women into the general development activities
      of the project, and
(b)   special activities in response to special needs of women.

The general program activities which serve women clientele or have sub-stantial involvement of women in one form or another are functional education, agricultural and horticultural extension, family planning, and health care. Activities which respond to special women's needs include mother and child-care clubs, skill training for women, women's cooperatives, women staff develop-ment, and the women's project in Jamalpur.

Serving Women Through General Programs

Functional Education

Women have participated in a major way in the functional education program. In the Sulla Project, of over 1,100 completers in the first two cyclces of courses in 1975 and 1976, about 400 were women. One-half of the centers were for women and the number of women instructors was of the same proportion.

The project in Jamalpur with functional education as the key element serves exclusively the low-income rural women in a cluster of 29 villages. This project, as noted earlier, originated from a project to help destitute women in the   same area.

The content of the functional education lessons also attempts to reflect women's needs and interests. While 70 percent of the content are of   general interest, 30 percent are differentiated for men and women. The special lessons for women cover such topics as women's contribution to agricultural production; food processing and preservation; nutritious cooking; savings habits; survey of the community birth, pregnancy, and family planning status; family planning methods; cooperation among women; nutrition surveys; breast feeding; and fire hazards in the kitchen. Some of the general lessons which are designed   for both men and women also include topics of special significance in improving the condition of women; for example, equal rights for men and women, cooperatives for women, nutrition topics, family planning methods, survey of family planning and nutrition status in the community, pregnant mothers' health, plight of widows, evils of early marriage, and child care.

Agricultural and Horticultural Extension

Women have a traditional role in Bangladesh in the horticultural activities around the home. BRAC extension service in horticulture, therefore,
serves both men and women. As noted in chapter 4, about 10,000 families in
the Sulla Project area benefited each year by the distribution of vegetable
seeds and by technical advice, and up to 800 acres of land were put   under
vegetable cultivation, including such newly introduced items as carrots,
broccoli, Chinese cabbage, as well as the more traditional vegetables. BRAC
also provided seedlings of fruit plants such as coconuts, bananas, mangoes,
guavas, and papayas, which were planted and reared to a large extent by the
women.

In the Jamalpur Project one of the major activities is to encourage
and assist women in undertaking vegetable, fruit, and other crop cultivation collectively as well as individually. This young project, only   in
its first year of operation in 1976, has yet to yield substantial results
in the horticultural area. Future plans for Jamalpur as well as   other
areas include efforts to design extension services for economically viable
collective or individual projects on grain processing, poultry and duck
raising, and animal husbandry. Another area to be examined is those technologies that will reduce the drudgery and increase the productivity   of
routine chores around the home: grain processing and storage, food preparation, water collection, household cleaning and sanitation, and so forth.

Health Care and Family Planning

Women constitute a specially vulnerable group in regard to health.
The BRAC health care program, important for the whole population, meets
a special need for women.   Bringing health care directly to the   rural
homes through the paramedics also facilitates women's participation in
the program. Special measures to improve the health care provisions for
women through staff development and village women's assemblies are mentioned below.

The family planning program in BRAC, following nearly universal
practice, uses a female-oriented approach: persuasion of women   to
take contraceptive measures. BRAC also encourages male vasectomy because of the simplicity of the procedure and the relatively smaller
medical risks involved. Furthermore, it shows that the responsibility
for family planning lies in a direct personal sense as much with   the
male as with the female population. The BRAC clinics in the Sulla Project also perform tubal ligation operations. However, these terminal
measures are resorted to by only a small number even when
family planning practices are widespread. Without underestimating the
importance of educating men about family planning, it can be said that
the success of the family planning program of BRAC depends very much on
how effectively the female population is reached with the message and
the services of family planning.

The use of female workers in the family planning program and the
related program of mother and child care education are discussed below.

Mother and Child Care Clubs

Widespread health and nutrition problems of pregnant and lactating mothers and children observed in the Sulla Project area led to a special effort to reach this group. The paramedics in their respective villages organized "mothers' clubs" or a monthly discussion group of the pregnant and lactating mothers in the village.   This group meets in the village gonokendra or a suitable home, where health problems and preventive and curative measures for mothers and children are discussed under the paramedic's guidance and certain services are provided. The services include blood pressure check, iron and vitamin supplement for pregnant mothers, weighing the children and recording their weight on "Road to Health" cards.

In the Sulla Project area 73 mothers' clubs were functioning in mid-1976, with attendance in each ranging from 10 to 20 mothers plus their children. About 15 other clubs have been organized in the Jamalpur Project area.

A series of posters and a discussion guide keyed to the posters have been produced by the BRAC materials development unit in order to provide some structure and guidelines for the mothers' club meetings. Another purpose of the materials and the discussion guide is to enable field workers, such as functional education instructors without paramedic training,   to conduct mothers' club discussion groups.

The multicolor wall poster set prepared for the mothers' clubs contains 15 posters on nutrition, care for pregnant and lactating mothers, child care, family planning, common diseases, and vaccination and inoculation. Each   of the wall posters is used as the main visual aid for conducting one discussion session. The discussion guide, compiled in the form of a mimeograph booklet, explains the basic principles to be observed in effective group   discussion, the objectives of each session, the main message or information to be conveyed to the group, the leading questions arising from the wall poster designed for the particular session, and other questions to maintain the momentum of   the discussion, with possible follow-up actions to be engaged in by the group   and the discussion leader.

The mothers' club as a device for organizing mother and child health care is a recent BRAC activity that began in the Sulla Project area   only in the latter part of 1975 and even more recently in the Jamalpur area, where the discussion groups are led by the women field workers (experienced functional education instructors who are serving as multipurpose motivators/organizers and supervisors of functional education).

It is too early to assess the effectiveness of the clubs. Discussion with the field workers in Jamalpur revealed a number of problems. Although a sizeable group gathers on the appointed day, there is often a lack   of continuity because the same person does not come on a regular basis. There appears to exist a superstitious belief that weighing a child attracts the evil eye and causes harm to the child's health.   Some of the field workers decided to counteract this belief by taking their own little children   to the village discussion meetings and weighing them in front of the   village mothers.   It is also often found that some members of the group want   to discuss problems and topics other than mother and child care. The meetings

are also frequently attended by a few women who are not pregnant or lactating mothers. They come sometimes as chaperons   of the young mothers (especially if a male paramedic is the discussion leader) or just as curiosity
seekers.

In the light of the experience with the mothers' clubs the BRAC
discussion leaders have accumulated some ideas for the future development
of this activity including the following:

(1)   converting the mothers' club into a more general forum for
      village women concerned with health and nutrition and re-
      naming it   the women's assembly (Mohila Shobha)

(2)   broadening both its membership and scope and using it as the
      vehicle for discussion, education and planning for   general
      development activities that are of interest to the group or
      emerge out of the functional education program.

It is interesting that both of these possibilities involve broadening the role and function of the women's forum and a departure from   a
rigidly structured and imposed discussion session. The participants, it
appears, are interested in setting their own agenda, pace,   and ground
rules. It is also noteworthy that BRAC field workers on their own have
detected and recognized these tendencies. However, how these needs would
be handled and what steps would be taken to prepare the discussion leaders to meet this demand, to provide the learning materials, and to   link
up the assemblies with other economic and educational activities   were
still to be worked out.

Vocational Training and Cooperatives

In its effort to help destitute women (without a male breadwinner
in the family) earn a living and enable other women to supplement the
family income, BRAC began a vocational training program in Sulla.   The
original ambitious plan envisaged four vocational training centers for
women in the project area teaching many types of productive skills.How-
ever it was possible to open only one sewing center in Derai, and the
plan for a weaving center had to be abandoned because of problems faced
in procuring cotton yarn that had even made many professional   weavers
unemployed.

In the sewing center 89 women in three batches received training
for three months in tailoring. UNICEF donated sewing machines and cloth
which were used to train the women in making children's clothing.   The
training, however, did not lead to the establishment of economic enterprises that provided employment and income to the trainees.   Apparently,
the local demand for commercial tailoring was being met by the existing
tailors in the bazars, and none of the trainees could afford to invest
in a sewing machine for meeting only the family clothing needs.

BRAC learned from the experience that the problem of unemployment
and absence of earning opportunities in a poor rural area could not be
solved by a skill training effort alone. It decided that "the training
of women in skills which require assistance of male members in such matters as the procurement of raw materials, marketing of finished   goods,

etc., would not be the right approach for ensuring their economic independence."[1]
BRAC's emphasis, therefore, shifted from skill training to promotion of collective economic projects by women compatible with the local market demands.   The
women were brought together through functional education groups and the formation of women's cooperatives.

In the Sulla area, some 30 women's cooperatives had made an embryonic
beginning by mid-1976 and were engaged in collective projects in agriculture
(growing of rice, potatoes, legumes, and vegetables), making fishing nets,
and pond fishery. BRAC Field Motivators helped in the initial formation of
the groups, advised the groups about the principles and practices of cooperatives, encouraged them to accumulate capital by regular (though small) saving,
and provided them with small credits with which to launch their projects.

In the newly initiated Jamalpur Project, by October 1976, there were 29
women's cooperative societies with a total membership of 353, mostly destitute
women or members of the poorest families. Their savings in less than six months
had approached Tk 1,000. With the assistance of the women field workers   of
BRAC and the promise of small loans from BRAC, the group had already launched
or were planning projects in block-printing of cloth, weaving, silkworm raising, oil pressing, running grocery shops, bamboo crafts, poultry, pond fishery,
and farming.

A comparable approach is proposed in the plans for the Manikganj Project:

BRAC's functional education classes will be the initial media
to bring women together. These classes will stimulate women to
think creatively about their environment and to develop their decision-making powers. The learners from these functional education
classes will become the potential core membership of women's societies.... Those members interested in savings and loans will   set
rice saving targets, and with the amount saved credit unions or rice
banks will be established. Loans will then be given to finance small-
scale, village-based economic activities.... The choice of activities
by the women will depend in part on local availability of raw materials
and marketing facilities. Certain activities will generate cash incomes for the women; others will add to the nutritive value of their
families' diets.[2]

Women Staff Development

Very often in rural development programs, even when special needs and
problems of women are addressed, the responsibility for carrying   out   the
development activities is in the hands of men, and the women become passive
beneficiaries of the project activities and services.

In BRAC, women workers had been employed as functional education instructors and Lady Family Planning Organizers. However, the Field Motivators

---

[1]BRAC, Sulla Project Report on Phase II, p. 19.

[2]BRAC, Manikganj Project, p. 15.

and the paramedics--the personnel responsible for organizing and initiating the functional education and family planning activities in the villages, supervising and guiding the instructors and the LFPOs, and providing back-stopping to these frontline workers often by direct contact with the rural residents--were all male. As noted elsewhere, the effectiveness and expansion of the health program suffered because all the paramedics were   men with whom the village women hesitated to communicate freely.

In 1976, BRAC initiated a number of steps to remedy this situation and to establish a parity of esteem and responsibilities between men and women among the BRAC personnel.

As noted in the chapter on health and family planning, all or nearly all frontline health and family planning workers--the village-based auxiliaries or the shasthya shevikas (with or without the duties of the family planning organizer)--would be women from the respective villages.   This was more than adding another tier of workers in the hierarchy; it signified a change of approach in the delivery of health service that made the village-based shevika the key link in the chain that connected the health program and the rural people.

The third phase of the Sulla Project (beginning in 1976) included the provision for training and recruiting 15 female paramedics. The training of these paramedics, besides the subjects contained in the regular paramedic syllabus, would include midwifery, mother and child care, and certain women's diseases. The female paramedics were also to be trained in IUD insertion and tubal ligation in order to reduce further the dependence on qualified doctors.

With the goals of training women program personnel, transfer-ring to women the direction of women-related activities, and exploring   new program ideas for improving the social status and economic condition of rural women, BRAC decided to open one camp in the Sulla Project area to be directed and staffed entirely by women. It was felt that in an all-female environment some of the housing problems and social obstacles in recruiting female full-time staff might be overcome. The women's camp in Anandapur, with a direct responsibility for programs in a cluster of 10 villages and indirect responsibility for support of BRAC activities affecting women in the whole project area, opened in March 1976 with a female Area Manager and three Field Motivators (two local and one outsider). Nine other women joined the camp   as trainees who would serve as BRAC personnel in Sulla or in other locations. The women in BRAC who conceived the idea of the camp (and one of whom serves as the Area Manager) describe the role of the camp as follows:

These staff [in the camp] carry out the female segment of BRAC's ongoing activities: functional education,   public health, family planning, cooperatives. They will also experiment with and demonstrate potential economic activities   for women: poultry and duck farming, food processing, intensified horticulture, manufacturing of utility items, etc. Eventually it is hoped they might design extension services and appropriate technologies to improve women's grain processing,   fuel processing, water collection, etc.

Anandapur Camp will serve also as a training centre for prospective female leadership from other areas. Each camp's staff

members [there are eleven other all-male camps in the Sulla
Project area] are being encouraged to locate a core of motivated and interested women from their camp areas to facilitate
some of the development activities now being facilitated by
male staff. Anandapur camp will serve both as an experimental laboratory (in which various ideas for women's development activities can be tested and evaluated) and as a training
centre (for local female leadership).[1]

The Jamalpur Project

In the Jamalpur Project of BRAC, which evolved from an ad hoc functional
education component in a UNICEF-sponsored "food-for-work" scheme for destitute
women into a special women's project of BRAC, the women functional education
teachers took the initiative and assumed responsibility for planning, managing, and implementing the whole project. When the UNICEF-assisted   project
came to an end in November 1975, the 15 women instructors decided to continue
the functional education courses and to expand the scope of their activities
to village-based women's development work in the villages of the functional
education participants. The women teachers, with the assistance of BRAC headquarters staff, prepared the project plans for poor rural women in 28 villages
of the Jamalpur subdivision. The objectives of the project, as formulated by
the women after investigating the needs and priorities of the potential participants in the villages, were as follows:

1. to make village women conscious of the root causes of their problems
    and to help them seek solutions;

2. to control population growth through family planning movitaion   and
    delivery of services;

3. to encourage joint savings and cooperative economic activities   by
    village women;

4. to educate village women in hygiene and nutrition;

5. to encourage horticulture and poultry raising by women;

6. to encourage village women to utilize fallow land surrounding their
    respective villages;

7. to intitiate women's organizations in the villages; and

8. to educate village women.

The 15 women set up their headquarters and a dormitory facility (for those
not resident of the town) in a rented house in Jamalpur town and launched   the

---

[1]Khushi Kabir, et al., Rural Women in Bangladesh: Exploding Some Myths,
Dacca, The Ford Foundation, May 1976, Appendix A, p. 5.

project in January 1976.   Most of them came from the general area.   Ten of them were married and were in the age-range of 19 to 25 years (except one who was 45).   Their formal educational achievement varied from eighth grade to twelfth grade.   They came to BRAC as candidates for the instructor's position in UNICEF-assisted functional education without any previous development work background and were chosen from a total pool of 60 applicants   on the basis of an interview by the BRAC functional education coordinator. After their selection, the women went through a five-day training course for functional education instructors.   This training, the experience of conducting the functional education courses with the destitute women, and two short evaluation and planning workshops (organized for them by BRAC to help evaluate the results of their work with the destitute women and to consider the issues in planning the future Jamalpur Project) were the women's main training and professional development exposure before they embarked on the new project.

By November 1976 the 14 women and one team leader were working in pairs five days a week in the 28 villages (with a population of 36,000 and 6,400 families).   In 15 functional education centers, close to 200 women attended courses three days a week.   As mentioned earlier, 29 women's savings groups were engaged in or planning group economic projects.

In 32 mothers' clubs, women discussed once a week (average attendance of 10-15) health, nutrition, hygiene, sanitation, and child care   problems and actions.   Over 550 acceptors of family planning measures were recruited (including 170 tubal ligation and 29 vasectomy cases).   Each Saturday   the women instructors/field workers met to report and discuss the previous week's activities and to plan for and discuss the next week's activities.   The teachers formed their own savings society and opened a joint bank account. The teachers together with selected village women received training   with BRAC headquarters assistance in public health and nutrition, duck and poultry raising, composting, and horticulture.   (For instance, two rural women from Jamalpur were sent to Sylhet, 200 miles away, for a six-week training course in duck farming conducted by a church organization.   On their return, these women started demonstration duck farms and were ready to advise others interested in raising ducks.)   In the course of a few months the team   of functional education teachers were maturing into a team of development workers.

Concluding Points

The relatively new and exploratory activities related to the improvement of economic condition and social status of women and making women partners in the overall rural development efforts already succeeded in indicating the potentialities of these activities and in demonstrating the promise of specific program approaches.[1]

It is evident, in the first place, that rural women, even those without formal education and experience in roles outside the family environment, can serve effectively as frontline workers in such roles as those of Shasthya shevikas, Family Planning Organizers, and functional education

---

[1]See Khushi Kabir, et al., Rural Women in Bangladesh...., op. cit.

instructors (who, of course, must have some formal education).

Second, women with some educational achievement and an interest in assuming a role outside home—irrespective of whether they are from a rural   or   a semiurban background—may be motivated and trained to take up supervisory, leadership, and field operation responsibilities involving extensive travel, public contact, and personal initiatives (as in the position of paramedics and   the Field Motivator).

Third, relatively inexperienced women with appropriate motivation, interest, and training, are able to plan, design, manage, and implement a development program designed to benefit rural women.

Finally, social constraints and inhibitions can be overcome if female workers live and work in teams. Village women also respond to female field workers and are willing to travel from their homes to attend meetings, form cooperatives, and participate in collective activities.

Despite the promising leads given by the BRAC efforts, many of the most apparent economic and social problems of the women participants in the various projects are by no means about to be solved.

The capacity to save money among the members of the cooperative groups is very small, and it cannot begin to provide the necessary capital even for modest economic ventures. For the limited number of groups with economic propositions in Sulla and Jamalpur, BRAC has given the seed money. But with a larger number of groups in the two areas and particularly if the approach is expected to expand to other areas, the demand for capital funds and the problem of managing and monitoring the use of these funds will be beyond the capacity of BRAC as well as that of other agencies, including the government.

Identifying and designing viable economic projects ensuring a reasonable return to each member of a group have been found to be extremely difficult. The experience to date in BRAC suggests that for maintenance of motivation and effort, it is crucial that an individual's return is sufficient to make   at least a small impact on his economic position. It is not enough for a   group project's total return to be relatively large, if the total when divided among members becomes insignificant.

Even if projects are theoretically sound, they need management and supervision that is not always within the competence of BRAC field workers. Anything beyond extremely simple and primitive production or processing activities often requires complementary inputs and support beyond the means of the project. These are difficult to organize.

Besides these obvious difficulties, the fundamental problem lies in the subsistence character of the rural economy with its extremely limited effective demand for commercial products and services. This situation severely limits the opportunities for families without access to agricultural land. A general improvement in the economic situation, spurred by higher agricultural production and better distribution of income, will generate the demands for nonsubsistence goods and services and create a more conducive environment for the poor women's economic ventures. Improvement of the women's situation beyond a certain point and beyond small numbers included in special "hot-house" projects is inextricably connected with overall rural development with equitable distribution.

It bears reemphasizing, however, that a lot more can be done to involve women prominently in health, family planning, education, and other social development efforts for rural families. This involvement will not only enhance the social status and self-esteem of women, but also help make the development activities more effective.

CHAPTER 6

RECRUITMENT AND TRAINING OF STAFF

A difficult problem in all rural development programs is the recruitment of field workers and supervisory people who not only are well-motivated,
dedicated, and willing to give up the attractions of the city, but are also
perceptive about rural problems, sensitive about pride and values of the rural
people, and above all, willing to learn from their experience. A difference
is usually noted in spirit and motivation between the personnel in the government agencies and those in nongovernment voluntary agencies--often because of
the close-knit interpersonal relationships in a small organization,   the influence of ideologically motivated leadership in voluntary programs, and the
fact that voluntary organizations tend to attract idealists. However, voluntary organizations have their own share of personnel problems in finding the
right people for the right tasks, helping the workers develop the necessary
skills and competence, and maintaining their motivation and confidence in the
face of frustration and failures. Any program past the stage of a small shoestring operation and employing paid workers needs to be concerned about   the
questions of recruitment, staff development, and efficiency of performance.
Another issue is to what extent and in what way government field agents   can
sustain the kind of motivation and enthusiasm that many workers in voluntary
programs apparently have.

BRAC Personnel

In July 1976, BRAC's personnel roll included 157 full-time members, excluding part-time workers in the villages such as the Lady Family   Planning
Organizers, and voluntary workers such as the functional education instructors,
and youth program leaders. By the end of the year, the total number of full-
time personnel rose to about 200 with the addition of 30 newly recruited shasthya shevikas and 14 trainee female paramedics.

Of the regular personnel, about 10 may be regarded as constituting the
directing staff of BRAC, including the Executive Director, the coordinators of
different administrative functions, the Program Administrators for Sulla   and
Manikganj, and the Medical Officers. The support staff including the training
and materials personnel, staff writers, clerical workers, drivers and mechanics, custodial staff, and office helpers numbered about 50. The number of paramedics including the trainee women recruits was 45. The main workhorse   for
BRAC's field activities with direct and multiple responsibilities for identifying and assessing opportunities and needs for field activities and initiating,
guiding, and supporting them, is the Field Motivator, 49 of whom were in employment in mid-1976. Directly above the Field Motivators, with immediate responsibility for guiding and assisting the Field Motivators, were 19 Program
Supervisors (also known as Area Managers).

The Field Motivator is the basic rank to which new multipurpose field
workers are recruited, and at this level the BRAC personnel receive   their

orientation and experience in the rural development approach of BRAC. Although lateral entry at the higher management levels has been necessary initially and still continues to some degree in the headquarters, a career ladder appears to be emerging as more workers are promoted to higher levels in the hierarchy from the rank of the Field Motivators. Recruitment   and training of specialized BRAC workers in health and education has been discussed in other chapters. This chapter will deal mainly with the   Field Motivators--the backbone of the BRAC personnel structure.

Recruitment Criteria and Procedure

There was initially a heavy emphasis on high formal education qualification in the recruitment of BRAC personnel; this emphasis still persists although its application appears to be somewhat less rigid now. At   the beginning of the Sulla Project, when BRAC had to recruit both the field level workers and the supervisory personnel (at that time there had been no opportunity to appoint supervisors by promotion), the basic requirements for Field Motivators were college graduation (two to three years of college education after the higher secondary stage), and the candidates for supervisory positions such as Area Managers (also called Program Supervisors) were required to have a master's degree. The emphasis was on the level of college qualifications rather than on a specific disciplinary background because a master's or bachelor's degree in any subject was acceptable   as the requisite qualification.

The argument for the high value attached to formal education degrees (irrespective of the subject of study) as put forth by BRAC was that a high level of formal education was likely to be associated with an adequate level of intellectual competence, leadership qualities, and an ability to analyze and learn from new experiences. The possible alienation of the educated youth from the rural environment and the difficulties in establishing a bond of empathy and rapport between the rural people and the urban-educated youth were apparently not a great concern to BRAC. The feeling was   that with its very low level of urbanization, Bangladesh was essentially a "rural" country and even the university-educated young people were not completely severed from their rural roots. The most important reason for insisting on high educational credentials probably was that with the prevailing high level of unemployment among the college educated there was an ample supply of these candidates for BRAC jobs.

As it turned out, the university degree was not actually the determining factor in recruitment. In selecting the personnel from the large   pool of available candidates, all with university degrees, BRAC management   used other criteria. Assessment of the candidate's suitability for the Field Motivator's job, determined through personal interview and personal recommendations about an individual's qualities and aptitudes, was really the decisive factor. It was all quite subjective--contingent largely on the notion of the qualities and competence considered necessary for the field worker's job by the person conducting the interview or making the recommendation.

It is difficult to make a judgment on the formal qualifications and the selection procedure followed, because there is really no benchmark for comparison. The Executive Director of BRAC considered the process as "hit or miss" and found the attrition rate among workers as relatively

high. He pointed out that, out of hundreds of job applicants who submit
their applications whenever new recruitment is announced, ten might   be
selected. Out of the ten, two would not turn up, two would leave during
the first two months, two would be asked to resign as incompetent within
the first few months, two would continue as "plodders" in their level of
performance and motivation, and two would turn out to be effective, well-
motivated, and enthusiastic. Most of the workers would stay on if they
survived the first six months.

       In order to improve on the "hit or miss" results described above, a
new selection procedure was introduced in 1976. This procedure consists
essentially of a two-day group interaction session of the applicants retained on a "short list" after preliminary screening of the written applications. The group session, called the "selection course" requires   the
applicants to engage in a series of exercises selected from BRAC training
modules (see below) involving communication, planning, and analytical skills.
The exercises offer the opportunity to BRAC management to observe and assess
the applicant's personality, perception of rural development problems, leadership qualities, analytical ability, and planning capability. The applicant also has the opportunity to get a taste of what might be required of
him as a BRAC worker and whether the job suits his own expectations   and
temperament.   The procedure is applied in selecting new male and female
Field Motivators. This procedure makes the selection process more systematic and permits at least an attempt to relate a potential recruit's competence, aptitude, and personality traits to the tasks required to be performed by the Field Motivator. The process, however, is yet to undergo
sufficient trial to warrant any definitive judgment.

                              Staff Training

       The training and orientation of the Field Motivators and other non-
specialized BRAC personnel have been dependent on a combination of brief
orientation sessions and the initiation of the workers into the   methods
and approaches of BRAC through practical experience.

       The new recruits go through an initial orientation course for about
a week in which the new personnel become familiar with the BRAC development approach, an overview of the program activities, specific responsibilities and assignments of field workers, and the work procedures   and
the administrative routines. After they are dispatched to the field, the
apprenticeship continues at least for a three-month period when the   new
recruits are accompanied and guided by their senior colleagues.   After
this apprenticeship period, the new Field Motivators are given independent
assignments and increasingly greater responsibilities. The Program Supervisors (previously known as Area Managers), each one of whom supervises no
more than four or five Field Motivators, are always at hand to assist and
advise the latter. Moreover, the full-time field workers of BRAC (Program
Supervisor, Field Motivators, and paramedics) usually reside in a communal
style in camps.   This leads to a close association with almost daily
comparison of notes and ideas, both formally at the Program Supervisor's
initiative as well as informally.

Problems and progress in field activities and plans for the subsequent months are taken up at monthly meetings at the project level (e.g., in Sulla, Manikganj, and Jamalpur), attended by all Program Supervisors and selected Field Motivators in turn. These meetings serve as a learning experience for the Motivators and they provide training and supervisory guidelines for the Supervisors.

In addition, special training opportunities are organized on specific topics. For instance, before the introduction of the second cycle of the functional education course and after the revision of the course content and methodology at the end of the first cycle, all field staff in the Sulla Project went through a five-day training session on the implementation of the functional education program. The Sulla Project staff attended special training sessions on cooperative principles and practices organized in Comilla in cooperation with the Cooperative College and the Academy for Rural Development. A month-long staff development workshop was conducted in the Sulla Project in July-August 1976, in which BRAC headquarters personnel, training staff, and field staff deliberated on seven selected topics--reorientation of functional education instructors, functional education methodology, BRAC approach to development, "consciousness raising" among the rural people, human relations, leadership and communication, and the third phase strategy for the Sulla Project. Similarly, a week-long evaluation and planning workshop was organized for the functional education teachers in the Jamalpur Project before they launched the special women's project there.

A small training team under a Chief Trainer was put together in BRAC headquarters early in 1974 and given the responsibility for arranging the special training and orientation sessions for the BRAC field personnel and for developing a portfolio of training materials and methods on specific topics called training modules. BRAC received assistance from a training expert provided by the Ford Foundation in the preparation of the training modules. The modules are resource materials on a specific subject that can be drawn upon in organizing a training session on the subject. These can be modified, adapted, and combined for specific groups, depending on their needs and the available training time. In fact, for each group of trainees, a special training program that may vary from a day to a month is worked out by adapting and combining the modules.

The training modules developed so far are the following:

1. Communications. There are three modules in the communications area--(a) teaching of methods for dissemination of ideas in a way that creates a sense of participation from all parties concerned; (b) organizational analysis and needs assessment to understand exactly what the organization desires from its workers, what the workers expect of the organization, and what they together expect their accomplishments to be; and (c) program planning where all members are involved in the process of establishing the goals and objectives of the program leading to plans and objectives to which all parties are committed.

2. Group dynamics. Establishing a sense of team effort through genuine interaction, teaching how to work together for common goals, and reaching consensus.

3. <u>Leadership</u>. Helping trainees to be self-confident and identifying and helping develop qualities and skills needed to achieve leadership status that is freely accepted by the people concerned.

4. <u>Consciousness raising</u>. Helping trainees develop analytical skills to understand why certain conditions and situations exist in the rural areas and to formulate and assess alternative approaches to solving specific rural problems.

5. <u>Functional education</u>. Training instructors in methodologies developed specifically for use with BRAC functional education material.[1]

Training and Resource Center (TARC)

With the establishment in mid-1976 of a Training and Resource Center consisting of six full-time staff members, the staff training program has become a systematic and regular activity and has developed into a service that is available to other organizations and groups interested in rural development and the BRAC program approach. The establishment of TARC does not mark any basic change in training content and methodology, but it permits orderly planning and management of the training activities and provides some assurance that the necessary staff and resources are devoted to training. An important motivation for setting up the center was also the growing demand by many voluntary organizations in the country for training assistance from BRAC for their own workers. Another reason was a new emphasis in BRAC's own program strategy on rural youth "self-starter" groups and youth leaders who might be trained and supported to initiate rural self-help projects without building a heavy staff and organization structure maintained by BRAC (see the chapter on institutional structures).

In 1976, about one-half of TARC staff time and training activities was spent in providing services to other voluntary organizations. They were charged fees roughly on the basis of actual costs for the services provided. The rest of TARC activities were devoted to training BRAC's own staff and rural youths identified as potential leaders of "self-starter" groups. A program timetable of TARC for one month (December 1976) indicates the typical scope and nature of TARC activities (see Table 6.1).

The Training and Resource Center was located in Dacca in 1976 in a rented building adjacent to the BRAC headquarters. It is planned, however, that the center will be set up in a rural location with residential accommodation and run like an <u>ashram</u> where trainees and trainers together form a community, meeting their basic needs through necessary manual labor and creating an environment for a total living-learning experience.[2] It is also planned that the training staff will alternate between training work at the center and regular field assignments in BRAC projects.

Six acres of land have been purchased at a cost of Tk 400,000 in Savar, 20 miles west of Dacca, for the site of the training center. The dormitory, staff

---

[1]BRAC, <u>Training and Support Programme for Rural Development</u>, n.d., pp. 2-3.

[2]BRAC, <u>Training and Support Programme</u>..... p. 5.

Table 6.1

TARC Program for the Month of December, 1976

Trainer	Date/ Period	Assignment	Organization Providing Trainees	Venue
Mijanur Rahman	13th–17th	Youth leaders' training	BRAC/Manikganj	Manikganj
Selim Ahmed Shahid Talukder	8th	Project planning workshop	Community Development Foundation	CDF-Dacca
Selim Ahmed	9th–17th	Management of works program	BRAC	Dacca & Savar
Rafiqul Islam	9th–20th	Works program	BRAC	Savar
Mijanur Rahman Selim Ahmed	19th–24th	Motivation and communication training	Swallows of Sweden	Dacca & Shaturia
Mahbuba Karim	7th–9th	Follow-up of previous trainees and consultancy	UNICEF	Gaibandha
Mijanur Rahman Selim Ahmed Rafiqul Islam	27th–31st	Youth leaders' training	BRAC Manikganj	Manikganj
Shamsul Huda	8th–16th	Poultry extension	BRAC/Jamalpur	Jamalpur
Shamsul Huda	20th–31st	Poultry complex construction	BRAC/TARC	Savar
Gishpoti Roy	6th–12th	Pond fisheries	BRAC/Sulla	Sulla
Gishpoti Roy	18th–31st	Duck hatchery construction	BRAC/TARC	Savar

Source: Training and Resource Centre, Bangladesh Rural Advancement Committee, Dacca.

residences, meeting rooms and other facilities are expected to cost a similar amount. The annual recurring expenses for running the center is estimated to be about Tk 350,000--a part of which will be recovered from fees for services provided to other organizations.

Maintaining Motivation and Morale

Persistence in rural development work and efforts to improve the condition of the poorest in a political climate and socioeconomic environment not particularly conducive to rapid social change takes a high level of stoic fortitude and a certain philosophical disposition. Successes when achieved are small and slow to come, and frsutrations and failures are frequent. A consistently high level of enthusiasm among rural development workers is unrealistic to expect. A high degree of "achievement motivation" gratified by quick and visible accomplishments is probably not as helpful to a rural development worker as it might be in McClelland's entrepreneurial world.[1] Morale and enthusiasm among the BRAC workers, therefore, have their natural "ups and downs," as the Executive Director put it. It is also likely that a number of the BRAC workers would prefer to have remained in the city with a desk-bound job in a government or commercial office and have come to BRAC only as a second choice.

On the whole, however, the level of enthusiasm and dedication among the workers is regarded as high by the BRAC leadership--an assessment confirmed by ICED researchers' impressions from visits to project sites and discussions at field camps. This is attributed to a number of factors by the Executive Director of BRAC:

1. Friendly interpersonal relationship among the workers is emphasized and the leadership pays attention to and helps resolve any interpersonal problems among workers.

2. There is a high level of flexibility in administration and management of program activities. Workers have a great deal of freedom about taking initiatives and making decisions and usually would receive backing from the leadership in their decisions and judgment.

3. There is an informality in relationship between the workers and the program management. The Executive Director and other program leaders are freely accessible to all workers.

4. The communal environment of camp living generates an organizational spirit and helps to protect the workers from the sense of isolation and frustration a conscientious rural development worker may feel.

Concluding Comments

It is not clear what the dividends have been in terms of performance and motivation because of the emphasis on formal education credentials in the recruitment of Field Motivators and higher level personnel. A variation seems to persist among personnel in performance and commitment to program goals as indicated by the "hit or miss" character of the results obtained from the re-

---

[1] David W. McClelland and David G. Winter, Motivating Economic Achievement: Accelerating Economic Development through Psychological Training (New York: The Free Press, 1971).

cruitment process. The new recruitment approach through group interaction
exercises is an interesting innovation and represents an attempt to make
the selection of personnel more rational and less intuitive. However, if
this approach proves to be more satisfactory, it would only indicate   the
importance of assessing personal traits and qualities of individuals rather
than placing a premium on university degrees.

Apparently little weight is given to the local background of the work-
ers--the project staff being drawn from all over the country. The educational requirements, in a sense, restrict the possibility of local youths
being employed as Field Motivators, because very few university-educated
young men can be found living in their own villages. There are both advantages and risks in giving a preference to the local candidates in recruitment. The local youths are likely to be acquainted with and sensitive
to local social and cultural characteristics and capable of identifying
with the aspirations and values of the people in the area. On the other
hand, in a social structure marked by inequity, the most likely candidates
for a development worker are apt to be members of the local "gentry," or
similar privileged groups, and they may not be effective in serving   and
safeguarding the interests of the local poor. A Field Motivator from
another district, even if he comes from a class background similar to that
of the local workers,will probably not be inclined as much to identify
himself with or to be sympathetic to the local power structure. Generalizations, of course, are inappropriate because the determining factor is
each individual's own attitudes and level of awareness of the rural socioeconomic condition.

In the light of recent shifts of emphasis in BRAC program strategy
towards stronger local organizations and less reliance on a large BRAC
staff for local project management, the pros and cons of recruiting local field workers need to be reexamined. There may be significant advantages and far-reaching consequences of recruiting and training local Field
Motivators who may, after a stint with BRAC, pursue a career in politics
and local government and carry over the BRAC experience and outlook to
their new vocations. Such workers would not become professional BRAC
field workers, and their life's ambition and the rewards and incentives
would not be tied to the career ladder held out by BRAC. Obviously, it
is not necessary or appropriate to apply the principle of local recruitment rigidly, even if it is found to be generally desirable.

The establishment of a training center and setting up courses ready
to be offered on request may have led to a process of growing formalization of training and an abstraction of training from the essence of program activities. Formal training sessions on specific topics and skills
as well as for general orientation can be extremely valuable. However,
the practical insight into the intricacies of rural life, the perception
of the problems of the rural poor, the approaches to dealing with them,
and the skills and understanding necessary for effective human relations
are developed through practical experience and are very much affected by
the program objectives and rationale. The training modules will   never
replace the learning experiences of the field worker during his   initial
apprenticeship and as he begins to take on independent assignments   and

responsibilities; but the training sessions and the refresher workshops can be invaluable as complements and stimulants to further learning.   This complementary and catalytic role of a training center needs to be recognized as   TARC continues to provide its services to BRAC and other organizations.

If indeed it is desirable in voluntary organizations to have field workers whose life's ambition does not lie in climbing the career ladder   in a rural development program and if the skills as a rural development worker cannot   be abstracted from the substance of the program to be put into the content of   a training course, then approaches followed for staff development and utilization in large public programs and small voluntary agencies must be somewhat divergent. Centralized planning and decisionmaking, larger bureaucracies, standardized personnel management and administrative procedures, while understandable in large public programs, do not readily lend themselves to the improvisation, individualization, and destandardization possible in recruitment, training, interpersonal relationship, and administrative procedures in small voluntary programs.   The public programs also would have these advantages to the extent that the nature of the public programs change in the direction of greater decentralization, local integration of development efforts, and local flexibility.

Creation of appropriate institutional infrastructures is both a pre-condition for effective rural development programs and an objective of such programs. The organizational and staff structure of a program and the concomitant mobilization of the beneficiary population into participatory institutions make it possible to carry out the program activities. This process of participation at the same time can help the beneficiary popula-tions develop their own capabilities to control and manage the development activities in a locality--growing increasingly less dependent either on outside voluntary organizations or a centralized government bureaucracy.

BRAC's approach to rural development attaches a high value to the growth of local participatory institutions and self-sustaining and self-managed rural development. However, in the short span of time since the inception of the BRAC development program, there has been an evolution of concepts and strategies about creating and strengthening institutional structures for rural development. Definitive solutions to the problems of institutional structures have not been found by BRAC and probably should not be expected; nevertheless, the BRAC experience with these problems and its continuing efforts to deal with them are instructive.

BRAC Organization and Staff Structure

In 1976, the BRAC organization was physically spread out in Dacca, where the central offices were located, and in three project locations--Sulla, Manikganj, and Jamalpur.

The central offices consisted of the Executive Director's office, the administration and accounts departments, the materials development unit, the Gonokendro editorial office, the research and evaluation unit, and the Training and Resource Center (until the Savar site for the cen-ter is fully developed).

The field organization was most elaborate in Sulla where BRAC was born and where the project had been in operation the longest. The Sulla Project area was divided into 11 sectors under 2 zones. Each sector was headed by an Area Manager (also known as a Program Supervisor) who had an average of 4 Field Motivators and 3 paramedics working under him. The Area Managers reported to the two Program Coordinators in charge of the two zones, and they in turn were supervised by the Field Coordinator for the Sulla Project. There were also three Medical Officers in the project area in charge of three clinics and responsible for providing technical support to the health workers in the area. In mid-1976 there were 42 Field Motivators and 31 paramedics in the Sulla Project area (in addition 14 women paramedics were under training). There were also 30 newly ap-pointed shasthya shevikas functioning as full-time village health

Figure 1.

Simplified Organization Chart of BRAC

January 1977

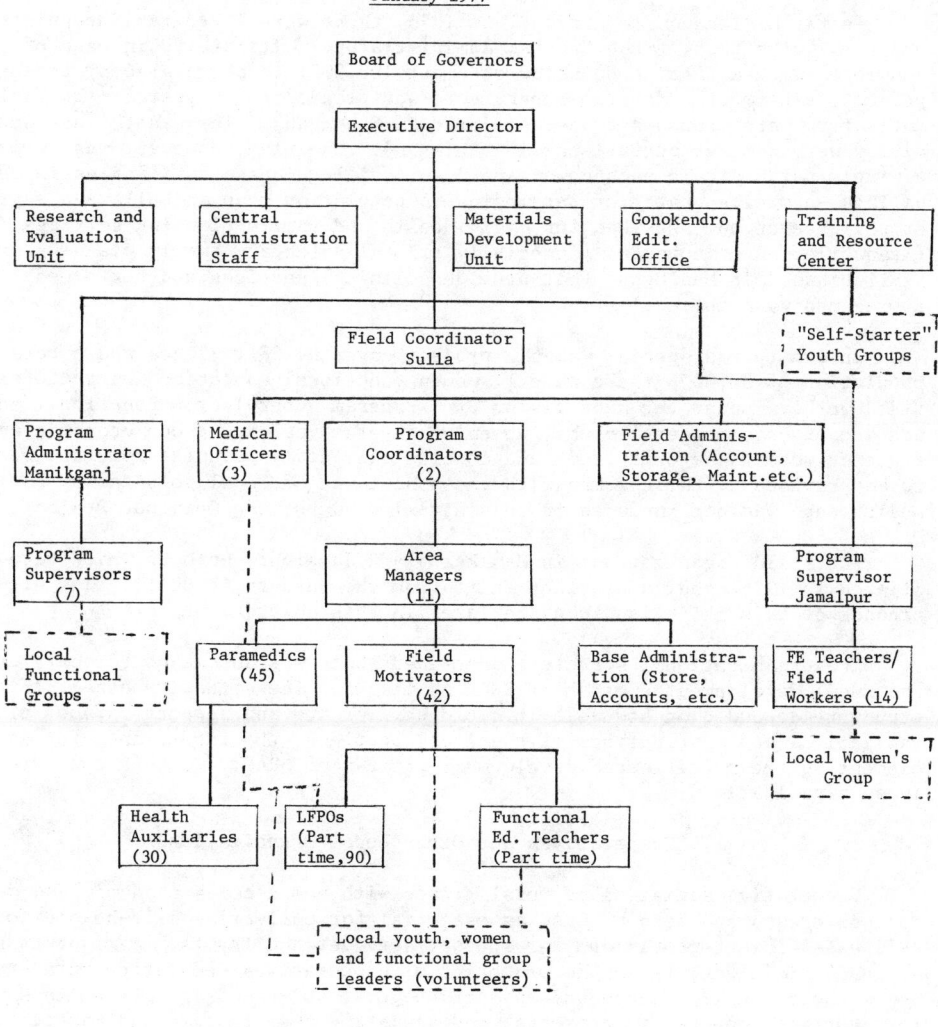

_____ Line of administrative control

- - - - - Line of technical support

auxiliaries in 30 villages; shevikas were to be ultimately appointed in each village in order to intensify the coverage of and improve the access to the health services in the area. There were also about 90 part-time Lady Family Planning Organizers and an unspecified number of volunteer and unpaid functional educational instructors and youth workers in the project area.

In the Manikganj Project in late 1976, there were 7 Program Supervisors under the direction of the Program Administrator. Ultimately, in each of the 8 unions (with a total population of about 100,000) to be covered by the BRAC project, a team of 2 Program Supervisors was planned to be posted. No Field Motivators were proposed to be appointed in Manikganj. The health care activities were not yet operational in Manikganj. The plan, however, was to post a single paramedic in each union and 3 to 4 village-based auxiliaries in each village--a smaller ratio of paramedics to population than in Sulla and a greater reliance on the shevikas for basic health and family planning services. (Meanwhile, BRAC supported financially a local voluntary family planning organization based in Manikganj that provided clinical services and performed tubectomies and vasectomies.)

In Jamalpur's special women's project covering 28 villages and a total population of 36,000, there were 14 women functional education instructors/ field workers under the supervision of a Program Supervisor. Functional education groups, mothers' clubs, women's cooperatives, and group economic activities were to be organized, and nonclinical family planning services were to be provided by these women with the assistance of local volunteers. Basic health care was not included in the initial phase of the Jamalpur Project.

The field organizations in Manikganj and Jamalpur, both of which were initiated in 1976, show a distinct shift from the pattern in Sulla. The significance of this shift is discussed later in this chapter.

The organizational structure described above was not meant to carry out the rural development program of BRAC by itself. The effectiveness of this structure depended on how well it could help create and support various organizations and institutions of the local people as the instruments for implementing the multifaceted development program of BRAC. We turn now   to these organizations.

Cooperatives and Other Local Organizations

Cooperative societies of rural groups with homogeneous economic and develo[p] ment interests are seen by BRAC as essential for collective self-help efforts a[s] well as efficient provisions for support services and inputs. A major task   o[f] all BRAC field workers is the promotion of cooperatives--educating rural residents about the importance and ways of cooperation, encouraging them to save an[d] to undertake cooperative projects, and assisting them to form and manage cooper[-] ative societies.

BRAC was interested in forming new societies as well as rejuvenating exist[-] ing farmers' and fishermen's cooperatives in the Sulla Project area. Many of th[e] old societies had become ineffective, having fallen into the hands of powerful groups in the village such as the larger landowners and moneylenders.   Input allocations, credit facilities, and other benefits of cooperative societies available from the government were monopolized by members of the managing grou[p] to the detriment of general members' interest. Furthermore, corruption and mis[-] management at the top were a common feature of the cooperatives.

One of the first tasks before BRAC was to rid the cooperatives of their unsavory image. It was necessary to restore the confidence of the general members in cooperative societies and eliminate the prevalent corruption and bad management. BRAC emphasized the importance of cooperative spirits, savings habits, collective responsibility, and cooperative projects, rather than achievement of legal status as a registered society under government regulation, although this was not discouraged. All Field Motivators were trained in cooperative accounting practices, and books of accounts of the societies were updated and regularly maintained. BRAC arranged with government cooperative inspectors for audit and regular inspection of the societies' state of affairs. The societies were encouraged to hold regular weekly meetings, and the members were encouraged to attend these meetings. BRAC field workers attended many of these meetings. New management committees were elected for many societies in a democratic manner. A training session was arranged for 154 chairmen and secretaries of the cooperatives by the joint efforts of the BRAC staff and the extension officers of the cooperative department.

About 120 primary cooperative societies were active in the Sulla Project area in 1976. About 80 of these were farmers' cooperatives, approximately 30 were fishermen's cooperatives, and the rest were societies formed by women's groups and landless laborers. The combined savings of these societies had exceeded Tk 200,000 by early 1976. Following the national pattern under the Integrated Rural Development Program (IRDP) of the government, the Sulla Thana Central Cooperative Association (STCCA) was formed in early 1974. The role of the central association is to serve as a channel   for credit funds and inputs available from the government for the primary society's members, to provide common services to the small primary societies they are unable to arrange by themselves, and to maintain liaison with government departments on matters of common interest to the rural cooperative members.

Interference by a prominent member of the ruling political party, who was interested in controlling the government patronage offered through the central association and was opposed to the prominent role of BRAC in the local cooperative movement, gave the STCCA an inauspicious start.   The situation improved, however, after the change of government in August 1975. The government appointed a Project Officer under the IRDP whose job was to provide technical assistance and management advice to STCCA.   The STCCA and through it the primary societies received the exclusive fertilizer dealership for the thana, and a credit fund of Tk 500,000 for lending to members of the primary societies was made available by the government. A central association was also formed in 1976 in Derai thana, part of which is included in the BRAC project area.

Deviating somewhat from the IRDP national pattern, the Sulla central association decided to decentralize its activities by forming another tier of association in each of the four unions in Sulla thana with all the primary societies in the union as its members. There was an enthusiastic response to this idea from primary societies, and land and money were donated by the local people for erecting the STCCA office.

In the Jamalpur Project some 29 women's groups were engaged in collective economic projects. (See discussion in the chapter on women's programs.) In Manikganj, during the first year of its operation in 1976, 27 groups of women and landless laborers with a total membership of over 400 were being assisted by BRAC field workers in group economic activities, including hand-husking and marketing of rice, farming, weaving, and pottery. These groups in Jamalpur and Manikganj were at a pre-cooperative stage in the legal sense and were entirely dependent for credits and inputs on BRAC, not being eligible for support from the government sources. In addition to the above, in November 1976, there were 19 other groups in Manikganj with 339 members which had made more progress towards becoming full-fledged cooperative societies with elected managing committees, regular membership meetings, and weekly thrift savings. Among these groups were 10 women's cooperatives with 158 members, 6 landless farmers' groups with 138 members, 2 weavers' societies with 24 members, and 1 potters' society with 19 members.

As the description of the Jamalpur and Manikganj efforts in the development of cooperatives (and collective economic enterprises) indicates, there is a deliberate emphasis in these projects to concentrate on helping the underprivileged groups organize collective self-help efforts through cooperatives--in contrast to the general cooperative development effort in the country by such agencies as the IRDP and the cooperative department, both of, which have concentrated on cooperatives of landowning farmers.

The cooperatives and pre-cooperative groups were seen as the institutional means for economic improvement. For the purpose of mobilizing people's initiative and motivation, creating a conducive environment for self-help efforts, and raising the level of awareness about the roots of rural problems and ways of dealing with them, BRAC introduced two kinds of institutions--the Gonokendro (people's center) and the functional education groups.

The Gonokendro, a modest building established in each village as a center of village community life and a physical base for various development efforts, was given a high priority in the second phase of the Sulla Project. Construction of 175 Gonokendro buildings were planned through joint contributions of BRAC and the individual village communities. BRAC was to supply the building materials and the villagers were to provide the land, labor, and the furniture. Actually 129 buildings were constructed by the end of 1974--mostly modest bamboo and timber structures.

While the accomplishments in physical construction of the buildings were relatively good, the experience of Gonokendro was an eye-opener for BRAC. In many instances, it was found difficult to overcome the rivalry of opposing factions, patronized and supported by influential families in the village. Many of the village committees formed for directing the Gonokendro did not have the support and confidence of the whole village. In at least one-third of the villages, it was not even possible to agree on a site for the center.

Apparently, the Gonokendro as a focal point for village organization and activities was BRAC's own concept of how the villagers could be organized and mobilized for development efforts. This concept ignored the reality of conflicts of interests among the village residents and the fact that the village community was not really one entity. The Gonokendro, an attractive idea on the face of it, did not live up to BRAC's expectations. BRAC concluded: "Despite the fact that this programme accounted for a substantial part of BRAC effort the achievement of the programme was not commensurate with the effort."[1] While building a community center in the village was not ruled out if the village desired it and was willing to contribute to its building and upkeep, it was not included as a project item in the third phase of Sulla or in other BRAC projects.

The role of the functional education groups in helping self-help efforts and in supporting the total rural development efforts has been discussed elsewhere in this report.

The group health insurance scheme and the mothers' clubs also have been described in other chapters of the report. The insurance scheme is intended to mobilize local financial support for the health care and family planning services, distribute the cost burden of health care evenly among the population and keep it within acceptable limits, and eventually be a mechanism for substantial participation of the local people in the management of the health program. The mothers' clubs are designed to facilitate health and nutrition education and to serve as a forum for collective and individual actions for the improvement of mothers' and children's health.

Important questions about the institutional and organizational arrangements of a rural development program are to what extent these arrangements facilitate community participation in its various dimensions and promote better integration of the program activities among themselves and with other rural development efforts.

Community Participation

Two main aspects of community participation are the distribution of the benefits of the development program among the various segments of the community population and the degree of active involvement of the beneficiary population in managing and carrying out the development activities.

Since BRAC has been in operation for some length of time only in the Sulla Project area, ICED attempted to determine to what extent the benefits of BRAC activities reached the poorer and the more underprivileged groups. A random sample of 240 households from 11 villages where BRAC had been active were asked about the number of instances they had benefited from various BRAC activities since the inception of these activities in the respective villages. The responses were classified according to the level of education and landholdings of the heads of the household. (See Tables 7.1, 7.2, and 7.3.) It was found, somewhat unexpectedly, that the overall

---

[1]BRAC, Sulla Project Report on Phase II, p. 7.

Table 7.1

Distribution of Benefits Related to the Level of
Education of the Head of the Household

Level of Education	Total Respondents Heads of Households		Frequency of Mention of Benefits									
			Health		Agric. Coop.		Family Planning		Other*		Total	
	#	%	#	%	#	%	#	%	#	%	#	%
Illiterate	105	44	56	34	28	29	26	38	210	37	320	36
Less than Complete Primary Ed.	66	28	46	28	32	33	18	25	172	30	268	30
Primary Ed. and above	56	23	50	31	30	31	20	29	149	26	249	28
Complete Secondary School and above	13	5	10	6	7	7	7	9	36	6	60	7
TOTAL	240	100	162	100	97	100	71	100	567	100	897	100

*See first footnote of Table 7.2.
SOURCE: ICED Field Data

Table 7.2

Distribution of Benefits Related to Land Ownership

Size of Landholdings	Total Respondents Heads of Households		Frequency of Mention of Benefits									
			Health		Agric. Coop.		Family Planning		Other*		Total	
	#	%	#	%	#	%	#	%	#	%	#	%
No land	62	26	33	20	8	8	21	30	111	20	173	19
Less than 1 Acre	130	54	10	6	6	6	10	14	44	8	70	8
1 to 3 Acres	40	17	52	32	40	41	7	10	164	29	263	29
3+ Acres and above	8**	3	67	41	43	44	33	46	248	43	391	43
TOTAL	240	100	163	100	97	100	71	100	567	100	897	100

*Other activities include fisheries cooperatives, youth groups, women's groups, functional education, providing power tiller and water pump, supply of seeds, and useful literature and advice.

**Many of the larger land-owners' families are joint families with several nuclear units within the joint family structure, which partially explains high frequency of mention of benefits from the various BRAC activities.

Source: ICED Field Data.

Table 7.3

Contribution to BRAC Project Activities by Level of Education
and Land Ownership of Head of Household

| Level of Education | Frequency of Mention of Contribution | | | |
	Participation in Planning and Management	Voluntary Service	Paid Services	Donation: Cash or in Kind
Illiterate	4	16	2	1
Less than Complete Primary Education	4	15	1	-
Primary Education but less than Complete Secondary Education	7	17	1	3
Secondary Education and above	6	3	1	1
Land Ownership				
No land	1	13	1	-
Less than 1 Acre	-	2	1	-
1+ Acre to 3 Acres	5	15	2	-
3+ Acres and above	16	21	-	3

N=240.

Source: ICED Field Data.

benefits as well as the specific benefits from the health activities, co-operatives, and the family planning efforts (as the respondents perceived the benefits) were distributed more or less evenly among the groups with different educational levels. Groups with higher levels of education were not enjoying a disproportionate share of the benefits.

The findings were quite different when the benefits were related to the landholding pattern. Households with no land or less than an acre of land revealed themselves to be recipients of benefits much less frequently than their share in the sample population and those with three acres or more land mentioned instances of benefits totally out of line with their proportion in the sample. The totally landless households fared somewhat better than those with less than an acre of land, apparently because of some special efforts to help landless laborers and destitute women, though even in this case the frequency of mention of benefits was less than pro-portionate to their number. The most "discriminated" group was also the largest group of households--those with less than one acre of land. The pattern of benefits according to landholdings for specific sectors was not the same for all sectors. (Table 7.2) The distribution of health care benefits was similar to the skewed pattern of overall benefits. In agri-cultural cooperatives it was more skewed in favor of the larger landowners than the overall pattern. The distribution of benefits was somewhat more favorable for the two poorer groups in regard to family planning.

The specific quantitative dimensions as shown in the table may not reflect a high level of precision, because the investigators in the sample survey relied on the verbal responses to their questions and were not able to apply any independent verification to the responses.[1] The investigators believe, however, that the main findings of the survey regarding the direc-tion of bias in the distribution of benefits are valid.

The absence of a relationship between educational distribution and the distribution of BRAC benefits and the positive relationship between landholding and benefits apparently mean that ownership of land is a more important determinant of economic status and social influence than educa-tional achievements and that distribution of education does not have a high correlation with the distribution of land ownership. These cross-relation-ships, however, need further investigation, especially for the purpose of assessing the role of education in rural development and determining educa-tional policies.

The heads of the same sample of households were asked about their contribution to BRAC activities by means of participating in program plan-ning and management, providing voluntary services, providing services for

---

[1]The landholding pattern, for example, indicated by the survey is some-what at variance with the findings of a BRAC survey in 1975 of 2300 households, which shows that 34 percent of the households are totally landless, 18 percent have one acre or less land, and 25 percent possess between 1 and 5 acres. The discrepancy, however, does not alter the basic characteristics of the ownership pattern.

payment, and offering cash or in-kind donation. The responses were predominantly negative for all educational groups and land ownership groups.
(See Table 7.3) This apparently was not because they were unwilling to
contribute. In response to queries, 90 percent of the sample household
heads expressed the willingness to commit labor and time to support BRAC
activities and 8 percent said they would contribute cash and materials to
help BRAC. The lack of contribution, at least in part, was due to the
organizational structure of the BRAC program that did not create conditions
for mobilizing local contribution.

     The overall picture that emerges regarding community participation is
that the benefits of BRAC activities in Sulla were enjoyed disproportionately
by the relatively better-off families with larger landholdings and that the
institutional structure of BRAC did not exploit to the full extent the
latent potentials of engaging the beneficiary population in planning and
managing the program activities and of mobilizing the community resources.

     On the question of the integrated approach, the Sulla experience points
to a number of problems that defy easy solutions. Having decided to address
various urgent rural problems in the areas of health, family planning, farming, fisheries, the landless, women's situation, and education, and lacking
the human and material resources to provide a reasonably comprehensive coverage of the entire project area population, BRAC scattered its sectoral activities among certain villages and certain population groups, making none the
true beneficiary of an integrated approach. As we have seen in the discussion
of the major sectoral activities, any overlap of participation among different
activities was coincidental rather than central to the program approach followed in Sulla. There was no central organizational mechanism that mobilized
groups of population to assess their own development needs and priorities and
to launch a multifaceted self-help program. The functional education groups
might have been the institutional means for homogeneous interest groups to be
organized for improving their own condition. But functional education in
Sulla, as we have noted earlier, was not linked directly to development action,
and the instructors and the BRAC field workers did not view functional education as the prelude to collective and organized action. The sectoral activities together constituted an integrated approach in an abstract sense from the
point of view of BRAC as an organization, since these appeared to complement
each other, but they remained somewhat compartmentalized for the beneficiary
population.

     The links of BRAC activities with nonBRAC development efforts--mostly of
the government agencies--were tenuous. As noted in the chapters on the major
sectoral activities, the differences in program approach and objectives, the
inadequacies of resources and personnel in national programs, and sometimes
the inclination to compete rather than to cooperate on both sides stood in the
way. The lack of resources for comprehensive service coverage either by BRAC
or by the government agencies left room for a tacit territorial and jurisdictional division of labor.

     Cooperation between BRAC and other agencies had been most pronounced in
respect of the agricultural cooperatives and the formation of the thana central
associations. After initial political problems the central associations,
formed with BRAC encouragement and support, received the standard financial
and technical support and the government allocation of agricultural inputs

available to all IRDP sponsored central associations. There was apparently
a sufficient commonality of objectives and approach between IRDP and BRAC
in this respect.

The problems of the institutional structure and organization in the
Sulla Project were apparently recognized by the BRAC leadership. In attempts
to deal with these problems, new program strategies and institutional approaches emerged, as the plans for the third phase of Sulla and the new Manikganj
project were prepared.

New Organizational Approach in Sulla

The main organizational goal for the third phase (1976-1978) of the Sulla
Project as stated in the project proposal is as follows:

> to organise and develop appropriate village and local level
> institutions, in order to effectively involve the masses of rural
> population in mobilising the communities' resources for their own
> development and to provide services to those whose needs are
> presently being ignored.[1]

The major features of the third phase plans, from an organization and institutional point of view, are the following:

1. The third phase puts special emphasis on organizing disadvantaged
rural groups with homogeneous development interests, such as landless laborers, small farmers, destitute women, fishermen, artisans, and the youth. The
functional education courses are to be organized for such homogeneous groups
and are to be used for planning and implementing group projects rather than
only for literacy teaching and "consciousness raising" in an abstract sense.

Another device to be used for spurring group action is the village workshop. These workshops, conducted by BRAC staff and local youth group members,
are to be a series of "conscientization" sessions with all the members in a
village community. In these sessions, a critical analysis of the village
socioeconomic structures and problems is to be made and action plans formulated for social and economic change.

As a result of the village workshops and the functional education program,
village organizations such as youth groups, women's associations, and cooperative societies of different types are expected to emerge, and a village development committee with the representation of these organizations is likely to
be formed. The village development committee is to plan and guide the broader
community-wide development services in such areas as those of health, sanitation, family planning, and education. BRAC staff and the youth groups are to
monitor the progress of the action programs of the village organizations and
the village development committee and provide critical support.

2. The BRAC field staff that was operational during the second phase is
to be maintained during the following three years or even slightly increased
with the addition of women Field Motivators. However, the main energy and
time of the field workers are to be devoted to "institution-building"--forma-
tion of homogeneous action groups of women, youths, landless laborers, fishermen, and so on, and supporting the plans and activities of these groups rather

[1]BRAC, Sulla Project Report on Phase II, p. 1.

than just organizing and carrying out sectoral activities initiated by BRAC
itself.

    3. The sectoral activities are to be used not only to provide needed
services but also to enhance the formation of organizations and institutions
that can help make the sectoral activities more self-sustaining and self-
managed. This is to be achieved by drawing up sectoral plans and objectives
with the involvement of the homogeneous interest groups and channeling the
services through the groups.

    4. The central association of cooperatives at the thana level is planned
to be more broad-based to include all cooperative groups rather than only agricultural cooperatives. The capacity of the central association is to be developed to service and support the various primary groups and to coordinate and
guide development efforts that affect the different village level societies.

    5. The BRAC organizational structure is expected to withdraw gradually
at the end of the third phase leaving probably only a skeleton staff for
technical support to the central association. The roles and functions that
BRAC is performing are to be taken over by the central association or a
similar central body and the village development committees.

    At the time of collecting materials for this report in late 1976, some
progress had been made in moving towards this new institutional approach.
The formats and procedures of conducting the village workshops had been prepared, BRAC field staff had been briefed about the workshops, and a small
number of the first round workshops had been conducted. The reorientation
of the functional education courses was under way, but the full implications
and the operational consequences of the new role of functional education were
yet to be fully worked out. It was apparent that no systematic planning and
thinking had yet gone into broadening the central association and building
its strengths for ultimately taking over many of the BRAC organizational roles.

Local Self-Sustaining Institutions in Manikganj

    The new BRAC project in Manikganj initiated in mid-1976 may be regarded
as a testing ground for the lessons learned from the Sulla Project. From the
very beginning, the emphasis in Manikganj was on keeping BRAC's own staff at
a minimum level, forming local organizations of homogeneous groups for collective development action, and using youth groups as a catalyzing force for
local activities.

    The initial preparation for the Manikganj Project was done through a food-
for-work program (FFWP) designed to attack three physical constraints to agricultural development in the area--early monsoon flooding, drainage, and irrigation in the dry season. Members of the local youth organizations participated in the FFWP by working with BRAC personnel to establish contact with the
people, select FFWP sites, motivate the people living adjacent to the sites to
give additional voluntary labor to the scheme, supervise the work, organize the
transportation of wheat to the sites, and make payment to the laborers. The
food-for-work program carried out between November 1975 and April 1976 not
only improved the physical infrastructure for agriculture and provided food
and cash to the vulnerable groups at a time of food scarcity, but also helped
identify promising youths and youth groups for future BRAC work, involved local people in planning and implementation of development schemes, helped BRAC

to be acquainted with the local development problems and prospects, and enhanced BRAC's credibility with the local people.

BRAC is of the view that throughout rural Bangladesh there are hundreds of rural youth groups, educated but unemployed,who can act as catalytic agents for various development oriented organizations and programs.[1]

From the youth group identified in each village in Manikganj, two to three are to be selected to undergo functional education instructor training, and then the group is to open a functional education center in its own community. As mentioned in the chapter on functional education, the functional education program is to be used as the main initial thrust for organizing groups for planning and carrying out self-help activities in Manikganj. As the groups begin to express the need for other programs, other youths are to be trained as paramedics, family planning workers, and motivators to assist in cooperative formation and other developmental activities.[2]

The strategy of supporting local youth groups is also being tried in Shaturia, the thana adjacent to Manikganj. A dozen members of local youth groups spent several months in Sulla acquiring practical experience of the BRAC development approach. On their return to Shaturia the youth trainees formed an alliance of 13 local youth groups and planned development activities in the areas of public health, family planning, functional education, fisheries, agriculture, and formation of cooperative groups. They were assisted by a BRAC staff member and received a limited financial support from BRAC. The Shaturia experience prompted BRAC to explore the prospects of a spcial program of training youth leaders of "self-starter" development programs and supporting such programs with small financial grants and technical advice.

The sectoral activities in health, family planning, and extension services for agriculture and fisheries in Manikganj are to be channeled and carried out through the local groups emerging from the efforts of the youth workers and the functional education program. As in the third phase of Sulla, ultimately the responsibilities for coordinating and supporting the development services are to be taken over by a thana level association of the primary groups.

Concluding Comments

In BRAC's efforts to create a viable institutional structure for its rural development program, a change of approach is readily discernible. Originally the pattern was characterized by a large paid field staff, BRAC-initiated and managed sectoral activities not fully integrated with each

---

[1]BRAC, Manikganj Project, p. 9-10.

[2]Ibid., p. 10.

other, a low level of community participation in planning and managing activities, and insufficient positive discrimination in the program in favor of
the poorest people. This had changed to a pattern marked by a small number
of full-time and paid field staff, reliance on members of local youth groups
for field work, emphasis on building organizations of disadvantaged groups
with homogeneous development interests, and a more prominent role given   to
functional education and village workshops in forming primary action groups
and in planning and carrying out the combination of sectoral activities
through the local organizations.

The new approach began to be reflected in BRAC activities and project
proposals in 1976 and is still in the process of being shaped and elaborated.
It is certainly compatible with BRAC's basic goals of promoting self-sustaining rural development, creating and strengthening local institutions,   and
helping improve the living condition of the most deprived and the poorest. It
is too early to tell how this approach will fare in reality and how effectively
BRAC will be able to put it into practice.

Two critical questions in relation to the growth of the local institutions
are how the local power structure will be dealt with and how the local institutional structure can be made strong enough to permit the "withdrawal" of BRAC.

What will be the response to BRAC's organizational efforts of the incest-
uous alliance of the larger landowners, moneylenders, and influential   families whose power, influence, and privileges are certain to be threatened? During the second phase of the Sulla Project BRAC had infringed on the vested interests of the local power structure only marginally; there was no concerted
and broad-range effort to organize the various deprived groups and to utilize
the idealism and the receptivity to change of the youth in this effort.   In
many instances the benefits of BRAC activities were enjoyed as much or   more
by the better-off families as the poorer families.

It might be noted here that a somewhat dramatic brush with the local power
structure came early in BRAC's life in a project in Rowmari in the northern
district of Rangpur. This ended in a BRAC retreat and eventual abandonment of
the project.

In the wake of the 1974 floods and famine, a famine relief project   was
launched in Rowmari with Oxfam-UK aid. BRAC also decided to initiate a multipurpose rural development program in the area, capitalizing on its association
with the local people and on its familiarity with the local situation. However,
soon after the relief operation began, BRAC faced a boycott and ostracism from
the carpenters who refused to build the BRAC office building, the local   bank
manager who refused to release funds from the BRAC account, the bullock   cart
drivers who refused to transport BRAC supplies, and the firewood merchants who
refused to sell their firewood to BRAC. A BRAC worker was assaulted in   the
night and was accused by village leaders of rape, even though he was not in the
locality at the time of the alleged "incident." It turned out that all   this
activity was orchestrated by an influential local man who was chairman of the
board of the IRDP-sponsored Thana Central Cooperative Association, a   wealthy
landowner, a jute exporter, and a former member of the parliament from   the
locality. He and his allies were apparently afraid of losing control of   the

local TCCA and other local institutions and also the system of patronage, influence-peddling, and corruption that went with this control.

With the intervention of government officials from the district, the relief operation was salvaged and BRAC brought it to a successful conclusion. It had fed 8,000 to 13,000 children for up to four months, averting malnutrition and many probable deaths. BRAC and its financial sponsor Oxfam-UK decided, however, to pull out from the development program in Rowmari when it became obvious that BRAC and the local TCCA were unable to work together.[1]

In order to have a better insight into the mechanism of social change in the village in the face of numerous obstacles, BRAC is supporting with a grant from the Ford Foundation an anthropological study of two villages in the two project areas of Sulla and Manikganj. Two research assistants have been hired to apply the "participant observation" techniques in the two selected villages. An anthropologist from the Marga Institute in Sri Lanka has been appointed as a consultant for preparing the research design, training the researchers in methodology, and supervising the study. The study is expected to provide useful policy guidance from a disciplined observation of the interplay of the "system" of values, resources, and social and economic relationships in a village. Preliminary results of the study are expected in late 1977.[2]

The reaction of the local power structure is only one element in the process of nurturing and strengthening local organizations of deprived groups and building an institutional structure for self-sustaining development. Another important element is the intention and attitudes of the national government in regard to the local government structure and the degree of decentralization and sharing of authority considered necessary or desirable. The BRAC efforts might be seen by the government as a useful trial with important lessons for the national rural development program. In this case a favorable climate of support and cooperation from the government agencies, particularly the local and district officials, can reinforce and accelerate the process initiated by BRAC. Alternately, the BRAC activities may be viewed as well-intentioned efforts of a voluntary organization that the government would tolerate as long as no laws are violated. In such an atmosphere, BRAC and the local organizations would be up against the added obstacle of noncooperation and foot-dragging of government agencies and their local agents. BRAC's experience and lessons would also have that much less impact on the government rural programs and the national rural development policies and strategies.

In fact, while at the field level the interaction between the BRAC activities and the government rural services have not generally been close if only because the thin spread of the government activities leave plenty of room for voluntary agencies to function, at the national level there appears to be a

---

[1]See BRAC, Report on Rowmari Thana Childfeeding and Nutrition Programme, Dacca, n.d.
    Also Cole Patrick Dodge and Paul D. Wiebe, "Famine Relief and Development in Rural Bangladesh," Economic and Political Weekly, Bombay, May 29, 1976, pp. 809-817.

[2]BRAC, Newsletter, vol. 1, No. 3, May-June 1976, pp. 6-7.

general awareness and appreciation of BRAC's useful work and bona fides
among government leaders and officials involved in rural development. A
member of the BRAC governing body is a member of the Council of Advisers
to the President (i.e., a member of the President's Cabinet equivalent to
a Minister) and there are other well-wishers of BRAC in influential official positions. There is increasing interest from relevant government
agencies in BRAC's functional education and health care efforts. For
instance, the Integrated Rural Development Program in launching a project
for women's cooperatives has called upon BRAC's assistance for developing
the educational components and training the field workers. The Division
of Population Control and Family Planning has often cited the Sulla Project of BRAC as an example where a family planning effort integrated with
a broader rural development program has demonstrated encouraging results.
However, a sense of goodwill towards BRAC and appreciation of its efforts
among individual government leaders do not necessarily translate into the
adoption of appropriate lessons from the BRAC experience in government
programs, which would often call for basic reorientation of objectives and
policies in government programs rather than the transplantation of certain
methods and techniques.

CHAPTER 8

COSTS AND FINANCES

The Pattern of Costs

Available information about the budgets of the various components of BRAC indicate the magnitude of the different project activities, the breakdown of the total costs into major cost categories, and the relative proportions of the cost categories compared to the total or to each other. The cost data are based on the proposed budgets for each of the major projects for the planned duration of the project, which varied from one year to three years. Actual expenditure data were not available as these projects were yet to come to a conclusion at the time of collecting the cost data (excepting the Functional Education Development project for which the data in Table 8.1 represents actual costs). However, major deviations from the budget in the total expenditures or in the relative proportions among cost categories were not expected. (Unfortunately, the breakdown of budget according to the categories in Table 8.1 for Sulla Phase II--the one major project that came to a conclusion at the end of 1975--was not available. This would have permitted a comparison of the pattern of expenditure between the early Sulla phase and the later projects.) All of the projects included in Table 8.1, except Functional Education Development, had their beginning in 1976 and they presumably reflect the changes in program approach following the early Sulla experience.

Among the six projects included in Table 8.1, the first three (Sulla Phase III, Jamalpur and Manikganj) are more representative of the normal and major activities of BRAC. Among the last three, the Training and Resource Centre is unusual because it has a large capital component (training facilities, dormitories, etc.) because of the nature of the project. The last two projects--Research and Evaluation and Functional Education Development--include provisions for foreign consultancy that consume a very large chunk of the total budget in each case and distorts the relative shares of the different cost categories.

Table 8.1 shows that in all of the projects the staff cost is a major item if not the largest item in the total budget. The field staff and head office overhead (which is essentially the head office staff salaries and the staff support and logistics costs) together accounted for 49 to 72 percent of total recurring costs in the different projects. The capital costs (land, building, transportation, equipment, and furniture) are relatively low or even nil in all the projects except the Training Centre project. In the two major projects--Sulla Phase III and Manikganj, they are 5 percent and 15 percent respectively. The lower figure in Sulla is explained by the fact that it inherited capital assets from the previous phase of the project.

Table 8.1

Categories of Budgeted Expenditures for Major BRAC Project Activities

(Taka)

Items	Sulla Phase III[1] (3 Yrs.)	Jamalpur (12 Mos.)	Manikganj (3 Yrs.)	Training & Resource Centre (3 Yrs.)	Research & Eval. Proj. (2 Yrs.)	Functional Ed. Dev. (19 Mos.)
Capital Expenses	310 000	--	605 000	723 000	--	--
Recurring Expenses	5 260 000	150 000	2 383 000	1 222 000	204 000	357 000
Field Staff	2 727 000	78 000	1 224 000	380 000	114 000	122 000
Head Office Overhead	521 000[2]	24 000	491 000	216 000	--	54 000
Materials & Supplies	1 164 000[2]	18 000	314 000[2]	50 000	--	120 000
Other Costs: (Travel, logistics, training, data processing, reports, etc.)	848 000	30 000	354 000	576 000	90 000	61 000
Special Costs	361 000	--	965 000	--	255 000	208 000
Loan Fund	111 000[3]	--	500 000	--	--	--
Grants to Local Organizations	250 000	--	465 000	--	--	--
Foreign Consultancy	--	--	--	--	255 000	208 000
Total	5 931 000	150 000	3 953 000	1 945 000	459 000	565 000
Capital Cost as % of total	5.2	0.0	15.3	37.2	0.0	0.0
Staff + Overhead as % of total	54.8	68.0	43.4	30.6	24.8	31.2
Staff + Overhead as % of total recurring	61.7	68.0	72.0	48.8	55.9	49.3

[1]Indicates duration for which the budget allocation has been made.

[2]Excluding part of the medicine costs to be recovered from patients.

[3]Only loan guarantee expenses assuming availability of loan funds from commercial sources.

Source: BRAC Project Documents.

The large difference in materials and supplies costs between Majikganj and Sulla Phase III is largely because of the plan to provide an intensive health and family planning coverage in Sulla and to build a base stock of supplies prior to BRAC withdrawal from the area at the end of Phase III. In both cases, the costs under this category would have been higher without the provision for recovery of drug costs from the patients. (Total drug costs are to be recovered in Sulla and 50 percent in Manikganj through insurance charges and service fees.) Without these provisions the costs would have gone up to Tk 1.6 million and Tk 250,000 respectively in Sulla and Manikganj.

The category "other costs" includes two major items--staff travel and staff training. Staff travel is generally calculated to be about 20 percent of salaries for all personnel with supervisory roles. Training and retraining constitute a substantial expenditure item for all field level personnel. In the case of Sulla Phase III this category includes the costs for functional education and village workshops, whereas functional education costs at least partially fall under "grants to local organizations" that are expected to carry out this activity in Manikganj. The large expenditure under this category for Training Centre obtains because the maintenance of trainees while resident in the Centre is a substantial cost item.

The loan fund for cooperatives and other group economic enterprises is smaller for Sulla than for Manikganj because it is expected that commercial banks will be found interested in extending credit to groups in Sulla under BRAC guarantee. The amount provided in the budget represents the write-off cost for bad debts (up to 20 percent of the total loans). In Manikganj, the loans are to be provided from BRAC's own funds.

Grants to local organizations of youth, women, and landless represent a new program approach that emphasizes the important role of local organizations and local self-management of group activities. The grants are to be provided as seed money for projects to be planned and implemented by the local organization. This approach, according to the budget figures, seems to be more vigorously pursued in Manikganj.

Major Program Items

Table 8.2 shows the major program items in the budgets for the three main sub-projects of BRAC--Sulla Phase II (concluded in 1975), Sulla Phase III and Manikganj (both begun in 1976). Health care and family planning clearly constitutes the most important component in all three sub-projects judged by budget expenditures. The budget for this component has gone up from under 21 percent of the total in Sulla Phase II to about 36 percent in Sulla Phase III. It is comparably high in Manikganj with 29 percent of the total allocation.

A comparison of the budgets of Sulla Phase II and the two other sub-project budgets indicates a trend toward a diffusion of the demarcations of sectoral activities and more emphasis on organizations and groups of the beneficiary populations rather than separate sectoral activities. This trend is more marked in Manikganj than in Sulla Phase III, probably because it was more difficult for Sulla Phase III to depart radically from Phase II patterns than for Manik-Ganj, a new sub-project.

Table 8.2

Major Items of Expenditure for
Three BRAC Sub-Projects

Sulla Phase II (Actual Nov. '72-Dec. '75)		
Items	Taka	Percentage
Construction of Community Centers	304 308	7.9
Functional Literacy	428 825	11.1
Cooperative Development	400 831	10.4
Agriculture	683 466	17.6
Fisheries	132 460	3.4
Health Care	438 254	11.3
Family Planning	367 371	9.5
Field Organization (Salaries and Staff Support)	445 301	11.5
Head Office (Staff and Logistics)	545 063	14.1
General Capital Expenses	125 779	3.2
Totals	3 871 658	100.0

Sulla Phase III (Budget for Jan. '76-Dec. '78)		
Institutional Development (Functional Education, Village Workshops and Staff Support)	930 240	15.4
Health and Family Planning	2 160 140	35.9
Disadvantaged Groups Programs (Landless, Women, Fishermen, Loan Guarantee Schemes, Grants, Staff Support)	931 240	15.5
Agricultural Development (Seed Multiplication, Veterinary Service, Staff Support)	636 080	10.6
Field Organization (General Staff Salaries and General Costs)	794 880	13.2
Head Office (Staff and Logistics)	520 992	8.6
General Capital Expenses	50 000	0.8
Totals	6 023 572	100.0

Manikganj (Budget for Jan. '76-Dec. '78)		
Health and Family Planning	1 136 400	28.7
Grants to Local Organizations (Youth, Landless, Women)	465 000	11.8
Cooperative Loan Fund	500 000	12.6
Field Organization (Salaries, except Health and FP Staff, Staff Support and other General Field Costs)	880 920	22.3
Head Office (Staff and Logistics)	491 000	12.4
Capital Costs (other than Health)	480 000	12.2
Totals	3 953 320	100.0

Source: BRAC Project Documents.

Functional education and other training and educational activities (including village workshops in Sulla) remain a central element in the two recent sub-projects. It is not a separate line item in Manikganj budget because
much of the educational activities, as noted above, are to be carried out by
local organizations with BRAC staff support; hence the costs are included under organizational grants and general field organization costs.

The field organization costs in Manikganj are relatively larger than the
others because all staff costs in Manikganj (except health workers) are included under this item, whereas some of the staff costs in Sulla Phase III are
shown under separate program costs. Manikganj actually has, on the whole, a
smaller paid staff relative to the size of the sub-project.

Overall Size of Operation

Overall size of the BRAC operation is indicated by the total annual noncapital expenditure during the financial year 1975-76. The total came to
approximately 4.9 million Taka with the following breakdown:

Sulla Project	Tk 1 600	Thousand
Manikganj Project	1 000	"
Works Program	545	"
Jamalpur Project	130	"
Shaturia Youth Project	175	"
Gonokendro (monthly publication)	430	"
Materials Development Unit	400	"
Research and Evaluation	200	"
Mothers' Club Development	120	"
Training Program	300	"
Total	4 900	"

The capital assets of BRAC in early 1976 were valued at approximately
1.8 million Taka, divided equally between fixed assets in the form of land
(on the project sites and land purchased for the training center, the future
BRAC head office and the BRAC printing plant) and movable assets. The capital assets in 1976 included the following:

Land	Tk	922 000
River Crafts and other Vehicles		87 000
Camp Houses		388 000
Furniture		109 000
Office Equipment		148 000
Other Equipment and Machinery		232 000
Total		1 836 000

The above figures do not include approximately 400,000 taka spent toward
site preparation and construction of the training center and the printing
press building in 1976. BRAC also received shipment of the printing plant
equipment worth US$117,000 in 1976 which was still to be installed.

Dependence on External Sources

BRAC--of which the staff, management and leadership are wholly indigenous--is totally dependent on external support for both the operational expenses of all of the project activities and for building up the capital assets. The organization, as we have noted, originated as an instrument for distributing relief supplies provided by private relief organizations from abroad; but as its role changed into that of a rural development agency--with sympathetic backing and encouragement of the donors who originally supplied the relief materials--BRAC remained dependent on the outside donors for carrying out the new development-oriented activities.

BRAC has succeeded in attracting the support and assistance of a large number of external assistance agencies of different types which include secular philanthropy, religious charity, foundations, international agencies, and government aid agencies. The most consistent and the largest donors have been the different branches of Oxfam in U.K., USA, and Canada. The religious charities include Novib of Holland and Bread for the World of Germany. Inter Pares of Canada, a secular philanthropy, has also provided funds. The Canadian International Development Agency (CIDA) has given support towards establishing the printing press. United Nations Children's Fund has financed the publication of the monthly Gonokendro. The Ford Foundation has given a grant for carrying out a research and evaluation project.

Overall Cost Feasibility

The cost of the second phase of Sulla, as we have noted, was about Tk 4 million over three years; or about Tk 11 per capita per year for the 120,000 people in the project area. The budgets of Sulla Phase III and the Manikganj project are of the same order of magnitude (Tk 6 million and Tk 4 million respectively over three years with 100,000 people in the BRAC project area of Manikganj thana).

The absolute per capita amount of money spent in the projects, given their scope and objectives, is obviously small. It may be argued that the project activities do not directly benefit the total population of the respective areas and, therefore, the denominator in the calculation of per capita cost should not be the total population of the area. On the other hand, the same argument is applicable to most rural development programs including the government ones. By way of comparison, it may be noted that per capita government expenditure for the whole country in 1975-76 for health and family planning was Tk 10.[1] Since then, the government budget, particularly for family planning, has been boosted substantially by external assistance. The proposed population control and family planning budget of the government for a two-year plan covering 1978-79 and 1979-80 announced in September 1977

---

[1]However, most of this amount was spent for curative services and medical facilities in the urban areas. See Oscar Gish, "The Development of Health Services in Bangladesh," Institute of Development Studies, University of Sussex, February 1976.

is Tk 3,040 million or about Tk 20 per capita per year. BRAC activities cannot be seen as supplanting government agencies and services, but BRAC has attempted to fill critical gaps in rural services and institutional development at costs that appear to compare favorably with the costs of government programs.

It has been noted in chapter 7 that the organizational approach envisaged for primary health care including family planning, if implemented successfully, will permit the health care program to be self-financed to the extent of two-thirds of the cost at the community level. The remaining one-third (about Tk 6) needed from extra-community sources is well within the range of the growing per capita health and family planning expenditure of the government, if the government funds are redirected towards the provision of primary health care in the rural areas.

Mobilization of financial, material, and human resources from the communities for community programs is a principle to which BRAC has been attaching increasing importance and which it has been attempting to apply with vigor in the newer projects as the discussion of the institutional structures in chapter 7 shows. It is, however, not BRAC's premise that rural people living in absolute poverty can lift themselves up from their condition by their own bootstraps without substantial assistance from outside the rural community.

Future Outlook

What is the future resource outlook for BRAC? Is BRAC to be permanenly dependent on external sources of support for carrying out its development activities?

It has been noted that in the Sulla II health care program BRAC has recovered about half of the cost of drugs--the major cost component of health care--through the insurance scheme. The goal for the third phase of Sulla is to recover the total drug cost by improving the coverage and operation of the insurance scheme. The Manikganj project has a similar eventual objective.

As the third phase plans of the Sulla Project indicate, it is BRAC's expectation in each project area to develop the local institutional structures to a level that will enable BRAC to withdraw its own personnel from the project, letting the local institutions manage the development and service activities with their own resources and such government and outside subsidies as they can attract on their own. The problems and prospects of realizing this outcome are discussed in other parts of this paper.

Another important step taken by BRAC is to build an accumulation of capital assets that will provide a core of permanent financial support. To this end a relatively large printing press is being set up at a total cost of approximately US$170,000 (site, plant and machinery), which will serve BRAC's own printing and publishing needs and is expected to generate an annual net earning of Tk 1 million for BRAC. This site will also house BRAC's head offices, effecting substantial savings in costly rentals.

With the establishment of the new Training and Resource Centre facilities outside Dacca, including residential accommodation for trainees, the center is expected to devote at least one-half of the training activities to serving other organizations in Bangladesh and to exact appropriate fees for these services.

If these expectations are fulfilled, it will mean that BRAC will be able to maintain from its own resources its organizational existence, support a core of permanent professional staff, and carry on essential follow-up of its earlier projects. This will be no small achievement. However, it also means that for undertaking new development projects or extending the scope of present activities geographically, BRAC will have to depend on external sources of support.

This situation does not necessarily portend a bleak future for BRAC. If philanthropic assistance from the industrial countries to the poor nations continues at least at the present level and if BRAC continues to prove itself to be a relatively effective voluntary agency capable of making good use of resources entrusted to it, it should not have any great difficulty in attracting sufficient financial support.

The purpose of our review and analysis of the BRAC rural development activities is to draw appropriate conclusions and lessons about the important questions that inevitably arise in the course of designing and implementing programs to serve the rural poor. As a rural development program focusing on the disadvantaged groups in the rural population, BRAC's own efforts to tackle the problems of planning and managing a multifaceted program are expected both to clarify the nature of the issues relating to these programs and to indicate the approaches to resolving the issues.

The questions that prompted this case study and others in the ICED series, we might recall, are the following:

-- How can the individual and fragmented activities be integrated into a concerted development process aimed at improving the life of rural families?

-- How can the usual "top-down" approach of rural programs be reversed and how can the rural people and communities effectively participate in the programs?

-- How can the educational processes be effectively used to improve the performance of the development programs and to enhance integration and community participation?

-- How can the development programs extend their reach and benefits to the poor and the underprivileged segments of rural communities?

-- How can voluntary organizations best utilize their unique advantages and become the precursors and demonstrators of new approaches for larger public programs?

In attempting to arrive at answers to these questions, one cannot help asking what difference the BRAC efforts have made to the life of the people in the project area. As the preceding sections of this report must have indicated, this straightforward question does not have a simple answer because the BRAC undertaking is complex, its goals are diverse in scope and quality, it has been in existence for a relatively short time, and the one-to-three-year time-scale of the financial donors supporting specific project activities does not provide an adequate basis for judging the impact of the program. One may, however, appropriately point to the factual evidences relating to BRAC performance in the Sulla Project area where BRAC has functioned the longest and where, at the time of this writing, one development phase has been concluded and another phase is well underway. The important indicators of BRAC performance during the three years of the second phase in Sulla are noted below.

At the cost of a major share of the total financial resources and over one-half of the manpower in the project area, the health and family planning program achieved the participation of approximately 15,000 residents (out of a total of over 120,000) in the health insurance scheme and reached a level of about 2,000 (out of an estimated potential number of 20,000) married women of child-bearing age as acceptors of a family planning method. The tangible impact of this service coverage after three years of operation in terms of health and family planning status of the population appears to be marginal. Although pre-project benchmark data were not available for comparison, statistical evidences of mortality and morbidity for mid-1975 and demographic information for early 1976 do not suggest a significant improvement when these indicators are compared with national statistics. Obviously, the health care program has not had the opportunity by 1976 to provide a sufficiently widespread, sustained, and intensive service to make a dent on the health situation. Similarly, the cumulative acceptor figure in the family planning program is not large enough or does not represent a retention pattern of sufficient duration (most being acceptors for less than a year) to mark an impact on the demographic situation.

About 2,600 project area residents participated in the functional education program and about one-half of this number is reported to have completed the lessons. We are not sure, however, what the completion of the course means in terms of new skills, knowledge, and attitudes. Most of the completers do not appear to have acquired a usable level of reading and writing skills, nor is there evidence (as far as the implementation of the program in Sulla Phase II is concerned) that any systematic effort was made to help the learners make the connection between the lessons and individual and collective self-help projects. Methodology and content of the functional education program was a distinct improvement over the traditional adult literacy efforts, but during Phase II of Sulla an effective approach was yet to be developed of making functional education truly functional, that is of its having a significant bearing on the current circumstances and future life prospects of the participants.

The agricultural promotion activities benefited less than 1,000 households, including 600 farmers in the "support blocks" and 300 landless laborers, although the extent of improvement in the economic status of these households was not clear from available information. Another 10,000 families were reported to have benefited from the distribution of vegetable seeds and fruit plants and saplings.

The effort to help improve the status of women through conventional skill training did not succeed and was abandoned in favor of more systematically organized collective economic and self-help projects through cooperatives and joint savings. It was possible to organize only a small number of such group activities by the end of the second phase of Sulla. BRAC also encouraged the

formation of more traditional farmers' cooperatives and assisted in improving
the performance of the existing ones. BRAC's efforts created a firm base for
the extension of the government's Integrated Rural Development Program (centered on a two-tier structure of primary cooperatives and a central association
of the primary societies) to the project area. The cooperatives facilitated
the supply and distribution of agricultural inputs for the members; however,
the total number of beneficiaries was small and the cooperative structure was
yet to take a firm root, expand its coverage, and become the main instrument
for agricultural and rural transformation that it was intended to be.

It should be noted along with this catalog of achievements and nonachieve-
ments that the total time-span of the second phase of Sulla was about three
years (and considerably less for some of the component activities), the total
financial resources committed were less than Tk 4 million, and the involved
BRAC staff comprised less than 100 young people--most without any professional
expertise or high level training.

The most enduring achievement of the Sulla project so far is to be found,
not in the quantitative record of performance of the sectoral activities, but
rather in the fact that it brought to the surface various problems of development programs intended to help the rural poor, established a base of institutional structures and experienced personnel, and pointed the direction to be
taken in reshaping and reorienting the program during the third phase of Sulla
and in other new projects. The questions raised above can be fruitfully explored if we look at the BRAC experience in this light--as a continuous striving towards the development of a viable integrated approach for helping the
needy and disadvantaged to help themselves through collective efforts.

The Integrated Development Approach

BRAC recognized the need and significance of an integrated approach and
in pursuing this approach put different rural development components together
in the Sulla Project. However, the resources and manpower committed to   the
project did not permit a sufficient participation of the people in the project
area needing the various services offered by the project. The program management also did not provide for the mutual linkages and reinforcement of   the
different program activities essential for an integrated approach. The result
was a series of parallel sectoral activities with only incidental overlap   to
the beneficiaries.

The program approach taken was an identification of certain general needs
of the population and an attempt to meet them with a number of sectoral activities devised by the prevalent conventional wisdom about what constituted   a
rural development program. The needs that were identified (such as basic healt
care, agricultural development, functional education, cooperatives and so on)
were genuine enough in a general sense, and a certain number of the project
population undoubtedly benefited from the services provided; but, as we have
seen, the program after three years of operation of its developmental phase has
not brought about a major improvement in the quality of life of a significant
proportion of the population--least of all, in the life of the poorest groups.
Evidently the project activities needed to be tailored specifically to the
needs of specific groups (especially if the purpose was to help the economically weaker and the disadvantaged sections of the community) but also made
flexible enough in different combinations of components for a variety of groups

Apparently the assumption behind the sectoral activities undertaken was
that the individual participant, in assimilating their separate benefits
would somehow effect an integration of them in terms of his own plan for
managing his resources and improving his socioeconomic situation.   This
assumption was probably valid for those who were economically and socially
in a relatively advantageous position. The sectoral approach (in contrast
to the "people approach") inevitably gravitated towards a norm of operational goals and patterns that benefited the easily reachable and the relatively better-off at the cost of the disadvantaged.

In operational terms, a shift of emphasis from separate sectoral activities to an integrated "people"   approach means that different relatively
homogenous socioeconomic groups have to be identified and organizational
structures developed accordingly. This is the logical approach when the
goal is to help the disadvantaged groups rather than to offer a series of
services for the benefit of the general public. This is the approach towards which BRAC appears to have moved for the third phase of the Sulla
Project and for other new projects.

Integrated rural development (in contrast to the parallel functioning
of sectoral activities in the same geographical location or the coordination of different sectoral activities through various administrative
devices) requires a focus on the participant population--their circumstances, their own perception of their critical needs, and their preference
and values. The implication of this premise for national rural development
efforts is that, instead of attempting to reach the rural population   with
vertical sectoral programs, a means must be found to form local organizations of homogeneous interest groups and make them serve as the instrument
for integrating and managing the sectoral activities of the beneficiary
population. A strong local government structure, adequately representative of the total rural population, can become a mechanism for coordination
among the network of local organizations and institutions and for mediation
between the local groups and the higher tiers of government agencies at the
regional and national levels.

Since health care and family planning have been implemented in BRAC virtually as one sub-program, a question of particular interest is how this
integration has affected the performance of both health care and family planning activities. One may also ask what the consequences might be for health
care and family planning performance under a more effective overall integration of the different components of BRAC.

We have to admit that a definitive and totally unequivocal conclusion in
this regard cannot be drawn from the BRAC experience. BRAC obtained certain
results by organizing the health care and family planning services in a particular way, important features of which were the following: (a) the medical
and clinical backup of the family planning services was provided by the health
care staff and facilities; (b) at the field level, special family planning
workers were used for contact with clients and distribution of contraceptives
but they were under the direct and close supervision of the paramedics who
also played an important motivational role regarding family planning;   and
(c) the local people perceived the two activities as related--BRAC's medical
services being the most well-known and widespread of all BRAC activities--
and knew that for any medical problem arising from the acceptance of family
planning, they could get help from BRAC medical service.

We do not know what the results would be if a family planning program were
not backed by the health service, not identified with a multifaceted rural development program, and only had community-based field agents with supervision
and backstopping provided by the family planning organization itself. The government family planning program is run along this line (though, in principle,
maternity and child health care is regarded as a part of the family planning
program), and its performance so far compares less than favorably with the BRAC
program. But because of its many management and logistical problems, the government program, at least at the present time, is not a good example of a "single-
purpose" family planning program and does not provide a good basis for comparison

While a "proof" cannot be offered on the basis of BRAC experience in favor
of or against a combined health and family planning program or a more integrated
approach, a number of pertinent factors must be taken into account in considering the issue. First, given the evidence regarding prenatal deaths of women and
high postnatal infant and children's mortality, a high rate of births per child-
bearing age women, and a large family size are themselves serious health problems
as far as the mothers and children are concerned. Second, it imposes an unafford-
able and unnecessary economic burden on poor countries to duplicate the technical
and professional support manpower and support facilities for both family planning
and primary health care. Third, the problem of establishing credibility and inspiring confidence about the family planning program is more easily overcome when
it is offered in conjunction with activities that meet the perceived needs about
health problems.

The basic question, however, is not one of the technical efficiency of the
single-purpose approach (on which ground alone the case for it is argued), but
of values regarding all development efforts--whether the concern is about meeting certain sectoral quantitative targets or improving the welfare of people.
The question needs to be posed in this stark form to get at the heart of the
integration issue, and it needs to be underscored that reduction of population
growth and gaining acceptance of the norm of a small family size are not ends
in themselves. (It is, by no means, certain that even on technical efficiency
grounds the single-purpose approach is superior.)

In a similar vein, it may be argued that health and family planning efforts
will be better accepted, will have a more sustained impact, and will achieve
goals in line with the preference and the value system of the beneficiary population if implementation of these efforts is made a component of the collective
and organized self-help activities that improve the socioeconomic situation of
homogeneous rural interest groups. In other words, the health care and family
planning program is likely to be more effective if the rural communities themselves can take charge of planning and managing the delivery end of the services,
in the context of tackling other survival and development problems, with appropriate technical assistance and resource support from the higher tiers of government and other external sources.

Community Participation

Despite the intentions and efforts behind the functional education program
and the formation of cooperatives, community participation was not   a strong
feature of the early phase of BRAC. The sectoral approach it adopted and the
heavy reliance on its own relatively large field organization for management

and implementation of the sectoral activities undermined the principles of
community participation.

Community participation has many dimensions which, in the context of
a program to help the disadvantaged sections of the rural community, might
well include the following: (a) organizing services in the community on a
community basis and making the services widely and easily accessible; (b)
contribution by the community to the operation and maintenance of the services; (c) participation of the community in planning and management of the
services within the community; (d) community input in overall strategies,
policies, and work plan of the development program transcending individual
communities; and (e) overcoming factionalism and interest conflicts in the
community to achieve broad-based participation, particularly of the disadvantaged groups.

Participation of the beneficiary population in a development program
along these dimensions is essentially a problem of building local organizations and institutional structures in such a way that participation is
a significant and meaningful contribution rather than a token gesture.
This in turn raises the problems of rationale for forming viable local
organizations, the best approch to mobilizing people for collective action and creating a "consciousness" about collective or class identity
and class interests, and the best means for building the necessary competence and capacity for collective action.

In rural societies characterized by peasant farming and large segments
of landless and other disadvantaged groups, creation of participatory institutions and promotion of the participatory process require basic changes
in the overall configuration of the intergroup social and economic relationships. For instance, the participatory institutions must overcome the entrenched factionalism in village communities that are nurtured by powerful
and influential families and groups; break the semi-feudal patron-client
bondage; and give the disadvantaged groups the self-confidence, hope, and
courage that will convince them of their collective strength.

There is need for a clear conceptualization of the participatory process and its goals in a given rural context. A strategy for identifying
and forming the homogeneous interest groups must be determined, activities
must be devised and implemented that are within group capacity but also
strike at the root of their subjugation and deprivation. The educational
process becomes a central element in this strategy.

Ensuring participation in all its dimensions, as the evolution of the
Sulla Project and the plans for other new projects indicate, calls for a
lessening of emphasis on the sectoral approach and building an organizational
structure that, instead of managing the program for the beneficiary population,
permits the growth of the local groups towards greater self-reliance and autonomy. As we have noted earlier, the sectoral approach and an organizational
model that inhibits popular control of the development program tend to go
hand-in-hand; conversely, effective integration and meaningful participation
are like two sides of the same coin.

Finally, the efforts to promote participation can succeed only with
unambigious commitment on the part of the development agency, whether a
voluntary organization or a government department, to serve the interests

of the disadvantaged groups--the landless farm workers, women from poor families, young people, small farmers, and rural artisans struggling to eke out a   living from traditional occupations.

Education

BRAC's program approach is distinguished by the systematic use of varied educational approaches in support of its objectives. Three major categories of educational activities in BRAC are: (a) programs for the beneficiary population with the aim of raising their levels of awareness and understanding and making them better participants in the development activities, such as functional education and village workshops; (b) devices that develop the special skills and competence of specialized program workers, such as paramedics, village health auxiliaries, family planning workers, cooperative accountants, instructors for poultry raising, functional education teachers, and so on; and (c) training for general BRAC field workers and potential youth group organizers.

Given the overall goals of supporting self-sustaining development and helping the rural poor, it was no surprise that the conventional literacy program launched by BRAC did not serve its purpose. The program was quickly abandoned and a new functional education approach was introduced. The new program was marked by substantial innovation in methodology, content material, and relevance to the learner's life. Apparently, even this, a series of prestructured lessons taught through a relatively standardized pedagogical approach to a group formed without any specific rationale, was not adequately functional as far as the life of most of the learners was concerned. BRAC recognized that the functional education learning groups had to be formed with people who had common socioeconomic interests and that the educational program must be linked more directly and intimately with collective development action. This is the direction that had been taken by the functional education activities in the newer BRAC projects. "Consciousness raising" and engaging in collective self-help action had gained precedence over the traditional goals of acquiring literacy and numeracy skills, although these were not seen as alternatives. Village workshops introduced in Sulla could be described as a form of relatively unstructured functional education without the literacy and numeracy content and reflected a concern about making the educational program an active instrument for promoting development action.

The evolution of the functional education program in BRAC suggests that the lessons and the methodology of the functional education course cannot be inserted into any situation and expected to promote development, unless the particular situation permits the formation of relatively homogeneous interest groups and unless the atmosphere exists for using the educational program to plan and initiate collective self-help activities.

In the training of health workers and other field-level specialized personnel, BRAC evolved a low-cost but effective formula by shunning the trappings of such conventional training programs as classroom lectures, theoretical studies, highly structured syllabuses, full-time professional trainers, and special training facilities. It relied on supervised apprenticeship in real-life work situations followed by adequate technical support when the apprentices took independent responsibilities. BRAC also demonstrated that with continuous technical backup, people of both sexes, varied socioeconomic background, and little or no formal education could be entrusted with specialized development functions. Even with the "informal" training approach, a large variety of com-

petence and skills (such as those of paramedics, shevikas, and LFPOs) could
be differentiated and developed as demanded by the circumstances.

It might be noted that paramedics, with their short informal training,
would probably not be recognized as "paraprofessionals" by government standards, although even they could not be afforded at the base of the service
delivery system--hence another layer of auxiliaries, the shevikas.   This
raises questions about the manpower policies and training requirements of
government programs that raise public costs and make services out of the
reach of the rural people. An alternative model of manpower development
and utilization deserves serious consideration and trial, one that relies
on practical apprenticeship and relatively intensive technical supervision
as the basic approach for all field level workers of development services.

For the improvement of skills and competence of general field level
workers BRAC has moved from an informal   on-the-job learning approach to
a more systematic training program. This appears to be in part the result
of the accumulated BRAC experience in the field that has led to the identification of certain skills and knowledge that need to be developed by all
field workers and for which a training process may be devised. The emphasis on a special training program also reflects a shift in the program
approach away from a large BRAC field organization to a greater reliance
on the leaders of local organizations. The local group leaders are not
full-time BRAC workers and, unlike BRAC's own full-time field agents, are
not under the continuous supervision and guidance of BRAC personnel.

It is evident that the rural development approach of BRAC requires the
field workers--whether full-time members of BRAC staff or members of local
organizations--to acquire basic skills and understand the communication
process, group dynamics, survey and analysis of the local socioeconomic
situation, planning group projects, following through the implementation
steps of a plan and assessing results, and the use of the functional education approach for initiating and organizing collective self-help efforts.

Programs that are relatively large in size or are expanding to new geographical areas and programs that are concerned with developing local leadership and agents of change cannot entirely rely on an informal apprenticeship
approach. A more systematic and somewhat institutionalized training process
becomes inevitable. Any application of the BRAC program strategies in government programs is hardly possible without a well-organized training program
for workers.

What needs to be watched is that the training program, with special
physical facilities and a full-time staff, does not become an artificially
contrived and sterile process removed from the realities that the field
workers would face in the villages. As for the skills and understanding
required to be developed by field workers, institutionalized training cannot be seen as a full substitute for learning from practical apprenticeship and experience. The training program can at best complement such
learning or prepare the new field workers to benefit more fully from on-
the-job experience. The training programs, therefore, are likely to be
effective only under certain conditions: if the inherent limitations of the
structured training courses are recognized, a balance is maintained between
institutionalized training and the practical apprenticeship approach, and a
recurrent approach is followed through short intermittent courses permitting

the field workers to come back periodically to the training center and the
trainers to rotate between field work and training. In such a scheme, the
training interlude can be the occasion to analyze the collective experience
of the field workers, to examine the applicability of general principles in
specific situations, and to devise new solutions for specific problems.

If the training program for general field workers--as opposed to specific
training for technical skills such as maintaining the books of the cooperative
society or artificial insemination of cattle--is seen as an integral and inter-
acting element of a development program, it would be difficult to offer "pre-
packaged" courses for the workers of different organizations with varying objectives and philosophic rationale. There are, of course, certain technical
contents in training "modules" on communication or group dynamics that may be
helpful for all rural development workers. However, as in the case of functional education, the effectiveness of the training of field workers is bound
to be minimized when training as a recurrent process is not linked directly
with the development actions in which the field workers are engaged.

Reaching the Poorest

Poverty, whether defined in terms of a minimum per capita income or access
to a set of basic goods and services, is pervasive in rural Bangladesh.   One-
half to three-quarters of the rural population, depending on the estimate of income or consumption level considered necessary to rise above the poverty line,
live in poverty. But among the poor, some are poorer than others. The hardest
hit groups, living virtually on the fringe of physical survival, are the families of the landless farm laborers, the destitute women without able-bodied
males in the family, and members of certain traditional artisan castes (such
as potters, weavers, cobblers) for whom the economic base of the occupation has
eroded because of problems of market, raw materials, and competition from industry

Despite the avowed concern for the poorest, in the early phase of Sulla
there seems to have been insufficient attention to the differentiation of the
relative levels of poverty among the total population; the varying socioeconomic circumstances of such groups as the landless laborers, the destitute
women, and the unemployed artisans; and the need for different program strategies for improving their situation. In the later phase of Sulla and in the new
project activities of BRAC, there is a much greater awareness of the relative
levels of deprivation among the poor and the need for a sharper focus on the
most deprived groups as reflected in the emphasis on mobilizing functional interest groups for collective self-help activities.

Available evidence, as we have noted earlier, shows that the general development services of BRAC--health care, family planning and functional education--as
sectoral activities (and not integrated with the collective self-help projects of
homogeneous interest groups) have benefited the relatively better-off sections of
the rural population more than the poorest. The agricultural support activities
and the promotion of farmers' cooperatives, for inherent reasons, have also helped
the less poor among the rural population.

Given the fact that cultivable land, the most important productive resource
in the rural areas, is owned and controlled by a relatively small minority that
also enjoys the social, economic, and political power derived from this control,
it is inevitable that the benefits of any general development program will be
shared disproportionately by the powerful minority, unless ways are found to con-

centrate the program efforts on the specific needs of the poorest. A general
development program for improving agricultural production and providing essential social services can benefit the total rural community only if a large
section of the community is not left out of the control and utilization of the
productive resources of the community. This apparently has been recognized by
BRAC, and its project activities have shifted towards more selective activities
focusing on the most disadvantaged and deprived groups of the rural population.

The selective focus on the poorest groups has its inherent limitations as
long as this happens in the context of existing production and power relationships in the rural community. It will take hard work and imaginative approaches
to make the poorest groups participants and beneficiaries of the social services
such as health care, family planning and education. But with the scarce productive resources (land being controlled by a section of the community and economic opportunities in general being limited), it is difficult to visualize more
than marginal improvement in the economic situation of the most deprived groups.
Insignificant progress on the economic front, in turn, is likely to undermine
the efforts to widen participation in the social services. This is the fundamental reality that BRAC efforts bring to the surface and has to be faced by
all rural development agencies and the national policymakers.

Special Role of Voluntary Organizations

Small-scale development programs managed by voluntary organizations have
well recognized advantages of flexibility and freedom from bureaucracy   that
large public programs normally do not enjoy. Voluntary organizations are also
able to select the scope of their activities, the geographical locations   for
the programs, and their participants to a much greater extent than public programs. Voluntary agencies also tend to attract idealistic and well-motivated
people as paid and unpaid workers in their development activities. All   of
these favorable factors make it possible for voluntary programs to vary program approaches for specific locations and clienteles within the same project,
modify initial plans in the light of experience, and take quick policy decisions when necessary. The evolution of BRAC's program approach from relatively
conventional sectoral activities to a development approach concentrating on the
promotion of local self-help groups on the basis of the early Sulla experience
is a demonstration of the special strength of the voluntary programs.   This
change came about without the fanfare of formal evaluation studies or   review
missions of international experts—not that systematic evaluation of projects
is unnecessary.

The unique characteristics of the small-scale nongovernment programs make
them good instruments for testing and developing innovative ideas and approaches
that may be difficult to try within the constraints of public programs. Many
program ideas already applied in the various sub-projects of the multifaceted
BRAC program suggest themselves as good candidates for testing for their potential adoption or adaptation into government programs on a large scale.   Of
course, apart from their inevitable bureaucratic tendencies, the government
programs do not enjoy the flexibility of the voluntary organizations; therefore, straight transplantation of certain elements of the voluntary program
into the government program is almost never advisable.

A practical way of transferring lessons learned in voluntary programs
to government programs would be for the government and the voluntary organization to embark on a kind of "joint venture" in the shape of pilot

projects in one or more specific locations.

Once the viability of an approach is demonstrated in small-scale programs and some basic criteria of viability and feasibility (such as compatibility of objectives between the private program and a national program) for a large-scale expansion appear likely to be met, a pilot phase can be initiated on the basis of close collaboration between the government and the voluntary organization in a limited area (preferably in a standard territorial unit of administration, such as a thana). The objective of such a venture would be two-fold: first, to test and develop the specific adaptations and modifications of the approach of the small program inevitably needed for a national and public program; and second, to work out the operational steps for moving beyond the pilot phase and to use the pilot phase for training and orientation of the government functionaries in anticipation of further expansion of the approach. The government, obviously, has to be enthusiastically committed to giving the pilot project a fair trial and to following it up appropriately. The voluntary organization, on its part, should be appreciative of the problems of national programs and large bureaucracies and be willing to be flexible without sacrificing the essence of its own approach.

Besides being the testing ground for innovative techniques in integrated rural development, an equally significant potential role of voluntary organizations is that of an institutional mechanism complementary to the local government structure. The government rural development approach in Bangladesh, represented by the Integrated Rural Development Project (IRDP), visualizes a strong thana-level development guidance and coordination body composed of elected representatives and government personnel as the means for decentralizing development responsibilities. As we have noted, it is also BRAC's expectation that a thana-level apex organization representing various primary cooperatives and organizations in the villages will eventually take over the support and coordination of local development projects and services, permitting BRAC to dismantle its own field organization. Whether this institutional design for rural development will be effectively established and whether it will serve the interests of all the rural people including the poorest instead of being captured by the powerful minority will depend on the success of the efforts to mobilize and organize the local interest groups of the deprived and the disadvantaged.

If BRAC, through its projects for "conscientizing" and generating homogeneous interest groups of the poor for collective self-help activities, can demonstrate a feasible approach for organizing the poor into constituent primary interest groups (and, to a degree, a countervailing political force) for the local government and local development coordination body, it will be a far-reaching contribution to building an effective rural development strategy. The mobilization of the poor for self-help also opens up the possibility of conflicts between the organized poor and others who would want to retain their control over the local institutions. The rights and interests of the poor majority cannot be safeguarded without facing this possibility.

7 The Sarvodaya Movement: Self-Help Rural Development in Sri Lanka
Nandasena Ratnapala

EDITOR'S NOTE

This case study examines the well-known Sarvodaya Shramadana Movement in Sri Lanka from an unusual angle of vision—namely, from the village level looking up, rather than from the headquarters level looking down. This grassroots perspective provides unique insights into why the impact and staying power of the Sarvodaya Movement has been quite substantial in some villages but relatively limited in others. It also reveals how various features of Sarvodaya's administrative arrangements and staff training provisions have either helped or hampered its effectiveness at the village level. Although the findings are critical in certain respects, they in no way detract from the impressive overall record of achievement of the Sarvodaya Movement. Indeed, it is hoped that these findings may, in a modest way, contribute to making the future performance even more impressive.

When ICED's Pratima Kale first proposed this unconventional research approach to Mr. A. T. Ariyaratne, President and inspirational leader of the Sarvodaya Movement, he welcomed it enthusiastically, observing that his organization's structure and activities had never been assessed from this angle and that the findings would undoubtedly be useful.

The sample of seven villages selected for intensive study reflected wide differences of local conditions and a similarly wide diversity of Sarvodaya's experiences and impacts. Household surveys and interviews conducted in each village revealed, among other things, how various local residents perceived Sarvodaya's efforts and what value they placed on them. The local investigations also examined the historical evolution of the Movement in each village, how and to what extent it had taken root, what principal Sarvodaya activities had been initiated and how well each had prospered, who had provided the local leadership, what role Sarvodaya's trained workers had played, and other factors that appeared to have had a positive or negative influence.

In addition to the village studies, the research team observed activities and reviewed relevant documents and data at the Sarvodaya headquarters, the Research Centre, the Development Education Centre, and selected Gramodaya extension centers. They also held extensive discussions with Sarvodaya workers at all levels, with members of the Executive Council, and with Mr. A. T. Ariyaratne,

469

Sarvodaya's president.

The chief investigator and principal author of the report, to whom ICED is deeply indebted, was Dr. Nandasena Ratnapala of the Department of Sociology and Anthropology at the University of Sri Lanka's Vidyodaya Campus. His main assistant was Indra Wickramaratne, seconded from Sarvodaya's Research Centre in Colombo. Other members of his field research team included: H. Wijesuriya, Project Director, Family Planning Association, Colombo; Mahinda Ratnapala, Lecturer, Teachers Training College, Polgolle, Kandy; Edwin Ganihigama, Assistant Lecturer, Department of Sociology and Anthropology, Vidyodaya Campus, Nugegoda; Nandasena Gamachchige; Upali Mahagedaragamage, Research Assistant, National Heritage, Colombo; Daya Perera and H.M. Dharmadasa, Research Assistants, Sarvodaya Research Institute, Colombo; Devaviraj Peiris; and Wilbert Samarasinghe.

Manzoor Ahmed of ICED edited the final report as it appears here, based on Dr. Ratnapala's draft and the individual village studies. He also wrote the introductory chapter.

Although responsibility for the contents of the report rests solely with the author and ICED, it is appropriate here to acknowledge and express ICED's deep appreciation for the important contributions made by many others--including the various members of Dr. Ratnapala's team, Mr. Ariyaratne and various Sarvodaya staff members and, not least of all, the many Sri Lankan villagers who opened their hearts and minds to the visiting researchers.

INTRODUCTION*

Origins and Emphasis

The Sarvodaya Shramadana Movement of Sri Lanka has earned a well-deserved international reputation as a national development organization with many accomplishments. It originated some two decades ago from the sense of social responsibility and moral obligation of a small group of young teachers and students from Colombo who organized the first shramadana work camp in a "low-caste" village 58 miles from the capital city. Since that small beginning the Movement has grown into a national organization, articulated the philosophical basis and moral principles for a national development program, persuaded some 300,000 people to volunteer their time and labor for the Movement, and reached out in one form or another to 2,000 village communities all over the island.

The literal meaning of the organization's name--universal awakening through sharing of time, thought, and energy-indicates the emphasis placed on the spiritual and moral aspects of development at every level: the individual person, the community, the nation, and the world. It is recognized, however, that spiritual fulfillment cannot be achieved without meeting basic mundane needs. As A.T.Ariyaratne, the president of the Sarvodaya Movement, put it:

> In the ultimate analysis, the end result of social
> development is optimum happiness of man through spiritual

---

*The main body of this report was prepared by Nandasena Ratnapala of the University of Sri Lanka. This introductory chapter, however, was prepared by Manzoor Ahmed, Deputy Director of the ICED project.

fulfillment. But spiritual fulfillment can never come
about without adequate satisfaction of basic human needs.
Hence the Sarvodaya Shramadana Movement has harmonized
these two, by placing before the individual four principles of personality awakening; namely, respect for
life, compassionate action, joy of service and mental
equipoise. These principles are always applied to and
integrated with all developmental actions undertaken by
the Movement.[1]

Sympathetic observers of Sarvodaya admire the strength of the
Movement that is derived from spiritual and moral foundations
anchored in Buddhist philosophy and traditional cultural values
leavened by the principles of the Gandhian Independence Movement in
India. They also ask whether and to what degree spiritual fulfillment
and basic human needs have indeed been harmonized and whether and
how effectively the moral principles have been translated into
appropriate forms of development action. This case study of the
Sarvodaya program attempts to answer these questions, and in doing
so sheds light on some major concerns in all programs aimed at inducing self-sustaining socio-economic development among the disadvantaged segments of the population. A few of the major points
that emerge from the case study and are likely to be of interest
to readers are presented in these introductory comments.

It should be said at the outset that the founders of Sarvodaya
set for themselves an excruciatingly difficult goal--the goal of
elevating the condition and lifting the spirits of the poorest people
in the poorest village. In relation to today's internationally popular
rhetoric on improving the lot of the rural poor, Sarvodaya's experience
teaches one important lesson above all others. It is the simple but
profoundly important lesson that translating this rhetoric into
practical deeds and meaningful results is a far more difficult and
painstaking task than many users of this rhetoric may realize. Although the Sarvodaya Movement's progress toward this goal has been
outstanding by any normal standard, it has been a hard road and
the negative lessons of the experience are no less valuable than
the positive ones.

DECENTRALIZED PROGRAM MANAGEMENT, COMMUNITY PARTICIPATION AND SELF-RELIANT DEVELOPMENT

The principle of self-reliant development for communities is an
extension of the moral principle of one's personal obligation to
strive for self-fulfillment and to take responsibility for his spiritual and material well-being. The aim of promoting self-reliance
obviously requires a decentralized planning and management approach.
The management structure of Sarvodaya, however, is centralized with
major policy and program decisions concentrated in the central headquarters. The activities of the regional centers and the local
Gramodaya extension centers are guided and controlled by the central
program coordinators. This control has created a uniformity of program
approach and content, with an apparent dampening effect on local
initiatives.

In the sample villages examined by this study we see an almost
mechanical repetition of a pattern of program activities, clienteles,

---

[1]Ariyaratne, A.T., "Sarvodaya Shramadana Movement for Social
Development in Sri Lanka: A Study of Experience in Generating People's
Participation." Working paper prepared for United Nations Children's
Fund, April 1977.

methodologies, and organizations. The village activities are initiated and sustained by an alliance of the Sarvodaya worker from the regional extension center (or sometimes posted by the headquarters) and the village monk or priest. As long as both of them (or at least one of them) have a genuine interest in the Sarvodaya activities and can command confidence and respect among the village people, the Sarvodaya program continues with relative vigor and provides useful services to the villagers. However, when this external leadership is removed, the village program often loses vitality or continues in a somewhat moribund fashion. Rarely do the institutional capacities in the village community itself develop sufficiently to take over and run the program. The leadership training activities and the elaborate efforts to form various village organizations do not seem to have made a sufficient difference in this respect in many of the Sarvodaya villages.

The education and training activities of Sarvodaya are commented upon below. The village organizations for children, youth, mothers, farmers, family elders and so on--the ostensible vehicles for participation and self-management--do not appear to have matured as yet into viable instruments for self-management of community programs. Often only a fraction of the eligible community people has participated directly in the several group activities; indeed, most of the participants have remained only passive beneficiaries of services, and the organizations and their programs have been kept propped up by the Sarvodaya staff and the local monk rather than by the initiative of the local people.

The Sarvodaya experience, therefore, offers negative as well as positive lessons regarding community participation and self-reliant community development. The essence of these lessons is that mere leadership training courses for youth and a predetermined pattern of local organizations formed at the instigation of a voluntary organization that is external to the village community do not necessarily result in meaningful forms of community participation, nor do they initiate a self-reliant development process.

What might have been done in the situation Sarvodaya found itself in--a situation typical of rural areas in many poor countries--can only be speculated upon. One can seldom be sure of the right course until it is tried out, tested, and found to be working. We suggest three propositions.

Despite the universalist preachings of Sarvodaya, the rural participants in the village organizations have not been able to transcend their factional vested interests and conflicts to rally behind programs that make a real dent on the life of the disadvantaged members of the community. That is why there is much emphasis on innocuous and "harmless" service activities and not enough on significant economic programs that rescue the disadvantaged from their grinding penury and successfully combat the interests of the local traders, moneylenders, and landowners. It seems that some clear-cut choices will have to be made. To the degree that Sarvodaya seriously backs the poor, it will have to face the risk of opposition from the wealthy. Program activities that offer hope of substantial socioeconomic change in the lives of deprived groups will command their active support and very likely lay the basis for strong local organizations.

Organizations concentrating on social service activities that do not
address needs perceived to be critical by the deprived population
cannot attract the support and involvement necessary for building
effective self-management institutions.

As the author of the case study has suggested, decentralization
and capacity for local level management can probably be promoted by
identifying entrepreneurial skills in the communities, putting the
competent local people with such skills to work in program activities,
and utilizing them for developing further skills and competence among
other local personnel. This is not an easy task.

Certain changes can be adopted in the Sarvodaya organizational
structure to establish a greater measure of collegial relationship
between the headquarters coordinators and the field staff by delegating authority and responsibility, posting really outstanding personnel in the field, giving the field personnel status and rewards comparable to those of headquarters personnel, and by rotating personnel
between the field and headquarters.

IN PURSUIT OF AN INTEGRATED APPROACH

If the concept of integrated development embraces such elements
as an overall development strategy, a relationship of mutual reinforcement among different development activities, mobilization of all available resources, and participation of the beneficiary population in
planning and managing the activities, then the organizational structure Sarvodaya tries to build in each village should provide an ideal
setting for pursuing the integrated approach. Various functional groups
and the overarching village reawakening council, representing all
interest groups and all development and service agencies in the community including the government ones, in principle, create the participation and mobilization mechanisms for pursuing the goals of
integrated development.

For example, one notes with satisfaction that in some of the more
active Sarvodaya villages the organizations for youth and mothers have
become instrumental in initiating diverse community services by drawing upon the voluntary labor and enthusiasm of these groups. The
mothers' group and the preschool center have often brought the services
of the government health department to the village. The government
agricultural extension service has sometimes found a vehicle for
serving the rural residents in the young farmers' groups. The Sarvodaya
village council has sometimes served as the unofficial coordinator of
development activities undertaken by different government and private
agencies.

On the whole, however, the strength and character of the local
Sarvodaya organizations vary widely and achievement of an integrative
role has not been fully realized. The factors that have impeded the
growth of strong local organizations and discouraged autonomy and local
participation have also become obstacles to the integrated development
approach. For the absence of a broad community consensus about priorities and goals and commonality of interests, it is difficult to come
up with a village-wide development plan as the basis for an integrated
development program. Again it appears that Sarvodaya has first to
identify the disadvantaged groups in the rural areas, align itself
with these groups, and then develop concrete strategies to safeguard
and promote the social and economic rights and interests of these

groups. This means nothing less than facing the risk of opposition from other groups in the village. The integration of activities had to be predicated on the needs of the specific deprived groups rather than on much broader village or regional needs because the needs and interests of all the groups in the village are not the same. The application of the universalist principles of Sarvodaya has to be reassessed in order to make its development activities practical and truly effective.

A voluntary organization like Sarvodaya is subject to obvious limitations of resources, authority, and responsibility in pursuing an integrated development strategy. The most fruitful role it can play is to help build the institutional structures for participation of the local people and mobilization of the local resources. Local government bodies backed by appropriate national policies and programs must bear the burden of carrying out the development program. In Sri Lanka the national government is still in the process of evolving the structure, development functions, and authority of the local government bodies; and the priciples of a mutual working relationship between the local authorities and Sarvodaya are yet to be formally worked out. The relationship that exists now is contingent almost entirely on the individual personalities and attitudes of local government officials and Sarvodaya workers. The change in government in 1977 may have created an atmosphere for evolving a closer and more systematic working relationship at the local level between the government and Sarvodaya. It is reassuring that some thought is now being given by Sarvodaya leaders to collaboration with the government on preparing and implementing comprehensive development plans for Sarvodaya villages.

ROLE OF EDUCATION AND TRAINING

Inculcation of Values and Attitudes

As an ideological movement concerned with changing people's attitudes and values, all Sarvodaya activities are frankly educational. All components of the Sarvodaya program include elements of "consciousness raising," transmission of new information, and dissemination of new social attitudes and perceptions. The more the leaders and workers of the program are aware of the educational nature of the program and their own educational role, the more likely it is that the educational objective will be served. Effectiveness of the educational function in each program activity, whether it is a community kitchen or a young fishermen's group, affects the overall performance of the particular activity. On the other hand, the validity of the activity itself (for example, in terms of its objectives, clientele, and feasibility) and how successfully it is managed determine whether the activity will have an educational impact. A community kitchen, run poorly and irregularly, not perceived as an important need by the local people, cannot be a vehicle for spreading ideas of nutrition and sanitation, nor a means of stimulating local initiatives, community cooperation, and other useful ideas and practices.

Shramadana--the work camp through which Sarvodaya volunteers and villagers join together in an essential construction project--is the basic means for learning about village life, analyzing village problems and possibilities, and introducing Sarvodaya ideals and objectives to the villagers. With planning and guidance, it can be an intense educational experience for all concerned and exert a

strong impact on the nature and quality of the development efforts that
may follow in the village.

Besides the general "consciousness raising" and educational role
of the total Sarvodaya program, there are also three main categories of
specifically organized educational activities to which a large   proportion of the Sarvodaya resources and efforts are devoted. These are the
training of women for managing preschool centers and community kitchens,
the training of youth for community development work, and skill training.
Only one of these, training for the management of preschool centers and
community kitchens, is linked directly with a definite program for   actually utilizing the trainees in Sarvodaya villages where preschool centers and community kitchens are such distinguishing features of   the Sarvodaya program. In their training course, the young women trainees
are given a clear view of how and where their new knowledge and   skills
will ultimately be used. This cannot be said of the other training activities.

Community development training for youth appears to be   a hold-
over from the early days of the community development movement   when
leadership training courses sprouted up everywhere and reflected a naive
faith in training as the means for promoting local leadership and initiative. There are manifest weaknesses in the Sarvodaya training course, as
the author of the case study points out, with respect to such considerations as course content, competence of instructors, and teaching methods.
These can be readily remedied if the basic approach is valid.   But
whether the approach is valid is questionable, when, for example,   a
group of rural youth selected rather indiscriminately is brought to one
of the Sarvodaya centers and for a period of three to six months   is
subjected to a series of lectures about Sarvodaya principles and   goals
and exposed to some of the Sarvodaya activities in the village.   It is
intended that this contact with Sarvodaya and the experiences of   community living in the Sarvodaya center will turn the youngsters   into
zealous agents of social change and initiators and organizers of development activities when they return to their villages.

QUESTIONS ABOUT THE EDUCATIONAL APPROACH

Many questions arise about Sarvodaya's approach to training for
the youth. What are the real motivations and interests of the   youngsters? Do they have the motivation to be Sarvodaya workers in   their
own villages or do they come to the training course only because   they
have nothing better to do? How can the motivated ones be identified or
the motivation created? To what extent can the young trainees fit into
the social structure and the traditional leadership hierarchy in   the
villages and do something of significance? To what extent can qualities
of leadership, dedication, and ingenuity be developed through a training
course? What follow-up and backstopping are needed once the trainees return to their villages, and how can these effectively be provided?

These are just some of the questions that have to be   resolved
before a training program for community development workers   can   have
positive results. A minimum need, it appears, is a definite   follow-up
program that reinforces training and gives specific and continuous sup--
port to the trainees when their formal training is over.   Training, by

itself, even if it is carried out well, cannot be very effective unless its fruits are nurtured in ultimate community development activity.

In skill training Sarvodaya has attempted to introduce realistic approaches by relying heavily on on-the-job experience and apprentice-ships with village artisans. Yet the training effort does not   often achieve the goals of opening up productive employment opportunities and increasing the income of the participants. Reasons for this   abound. There may indeed be a lack of knowledge about specific production skills, but this is the least of the obstacles, and it can readily be overcome. More serious are such considerations as demand and market for the pro-ducts, supply of raw materials, availability of capital, and management efficiency. In the rural economy functioning at a near-subsistence level, economic opportunities are indeed limited. Once opportunities   are identified, various alternatives for skill development, if that is needed, can be found even without setting up special training courses. Organi-zing training programs without proper attention to the opportunities for utilizing the skills they teach may create new problems, particularly when those already practising certain trades and occupations are living on meager earnings.

The combination of the preschool center, community kitchen, and mothers' group--the hallmark of Sarvodaya programs--not only opens up a unique opportunity for educating the mothers and the community at large about the social and physical development of children and basic health care for the entire family, but at the same time, makes important educa-tional, nutritional, and health services available to both mothers and children. The women workers involved in these activities--young women recruited from the same village in which the activities take place and given a short training at a Sarvodaya center--have generally proved to be able and dedicated workers who look upon their responsibilities, not as just another job, but as a service to their communities at large. This experience demonstrates the potentiality and promise of utilizing women extensively as community development workers and agents of social change.

The opportunities created by the children's and mothers' acti-vities, however, cannot be realized if and when the local leadership, such as the Sarvodaya council and the Sarvodaya representative in the village, does not or cannot create a favorable climate of support. In a good climate a high ratio of attendance among eligible children is achieved, many mothers become active and interested participants, and local resources become more abundant.

Sarvodaya has paid considerable attention to getting the chil-dren of compulsory schooling age, years 6 to 14, to attend school, al-though this is not discussed in this report. Several school buildings have been constructed through Sarvodaya efforts and have been handed over to the Ministry of Education. Among the schemes implemented by Sarvodaya in support of primary and secondary education are supplying textbooks to rural children, opening up village and school libraries and book-banks, buying clothing for children, conducting special reme-dial and tutorial classes for children after school hours, organizing

shramadana to construct school playgrounds and wells and so on. A recent
program calls for Sarvodaya to work with the Ministry of Education   in
improving the physical condition of 2,500 most backward schools   in   the
island. All of these efforts, however, are carried on very much   in   the
context of the conventional, formal school system which do not seem   to
serve well the most disadvantaged groups of children. In the "low-caste"
Sarvodaya villages,described in this report, various social and economic
factors have caused a high rate of nonenrollment and early dropout. Opening up educational opportunities for the children of these villages calls
for changes in the organization and content of schooling that would   fit
education to the work cycles and economic circumstances of the poor families in these villages. Ensuring access to and effectiveness of   basic
educational opportunities for all requires more than sprucing up the existing school system. Sarvodaya, which devotes so much attention to children, probably has to be more concerned with the larger issues of educational
reform.

LOGISTICS AND STRATEGY OF EXPANSION

        A common question regarding most voluntary organizations is   how
its program activities, effective on a small scale for a limited   number
of participants, can be multiplied and given a wider, even national, impact. The Sarvodaya organization has attempted consciously to reach out
to as many village communities as possible in all corners of the   island
and has encouraged the involvement of as many people as could be   persuaded in the shramadana voluntary labor projects. During the decade
since 1968 the number of villages that Sarvodaya has reached in one form
or another has increased ten-fold without a commensurate increase   in
resources and personnel that were rather thinly spread in the first place.

        It is natural for an ideological movement to attempt to spread its
message widely, to generate a psychological momentum, and to create   a
favorable environment for its acceptance. However, when the ideology   is
translated into an operational program for socioeconomic development, mere
transmission of ideals and values is not enough. At this stage, resources,
personnel, logistics, and management come into play, and all of these factors set a limit to the expansion that can be prudently undertaken.

        It may well be necessary for a development organization to   make
a distinction between a general "consciousness raising" phase which may be
aimed at the total population and a more limited operational phase that is
subject to relatively rigid logistical, management, and resource   constraints. The implication for Sarvodaya is that the ideological message
of Sarvodaya can be spread nationally, even internationally, through all
appropriate and available forums, but that village level Sarvodaya organizations should not be set up indiscriminately until a minimum level   of
effectiveness and performance can be reasonably assured. This will   require the formulation of criteria that can be applied to villages before
their inclusion in the program and a careful assessment of the preparatory
steps and the process of program development in the villages.   A further
implication is that the Sarvodaya leadership should embark on a consolidation program to bring the present 300 or so villages with the Sarvodaya

organizational structure to a minimum level of performance before other
organizations are set up in new villages. Such an effort may require a
shift in the allocation of authority and responsibility from   headquarters to the field, a redeployment of personnel, identification and
provision of forms of guidance and technical assistance needed for the
village organizations, and discovery of new and effective economic projects, probably in collaboration with the government, that tackle with
determination the problem of absolute poverty.

        A final point to put the Sarvodaya performance in perspective:
it must be remembered that Sarvodaya has deliberately sought out some
of the most difficult rural communities as its program locations--vil-
lages that are victims of age-old social discrimination and economic
oppression, villages that have few economic resources or natural en-
dowments on which to build the foundation of anything developmental at
all. In these villages Sarvodaya has helped to soften the harshness
and to moderate the cruel aspects of the most invidious forms of caste
discrimination. It has helped to provide some essential   community
services, even when it has failed to make a dent on the economic situation of the poor. As is pointed out in the case study, the capacity
of a voluntary organization is obviously limited in effecting   basic
changes in the economic structure at any level, unless a favorable climate is created and a collaborative hand is extended by the   national
government. The significance of the accomplishments of Sarvodaya and
the reasons behind the unfulfilled expectations can be properly understood only by comparing them with the nature of the obstacles   that
Sarvodaya faces. These factors also explain why Sarvodaya survives,
expands, draws national and international support, and continues   to
stir the idealistic spirit among its devotees in Sri Lanka and abroad.

CHAPTER 2

BACKGROUND AND OVERVIEW

THE NATIONAL SETTING

Sri Lanka is an island in the Indian Ocean having an area of 25,332 square miles and a population of 13,393,000.[1] The island may be divided geographically into four different zones--the wet zone, dry zone, arid zone, and the hill country. The southwestern and central parts of the country comprise the hill country, while the rest, except for a few elevations, is comparatively flat. The rainfall of the island varies from 100 inches or more in the wet zone along the southwestern coast to 25-50 inches in the arid and dry zones in the northeastern part of the country. Rain is received by means of southwestern (May-September) and northeastern (October-December) monsoons.

The island has a recorded history from the third century B.C., when Buddhism was introduced to the island. The early settlers from India settled in the northeastern and north-central areas of the country where they developed agriculture by means of an ingenious system of storing rain water in man-made ponds and canals. Ancient and medieval kingdsom flourished in the north-central and also southern areas of the island, but with the progress of time, because of the influx of South Indian invaders and also perhaps of epidemics such as malaria, the population was driven towards the south until finally the last royal city came to be situated at Kotte (near Colombo) and then at Kandy.

The island ruled by Sinhalese monarchs following a feudal system of government retained its independence but suffered various vicissitudes, until finally the maritime provinces were conquered by the Portuguese, then the Dutch, then the entire island in 1815 by the British. The island regained its independence in 1948 choosing to remain a member of the Commonwealth. In 1972 with the promulgation of the new Constitutions, Sri Lanka became an independent republic while retaining its Commonwealth membership.

The island is inhabited by different races: of them the Sinhalese tracing their ancestry to Aryan stock are in the majority (71.9 percent); next come the Tamils of whom there are two distinct groups. The Jaffna Tamils (11.1 percent) are the descendants of Dravidians who came to the island from time to time either as invaders or peaceful settlers. During the British times cheap labor from South India was introduced into the island in order to assist in the cultivation of first coffee and then tea. Such laborers, found mainly in the hill country and employed on tea and to

---

[1]Census of 1974.

a lesser extent on rubber estates, are known as Indian Tamils (9.4 percent). Next in importance are the Moors, descendants of Arab traders who settled down in the country. There are scattered groups of Malays, Burghers, and Europeans who constitute an insiginificant portion of the island's population.[1]

The Sinhalese are predominantly Buddhists, although a small portion of Christians may be found among them. The Tamils are again mainly Hindus, yet even among them adherents of Christianity are found scattered throughout the island. The Moors and Malays are as a rule followers of Islam. According to the census of 1974 the breakdown by religion is as follows: Buddhists--67.4 percent; Hindus--17.5 percent; Muslims--7.7 percent; Roman Catholic and other Christians--7.7 percent.

The island's economy is mainly dependent on agriculture. Main commercial crops are tea, coconut, and rubber. Gems, spices, and plumbago are other significant exports that bring revenue to the country. In the past during the reign of Sinhalese kings rice farming was the main economic activity, done collectively in each village. Tanks, or man-made water reservoirs, were used to collect rainwater for irrigating the rice fields. During foreign rule the cultivation of rice was relegated to the background in favor of plantations of tea and rubber. Tanks were willfully destroyed or neglected. With the neglect and destruction of tanks and the decline in rice cultivation the cooperative pattern of village life was discontinued.[2]

There are approximately 24,000 villages in the island in which about 78 percent of the people live, although the towns are now experiencing a heavy influx of migrants. Among the rural residents 70 percent are estimated to be unemployed or underemployed. Only 3 percent of their housing units possess electricity and 5 percent have tap water. The literacy rate is relatively high with 65 percent of the rural children attending school.

National development efforts and resources have generally been concentrated in the cities, although less than a quarter of the people are city dwellers. For instance, the capital city of Colombo has 15 percent of the nation's population and 125 hospitals with 26,254 beds and 60 percent of the medical specialists, for all of which the government spends Rs. 225 million per year. By comparison the rest of the country has 308 hospitals with 7,044 beds and 40 percent of the specialists, for all of which Rs. 24.6 million is spent in a year.[3]

The attention paid to urban areas by the central government is not confined to the sphere of health. It is the same picture in other areas of development. Some efforts have been made since the early '70s to remedy obvious imbalances, yet the scene, except for certain details, remains very much the same.

---

[1]Sri Lanka Moors 6.3 percent, Indian Moors 0.3 percent; Burghers and Eurasians 0.3 percent, Malays 0.3 percent.

[2]For details on ancient and medieval system of irrigation read: R. L. Brohier, "Ancient Tanks and Canals" in Journal of The Royal Asiatic Society (Ceylon Branch) XXXIV, 85.

[3]Budget estimates in 1977.

The Sarvodaya Movement is significant when viewed in the above perspective because it lays emphasis on the development of the village.   The
cooperative life of the village that was centered on rice cultivation during the medieval period inspired the movement to incorporate in its philosophy those significant features that had sustained village social   and
economic life in the past.   It is Sarvodaya's belief that without   the
development of the village in all its spheres--the social, economic, religious, and cultural--the resurgence of the nation as a whole is impossible.
In order to work for such an economic and social resurgence in rural   life
the Sarvodaya Movement delved deep into the sociocultural roots that   once
gave birth to a self-sufficient economy and sought to draw from these whatever seemed relevant, significant, and useful for modern times.

ORIGIN AND GROWTH OF THE MOVEMENT

The beginning of the Sarvodaya Movement in Sri Lanka can be traced
back to 1958 when A. T. Ariyaratne, a young teacher in a Buddhist college
in Colombo, and a band of his colleagues and students spent a holiday in a
village in order "first, to learn from the village and then utilise   the
knowledge gained to improve rural life."[1] The selected village was inhabited by one of the lowest castes in the country known as the Rodiyas.   These
people, condemned to live as outcasts in their isolated hamlets, eked   out
their existence largely by begging.   They were not even allowed to   cover
the upper part of their bodies, and even Buddhist priests refused to   perform religious rituals on their behalf or to receive alms from them.[2]

The village selected by the Sarvodaya pioneers led by   A. T. Ariyaratne was Kanatholuwa, near Kurunegala (58 miles from Colombo). They went
to the village, lived with the villagers, shared their food, learned   from
them, and helped them construct houses, lavatories, and other needed physical facilities.

At that time the pioneers named their project after the selected
village, the "Kanatholuwa Development Educational Extension and Community Service Camp."   The experience of the first "village camp" encouraged the group to continue its work in other villages.   As a result, by
1961, 26 villages were covered in which 36 work camps were held.

The young pioneers of Kanatholuwa were deeply influenced by the
struggle for freedom and social change in the Indian subcontinent   and
drew their ideals and inspirations from the Sarvodaya (spiritual reawakening) movement led by Mahatma Gandhi and Vinobha Bhave.   The young
pioneers even began to call their own activities the Sarvodaya Movement
of Sri Lanka.   The movement came of age with the increase of its   activities to various parts of the island; and as the leaders began to see
the roots of their own culture, they began to develop an indigenous philosophy, widening the purpose of their efforts and looking   for   new

---

[1]For details of the pioneer work in this village see: "Kanatholuwa
Village File PK/65. Report of the holiday camp in a backward community."

[2]For information on Rodiyas (the backward community at Kanatholuwa)
see M. D. Raghavan, Handsome Beggars, the Rodiyas of Ceylon, Colombo, 1957.

horizons. The rural life of Sri Lanka, having imbibed the Buddhist culture
for 2500 years, is essentially a society based on Buddhist principles.   It
was these principles that in the past had helped the rural community   to
knit itself into a close cooperative unit, self-sufficient and creative. The
widening of the philosophical base of the movement was sought by synthesiz-
ing the Buddhist cultural pattern in rural life with the Gandhian ideals that
had inspired the pioneers.[1]

        The new philosophy fashioned largely from living and working   with
villagers (by 1968, the movement had attracted 250,000 volunteers to work in
125 villages) emphasized the involvement of the rural communities, especially in the most underprivileged areas, as direct participants in the struggle
for social change. The adherents of Sarvodaya hoped to achieve   national
integration by inspiring people to think as 'one' and not as members of one
individual community, religion, or race. They expected to foster a   spirit
of brotherhood among the people by bringing home to them the advantage   of
relying on their own strength and cooperative effort rather than on   outside
help. The shramadana (literally, gift of labor) camp was the device   that
united the Sarvodaya volunteers and the villagers in pursuit of a   tangible
common goal and also became the means for learning and "consciousness-raising" of both the volunteers and the villagers.

        In these experiences involving villages in all parts of the island,
where for a long time the folk had practised an agricultural way of life
that was traditionally based on mutual cooperation and rooted in Buddhist
principles, the Sarvodaya workers were able to understand the underlying
motivating forces and simply philosophy of the rural people. Respect for
life in all its forms, universal compassion, joy that emanates   from service to one's self and others, and psychological and physical stability
were the cornerstones of this simple but very practical philosophy.[2]

        To this was added the Buddhist-inspired practices of sharing,
pleasant speech, creative or constructive activity, and the idea   of
universal equality. This philosophy had as its immediate aim   the
liberation of man, then his community (village), and as its final aim
the liberation of the country and then the world. The liberation idea
had as its basis the freedom of the individual from fetters of both economic and social bondage and self-realization in the total development
of his personality. The synthesis achieved between the Gandhian philosophy and the Buddhist philosophy provided a basis as well as a motivational force for the extension of the services rendered by Sarvodaya in
the 1960s.

---

        [1]"Though the Movement was inspired by the thoughts of Mahatma Gandhi
and Vinobha Bhave in its formative step, it gradually developed a   distinct
philosophy of its own. Even though the word 'Sarvodaya....' was adopted from
India, the interpretation of its deep meaning in the context of Sinhalese
Buddhism and as relevant to our nationals is completely our own." A. T.
Ariyaratne, "Sarvodaya Shramadana. A Growth of a People's Movement" (quoted
in the Study Service) p. 26.

        [2]See Sarvodaya Shramadana Movement--at a glance, Sri Lanka, 1976.

In 1971 a violent insurrection of youth throughout the island
ushered in a period of instability and suffering. The revolt   was
engineered by Marxist-oriented educated youth and the participants were
primarily rural, unemployed young people. The Marxist youths had helped
the United Left coalition led by Mrs. Bandarnaike to win the   election
in 1970 but soon found that the government had little inclination   to
bring about the radical reforms they desired. They decided to take the
path of insurrection. The participants in the revolt felt that the prevailing social, economic, and political condition denied them any opportunity for the fulfillment of their life purposes. They came from   the
lower middle class and working class background and many belonged to the
low-caste groups. The insurrection was ruthlessly put down by the government and youth leaders in large numbers were put in prison. Although the
insurrection was controlled by the government, the fundamental questions
raised by the upheaval about the need for radical change in the   socioeconomic structure remained unresolved, and the suppression of youthful
activism left the youth without leaders and outlets for venting   their
energies and grievances constructively.

The rise and expansion of Sarvodaya from 1971 onwards   can   be
attributed to its ingenuity in filling the gap created by the   suppression of the youth revolt and providing alternative leadership   to   the
rural youth who were looking for nonviolent and pragmatic ways to   challenge the old order. Sarvodaya, strengthened by its outlook   and
philosophy formulated through nearly two decades of work among   rural
people, managed to identify itself with the aspirations of the   rural
people.

In 1972 the villages associated with the Sarvodaya effort reached
1,000 from a mere 100 villages in 1968 and only one in 1958. By the   end
of 1977 the number was nearly 2,000, although the program and the organization existed on a relatively permanent basis in only about 300 villages.

GOVERNMENT EFFORTS TO SPUR RURAL SELF-HELP

Beginning in the 1950s, but particularly in the early 1970s, some
efforts were made by the Sri Lanka government to accelerate   development
activities in the rural areas, to extend the reach of government services
and agencies more widely into the villages, and to facilitate   meaningful
participation of the rural people in the national development process.

A significant recent move was the introduction of a system of "decentralized budget" by which in each parliamentary district the so-called
district political authority comprising the members of the Parliament and
the district officials plans its own development program and receives   an
allocation from the central government to implement it. This arrangement
does not necessarily mean that the right priorities are applied in   program choices, that the interests of the common people are served, or that
the programs are effectively implemented. But it does mean that the mechanism has been created for meaningful popular participation in   local
development and the people given the opportunity to take control of their
own development programs and resources, if indeed they are prepared   and
willing to do so. An organization like the Sarvodaya movement can play a
crucial role in educating and mobilizing the people at the local level
for taking advantage of such opportunities created by governmental decisions and policies.

There are other instances of governmental effort being impeded by the inability of the rural people to reach out to take what rightfully belongs to them. The government health facilities and health workers, for example, cannot possibly cover all the remote villages in the country by offering curative care, preventive service, health education, inspiration, and advice for self-protection measures. However, this gap can be bridged if under the auspices of an organization like Sarvodaya the villagers are organized to help themselves and to appoint health auxiliaries from among themselves to serve as links between themselves and government personnel.

Following the nationalization of the banking service, the government opened a new chain of banks called the People's Banks to serve rural needs. Again the inability to prepare, plan, and organize for this new opportunity on the part of individual communities has meant that the vast majority of the rural people cannot benefit from this desirable service.

The Rural Development Societies, sponsored by the Rural Development Department of the government, are seen as another means by which the people can participate in village development activities. These voluntary societies, comprising villagers and local-level government officials, can in principle plan development programs of their own and receive government funds and technical assistance to supplement their own resources which, by the way, need not be confined to physical construction alone. The bureaucratic process of government fund disbursement, the recalcitrant attitudes and behavior of the local officials, and the inability of the community people to unite for self-help action have generally turned the Rural Development Societies into another government agency controlled by the local officials. Other rural participatory organizations formed under statutory provisions--the Cultivators' Committee and the Productivity Committee--for the purpose of encouraging all the farmers in a village to plan together for the improvement of agricultural productivity have also proved to be ineffective, partly because the farmers have not been able to organize themselves collectively.

The government has attempted to utilize institutions similar to shramadana to rehabilitate the old water storage and irrigation system in the dry zone through "tanks" (small water reservoirs). In this effort the government makes grains and other food items available to people who participate in the reconstruction or renovation of tanks. The officially-organized program, however, has produced many ill-constructed tanks and half finished waterways, many of which can be of little use for irrigation. The program has failed to evoke the involvement of the people and the spirit of dedication that normally should characterize shramadana projects. It has become a relief program for the distribution of donated grains.

Be that as it may, the government efforts to create rural institutions and to expand development services in the rural areas and the relative lack of effectiveness of these efforts give voluntary organizations like the Sarvodaya Movement the opportunity and responsibility to organize and educate the rural people to help themselves by combining their own resources with those of the government.

CHAPTER 3

ORGANIZATIONAL STRUCTURE
AND MANAGEMENT

CENTRAL ORGANIZATION AND STAFF

The Sarvodaya Movement was sanctioned as an approved charity in 1965 and gained full official recognition in 1972 when the charter of incorporation was approved by an act of the Parliament. Over the years the expansion of the movement's work and the additions to the scope of its program have necessitated the growth of a complex organizational structure.

The general membership of the movement consists of various categories of dues paying members (Life, Honorary, Ordinary, Donor, Youth, and International), members of Sarvodaya groups (children 7-16; youth 16-35; mothers; farmers; general) in the villages, the members of Sarvodaya Bhikku (monks) Conference, members of the Sarvodaya branch societies; and members (or representatives) of organizations affiliated with Sarvodaya.[1]

The Executive Council, the policymaking body of the movement, consists of the president, two vice-presidents, the general secretary, the organizing secretary, two assistant secretaries, the treasurer, the assistant treasurer, an elders' council comprising 15 individuals and 11 other Executive Council members; all of these are elected by the general body of members. In addition, there are 35 invitee members (all from Sri Lanka) of the Executive Council, who are asked by the Council to become members because of their special knowledge and experience in the development field. The appointment of 35 invitee members is a strategy introduced in order to secure the services of experts in various fields who would not ordinarily be elected to the Executive Council or who for personal reasons would not like to be officially elected in this manner.

The Executive Council is assisted by a number of advisory committees, such as those on general administration, finances, projects, development education, and village reawakening. Recently two more advisory committees on appropriate technology and national unity have been appointed.

The administration of the program is carried out by a team comprising a general administrative secretary, finance secretary, project secretary, development education secretary, and village reawakening secretary. There is also a team of coordinators for implementation of plans with a coordinator

---

[1]See Sarvodaya Shramadana Movement at a Glance, Sri Lanka, 1976.

each for (1) general membership, Executive Council, and Movement affairs; (2) management of personnel; (3) finance management and accountability; (4) general   services; (5) production and marketing; (6) projects; (7) development education; and (8) village reawakening.

The national and international headquarters of Sarvodaya is at Meth Medura in Moratuwa district near Colombo. In addition to administration and associated activities one also finds at Meth Medura (1) the Sarvodaya Development Education Institute, (2) the Sarvodaya Community Living Programme (for 300 youths), and (3) the   Central Sarvodaya Services.

In addition to Meth Medura there are five other important centers of Sarvodaya work scattered throughout the country: the Sarvodaya Development Education Centres at Tanamalwila in Monaragala district, at Baddegama in Galle district, at Panwila   in Kandy district, and at Karativu in Jaffra district; and the Sarvodaya Community Leadership Training Institute for Buddhist monks at Pathakada in the Ratnapura district.

The Development Education Centres, beside acting as the educational base for Sarvodaya regional services, have the following components: (1) a community leadership training program, (2) a training program in agricultural and technical   skills, and (3) community living facilities for the trainees and the Sarvodaya workers. The center at Tanamalwila has an Appropriate Technology Development Unit. The center at Karativu is the only such center in the Tamil-speaking areas; it has started   relatively recently with a community development training program.

The center for the monks is for the purpose of preparing monks for community leadership. The important role that the Buddhist monk plays in the rural areas as a community leader and the role of the temple as a pivotal point for social, cultural, and economic development have always been recognized by Sarvodaya but not sufficiently understood by those who plan and execute governmental programs.

There is also a Sarvodaya Research Centre situated in Colombo. Started as a "study service scheme," it has grown into a center where numbers of qualified young men and women are trained to do research on many aspects of Sarvodaya activities and rural development. Their findings are expected to provide the basis for   evaluating Sarvodaya programs, formulating policy, and developing strategies and designs   for future programs. A vishvodaya ('awakening of the world') center, to serve as   the base for the international aspects of Sarvodaya, is planned to be opened   in   the near future.

The regional centers are linked with the villages through seventy-four extension centers known as Gramodaya Centers. An extension center may serve from two   to thirty-five villages, the average being around ten. Through the extension centers, the headquarters and the regional centers provide services, advice, and   material assistance, such as the provision of powdered milk for the community kitchens. It is the base, often the residence, of the Sarvodaya workers assigned to the   villages. Some of the training programs are also held at the extension center instead of   at the regional center.

Most of the Gramodaya extension centers are located at the temple or in church premises or in some other community building. The centers are manned by two or three Sarvodaya workers who have gone through Sarvodaya community leadership and community development courses and may also have had some training in agriculture. The volunteer workers, as they are called, are paid an allowance (average of Rs. 150 per month, equivalent to US $18) by headquarters. The worker at the extension center is an all-purpose individual who remains in close touch with his villages, works with the villagers in developing their own Sarvodaya programs, identifies specific forms of help that Sarvodaya can offer to the villages, and tries to be generally available and helpful in the villages. The success of the village program depends heavily on the personality, dedication, and competence of the worker at the extension center. Usually, one worker handles one village, but occasionally more than one volunteer may work in one village or a group of volunteers may be responsible for a cluster of villages. The volunteer workers are selected by the village Sarvodaya Group and sent for training at the Gramodaya center or at one of the regional education centers. The training may vary from two weeks (basic training) to three months and is followed up by refresher courses from time to time.

ORGANIZATION OF THE VILLAGE ACTIVITIES

The organization and institutions described above form a superstructure that exists to support Sarvodaya activities in the villages. Sarvodaya activities are introduced into individual villages in various ways. In many cases it is the village monk who takes the initiative by writing a letter explaining the desire of the village to join Sarvodaya or perhaps his own interest in getting the people interested in Sarvodaya. Sometimes a villager himself finds the Sarvodaya program appealing, stirs up interest among some of his peers, and communicates with Sarvodaya headquarters. Once such a communication is received, the village is advised to form a Sarvodaya organization, in most cases a youth group. A volunteer worker from headquarters is sent to advise the villagers and to enable them to take the initial steps in introducing Sarvodaya there. The initial steps often include one or more shramadana projects which become the occasion for Sarvodaya workers to work and live with the villagers and discuss the Sarvodaya principles as well as make plans for future activities in the village.

Another early step that usually follows the formation of a society in a village is to conduct a survey of the socioeconomic situation of the village. Sarvodaya workers and the leaders of the newly-formed village organization jointly carry out the survey, guidelines for which are provided by the Sarvodaya Research Centre in the form of a questionnaire that tries to assess the manpower situation, economic resources, social characteristics, basic health situation, and important cultural traits. If it is properly conducted and if the Sarvodaya workers and village leaders know what to do with the information, the socioeconomic survey provides the basis for future Sarvodaya programs in the village. Often, however, useful information is not adequately collected, and there is insufficient understanding of how to use the information for planning purposes. Therefore the program that is set up is apt to follow a stereotyped pattern as seen in many other Sarvodaya villages.

Ideally, the Sarvodaya organization in a village includes a youth group (16-25 years), mothers' group, farmers' group, children's group (7 - 10 years), and a preschool group connected with the mothers' group. The ideal model is completed with the inclusion of an elders' group and sometimes the Samudan group. The elders' group obviously enrolls the village elders, and the Samudan group taps the expertise, special talents, and experience of certain village residents who for one reason or another are not included in any of the other groups. In practice there are few villages where all these groups function in full capacity. In many villages one may find only one group functioning. In others two or three or, at the most, four are at work.

According to a 1976 Sarvodaya count, 961 villages were contacted by Sarvodaya under its proposed 1,000 village development program. Details of these 961 villages were not at that time available, but a December 1975 report provides information about 804 villages then included in the program. Of this number, 334 villages were at the first stage: i.e., they were about to enter the Sarvodaya program. The initial socioeconomic surveys had been conducted in these villages with the purpose of ascertaining the problems at hand. There were 380 villages at the second stage, or the shramadana stage Usually after the socioeconomic survey has identified the problems of the village, steps are taken to organize Sarvodaya activities, the initial step being the holding of a shramadana, or work camp.

Shramadana is a work camp for physical construction for which labor and skills are donated by volunteers. Since time immemorial the donation of labor for individual or social purposes had been regarded as an action that accrued religious merit. In the village people donated their labor for the construction of houses, digging wells, ploughing the fields, harvesting and so on. Sarvodaya has resurrected this customary practice by motivating people to donate their collective labor for the construction of much needed roads, wells, tanks, and similar community projects. In such work camps villagers and Sarvodaya volunteers work together.

The third stage is the stage of gramodaya (the awakening of the village). By this time Sarvodaya organizations are formed, the village people begin to understand the principles and philosophy of Sarvodaya, and they begin to make their own plans and put them into action. The Gramodaya Mandala (council) is the apex organization in a Sarvodaya village. It consists of representatives from all Sarvodaya groups (children, youth, farmers, and so on) and is the local "supreme authority" for Sarvodaya development work. It is the coordinating body for the village for Sarvodaya activities (and sometimes for rural development activities of the government and other voluntary agencies as far as the village is concerned). There were 94 such gramodaya villages in 1975. By the end of 1977, it is estimated that about 2000 villages had some association with Sarvodaya, and that about 3000 villages had reached the gramodaya stage, having formed a gramodaya council and initiated some program activities on a continuing basis.

How the organizational structure described above has served the Sarvodaya objectives and to what extent it has facilitated the various program activities at the grassroots level can be assessed only by examining the field operation at the village level. A close-up view of some Sarvodaya villages presented later in this report will provide some clues to its overall effectiveness. An observer of the headquarter's operations, however, comes away with some impressions that may have a bearing on the general effectiveness of the organization and its program.

CENTRALITY OF CONTROL

In contradiction to its goal of creating self-reliant and autonomous rural communities, the Sarvodaya organization seems to function in too centralized a manner. Substantially all policy and program decisions are made at the central headquarters, and the sectional coordinators exercise control over all aspects of the program within their respective jurisdiction.   The regional centers and the extension centers are essentially channels for transmitting and carrying out directives from the central level. Decisions needed to be taken at the field level, sometimes even decisions regarding individual

village programs, are referred to the central office. One reason for this
in the past has been the irresponsible behavior of some of the field personnel who have mishandled funds and other resources.

Another reason for the "centralized" character of the organization
is the towering personality of the movement's leader, Mr. Ariyaratne, and
the central role he has played in building up the organization.   The
impulse to look up to the headquarters, particularly to the leader   and
the people who are in close contact with him, is pervasive in the   whole
organization. This tendency is probably a cultural trait in the hierar-
chic social structure of Sri Lanka that encourages unquestioning obeisance
to anyone regarded as superior in some respect. The net result of this
situation is an overburdened central management, a stunting of initiatives, and a less than ideal atmosphere for the growth of new leadership.

An outgrowth of the centralization in management is the tendency
of the sectional coordinators to maintain a tight rein over   their
respective fields of activity to the detriment of essential interaction
and cooperation among different activities within the organization itself. This is the impression the author of this report formed from personal observation and interviews conducted with the coordinators.   It
also appears that the coordinators have not made full use of the knowledge and experience of the invitee members of the Executive Council,
although their special expertise is the reason for including them as
members.

As one enters the Meth Medura complex of Sarvodaya headquarters
and encounters the array of buildings, officials, trainees,   camp
organizers, group leaders, and other paid workers, one cannot help
thinking of the simple early days of Sarvodaya when it was essentially
a dedicated band of volunteers living and working with villagers   in
village shramadana camps. The extension of the movement to different
parts of the island and the increase in personnel and scope of   activities have invariably created a bureaucracy and a style of operation
that may have to some extent enervated the original spirit of   the
movement.

CHAPTER 4

EDUCATION AND TRAINING ACTIVITIES

As has been noted previously, a high degree of emphasis is placed on education and training in the Sarvodaya movement. Much of the bustle   of activities noticed at the Sarvodaya headquarters at Meth Medura and at the regional centers is related to education and training courses of one sort or another. Education and training for the Sarvodaya volunteers, the monks,and selected villagers are seen as the means of awakening the latent capacities and strength of the people and inspiring them to proceed in the direction of self-reliance and collective self-help. The major organized educational ac- tivities carried out at the headquarters and the regional centers are: (1) community leadership training of various duration, (2) training for preschool instructors, (3) training in crafts and skills, (4) agricultural training, and (5) leadership training for Buddhist monks.

A close look at the education and training activities in one of the regional centers at Baddegama in the southern district of Galle will   be helpful in appreciating the nature and effectiveness of these   activities. The center served a territory comprising 87 villages with a population of 114,000. The center is located in a building leased on favorable   terms from a Sarvodaya sympathizer. The center began operation in 1974 with   a preschool center, a batik-making section, a carpentry section, and   agri- cultural training. Training in arts and crafts began in 1975. Output from the training program until the end of 1976 was the following:

> 1974--30 agricultural trainees
> 1975--15 agricultural trainees, 10 from the batik unit,
>   5 in indikola weaving and other crafts,   15   in
>   carpentry, and 15 in other rural skills, including
>   blacksmithy
> 1976--21 in carpentry, 12 in metal work, 7 in batik,
>   14 preschool instructors, and 17 in indikola
>   weaving crafts. In addition there were trainees
>   in community development and leadership courses.

The selection of trainees is done by issuing application forms to the villages linked to Sarvodaya and asking the applicants to send in their ap- plications. The village organizations sometimes select the applicants   and send in the names of the nominees, or else the center itself will go through the application forms and select the best qualified to be trainees.   There are no rigid criteria for such a selection, but the applicant's aptitude for development work and his association with the movement necessarily are fac- tors that are considered in the process of selection.

COMMUNITY LEADERSHIP TRAINING COURSES

There are courses on community leadership at Baddegama for different durations of time: (1) two weeks; (2) three months; and (3) six months.

The two weeks' course is devoted largely to lectures and discussion sessions at the center, at the end of which the trainees are sent to take part in a shramadana camp. The lectures, besides expounding Sarvodaya philosophy, cover the organization of shramadana projects, such as community kitchens, and the dealings with community leaders. This type of short training was considered necessary at the early phase of Sarvodaya when it did not have the resources to offer a much longer period of training, and when trained volunteers were in demand for the expansion of the program. This short training cannot do much more than provide a "foretaste" of what Sarvodaya is all about.

The three months' training course begins with lectures on Sarvodaya for two days to initiate trainees into the movement and to provide a general orientation for the work to follow. Then the trainees are sent to a farm associated with Sarvodaya to acquaint them with strictly practical work. They are brought back and kept for two days at the center. After lectures and discussions again they are asked to go to their own villages for a week with a set of questions and guides for studying and analyzing the village situation. They then come back to the center for more instructional sessions.

The particular group of trainees observed by us in May 1977 consisted of sixty participants. After the lectures the trainees were divided into three groups and sent to three villages (Ginimellagaha, Talawa, and Akuressa). Here they were to take part in formulating a developmant plan and as a group to discuss its feasibility and implementation. After the stay in the villages they were again brought back to the center for a critical group assessment of the experiences encountered, the work already done, the problems faced, and the methods adopted. At the end of this session they were sent to their own villages and asked to continue Sarvodaya activities there. They were encouraged to start such organizations as youth groups, mothers' groups, and so forth. Each volunteer was also asked to bring to the center up to five individuals from their respective villages in order to take part in a seminar which lasted for three days. Towards the end of the seminar all of them (60 volunteers and 100 newcomers) were divided into small groups of five each and informal discussions on Sarvodaya and development were carried out.

The six months' course is an innovation begun for the first time at Baddegama. For this course only those who have already given some time to voluntary village work are selected. It starts with two weeks of lectures, and then the trainees are asked to draw up a program for "development" of their village which is to be put into action during the training period.

The "development program" usually concentrates on the creation of basic Sarvodaya units such as the youth group and mothers' group, or on improving the effectiveness of these groups where they already exist. The trainees are brought back to the center after an initial stay of three weeks in the village. In the lectures and discussions that follow they learn more about how to put the Sarvodaya plan for the development   of   the village into action. At this time the trainees begin to alternate with   two weeks at the village and two weeks at the center. When they come to the center every alternate fortnight the lectures and discussions about all aspects of Sarvodaya and development continue.

The effectiveness of a training program for community development workers depends not as much on the conduct of the training course itself as on the motivation of the trainees, what setting they return to after the training, and what kind of support the workers can get from the sponsoring organization.

Discussion with a group of twenty trainees in the three months' course who were on their village assignment provides some clue to the motivation and expectations of the trainees. Of the twenty trainees, ten were from villages with Sarvodaya organizations and all of them had completed the first series of lectures in the training course. Yet only three trainees were able   to explain Sarvodaya's philosophy and objectives even in a general way, nine of them saw the course as a possible extra qualification for landing a government job, and eight expected to work in the Sarvodaya program   as   paid employees. More than half of the group thought the course was "unfruitful" to them personally. Most of the group members found the village assignment not adequately organized and not sufficiently instructive.

The trainees for the six-month course are expected to have better motivation and clearer personal goals because they would have already devoted considerable time to voluntary work and have had an opportunity to demonstrate their aptitudes and personal commitment.

TRAINING FOR PRESCHOOL INSTRUCTORS

The preschool center, the community kitchen, and the mothers' group constitute a complex of institutions in Sarvodaya villages that together cater to the needs of young children below the schoolgoing age of 7 and to some extent the needs of mothers. The worker in charge of these activities is a young woman from the village who is given a preparatory training by Sarvodaya. Two kinds of training courses are run--one fro two weeks and the other for three months--at Sarvodaya headquarters and the regional centers, including the one at Baddegama.

The short course of two weeks was initiated to alleviate the financial and other constraints that a longer course would impose and to meet the rising demand for preschool instructors. The three-month course was later begun as the need for a more thorough preparation became apparent.   Both courses, however, continue at present, and some trainees of the shorter course eventually join the longer course.

The trainees are, in principle, selected by the village Sarvodaya organization on the basis of their individual qualities and commitment to serve the community. They usually have comparatively low secondary level education (nine to ten years of schooling). Occasionally the trainee has joined the course on her own initiative or at the recommendation of some influential individual. The motivation of these trainees, as revealed from interviews with a number of them, is sometimes a desire to qualify for employment as a preschool instructor under the government or some other program.

The courses cover subject matter related to child development, principles of nutrition, organization of community kitchens, basic health care for children and mothers, preventive measures, and the principles and goals of the Sarvodaya organization.

A course for training village health auxiliaries was opened at one stage, but soon discontinued. Apparently it was decided that training and maintaining its own cadre of village level health workers was not the best possible use of the limited resources of Sarvodaya in the face of competing demands.

COURSES IN CRAFTS AND SKILLS

A number of courses in arts and crafts for village youth are being carried out at Baddegama. Applications are invited from those with the necessary aptitude from the villages associated with Sarvodaya. The following training courses are available at Baddegama and are represesentative of skill training in other regional centers and at headquarters.

Batik. There is a batik training unit attached to the Baddegama center where training, usually for girls, lasts for six months. After the six months, the girls are encouraged to set up a batik center in their own villages, train other girls there, and make batik products for sale. Capital in the form of cloth, dyes, and other necessities for the village centers are loaned by the Sarvodaya center, which also buys the finished product. There are two villages where batik centers have been opened by trainees from Baddegama.

The problem with batik-making is the uncertain market. The center at Moratuwa collects the products from the villages and tries to find overseas markets for them, but we were informed that no outlet had been found for the work completed at Baddegama. Consequently the girls at the village centers often have to sell their products locally, and this is a difficult task.

Painting. Painting as a profession is not very promising unless one is exceptionally talented. Sarvodaya has encouraged some village youth with talent to become designers for batik products, but this effort has not been very successful.

Indikola craft. Indikola is a type of reed out of which various items such as baskets are woven. The course on indikola weaving, like that on batik, lasts for six months. A qualified teacher from outside is engaged to teach the skills to a number of girls from the neighboring villages. As the raw material is found in certain villages, women in those villages produce various items such as table mats and baskets, thus supplementing their own meager family income. Because skills are transmitted to younger girls in the same villages, the need for a special training course at the center is not as great as for other skills. The difficulty again lies in marketing the product, and no systematic plan for this purpose has as yet been evolved.

Rural industrial skills. The purpose in teaching rural industrial skills is to train youngsters in a skill or skills that can be used   to produce materials for local use in the village itself. The training covers basic skills in woodwork, ironwork, and building construction. The course lasts for six months and youths, qualified in S.S.C. (ten years of school- ing) and nominated from the youth groups in the village, are enrolled   in this course. Some of the youths have entered government service by virtue of the training recieved; still others have been sent to other Sarvodaya centers as instructors.

This training is useful to a village only if its youthful trainees elect to return to their village. There are, of course, several difficul- ties to be encountered here. In the first place the youths need a sizeable capital with which to start a business, even a small smithy. Even if the necessary capital were to be provided by a loan from Sarvodaya, the problem of marketing the products still remains. Demand is relatively slight and the income that such work provides is low. There is a small industries pro- ject run by the government that encourages youth in self-employment enter- prises: raw materials are provided and some help is offered in marketing the products. If the Sarvodaya training could link up with the government project, it would have a better chance of success. In the government plan for the development of rural industries there is apparently no provision for linkage with a nongovernmental body, even if it is a rural voluntary organization. Possibly a dialogue on this subject between the Sarvodaya leaders and the government would help solve this problem.

There are also sociocultural barriers to the promotion of rural in- dustrial skills. Blacksmiths, for example, are people belonging to a caste that is considered low in the caste hierarchy. High-caste persons in the rural areas would consider it demeaning to be associated with such an occu- pation, in which the skills, like those of carpenter and builder,   are passed on in the family through an apprenticeship system. Even when Sar- vodaya trains youths at Baddegama for various industrial skills, it   takes high financial and other incentives before the trainees will break   with caste tradition and start, for example, a blacksmithy in the village.

At the Panwila regional center an apprenticeship scheme in ironwork has been started recently. Under this scheme selected youths live in their own villages and work as apprentices with the village blacksmiths. The village "meister" receives improved equipment and the free labor of the apprentice for his services. This scheme has the advantage of keeping the trainee in his own setting, but the basic economic constraints to   the growth of rural skills still remain.

Agricultural training. An agricultural training course was activated with the intention of providing a basic knowledge of agriculture to youth in order to engage such youth in land development projects in the villages. The course was discontinued after training 30 youths in 1974 and 15 in 1975. Some of those trained were able to find employment on government farms, but others found it difficult to use their skills as they had no access to land. These constraints prompted the closure of the course.

An interesting agricultural training program combining community development training and farming skills has been begun at the regional center at Tanamalawila, where a 500-acre stretch of land has been cleared to set up a farm for seasonal crops, plantation crops, and the raising of dairy cattle. The farm is expected to provide the training facilities for youth trainees, resident on the farm, and to serve as a demonstration project for neighboring village farmers who would contribute their labor along with that of the youth trainees and share in the profits. The project is seen as a means of learning from   the traditional wisdom of rural farmers and of enabling the young trainees to become intimately familiar with the problems of farmers.   The trainees would also learn farm management and optimal utilization   of available land resources. Apparenlty some of the trainees are expected to work in the movement; others may become settlers in new areas   or become change agents in their own communities as individual farmers. The program has not been in operation long enough to warrant any conclusion about its performance.

TRAINING FOR BUDDHIST MONKS

The program for Buddhist monks at Pathakada was begun with the idea of utilizing the services of monks, still the traditional leaders in villages, for village development. In medieval times the temple was   the focal point of all religious, economic, social, and cultural activities. During the period when Sri Lanka came under foreign rule this vital function was almost destroyed. If the monks could be made aware of   these cultural roots and the important role they could play in village development, with some knowledge of modern technology, they could very well become instruments for transforming village life. It was with this purpose in mind that a training program for monks was started at Pathakada. The duration of the program was six months. It was started in 1974 and   was expected to train 120 monks a year.

Fifteen subjects, including Buddhist philosophy and Sarvodaya philosophy, are taught in the course. The content of the syllabus includes "the village and its structure"; social service; social relations; community development; health; village and government institutions; psychology; astrology; English; and program planning, management and implementation. The syllabus is impressive, but actual teaching is reported to have suffered from the lack of qualified teachers. Another problem is insufficient provision for effective follow-up of the trainees; there is no means of knowing whether the knowledge acquired from the training is put to effective use. A plan for systematic follow-up and support does not seem to exist. A complete review of the training course, including follow-up and ways of enhancing the impact of the training, is currently under consideration.

CHAPTER 5

RESOURCES AND COSTS

THE ANNUAL BUDGET

The finances for the movement in its early days came from small donations of well-wishers in the country. As the movement increased its sphere
of activities, it attracted support from both local and foreign well-wishers
and philanthropic organizations. At the moment various foundations   from
abroad are financing the bulk of the costs for different projects.   Among
them are NOVIB of Holland, OXFAM of the United Kingdom and United States,and
Friedrich Neumann Stiftung of the Federal Republic of Germany.

According to the budget prepared for the financial year 1977-78, total
expenditures for the year come to Rs. 34 million.   [US$1 was approximately
equal to Rs. 8 under official exchange rate in late 1977.] This is   divided
into different items in the following manner:

1.	Shramadana Camp Organization	Rs.	2,862,972.
2.	Preschool Program,		
	Community Kitchen-cum-Health Care		6,787,225.
3.	Gramodaya Revolving Fund		6,458,500.
4.	Development Education Activities		149,290.
5.	Development Education Center (Meth Medura)		607,819.
6.	Development Education Center (Tanamalwila)		7,367,670.
7.	Development Education Center (Baddegama)		460,150.
8.	Development Education Center (Kandy)		979,937.
9.	Development Education Center (Pathakada)		610,340.
10.	Development Education Center (Karativu)		349,797.
11.	Sarvodaya Library Service		218,450.
12.	Gramodaya Centers		1,721,030.
13.	Finance and Accountability		334,960.
14.	General Support Service		1,503,110.
15.	Production and Marketing Unit		1,597,335.
16.	Sarvodaya Research Centre		534,015.
17.	Visvodaya Building--Capital Expenditure		1,500,000.
	TOTAL . . . RS		34,042,600.

---

[1]See Sarvodaya Shramadana Movement, Revised Budget Proposal for the
Financial Year 1977-78.

The single largest item of expenditure in the budget is the regional Tanamalwila Development Education Centre, because it   includes
the capital expenditures for a 500-acre mixed agricultural and   dairy
farm. Second to this item is the budgeted amount for the   preschool
centers and the community kitchens which are so central to the   Sarvodaya village effort. The movement provides an allowance for the instructors, arranges preparatory and refresher training for them,   and
bears the transportation cost for the distribution of donated   milk
powder in the community kitchens.

Another large item is the Gramodaya Revolving Fund, from which
loans are made to projects submitted by villages through their gramodaya councils. This is not strictly an expenditure item, as the   loaned amounts are expected to be repaid and the fund replenished   for
further use. The loan fund began operation in 1975 with 13   small
loans for projects prepared by individuals and groups. This was made
possible by a grant of two million rupees by NOVIB for this purpose.
The fund is expected to help develop a rural credit system to provide
capital for small-scale rural enterprises. The fund will grow in size
as Sarvodaya develops its own capacity for helping villages   identify
economic opportunities, draw up schemes, and assess the feasibility of
such schemes. Sarvodaya also has to ensure a reasonable rate of recovery of the loans so that the fund remains solvent.

If the revolving fund is excluded from the annual budget,   the
total for 1977-78, including both capital and current expenditures,
comes to about Rs. 27.5 million. More than half, or about Rs. 14 million, of this amount is allocated to the two items mentioned above: the
Tanamalwila center with its agricultural farm and the preschool center-
cum-community kitchen program. Understandably, another sizeable   item
is for the organization of shramadana camps, the main vehicle for introducing the Sarvodaya program in villages and involving villagers directly in the program. The amount devoted to this item for 1977-78   was
Rs. 2.9 million, or over 10 percent of the total budget, excluding the
revolving loan fund.

Cutting across the major line items, two major categories of
expenditures are maintenance of building, equipment, and vehicles
(including the staff salaries related to maintenance) and training
activities of different kinds. The total maintenance budget for 1977-
78 was about Rs. 12 million. The amount allocated to all forms   of
organized training in 1977-78 was approximately Rs. 3 million.

It should be noted that the budget discussed above was only the
indicative target based on the year's plan of activities. We are informed that the actual amount of funds raised and spent would probably
be no more than one-half of the target and would probably affect relative allocations under different heads. Actual revenue and spending
figures were not available at the time of this writing.

NONBUDGETED RESOURCES

Among nonbudgeted resources are the land and buildings donated free of cost and the volunteer labor. Sarvodaya has received free gifts of land and buildings in most villages. The centers at Baddegama, Kandy (Panwila), and even the headquarters at Meth Medura are situationed on donated land. The main buildings at the headquarters now reconstructed and renovated are also donated. The volunteer labor falls under different categories: (1) the Shramadana, or gift of physical labor: volunteers are involved in such activities as the construction of roads, buildings, farms, lavatories, and wells; (2) Buddhidana, or the gift of knowledge: volunteers sometimes contribute their knowledge by teaching skills to others; (3) Saukya-dana, or the gift of health: volunteers devote their time and energy by providing first aid and meeting other needs pertaining to health and sanitation; and finally, (4) Dhamma-dana, or gift of knowledge pertaining to spiritual welfare: volunteers organize, according to each one's religion, religious activities that contribute to spiritual welfare. By 1978, the number of volunteers who had donated their labor or time for various periods of time had reached 300,000.

There is also in-kind contribution. The most prevalent and typical form of such contribution is the donation of food items for the community kitchens; for example, the fistful of rice brought in by each child. Kitchen equipment, furniture, and equipment for community facilities and construction materials are other common items of contribution.

COST COMPARISON

How do Sarvodaya program costs compare with similar government programs? Strict comparisons are not possible, since the programs are not quite similar and details about costs of both kinds of programs are not available. Yet, generally speaking, one may venture to say that similar government programs incur greater expenditure with lesser results. Government programs rarely take into consideration the use that can be made of the cultural and social foundations that exist in a village. A case in point is a government reforestation campaign carried out some years ago in which plants or seeds were distributed and government officials initiated shramadana programs to plant them. Unfortunately, many of the plants died for lack of attention: the people simply had lost interest. In contrast seeds were distributed in Sarvodaya villages and the normal involvement of community elders awakened in the workers a sense of common responsibility, self-interest, and pride. Expenditures involved in the project had been minimal, and the plants were well cared for.

The most important feature of Sarvodaya projects is that the community's own resources of different kinds invariably supplement the resources provided by the Sarvodaya organization and raise the total "productivity" of the resources used in these projects. This rarely happens in government projects.

DEPENDENCE ON EXTERNAL AID

The dependence of Sarvodaya on external assistance has often been criticized both by Sarvodaya people themselves and by outsiders.   Sarvodaya leadership is conscious of the dilemma of an organization preaching self-reliance for rural communities, but itself palpably dependent on external assistance. On the other hand, Sarvodaya's ideal   of universal brotherhood and cooperation supports the notion that the more fortunate ones should extend a helping hand to their less   fortunate brethren, wherever they are. But help is most fruitful where the   recipients of help are determined to help themselves.

Sarvodaya has taken some steps to become increasingly self-reliant, and other steps are under consideration. In principle, the skill training activities of Sarvodaya should not only be self-sufficient but should also generate some income for the movment, inasmuch as all training activities are conducted with commercial production in mind. In practice, as   we have seen, the expectation has not always been fulfilled. More careful selection of skills to be taught, greater management efficiency in   the programs, and more imaginative marketing efforts might make the   learning-cum-production feature of skill training a paying proposition.   The agricultural farm at Tanamalwila, for example, is viewed as an   economic enterprise that could make the regional center self-sufficient.

Decentralization of the entire organization with regional centers and individual villages in charge of planning and implementing   programs is also seen by some as a move towards self-sufficiency. It would   eliminate many of the heavy costs of the central superstructure, both administrative and supervisory; it would obviate the necessity of a continuous two-way movement of the fleet of vehicles and personnel. Some of the central activities, particularly certain training courses, seem to have a momentum of their own and can go on indefinitely without being subjected to a critical assessment of their utility and justification. Decentralization would ideally invite a reassessment of program activities, each one requiring justification in terms of genuine local needs,   and it would impose a discipline by requiring the regional centers and villages to undertake only those activities that resources in their control   can support.

In the meantime, Sarvodaya appears to be able to attract assistance and support from diverse sources both in and out of the country.

CHAPTER 6

A CLOSE-UP VIEW OF

SEVEN SARVODAYA VILLAGES

The seven villages associated with the Sarvodaya movement described in this section represent a spectrum of the 300 or so villages in which the Sarvodaya program has reached the gramodaya stage. Organizations of different interest groups have been established in these villages along typical Sarvodaya lines and an overall directing body of the village Sarvodaya council has been formed; or, at the very least, the villages are in close contact with a nearby Sarvodaya Extension Centre or a regional Sarvodaya Development Centre and usually one or more Sarvodaya volunteer workers deputed from headquarters are posted in each of the villages. By contrast, there are about 1,700 other villages in which Sarvodaya has merely established a rudimentary presence, by undertaking a shramadana project, by holding a meeting with some villagers about Sarvodaya objectives and ideals, or by selecting some village resident for one of the Sarvodaya training courses. No real progress has been made in these villages in setting up permanent village organizations or in launching program activities on a continuing basis.

Whether seven, somewhat arbitrarily selected, villages can serve as an adequate sampling of three hundred villages is a valid question. Geographically and culturally they reflect at least a pattern of the total program. Four of the villages are located in the coastal and southern wet zone, two in the dry zone, and one in the central hill country. Four of the villages are primarily farmers' villages, two are mainly fishermen's, and one is inhabited by people with a caste occupation of mat weaving. People of the Sinhalese-Buddhist origin live in six of the villages, one village is occupied by Sinhalese-Roman Catholic residents. No Tamil, Hindu, or other minority groups are included in the village sampling.

However, the fact that personnel of the Sarvodaya Research Centre were instrumental in the selection of villages and the gathering of information about them makes it likely that the selected villages are fairly typical of other Sarvodaya villages. The general similarity in the pattern of program activities, the organizational approach, the degree of participation of the villagers in the activities, and the evolutionary process of the program in each village also suggest that the selected villages provide a reasonable picture of the accomplishments and shortcomings at the village level of the movement as a whole.

TUNNANA

Special Characteristics

Tunnana is a wet zone Sinhalese-Buddhist village situated 28 kilometres away from Colombo on the Avissawela Road. The village had a population of 3,202 at the end of 1977 with 520 households. Three-quarters
of the 800 acres of farm land in the village are used for rice.   Other
main crops are rubber and coconut. One-half of the adult males in the
village are farmers either owning small plots of land or working as farm
laborers. The rest of the work force is engaged in diverse activities,
including such skills as carpentry and masonry, petty trading,   casual
day-labor, and work in the nearby rubber estates. Three percent of the
workers are regular wage-earners as government, semi-government   and
modern industrial or trade employees.

The villagers form a homogeneous cultural entity: all belong to
the same ethnic and religious group and the same Padu caste considered
to be one of the inferior castes. Poor self-image born of inferior
caste status and social and economic discrimination by neighboring high-
caste villages that surround Tunnana have greatly contributed to the
relative backwardness of the village. The educational level of the village compares unfavorably with the national average. About one-half of
the adult population is literate, 28 percent of the 6-15 age group do
not go to school, and the school dropout rate is high mainly for economic
reasons. Only four people in the village have completed the General Certificate in Education (9 years of schooling).

Although farming is the main occupation, cultivable land is scarce.
Very few families, probably two or three, own over four acres of land and
about 20 percent own less than one-fourth of an acre. The small plots of
land are usually owned jointly by families without clear individual title
of ownership, because establishing individual inheritance would so frag-
ment the land as to make it virtually useless. The average monthly income
of a family is estimated to be Rs. 150 (US$18.00).

The Influence of the Temple

Tunnana is the seat of a respected Buddhist temple established some
forty years ago. The temple and the two resident monks have become   a
powerful influence in the life of the village and have been instrumental
in fostering a sense of community and in taking many social and community
development initiatives. It was one of the monks, the Reverend Tunnana
Sumanatissa, who introduced the shramadana concept of the Sarvodaya movement to the youngsters of the village. The monks actively associated
themselves with the movement and permitted the temple to be the center
of village Sarvodaya activities as well as the seat of a Sarvodaya
extension center that serves 21 villages in the vicinity.

At the initiative of the temple authorities, the government rural services, voluntary activities other than Sarvodaya, and the Sarvodaya program function in close collaboration with each other. Various government-sponsored rural organizations, such as the Rural Development Society, the Death-Aid Society (a traditional mutual-help body), the Sumana Praja Mandalaya (a farmers' association), and the Children's Welfare, are based at the temple; and a monk is the chief patron of all of the societies. The Grama Sevaka, the chief government agent in the village, maintains close liaison with the monk and is an enthusiastic supporter of the Sarvodaya movement. This framework of mutual linkage and cooperation established under the auspices of the temple has proved to be beneficial to all of the organizations and to the people of Tunnana. Often this has meant that government funds and resources--such as concrete slabs for latrines, money for the preschool program, seeds and saplings for reforestation, and anti-rabies vaccine for dogs--have been channeled through the Sarvodaya organization. This has resulted in an effective use of these resources when they have been mobilized with those in the villages.

The apex of the Sarvodaya organizational structure in Tunnana is the Gramodaya Mandalaya (the village reawakening council) consisting of village elders and representatives from other groups such as the mothers' guild, the youth group, and the farmers' club. The Gramodaya Mandalaya, embracing both the traditional and formal leaderships as well as the emerging informal leadership among different interest groups, provides a "social legitimacy" to the Sarvodaya activities and helps to promote a cooperative and integrated approach.

The Preschool Centers and Community Kitchens

Two preschool centers and the attached community kitchens, the most visible parts of the Sarvodaya program in the village, have satisfied an obvious need in Tunnana. About two-thirds of the 100-odd preschool age children attend the two centers and a third is being contemplated to include the others. The "teachers" of the centers are village girls trained in a brief course at the Sarvodaya Training Centre at Meth Medura. The teachers are assisted by two other girls from the village. The teachers are paid a small monthly allowance (Rs. 40) by the central Sarvodaya office.

While the preschool centers look after the socialization process of the children and keep them usefully occupied, the attached community kitchens serve their nutritional needs. The children get a drink prepared with powdered milk donated to Sarvodaya from abroad and a snack made from fistfuls of rice, vegetables and legumes that the children themselves or their mothers bring to the kitchen. The "teachers" also try to promote healthful habits among the children and their mothers and arrange for preventive vaccinations and health inspection on the part of government health personnel.

The mothers' group, scarcely less important than the preschool program and the community kitchen, functions essentially as a support organization for both of them. Prenatal and postnatal care and a more healthy upbringing of children are also its concerns. The preschool teachers and their assistants are the guiding spirits behind the mothers group. One recent development is a plan to set up a mothers' clinic for prenatal check-ups that would be serviced by the government midwife on fixed days of the week. This would save long walks to the government clinic, which have discouraged many mothers from visiting the clinic.

Activities of Youth

The youth group is an informal forum for organizing needed services for the group itself and for the community as a whole. The prime concern of the young people in Tunnana is to find gainful employment and generally to improve their life prospects. Sarvodaya's efforts in this regard have consisted of a training project in batik making and training courses for a small number of village youths in its Meth Medura center in such skills as carpentry and masonry.

About 20 young people have been involved in batik making, but the economic prospect for this skill is somewhat cloudy. The output of the center is now sent to Sarvodaya headquarters for sale, but this does not necessarily hold promise of much income to individual trainees. It is not known what use the trainees at the Meth Medura center are making of their skills; apparently, there was no well thought out plan for gainful utilization of the skills. A government weaving center in the village has not fared much better in solving the livelihood problem of the youth. Training programs in cottage crafts and other common trades generally do not seem to be of much help to the village youth. Some members in most families in the village are adept in one or more crafts or skills and are able to satisfy their own meager needs. What is needed is not so much training but help in opening up new markets for the villagers' products. One step in this direction contemplated by Sarvodaya, but yet to be implemented at the end of 1977, is setting up a shop on the main road to display and sell the village products.

Cooperative Effort

Scarce farm land, highly fragmented landholdings, and dependence on seasonal rainfall leave very limited opportunities for raising the villagers' income through agricultural development. One of Sarvodaya's efforts in this area has been an attempt to revive the now forgotten "kaiya" system by which all the villagers help each other by working together in all of the major steps such as ploughing, planting, and weeding. This process utilizes labor more efficiently, gives a lift to families with fewer working hands, conserves water, and facilitates crop protection. The single wealthy family (the Mudalali) of the village took leadership for this initiative, but, unfortunately, it made others somewhat suspicious of this effort. Furthermore, the advantages of the approach were not sufficiently self-evident to the families with only small plots of land.

Labor intensive commercial crops such as cloves, coffee, and spices are cultivated in small amounts by some of the families. In a land scarce situation, probably more attention could be given to these crops, and appropriate forms of assistance from the government's Department of Agriculture could be sought. Animal raising on a household basis is another possibility. It should be noted in passing that cattle-rustling has been a serious problem in the village, and this naturally discourages the villagers from raising cattle. Sarvodaya, at one stage, with the cooperation of the local authorities, organized a village watch operation and successfully stopped cattle-lifting and robbery, but the arrangement somehow broke down and the project was discontinued with a change in the local police personnel.

The Gramodaya Mandalaya and other subsidiary bodies created by Sarvodaya and the enlightened leadership of the monk have provided mechanisms for orchestrating the different government and voluntary community development actions and for deriving maximum benefit from them. As a consequence whatever meager resources and assistance have been available from various government sources have gone further in eliciting popular response, and in supplementing local resources. The benign influence of the temple and the wide acceptance of the monk's leadership have been crucial factors in the development of the Sarvodaya program in the village and have gone far in making the coordination of effort possible.

Economic Constraints

On the economic front there is perhaps less concrete achievement to show for all the efforts of Sarvodaya. Young people have been attracted to Sarvodaya in the hope of finding an escape from a life of grinding poverty, but most   of them have soon become discouraged because Sarvodaya cannot seem to show them the way out. In spite of the movement's effort to work with the most deprived   elements of society, its uncertainties on the economic front have kept these elements out of the fold. Almost all the families in Tunnana are desperately poor by any standard of measurement, but it is the relatively better off families among the poor who seem to be the principal participants and beneficiaries of the Sarvodaya activities. It comes as no surprise that the cattle-rustlers, the makers of illicit liquor, the gamblers, and the petty thieves, who comprise a sizeable number of Tunnana inhabitants and more of them "bred" naturally in an environment of social and economic deprivation, find the moralistic stance and high ideals of the Sarvodaya organization incomprehensible.

Yet it must be recorded that Sarvodaya in Tunnana has helped to change the self-image of a group of people burdened by a fatal sense of inferiority; it has shown that substantial progress can be made in the right direction through collective efforts; and it has built an institutional base that may prove to be very significant,particularly if the recent national decision to hand over control of development plans and funds to the local people is put effectively into practice.

KIVULEKELE

Special Characteristics

Kivulekele is located in the northeastern dry zone near the town of Puttalam, 82 miles to the north of Colombo. The 454 people of Sinhalese origin belong to 84 families, mostly Buddhist, and a few Christian.

The village in its present form came into being about ten years ago when the government decided to open new settlements in the area by offering plots of land to young people with a secondary school certificate (ten years of schooling). Later, others from the nearby towns and villages also came to   settle there, attracted by logging and timbering opportunities in the surrounding forests.

Land in the village is not as scarce as in many of the other rural areas, and each family owns five or more acres. The land, however, is unsuitable for rice and the usual crops are coconut, tapioca, spices, and certain vegetables. Yields of these crops also depend on a rainfall that can be very erratic; drought has seriously affected the area during the past four years, although a normal rainfall in 1977 was marked by a fever-ish pace of farming activities.

A distinctive characteristic of the village is the absence of caste consciousness because the families have come from different caste back-grounds and different localities, a phenomenon that has prevented   the formation of a well defined caste hierarchy.

Early Beginnings

The village monk invited Sarvodaya to come to the village in 1974, partly as a reaction to the activities of another Colombo-based social service organization. The conduct of the city-bred young men and women of that organization had met with the disapproval of the villagers and the monk. A Sarvodaya worker from headquarters arrived in the village   and several shramadana projects were organized as a means of introducing Sar-vodaya ideals to the villagers. These projects were the construction of two buildings and an approach road into the village, the repair of a "tank" for conserving water for irrigation, and the preparation of land for   a farm that the Sarvodaya organization had acquired.

The initial enthusiasm and high spirit in the village about Sarvo-daya did not last very long, however, mainly because the monk who brought Sarvodaya into the village moved to another temple and the new monk   and the Sarvodaya representative did not get along very well. The situation did not improve much, even after headquarters replaced the Sarvodaya work-er with another.

At the present time (late 1977) the preschool center and the farm are the only visible symbols of Sarvodaya's existence in the village. The preschool center and attached community kitchen were originally set up at the temple, an appropriate location because the temple is in the   center of the village and is regarded as a natural place for community activities. In any case it is visited almost daily by members of the mothers' group, who are supposed to be closely involved in the running of the preschool center and the community kitchen. The Sarvodaya worker, for some reason, perhaps because of a mutual antipathy between himself and the new monk--decided to move himself and the preschool center from the temple to the Sarvodaya farm at the outskirts of the village. This action severed the close connection between the mothers' group and the preschool center-cum-community kitchen. Now the preschool center functions as another kinder-garten without much direct involvement on the part of the mothers. It is to the credit of the preschool teacher, a village girl trained at the Sarvodaya Training Centre as a preschool instructor, that the center and the kitchen still continue to serve about 30 children of the village, though the previous close relationship with the mothers has not continued.

The Farm and Its Management

        The farm, started on a plot borrowed from government reserve land, is
run by two Sarvodaya volunteer workers sent from headquarters along   with
five youths (three girls and two boys) from the village. Although 35 acres
of land were acquired for the farm, only 17 acres are used now. The rest is
in the illegal possession of some of the villagers and is a source of   conflict and ill-feeling between Sarvodaya and the villagers.

        The purpose of the farm and its management by Sarvodaya is not   abun-
dantly clear. Although two full-time Sarvodaya workers, a tractor,   and
other equipment have been made available to the farm, there appears to be no
well thought out management plan. The farm is badly kept, its yields   are
low, and some of the young workers from the village who came to the farm   to
learn new skills and earn a reasonable income have left it in frustration.
It is neither a demonstration and experimental farm for dry zone agriculture
nor a means of income generation for the local Sarvodaya or its young   workers. Ostensibly, the farm is the seat of a Sarvodaya Extension Centre   for
the neighboring villages, but the way the farm functions and serves   the
youths of Kivulekele make it an ineffective extension base.

        In contrast, however, one might mention that in another nearby settle-
ment village, Wanatawilluwa, it is reported that under Sarvodaya auspices a
cooperative land utilization plan involving dairy farming, mixed cropping,
and tapping of underground water resources has been successfully worked out.

Other Projects

        Among other projects of Sarvodaya in Kivulekele are a village market,
set up in collaboration with the Rural Development Society. This market enables villagers to exchange products and commodities within the village instead of travelling several miles to the town. At Sarvodaya's initiative, a
weekly clinic has been arranged in the village in which the government doctor and the public health inspector take care of primary health needs of the
villagers, including vaccinations and inoculations. An effort to bring   in
the extension agent of the agricultural department to instruct   villagers
about improved techniques did not work out very well when the farmers   found
out that some of his advice was clearly wrong. Under Sarvodaya auspices the
youth group prepared a volley ball court and acquired the necessary equipment.

        Although the economic situation in Kivulekele is relatively   homo-
geneous, with most families owning between five and ten acres of land,   there
are three patriarchs of joint families who are very powerful, each one   of
whom owns over 25 acres of land besides having other earnings from trade and
government contracting. The positions of presidents, or patrons, of   such
village organizations as the Rural Development Society, the Death-Aid Society,
and the Buddhist Association, rotate among these three people.   They were
initially supportive of Sarvodaya and encouraged the early shramadana   projects. But later they apparently detected some threat to their own   positions of leadership when a new and younger generation of leaders   emerged
through Sarvodaya activities. The traditional leaders also viewed   with
suspicion the fact that the base of Sarvodaya activities was moved from   the
temple, the domain of the traditional leaders, to the farm, presumably   outside their full control.

Loss of Momentum

It appears that the Sarvodaya organization has lost its early momentum in Kivulekele and faces an uncertain future. The lack of   sympathy of the new monk and the powerful village leaders has contributed to   the lack of effectiveness of Sarvodaya. This suggests that the lack of   enthusiasm, actually the resistance, of the traditional leadership is something Sarvodaya should be prepared to encounter if it wants to serve   the disadvantaged and bring about social change. In any event, uninspired and incompetent leadership on the part of Sarvodaya village workers,   vividly symbolized by the haphazard management of the Kivulekele agricultural farm, cannot long be sustained. An observer comes away with the impression that many opportunities to work with the villagers, to gain their trust, and   to lead them in the path of self-reliant development have been missed by Sarvodaya. It is reported, for instance, that there are sources of   underground water in the village. An organization like Sarvodaya could attempt to tap these sources, probably with the assistance of the government   or other voluntary agencies, and compensate in some part for the aridity   of the land. There is, in fact, the living example of a villager who improved his own fortunes dramatically in the course of a few years by pumping   his own underground water for farming. Sarvodaya has failed to utilize   the mothers' group and the shramadana institution to remedy the deplorable sanitary and hygienic condition of the village: six latrines for 84 families and unprotected dug wells as the source of drinking water.   Sarvodaya's organized self-help approach would make a dramatic difference in the marketing of such Kivulekele products as cassava and coconut. As most of the villagers find it difficult and even unprofitable to carry their   individual small quantities of marketable produce to the town seven miles away, they are at the mercy of itinerant merchants who buy the produce at   a high discount. A cooperative marketing project in this situation   might ensure a fairer deal for the small village farmers.

GINIMELLAGAHA

General Features

Ginimellagaha is a small farming village in the wet southern zone of the island, about 80 miles from Colombo. Baddegama Educational Development Centre of Sarvodaya, one of five such regional centers, is about four miles away from the village.

Ginimellagaha had a population of 2,662 of Sinhalese-Buddhist origin at the end of 1976; it has a land area of about 640 acres, one-third of which is used for growing rice. Rubber is the other principal crop. Only four or six of the 509 families own more than four acres of land. The river Ginganga passes by the village and overflows two or three times a year disrupting communication and damaging crops   and property. From a social point of view, the village is divided between the original residents and the settlers who at one time were   allotted land by the government (during the late 1950s and the early 1960s)   to settle in the area and came from the neighborhood as well as from some distance. The settlers do not have the kinship and caste affinity among themselves as do the   old residents of the village.

About 70 percent of the village people can read and write. A quarter of   the youth population has completed the General Certificate of Education (ten years   of schooling). The village has a primary school that offers instruction up to the eighth standard. A secondary school exists in a neighboring village. The village also has a religious school run by the monk that meets once a week, where nearly 60 children learn about religion. A few of the villagers work as clerks, teachers, traders, and similar occupations. All others are farmers. Most of the farming families attempt to supplement their earnings by some nonfarm activities--such as weaving, brick mak- ing, and collecting latex. The products of these labors are sold to local merchants for a very small return.

The Influence of a Family

A shramadana project for the purpose of building an approach road was organized in Ginimellagaha in 1966 by a service organization called the Perakum Shramadana So- ciety. A local leader of that project, Mr. Amara Pennappurema, became interested in Sarvodaya and joined forces with the monk of Baddegama to bring Sarvodaya to   the village. Soon after a Sarvodaya youth group was organized, other collective activi- ties such as a mothers' group, gramodaya, preschool, and the community kitchen came in its wake.

Mr. Pennappurema and his family have played a dominant role in organizing the Sarvodaya activities in the village. Their home is the meeting place for the youth group, the mothers, and the gramodaya council; even training sessions for youths have been held there. The Pennappurema family, by virtue of its leadership and common memberships, is also the link between the Sarvodaya and other traditional community organizations such as the Death-Aid Society, recreational and cultural groups, reli- gious organizations, and such government-sponsored bodies as the Rural Development Society, and the Agricultural Productivity Committee.

Major Activities

The major Sarvodaya activities in the village, in addition to shramadana, are the preschool group and community kitchen, the mothers' group, skill training, the industrial unit, shanti seva (community service), the youth organization,   and the gramodaya village council.

In keeping with the classic organizational approach of Sarvodaya, shramadana has been used to introduce the movement into the village and to build up the insti- tutions and the programs. Through shramadana projects, the villagers have built a one-and-a-half mile long road, buildings for the gramodaya council and the industry and carpentry centers, a dwelling for the monk, a classroom for a Methodist school in a neighboring village, and the community kitchen; they have prepared the   land for construction of a rubber processing plant; and they have farmed the land attached to the community kitchen to provide supplies for the kitchen.

The preschool program and the community kitchen began with 54 children but that number was reduced to 25 children in 1977, mainly   because a government pre- school facility was opened in the neighborhood. The preschool teacher, a young woman from the village, was trained in a three-month course at the Sarvodaya head- quarters. She is assisted by two other girls from the village. The activities for the children are conducted for three hours in the morning,   five   days   a week. The   mothers'   group   is actively involved   in the   program,   and

once a month the mothers formally meet the teachers to discuss the management of the program. The attached kitchen serves over 1500 meals a year
prepared with general provisions donated by the villagers   and powdered
milk supplied by Sarvodaya. Physical and social development,   nutrition,
and elementary health care for the children are the primary concern of the
preschool program.

The carpentry workshop and the industrial unit are training-cum-pro-
duction facilities where skilled workers as well as learners participate.
The skilled workers from the village use the facilities and the equipment
for supplementing their own incomes, while at the same time they teach the
skills to other youths in the village. As timber is available at little or
no cost from nearby forests, the carpentry project has done relatively well
in both carpentry production and training of carpenters.

Youth Groups

About 18 members of the youth group have also been engaged in other
production activities such as basket and mat weaving, and making   tooth-
powder (substitute for toothpaste). In all of these manufacturing   activities there are two unsolved problems. The marketing of products   is
uncertain at best, and it is difficult for the young learners to   advance
from apprenticeship to ownership of an economically viable enterprise. An
effort to run a cloth weaving center and a latex processing plant   failed
because the program could not supply the raw materials and could not   ensure a ready market for the products.

Shanti seva (literally, service to promote happiness   and   peace),
another aspect of the local Sarvodaya program, involves the youth   and
other villagers in organizing religious, cultural, and recreational activities in the village. A small lending library is also included in   the
service program of shanti seva.

The youth organization consisting of over 80 members is the motivating force behind all of the activities described above. The youths   are
the participants and direct beneficiaries of many of the activities,   and
they provide both the manpower and the leadership. About one-fourth of the
total membership is considered to be highly active in Sarvodaya   affairs,
while others participate less actively and more intermittently.

The Gramodaya Council, representing the village elders, is somewhat
informal in character and provides social legitimacy, sponsorship,   and
protection to the Sarvodaya activities by offering its general approval of
youthful initiatives.

Tangible Achievements

Some of the achievements of the Sarvodaya movement in Ginimellagaha
are tangible and readily evident. Physical infrastructures such as   roads,
community buildings, and leveled land for community use have certainly been
facilitated and expedited by Sarvodaya-inspired shramadana.   The preschool
program and the community kitchen serve the obvious needs of a large number

of young children. The shanti seva activities enrich the social and cultural
life of the village. Less tangible results of the Sarvodaya efforts are no
less significant. The movement has helped to mobilize the resources of the
village for common purposes and has given villagers a sense of   collective
strength and confidence. The Sarvodaya activities have provided an outlet for
the idealism and energy of the young people in the village.   The collective
activities of mothers, youth, and elders have created a mechanism   for   the
potential integration of traditional, governmental, and communal   initiatives
and for the participation of the villagers in the programs inspired by them.

Clouds of Uncertainty

These results, important by themselves, should probably be seen from a
broader perspective of the overall development needs and prospects of   the
village. Sarvodaya has not really alleviated the economic situation of   the
village. The skill development and manufacturing activities have   involved
small numbers of youth and do not appear to offer an economically viable solution to the employment problem.

In Ginimellagaha the role of the monk at the village temple as organizer and guide of Sarvodaya activities has been taken over by Mr. Pennapperuma
and his family. However well-intentioned and responsible the members of this
family are, it is they who dominate the movement and probably most   other
affairs in the village. The small number of low caste washermen and fishermen families (about 25 out of over 500 families) appear to be neither participants in nor beneficiaries of Sarvodaya activities. Activities   on   the
whole are restricted to the relatively prosperous original settlers of   the
village. The "colonists," economically worse off, educationally   backward,
and without the homogeneity of kinship ties, have generally remained   aloof
from the movement. Sarvodaya at one time made an effort to run a preschool
center in the "colonist" section of the village, but it closed down when for
some reason the Sarvodaya headquarters failed to supply the powdered   milk
for the center and the parents very likely in consequence lost interest in it.

At this time of flux it is difficult to visualize if or what changes in
strategy and policies of the Sarvodaya activities in the village will   make
Sarvodaya more effective in serving the needs of the more disadvantaged sections of the village population.

TALAWILA

A Seacoast Village

Situated on the seacoast 98 miles north of Colombo, Talawila is a dry
zone Sinhalese-Roman Catholic village of about 1500 people. About 160   of
the 280-odd families depend on fishing for a living; about 100 are   farmers;
and the remainder are engaged in diverse occupations.

The village has a total land area of 1500 acres. In addition to rain-
fed rice the farmers of Talawila grow tobacco, onions, and chillies. Fishing
is done mostly in wooden rowboats and by hauling nets during the months from
September to April when the sea is not too rough. A few of the   fishermen's
families own motorized boats. Though the rewards are not always   adequate,
fishing and farming provide ample employment opportunities to all the able-

bodied workers in the village. This is in contrast to many rural areas in the country.

Church Influence

Talawila is the seat of an old Catholic church and the site   of twice-a-year religious festivals to which come devout Catholics from   all over the island. The priest at St. Anne's church was instrumental   in bringing Sarvodaya to the village. He is also the patron of the government-sponsored Rural Development Society, the local branch of the   church-organized Socio-economic Development Committee (SEDEC), and the   Sarvodaya. All of these organizations have been brought together in the village in an apex organization called the Talawila Committee for Rural Development (comparable to the village reawakening councils in other Sarvodaya villages). At the initiative of the priest, the first Sarvodaya shramadana project to build a road in the village was undertaken in 1974. (Other later   shramadana projects included public and family latrines and wells for   drinking water.) At the same time, the preschool center of the village run by   the church was handed over to the local Sarvodaya committee, a mothers' group was formed, and a village girl was sent to a Sarvodaya training center for preschool training. A full-time worker from Sarvodaya headquarters   was also sent to the village.

Preschool Center and Kitchen

About one-half of the village children (an average of 60)   between three and six years of age attend the preschool center.   The preschool teacher, a very energetic and personable young lady,   has managed   to establish a very close and personal relationship with the children   and their families. The mothers gladly receive her advice on their children's nutrition and health problems and even consult her on other family matters. The teacher is paid an allowance of Rs. 75 per month by Sarvodaya   headquarters; this is half the amount a government preschool teacher   is paid. However, the teacher's own identification with the village children and the supporting role of the mothers' group make the Talawila preschool   center much more effective than the usual government kindergarten.

The community kitchen attached to the preschool center serves   five days a week a nutritious meal prepared with donated powdered milk supplied by central Sarvodaya, fistfuls of rice brought in by the children,   other vegetables, coconuts and dried fish contributed by the mothers' group,   and food items put aside by the priest from offerings made to the church. The preparation of the community kitchen meals and the involvement   of   the mothers' group in the community kitchen project have become a means for the introduction of basic nutrition concepts and practices in the village.

Other Enterprises

The most important economic project of the village is the   young farmers' club and its three small farms that are run on a cooperative basis by the youths themselves on about 15 acres of leased land.   High priced commercial crops such as tobacco, chilli, and onions are grown   on   these farms. The priest serves as a management adviser to the farms and has arranged for production loans from SEDEC that are repaid from the profits after the produce is marketed. About ten young men are participants in this project.

Other economic enterprises engaged in by the village youth   include making handicraft items, drying and packaging cashew nuts, and packaging shrimp powder from shrimps too small to be sold in the market. These items find   a ready market during the semi-annual religious festivals when many visitors come to the village. The possibility of exporting powdered shrimp is being explored by a Dutch voluntary organization. A training project in basket weaving   has also been initiated in the village and ten young people have joined it.   However, the marketability of the baskets is uncertain.

The economy of the village can be greatly improved if technological innovations can be brought to the fish-catching enterprise: mechanization of the catching process; improvements in packaging, transporting and marketing,   and the introduction of better storage, preservation, and processing   facilities. Greater promise lies in having the fishermen themselves   control their   business through cooperative ownership. All these, of course, take capital investment and special knowledge far beyond the means of Sarvodaya or the   local church. A small effort in this direction was made by the priest by   arranging for small loans to young fishermen for the purpose of purchasing their   own boats, nets, and other equipment. Even this rudimentary effort provoked   the antagonism of merchants in the village and outside who owned the fishing gear, in general monopolize the marketing process, and in effect allow   a   mere subsistence wage to the fishermen themselves.

Implications of Priestly Leadership

Community development activities in Talawila owe their existence to the dynamic leadership and devotion of the priest, the Reverend Emmanuel Fernando. Father Fernando and his church in Talawila, it might be said, are   counterparts of the monk and the temple in the Sarvodaya villages with a Buddhist population. In any event he has committed the resources and influence of the church to the cause of welfare and development of the entire village. He has induced the Grama Sevaka, the government representative in the village, to become an active member of the Village Development Committee--a significant fact because in most   other Sarvodaya villages the Grama Sevaka has not become identified with the Gramodaya Council or its equivalent. The priest has tried to overcome the conservatism of the local Roman Catholic families by sponsoring youth group activities   under church auspices for boys and girls. When the fishermen's irregular working hours during the fishing season prevent them from coming to the village gathering, the priest keeps in touch with each family through personal visits.

It is noteworthy that the priest's breadth of mind and outlook had made it possible for the Roman Catholic village to be associated with Sarvodaya,   a movement generally identified with the Buddhist faith and tradition. The   Roman Catholic hierarchy has apparently not been entirely happy about the association-- particularly because some village activities regarded as inspired by Sarvodaya have received small financial support from the SEDEC church fund.   Sensing this sentiment, the Sarvodaya headquarters has lately withdrawn its own representative from the village. Sarvodaya, in a formal sense, therefore, does not exist in the village. Nevertheless, the Sarvodaya activities and spirit live on under   the able guidance of Father Fernando.

The dominant role of a single towering personality in Talawila raises a question that might just as well be raised here: what would happen to all the community development and self-help initiatives if the priest were to be moved to another parish? This is not an uncommon problem in several Sarvodaya villages. Another common Sarvodaya feature found in Talawila is that the movement has remained confined to a few regular activities such as the preschool group, community kitchen, and some skill training and crafts projects. Its achievements in the economic field have been limited as in other villages, although the cooperative farm project for the youths is a notable exception. One problem in the village that neither Sarvodaya nor any other agency has tried to do anything about is the very high school dropout rate of children. The main reason appears to be the seasonal character of the fishing operation, in which all male members of the family including adolescents are involved on a 24-hour basis during certain parts of the year. A school program designed to accommodate this special feature of the local fishing occupation could probably cut the dropout rate substantially.

ATULUGAMKANDA

The First Sarvodaya Village

Atulugamkanda is a wet zone Sinhalese-Buddhist village situated on the Avissawella-Kegalle road, about six miles from the town of Dehiowita and 44 miles from Colombo. The village has 98 families (78 homesteads) with a total population of 427 (late 1977). It is a village of craftsmen and laborers; most adult males work as masons, carpenters, and laborers in the nearby rubber plantation. The entire village (except for four high caste families) belongs to the same Padu caste, regarded as inferior in the caste structure.

The village has been associated with the Sarvodaya movement for several years, being the first of the planned 1000 village development scheme. The village came into the Sarvodaya fold through the initiative of Mr. P. A. Kiriwandeniya, one of the current leaders of the movement. When Mr. Kiriwandeniya was a teacher in a nearby monastic school, the village was hit by a severe flood and threatened by epidemic diseases in the wake of the flood. Mr. Kiriwandeniya persuaded the local authorities, the monks, and the local people to engage in a shramadana project to clean up the debris left by the flood and to take preventive measures against diseases. This self-help effort impressed the villagers with their own potentialities and other small shramadana projects followed, leading to a more formal association of the village with the movement.

As in other Sarvodaya villages, the movement's programs have been put into action through various groups, such as youth groups, the workers' groups, and elders' groups. The specific activities follow the pattern of Sarvodaya programs elsewhere and include a preschool center, a community kitchen, skill training in batik and printing and masonry, and a shop for selling both village products and the essential consumer items of the villagers.

Eclipse of a Promise

The Sarvodaya program in Atulugamkanda has to be described for the most part in the past tense because the program has been on the wane and many of the activities have lapsed since the original initiator of the program in the village, Mr. Kiriwandeniya, left the area to join the headquarters staff of Sarvodaya. The two volunteers selected from the village also moved to the headquarters and others who replaced them failed to rejuvenate the program. The absence of a temple and a resident monk in the village has also meant that there has been no rallying point or leadership in the village itself for community development activities. A temple has recently been built in the village, but a monk has yet to be found to take residence in the temple.

During the more active days of Sarvodaya in Atulugamkanda, about 50 youths belonged to the youth group and about 60 children attended the pre-school center. At the end of 1977, only 10 or 15 young people were reported to be active in the program; only 30 or so children benefited from the preschool center and the community kitchen. About 20 mothers belonged to the mothers' group, and this meant essentially that they helped in keeping the community kitchen running. Up to 20 heads of families were reported to gather irregularly for the elders' meetings.

The skill training effort did not prove to be successful. Training in batik printing did not evince enthusiastic response from the village youths because they saw little economic gain in it in the absence of a proven market for the products. A group of 15 youths from the village were sent to the Sarvodaya training center at Moratuwa for training in masonry, but again, it appears, without much thought for the market this skill would command after completion of their training. None of the trainees has found it possible to take up masonry as a means of livelihood. Another group of youngsters from the village were sent to a Sarvodaya-sponsored settlement about 140 miles away to learn to become farmers and eventually to settle there as farmers. This venture was disappointing, even frustrating, to the youngsters. The land lacking sufficient water was not particularly productive. There was very little help or encouragement available to the youngsters when they arrived, and there was apparently very little advance planning on the part of the Sarvodaya workers. Another project to help villagers raise commercial crops was launched, and a supply of pepper and clove saplings were received from the Department of Agriculture. Again the project failed for lack of systematic follow-up and support efforts.

The shop established by Sarvodaya turned into a little grocery store for the villagers--a convenience but hardly a vehicle for promoting the sale of village products.

Atulugamkanda seems to be one story of the partial extinction of the flame of hope kindled by Sarvodaya some years ago. It is apparent that the project here faltered because unimaginative and run-of-the-mill workers from Sarvodaya failed to follow up the pioneering work of the first leader. In any case able leadership somehow did not emerge from the village itself.

HENAWALA

A Mat-Weaving Community

Henawala is a Sinhalese-Buddhist village in the central hill country about ten miles from the town of Kandy. Fifty-three families consisting of about 250 people live in the village. They belong to the Kinnara caste, regarded as one of the lowest in the Sinhalese social structure. The families own little or no farm land, which amounts to a total of 9 acres of rice land and 15 acres of land in which cocoa, cloves, and coffee are grown for the whole village. Weaving mats from a burlap-like plant fibre that grows wild in the area is the main occupation of the people.

Mat weaving is a caste occupation in which the entire family participates. In ancient times, the mats were prepared and used for ceremonial purposes in the king's court, and the villagers in return were looked after by the court. Today these mats are just another product without much commercial value, and the families engaged in this occupation can hardly make more than Rs. 100 (about US$12.50 in 1977 exchange rate) per month.

Sarvodaya Beginnings and Problems

The monk, the Reverend Premavansa, living in the neighboring village of Hurikaduwa where a Sarvodaya extension center is located, conceived the idea of bringing Sarvodaya to the extremely poor and "lowly" Kinnara people of Henawala. The monk took residence in the village in 1973 and initiated a shramadana project to build a road into the village. The expectations generated by the monk's initiatives, however, were short lived, because he ultimately decided to go to a Bhikhu Training Institute, and the volunteer workers sent from Sarvodaya to carry on the initiative the monk had begun proved to be ineffective.

The usual Sarvodaya institutions such as the preschool center, community kitchen, mothers' group, and the youth group were not attempted here. Apparently, the village was economically and socially too deprived to mount the minimum effort needed to launch such activities. It was, for instance, difficult to find a village girl with the minimum educational background to be trained as the preschool instructor or to persuade the villagers to contribute to the community kitchen from their meager family food supply.

Under Sarvodaya auspices, a plan to grow the plant that provides the fibre for the mats (instead of relying on the unreliable wild growth) and to establish a training center to improve the skills of the mat weavers was initiated. The plan was not thought out thoroughly and ran into various snags. In essence the village had no land to spare for growing the fibre plant. Probably a solution could have been found by working out an arrangement with the government authorities to use nearby reserve land, but this was not pursued. The skill center idea was also not very well conceived, because the villagers had perfected the traditional weaving skill through generations of practice, and every family had one or more skilled craftsman who passed on the skill to the younger generation. In fact, the problem was that the mats were too highly artistic and their time-consuming production by craftsmen of exceptional skill made them too costly for the local market. What the villagers needed most were strategies of marketing their art-quality products outside the locality and of making economically priced items for local consumption. Possibly a close liaison with the small industries de-partment, the tourist board, or other agencies of the government would have been helpful in formulating a plan to vitalize this village's economy.

Alleviation of Caste Prejudice

The Sarvodaya movement, to its great credit, has attempted to erase the stigma of caste inferiority and the attitude of subservience and fatalism it has engendered among the Kinnara people. By paying attention to the plight of these people, by associating with them, and by living and eating with them, the Sarvodaya volunteers in the village and in the Sarvodaya extension center in the nearby high caste village have helped to soften the harsh prejudices against the people in Henawala. Only recently it was considered inappropriate for a monk to visit the village or to receive the traditional alms. Now the situa-tion has changed, but still there is a long way to go before the villagers find themselves free from the burden of caste prejudice and other forms of social and economic deprivation. In spite of obvious gains, Sarvodaya's pre-sent lack of effectiveness in Henawala does not portend a very prominent role for Sarvodaya in any struggle for social and economic emancipation for the vil-lagers.

YAKDEHIMULLA

Fishing for a Livelihood

Yakdehimulla is a tiny fishing village at the southern tip of the is-land, five miles from the town of Galle. The Sinhalese-Buddhist population of about 300 belong to 52 families huddled together on a 2.5 acre strip of land along the coast. Possessing no farm land and having no other occupational op-portunity available, all of the families depend on fishing for their livelihood. Fishing, however, is carried out in a primitive way with small rowboats and simple nets. It can be undertaken without risk of life for only about six months in a year when the sea is relatively calm. Fishing, therefore, offers far from an adequate living for the Yakdehimulla villagers. The socioeconomic situation of the village is reflected in the fact that the village has no pri-mary school or any other community facility except a temple. There are only three latrines for all 52 families and a single dug-out well for drinking water.

Preschool Center and Community Kitchen

The complex of the preschool center, the community kitchen, and the mothers' group is designed to serve the health and nutrition needs of children and mothers in the village. The preschool teacher, a local girl trained at Sarvodaya headquarters, takes an active interest in the physical development and health habits of the children in her charge. She also acts as an "inter-mediary" in getting the public health inspector to distribute vitamin tablets. She encourages the mothers to have their children take the triple antigen in-jections from the nearby health center. The community kitchen provides por-tions of rice and other food items brought to the preschool center by the children or donated by the villagers. This contribution is supplemented by powdered milk supplied by Sarvodaya. All the children, whether enrolled in the preschool center or not, pregnant mothers, and invalid and needy adults share the meals of the community kitchen.

In Yakdehimulla Sarvodaya is identified most prominently with   the preschool center-cum-community kitchen, which fulfills an extremely   important need and has generated much goodwill for the movement.   This goodwill, however, does little to improve the precarious economic situation of the villagers, which is the main concern of all the village households. Sarvodaya does not appear to have any definite plan to address this   main economic problem of the village; it is by no means clear what Sarvodaya can really do about it.

CONCLUSIONS AND LESSONS

ACCOMPLISHMENTS OF SARVODAYA

It is difficult to judge the impact of the Sarvodaya program because its objectives relate to spiritual reawakening,   inculcating moral values, promoting certain personal habits and conduct, and--secondarily--undertaking certain social services and economic activities for collective   and indivi- dual benefit. The problem of development is seen by the leaders   of Sarvodaya, not so much in terms of the production and distribution of goods and services and building the institutional structures for that purpose   as in terms of awakening the innate goodness in the heart of man and returning to traditional values and codes of conduct which essentially can provide so- lutions to the problems of society. Social services and economic projects, as it were, are occasions for practising loving kindness, sympathetic   joy, equanimity, and pleasant speech, and, only incidentally, the means for meet- ing obvious needs. It is important that observers of Sarvodaya   understand these objectives in the order of their importance.

It has to be assumed that the immediate results of the effort   to adopt and practise the philosophical ideals and moral   principles   find tan- gible expression in the social and economic program activities in   the   vil- lages, and one has to assess the impact of the Sarvodaya movement   on   the basis of these activities, however inadequate such assessment may be.

As we have noted, the shramadana projects of Sarvodaya   have attrac- ted 300,000 volunteers from all walks of life and from all parts   of   the island for various durations. This widespread participation in   development projects and exposure to the Sarvodaya values cannot be taken lightly.   They have presumably made the participants better human beings and have given them a better understanding of rural life and its problems.   Shramadana projects have also constructed badly needed roads, canals, and community   facilities; they have built houses for poor and disabled families, lavatories, wells, and buildings for farms and factories. In short, they have addressed   themselves to human needs.

Some 2,000 villages, out of a total of 24,000 in the country,   have come in contact with Sarvodaya. About 300 of these villages have   reached what is called the gramodaya stage. In the gramodaya village, an   organiza- tional structure for community development action has been established,   and one or more projects--a preschool center-cum-community kitchen,   a skill training project, a cultural and religious group, or a farm--continue   to function. The Sarvodaya councils representing the village elders and   other interest groups provide not only the forum for collective planning   and decisionmaking on matters of common interest, but also--at least in some   in- stances--they have become the machinery for helping the effective implementa- tion of government development services in the locality, pressuring   and

keeping a watch on government agencies where this is necessary, and mobilizing local resources to supplement government inputs.

The Most Distinctive Sarvodaya Effort

The preschool group-community kitchen-mothers' group complex--   the
most widespread community service in Sarvodaya villages--caters to   the
health, nutrition, and social development needs of thousands of   children
throughout the island. To a lesser degree, this complex also   provides
health education and some health care to mothers at prenatal and   postnatal
stages. This program has served as liaison with the government health service in bringing immunization and basic health care within the reach   of
children and mothers in many Sarvodaya villages.

Participation of Youth

Thousands of youth in the rural areas have found a constructive outlet for their idealism and energy through the youth organizations in   Sarvodaya villages. These organizations have been the vehicle for introducing
Sarvodaya values to the youth and to engage them in community activities of
a cultural, recreational, and religious nature. Sarvodaya villages   with
youth organizations have proved to be of great value in facing emergencies
or even natural calamities, such as floods and cyclones. At times of social
tension--for instance, during the 1971 youth insurrection and 1977   ethnic
conflicts--villages with well-established Sarvodaya organizations have retained their poise and remained peaceful in a time of destructive turbulence.

The youth have been prominently involved in shramadana projects and
other economic projects for their own benefit. Various skill training programs found in all Sarvodaya centers and in many villages and other economic projects that combine production and learning are primarily aimed   at
the youth. On the whole, these activities have fared less well   largely
because they have paid attention mainly to the teaching of skills and have
ignored or failed to solve problems of marketing and allied barriers to the
growth of rural production. As a result, many young men who have been attracted to Sarvodaya with the hope of improving their economic lot   have
become disappointed and even frustrated.

Agriculture

Similarly, in the field of agriculture, the main approach   followed
by Sarvodaya has been to engage youths in farm work to teach them the necessary skills. In most cases, however, insufficient attention   has   been
given to the problems of access to land for the youths, of fragmented landholdings that prevent farming on an economical scale, of questions of overall
utilization and management of land either of a family or a community, and of
workable provisions for inputs and markets. Management of the farms   under
the control of Sarvodaya organization has been generally poor, and economic
satisfaction both for Sarvodaya and for participant workers has been low.

The Backdrop of Caste and the Persistence of Poverty

Sarvodaya has deliberately concentrated its program efforts among the
lowliest of the low caste villages beginning from the very first village of
Kanatholuwa in 1958, thus taking on the most difficult development tasks of

all. In many of these villages the community infrastructure such as roads,
wells, latrines, and community buildings has improved; the cultural   and
recreational life has brightened; and useful services such as preschool centers and community kitchens have been established. In spite of Sarvodaya's
concentration on the depths of poverty, the economic situation of the families and the life prospects of the young people in these villages   have
remained essentially unchanged as the close-up view of selected   villages
indicates. At Atulugamkanda, for instance, the first of the 1000   village
program, which is considered to have reached the gramodaya stage,   the
tangible evidence of Sarvodaya efforts are the preschool center, the batik
center that cannot readily sell its product, and a grocery stall.   The
village remains steeped in poverty and there is no effective program   to
lift it from this state.

        Another example, regarded as representing a more successful   Sarvo-
daya effort, is the village of Tunnana; but even here Sarvodaya has   made
little difference in the standard of living of most of the village families.
It is true that some families here attend the gatherings of family elders,
take part in shramadana, and send the children to the preschool center with
more enthusiasm than is generally found; but then there are many families
who do not participate in Sarvodaya activities at all and are oblivious to
the Sarvodaya presence in the village. It is likely that for the lowliest
groups, such as the mat weavers in Henawala, the Sarvodaya presence   has
helped to soften the harshness of the most invidious caste prejudices (now
at least the monk receives the offerings of the people of Henawala),   to
highlight the seriousness of the caste problem, and to give the suffering
people some inducement not to accept injustice with unquestioning submission.

Theory and Practice

        The preaching of universalist values and the harking back   to the
ideals of the past by Sarvodaya do not appear to have transformed   individual villages into cooperative communities pooling their resources   and
labor to help all the residents of the community. The old conflicts   of
divided interests, factionalism, the socioeconomic relationships, and the
relative level of deprivation persist. In most villages the Sarvodaya organization and its activities are sustained by the interest and influence
of the monk, whose transfer to another temple (as we have seen) brings the
organization to a near collapse. The focus on spiritual development   and
the reliance on the monk, generally a symbol of conservatism, are viewed
by many as a deliberate rejection on the part of Sarvodaya of the realities
of the structure of economic exploitation. These critics of Sarvodaya are
found among both the educated elites and the politically conscious   elements in the rural areas aligned with certain national parties.   These
critics see the solution to the problems of deprivation and   exploitation
in vigorous political and economic action and not in preaching messages of
brotherhood and love. They find Sarvodaya's spiritual leanings and reformist stance essentially retrograde, and therefore they identify   the
Sarvodaya movement with the rightist and conservative political forces in
the country. Whether they are justified or not in their assessment   and
characterization of Sarvodaya, this attitude has the result of dividing and
polarizing public opinion even in remote villages with a highly politicized

citizenry and of impeding participation of all the people of a village in Sarvodaya activities.

GENERAL LESSONS

Some general lessons from the Sarvodaya experience for community development programs are presented below.

1. As we have seen, planning and management of the total Sarvodaya program controlled from the Meth Medura headquarters, has created a monolithic structure that does not serve well the purpose of the movement. In the largest part because of the lack of qualified men in the field where local planning could be carried out, planning and management has become the prerogative and the burden of the Meth Medura headquarters. Plans now take shape at central headquarters; they are supervised by headquarters, and they are controlled by headquarters--and with a tight grasp on the budget. The enforcement of central control also requires personnel and time, as well as money.

Planning at the grass roots level can take place only if villagers are enabled to develop a capacity for their own planning. Villagers need outside help in developing this capacity. It is in this much needed enterprise that workers of voluntary organizations like Sarvodaya can play a crucial role. But these workers themselves have to understand and learn about the realities of planning projects and programs at the local level. The kind of training Sarvodaya volunteers receive in farming or community development is evidently inadequate and not attuned to actual circumstances. When a volunteer returns to his or another village he is not equipped to plan a farm, much less to manage it. Perhaps rural people themselves, those who manage small farms and other enterprises, can be a more fruitful source of knowledge for the volunteers. Some of the rural practitioners could be brought together to analyze the planning and management processes they themselves have been applying in managing their own enterprises. In any case making planning and management decisions in a central headquarters far away from the village is a poor substitute for learning from the local situation and generating competence at the local level.

2. Without an integrated approach the implementation of any aspect of rural development becomes difficult. As economic factors are closely bound up with social, religious, and cultural factors, the preparation of one program and its effective development presupposes the presence and development of other related programs. For example, a health program cannot be developed, say, by the building of village latrines; because, without an economic program there may be no land to build even a latrine as at Yakdehimulla, without an educational program the people may not be motivated and trained to use the latrines, and without a cultural or social program the cultural or social patterns of behavior may be incongruous with the use of such latrines. Although different interrelated needs require diverse programs especially tailored to suit the exigencies at hand, the needs are inextricably interwoven with one another and the solution of one depends on the solution of others.

Integration of programs in the village is helped by some commonality of leadership in the different organizations and programs. At Ginimellagaha, for instance, whatever success Sarvodaya has achieved is due to the fact that the same group of ardent youths are represented in different village organizations. This does not mean that the same clique must control the entire set of organizations. It simply means that the same group of people in the community have different needs and problems that in turn are handled by different organizations.

Utilization of the sociocultural pattern in organizing different activities contributes to integration. The central place of the temple or the church in village life and the respect and trust enjoyed by the monk or the priest can be used to great advantage when the temple or church becomes the base for different activities and the monk or priest is assured of a prominent role in these activities.

3. It is universally accepted that an effective community development strategy requires an intimate understanding of the community. Sarvodaya experience shows that this understanding has to be achieved by truly being "immersed" in the community. The Sarvodaya pioneers, motivated by the simple purpose of doing something "useful" for the backward communities, lived in these communities and identified themselves with the people. This experience over a number of years has gone far in helping Sarvodaya to develop an authentic and indigenous strategy for community development. The people understand and accept Sarvodaya principles and philosophies when they are seen to be consonant with their own customs, traditions, and values. Sarvodaya, of course, has to disavow the obscurantist and antiquated social customs and appeal to the more universal and progressive values in the religious and cultural tradition of the people.

4. Another Sarvodaya lesson is that a community development program must cater to different sexes, age groups, occupations, and interests in the village. Among these groups the youth need and deserve special attention, both because young people bring vigor, enthusiasm, and idealism to community development activities and because, standing at the threshold of their own adult roles and responsibilities, they need special help in shaping their own future.

5. Sharing experiences in different program activities is a vital informal process of education encouraged by Sarvodaya. In fact, shramadana is an informal sharing of experiences. Similarly, all other activities involve a sharing of experiences and learning for all concerned. This learning is not just the acquisition of new skills and information, but is the formation of new attitudes, the acquisition of new vision and insight, the achievement of a consensus about common objectives. The informal learning process through which the organization's principles and values are internalized and common goals are accepted is eventually more important for the success of the organization than the more direct and formal educational activities, such as skill training and preschool centers.

6. The poorest segments of the rural society can be reached only by initiating programs that have a direct relevance and immediate meaning to them. The poorest families in Sri Lanka villages are usually unaware of the existence of many organizations such as the rural development society, Praja Mandalaya, and religious societies, although the majority of

them participate in the Death-Aid Society and Debt Reconciliation Society--
two societies dealing with two vital concerns of the poor.

Many activities that are intended for the poor, such as various government services, can reach them only if they are organized as collective
entities ready to demand what belongs to them. Once the people are made
aware of their rights and privileges, it is no longer possible for a government official, or even the worker of a voluntary agency, to act according to his whims and fancies. Raising the level of consciousness about one's
worth as a human being, the roots of injustice, and the possibilities for
change, is particularly important for groups of people oppressed for generations in a caste system sanctioned by tradition and cultural values.

8 Planning from the Bottom Up: Community-Based Integrated Development Rural in South Korea

Vincent S.R. Brandt
Ji Woong Cheong

EDITOR'S NOTE

This report is the result of a collaborative effort by two social scientists--an American social anthropologist and a Korean rural sociologist--who were exceptionally well-qualified for the assignment. Professor Vincent S. R. Brandt had studied Korean society for many years and just prior to the present case study had engaged in an extensive case study of the Saemaul Undong (New Community Movement), which forms an important part of the context of the CBIRD program. Dr. Ji Woong Cheong, Professor of Community Development at the College of Agriculture of Seoul National University, had done numerous previous field studies of rural development in both Korea and the Philippines and already had a first-hand acquaintance with the CBIRD program.

These researchers were encouraged by ICED to give special attention to qualitative evaluation of the CBIRD projects in terms of organizational and interpersonal relationships and environmental adaptations. At the same time they included extensive quantitative evidence of improvements in productivity, income and social welfare in the impact areas. Of the six CBIRD rural impact areas in Korea, four are described here in some detail. Each of the authors, while responsible for writing about two areas, visited all four in order to obtain a general, comparative perspective.

The data on which the report is based comprise extensive personal observations at the village level, numerous interviews with local leaders and ordinary farmers and fishermen, and long discussions with CDF Coordinators in the field and with the Director and Staff of the SCF/CDF office in Seoul. In addition the authors have consulted and drawn upon the large body of descriptive and statistical documentation compiled by SCF/CDF.

The field research was carried out over several weeks between August and October 1978, during which time the researchers worked closely together exchanging data and observations and discussing conclusions. For logistical reasons, however, the report itself was drafted mainly by Professor Brandt, working on his own, after returning to the United States. Thus, while Dr. Cheong contributed importantly to the substance of the report, Professor Brandt has asked that it be made clear that he personally accepts final responsibility for the views and interpretations expressed in it.

The conduct of the study was greatly assisted by the Director of the SCF/CDF Field Office in Seoul, Dr. Melvin E. Frarey, and his staff; by other SCF/CDF officials and staff in Westport, Connecticut, especially Dr. Pratima Kale, a former ICED staff member who is currently SCF/CDF's Program Director for Asia; and not least of all by the CDF Coordinators, Community Committee members and other villagers in the project areas.

The views expressed in this report are solely the responsibility of ICED and the author and do not necessarily accord with those of the SCF/CDF or of any of the organizations that have co-sponsored and provided financial support to this ICED project.

EDITOR'S COMMENTARY*

CBIRD (pronounced sea-bird) is the acronym for a development concept devised in the early 1970s by the Save the Children Federation/Community Development Foundation (SCF/CDF) on the basis of their many years of experience with helping the underprivileged in a variety of developing countries.** CBIRD is actually not a "model" in the strict sense; it is more in the nature of a particular strategy, based on a certain set of principles and goals, that can be flexibly applied in different situations in a wide variety of ways.

The CBIRD idea was first introduced in South Korea where SCF/CDF had operated for many years, but it is not limited to South Korea. In recent years SCF/CDF has sought to introduce the same strategy--though in very different specific forms and on a more modest scale--in 17 other less developed countries in Asia and the Pacific, Africa, the Middle East and Latin America. The South Korean version, however, represents the most comprehensive, sophisticated and ambitious application of the general approach thus far.

---

*By Philip H. Coombs, ICED Project Director.

**Save the Children Federation (SCF) began as a voluntary children's relief organization in the USA during the Great Depression of the 1930s. After World War II, SCF extended its child relief activities overseas to several developing countries--one of the first being South Korea in the immediate wake of the Korean War. After the mid-1950s SCF expanded its program scope beyond simple relief to individual children and began supporting self-help development efforts by poor families and communities that could bring about more lasting improvements. To promote and implement these broader self-help projects in the field, SCF created the Community Development Foundation (CDF) in 1957 and established the first CDF field office in South Korea--which later became the sponsor and manager of the CBIRD Project. The two names have since been merged--the official name of the parent organization now being Save the Children Federation/Community Development Foundation (SCF/CDF). But since most Koreans still associate the separate CDF name with CBIRD, the authors of the   case study have used this shorthand identification except when referring to the parent organization (as SCF/CDF).

The architects of CBIRD believed that the serious deficiencies of the conventional top-down, fragmented approach to rural development, described in the introductory chapter of this volume, could be substantially remedied, if not entirely overcome, by creating an integrated, bottom-up development system, managed by local community committees, that could be linked, close to the grassroots level, with centralized government services.

In the context of South Korea, the new CBIRD initiative happily coincided with a strong commitment by the central   government to promote and invest substantial amounts in rural development under the aegis of the *Saemaul Undong* (New Community Movement). This strongly top-down campaign put great pressure on all the lower echelon administrators of various bureaucracies to coordinate their rural activities. It also, paradoxically, put great pressure on the villages to engage in bottom-up community planning and extensive self-help efforts. The promoters of CBIRD took skillful advantage of these circumstances and tailored their strategy to harmonize with the Government's efforts, but going substantially beyond them by establishing much stronger and more sophisticated mechanisms for local planning and development management.

The evidence in the case study portrays an impressive record of accomplishment, but also some notable shortfalls. The CBIRD community-based system, all things considered, is working remarkably well in the six selected rural "impact areas". It has clearly contributed significantly to increased productivity and income and to improved living standards in these areas. Its largest and most visible achievements have been on the economic side. The main weaknesses in the performance record, according to the case study's evaluation, are in the area of social welfare services and help to the poorest 20 percent or so of the population. But this, according to the analysis, was not for any lack of trying on the part of CBIRD's sponsors and field personnel. The main causes of the imbalance between income-increasing projects that would benefit mostly the middle and higher level farmers, and social welfare and other efforts designed to benefit the poor, the women and the young children, were rooted in the traditions and social structure of the communities themselves and reflected the felt needs and ordering of priorities as seen by the local decision-makers.

This phenomenon is not unique, of course, to the Korean context; it can be found in a great many rural societies. But it happens to be unusually well analyzed and brought into focus by this particular case study.

The findings of this study, though confined to South Korea, lend support to the following general propositions that have relevance for rural development planners in many developing countries.

1) If any externally designed rural development model is to have a reasonable chance of success, its original basic assumptions, goals, and strategy must come to terms with the traditional value system, human relationships and felt needs of the rural society into which it is being introduced. This requires a process of sensitive and skillful compromise and adaptation; otherwise the alien scheme will be rejected like an incompatible heart or liver transplant from

the human body. The CBIRD experience in South Korea offers useful
lessons on how such a process can be successfully conducted, and on
why the necessary compromises are likely to result in a significant
gap between the originally proclaimed goals of the imported model and
the realities of its actual accomplishments.

2) It would be unrealistic to expect an intervention of this sort
in a few pilot areas to bring about, all by itself, a fundamental transformation of the existing socioeconomic structure, traditional values,
and pattern of human relationships in these areas. If properly adapted
to locally felt needs, preferences and mores, as well as to prevailing
government policies and programs, such an intervention--as the CBIRD
experience demonstrates--can result in impressive improvements. But
a fundamental transformation of existing village structures and
behavior patterns can only be brought about by broader and deeper
nationwide economic, political and social changes. South Korea in the
1970s was a textbook example of such broad dynamic changes and
provided a highly favorable climate for the CBIRD projects.

3) The rate and extent of local improvements that can be brought
about by an innovative rural intervention--such as CBIRD--also
depend heavily on the development potential of the particular rural
areas to which it is applied. This potential is determined by a
combination of factors such as topography and natural resources,
social cohesiveness or divisiveness, physical access to markets, the
nature and strength of local institutions and traditions of cooperation,
and the availability of dynamic local leadership. The importance of
these factors, as well as their geographic variations, are well
illustrated by the different CBIRD impact areas.

4) Achieving a sizeable and permanent improvement in the
position of the poorest families in virtually any rural area--as distinct
from temporary infusions of charitable relief--is a far more difficult
task than the currently popular rhetoric suggests. This proved to be
the case even in the unusually prosperous circumstances of rural South
Korea in the 1970s, despite the best efforts of CBIRD's sponsors. This
in no way diminishes the importance of the goal of helping the rural
poor, but it does caution against creating unrealistic hopes and
expectations that in the end can only lead to disappointment and dis-
illusionment and to making the task even more difficult the next time
around.

5) The pressures from many quarters on the managers of rural
development projects to produce quick, visible and *quantitatively*
measurable results tend to create program distortions and to become
a major obstacle to achieving equally important *qualitative* changes
and improvements. There is a crucial message here for decisionmakers
and quantitatively-minded program analysts and evaluators of major
bilateral and multilateral assistance agencies!

The above observations are in no way intended as criticisms of
the CBIRD program in South Korea. On the contrary, the fact that
CBIRD's managers were able to cope with the realities of the situation, to take such good advantage of the favorable factors in the
South Korean context, and to navigate skillfully around the obstacles,
is a tribute to their sensitivity, ability and devotion.

CHAPTER 1

THE CBIRD CONCEPT AND GOALS

The Save the Children Federation/Community Development Foundation (SCF/CDF) of Westport, Connecticut, U.S.A. has been engaged since 1973 in an innovative, systematic, and highly organized effort to increase rural income and upgrade the quality of village life in South Korea. SCF/CDF, a nonprofit, sectarian, voluntary organization, has appropriately named its Korean program, "Community-Based Integrated Rural Development"(CBIRD).

Funds to support the CBIRD program are obtained from several sources: 1) SCF/CDF funds raised privately in the United States; 2) an Operational Program Grant from the United States Agency for International Development; 3) Republic of Korea Government funds; and 4) contributions and investments by the villagers themselves.

BACKGROUND

Save the Children Federation began its work in Korea in 1953 by providing aid to war orphans, widows and refugees. Money contributed by individual American "sponsors" and relief supplies were distributed to the families of needy Korean children during the period of extreme deprivation that followed the Korean War. In particular SCF focused its efforts on uprooted refugee groups in an attempt to preserve family cohesion and stability.

A transition took place after 1957 when SCF established an office of its newly created Community Development Foundation (CDF) in Seoul as its representative in Korea.*   Thereafter aid in the form of cash and relief goods was increasingly converted to self-help support, with CDF providing assistance to poor families in both urban and rural communities. Support spread to encompass children's educational scholarships, family self-help plans, and community improvement projects. In order to increase family productivity, CDF encouraged and assisted farmers in the raising of livestock and the cultivation of cash crop vegetables. For the community as a whole there was support for such public works projects as land reclamation, bridge and reservoir construction, and improved sources of drinking water. From the start SCF/CDF encouraged the maximum

---

*Although the organizational name has since become SCF/CDF, the earlier CDF name is used in this report in the context of CBIRD because this is how it is still popularly known in Korea.

amount of local participation and management in its development projects.   By 1972 various kinds of assistance--to individuals, to families, and to communities--had been furnished to about 7,000 people in some 400 communities.

In 1972 SCF/CDF decided, as the result of a thoroughgoing self-evaluation of its activities, to consolidate the various programs, focusing its main effort on promoting integrated development in clusters of cooperating villages that were called "impact areas." This integrated, "high impact" approach to community improvement was launched in the following three carefully chosen groups of villages: 1) Tong Myon (township or sub-county), Chunsong Gun (county), Kangwon Province; 2) Tong Myon, Yanggu Gun, Kangwon Province; 3) Sanbuk, Yoju Gun, Kyonggi Province.*

In June 1976 SCF/CDF received from the United States Agency for International Development (US AID) a sizeable Operational Program Grant in partial support of the Korea program. Under provisions of the grant CDF was expected "to establish pilot community-based integrated rural development projects as mini-regional (or small area) development management models, with an ultimate goal, over a five year period, of institutionalizing a process that will improve income, health, education, and community institutions and services for low income rural people." The US AID grant enabled CDF to select three additional island communities off Korea's southwest coast, so that in all there are now six "mini-regional" projects (three island areas and three in the mountainous north central region).**

The CBIRD Concept

In very general terms there are three main aspects of the CBIRD concept that, when taken together, distinguish it from most other development efforts:

1) The term, Community Based Integrated Rural Development, represents an attempt to combine the strengths of traditional community development theory and methodology with the advantages of a larger scale, systems oriented, carefully planned and integrated development strategy.

2) The unit of development or impact area comprises several villages, roughly corresponding to the lowest level of local bureaucratic administration.

---

*A fourth impact area, not considered in this study, is an urban, low income neighborhood on the outskirts of Seoul; it is inhabited by rural migrants to the city who were formerly squatters.

**US AID/Seoul's funding contribution for the island impact areas during the period June, 1976 through the end of 1978 equalled 16 percent of total investments (including villagers' contributions).

3) The CBIRD program is designed to supplement and be integrated with the *Saemaul Undong* (New Community Movement), an intensive program of rural development that is being promoted by the Korean Government throughout the country.

CDF has been prolific and articulate in documenting the aims, methodology, and results of its Community Based Integrated Rural Development (CBIRD) projects.[1] A typical statement follows:

Small area community-based development involves building upon the experience of individual village development with wider concern for inter-village cooperation and systematic planning to create and expand market and employment possibilities, for improvement and utilization of health and educational systems accessible to the villagers, and expansion of credit systems to recycle rural income back into the rural economy. The area size is determined by the linkages, administrative, economically, and socially that are important to the people for a broader development outlook on their needs and resources. Generally, the size of the area encompasses a whole 'myon' (township) including eight to twenty villages and populations from 3,000 to 8,000. CDF has established the project in three island myons off the south-west coast of Korea and in three mountain-ous areas of the north-east and north-central region of Korea.

In implementing a community based integrated area development program, CDF is introducing and demon-strating skills for improved planning, management and evaluation of economic and social development projects to link macro level development objectives with speci-fically targetted community goals. The project is designed to involve bottom-up planning and grass-roots representation in the planning process and the implementation of projects with long-range and short-term objectives that reinforce national development plans for increased productivity, income, and improvement of the quality of life for Korean people.[2]

---

[1] SCF/CDF, Korea Field Office, *Semi-annual and Annual Reports,* Seoul, Korea, Jan.,1977; July, 1977; Jan., 1978; August, 1978. SCF/CDF Korea Field Office, *Application to AID for Operational Program Grant in Korea,* Seoul, Korea, 1975.

[2] SCF/CDF, Korea Field Office, *Third Semi-annual Report,* Jan., 1978, pp. 1-2.

The general scheme tries to profit from the insights and techniques of the hard-headed economist or systems analyst, while
remaining true to basic community development principles.   The
community development approach has traditionally been people-
oriented, with an emphasis on changing values and relationships
within a small face-to-face community in order to get things moving.
CD practitioners insist that development efforts should be directed
at the "felt needs" of a community, and that this can only be achieved
by maximizing local participation in decision-making--in the planning
and direction of projects. Self help through cooperative effort and
the investment of local resources is stressed. And finally there is
usually an emphasis on egalitarianism and improving the quality of
community life, particularly with regard to the situation of the
poor and other deprived groups.

The economist's planned approach to rural development, on
the other hand, usually involves both capital inputs and direction
from outside the local community, in accordance with a large scale
plan that is more concerned with increasing quantifiable measures
of production than with such intangibles as human motivation and
satisfaction. The plan, which usually covers a relatively large
geographic area, is formulated on the basis of more or less rigorous
surveys and sophisticated economic and technological analyses of
problems to be overcome.

The CBIRD concept combines what are regarded as the
strengths of both methodologies. At the same time it recognizes
that the actual program operation must take place within the
political context of a highly centralized, authoritarian bureaucratic
administration. The term, "integrated", in the CBIRD title, then,
can be taken to mean that a variety of problems at the village level
should be attacked simultaneously, and that local development
projects should be mutually reinforcing; but also it encompasses
the adoption of a holistic view of village problems within the regional
and national economic, sociological, environmental, and administrative setting.

In its theoretical formulations SCF/CDF places great emphasis on
local decision-making, and self help. The creation of permanent
local organizations capable of planning and implementing various
kinds of development projects is regarded as just as important as
the actual end results achieved by such projects. This process
of "bottom-up" decision-making and management is believed to be
superior to centrally planned and directed "top-down" systems
imposed on farmers by bureaucrats from outside the villages for
two principal reasons: 1) it is alleged that only grass roots
participation in the entire process can ensure enthusiastic widespread involvement, a correspondence of project goals with locally
felt needs, and an equitable distribution of benefits; 2) in the
longer term after CDF capital and advisors are no longer available,
local initiative and control are necessary in order to ensure that
developmental momentum is maintained.

In CBIRD terminology, the "development management model" requires that villagers receive various kinds of training in order to be able to survey local needs themselves, assess capabilities, reach reasonable decisions and carry them out effectively. Accordingly the CBIRD projects all involve extensive programs of nonformal education. In addition to courses in leadership, planning, evaluation and agricultural (or fishing) technology, CDF also trains villagers to manage local credit unions and to operate a system of development loans through a revolving fund, by which increased farm income is recycled into the local village economy. While it is recognized that increases in productivity and income should probably have priority at the initial stages of a rural development program, CDF tries to attack all the major constraints on improving village life, rather than concentrating on any single sector or set of problems.

Thus health care, nutrition, child care, family planning, sanitation, and social/cultural/recreational activities are as much a part of the overall design as projects designed to increase productivity and incomes. In particular, CDF has stressed, both in its general announcements and in formulating specific planning goals, that the CBIRD projects are designed primarily to assist the rural poor, with women and children singled out as the principal beneficiary groups.

These are all conventional community development goals. What is innovative about the CBIRD program is that it is organized to provide an integrated development approach for larger areas, comprising from six to twenty-one villages with populations of from 2,000 to 9,000 persons. There seem to be two main, interrelated advantages to increasing the size of the impact area: 1) it becomes feasible to undertake more ambitious projects in such sectors as public works, education (both formal and nonformal), and health care where large initial investments in trained personnel and facilities are usually required. Also, there is a much larger local resource base to support such projects, both in terms of labor and material contributions; 2) the "mini-regional" area corresponds roughly to the sub-county or myon, which is the lowest Korean administrative unit staffed by full-time government employees. The fact that the local cooperatives and extension service also have offices at the myon level is of great importance. Once a measure of consensus and a willingness to participate in achieving joint goals has been established beyond village boundaries within the impact area, then local leaders can work together with officials in formulating development plans and obtaining additional funding or other kinds of governmental assistance.

Close collaboration with governmental administrative agencies and other outside institutions, both public and private, is an integral part of CDF's method in Korea. The integration of village economies with national markets, the introduction of the latest agricultural and fisheries technology, and the inculcation of efficient methods of local planning and financial management, all require close and constant ties with the more modernized sectors of Korean society.

CBIRD goals in Korea can be summarized then as follows:

a) To expand the boundaries of the cohesive, cooperating, and developing community from the village to the subcounty or township.

b) To focus assistance efforts on the rural poor, both by raising incomes and by improving the quality of life through social welfare programs.

c) To maximize local participation in development planning and management initiatives by mobilizing local energies and resources through effective organization and training.

d) To integrate rural development efforts with on-going governmental programs and other sources of help outside the village.

e) To develop techniques that can be applied elsewhere.

The last goal listed above, (e), represents a somewhat different kind of objective as implied by the phrase, "establish... development management models," that was used as part of the rationale for obtaining an Operational Program Grant from AID. Here the emphasis has shifted somewhat from concrete efforts to improve the economic and social situation in particular communities to a more general and abstract goal, that of formulating an organizational structure and method that can be used or built on by those responsible for improving the condition of the rural poor elsewhere.

In analyzing the successes and shortcomings of the CBIRD program in South Korea, we have kept these goals in mind as the principal basis for our evaluation.

CHAPTER 2

THE ENVIRONMENTAL SETTING

AND IMPACT AREAS

South Korea (the Republic of Korea) has a total land area of about 38,000 square miles (98,500 square kilometers) and a population of about 37,000,000, making it one of the most densely populated countries in the world (374 persons per square kilometer). Less than 25 percent of the land area is arable, however, so that the actual concentration of people, even in rural areas, is much greater. Because winters are fairly cold and dry, double cropping is only possible in the southernmost provinces. However, winter vegetable growing in vinyl greenhouses has been widely adopted in recent years.

Since the Korean War, South Korea has undergone an extraordinarily rapid rate of industrialization, urbanization and economic growth.* Starting from a predominantly agrarian society, its urban population rose from 28 percent of the total population in 1960 to nearly 55 percent at present, with a corresponding decline in the rural population. The Gross Domestic Product (measured in constant prices) grew at an average annual rate of 8.5 percent between 1960 and 1970, and 10.3 percent from 1970 to 1976. Per capita real income rose at an average annual rate of 7.3 percent from 1960 to 1976, reaching an average of US$670 per person in 1976. Despite an absolute decline in the agrarian population (due to rapid urban migration and an increasingly effective birth control program), agricultural output grew at an average annual rate of 4.5 percent from 1960 to 1970, and 4.8 percent from 1970 to 1976. However, its share of the total GDP fell from 40 percent in 1960 to 27 percent in 1976 because in the same period industrial production was growing at more than 17 percent a year, bossting its share of the GDP from 19 percent in 1960 to 34 percent in 1976. At present there is an actual shortage of agricultural labor in South Korea--an unusual phenomenon in the developing world.

---

*The statistics in this paragraph are from the World Bank's *World Development Report, 1978.*

In contrast to most other Asian developing countries, the distribution of wealth in South Korea is fairly equitable (comparable to that in the United States).

RURAL DEVELOPMENT

A thoroughgoing land reform program was carried out in 1949/50. As a result, while over 83 percent of farm families depended to a greater or lesser extent on landlords in 1947, in 1964 (after the reform) the figure had dropped to about 30 percent. During this same period the percentage of completely landless households in the farm population fell from more than 45 percent to about 7 percent.

Although agricultural production rose in the 1960s, its pace picked up in the early 1970s. Grain production since 1973 has increased at a rate of about 7 percent annually, mainly due to the successful adaptation of new varieties of rice and barley to Korean soils and climate. Urban and export demand for agricultural products, particularly cash crops such as fresh vegetables, fruit, and meat, stimulated even greater increases in productivity in some of these crops. While demand is, of course, an essential stimulus, the rise in farm production has only been possible because more fertilizer and pesticides, improved irrigation systems, greatly increased amounts of rural credit, and improved technical knowledge have been made available in recent years.

Increased productivity and rising prices for agricultural products have improved farm income and the farmers' terms of trade. Better transportation, rural electrification and a rapid expansion in educational facilities have also contributed to the rising quality of rural life. In summary, there has been since 1971 a real transformation in rural living standards with average farm household income approaching that of urban workers. Development is the main preoccupation of most Koreans today. In rural areas new crops, new agricultural methods, and dramatic improvements in social infrastructure are characteristic of most villages.

THE SAEMAUL UNDONG

While the economist tends to see the causes of this rural economic growth and social transformation in such factors as market incentives, improved seed varieties, and the greater availability of agricultural raw materials and services to the farmer, the Korean Government attributes most of the recent progress to the successful implementation, starting in 1971, of its *Saemaul Undong* (New Community Movement). Although the main focus of the New Community Movement has been rural development, it also has another dimension--the fostering of a new ideology.

In recent years social commentators as well as political scientists have deplored the lack of a genuine national ideology in South Korea, maintaining that anti-Communism and the pursuit of material progress were not enough to provide inspiration as national goals and symbols. By 1972 it was apparent that the New Community Movement in its broadest context constituted part of a determined attempt by the Government to fill this ideological gap. The attempt is still being pursued, and strenuous efforts are made to infuse every aspect of life--from garbage collection to poetry writing--with the Saemaul spirit. The Movement adopted "self help, cooperation, and diligence" as its motto, and the President's frequently repeated words, "Let's live better," became a kind of slogan. Building on both the hierarchical and collective traditions, the Movement stressed obedience to expert, paternalistic administrative leadership and an extension of the idea of community to encompass the entire nation. The ideological component was, of course, closely related to the Park Government's objective of expanding and consolidating grassroots political support.

By the winter of 1971-1972 a major effort had been launched to get the majority of farmers in all 35,000 South Korean villages involved in cooperative village improvement projects. Supplies of cement and steel reinforcing rods were made available by the authorities, and villages were encouraged to use them to improve roads, bridges, wells and sanitation facilities. A major program was also launched simultaneously to persuade farmers to replace their thatched roofs with tile, metal or composition. The expectation was that through participation in projects having an immediate impact on the village environment, farmers would realize the benefits of working together during the off season, and a spirit of progressive community activism would be fostered.

Because of unrelenting pressure from the top, bureaucratic efforts to achieve the movement's goals were intense. Saemaul became the main focus of activity for all local administrative agencies, and thousands of other officials from the capital descended on the provinces to inspect, exhort, direct operations, and, to some extent, compete with local officials. The result initially was often confusion and bureaucratic overkill, while the astonished villagers struggled to comply with mounting and sometimes conflicting demands for compliance with various aspects of the overall plan.

In the beginning most farmers distrusted the motives of officials and resented their constant interference in village affairs. After all, nothing good had ever happened to rural society before as a result of closer contacts with the bureaucracy. Where villagers were slow or reluctant to organize for carrying out suggested projects, official pressures were applied that often amounted to direct coercion. For example, if several farmers in a village were reluctant to replace the traditional brush fences around their houses with cement walls, jeep loads of men from the county seat might arrive and simply tear them down. Similarly, there were occasions when house owners who were unwilling to make the substantial investment necessary to replace their thatched roofs with composition or tile might return home from a market trip to find the thatch gone and their homes open to the sky. Such excesses, which reflected the concern of local officials with producing quick results to please superiors, generated a lot of resentment and cynicism during the first two or three years of the movement.

But since 1973 attitudes in most places have gradually shifted, as farmers discovered that all the excitement and effort did, in fact, result in substantial benefits. Each village is given a rating by the county chief in accordance with its accomplishments, and local pride has in many cases been stimulated to a high competitive pitch among neighboring communities. Where village leadership is in the hands of determined activists, who are also skillful in maintaining good relations with other members of the community, a considerable degree of constructive enthusiasm has usually been generated and sustained. Once the most influential men in a village are committed to pursuing the Movement's goals, others will nearly always follow, and non-conformists are subjected to subtle but extremely effective social censure. As a result, although distrust and reluctance prevailed a few years ago, now most village councils are eagerly drawing up ambitious development plans and begging for official support to help carry them out.

There is a good deal of variation from one village to another, and while some degree of participation exists everywhere, such factors as the quality of leadership, geographic accessibility, the degree of village cohesion (or conversely, of internal division, usually along kinship boundaries), the distribution of wealth, and commercial opportunities for individual profit, all vary from place to place, and all affect the extent and intensity of involvement in collective community efforts.

Nevertheless, in spite of the uneven performance it is undeniable that the Saemaul movement has transformed the appearance of Korean villages, fostered the successful completion of a large variety of cooperative, self-help projects, and promoted more effective working relationships, both among farmers and between farmers and local officials. It has also given villagers a sense of participation in a momentous national effort, with strongly patriotic overtones. Any visitor to rural Korea today can observe the pride in recent achievements and a confidence in the future that were almost entirely absent ten years ago.

The government's claim that it is the New Community Movement that is responsible for bringing about the new rural prosperity, is not entirely convincing. Actually, it has become increasingly difficult to analyze cause and effect in rural development, because the dimensions of the movement as a "nation building" ideology have been expanded to include everything positive that happens in rural society. It seems clear, however, that it is not so much that Saemaul has sparked rural prosperity, as that it has been pushed in a context of relative rural prosperity that is the result mainly of other factors: 1) the widespread successful adoption of new, high-yielding

varieties of rice and to a lesser extent barley;   2) the maintenance of
favorable subsidized grain prices by the government;   3) the increased availability of more effective agricultural extension services;
4) the greatly expanded urban market for a wide variety of new cash
crops;   and 5) improvements in transportation and storage facilities
that have made it possible for farmers to engage profitably in
commercialized agriculture.

    It is in the upgrading of administrative performance by local
governmental and semigovernmental agencies and the improvement
of institutional linkages and communications between village and city
that the Saemaul Movement has probably made its greatest contribution. Pressures from the top to achieve rapid, concrete and dramatically visible results have been so great that in six years the mass
of provincial, county and sub-county officials has been forced to
change their outlook and working style from that of conservative,
self-seeking, formalistic control and *status quo* oriented bureaucrats
to that of relatively enthusiastic activists dedicated to a transformation of the countryside. Their careers have been at stake. The
highly centralized, authoritarian political system of South Korea has
proved to be well adapted for accomplishing this transformation, even
though it has never been specifically enunciated as a goal of the
Movement.

    The Ministry of Home Affairs and its local agencies, the pro-
vincial, county and sub-county administrative offices, have generally
exercised effective supervision, making sure that the efforts of
various other concerned government agencies were integrated in the
overall Saemaul Movement. After many years of "fragmented hierarchical programs" South Korea has finally achieved a coordinated
administration of rural development policies. The implications for
future rural development of such increased local administrative
effectiveness are great. In addition there is now a recognition by
villagers that technological advice, capital and improved marketing
facilities can best be acquired through official channels and the
expansion of ties with the national economy. Officials are no longer
feared and avoided as in the past, and the social gulf between farmers
and bureaucrats has noticeably narrowed.

    Some persistent problems remain, however. The poorest
farmers and laborers, who have no land or very little land, and who
make up about 15 percent to 25 percent of the rural population, are
not particularly enthusiastic about the New Community Movement.
They complain that while obliged to participate in village public works
projects, usually without pay, they receive no benefits comparable
to those of landowners whose property is being improved. They must
live by their labor, and they insist that "voluntary" collective work is
an unfair burden. Also, higher grain prices are of little help to the
40 percent of all farm households whose land holdings are so small
that they have little or no marketable surplus.

    The long run future of the Movement is somewhat problematic,
because of a potential contradiction in values and organizational
structure that is inherent in contemporary Korean society.   The

Movement's success (but not necessarily further rural development) depends on continuing community solidarity and cooperative effort at a time when individualism and materialism, both as personal ideologies and as patterns of economic behavior, are challenging tradition in every social sector. So far, although exceptions exist in most villages (particularly those near urban areas), traditional patterns of interaction reinforced by outside official support for collective organizations and cooperative effort seems to have resisted or contained the divisive effects of commercial individualism.

The CBIRD program began some two years after the start of the Saemaul Undong, and it would not be an exaggeration to state that it has managed to embed itself within the Saemaul Movement, both at the village level and in terms of the local administrative environment. In any case it is not possible to understand the CBIRD method of operation or evaluate its achievements without considering the general context of contemporary rural development in Korea as outlined above.

THE CBIRD IMPACT AREAS

Two inland and two island groups of villages are considered in this report. The unit of "community" in the CDF community-based integrated rural development (CBIRD) program ranges from about one-half of a myon (township or sub-county)* with six villages to a full myon, with twenty-one villages. The two inland or mountainous pilot areas examined here are both parts of a myon, while the two island areas comprise entire myons.

CDF had two criteria for the selection of its impact areas: 1) that they be isolated and "deprived", i.e., relatively impoverished by Korean standards; and 2)that they possess a good potential for development with regard to such factors as cooperation, leadership, and resources.

CDF has been working in the three inland or "mountainous" areas, Yanggu, Chunsong and Sanbuk, since 1973. Of these, all of which are in north central Korea, the latter two are described below. All three of the island projects, Jeungdo, Yaksan, and Wido, were first implemented by CDF in 1977. An account of the programs in Yaksan and Wido is included here.

Sanbuk Area

This area comprises eight administrative villages *(ri),* each of which is made up of several hamlets or small natural communities.

---

*The myon office with 15 or 20 full time employees is the lowest level of bureaucratic local administration.

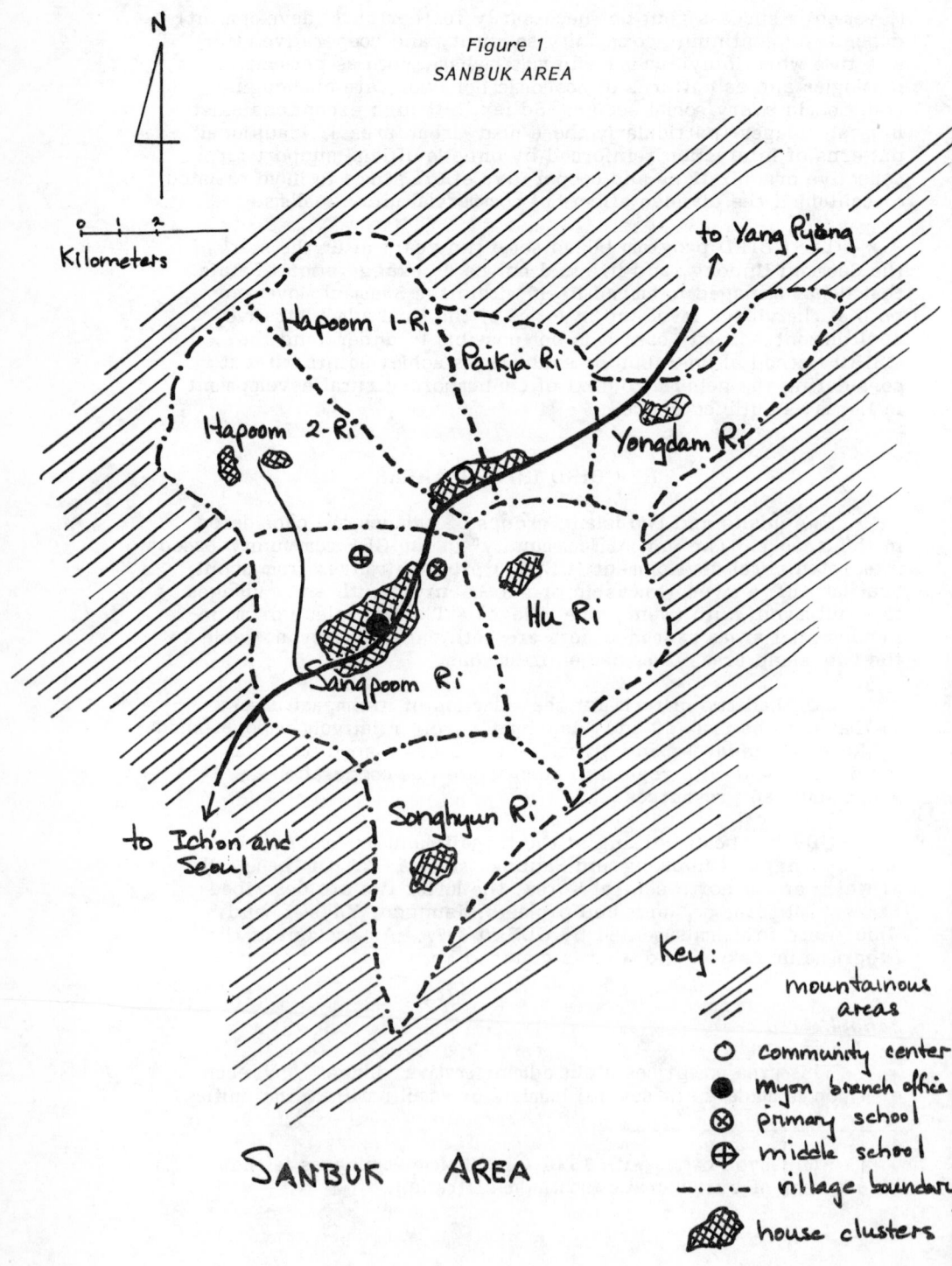

Figure 1
SANBUK AREA

Key:
///   mountainous areas
○   community center
●   myon branch office
⊗   primary school
⊕   middle school
-·-·   village boundary
house clusters

There are 562 households with a total population of 3,134. The main occupation is agriculture on some 539 hectares of land, of which only about one-third is irrigated. In addition an important cash crop-- fragrant mushrooms--is harvested on the wooded mountain slopes, which make up 83.5 percent of the total land area. The average holding per farm household of arable land is 1.17 ha., which is above both the national average of .94 ha. and the provincial average of 1.14 ha. Yields per hectare for rice are below the national average, however. Average farm household income (some 95 percent of Sanbuk households are agricultural) was about 1.3 million won or $520 per capita in 1977, which was also below the national average. Land distribution is relatively equitable with the largest land holding amounting to only 4 hectares.

The Sanbuk area is unusual in that the eight villages are sur- rounded by high mountains, and therefore, although there is easy access from one village to another, the entire district is somewhat isolated from the rest of the myon and county. In fact, because of the mountains and bad bus connections it takes nearly an entire day to reach the myon office (including a ferry ride across the Han river). The county seat, Yoju, is approximately 30 km. to the south, while Seoul is 60 km. to the northwest. Actually, it is easier for Sanbuk residents to travel to two other county seats, Ichon and Yangpyon, than to their own. Because of this geographic isolation and as a result of CDF initiatives, a branch of the Kumsa myon office has recently been established in Sanbuk.

Several observers as well as most of the local residents them- selves attribute their readiness to cooperate and the widespread sense of community encompassing all eight villages to the common heritage of deprivation in a context of geographical isolation. There was no regular bus service until 1963, and residents had to walk 12 kilometers to reach the market in the nearest town. Today, however, busses pass through Sanbuk six times daily, so that transportation with the outside world is no longer a significant problem.

Kinship ties among members of a single predominant lineage that includes nearly forty percent of the area's population provide another source of cohesion among the various villages. A dispro- portionate number of leaders and wealthy farmers belong to this lineage.

In a mountainous country like Korea the grouping of villages in relation to land, as well as the clustering of houses within a village, have an important influence on patterns of interaction and cooperation. In the case of Sanbuk, kinship ties, both through membership in a common lineage and as a result of marriage, provide a structural channel for frequent interaction among the villages. What was previously a sense of solidarity in terms of shared poverty and isolation has been transformed during the past several years into an extraordinarily dynamic cooperative spirit for self improvement. The special topographical situation of Sanbuk as well as the cohesive spirit of its inhabitants were important factors

in its choice as an impact area. While admirably fulfilling the requirements for development potential, it is somewhat difficult to duplicate
this situation in other parts of the country.

Chunsong

This impact area includes six administrative ri (twelve natural
village communities) located in interconnecting mountain valleys
(see map). Jinaeri 1, which is the administrative center of the
myon as well as of the CBIRD impact area, is only about 8 kilometers
from the provincial capital, Chunchon, a city of more than 250,000
people.

There are 393 households in the area with a total population
of 2,080. More than 100 residents work outside the Chunsong area;
most of these commute to the nearby capital city.

Of the 394 hectares of arable land, about one-third are
irrigated rice fields. The average land holding per farm household
is 1.06 hectares, which is a little more favorable than the national
average but less than the average for the province. Yields are
still rather low, however, because of the relatively severe climate,
poor soils, and lack of advanced agricultural technology. The most
important crops raised are rice, tobacco, corn, beans, peanuts,
and green onions.

Farm household income averaged 1,590,000 won or US$515 per
capita in 1977, which is almost exactly the same as that of Sanbuk.
Although this amount is still less than the national average, the
gains for both areas in recent years have been slightly better than
the average increase for the country as a whole.

The county seat is in the nearby capital city of Chunchon,
and transportation is excellent, with buses running every hour
from Jinaeri. The other villages are all fairly close and are
connected by reasonably good roads. In addition to the myon
administrative office, there are offices of the agricultural cooperative,
the extension service, and the health service nearby. A primary
school is also located in the same village.

The distribution of wealth is fairly equitable except for one
village, where it is concentrated in the hands of a single dominant
lineage. This village has generally demonstrated less enthusiasm
for participation in CBIRD activities than the other five communities.
Two of the villages, Jinae 2 and Jinae 3, have cooperated closely
with each other and been particularly active in planning and implementing a wide variety of self-help projects under CDF auspices.

While they have not displayed the same sense of community
and cooperative spirit at the "mini-regional" level as in Sanbuk,
most of the people in the Chunsong area have been taking advantage
of available opportunities, particularly in the economic and
educational fields. If the most isolated and least progressive

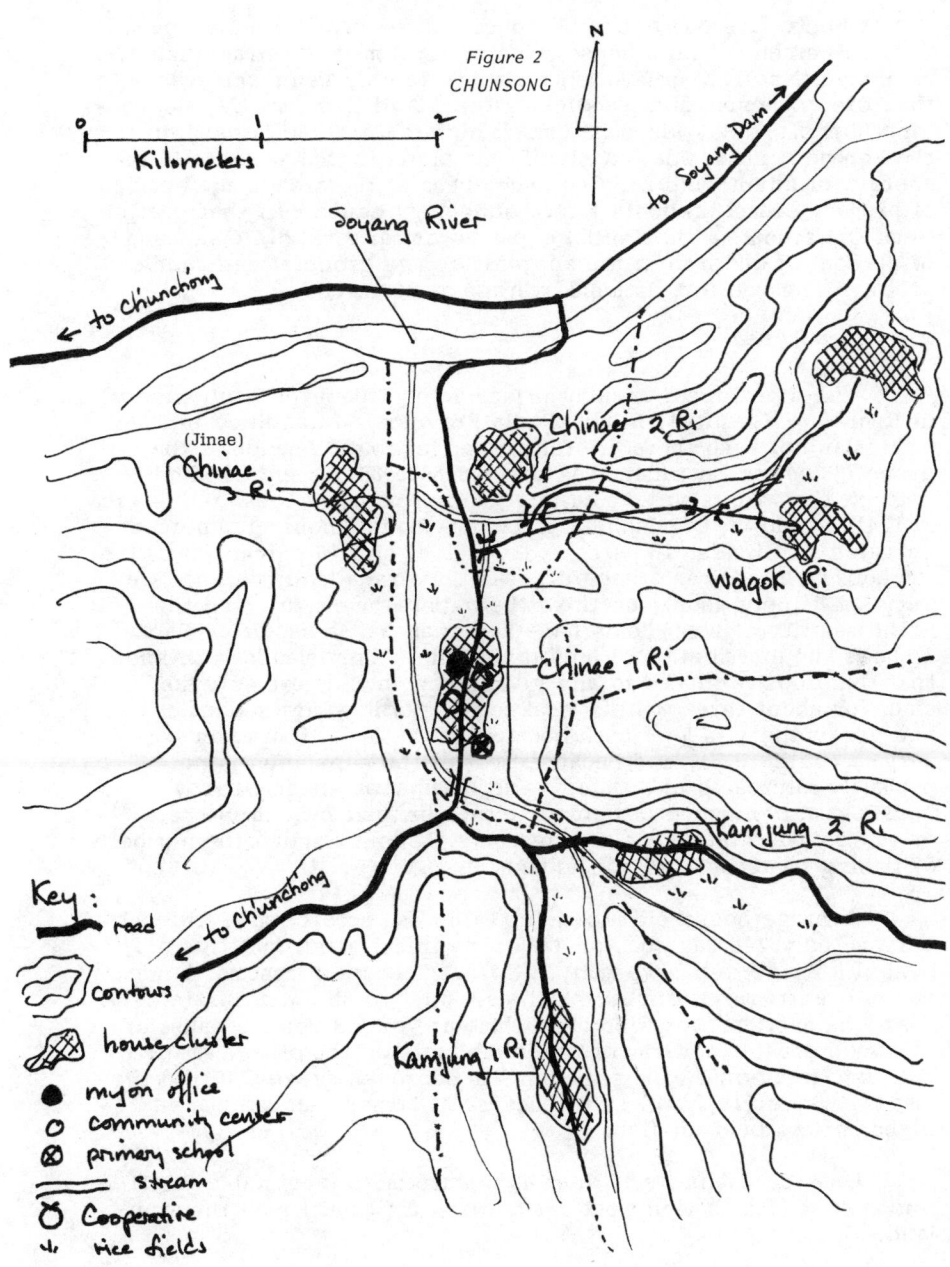

Figure 2
CHUNSONG

village--the one with a single dominant lineage and particularly unequal land distribution--is omitted from the averages, then the pace of development for Chunsong is well above the national average, despite disadvantages of the environment.

Ninety-five percent of all houses in the area have electricity. Only 12 percent of farm house roofs are still made of straw thatch; more significantly, composition roofs are rapidly being replaced with the more expensive and prestigious tile. And there are 71 telephones for 376 households, which is a much higher rate than is usual in the Korean countryside. A significant statistic that testifies to the energy, ambition, and solid economic base of the area is the number of primary school students (free, obligatory education) that goes on to middle school, a substantial expense for farmers. In Chunsong 87 percent of children in the appropriate age group attend middle school, compared to a national average of 79 percent.

Wido Island Area

The Wido impact area comprises all of Wido myon (sub-county) in Buan *Gun* (county), North Cholla Province. In addition to the main island of Wido there are four other inhabited islands in the group. The total population is about 4,500, 80 percent of which lives on the main island. The total land area of the inhabited islands is 1,414 hectares, of which 76 percent is mountainous, 1.3 percent irrigated rice fields, 13 percent dry fields, and 10 percent is used for houses, roads, or other purposes. Average land holdings are very small (only about one-third the national average), and the great majority of households have less than half a hectare. Table 1 shows the distribution of land ownership. The islanders all know that the crops produced in any given year on Wido are only suffi- cient for about three months local consumption. Farm technology and productivity is low, both because of the lack of an extension service (until 1977), and because most of the population is not primarily interested in farming as an occupation: nearly every houshold also engaged in fishing, either in their own small boats or as employees on larger fishing boats. Table 2 shows the number of fishing boats by kind and village.

Average household income in 1976 was, according to CDF's 1977 survey, only 748,000 won, or $275 per capita, about half that of Sanbuk. Fishermen have many different sources of income, however, and it is extremely difficult for the outsider to obtain accurate data. Also, the averages for Wido as a whole are pulled down because of the much greater poverty of the inhabitants on the other, smaller islands. In any case the situation has improved greatly during the last two years (1977 and 1978) because of larger fish catches and higher prices paid for fish.

On Wido island itself there is a much more inequitable distri- bution of wealth than in most agricultural communities on the main- land.

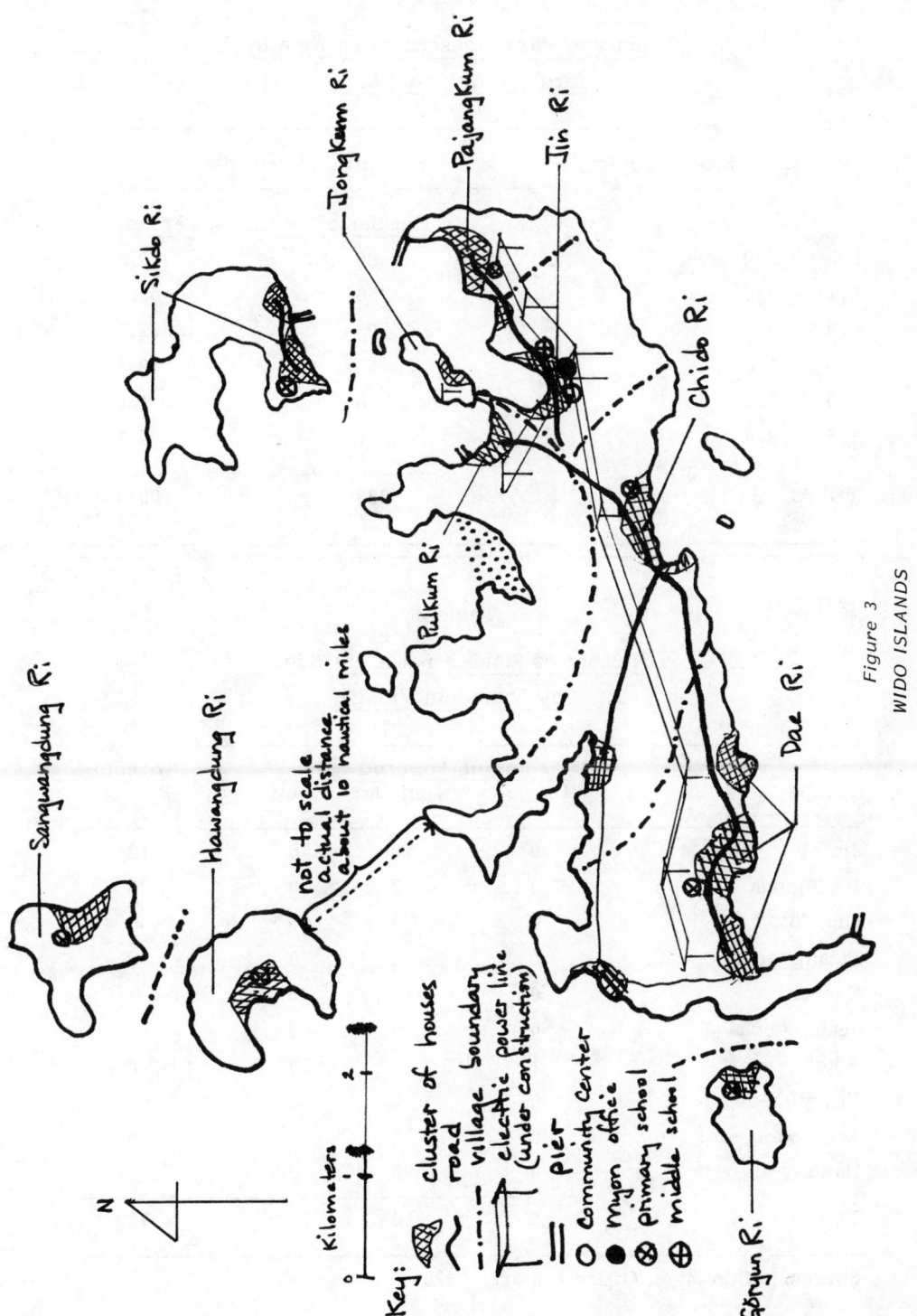

Figure 3

WIDO ISLANDS

Table 1

Number of Farm Households on Wido by
Size of Cultivated Land

Land Size (hectare)	Farming Households	
	Number of	Percent
less than 0.1	66	10.6
0.1 - 0.3	266	42.6
0.3 - 0.5	203	32.5
0.5 - 1.0	83	13.3
1.0 - 1.5	6	1.0
1.5 - 2.0	1	0.2
TOTAL	625	100.2

Table 2

Number of Fishing Boats on Wido,
by Type and Village

Village	Engine Powered			Without Power
	Large	Medium	Small	
Jin-ri	0	10	5	18
Beol-geum	4	7	0	26
Chi-do	0	0	20	0
Pajang-geum	0	3	0	9
Dae-ri	0	17	43	0
Jeong-geum	0	0	0	7
Sikdo	1	11	10	0
Georyun-do	0	2	0	2
Sang-wang-do	0	0	1	9
Hawang-do	0	0	0	2
TOTAL	5	50	79	73

Source: Wido Myon Office Report, 1978

The ten *ri* (administrative villages), five of which are on the main island, are quite distinct from each other in terms of their topographical situation, amounts of arable land, access to marine resources, community cohesiveness, and other aspects of local tradition. For example, Jinri is the myon's administrative center where public agencies are located. Nearby Polgum has a deep water harbor and a good beach with considerable potential for tourism. Pajangum is two kilometers to the northeast and has a large sheltered harbor used by hundreds of mainland boats as a base during the fishing seasons. As a result there is a large and prosperous entertainment industry located there. Daeri, six kilometers southwest of Jinri has the best anchovy resources of the island and a somewhat closed solidarity that is expressed in strong folklore traditions and a reluctance to cooperate with other communities. Jonggum, a presque isle connnected to Wido by a narrow strip of land at low tide, and Sikdo have demonstrated strong collective efforts in accomplishing self help projects. The small communities on the other islands are also distinctive, but they are insignificant both in size and in terms of the CBIRD program. (See map.)

There is a regular daily ferry service between Wido and the mainland that takes two to three hours depending on the weather. The mainland port is also rather isolated, however, and another seven hours of travel is necessary to reach Seoul. Transportation on Wido is poor, as there are only narrow steep rocky paths and roads. There are no motorized vehicles and only a few bicycles. It takes about 1-1/2 hours on foot to go from Daeri to the boat landing at Beolgeum. Except for the three villages that surround the main harbor, regular ferry transportation among the villages by small boat is impracticable, because of the lack of landing piers.

Although there are widespread kinship ties among the villages as a result of intermarriage, there are no strong cohesive lineage organizations on Wido.

Yaksan

Yaksan myon is a single island about 9 kilometers long and 5 kilometers wide off the South Coast of Korea in Wando county, South Cholla Province. It comprises 21 villages with a total population of about 9,000 persons. Even though the island is extremely mountainous, the population density of 376 persons per square kilometer is higher than for the county or for the nation as a whole. The average arable land holding is less than half a hectare, of which about 40 percent is rice land. Most households (1,299 out of 1,478) are engaged in both farming and fishing.

Because of the shortage of land and a consequent concentration on fishing, agriculture is not particularly well developed. The major crops are rice, barley, soy beans, potatoes, and vegetables, but production is insufficient for the island's needs. In addition, pigs and goats are raised. The average income per farming household from agriculture is about 500,000 won (US$1,000).

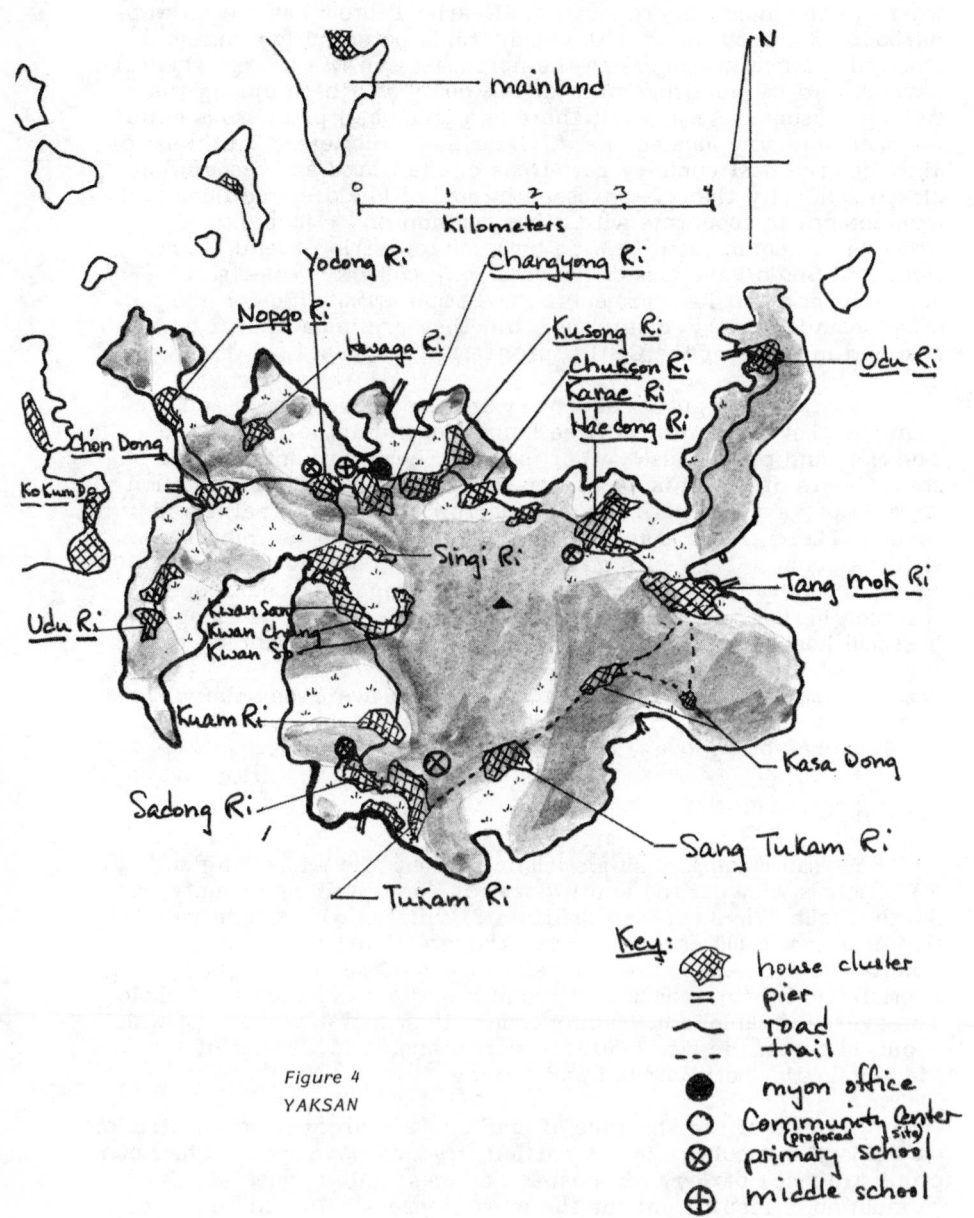

Figure 4
YAKSAN

Income from ocean products--the cultivation and gathering of seaweed is more important than fishing--is much greater than from agriculture. The average per household income from this source is over 1,300,000 won (US$2,700). This average figure is misleading, however, because much of the income from seaweed production goes to large, wealthy operators.

With only 15 households owning more than 1-1/2 hectares, the land distribution is relatively equitable for the island as a whole. As a result of the varied topographical situation, however, some villages, particularly the eight prosperous communities on the northern side of the island, have much more land than the others. So here again average figures are misleading. The same situation exists with regard to fishing and seaweed cultivation. Some areas have access to much better ocean resources than others. As a result there is, with a couple of exceptions, a relatively sharp division on the island between the poor villages along the west and south coasts and the prosperous villages (which have average household incomes much higher than the national average) to the north and northeast (see map where the names of the prosperous villages have been underlined).

There are also differences among the villages with regard to the distribution of income gained from the sea. While there are many small cultivators of seaweed, its processing is mostly in the hands of a relatively few wealthy men. On the other hand, the ownership of small motor boats for fishing is widely distributed.

Over 90 percent of the houses have electricity, and in 1978 there were 637 television sets or one for every 2-1/2 households. Although the island has 75 telephones, they are unevenly distributed, so that some villages are still without telephone communication.

In addition to the myon office, there is a farm cooperative and a fishery cooperative on the island. A public health office building exists, but at present (1978) it is not staffed.

There are 3 primary schools, 3 small branch primary schools, and one middle school on Yaksan. Just under 80 percent of eligible students attend middle school, which is close to the national average.

GENERAL OBSERVATIONS ON THE IMPACT AREAS

If we are to evaluate CDF's contribution to development through its CBIRD program, some allowance must be made for various aspects of the natural setting. Or to put it somewhat differently, the process of change in each area must be examined in relation to environmental factors.

In addition to their later start in the CDF program (only two years ago) the island communities present some special problems that make rigorous comparisons with the mainland areas difficult.

Koreans have traditionally regarded fishermen with contempt, and most small island villages have with few exceptions been relatively poor. In recent years, however, the higher demand and better prices for sea products have brought relative economic prosperity wherever ocean resources are abundant. But the distribution of wealth is generally somewhat more uneven in Korean fishing communities than in inland agricultural areas; and this tendency has been reinforced as owners of boats, nets, and seaweed producing facilities have taken advantage of the improved opportunities. Accordingly, the gap between rich and poor has widened. It is axiomatic, in Korea at least, that such concentration of wealth within small communities makes the organization of cooperative self help activities more difficult.

Another set of more general and intangible contrasts can be hazarded to distinguish the inland and island areas. Farmers tend to be less geographically and occupationally mobile, conforming more to tradition in a variety of economic and social matters. Accordingly the pace of change in agricultural villages is relatively slow and consistent, if not predictable. Fishermen, whose livelihood is closely tied to mainland markets, are less committed to any particular activity or place. In addition to small scale subsistence farming they are engaged in seaweed cultivation, the gathering of oysters and various kinds of fishing, depending on available resources and current market opportunities.

The potential economic rewards for inter-village planning and cooperative effort in building, for example, a reservoir, irrigation or flood control facilities, or roads and bridges are immediately apparent to the farmer. In the two CBIRD island areas, however, the current prosperity of the fishing sector is absorbing much of the available energy; the fishing economy tends to focus villagers' attention on their own harbors, boats, nets, fishing grounds, and markets rather than on the need for cooperation with neighboring communities. At the same time the fisherman's lack of strong ties to the land, his dependence on manufactured goods (engines/fuel/nets) and his involvement in national and export markets, make him particularly sensitive both to the need to acquire the latest technological skills and the requirement that he engage in capitalistic entrepreneurship. Thus, there is a real sense in which fishermen, despite their physical isolation, are being swept along by the processes of social change accompanying economic development even faster than farmers. There seems to be a paradox, however. On the one hand fishermen are more mobile physically in the sense that they are usually more willing than the farmer to change their residence and occupational activity according to economic exigency, while on the other hand fishing villages tend to retain a more closed and ingrown type of isolated solidarity.

The importance of mass communications and transportation for development, particularly in relatively inaccessible areas, is undoubtedly great. The fact that Yaksan is almost completely electrified, which permits the operation of large numbers of television sets, means that island residents are being rapidly indoctrinated in

national popular culture. Even on Wido the isolation is far from
complete, since almost every household possesses a transistor radio.

Transportation to and from the island areas is a good deal more
difficult, of course, than in mainland rural areas, because passenger
boat service is limited. Yaksan, however, is fairly close to the mainland and to other well populated islands, so that ferry service to
several different villages is quite frequent. Also, the fact that so
many households have boats, while the surrounding waters are mostly
sheltered, means that transportation is not a serious problem. Wido,
however, is much more inaccessible.

The Yaksan and Wido islands are both mountainous, so that
land travel among most of the villages is difficult. While roads
have been improved recently as a result of Saemaul and CDF initiatives
(using local cooperative labor), there has not yet been time to
observe how much this has helped to broaden traditional village
feelings of solidarity so as to include a larger geographical area.

South Korea is a small country with a racially homogeneous
population. Throughout the peninsula people speak the same
language, share a common belief system, wear the same clothes,
eat the same kinds of food, and observe most of the same customs.
There is a general pattern of rural social organization that is, with
few exceptions (e.g., Cheju Do), repeated everywhere. Yet the
variations--economic, environmental, social/psychological, and
structural--that distinguish different regions as well as communities
within the same region have a significant relation to the pace and
kinds of developmental processes that are going on.

CHAPTER 3

ORGANIZATION: STRUCTURE,

LINKAGES AND ROLES

Local Administration

As noted earlier, CDF decided in 1973 that its development effort should be organized on a larger scale than the single agricultural village. One important reason was the need to establish and maintain close ties with local administrative agencies in planning and implementing projects, since integration with the Saemaul Movement was a necessary condition for success on both political and economic grounds. The myon (township or sub-county), which is the lowest level of local administration, was a logical and, in terms of size, manageable unit on which to base the CBIRD structure. The myon usually comprises anywhere from eight to twenty-one administrative villages with a total population of from 3,000 to 10,000 persons. In each myon there is an administrative office (Home Ministry), an agricultural extension office (Ministry of Agriculture and Fisheries), an agriculture and/or fisheries cooperative (National Cooperatives Federation), and a health office (Ministry of Health and Social Welfare). In addition there are the primary schools and a middle school (Ministry of Education), the post office, and a unit of the national police. Each of these agencies is the bottom link of a large national bureaucracy with its own chain of command, system of communications, and operating procedures that extend from Seoul down through the provincial and county administrative levels. There are also local political party heads-- wealthy and influential residents--who have their own formal and informal links to the sources of authority in Seoul.

All of these representatives of the central power structure (except for the outlying primary schools) are grouped fairly closely together near the myon administrative office *(myon samuso)*. The head of this office, the *myon chang,* has the highest formal, bureaucratic prestige and authority in the area.   It is his responsibility to coordinate the efforts of all the agencies within his jurisdiction in order to promote the development and economic well being of the myon. Since the beginning of the New Community Movement (Saemaul Undong)in 1971, he has been under intense pressure from his superiors at the county administrative office *(gun ch'ong)* to produce fast results in readily observable, quantitative terms. To the extent

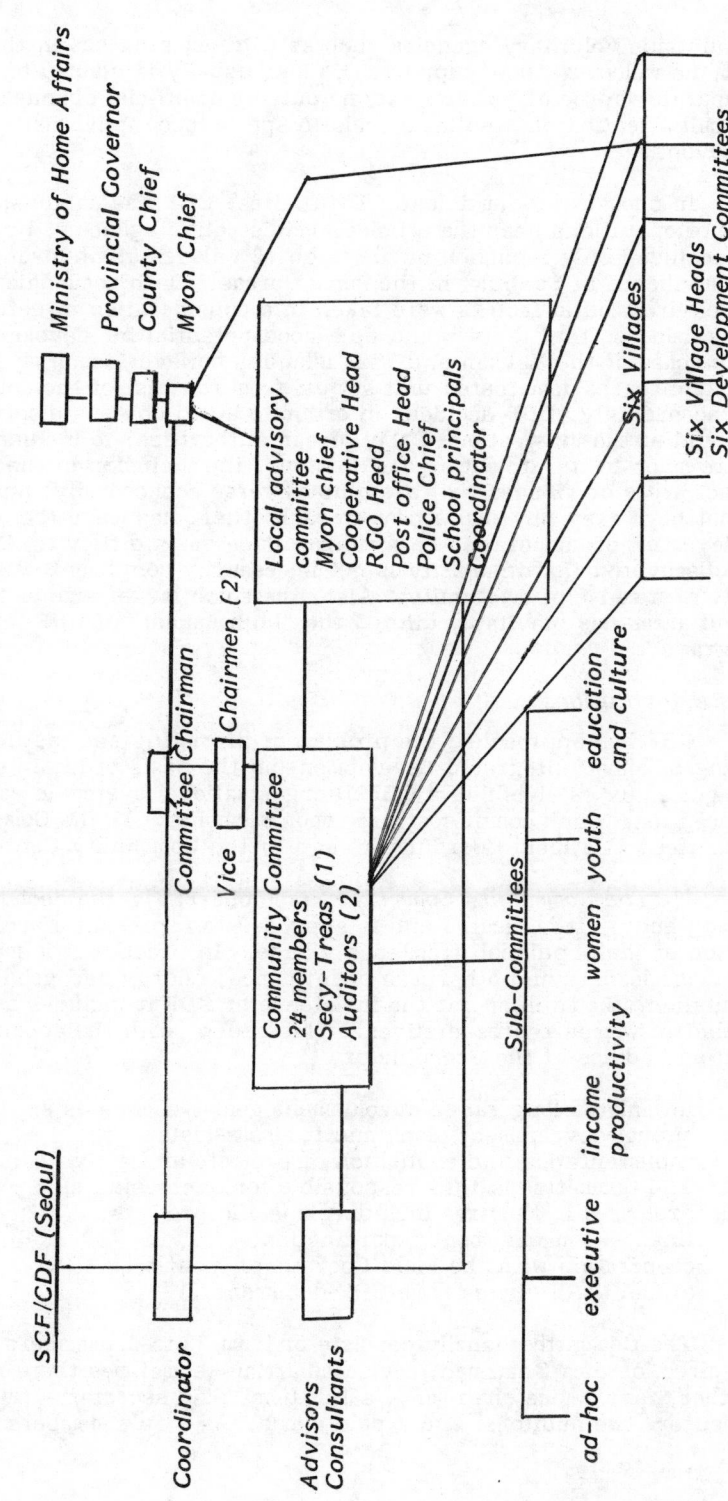

Figure 5

ORGANIZATION OF CHUNSONG COMMUNITY COMMITTEE

that outside voluntary agencies such as CDF assisted him in this task, he welcomes their support. He also usually is glad to have a separate source of public relations outside of official channels that can call attention on a national scale to special accomplishments in his myon.

In choosing the mainland CBIRD sites, CDF has established its base of operations near the official administrative agencies, but has included only a portion of the myon (6 villages at Chunsong and 8 villages at Sanbuk) in the impact areas. Both sociological and environmental factors were taken into consideration in defining these limits so that there would be a good potential for development. In the case of the Yaksan and Wido islands, however, each myon was a single clearly demarcated unit set off from the rest of the country, and accordingly, CDF decided, in order to avoid obvious discrimination and at the suggestion of the Korean authorities, to include the entire myon in its project area. However, the inclusion in the island impact areas of villages that are quite diverse economically, and that do not have easy physical access to each other, has made the achievement of cooperation on a multi-village basis difficult. CDF has discovered that insularity is not necessarily congruent with unity or a sense of community. Also, the much larger size of the island areas has inevitably diluted the "high impact" of CDF programs.

CBIRD Institutions

CDF has approached the problem of promoting and instutionalizing balanced integrated development on the basis of local needs and goals, by establishing a CBIRD organizational system in each impact area, which comprises three main elements: 1) the Community Committee, 2) a Field Coordinator, and 3) the Community Center.

1) *The Community Committee* (see chart) is the decision-making body. It is elected and is supposed to represent a cross section of the population from each village. In practice it is made up of village leaders and other men of influence, energy and good reputation. In addition, at the insistence of CDF it includes a number of women representatives. This group, with the encouragement and advice of the Coordinator,

> formulates long range development goals, as well as an annual development plan, and it also assists in the implementation and evaluation of projects and activities. The Committee is thus responsible for overseeing all programs in the area including specific projects, finances, management, coordination, etc., in cooperation with the Field Coordinator sent from CDF office. (All quotes from CDF documents.)

The Committee usually consists of from 20 to 25 members under the direction of a Chairman, a vice chairman (sometimes there is another, female vice chairman), a full time, paid secretary-treasurer, two auditors, and a paid clerk. As a rule members serve for two years, and the Committee meets once a month, but such procedural matters are determined by the Committee itself.

Annual meetings, at which project planning and budgeting for the subsequent year is determined, may go on for two days or even longer, while the monthly meetings to cope with the various problems and changes that occur in the course of the year may take only a half day. "The committee formulates regulations for organization and operation which are submitted to the people along with financial statements in annual general meetings."

The actual composition of the Community Committee is determined locally in accordance with what appears to be the most equitable representation of village opinion and interests. At Yaksan the Committee is made up of the village heads of all 21 villages on the island plus the Chairman and Vice Chairman. In Wido there is a kind of proportional representation with three committee members from each of the three largest villages, two from each of the other villages on Wido itself, and one each from the four small communities on outlying islands. On the mainland Chunsong and Sanbuk both have the same system. Each village has two committee members (three for Chunsong), and in addition there are the two officers and several women representatives. For each village with more than one member the village head is invariably included, and the other representatives are "elected", which usually means appointment by consensus decision rather than formal vote.

The four permanent sub-committees of the Community Committee are, Children, Youth, Women, and Income Increase (or productivity). The sub-committee on children supervises the operation of day care centers for pre-school children, and the youth committee assists the various 4H clubs of member villages, also organizing sports events between villages or local associations. The women's sub-committee encourages such programs as "rice saving" (building up small family savings by decreasing daily rice consumption), the operation of a women's credit union, the provision of meals for day care centers, and in some areas women's joint, cash crop farming. In implementing projects that deal with health care, nutrition, and family planning, the women's sub-committee either organizes its own meetings and training sessions or tries to revitalize such existing organizations as the Mothers' Club and the Women's Club. The income increase sub-committee provides organizational and material support as well as advice to a number of individuals and local groups, e.g., associations for cattle and pig raising, dairy farming, seaweed cultivation, mushroom growing, apple cultivation, green house construction, credit unions, and other financial organizations.

Special temporary sub-committees are established to deal with currently urgent projects such as electrification, flood control, irrigation, bridge construction, and telephone installation. These sub-committees must approach the appropriate government authorities for approval and financial support; in addition they seek advice and assistance from non-governmental experts.

2) *The Field Coordinator* is "a qualified and trained field worker of CDF" who is chosen in consultation with the local administration.

> He organizes the Committee initially and works in
> close cooperation with it subsequently, providing
> continuing advice on the planning, implementation,
> and evaluation of projects, as well as on finances.
> He gives continued support and guidance to facili-
> tate the effective operation of the program and tries
> to better acquaint the community with available
> outside resources and ideas.

It is essential that he provide an effective link between the Committee and local official agencies, so as to obtain their support and make sure that the Committee's efforts are integrated with other developmental goals. He also has responsibility for organizing training programs, and he supervises the keeping of descriptive and financial records, making periodic reports to the CDF field office in Seoul.

New recruits for the job are ordinarily given three months intensive training by CDF followed by a period during which they work under an experienced Coordinator in an established impact area. The coordinator lives in the impact area during the first few years of operation of the CBIRD program, until the Community Committee and its chairman are able to function without constant supervision and guidance. Thereafter, he visits the area frequently, consulting with local officials and committee officers as well as participating in important meetings and social events. Successful implementation of the CBIRD program probably depends more on the Coordinator's skill than on any other single factor. Ideally, he should be a diplomat, a charismatic mobilizer of men and women, and a practical trouble shooter. Further discussion of the Coordinator's role follows below under *Roles and Relationships*.

3) *The Community Center* is a building or group of buildings that is owned by and registered in the name of the Committee. It is located near the myon office and other administrative agencies so as to be as accessible as possible to all people in the CBIRD area. The design and construction is carried out with the idea that future additions will be made to the building as the Committee expands its activities and the number of community organizations under its aegis increases. In addition to the office of the Coordinator and full time Committee officials, the center is used for committee meetings, training sessions, workshops, ceremonies, and recreational events. It may also house a day care center, a credit union, a club for the elderly, a small factory, or an official agency such as the extension service branch. It is up to the Committee to determine how best to use the Center so as to make it the focus for developmental activism in the wider community.

The Korea Office of SCF/CDF has strongly urged the Community Committees to build their Community Centers in traditional style with heavy curving tiled roofs, even though this type of construction is more expensive. The general idea seems to have been that such a uniquely Korean building with all its associations of upper class authority and aesthetic beauty would inspire a great pride in local citizens. And in fact the Community Center at Sanbuk, which is built in this style, is the most intensively and constructively utilized of all the Centers. Its functions have been incorporated into the daily lives of local residents, who for the most part do appear to have a sense of proprietorship--a feeling that they share in its ownership and operation. Furthermore there is little doubt that Sanbuk Center is built solidly with local materials and will stand as either a monument or symbol to people of the village for generations to come.

On the other hand, pragmatic modernists (and there are a great many such people in the Korean countryside today) favor westernized efficiency--in this case maximum accommodation for the least cost. At Chunsong, for example, there is also, at least among the lite, local pride in the fact that the Community Center, a modern building, is able to house so many different organizations with so many different functions under one roof. Nevertheless, the mood of the center is somewhat more bureaucratic and formal than at Sanbuk, with fewer visits by ordinary farmers and women. While it is manifestly impossible to reach any solid conclusions with regard to the importance of an intangible factor such as building design in the mix of variables that contribute to community spirit, there is a hint here that greater attention should be paid to the subtler, psychological ingredients of local morale, instead of concentrating entirely on concrete measures of social and material progress.

The following principles are stressed by CDF for the Center's operation: 1) The Center is to be used to promote the economic and social benefit of all the villagers in an integrated manner, without giving undue emphasis to any one area, group, or type of project. 2) There should be more emphasis on fostering self help efforts by the villagers than in providing services or aid from outside. 3) The Center should be used to encourage systematic cooperation and joint activities with other agencies in the area, rather than focussing on independent CDF projects.

As an example there are listed below the events taking place in a typical summer month at the Chunsong Community Center:

Date	Name	Sponsoring Agency	No. of Participants
July 9	4-H Club	Rural Guidance Office (extension)	15
12	Day Care Center Committee	Community Committee	10
14	Governing Board of Women's Bank	Women's Bank	12
14	Women's Bank Context	Women's Bank	80

Date	Name	Sponsoring Agency	No. of Participants
July 14	Welcome Party for University Medical Service Team	Community Committee	30
17	Tong Myon Integrated Development Conference	Tong Myon (Chunsong) Committee	13
21	Civil Defense Drill	Tong Myon (Chunsong) Office	70
23	Evaluation of Training Programs	Community Committee	8
24	Evaluation and Planning Meeting for Saemaul Activities	Tong Myon Office	70
27	Tong Myon Elders	Tong Myon Elders Committee	50
28	Mothers' Meeting for Day Care Center	Kasan Day Care Center	35
29	Monthly Meeting	Community Committee	16

One of the best indications of how effective the CBIRD program has been in any given area is the amount of activity that goes on in the Community Center. Where, in addition to regularly scheduled meetings, the Center becomes a place in which there is frequent informal personal interaction and an on-going exchange of ideas on a variety of matters affecting development in the entire area, then the Center's purpose as the focus of cooperative efforts is probably being realized. Both the sense of popular involvement and of common proprietorship are expressed through continuing, frequent use of the building.

RELATIONS WITH OTHER ORGANIZATIONS

One kind of formal linkage between the CBIRD structure and other organizations and agencies in the myon is provided through a local Advisory Committee, which is organized by the Coordinator and the Community Committee. (See Fig. 5.) It comprises the myon chief (myon branch chief in Sanbuk), the head of the agricultural cooperative and/or fisheries cooperative, the head of the Rural Guidance Office (extension service), the police chief, the post office head, the school principals, ex-chairmen of the Community Committee, and other influential men. The Coordinator is naturally anxious to obtain the administrative, material, and social support of such local dignitaries for the work of the Community Committee, and whenever a person is newly appointed to one of these offices, he is asked to serve on the advisory committee and then briefed at some length regarding the CBIRD operation.

The most crucial link for everyday implementation of the program is between the CBIRD structure and the myon office. The Coordinator tries to make sure that both the county (gun) and myon officials are involved with him in joint planning and funding for development, i.e., that CBIRD is incorporated in Sae-maul plans. In this way local officials can participate in and take some credit for CDF accomplishments, while Korean Government funding is made available to the Community Committee for multi-village projects. In 1978 the Korean Government contributed a larger share of outside funding support to CBIRD projects than did CDF. CDF comments, "this is an achievement of the joint planning efforts by local government and the people with motivational and technical support from the CDF field coordinator."

In addition to the Coordinator's diplomatic skill and persuasiveness in dealing with myon officials, constructive relations with the bureaucracy also depend on high level contacts with the national centers of power. The director and staff of the SCF/CDF Korea Field Office in Seoul maintain contacts with the President's office, the Economic Planning Board, and the Ministries of Home Affairs, Agriculture and Fisheries, Health and Social Welfare, and Education. As a result of these initiatives at the top, provincial, county, and myon officials have been instructed by the Home Minister to cooperate with CDF in local development projects, and petitions from CBIRD areas, particularly Wido, for larger scale government investments have been favorably acted upon. Officials at the provincial, county and myon levels have participated in CDF training courses and visited the impact areas to observe actual accomplishments. In this way, as well as through various kinds of mass media publicity, CDF has been able to focus attention on the special problems that exist in remote areas, particularly the islands. The institutionalization of local planning, decision making, and the direction of projects through the Community Committee has given provincial and county officials confidence that their investments will be effectively utilized.

The Korean Government is also interested in the CBIRD program as a source of new ideas and practices that might be incorporated in national development policies. CDF training methods, the mechanisms for establishing revolving funds and providing credit, as well as the overall concept of a small area or multi-village planning and funding unit, are under consideration as possible models for the modification of national programs.

ROLES AND RELATIONSHIPS

The new institutional structure created by CBIRD to achieve its goal of organizing integrated development on a multi-village or small regional basis, requires that villagers modify certain attitudes and roles, entering into different kinds of relationships. Previous patterns of authority, loyalty, and association had been closely integrated with the traditional, closed, cohesive village structure, and Coordinators encountered considerable initial resistance to change. In the beginning there was a tendency for relations between the Community Committee and the village power structures to reflect a certain amount of rivalry and jealousy, both over positions on the Committee and regarding the division of available funds. The idea that the total pie was limited, and that one village could only profit at the expense of another, was firmly rooted in rural thinking. Village elites, whose economic and social base had usually been narrowly confined to one small community, were reluctant at first to commit themselves to the new institutions. In addition to their farming tasks there were the incessant demands of the Saemaul Movement, so that established leaders were unwilling to take on new responsibilities. Where this occurred, the Coordinator usually had to go ahead with younger, less prestigious men who were more receptive to change.

Only very gradually as the Coordinator continued to preach his message, and as a few initial projects brought good results, was there increasing acceptance of the idea of several villages joining together in development efforts. Without substantial outside capital inputs from CDF it would have been much more difficult, if not impossible, to get things started. Some Coordinators found it expedient to direct the initial benefits from such projects as cow raising or house repair to village leaders, in order to ensure their enthusiastic participation in the program.

The construction of the Community Center as a tangible symbol of the CBIRD ideal appears to have been something of a turning point in overcoming village parochialism. The fact that the new centers involved joint planning, the mobilization of labor from every village, and the subsequent diversified use for the benefit of the entire impact area has helped to consolidate the idea of inter-village cooperation.

The role of the Coordinator is, of course, especially important during the early phase. He has great influence--amounting almost to control--over the Committee's decisions regarding the expenditure of CDF funds, and he must use this influence wisely, e.g., by urging the Committee to give the best cow to the chairman if necessary, or by opposing extravagant plans that have little prospect of immediate success.

On the other hand, as an outsider it would be counterproductive for him to take too strong a stance in dealing with local leaders. He should exercise guidance as indirectly and subtly as possible, so as to foster the Committee's ability to discuss projects intelligently, resolve conflicting claims, and take effective action on its own. The Committee should not only have responsibility for decision making; it should accept responsibility for failures. Too much dependence on the Coordinator is bound to inhibit the development of a self sustaining Committee that commands support and respect throughout the area.

If people think the Coordinator can do anything he wants, a number of aggressive individuals will invariably try to get him to support their own private goals, which are likely to be mutually contradictory. Or if local officials find that he is the key man in successfully carrying out Saemaul projects, he will be under intense pressure to achieve their targets for them at the earliest possible date. He must therefore maintain a certain distance as a neutral, objective advisor, guiding people to do things for themselves while avoiding direct responsibility.

The Coordinator cannot remain entirely objective and neutral in his personal relationships, however. The kind of influence over people that is described above is only possible if there is a considerable degree of genuine warmth and respect, and this takes time to establish. He must be able to get along with people of all types and social levels. His character and behavior are under constant, intense scrutiny, particularly when he first arrives in the area. Any moral lapse (one Coordinator was replaced because of a scandalous romance with the Committee clerk) or violation of etiquette will seriously impair his influence and effectiveness.

All of these personality characteristics, including even the Coordinator's style of speaking, are important. His role is to preach a somewhat radically new ideology to the effect that everyone in the larger multi-village community can benefit only if all work together for common goals rather than just for the advantage of their own households or village. For this kind of missionary activity a certain charisma is necessary; once the Coordinator has succeeded in gaining the respect and affection of local residents, then all aspects of the program seem to be easier to accomplish.

Another key role in the CBIRD system is that of the Community Committee Chairman. He is a prominent local citizen elected by the Committee to lead the village representatives in their effort to plan and carry out development projects on a regional basis. He is the main link between the Coordinator and the local population, and he also formally represents the CBIRD area in dealing with the bureaucracy or other outside agencies.

Each village chief in Korea has direct relations with the myon office on Saemaul and other administrative affairs, so that there is a built-in potential for rivalry between village heads and the Committee Chairman, who deals with the local authorities as the representative of several villages on CBIRD matters. If there is widespread confidence in the ability and fairness of the Chairman, however, the several village heads are usually glad to delegate as much of their time-consuming and onerous duties to him as possible, so that a respected Chairman becomes in fact a kind of *de facto* representative of the entire area on most development matters.

On the basis of CDF experience in Korea and by making very broad (and crude) distinctions, one can define four different general types of Chairman: 1) the authoritarian activist; 2) the

respected and energetic leader;   3) the ordinary farmer of good
reputation; 4) the honorary officeholder.   At various times Community Committees have chosen chairmen who represent variations on all
four types, but the job of the Coordinator is made much easier if he is
lucky enough to work with type number two, "the respected and
energetic leader."

Of course prestige is always an important incentive, since
Chairmen receive no salary.   It is appropriate in the East Asian
tradition that a man of means, ambition, and ability should, as he
gets older, devote himself to the general welfare without thought of
remuneration.   He and his entire family then receive added status
from this role.   But today the effective Chairman (or village chief
in most other Korean villages) must also be a determined activist,
deriving satisfaction from the achievement of practical development
goals.

Either of the first two types listed above can be effective as
chairman, although the authoritarian approach may provoke opposition and exacerbate existing divisions.   The third type, the
ordinary respectable farmer, may be too busy with his own farming
or fishing activities to devote the necessary time to CBIRD matters.
And such a person, if he lacks a high school education or special
strength of character, may depend too much on the Coordinator,
acting more as figurehead than as leader.

Unfortunately, candidates of the fourth type, the honorary
officeholder, are not lacking in Korea.   Such obvious and widely
recognized qualifications as wealth, higher education, and important
connections are hard to ignore when people are being chosen for
important or prestigious posts, even though the primary interest
or talent of such a person may have little or nothing to do with
rural development.

Once a progressive style of chairmanship has been firmly
established in an impact area, it seems to be easier to maintain
the momentum, even though the position itself is rotated every two
years or so.   It then becomes possible for the Coordinator to play
a less conspicuous role, as Chairman and Committee members learn
to plan and implement projects within the broader, multi-village
environment.   The start-up period, i.e., the first six months
or so during which CBIRD institutions are established, appears to
be crucial in determining local attitudes, procedures, and precedents.

It is an obvious condition for effective performance in planning
and implementing development projects that the three key figures
on the local scene--the Coordinator, the Committee Chairman, and
the sub-county chief (myon chang)--should get along well
together.   Unfortunately, interpersonal tensions do sometimes arise,
and the program invariably suffers as a result.

In contemporary Korea the government has promoted youthful,
dynamic village leadership as an integral part of the Saemaul

Movement. When innovations are introduced, there has been some
tendency for older, well-established, more conservative farmers to
hold back, waiting to assess the results. These informal leaders
tend to get more involved in community development efforts, only
as the success of the new methods becomes apparent. This same
linkage between the adoption of successful innovations and the
increased community involvement or public spiritedness of older
village elites is also evident in the CBIRD program. When it occurs
there is a significant strengthening of the institutional base for
development.

VILLAGE ORGANIZATIONS

In each village there are several organizations established by
governmental order to accomplish development   goals. The situation
varies, of course, from one place to another, but there is a strong
tendency for many of these, such as the Mothers Club, the Farm
Improvement Club, the Forestry Association, the 4-H Club, or the
Women's Club to exist only on paper, or when prodded into temporary
activity by local officials. CDF usually tries to encourage such
activities,   both at the village level and in a regional context, by
providing a meeting place, technical advice, and sometimes material
support.

As a result of the Saemaul Movement two organizations, the
Village Development Committee and the Village Bank or credit union
now function more or less continuously, depending on local leadership and the extent of activism in the community. Village Development Committees comprising both formal and informal local leaders,
have the main responsibility for planning and implementing   Saemaul
projects in accordance with the general wishes of the community.
The village representatives to the Community Committee are likely
to be also members of the Village Development Committee (the village
chief invariably is), and this overlap in membership linking the
village to the impact area helps ensure that decisions and commitments
made under CBIRD auspices will in fact be carried out.   It also
helps ensure that Community Committee decisions are based as much
as possible on responsible grass roots opinion.

The village banks usually suffer from lack of managerial skills
and a shortage of funds, forcing farmers and fishermen to continue
to rely on usurious loans for a portion of their credit needs. CDF
is encouraging the amalgamation of several such small banks into
stronger multi-village financial organizations. Training is provided
for the bank staff, while the Community Committee makes a portion
of its revolving fund available as bank capital.

RELATIONS WITH OTHER ORGANIZATIONS IN KOREA

CDF has been extremely active in developing contacts with,
and utilizing the services of, many other semi-public, and international organizations in the development field. There have been

numerous inspection trips, joint workshops and study groups with such agencies of the United Nations as the Economic and Social Commission for Asia and the Pacific, the UNDP Asia Center for Training, UNICEF, and UNESCO.

Discussions of particular problems have been held with experts from such national Korean Organizations as the Korea Development Institute, the National Social Workers Training Center, the Korea Institute of Family Planning, the National Agricultural Technical Association, and the Korean Society for the Study of Education. CDF has hired a number of university professors and their research assistants to carry out surveys and provide assistance in refining the CBIRD long term programs. Coordinators obtain help from expert consultants on the technical aspects of particular projects in their impact areas.

University medical teams have carried out surveys in the CBIRD areas on nutrition, public health and medical care. They have also operated temporary dental and medical clinics in the impact areas with a view to developing a comprehensive rural medical service program in the future.

There has been frequent discussion and collaboration with other voluntary agencies operating in the field of Korean rural development. Private business and trading (import-export) firms are consulted on a continuing basis with regard to the technical and economic feasibility of such varied matters as the introduction of new agricultural products, cattle breeding, and the installation of boat engines.

CDF has also established an advisory committee of prominent Koreans and Westerners in Seoul, which has been able to raise over $15,000 for CDF projects in 1978. Because of the interest that has been generated in the CBIRD development projects, CDF staff are obliged to spend a good deal of their time briefing foreign and Korean visitors and taking them on tours of inspection to the impact areas.

CHAPTER 4

THE PLANNING PROCESS

The CBIRD areas have from the outset been engaged in a relatively sophisticated planning process under the guidance of the CDF
Coordinator. In this respect, CBIRD is a sizeable step ahead of the
Saemaul Movement, which also encourages local planning but within
the framework of a standard, nationwide bureaucratic model that
often cannot be easily adapted to the varying needs, conditions and
capabilities of different villages. Moreover, the Saemaul approach
applies only to making separate plans for each individual village,
whereas the CBIRD approach applies to a consortium of neighboring
villages.

In principle, the CBIRD planning system provides all villagers
in the area, whatever their status, an opportunity to express their
views not only on their own priority needs and aspirations but on
what the priority development objectives of the whole area should be.
Since such views are bound to differ from family to family and village
to village, the system also provides for mediating these differences
through a give-and-take process until a generally acceptable consensus emerged.

This consensus gets expressed in the form, first, of a "long
term" development plan (3-year) and later in a series of short term
(1-year) development plans for each CBIRD impact area, itemized in
terms of specific "productivity" and "social infrastructure" projects
with corresponding investment requirements and sources. The
process imposes a strong discipline because the overall plan must be
cut to fit a clearly defined timetable and the set of resources
expected to be available from both local and outside sources. In
other words, it cannot be simply a list of dreams and compromises
that cannot possibly be implemented. Nor can the process end
simply with an overall plan; each individual project must also be
planned and properly prepared if it is to be effectively implemented.

Making such plans is inherently a very complex undertaking,
especially in a rural society unaccustomed to such sophisticated self-
diagnostic and decision-making methods. Not only must the
community's own needs, resources and potentialities be accurately
assessed and a meeting of minds achieved among conflicting interests,
but the local plan must also be compatible with the policies and
capabilities of outside supporting agencies--particularly Saemaul
and CDF. This requires skillful negotiation. Moreover the plan must

be sufficiently flexible and adaptable so that it can be altered on
short notice in response to unforeseen events such as droughts or
a serious delay in the delivery of expected outside assistance.

Types of Projects

To interpret a typical CBIRD plan it is necessary first to understand the various categories and terminology used in CDF plans and
financial reports.

Following Saemaul practice, all CBIRD projects are classified
under two headings: 1) "Productivity/Income-Raising" projects
and 2) "Social Infrastructure Projects" (sometimes also referred to
as "Environmental Improvement"). The *productivity* projects include
mainly agricultural (or fishery) improvements carried out by
individuals, largely with their own efforts and investments, though
often with temporary loans and technical assistance from CBIRD or
others. Typical projects in this category include: raising new livestock, building a vinyl greenhouse for cash crops, or improving
boat and fishing equipment. This category may also include, however,
certain economic infrastructure items of utility to the whole community,
such as a warehouse, local bank or cooperative store.

The *Social Infrastructure* category can be quite confusing to the
outsider because it combines several quite dissimilar sub-categories,
some of which are more closely linked in conventional parlance to
economic development than to social development. These sub-categories
include: (a) *household improvements* by individual families (largely
at their own expense, using loans where necessary) such as replacing
a thatched roof with tile, making kitchen improvements, building a
latrine or installing electricity, running water or a telephone; (b)
community *health and sanitation activities* such as nutrition, family
planning, medical insurance, water systems and parasite control
programs; (c) *education and culture* projects, such as day care
centers, school improvements, athletic and cultural programs, and
scholarships; (d) *public works* projects (with important economic
implications) such as road, bridge or dike construction, harbor
improvements, truck purchases and the like; and (e) *program management* including local administration of the CBIRD program, operating
the community center, technical and leadership training, and emergency assistance. The important point to bear in mind is that this
Social Infrastructure category includes a melange of projects, only
a few of which could properly be classified as social welfare under
customary usage.

CDF's Financial Strategy

The financial aspects of CBIRD plans and CDF summary reports
can also be confusing to the outsider who is unaware of CDF's basic
financial strategy. This rather unusual strategy has four main objectives: (1) to maximize self-help by individual farmers, fishermen
and households by providing easy access to loans at moderate
interest rates; (2) to recycle a substantial portion of CDF grant
funds back into the local economy in the form of loanable assets

under the control of the Community Committees; (3) to combine CDF project support wherever possible with substantial local and government support; and (4) to use a portion of available CDF funds--if need be without matching funds from other sources--to spearhead certain social welfare activities considered important by CDF but not yet considered high priority by the local community or the government.

Evidence presented in the next chapter sheds light on how effective this finarcial strategy has been. Before presenting this evidence, however, it is important to explain how CBIRD plans are made.

Making a Plan

Getting t! ϶ CBIRD type of planning process implanted is not an easy matter and requires great skill and ingenuity on the part of the Coordinator. It works somewhat differently in each area, but in principle the planning process starts with a survey of the impact area to obtain "baseline data." In addition to a general description of the area, the survey contains demographic data, lists of local organizations and institutions, and detailed quantitative information on land quality, ownership and use, crop yields, agricultural implements, household income, housing conditions, and facilities for health care and cultural activities. A parallel and somewhat more informal survey collects the views of people in the different villages on the most pressing needs and priority goals to which the plan should be addressed.

On the basis of all this information--and after extensive informal and formal discussions--the Community Committee with the help of the Coordinator draws up a *three-year plan* based on selected priority development goals and targets, with corresponding cost estimates and projections of anticipated "investment" resources from CDF, the local people, the Government (mainly under the Saemaul program), and any other outside sources. A sample of such a 3-year plan, from Chunsong for the period July 1976-June 1979, is shown in Table 3. This plan envisages 45 different projects and activities over three years at a total investment of nearly $270,000, equally divided between productivity and social infrastructure projects. Of this total, 52 percent would come from "self-help" (cash plus contributed labor), 17 percent from CDF, and 31 percent from Government.

The process of developing an *annual* plan, according to Coordinators, has proved to be a heavy and difficult task for the Chairmen and members of Community Committees, requiring continuous and extensive assistance by the Coordinators. A summary of the FY 1977/78 annual plan of the Chunsong Area is shown in Table 4.

The gestation period for an annual plan is usually about five months, starting in February and ending in late June with a new plan ready for implementation. At the formal level the Coordinator usually initiates the process by presenting the overall scope of the annual CDF grant to the Community Committee. He then suggests that the Committee draw up its development program, taking account of the villagers' most pressing needs and the extent of local resources

Table 3

Example of a Three Year CBIRD Plan

(Chunsong Impact Area)

Planning Period: July 1976 - June 1979

Type	Name of Project	Contents	Relative Investment (U.S. dollars)			Total
			Self-Help	SCF/CDF	Others	
Productivity	(Agriculture)					
	Water way	5 places	2,000		3,000 (Govt.)	7,000
	Water Lift System	1 place	1,000		3,000 (Govt.)	5,000
	Land Improvement	20 ha	2,000		2,000	4,000
	Seed Improvement (rice)	100 bag	1,200			1,200
	Seed Improvement (other)	100 bag	600			600
	Vinylhouse Culture	100 houses	6,000	1,000	2,000 (Govt.)	9,000
	Fruit Tree Plantation	20,000 trees	5,000	1,000	6,000 (Govt.)	12,000
	Warehouse Construction	6 places	5,000	5,000	7,500 (Agr. Coop)	17,500
	Cow Raising	278 head	13,900			13,900
	Milk Cow Raising	30	4,500	1,000	6,500 (Govt.)	12,000
	Bee Hives	50 boxes	1,000			1,000
	Deer Raising	10 head	3,000			3,000
	Fish Raising	1 place	5,000	1,500	2,000 (Agr. Coop)	8,500
	Sub-total		50,200	14,500	30,000	94,700
Productivity	(Commerce & Industry)					
	Cooperative Stores	10 places	2,000		2,000 (Agr. Coop)	4,000
	Village Bank	3 places	3,000	1,500		4,500
	Mine Development	5 places	30,000			30,000
	Village Industry	2 places	1,000	1,000	2,000 (Govt.)	4,000
	Sub-total		36,000	2,500	4,000	42,500
Social Infrastructure	(Environment Improvements)					
	Roof Improvement	110 houses	6,100	1,100	3,300 (Govt.)	10,500
	Kitchen Improvement	143 "	2,860	1,430		4,290
	Latrine Improvement	151 "	3,020	1,510		4,530

Table 3 (continued)

Type	Name of Project	Contents	Relative Investment (US dollars)			
			Self-Help	SCF/CDF	Others	Total
Social Infrastructure	Compost Places Constr.	147 places	882			882
	House Improvement	13 houses	2,600	1,300	2,600 (Govt.)	6,500
	Barrier Improvement	43 "	1,270			1,270
	Community Beautification	6 villages	5,000			5,000
	Sub-total		21,732	5,340	5,900	32,972
Social Infrastructure	(Health & Sanitation)					
	Running Water System	6 places	3,600	1,200	2,400 (Govt.)	7,200
	Nutrition Program	450 children	1,600	1,600		3,200
	Medical Insurance	6,000 people	1,500	1,500		3,000
	Parasite Control	2, times/yr.	300	300		600
	Family Planning	80 people	200	200		400
	Sub-total		7,200	4,800	2,400	14,400
Social Infrastructure	(Education & Culture)					
	Daycare Centers	4 centers	3,000	3,000		6,000
	Athletic & Culture	3 years	1,500	1,500		3,000
	Scholarship Program	10 students (10 y.)	3,000	1,000		4,000
	Amplifier System	6 places	600	600		1,200
	Playground	6 places	600	600		1,200
	Sub-total		8,700	6,700		15,400
Social Infrastructure	(Program Management)					
	Community Center Operation	1 center	1,000	3,000		4,000
	Village Centers	7 centers	700	700		1,400
	Training Programs (Leaders.)	21 courses	1,000	2,000		3,000
	Technical Training	30 courses	2,500	1,000		3,500
	Emergency Assistance	21 cases	500	420		920
	Administration	3 years	1,500	1,500		3,000
	Sub-total		7,200	8,620		15,820
	GRAND TOTAL		140,332	45,960	83,300	269,592

Table 4

Example of an Annual CBIRD Plan

(Chunsong Impact Area)

Period: July 1, 1977 - June 30, 1978

| Type | | Date: Month | | Relative Investments (U.S. Dollars) | | | | | TOTAL |
		Starting	Ending	Community Cash	Community Inkind	CDF Cash	Govt. & Other Sources Cash	Govt. & Other Sources Inkind	
A. Priority CBIRD Projects									
Tobacco Drying Houses	P*	Feb. 78	June 78		3,742	2,079	4,158		9,979
Cow Raising	P	Sep. 77	Nov. 77	4,158	2,599	4,158			10,915
Animal Pen Construction	P	Sep. 77	Nov. 77	4,158	2,079	4,158			10,395
Vinyl Houses	P	Jan. 78	Apr. 78	2,079	4,158	3,534			9,771
Project Bank	P	July 77	June 78		2,079	1,040			3,119
Community Center	S*	Ongoing			1,040	2,798			3,838
Leadership Training	S	Ongoing		416	2,911	1,663			4,990
Daycare Centers	S	Ongoing		1,247	3,119	2,079	1,559	2,275	10,279
Education & Culture	S	Ongoing		208	1,462	2,214			3,884
Health & Sanitation	S	July 77	June 78	1,871	1,558	1,736			5,165
Administration		Ongoing				1,341			1,341
Sub-total				14,137	24,747	26,800	5,717	2,275	73,676
B. Supplementary Projects						4,158	62,370		66,528
C. Locally Supported**				12,682	1,663		8,316		22,661
GRAND TOTALS				26,819	26,410	30,958	76,403	2,275	162,865

*P = Productivity   S = Social Infrastructure

**Projects not utilizing SCF/CDF Funding but which resulted directly or indirectly from SCF/CDF's assistance or involvement.

available for investment to supplement or match outside help. There
is continuing reference to the general guidelines and objectives
established as part of the area's three-year plan, although considerable flexibility in adjusting to changing conditions or in adopting new
and innovative ideas is encouraged.

The village chiefs, who are also members of the committee, then
convene a series of meetings at their own villages, where there is
discussion of which projects are particularly desirable and feasible
in the light of local capabilities. The projects may be either on behalf
of individuals, such as raising cows or installation of a fishing boat
engine, or a cooperative project such as the construction of a bridge
or piped water system.

A great deal of what eventually takes place is as much determined
by informal conversations among the Coordinator, local officials,
the Committee Chairman, the village heads, and farmers or fishermen as
by the deliberations in regularly scheduled meetings. Often the latter
merely ratifies what has been already worked out informally in
advance. Accordingly, the social skills, intelligence and good will
of the major figures involved are crucial factors in achieving results.

COORDINATION WITH GOVERNMENT

Once the Community Committee has settled on a *draft* of the
new annual plan, its members meet with representatives of government
agencies at the sub-county (myon) office to coordinate with the
Saemaul program and to request and negotiate for specific government
inputs. This is a time-consuming process and is considerably complicated by the lack of fit between CDF's fiscal year and that of the
Government of Korea.

There is considerable variation in the way this process is
carried out, depending on the method of operation of the myon
office chief. Saemaul projects are generally planned and implemented
as separate village efforts, and many are not included in the Community Committee's program. Conversely, some CBIRD projects,
particularly those dealing with education, day care centers and
health, but also some projects designed to increase income, are
excluded from the official Saemaul program.

The actual integration or linkage of CBIRD and Saemaul programs
usually takes place in one of two ways. First, the myon office
may decide to incorporate the CBIRD plan in its overall development
program for the area and retain responsibility for coordinating and
directing all the various projects within its jurisdiction--in which
case the Community Committee is subject to a greater degree of myon
office control and loses some of its autonomy. The second way,
practiced at Sanbuk, is for the Community Committee to review not
only the CBIRD projects but also the Saemaul projects of its member
villages, revising and eliminating some of them on the basis of its
own estimate of local needs and capacities, then submitting the
whole package for review. The advantage of this method for the
myon office is that instead of dealing with representatives from each

separate village on several different plans, it can discuss a single
unified CBIRD/Saemaul program with the Community Committee that
encompasses all the villages. The Committee benefits by retaining
more independence and gaining greater bargaining power with the
myon office concerning the amount and direction of governmental
inputs.

REVIEW BY CDF

When negotiations with local government agencies have been
completed, the projects are then divided by the Committee into those
that can be funded and carried out by the community alone and
those requiring outside assistance from CDF, the Korean Government,
or other agencies such as CARE. As the final step, the Committee
not only submits the plan as a whole to the CDF Seoul office for
review and approval but also a statement describing and justifying
each individual project. An example of such a Development Project
Description Form relating to the creation of a community bank in
Yaksan, is shown in Appendix I.   The plans for each impact area
are reviewed by the director of the CDF Korea program, a procedure
that requires a series of meetings in Seoul of the Coordinators and
other members of the CDF staff. There is heavy pressure to
complete this final clearance process before the end of June so that
implementation can begin in July.

PLANNING AND IMPLEMENTING SPECIFIC PROJECTS

Specific project proposals usually originate from four different
sources. 1) Local leaders and Committee members representing the
population of their villages are likely to bring up economic (i.e.,
income raising) projects. 2) The Field Coordinator tends to propose
projects dealing with training, welfare, and the development and
management of CBIRD institutions. 3) Local agencies such as the
schools, the extension service, or the myon office also make project
proposals from time to time. 4) Many project ideas arise from
discussions that take place in the course of various meetings. Most
project ideas are discussed informally with the persons or organizations most immediately concerned before being put to a formal meeting
of the Community Committee.

Once a project is adopted, its effective implication requires
further careful planning and preparation. For example, for
innovative projects on which local knowledge is inadequate, expert
advice is sought from a number of sources, either through such
governmental agencies as the extension service or the cooperative,
or through CDF. The Coordinator may directly seek out experts
in nearby towns or cities, or he may ask the CDF office in Seoul
to obtain the services of a specialist consultant. Coordinators find
that obtaining timely, expert, technical advice is often a difficult
problem. In Chunsong the fact that the local agricultural extension
office is located in the Community Center has made it easier to obtain
such help in introducing new kinds of agricultural practices.

THE PLANNING ROLE OF THE COORDINATOR

The CBIRD concept and methodology envisages an initial strong role for the Coordinator that gradually diminishes as the local population--particularly the local leaders--gain experience and competence and develop self-confidence in running their own program. Though in principle the Community Committee is responsible for the planning, scheduling, implementation and evaluation of projects, the ideas of the Coordinator and the main concerns of CDF inevitably tend to predominate in the formulation of plans during the first couple of years. In addition to promoting the proclaimed CDF goals of responding to local needs and helping the poor, the Coordinator endeavors to mobilize interest and involvement on the part of the local population that will produce sufficiently dramatic results to inspire confidence in the effectiveness of the CBIRD approach.

A comparison of the impact areas in Korea indicates that it is important right from the start for local leaders to be given as much responsibility as possible so as to acquire from the outset the conviction that they are operating their own program rather than one controlled by CDF. Once an initial habit of dependence on the Coordinator is established, it becomes more difficult later to promote local leadership and institutions on an independent, self-sustaining basis. There is a tendency for Koreans to adapt naturally and easily to hierarchical, paternalistic relationships, particularly where the patron possesses knowledge, relatively high status, and material resources. This kind of problem can arise not only where there is a particularly strong and competent Coordinator, but also if the Chairman of the Community Committee has a great deal of power and authority in the area.

If all goes well, the Coordinator gradually recedes into the background of the planning process and the Committee members take over increasingly. Nevertheless he continues to exert considerable influence in determining the actual mix of projects in the annual plans. He must occasionally discourage what he regards as excessive local enthusiasm for an impractical or risky undertaking, and he must also counter the local preference for income-producing or public works schemes by pushing social welfare projects that are considered by CDF an essential part of village development. Such projects, which include athletic and cultural events, film showings, day care centers, health clinics, meetings for the aged, and help for local education, are also designed to develop cooperation and community spirit among residents of the several villages that comprise the impact area. So far the greatest local enthusiasm for this kind of project has been demonstrated in Sanbuk.

The acid test of any planning process, of course, is the extent to which it ultimately gets translated into action and positive achievements. The next chapter examines the record from this point of view.

APPENDIX I

DEVELOPMENT PROJECT DESCRIPTION FORM

1. Name of Project_____Village Bank_____
2. Project Number_____
3. Name of Country___Korea_____ Name of Field Office___KFO____
4. Impact area number and name_____07 Yaksan_____
5. Village Name _____Jangyong area and Oedu-ri_____
6. Number of Beneficiaries - Direct __530__ ; Indirect __890__
7. Date of preparation____May 20, 1978____
8. When Will   When Will
   Project Begin___July 1, 1978___ Project be completed__June 30, 1979_
9. Problem - Why is the project needed?

   There are 2 financial organizations and a few village banks in Yaksan area. But since they fail to meet the islander's financial requirements, usurious debts are prevailing in this community. The said village banks have a little funds and are operated inefficiently. It is, therefore, necessary that there should be some measures to improve this discouraging situation.

10. Purpose - How will these conditions in your community be measurably improved during the next year by carrying out the project?

   This project is designed to help the islanders reduce their usurious debts and meet their fund needs by merging four village banks into one for its efficient operation--through reduction of operational expenses.

11. Activities - What will you do in order to make these changes?

   The 4 village banks will be merged by June 1979 with supporting fund of $4,158 to be made available from the revolving fund of the community committee. The staff members of the newly-established bank will be provided with training in management and they will observe the community which is operating the village banks efficiently and successfully. The training and observation will be carried out in cooperation with the village bank federation. Also, this project will place emphasis on Bank members' investments in order to increase its fund.

12. Inputs - What will you need in order to do these activities?

RELATIVE INVESTMENT

Community		CDF	Others			Total
Cash	Inkind	Cash	Cash	Inkind	Source	
$9,355						$9,355

APPENDIX I (continued)

BREAKDOWNS

Contents	Fund	Calculations	
Bank Merger	$9,355	Supporting fund:	$4,158
		Jangyong Bank:	$2,079
		Oedu " :	$2,079
		Kuseong/Yeodong	
		Banks:	$1,039
Total:	$9,355		

13. Assumptions - For what reason could your project fail or have only partial success?

Discouraging factors in operating this project could be failure to merge village banks, inefficient operation, slump in investments and failure to conduct training in management for the accountants and other staff of the village bank.

14. Goal - What long range social or economic problem in your community does this project help to change?

Improved management of the bank resultant from a merger would be able to help the population reduce or exterminate usurious debts by meeting partial or entier requirements of the islanders' funds. As a result people here would benefit by this project.

15. Benefits for Children - What benefits will this project provide for the target group of children and youth?

Children will benefit directly or indirectly by this bank. Because their parents are able to borrow some money from this village bank when they are in dire need of funds for their living earning business or for their children's schooling or clothes, etc.

16. Community Development - How will the community be able to continue this project after funding coming from SCF/CDF is no longer available to the community?

The Community Committee would continue this project with its own fund in cooperation with bank's members by expanding its fund.

17. The field coordinator should sign the copy of the Development Project Description From (plan) sent to the National Office to indicate approval. (In addition, copies of project descriptions retained by the community committee and/or field office must also be signed by the representative of the community. During field visits National Office staff will verify that the community representative has signed the project plans.

Oh Byung Sup
————————————————————   ————————————————————
Chairman on behalf of   SCF/CDF Field Coordinator
The Community People

CHAPTER 5

THE IMPLEMENTATION RECORD

In examining the implementation record of CBIRD plans it is important to bear in mind the following environmental factors, discussed in Chapter 2, that strongly influence the development capabilities, incentives and behavior of CBIRD and other Korean rural communities.

Rural development in Korea today--in contrast to earlier years-- is very much an active concern of both the farm population and local administration. The booming prosperity and industrialization of the urban areas and the rapid growth of the economy have created unusually favorable conditions for development in both agriculture and fishing. Villages have been carrying on extensive self-help projects since 1972 within this favorable economic climate and there have been significant increases in living standards and agricultural productivity. Expectations for further progress are high, and there is a general acceptance of the need for innovative change. In contrast to the suspicion and hostility with which officials were regarded in the past, villagers now tend to look to local administrative agencies for advice and material assistance. Although progress has been uneven, government planners are making efforts to provide more assistance to lagging areas.

Environmental factors, however, vary a great deal in Korea and play an important role in determining the developmental opportunities and constraints that any particular village or group of villages confronts. While the CBIRD areas all have considerable potential for development in terms of topography and arable land--or access to marine resources--the mainland farming communities have certain advantages over the island areas, at least at this stage. They are more homogeneous, both with regard to kinds of productive activity and the distribution of wealth. They are also more compact, comprising fewer villages, among which transportation is easier. Moreover, CBIRD programs were initiated in the mainland communities in 1973 and 1974 whereas the island programs have only been in operation since 1976.

These and other differentiating factors must therefore be taken into account in comparing CBIRD accomplishments in such disparate areas. Some--probably most--of the difficulties encountered in the island projects are attributable to aspects of the physical environment,

the amounts of investment, and the relatively short period since CDF
launched its project. In addition, the unfortunate tradition in Korea
of contempt by educated city dwellers for fishermen, whose characteristics are contrasted unfavorably with the sturdy virtues of the farmer,
still persists to some extent. Accordingly, there is some tendency on
the part of officials and other outsiders (sometimes even CDF coordinators) to attribute certain problems to the particular social organization
of island communities or the peculiar personality and customs of island
people.

THE EVIDENCE

CDF has developed an extensive statistical reporting system
designed to monitor and assess progress in project implementation in
each CBIRD area and to keep close track of financial flows. Although
the reports from different areas differ in clarity and comprehensive-
ness, and one encounters occasional puzzling discrepancies between
different reports from the same area as well as among the numerous
summary accounts of the Korea program, they nevertheless provide a
useful quantitative picture of the physical progress being made on
various types of projects and of their financial dimensions.

These quantitative statistics do not, however, shed much light
on significant *qualitative* changes taking place (which sometimes are
even more important than the quantitative ones). Nor do they reveal
what sorts of impact the successfully implemented projects are actually
having on the lives of various subgroups in the local population.   It
is especially difficult to ascertain from these quantitative data whether
and to what extent the poorer families are sharing in the overall benefits of the CBIRD program--a question we will return to later.

The present chapter draws upon a number of different CBIRD
statistical reports for quantitative purposes but relies upon the
authors' discussions and direct observations in the four selected
project areas with regard to qualitative and distributive aspects.

IMPLEMENTATION OF THE FINANCIAL STRATEGY

The CBIRD program has clearly made substantial progress in
implementing the financial strategy described in the previous chapter.
Cumulative CDF grants to the *six* rural CBIRD areas through June,
1978, totaled $683,000 (excluding expenditures of the SCF/CDF field
office in Seoul).* Investments in CBIRD projects by the Government of
Korea over the same period somewhat exceeded this amount. Community
self-help investments and contributions of materials and labor totaled
an estimated $1,500,000. (This figure, particularly the portion rela-
ting to contributed labor, is only a rough approximation and could be
somewhat inflated.) Thus it appears that, overall, each CDF dollar
has been matched by four to five dollars of local effort and government
funds. These figures do not mean, of course, that in the absence of
CDF grants and the CBIRD program none of the other investments
would have been made. There is good reason to believe, however,
that the CDF funds primed the pump for considerably larger
efforts by others--especially the communities themselves--than
would otherwise have occurred.

---

*See note on Table 8 for SCF/CDF Field Office expenditures.

The impressive local effort shown above is partly explained by the fact that 40 percent of the CDF grant funds were recycled back into the local economy as loan assets (controlled by the Community Committees), against which local people can borrow for their own private productive and household improvement projects. An additional 34 percent went into physical property and facilities (e.g., the Community Centers) vested in the Community Committees. These growing assets, summarized in Table 5, have given the Committees an increasingly stronger base of authority and viability.

We can reasonably conclude from the above evidence that CDF's financing strategy, calculated to produce a multiplier effect on total investment funds for the CBIRD programs and to build financial foundations for continuing the CBIRD approach after CDF's withdrawal--has been quite successful.

A COMPARISON OF TWO CBIRD AREAS

It is instructive to compare the FY 1978 record of one of the early mainland CBIRD areas, Chunsong, and one of the later island areas, Yaksan, in terms of their mix of planned projects and the extent to which they were implemented.

Chunsong

The projects planned for the Chunsong area for FY 1978 and the extent to which they were actually implemented are shown in the first two columns of Table 6. The next three columns show the relative investment of CDF, Community, and Government funds in each project. Out of a total investment of $94,800, CDF grants accounted for $29,400; community effort, $53,400; and Government contribution, $12,000.*

The annual plan as depicted in Table 6 originally provided for six productivity/income-raising projects and five social infrastructure projects. Two important modifications were later made, however. The project for building 20 tobacco drying houses was dropped because, even though local farmers had been heavily and profitably engaged in tobacco growing, increased problems with plant disease and falling prices convinced them that other crops would be more profitable in the long run. Hence, some of the funds earmarked for the tobacco houses were redeployed to irrigation pumps to counter the adverse impact of the 1978 drought on cash crops.

The striking fact is that, according to the year-end report to CDF, all the remaining 10 projects (except for Health and Sanitation) achieved or exceeded their planned targets during the year--an impressive record.

---

*These totals are taken from Table 8. The totals for community and government contributions shown on Table 6 are provisional and hence do not quite jibe with the corrected totals on Table 8.

Table 5

Community Assets Created by CDF Grants
as of 1978 (in U.S. dollars)

	CDF Grants	Community Committee Property	Revolving Fund Loan Assets
Sanbuk	165,135	78,703	70,157
Yanggu	167,131	66,112	56,694
Chunsong	125,042	63,027	48,422
Wido	74,552	--	29,923
Yaksan	76,639	6,570	36,417
Jeungdo	74,224	17,671	42,931
Totals	683,323	232,083	284,544

Table 6

Implementation Record of Chunsong
CBIRD Projects FY 1977-78

Projects	No. of Projects		Actual Investments[4] (US$)		
	Planned	Actual	CDF	Community	ROK Govt.
Tobacco drying houses	20	0[1]	--	--	--
Cows	10	10	4,158.	6,757.	
Cow pen construction	10	15	6,237.	9,356.	
Vinyl greenhouses	10	10	3,534.	6,362.	94.
Community center	ongoing	1 center	2,798.	1,040.	
Leadership training courses	16	16	595.	666.	
Day care centers	ongoing	4 centers	2,524.	4,366.	6,220.
Education & culture	8	10	2,144.	1,331.	
Health & sanitation	4	1	1,247.	7,445.	
Irrigation pumps		19[2]	2,219.	3,169.	561.
Administration			1,341.		
Totals			27,072.	40,492.	6,875.
Locally Supported Projects[3]					
Garlic planting	2 ha	4.2 ha		10,395.	
Truck purchase (co-op)	1 truck	1 truck		2,079.	8,316.
Women's Welfare Bank	1 bank	1 bank		1,206	
Totals			27,072.	54,172.	15,191.

[1]Cancelled; see explanation in text.

[2]Added; see text for explanation.

[3]Defined as "projects not utilizing SCF/CDF funding but which resulted directly or indirectly from SCF/CDF's assistance or involvement."

[4]The figures on this table for community and government contributions are provisional. The correct totals are shown on Table 8 below.

The emphasis of the Chunsong program is revealed by the allocation of expenditures. Two-thirds of the total expenditures went into economic projects (principally cattle raising, vinyl greenhouses for cash crops, garlic planting and purchase of a truck), reflecting a strong local preference for income-producing projects. Within the social infrastructure category the largest expenditures were for operating the four existing day care centers for children, a health and sanitation project, and the operation of the Community Center, all of these reflecting CDF priorities. Smaller amounts went to leadership training, education and culture, and administration.

Yaksan

This island area presents a quite different pattern than Chunsong in FY 1978. As shown in Table 7, the plan provided for 10 basically economic projects representing a wide assortment of activities (e.g., animal raising, vinyl greenhouses, growing medical herbs, kelp and seaweed, planting fruit trees, an abalone nursery, and an irrigation channel). The 12 planned social infrastructure projects were equally varied. They included, for example, building a community center, a public bathhouse, a consumer cooperative store, a road and ferryboat landing, kitchen and roof improvements on private homes, school supplies and equipment, athletic and cultural events, health (parasite extermination), and leadership training.

The actual implementation record was considerably poorer than Chunsong's. Of the 21 planned projects only ten met their target, five fell short, and six were delayed or cancelled, but four small unplanned projects were added. In the circumstances, however, this was actually not so bad a record. The CBIRD program in this area, after all, was quite new and the management inexperienced; expected government funds for some important projects failed to materialize; the drought upset certain other projects; competing Saemaul projects diverted funds and energies; market conditions for some agricultural products declined, and popular interest in certain projects evaporated.

Despite all these problems a total of $240,000 in cash and in kind was invested during the year, including $39,900 of CDF funds, $75,900 in local resources, and $108,100 in government funds and materials.* The largest single expenditure was on re-roofing houses ($24,000); the main agricultural projects together took $35,000, and public works over $11,000. Less than $5,000 was devoted to social welfare.

A puzzling contrast emerges when CDF grant funds to Yaksan on a *per capita* basis are compared to other CBIRD areas. As shown in Table 8, the FY 1978 figure for Yaksan is only $5.85 per capita compared to a range of nearly $12 to $14 for Wido, Chunsong and

*These totals are taken from Table 8. The investment figures on Table 7 for the community and government are incomplete. CDF actually granted $53,000 to the Yaksan Project for FY 1978 but $13,500 of this was not used due to delays in the community center.

Table 7

Implementation Record of Yaksan
CBIRD Projects FY 1977-78

Project	No. of Projects Planned[1]	Actual[1]	Actual Investments (US$)[2] CDF	Community	ROK Govt.
Animal Raising			5,925.	6,998.	
Cows	35	3			
Goats	100	50			
Pigs		60			
Medical Herbs (stavia)	.02 ha.	.02 ha.	1,663	3,746	
Consumers Co-op Store	1 store	1 store	1,040	946	120
Vinyl Greenhouse	0.3 ha.	0.2 ha	624	249	
Kelp Cultivation	3.0 ha.	delayed	4,158		
Women's Sub-committee	(various projects)		1,040	2,721	
Community Center	construc-tion planned	delayed	5,489		
Kitchen Improvement	30	30	624	936	
Abalone Nursery	2 ha.	cancelled			
Irrigation Well	not planned originally	½ acre irrigated	624	959	
Leaders Training			2,079	1,372	
Athletic & Cultural Events	cancelled because of drought				
Roof Improvement	41 houses	41 houses	6,819	17,364	
Seaweed (laver) Cultivation	1 nursery	1 nursery	2,079	6,237	2,079
Public Health	Parasite Extermination		1,040		1,040
Housing	30 houses cancelled				
School Supplies	Books & drawing materials		624		624
Telephone Line	1	1	520	21	
Public Facilities	bath house village hall	cancelled			
Road Construction	100 m.	100 m.	416	499	
Water Tank	not originally planned	1 tank	624	895	
School Drinking Fountain	not originally planned	1 system	2,017	1,490	
Administration			2,495		
TOTALS......................................			39,900	44,433	

Table 7 (continued)

Project	No. of Projects Planned[1]	Actual[1]	Actual Investments (US$) CDF	Community	ROK Govt.
Balance from previous page			39,900.	44,433.	3,823.
Locally Supported Projects					
Fruit Tree Planting	3,000 persimmons	3,000 persimmons		5,884.	
Irrigation Channel	400 m.	300 m.		1,238.	624.
Ferry Boat Landing	1500	150 m.		labor	10,400.
TOTALS			39,900.	51,555.	14,847.

[1] Additions and cancellations of projects explained in text.

[2] The figures on this table for Community and Government investments are incomplete. The correct totals are shown on Table 8.

Table 8

Funding Sources and SCF/CDF Grants

Per Capita, FY 1977-78

Impact Area (population)	Funding Sources (U.S. dollars)			
	SCF/CDF	ROK Govt.	Community	CDF Grants (per capita)
Yaksan (9058)	53,000.[1]	108,100.	75,900.	5.85
Wido (4500)	50,000.	78,100.	69,600.	11.84
Chunsong (2108)	29,400.	12,000.	53,400.	13.94
Sanbuk (3134)	43,000.	107,500.	196,300.	13.72

Sources: CDF Semi-annual Reports and Project Evaluation Summary
          Sheets, FY 1978.

[1]Includes $13,500 not yet spent because of delays in planning the
Community Center.

Note: Overall SCF/CDF expenditures in Korea for FY 1977-78
      included:

      1) SCF/CDF Field Office Budget
              Salaries (including CDF Coordinators)
              Transportation & Administration $231,777.
              Training   11,992.
              Consultants   4,318.
              Sub-total $248,087
      2) Grants to (7) Impact Areas   295,769
      3) Grand Total $543,856.

Sanbuk. The explanation may lie in the fact that Yaksan's population
is two to four times larger than the other areas whereas an equal
$50,000 of the US AID grant to SCF/CDF was arbitrarily earmarked
for each of the three new island areas regardless of their differing
population size. Or alternatively, perhaps the SCF/CDF office in
Seoul felt that Yaksan simply was not yet ready to absorb larger
funds. In any event, this marked discrepancy poses an interesting
question as to whether there may not be some "minimum critical mass"
in terms of the per capita grant below which a new CBIRD impact area
will have great difficulty "taking off." It also raises the question of
how the limited funds available to CDF in Korea can most effectively
be divided among relatively well established CBIRD areas, such as
Sanbuk and Chunsong, and new areas such as Yaksan and Wido
that are still in the early stages. A related question is, when should
CDF start phasing down its annual grants to the older project areas,
and when will it be prudent to pull out altogether?

        Another point of interest is the great variation in the amount of
government funds made available to the different CBIRD areas in
any year, the large annual fluctuation in these funds from year to
year, and the disruptive impact on local plan implementation when such
funds fail to come through. The instability of Government funds--and
the incompatibility between the Government's fiscal year and CDF's
fiscal year--clearly creates some difficult problems for making CBIRD
plans and implementing them.

EXAMPLES OF SUCCESSFUL AND
UNSUCCESSFUL PROJECTS

        It is helpful to get behind the cold statistics and discover why
some projects work out better than others. The following sample
cases illustrate some of the reasons.

Credit Union in Sanbuk

        In April 1976 the Sanbuk Coordinator, who happened to have
extensive experience with rural cooperative credit organizations,
introduced the credit union idea to the Community Committee. After
extended discussion the Committee adopted the idea and decided that
its permanent employee, the secretary-treasurer, should receive
intensive training as the credit union manager. On May 21 the union
was established with 87 initial members who invested a total of 44,510
won. With the strong backing of the Committee the credit union
prospered. By January, 1977 there were 119 members and by the
end of June, 1977 the membership had reached 200.

        During the first year of operation the credit union provided
low interest loans averaging $186 to each member household from
a total fund of about $18,000, of which CDF had contributed $7,732.

        Earlier, under the Saemaul program, each village in the impact
area had established an officially sponsored micro-bank. Since these
organizations had the same function and rationale as the credit union,

there was considerable competition--in which the village micro-banks were losing out. In order to solve the problem, a joint meeting was arranged in June, 1977, attended by the village micro-bank chairmen, the Sanbuk credit union chairman, Community Committee members, the Coordinator, and myon officials. It was decided to integrate the village micro-banks with the credit union on the condition that the new organization would retain the Saemaul name of *Maul Kumgo* (micro-bank), and that its operations would be reported through official channels, following the previous practice of the several smaller micro-banks. On August 23, 1977 the credit union in effect absorbed the micro-banks, while retaining its original organizational structure and method of operation. By June, 1978 when the former Chairman of the Sanbuk micro-bank was elected Community Committee Chairman, the credit union had 491 members and investments of about $33,000. During FY 1978 each member received dividends equal to 31.2 percent on his deposit, an impressive yield.

The new Sanbuk credit union has practically eliminated the dependence of farmers on usurious loans from private moneylenders. Members have utilized credit union loans for both home improvement and productive investments. Since the credit union is an integral part of the Community Committee, its success has helped to strengthen the Committee as a local institution. The Committee's secretary-treasurer is busy every day with credit union matters, and the Community Center has become the focal point of the area's financial affairs.

Electrification on Wido

Because of the strong desire for electricity on the part of all Wido Island villages, a sub-committee for island electrification was organized as soon as the CBIRD Community Committee was established in 1976. Soon thereafter an electrification project proposal was submitted, both to the local administration and to CDF. After a Coordinator was assigned to Wido in the spring of 1977 several meetings of the Committee were held to discuss basic strategy. The Committee selected eight members for an observation trip to study a model electrification project on another island. Other Committee members together with the Coordinator were able to obtain promises of technical and financial support for the project under Saemaul auspices from the local fisheries cooperative and the myon office. The Committee with the help of the Coordinator then submitted a detailed plan for electrification to the national government through the local administration.

As finally approved, seven out of ten villages on the island are included in the project. The plan provides for the construction and transportation to the island of concrete electric power poles, to be installed by contributed local labor. As part of the myon Saemaul effort, the Government is providing about $35,000 of support. The fishery cooperative is furnishing $10,000 more, and CDF's investment is $14,000. Each electrified household must pay $60.

As of late 1978 the project was being implemented under the supervision of an advisory team composed of the myon chief, the gun chief and the Coordinator. CDF employed an electrical technician and three assistants to direct the actual work, and village labor was mobilized as needed.

It was hoped that the completion of this project would not only raise the living standards and morale of the islanders but would also increase their respect for, and involvement with, the Community Committee as the key local development agency.

The project was originally scheduled for completion by June, 1979 but a number of problems have arisen and work has gone more slowly than expected. Some of the villagers have only been willing to work on the sections that directly lead to their own communities. Villages on the outlying islands and those individuals who are too poor to pay the 30,000 won are excluded from the project, and this has resulted in widespread dissatisfaction.

In retrospect, perhaps the initial planning should have taken these problems more into account. Possibly low cost, long term loans to the poor might have been arranged. Also, there might have been more discussion of the situation of the remote villages on outlying islands together with a stronger bid for aid from the authorities on their behalf. Even if unsuccessful, such actions might at least have given the disadvantaged persons and villages more of a sense of participation in CBIRD development efforts.

Livestock and a New Cash Crop on Yaksan

The original Yaksan plan was to buy black goats and Korean cows for distribution to selected farmers, since they were well adapted to local conditions, and the villagers were already familiar with their care and feeding. Just as this CBIRD project was getting underway, however, the market price of cows more than quadrupled. At the same time, the government together with the local fisheries cooperative decided to distribute 80 cows on the island. With such a large government cattle project under way it seemed unnecessary for the Community Committee to spend the limited amount of available CDF funds for the same purpose.

Accordingly the Coordinator looked into the possibility of raising pigs. About 80 percent of the farmers on the island were already raising the Korean variety of pig, but compared to western varieties the east Asian pig has a slower rate of growth and produces much less meat when mature.

The Coordinator consulted experts from the Office of Rural Development with regard to appropriate pig varieties, techniques for raising them, prevention of disease, and market conditions. He then presented all the information to the Community Committee, recommending that the project be adopted. The Committee decided to buy 60 pigs and selected 30 skilled, conscientious farmers from two villages who, it was hoped, would be able to raise the new varieties of pigs carefully according to instructions. The farmers were sent to the

county experimental livestock farm for two days of intensive instruction in pig raising, and the pigs were purchased through the good
offices of the county administration and the experimental farm. Since
the new pigs required more sanitary conditions than the Korean variety,
the selected farmers had to build concrete-floored pens at their own
expense.

The Yaksan extension office was able to arrange cooperative
purchasing of pig feed and immunization materials for the new owners.
Most other farmers had shown little interest in the project initially,
but after seeing the astonishing growth rate of the new pigs, everyone wanted to raise them. Those persons involved in the project thus
found themselves in a position to make substantial profits, both from
the sale of pork when the mature pigs were slaughtered and by selling
the piglets, now in great demand locally.

It is expected that eventually every household on the island will
be able to raise the new breed of pigs. There is a large national
demand for pork, and the Yaksan agricultural cooperative has agreed
to market the pigs so as to maximize profits for the farmers. Regular
courses of instruction in pig raising are to be held twice a year for
prospective new owners. A local pig raising association has been
formed, and there will be strict regulation to ensure that immunization and breeding are carried out properly.

An Ill-fated New Cash Crop on Yaksan

In contrast to Yaksan's highly successful pig project, an
attempt to introduce an innovative cash crop there in 1978 ran into
difficulties. *Stevia*, a plant of the chrysanthemum family originating
in Paraguay, has been developed in Japan as a sugar substitute with
a wide variety of uses. The Coordinator had heard a radio report
that the plant was successfully grown over a two year period on
Cheju Do (a Korean island province), and there was widespread
interest when he mentioned it at a Community Committee meeting.

The Coordinator then made inquiries at the provincial branch
of the Office of Rural Development, at large city nurseries, at the
Fishing Village Development Institute in Seoul, and at pharmaceutical
companies. He discovered that good profits could be made if sizeable amounts were grown for export to Japan. People with experience
in growing Stevia were asked to visit Yaksan where they explained to
the Community Committee that income from the plant, which is harvested three times a year, would be about double that from beans or
sesame on the same field.

The Community Committee selected 20 farmers as Stevia growers,
loaning them a total of $1,629, or about one-third the cost of the
seedlings. The other two-thirds of the cost was born by the individual
growers. Unfortunately, because of the severe drought in 1978, only
one harvest instead of three was possible, and the expected income
did not materialize. Even so, the return was better than for beans
under similar drought conditions, and most of the farmers want
to try again.

Vinyl Greenhouses in Chunsong

Some of the problems involved in introducing new agricultural technology, even under the most advantageous circumstances, are illustrated by the vinyl (polyethylene) greenhouse cash crop project in Chunsong. Until 1974, because of lack of confidence, resources and know-how, there were almost no vinyl greenhouses in Chunsong, although they were widespread and a source of good profits among the more progressive and prosperous farm villages in the neighboring myon just across the Soyang river. The Community Committee, having discussed the problem several times, finally decided to organize a training program, which took place in January, 1975. A specialist instructor from the provincial Office of Rural Development emphasized the profit-making potential of planting sweet corn in greenhouses, because this crop would reach markets early and command high prices. He also described the necessary techniques to the 80 farmers who had indicated a desire to participate.

Those attending the training program decided to go ahead with the project. CDF, in addition to arranging the instruction, was to provide loans covering one-third the cost of building the greenhouses. After returning home and discussing the project further, however, most of the farmers backed out, because they felt that the new techniques were too complicated.

The Committee then set up another training session. This time they invited two experts with more practical experience. Those attending listened closely and exchanged ideas and opinions. Once again they seemed to be confident at the meeting of their ability to engage in this kind of farming, but after more reflection at home they again felt they could not apply what they had learned.

In early March of 1975 the Committee organized a chartered bus study tour for direct observation of vinyl greenhouse cultivation techniques. The 40 people who took part were much impressed, and on their return more training sessions were held locally in cooperation with the extension service. Still there were objections that the cost of building the greenhouses was too high. So a revised construction method was devised by the Committee in cooperation with the extension service, using bamboo instead of steel ribs. Two demonstration greenhouses were built and more detailed instruction on setting out the plants and transplanting was provided. Finally, only twelve farmers actually undertook the greenhouse cultivation, and most of them failed, even though the Committee worked closely with them to make sure that everything was done properly. According to the Coordinator, the trouble was that farmers would not follow instructions exactly.

During the past three years the Committee has continued to encourage greenhouse cultivation, and the number of farmers successfully using this method has slowly increased, though with many ups and downs. In FY 1978 CDF supplied $3,534 in loans for vinyl house operations. In contrast to the original 1975 plans, however, the CDF loans covered about two-thirds of the cost, with farmers putting up

only one-third. It is expected that from now on the expansion of
this form of cultivation will be rapid.

AN IMPROVED MONITORING SYSTEM

A clearer picture of the progress being achieved in the impact
areas is provided by the new *Project Design Summaries* recently
adopted by CDF, based on the "Logical Framework" method of
project evaluation devised by U.S. AID. The Sanbuk version is
shown in Table 9.

Under this system a list of "objectively verifiable indicators"
is established under various program headings such as training,
agricultural improvement, health services and so forth. Quantitative measures of these indicators are provided for three different
dates: (1) the base year (1975), (2) the date of the most recent
survey (in this case May 1977), and (3) the target year (1980). A
comparison of the quantitative indicators for these three dates
reveals how far various parts of the overall program have
progressed since the base year toward the objectives set for the
target year.

To illustrate: one of the Sanbuk objectives under Agricultural
Improvement is to increase the number of milk cows from 400 in 1975
(the base year) to 800 in 1980 (the target year). By May, 1977 the
number of cows had actually increased to 467. Thus it was evident
that, although some progress had been achieved in two years, much
more would have to be made in the next three in order to reach the
target.

An examination of all the indicators on Table 9 reveals wide
variation in the rate of progress up to mid-1977 toward various 1980
CBIRD targets in Sanbuk. Projects under the Training Program
(except for youth training) scored consistently high. The Agricultural Improvement Program had made measurable progress but would
have to speed up to meet the 1980 targets. The Home Industry and
Off-Farm Employment Program was clearly in trouble. The record for
Health Services presents some puzzling paradoxes. On the positive
side dramatic reductions are reported in infant mortality, TB cases,
and the rate of population growth. By contrast, as of mid-1977
nearly one-third of the children had not yet received government
required immunizations; the proportion of preschool age children
receiving supplementary food had increased only six percentage
points; and less than one-quarter of the population was utilizing
public health services or was supplied with sanitary water. However,
household improvements (on roofs, kitchens, etc.) were making
substantial progress toward some very ambitious goals, as were
Public Services (new and improved roads, telephones, electrification,
etc.).

Overall, the Sanbuk implementation record between 1975 and
1977--notwithstanding the shortfalls in some program areas--was quite
impressive, considering that the momentum of the CBIRD program was

Table 9

Project Design Summary
Logical Framework

The Sanbuk Project

Narrative Summary	Objectively Verifiable Indicators	1975 Base Year	May 1977 Latest Survey	1980 Target Year
Outputs for Sanbuk Miniregional Development Area				
The expected functional output included the following components	a. 1 community committee established and functioning	1	1	1
	b. 20 committee members trained in develop. components	5	20	20
1. Training	c. 25 women trained in spec. dev. comp.	8	24	25
	d. 20 youth trained in spec. dev. comp.	0	5	20
	e. 8 trainees particip. in spec. dev. courses (e.g. credit, agr. tech.)	0	6	8
	f. 7 agriculture improve. club functioning	1	6	8
	g. 8 mothers clubs functioning	8	8	9
	h. 7 youth clubs functioning	7	7	8
	i. 24 community leaders trained in spec. comp.	10	17	24
	j. 3 local officials involved in dev. train. sessions	0	3	3
	k. 1 joint plan. session with local officials	0	1	1
	l. 1 field coordination placed	1	1	1
2. Agriculture Improvement Program	a. 200% inc. in food crop	1,460 ton	1,533 ton	1,753 ton
	b. 200% inc. in cash "	8.5 ha	10 ha	25 ha
	c. 100% inc in livestock	400 cows	467 cows	800 cows

Table 9...continued

Narrative Summary	Objectively Verifiable Indicators	1975 Base Yr.	May 1977 Latest Survey	1980 Target Yr.
3. Credit & Finance Program	a. 75% inc. in farm bank savings	$40,000.	$53,600	$70,000
	b. 150% inc. in low interest loans	$40 per household	$186 per household	$300 per household
	c. 200% inc. in aver. household income	$900	$2,000	$3,700
4. Home Industry and Off-Farm Employment	a. 50% inc. in home industries	10	0	15
	b. 36% inc. in off-farm employment	100 persons	105 persons	136 persons
5. Health Services Nutrition & Family Planning	a. 100% people utilizing public health services	0	20%	100%
	b. 1.5% population growth	2.0%	1.2%	1.5%
	c. 70% children achieving normal growth standard	50%	n.a.	70%
	d. 60% pre-school child. receiving supplementary food	30%	36%	60%
	e. 95% people sanitary water supplied	0%	23%	95%
	f. 70% non-parasite infected	30%	n.a.	70%
	g. 3.0% infant mortality	4.0%	1.4%	3.0%
	h. 100% child. receiving immunizations required by govt. standard	60%	70%	100%
	i. 2.0% active cases of TB	4.0%	1%	2.0%
6. Education	a. 95% eligible child. enrolled in middle school	75%	84%	95%
	b. 50% inc. in nonformal education activities	2	n.a.	3
	c. 100% inc. in daycare kindergarten programs	1 (program)	1	2
	d. 50% inc. in no. of child. attending voc. training	2 (programs)	1	3

Table 9...continued

Narrative Summary	Objectively Verifiable Indicators	1975 Base Yr.	May 1977 Latest Survey	1980 Target Yr.
7. Environmental Improvement	a. 90% of roofs improved	53%	81%	90%
	b. 90% of kitchens improved	136 houses	200 houses	539 houses
	c. 90% of toilets improved	92 houses	152 houses	543 houses
	d. 90% of chimneys improved	92 houses	126 houses	543 houses
	e. 90% inc. in no. of sanitary drainages	40%	50%	90%
	f. 10 community beautification projects	0	3	10
8. Public Services	a. 10 km of new farm roads constructed or improved	11 km	18 km	21 km
	b. 7 community cntrs in operation	7	8	9
	c. 8 projects of telephone	0 villages	4 villages	8 villages
	8 public speaker	7 villages	8 villages	8 villages
	d. 5 projects of embankments	0	0	5
	e. 1 community owned bath house per village	0	4	8
	f. 100% houses electri.	10%	98%	100%
9. Cultural Enrichment	a. 4 film showings annually	1	2	4
	b. 10 community libraries established	5	7	10
	c. 3 community playgrounds established	0	5	3
	d. 2 facilities for elders established	0	0	2
	e. 3 cultural events org. annually	1	2	3

just building up in this period and was likely to accelerate from 1977 to 1980.

As helpful as these quantitative indicators are for monitoring the progress of implementation, some important qualifications about them must be noted. First, they do not reveal important qualitative dimensions or changes, nor do they shed any light on *why* some projects are doing well and others poorly. Second, they provide little if any evidence of actual impact that successfully implemented projects are having on the lives of people, and no clues whatever on how the benefits are being distributed among different sub-groups in the population--especially the poor. Finally, some of the recorded improvements may be the result of separate Saemaul projects, individual initiatives or any other cause; hence it is not possible to determine how much is attributable specifically to CBIRD actions. However, every indicator listed corresponds to a CBIRD objective, and in many cases--such as, for example, women's training, day care centers, and technical training--CBIRD is probably the only organization sponsoring that particular kind of activity.

Despite these qualifications, the conclusion we draw from the evidence cited in this chapter is that the CBIRD program, viewed in the large and judged by any realistic standard, has achieved a remarkably good record of implementing its project plans. One can reasonably expect that as more experience is gained the record will become even better.

CHAPTER 6

THE SOCIAL WELFARE RECORD

The evidence examined in the previous chapter reveals a generally impressive record of achievement in terms of the physical implementation of local CBIRD project plans and the practical application of CDF's basic financial strategy. The evidence also suggests--even though direct measurements are not available--that the CBIRD program in combination with the Saemaul Movement is making a significant contribution to increased productivity and income and to better living standards in the rural impact areas, and that this contribution is likely to increase over time.

It is important, however, to ask a further question: How well are all these activities serving CBIRD's basic *social welfare goals*?

In examining this question it is important to bear in mind that the CBIRD approach and objectives are founded on a broad eclectic view of rural development which holds that economic and social development must go hand-in-hand. Economic growth, the argument runs, is essential to provide increasing support for meeting basic human needs and improving living conditions; but a strategy that focuses largely or exclusively on economic growth results in a lopsided and morally and politically unacceptable form of development that enriches the better off and may actually worsen the plight of the poor and disadvantaged. Moreover, widespread chronic ill-health, malnutrition and ignorance can be serious deterrents to increased rural productivity, and unrestrained population growth can offset the gains of economic development.

Taking this view, the CBIRD approach therefore calls for an integrated combination of economic and social improvement measures, with special emphasis on improving the welfare and status of the most disadvantaged families--particularly the women, the young children and the helpless who comprise the most vulnerable group. These humanitarian goals and principles are constantly stated and restated in CDF reports, evaluations and brochures prepared for outside visitors and supporters; they are also stressed in CBIRD training programs and by Coordinators in Community Committee meetings; and they get reflected in various social welfare projects within local CBIRD plans involving, for example, health, nutrition, child care, education and culture, family planning, and women's activities.

THE EXTENT OF CBIRD EFFORTS
TO HELP THE POOR

The previous chapter showed that large expenditures have been made under the rubric of "social infrastructure." But, as noted earlier, only a fraction of the projects within this category can be properly classified as authentic social welfare projects calculated to help the poor. For example, the investments going into home improve-ments--particularly new roofs, running water, latrines, tiled kitchens, electrification and telephones--have been quite sizeable, but such improvements are largely restricted to better off families with sufficient assets to afford the cost and are generally out of reach of the poorer families. Even the day care centers, which charge fees, are very difficult for the poor to patronize, except in special cases where scholarships for indigent children are provided by the Community Committee.

An analysis of the projects undertaken in the CBIRD areas shows that only relatively small investments are being made in direct social welfare services such as health, child care and nutrition, to which the poorest families are likely to have effective access. Precise calculations are difficult to come by, but our estimates indicate that in the three year plans for Chunsong and Sanbuk for FY 1976-79 no more than 15 percent of the overall projected investment appears to be earmarked for such social welfare programs.* Or, if we consider the annual plans for FY 1979 of Chunsong and Yaksan, the equivalent percentages are only 14 percent and 12.5 percent respectively. As a further check, the CDF project evaluation sheets for projects actually implemented in FY 1978 give the following even lower estimates for social welfare projects:

Chunsong	12 percent
Sanbuk	10 percent
Wido	5.5 percent
Yaksan	5.5 percent

The above expenditures, it should be noted, are not specially designed to benefit only the rural poor; rather they are for social welfare projects from which the poor as well as all others may have a real opportunity to benefit.

These facts are generally obscured by the way in which projects are categorized on the forms used for planning, reporting and evalua-tion; genuine social welfare programs are shown under the "social

---

*For purposes of this calculation, the running water systems under the category "health and sanitation," which require substantial invest-ment by the home owners, are excluded. Similarly, under "education and culture" the day-care centers, which charge a fee, and the athletic and cultural events that are enjoyed by the whole community, are excluded. Some small portion of the funds spent on home improvement may be of benefit to the poor, but there is no record of how much.

infrastructure" category which, as explained earlier, also includes such
items as public works, housing improvements, technical and leadership
training, the operation of community centers, and CBIRD program
administration. In order to permit analysis for review and evaluation
of projects in terms of their contribution to meeting basic CBIRD
objectives--particularly the objectives of improving the welfare of
children, women and the poor--there is pressing need for more
refined summary tables or graphs that would give a clearer picture
of which particular subgroups in the population are most likely to
benefit--or are actually benefitting--from particular projects.

There is no suggestion here whatsoever that any of this confusion represents a deliberate effort by CDF to mislead anyone. On
the contrary, it appears to be the result of determined, dedicated
efforts by everyone concerned to get on with the business of rural
development within the particular context and constraints of the
Korean milieu, without abandoning cherished humanitarian goals.

CONFLICTING VALUE SYSTEMS

It may be that South Korea is a special case, but it seems obvious
now in the light of both the Saemaul and CBIRD experience that rapid
rural development is possible without first or simultaneously attacking
the problem of primary health care, for example, or doing much about
the situation of the very poor. What has emerged from the Korean
experience is the fact that effective local planning and the mobilization
of local self-help efforts in conjunction with coordinated bureaucratic
help and a favorable economic climate has provided the formula for
progress. Increased purchasing power on the one hand and the greater
availability of goods and services on the other is contributing to higher
living standards and improved life chances pretty much in accordance
with the desires and aspirations of the rural population. Except for
the poorest 20 to 30 percent, farmers and fishermen are eating well,
dressing well, traveling a great deal, buying all sorts of personal
accessories and household appliances, sending their children to
higher schools, and investing in their own productivity. Their
behavior reflects Korean priorities and should not be thought of as
a distortion of some ideal conception of rural development. The focus
of government development policy has also been economic rather than
social, and integration has been achieved mainly in economic terms:
rural credit, technical advice, agricultural inputs, transportation,
storage facilities and, above all, increasing demand for the farmers'
crops at profitable prices, have all been made available more or less
simultaneously.

Slowly improving health care, more social services and a steady
but very gradual rise in the position of women--subject to the constraints of an evolving national cultural tradition--are following along
behind. With higher incomes farmers have been able to purchase more
and better services, both as individuals and cooperatively through
village organizations. The more able-bodied of the landless poor have
benefitted from the much higher wages paid for rural labor, thanks to
a labor shortage and the relatively high profits to be made from
commercialized agriculture. In other words, most of the social and

economic benefits for the poor are the trickle down effects of general
economic progress. In the mainland CBIRD communities, as a result
of several years of effort, it is now beginning to be possible to undertake more significant social programs on behalf of the entire local
population, using the revolving funds established through successful
economic projects. But it will evidently take a long time for the island
impact areas to reach this position.

From this perspective the CBIRD approach does not really appear
to differ so radically from the Saemaul model, except in the size of the
development unit and the sophistication of the planning and management
structure. Rather, it is a refinement of what appears to be a standard
pattern of Korean rural development with some supplementary emphasis
on cultural affairs, health, education, and family planning. The social
welfare side of the CBIRD effort, rather than being an essential aspect
of the integrated approach to development, appears more as an extra
benefit derived from increased economic productivity.

This is certainly the way the Korean farmer or fisherman views
the matter. Their strong preference--notwithstanding CDF's social
welfare objectives--is for productivity projects that will raise their
own income. The CBIRD impact area Coordinators are thus caught in
a dilemma between two value systems. In order to promote local
decision-making, to work towards the fulfillment of genuine locally
felt needs, and to win the enthusiastic support and participation of
those who count most in the community, most of the program's emphasis
must be on productivity and income-increase projects. But in order
to promote CDF's humanitarian principles and objectives and to satisfy
the sponsors, the Coordinators must also do their best to persuade the
Community Committee to devote a reasonable proportion of available
funds to genuine social welfare programs, aimed especially at the poor.
The result is usually a compromise strongly tilted toward economic
projects, which in the circumstances is undoubtedly the best that can
be hoped for.

Such projects as the construction of bath houses, toilet and
kitchen improvements, day care centers, improved nutrition, village
libraries, and cultural events do not really correspond to strongly
felt popular needs. Farmers and fishermen have to be taught to
value these projects, and even then they are likely to be more important as competitive status symbols--sources of individual and regional
pride--than for their inherent usefulness in improving the quality of
local life. This kind of project reflects the outside change agent's
view of the direction progress should take more than it does local
aspirations.

In spite of the intentions of planners, some social projects such
as day care centers, more sanitary kitchens and toilets, or the
installation of telephones actually increase the distance between poor
and well-to-do farmers rather than improving the position of low
income groups. In each case some contribution is required in order
to participate, and the poor either cannot afford to spend anything,
or they have different priorities for using whatever meager surplus
may be available. On the other hand, a shiny tiled kitchen or

private telephone gives added prestige to the more affluent house owner.

THE EXAMPLE OF RURAL HEALTH

Although lack of adequate health services is a major problem in most Korean villages, the perspective of outside observers and development agents, who usually have a particular solution in mind-- whether it be a proliferation of small rural clinics, the organization of para-medical services, or education for disease prevention--is likely to be somewhat different from that of the local population. Traditional attitudes, the lack of nearby medical personnel, and popular concep- tions of what constitutes adequate health care, all make it extremely difficult for CDF to achieve major results in this field.

Until quite recently most Korean farm families have been reluc- tant to seek medical help outside the village, partly because they were not entirely convinced of the efficacy of scientific medicine, partly because the fees charged by doctors in town were exhorbitant in proportion to rural incomes, and partly because of the poor quality of whatever health care was available closer by.

In the past, with most people's energies focussed primarily on survival, scientific medicine as practiced in towns and cities was an unattainable luxury, except for the richest farmers. Still today local remedies are tried first, and there is usually resort to a doctor only in desperation when the patient is very sick or badly injured. For these reasons health care still has a relatively low priority for much of the rural population, in terms of how people actually allocate scarce resources. The traditional practice of taking care of the sick at home without seeking expert treatment outside the village remains wide- spread, although it is often modified today by the more or less random purchase of antibiotics or other medicines on the advice of the drug- store owner in a nearby town. Or again, on the store owner's advice, injections may be administered by the village head or other reputable local figure. In any case, doctor's fees and hospitalization costs are still regarded as outrageously high by most ordinary farmers.

The farmer's relatively low priority attached to professional health care is mirrored in the meagerness of the Government's rural health programs. Part of the problem lies in the "Seoul-centered" attitude of most members of the central bureaucracy who, although they them- selves have access to the most modern medical facilities in the city, see no pressing need to tamper with the existing situation in the provinces. A perhaps even more difficult problem to overcome is the unwillingness of reputable doctors (and even many nurses) to live and work in small towns, let alone large villages such as the subcounty seat (myon). Everyone--even the farmer--is likely to think there is something wrong with a person who acquires so much education and expertise and then buries himself in a rural town. In any case, county and sub-county health clinics have a poor reputation among the rural population.[1]

---

[1]Peace Corps volunteers who have worked in these clinics are invariably appalled at the conditions and the poor level of treatment.

Rapid rural economic development is bringing many changes in this area as in most others. Farmers watch TV programs that show modern operating rooms in city hospitals; and increasingly they have money to spend. Nearly everyone has at least one close relative living in the city who consults professional medical practitioners as a matter of course. The result seems to be that while most people may continue to put off going to the doctor as long as possible, when they finally do go they prefer to make the journey to a nearby city and consult someone who inspires in them some degree of confidence.

Until very recently Korean doctors and nurses who did not work in large cities have usually gone abroad. Financial and social-psychological rewards are still not adequate to attract them in significant numbers to rural areas. The situation will probably improve in the future, however, as new medical and nursing school graduates find the Seoul job market completely saturated and opportunities overseas more restricted. Also, a gradual change in high level bureaucratic attitudes is taking place in the direction of providing more welfare services to ordinary people. This, combined with the greater availability of public funds, should eventually result in some sort of government subsidized health scheme. But since Korea is a small country with increasingly frequent and ubiquitous rural bus transportation, it seems more likely that adequate and relatively cheap medical care will be made available at the county seat level (usually towns with a population of 30,000 to 80,000), rather than that rural clinics will be established on any extensive scale.

Given the particular situation described above, the goal of establishing genuine rural health facilities must be regarded as out of reach for the foreseeable future. On this basis the fact that CDF has not made a major effort in the field of rural health must be seen as a wise acceptance of the realities of the situation.

Nevertheless, some of the CBIRD projects have made significant contributions to health improvement. The medical and dental schools of major Korean universities commonly send teams of doctors and students to the countryside during the summer to provide low cost health care, and CDF has arranged for such temporary clinics to be held in most of the impact areas. But farmers and their wives, even while taking advantage of the medical and dental services, invariably grumble because they believe that the treatment given by students is second rate.

CDF attempted in 1975 to set up modest health insurance schemes in Sanbuk and Chunsong, utilizing such intermittent clinics as well as government services. By the fall of 1977, 70 percent of the households in Chunsong were enrolled, but a year later the plan was no longer operating. No systematic investigation has been made into the causes of this failure.

CDF funds have also been used to try to revitalize family planning programs at the village level. Community Committees in several of the impact areas have sponsored lectures by well-known authorities on birth control, and expenses were paid for more than a hundred

women in FY 1977 who chose to have laparotomy tubectomies at provincial hospitals.

The Difficulties of Reaching the Poor

Due to the relatively equitable distribution of land and the
recent economic prosperity in the Korean countryside, the majority
of the population can be classified as self-supporting, middle level
farmers enjoying a fair degree of economic security. And, as was
pointed out earlier, the skilled agricultural laborer can now earn a
living wage, even if he possesses no land of his own. But the poorest
20 percent or so of the rural population--often comprising the sick and
physically or mentally handicapped, the widowed, the old and the very
young--remain in an extremely difficult and vulnerable situation. Some
meager welfare benefits are available through official channels and these
are increasing. But this sector of the population is genuinely deprived
and without real hope of improving its situation in the rural context.

It has proved extremely difficult for CDF to reach these people
because of a variety of structural constraints in the local environment.
The need to work with village elites in order to establish development
management institutions that can evolve in the direction of autonomy
has meant that most of the CBIRD program has been focussed on the
more prosperous sectors of rural society. Efforts to help the poor are
hampered by their lack of matching resources, low levels of competence,
and inferior standing in the community. Anyone who fails to attend
the separate village meetings at which individual "income increase"
projects are discussed, either through lack of interest and confidence
in the program or because he lives far away, loses his opportunity to
participate. Usually it is the poor who tend to live in the most
isolated and inconvenient areas, and they are the ones most likely to
be cynical and discouraged, because they do not have enough money
or other resources to make a significant matching investment of their
own.

Farmers and fishermen in the impact areas receive two kinds of
loans under the CBIRD system. The CDF money allocated for
income-increase projects is first loaned at low interest rates; then,
when it is repaid, a revolving fund under the control of the
Community Committee is established as a source of further credit.
As village leaders learn to manage these financial resources more
efficiently and rationally, the emphasis on raising productivity--on
obtaining a good return on revolving fund loans--increases. The
poor farmer is a bad risk, both because he needs the money for consumption, and because his productive capacity is lower. The
requirement that each borrower must have two guarantors willing to
sign his note effectively excludes most of the poor from access to the
revolving fund.

Coordinators have tried to get around the problem by developing
projects that are suitable for the poor. Korean cattle have been
provided to some poor farmers in mountainous areas where forage is
available to all. Similarly, various kinds of fishing equipment have
been furnished on a small scale in the islands. Efforts have also been

made to provide more loans to poor people by encouraging the formation of larger financial institutions, i.e., through merging the village
banks established under Saemaul auspices. CDF project funds have
been used in some instances to back these higher risk loans. In some
cases scholarships have been given to poor children, and in the long
run these may have the greatest effect. But overwhelmingly the main
thrust of the program has been to increase the earning power of middle
and well-to-do farmers and fishermen.

It is hard to imagine how a community development system could
function otherwise, with most really poor families today suffering
from various kinds of social/pathological problems that prevent them
from taking effective advantage of whatever opportunities exist.
Where genuine community spirit can be developed along with a widely
shared sense of social responsibility, Community Committees may elect
to do more for the poor. It should be recognized, however, that for
the most part such efforts will amount to charity, and there is no
special reason to expect prosperous farmers in a Korean CBIRD area
to be more charitable than people anywhere else. Thus, help for the
poor remains a minor and relatively ineffective part of the overall
program, despite the high importance attached to this objective by
SCF/CDF and its Western financial supporters.

THE EDUCATION
AND TRAINING RECORD

For over 1,000 years Koreans have valued learning above most
other activities, and during the past 500 years or so education has
been the main path to upward mobility and high social status. These
traditions are very much alive today, as they are in all countries that
derive their higher culture from the Confucian tradition.   Under
Japanese colonial rule most farmers in Korea had no schooling, but
after 1945 large investments were made in education; by 1960 nearly
everyone was attending primary school for six years. Today, with
relative rural prosperity, over 80 percent of rural primary school
graduates go on to middle school, and of this group 40-50 percent
continue their education in high school.

During the modern period, and especially since the Korean
War, educational aspirations have increasingly shifted from classical
and humanistic studies to science and technology. The ability and
eagerness of large numbers of students to absorb Western scientific
and technical knowledge has been one of the most important contributing factors to Korea's economic "miracle." Thus, not only is
the prestige of study both as an activity and as an end in itself
still very high, but more specifically, the acquisition of practical
technical skills for development is regarded as one of the most useful
and worthy activities that one can engage in.

These generalities also apply to the rural scene with certain
qualifications. In the past only a few village youths attended middle
and high school, and most of these moved to the towns and cities
after graduation. Those few who returned to their villages were
automatically regarded, upon reaching maturity, as being the best
qualified among the local population for leadership roles, regardless
of the nature of their education or their personal competence, simply
because of the social and ethical prestige inherent in education. One
problem in the past has been that not infrequently the high school
graduate who assumed such a role possessed neither leadership
qualities nor a dedication to public service, with disastrous results
for village development programs. Fortunately in recent years
much higher percentages of the rural school age population have
been going on to middle and high schools, so that in each village
there are many more persons in the 35 to 45 year-old group (the
usual age of active leadership) with some capacity to read technical

articles and administrative directives, keep financial records, and write reports. Such skills are increasingly necessary for village heads to enable them to cope with larger amounts of paper work and deal with officials and other townspeople without being humiliated. CDF leadership and management training has been primarily directed at this group.

While the rest of the rural adult population with only a primary school education or less may be only barely literate or illiterate, they are usually also eager to participate in whatever training possibilities are offered, even though nonformal education provides less prestige than the academic variety. In addition to the need for new skills there are important rewards in terms of self-confidence and standing in the community that derive from having completed any course of instruction.

CDF has taken full advantage of this extremely favorable situation to develop a large number of specialized training programs for the CBIRD areas. Some sort of nonformal and informal training accompanies virtually every specific project. The flexibility of the CBIRD program enables the Coordinator in consultation with the Community Committee to tailor educational programs to local require- ments. The Korean field staff has also recognized that even non- formal education has its formal aspects--that the special aura of prestige and confidence   bestowed by even a short course in leadership may be as important for subsequent performance as the contents of the instruction. Consequently such formalities as introductory oratory, group photographs, and closing exhortations are all utilized to reinforce the educational process.

CDF classifies its training programs according to three categories: 1) Community Basic Skills Training; 2) Intermediate Training; and 3) Advanced Management Training.

During FY 1978, a total of 8,520 persons participated in basic skills training at the community level, of whom 3,530 were women. Some 193 different courses were offered, lasting from one to three days.   Basic skills training accounts for the vast majority of all hours of instruction, total numbers of participants and numbers of courses. A descriptive breakdown for all six impact areas is shown in Table 10.

CDF has placed particular emphasis on the training of women, both in order to improve their standing in the community and to utilize their energy and abilities for development. In all, 3,530 women participated in some form of basic skills training during FY 1978. Another 34 women leaders attended leadership courses conducted in Seoul, while 76 women received special training in development planning in the island areas. If educational policy were determined solely on the basis of local initiative or Korean Government programs, there would be far fewer women enrolled in training courses.

Table 10

Summary of CBIRD Training Activities, All Areas, FY 1978

Type of Training	No. of Participants	Males	Females	No. of Courses
Agriculture	1,241	1,047	194	27
Animal Husbandry	216	147	69	15
Community Development and Planning	1,825	1,408	417	63
Cottage and Off-farm Industry	59		59	
Child Care	61	2	59	13
Credit and Finance	935	815	120	10
Family Planning	789	128	661	15
Nutrition	679		679	10
Para-medical	2,227	1,013	1,214	19
Water Resource Development	488	430	58	19
TOTALS	8,250	4,990	3,530	193

There are many different kinds of rural training institutions in Korea, both public and private. Coordinators can arrange to have selected trainees from their impact areas enrolled in appropriate courses, with the necessary funds provided either directly by CDF or through their Community Committees. The Saemaul Movement, the Office of Rural Development, the Federation of Cooperatives, the National Agricultural Technical Association and provincial universities all organize various kinds of training programs in which motion pictures, slides, charts, pamphlets and other kinds of visual aids are prominently used. The Korean concern--some might say obsession--with education is increasingly penetrating to rural areas, as funds have become available and organizational linkages established between the villages and national institutions.

Where Coordinators perceive that a need exists for specialized instruction, they can either invite experts to the community or arrange for villagers to attend regularly established courses of instruction (see the examples in Chapter V of pig raising on Yaksan and vinyl greenhouse construction in Chunsong). The Coordinators themselves, who usually have wide experience in teaching, conduct most of the leadership and management courses at the basic skills level. Some of them also have more specialized knowledge, for example, regarding such matters as cooperative financial organizations or particular aspects of animal husbandry, and they provide instruction and guidance accordingly.

In Sanbuk where the Committee has been particularly active in organizing training programs, an outside specialist is invited to come and instruct each time a new kind of project is adopted. For example, instructors in knitting as a cottage industry and in various kinds of food processing techniques were hired with money from the revolving fund to teach groups of women in FY 1978. In addition, using its own funds, the Committee has organized numerous tours, so that project participants can travel to other areas in order to observe similar, successfully functioning projects.

With the exception of technical subjects requiring qualified experts, most of the courses are taught by the Coordinator, local officials, knowledgeable Community Committee members, or other competent persons living nearby. In Chunsong, for example, officials of the agricultural extension service, which has its office in the Community Center, provide frequent instruction to farmers on technical matters, both in formally organized sessions and on an *ad hoc,* informal, individual basis.

In addition to carefully planned courses of instruction a good deal of informal training takes place. Frequently in the course of meetings or in casual conversations the Coordinator or members of the Community Committee will attempt to "correct" deep rooted values, attitudes, and patterns of behavior that are seen as limiting the effectiveness of developmental efforts. For example, the lack of punctuality, both in meeting deadlines for the submission of documents and with regard to attendance at meetings, is a persistent irritant and obstacle to getting things done. Older farmers in particular, who still own most of the land and therefore make many of the decisions, tend to retain a more easy-going, pre-modern sense of time. Another problem is the failure to comply exactly with detailed instructions as, for example, when raising a new variety of pig or planting vegetables in vinyl greenhouses. A particular innovation involving precise quantitative measures that are in fact crucial, may appear to farmers to be relatively trivial, so that they find it easier to retain their old ways or fail to follow instructions exactly. Then, when the project does not live up to expectations, there is likely to be general discouragement and a reluctance to recognize the real problem.

Another persistent cultural trait that sometimes interferes with the effective operation of CBIRD institutions is the belief by certain farmers--often influential ones--that a direct, informal approach to the Committee Chairman, the Coordinator or local officials is the best way to obtain special personal advantages from a given situation or opportunity. Sometimes the Coordinator does, in fact, find it useful to treat an important person with special consideration in order to ensure his whole-hearted cooperation. But as a rule Coordinators are likely to emphasize during training sessions as well as in informal conversations that the Community Committee must operate with objectivity and fairness, putting the general welfare ahead of personal interests in order to acquire and retain the general respect of the community. In other words, the Coordinator has the extremely difficult role of trying to inculcate universalistic principles of thinking and acting in a highly particularistic social environment.

In spite of its emphasis on training the "consumer" of developmental efforts, CDF has encountered some obstinate problems in mobilizing continuing enthusiastic participation in CBIRD activities. Often attendance at Community Committee meetings is no better than 60 percent. The reluctance of women to violate traditional norms of respectability by playing an active role outside the home has proved to be very hard to overcome. Significant progress is being made in both these areas, however, partly through the cumulative influence of repeated training courses, but also because of the more general effects of modernization--including the changing values and patterns of behavior that characterize younger generations.

CDF organizes more elaborate programs of instruction at its Seoul office for local leaders (usually Community Committee members) to broaden their understanding of CBIRD principles and to develop both leadership and management skills. The training periods vary from two to ten days and often include field trips to the various impact areas, so that participants may learn from each other's practical experiences. CDF staff, including the Coordinators, lecturers from universities or technical institutes, outside experts, and Saemaul or other officials, provide the instruction, which deals with such subjects as the planning process, financial management, working with other local agencies, relations with the Saemaul

Movement, record keeping and reports. There are also more inspirational sessions designed to increase motivation and the intensity
of participation in CBIRD activities.

A more complete breakdown for the 1977-81 planning period
of the contents of this kind of relatively highly organized and
centralized training follows: 1) specialized management training
for the Committee secretary/treasurer from each impact area;
2) further motivation and development training for all Committee
members (approximately 20 from each area); 3) special development
training for women (about 25 from each area); 4) special development training for youth (about 20 from each area); 5) specialized
technical training of various kinds (numerous groups with from
8 to 32 persons from each area); 6) training in agricultural techniques for Agricultural Improvement Club members (6-10 from each
area); 7) family life improvement for day care center mothers (10
from each area); 8) leadership training for youth (10 from each
area); 9) development training for local officials (3 from each area);
10) development training for community leaders (24 from each
area); 11) training for joint planning with local officials (1 or 2
from each area); 12) intensive training (three months) for new
Coordinators before they begin work in their impact areas.

Most of the trainees are selected at Community Committee
meetings, taking into consideration the interests, qualifications,
and place of residence of those who volunteer. Village heads and
other Committee members make recommendations, and in general
the Committee tries to select about the same number of trainees
from each village. The local institutional machinery for selecting
trainees appears to operate in a reasonably effective and democratic
manner, but inevitably the best qualified candidates tend to come
from middle level and well-to-do farm families.

Occasionally there will be joint training sessions organized
by local officials in cooperation with the Coordinator or Committee
Chairman, at which matters of concern to both CDF and the government are discussed. There have been occasions in the past when
officials used these meetings so blatantly for propaganda purposes
that the popular reaction was highly unfavorable. In this kind of
situation, when dealing with over-zealous local officials, great
diplomatic skill on the part of the Coordinator is necessary in
order to straighten things out.

Under the Saemaul Movement the acquisition of techniques
for the planning and management of development projects by village leaders has usually been a long and difficult process that
has slowed down community development in many ways. The CBIRD
approach of directly attacking this problem with well organized
training programs designed to give local leaders the ability to
operate their own institutions effectively represents an important
innovative advance.

The CDF principle that sustained, long run benefits depend
more on local mastery of the *processes* of development than on

immediate project success is supported by significant achievements
in all the impact areas, but most particularly at Sanbuk. There,
local leaders are intensely involved in utilizing the CBIRD institutions to promote development. They take their responsibilities
seriously and dedicate long hours to the practical nuts and bolts
aspects of getting things done. One result has been that local
participation, in terms of both labor and resource investment has
been consistently high, with a corresponding degree of success
in achieving project goals. Concurrently, participation in community-wide cultural and recreational activities has also been widespread
and enthusiastic. Chunsong leaders, while not generally as outstanding as those from Sanbuk in their desire and ability to take
over responsibility for running the CBIRD program, have nevertheless also acquired valuable experience and training in a variety of
management skills. The island areas are still at the stage where
Coordinators, local officials, and other important persons exert a
disproportionate influence relative to farmers and fishermen.

    Another CDF innovation has been the organization of special
training courses for officials concerned with development in the
impact areas. The job of the Coordinators and Committee Chairmen
is greatly simplified if the local myon and gun administration has a
sympathetic understanding of the CBIRD objectives and methodology.
The willingness of county and sub-county chiefs to send some of
their subordinates for CDF training has enabled the impact areas
to develop and improve working relationships with the local
bureaucracy.

    In addition this kind of training has provided CDF with a
means of getting its ideas on integrated community development
across to working levels of the Korean administration. Although
there is no evidence yet that CBIRD principles have been adopted
on a national scale, it is certain that they are being considered
in governmental circles as possible models for further developmental initiatives. And it can be expected that those aspects of
the CDF approach that are particularly successful will probably
be incorporated in some form in the Saemaul Movement. In any
event Korean Government policy for rural development appears to
be gradually converging with CDF ideas in two respects. There
is now somewhat greater emphasis on regional as opposed to village
projects, and slightly greater attention is being paid to rural
social welfare.

    In all the impact areas Community Committees, usually
working through an educational sub-committee, have used CDF
funds to improve the educational facilities provided by local
primary and middle schools. Various CBIRD projects have financed
classroom furniture, teaching aids, library books, and such ameni-
ties as school drinking fountains. In Chunsong, where collaboration
between the Community Committee and the Kasan primary school has
been particularly productive, CDF funds have been used, in
addition to the kinds of projects listed above, to support a
school newspaper and for the repair of a small educational greenhouse. In 1978 the Chunsong Community Committee Chairman

received a letter of commendation from the Minister of Education in
recognition of the Committee's role in raising the school's academic
performance. Where extensive day care programs have been underway for some years (Chunsong and Sanbuk), the beneficial effects
of pre-school experience in raising learning ability are now becoming
apparent, and the establishment of day care programs on a national
scale is under discussion by government officials.

In addition to the educational projects mentioned above, small
scholarship funds have been made available in all the impact areas
to help poor and worthy students.

There is another way in which collaboration between Coordinators and the primary schools helps to further CBIRD objectives.
Each school usually serves several villages, so that school activities
involving parents tend to promote inter-village contacts and to
some degree, cooperation. Where Community Committees actively
support and assist schools on such occasions as Children's Day,
athletic contests, the exhibit of agricultural products grown or
raised by students, and outings with parents, they are contributing to the creation of a larger community beyond single village
boundaries. The school, therefore, can serve as another focus
of multi-village activities in addition to the Community Center,
provided the Coordinator is able to establish appropriate relations
with local educational authorities. School teachers throughout
Korea have been commanded by the Saemaul authorities to contribute to development by helping raise the scientific and national
consciousness of the rural population, but often because of the
teachers' lack of practical knowledge, farmers and fishermen do not
take their efforts seriously. Nevertheless, school teachers are in
a position to contribute to leadership and management training
as well as the inculcation of a broader regional sense of community.
The fact that primary school teachers are somewhat overworked and
underpaid limits the extent of their participation in CBIRD activities,
however.

CHAPTER 8

SOME INTRACTABLE PROBLEMS

The CBIRD experience in Korea throws penetrating light on several deep-rooted problems that are generic to innovative rural development undertakings in many countries and therefore need to be understood by all who seek to bring about social and economic improvement in rural areas.

It is hoped that the discussion of these problems below will not be misconstrued as minimizing in any way CDF's impressive achievements in Korea, which are considerable. These achievements have been described and documented in the foregoing chapters, and indeed one wonders how it would have been possible to accomplish more with the available resources. The CBIRD program has been both innovative and flexible. Lessons learned in other parts of the world and through long experience in Korea have been incorporated in it, and the Korean Field Office director and staff have shown extraordinary dedication and ingenuity in pursuing both the basic goals and detailed practical procedures.

In spite of these positive factors, however, one lesson drawn from this study must be that, even under relatively ideal conditions, community and rural development is an extraordinarily difficult and complex undertaking, and we still have a great deal to learn about the best ways to carry it out.

INTERNAL AND EXTERNAL SOURCES OF DIFFICULTY

Part of the difficulty lies in the fact that so much of the community development literature--even including practical guides for use in the field--is tinged with missionary zeal born of Western humanitarian ideals. Expectations are high and there is so much at stake; upgrading the lives of unfortunate people is seen as a virtuous undertaking of such pressing importance that ordinary objections and constraints must not be allowed to stand in the way. But certain intractable constraints nevertheless do stand in the way, not least of all the traditional village social structures and patterns of behaviour that stoutly resist change in the face of outside blandishments and efforts. And to compound the difficulty, the proclaimed basic goals of the innovative model, reflecting the assumptions and value system of a distant "donor" society, may be quite incongruent with the current priority concerns, traditional value system and basic realities of the "recipient" society in which the new model is to be applied. In this event a sizeable gap inevitably develops between the stated goals and the actual accomplishments, and a distorted picture of the reality tends to emerge.

A further part of the difficulty is that once the new program gets underway, pressures mount steadily to produce quick, visible and measurable results. This pressure comes in part from a natural eagerness on the part of the project managers to prove to the local people and the host government that the particular innovative development model is indeed viable and capable of yielding sizeable benefits. But the pressure also derives from the need of the external sponsoring organization to demonstrate to its own constituency and major funding sources that their money is producing good results, consistent with the originally proclaimed priority goals. If a major funding source happens, as in this case, to be an official bilateral aid agency accountable to its national legislature for the effective use of the taxpayers' money in a manner consistent with the policy objectives set forth in its legislative mandate, then the pressure for demonstrable results becomes even more acute. Moreover, whether consciously or unconsciously, the bilateral agency's own evaluation staff, distant from the scene of action and unfamiliar with the surrounding realities, may exert a decisive influence on the project's built-in evaluation provisions and on the kinds of performance data that get periodically reported.

The inevitable net effect of these various constraints, incongruities, pressures and statistical reports is to build up a somewhat distorted picture of the internal realities of the project and its actual accomplishments, making them appear to fit the originally stated objectives more closely than the actual facts may warrant.

The point to be emphasized is that socio-economic change in any society has its own inner dynamic, patterns, and processes, and these often resist or even run counter to attempts by governments, voluntary organizations and local change agents to carry out programs of social engineering in accordance with predetermined ideas about where rural communities should be going. To a considerable extent the belief that one can transform local institutions, attitudes, relationships, and behavior is bound to be frustrated. For example, the whole complex of ideas, ideals, and rhetoric surrounding the concept of "community," which lies at the core of the CBIRD concept, appears on close examination to be fuzzy and somewhat unrealistic in the light of social reality (a point we will return to later). Or, to take an example at a different level, although the periodic CBIRD field reports have generally provided the types of statistics called for, they have devoted little attention to the analysis of problems; thus the failure of health insurance schemes, for instance, and of projects designed to promote small or cottage industry, have not been examined in a thorough, analytic fashion in order to determine what went wrong, and whether further efforts might be worthwhile. It is almost as if there were a general, informal agreement to the effect that there must be no dwelling on failures or concerns with problems that might interrupt the positive, optimistic momentum of the parent organization.

Anyone familiar with the financial and operational exigencies of voluntary organizations based in developed countries but seeking to assist developing countries will appreciate that the problems sketched above are by no means unique to SCF/CDF in relation to CBIRD; they are the common fare of virtually all such organizations, and they are well known also to official bilateral and multilateral agencies.

DILEMMAS IN THE SELECTION
OF PILOT AREAS

The first problem faced by any organization, public or private, that sets out to test a new rural development model is to establish appropriate criteria for selecting the pilot areas, then to select a manageable number of areas that fit the criteria. CBIRD's experience suggests that this selection process is likely to pose some difficult dilemmas.

In CDF publications two criteria for choosing the impact areas are stressed: 1) poverty and inaccessibility and 2) high potential for development. With regard to the first, it is observed that "all six project areas qualify as being among the most economically disadvantaged areas [in the country] with substandard conditions of economic and social needs." And, in fact, CDF base line statistics do show that income levels were somewhat below the national average at the time the areas were chosen.

Direct observation and further evidence now available, however, indicate that the levels of productivity and income in the selected impact areas are actually not greatly below the national average (in a period of rapid rural development), and that topographical constraints are not particularly severe. Although the mainland areas are characterized as "mountainous," this simply means that they are located in valleys with mountains rising up around them. The statement that "83% of the Sanbuk area is mountainous" should be compared with the fact that 68% of the entire country is too mountainous for agriculture. Sanbuk is only three hours by bus from the capital city of Seoul. The Chunsong area is very near a large provincial city with frequent bus service. In both regions the arable land per household is not significantly less than the national average.

In the island areas, there are a number of distinctly poor and relatively isolated villages, but the sharply rising prices for seaweed and fish in recent years and improving productivity have given many of the villages on Yaksan and Wido higher average incomes than nearby mainland communities. Nor is isolation such a severe problem any more, at least for most villages in the group. On Yaksan there are regular dialy ferries connecting several different island villages with each other, with the mainland, and with other islands. On Wido there is one large (100 ton) ferry making a daily connection with the mainland.

Thus the image of backward, isolated communities as the setting for CBIRD projects is somewhat exaggerated. Most of these villages are very much in the main stream of current Korean rural development, with the transition from a subsistence to a market-oriented economy

either well under way or virtually completed. Of course, CDF efforts
have helped speed the transition and decrease the degree of isolation,
but in the main it is rapid national economic growth, the Saemaul
Undong, and other governmental actions that are transforming Korean
rural society in this regard.

The other criterion for village selection was developmental
potential. CDF has reported that "cohesive areas" were chosen
"where linkages exist to market and growth centers," where there is
a "potential for investment," a "demonstrated willingness to learn,"
and the "potential for the development of leadership." Given this favorable constellation of attributes, it is almost inconceivable that in
contemporary Korea fairly rapid development would not take place
in any event. The CBIRD initiative, however, ensures that a few
clusters of villages will have an advantage, moving ahead faster
than others, with a more secure basis for managing their own affairs
and more effective procedures for linking their efforts with outside
resources, both private and official.

A number of questions can be raised about these procedures for
choosing impact areas. To what extent is it justifiable to "stack the
deck," as it were, in choosing villages that already have most of the
ingredients for successful development? Is there an element of discrimination against the "hard cases"--the *really* mountainous villages
or the *really* isolated islands--where outside help is much more
desperately needed? And how long should a voluntary agency assist
a carefully chosen community before seeking to extend its initiatives
to other less favored areas?

The dilemma here, of course, is that trying out a sophisticated
and complicated new approach such as CBIRD, even in relatively
favorable situations, is bound to entail unforeseen difficulties and
risks of failure. But to select the "hardest" cases will greatly
compound the difficulties and risks of failure, and even at best visible
results will come more slowly. Therefore prudence suggests the
initial selection of areas that lie somewhere between the most and
least promising situations, where the new approach will stand a
reasonable chance of success. But the further one moves in this
direction, the more one must stretch the criterion of "poverty and
inaccessibility," and the less relevant the experience may be to
truly disadvantaged and poverty-stricken areas, whether in Korea
or in lower income developing countries.

A further dilemma arises once an impact area is chosen and
actions get underway. Understandably, there is a compulsion to do
everything possible to promote its success, regardless of comparative
needs elsewhere. The success of that particular initiative becomes
almost an end in itself. Attention and resources are concentrated on
it without too much concern for whether similarly intensive assistance
is possible on a much larger scale. The Coordinator's personal sense
of mission and identity as well as his career reputation are linked to
successful project completion in one particular context. And to some
extent this phenomenon is reinforced at higher echelons, since the

SCF/CDF Korea field office is naturally anxious to report the successful achievement of its planned goals to the U.S. headquarters and its principal financial supporters.

These are difficult issues. CDF is confronted with the problem of proving its case in Korea. Unless there is fairly rapid, tangible progress in the CBIRD areas, neither the local population nor the Korean Government is going to become enthusiastically involved in furthering CDF objectives. Obviously results are necessary in order to make an initial impact, demonstrating to others that CDF innovative practices are effective. But the basic problem remains. If one avoids the "hard cases" not only in other parts of Korea but even the hard villages within the designated CBIRD impact areas, how relevant and useful will the lessons be to other countries where incomes and resources are much lower, and the rural economy is relatively stagnant?

For example, the Yaksan impact area, as noted earlier, is an island with 21 villages, some 12 of which on the East and North sides are quite prosperous, while the other 9 villages on the Western and Southern coasts are relatively poor, both in terms of amounts of arable land and access to marine resources. When questioned as to why so many of the CBIRD projects were clustered in the better-off communities, the Coordinator pointed out, quite rationally, that projects involving complex agricultural and fishery innovations were unlikely to succeed unless the farmers or fishermen in question are fairly well off, with resources of their own to invest and a reputation for competence. When it was suggested that some of the current projects in the more prosperous areas might be phased out to permit a greater concentration of effort in the poorer villages, there was immediate objection on the grounds that confidence in the credibility of CDF initiatives could only be established through continuing support of projects over a period of several years. Little could be accomplished, it was asserted, without this kind of follow-through. And without doubt the Coordinator was right!

The dilemmas are apparent. Conscientious, dedicated staff, both in the field and at higher levels, are committed to making certain development strategies work in the selected areas. But this process entails unforeseen consequences: there is a built-in tendency to favor places, projects, and persons where the risk of failure can be minimized. And the voluntary organization as a whole comes to identify its mission and accomplishments primarily with the ongoing progress of a few carefully nurtured impact areas. The more fundamental goals of 1) improving the situation of the "low income rural population" and 2) testing a "development management model" for eventual use in areas where development initiatives have been less successful, inevitably are relegated to a lower priority.

OBSTACLES TO CHANGING SOCIAL STRUCTURES
AND INCOME DISTRIBUTION

Throughout the international development community today there is a new emphasis on the humanitarian goal of improving the lot

of the rural poor. What this actually requires, of course, is
altering the social structures, the human relationships, and the
pattern of income distribution within rural communities. Again the
CBIRD experience demonstrates how difficult this can be, even in
an unusually dynamic milieu.

Despite the fact that Korean rural society is undergoing a process of extraordinarily rapid change and development, there is also
a great deal of social, political, and moral continuity. Contemporary
rural society is firmly rooted in traditional institutions, both the
cohesive natural community, which for more than 1,000 years has
supported itself by cooperative rice culture, and the beliefs and
patterns of behavior that are regulated in accordance with Confucian
doctrine. Thus the outside change agent, whether Korean or foreign,
who goes into a Korean village with a little capital and technical
advice, expecting to bring about planned "reforms" in the structure
of social relations, has little chance of success. Both the inexorable
changes associated with long term modernization and the deep-rooted
traditions are usually impervious to his efforts. But in Korea, at
least, development along economic lines does not require a thoroughgoing transformation. Fatalism, dependency, and lack of confidence
are being overcome within the context of a traditional social
environment that still emphasizes hierarchy, paternalism and
the subordination of individual goals and desires to the interests
of family, lineage, and community.

Historically, Korean villages have been left pretty much alone
by the central bureaucratic authority, and accordingly there is a
long tradition of self-government and self-reliance. Today the transition has been made nearly everywhere from leadership by an older
elite concerned mainly with survival and preservation of the *status
quo*, to leadership by younger activists determined to promote change.
But in other respects the traditional system is pretty much intact.

This system of authority and decision-making at the village
level can best be described as "consensus politics." There is extensive discussion among all those who are interested in any given issue,
and everyone's voice is heard. But it is the village elite--comprising
formal leaders, wealthy farmers and other influential men--who
actually determine (often informally) what decisions are reached and
how they will be implemented. It is their responsibility to make sure
that decisions are fair and equitable, and social censure is usually
effective in insuring a reasonable degree of conformity with the
ideal. Others are expected to go along once agreement has been
reached. Every man's voice does not have equal weight, and no
one, least of all the poor, expects that it should. Persons of education, wealth, high status, experience, and good reputation are
"naturally" regarded as more qualified to make decisions.

Land ownership is one essential attribute of status, respect,
and authority in traditional peasant societies. The landless poor are
dependent on the good will and charity of their neighbors (usually
relatives), and their influence on decision-making in village affairs

is slight. They are clients and go along with their patrons' wishes.

Twenty years ago 35 to 50 percent of Korean rural households could be classified as very poor--either landless or with so little land as to make them dependent on laboring for others. Today the combination of land reform, rural development, and very large scale rural/urban migration has probably lowered this figure to around 20 percent or even less. Another 20-30 percent might also be considered poor in the sense that they are barely able to make ends meet. But each year the "ends" in the sense of acceptable minimum standards for food, clothing, education, material goods, medicine, and so forth, become a little more ample.

Although wages and living standards of agricultural laborers have improved considerably (with the shortage of agricultural labor), the prospects for structurally altering the status of the rural poor are not particularly good. Land prices are well out of their reach, and without land they are unable to take advantage of most of the development projects that have been designed to raise productivity and increase income. An occasional competent, diligent, healthy, lucky, and austere individual will in fact succeed in breaking out of the category of the landless poor, but he is the exception. The hard core of the very poor are old, or young, or sick, or widowed, or lazy and incompetent; and the amount of self-help of which they are capable is limited. Except for the opportunity provided by migration and entry into the industrial labor force, the able-bodied rural poor are pretty well stuck with their role of agricultural labor, dependent for their well being on the trickle-down effect of increasing prosperity among their land-owning fellow villagers.

In the traditional village, kinship ties and a sense of communal responsibility provided a kind of primitive welfare system for the poor and unfortunate. With the exception of a few landowners, everyone's living standard was low, and the difference between the poor (ordinary farmers) and the very poor was as much one of status as of consumption levels. But as part of the modernization process there has been a weakening of kinship ties and communal responsibility during the past 30 years or so, with a corresponding development of individual initiative. Today, the attitude of middle-level and well-off farmers towards the village poor is not much different from that of Americans: they are necessary in order to perform manual labor, but their wages are regarded as outrageously high. Where personal ties exist, there are numerous individual acts of generosity. But most farmers still consider their own financial situation to be precarious, and they are primarily concerned with ways to take advantage of expanding markets and new technology in order to increase their own earnings. Any utopian notion on the part of change agents that such people are going to redistribute income in order to promote economic egalitarianism or operate a thoroughgoing communal welfare system must be rejected as utterly unrealistic.

It is within this context of traditional patterns of village
leadership and decision-making and in terms of the intractable
problems confronting the rural poor that one must consider CBIRD
objectives and accomplishments.

The Coordinator is obliged to work with local elites. Most (in
some cases all) members of the Community Committee are village chiefs,
while the Committee Chairman and Vice-Chairman are likely to have an
even more exalted status. The "felt needs" expressed as a result of
the Committee's deliberations are those of middle-level and well-to-do
farmers with capital resources in land worth from about $20,000 to
$50,000 or more (in 1976) and annual incomes ranging from $2,300
(average farm household income in 1976) to over $6,000 (on the
average, for that 5 percent of the farm population who owned more
than 2 hectares of land in 1976). These figures are, of course, much
higher today. To the extent that there is grass roots representation
in the planning and implementation process, these, then, are the
grass roots. The "bottom" in "bottom-up" planning comprises for the
most part agricultural or fishing entrepreneurs with considerable
capital, who are keenly cognizant of and participate in regional,
national, and overseas markets for their products, and who have
had rapidly rising incomes for the past ten years or more. The
rural poor, on the other hand, have neither the confidence, the
education, the status, nor the opportunity to participate, except
passively, in the planning or implementation of village self-help
projects.

Any program to redistribute land or provide long term low
interest loans for land purchases would require a major policy
decision on the part of the Korean Government (many such ideas
have been discussed) and an enormous capital investment. A
massive program along these lines is unlikely, however, because
from the economist's perspective--and economist/bureaucrats are
now the most influential technocrats in the Korean technocracy--
continuing economic development requires that more and more of
the rural population leave the land and join the industrial labor
force. Korean farms are too small to be really efficient, it is argued,
and to some extent current rural prosperity is indeed dependent on
artificially high (government subsidized) grain prices. It can be
expected, therefore, that in the future government policy will promote the increased mechanization of larger individual farms rather
than efforts to assist the lowest income groups to acquire land in
rural areas.

Such detailed background information regarding the rural
economy may seem irrelevant to an evaluation of CDF's highly
practical and effective initiatives in the six impact areas. But the
issue we are considering here is not whether the CBIRD system is
helping farmers and fishermen increase their productivity, incomes,
and quality of life, or whether it is helping them learn to manage
their own village affairs. It is doing this and doing it well. The
present issue is, to what extent is CBIRD reaching the rural poor?

It is our conclusion that, given the stage of development in Korea, the nature of village social structure and politics, and the direction of government policy, the capacity of self-help projects to improve the situation of the landless poor to any marked degree (except through charity) is quite limited.

If we examine the actual results in the impact areas, it is evident that most of the assistance and benefits are going to middle level and well-off farmers. Even the loan programs and most of the social welfare projects are relatively inaccessible to the poor. Loans from the village revolving fund require two guarantors. As a result the poor can borrow only very minor amounts. The fees of day care centers or health insurance schemes are too great for most poor families. And as we have shown earlier, except for a relatively few projects such as the raising of Korean cows, most of the efforts designed to raise icome have not been directed towards the poor.

In short, in the rural Korea of today there appears to be an inherent contradiction between the aim of improving the relative position of the poor and the aim of fostering a solidly-based, energetic program of development through self-help. CBIRD productivity projects are mostly geared to the requirements of independent cash-crop farmers or fishermen with some resources of their own to invest. By building up the economic base and supporting the authority of these village elites, CBIRD is in effect ensuring that the socio-economic structure of rural society will not be radically disturbed. If this is so, it is an important, albeit discouraging finding and should help to make the enunciation of future development goals and programs more realistic.

ACHIEVING A BALANCED "PROJECT MIX"

In the circumstances just described, achieving the "right" mix or balance in each CBIRD area between social welfare and productivity projects becomes very difficult. The fact that the direction of Community Committees is firmly in the hands of village elites means that there is a predilection for investment in projects that will increase incomes. The opinions or desires of women, children, the sick, or the old are not forcefully presented, yet one gets the impression that even if they were, village opinion would not differ drastically from that of their leaders. For the most part Koreans today seem to be strongly imbued with a capitalist, free enterprise mentality. They want to earn more money, and then from a position of relative economic independence decide themselves how to spend it.

On the other hand, there is in most places also a strong sense of communal responsibility and a tradition of cooperative effort. There is often great pride in successful cooperative undertakings and an improvement in morale as a result that goes far beyond actual economic benefits. This tension between traditional rural communalism on the one hand and the exuberant new individualist activism on the other is another factor contributing to the enormous complexity of contemporary Korean society.

In any case, among the projects requiring joint effort there seems to be more enthusiasm for building roads, dikes, bridges, and water supply systems than for day care centers or health clinics. And even when such social projects are carried through to completion, it is primarily the actual building that is the focus of popular attention and effort rather than the activity that is supposed to take place inside. All over Korea farmers have built village meeting halls at the urging of Saemaul officials, and there is often a good deal of local pride in the finished product as a monument to village cooperation and progressive spirit. But in many places the halls are seldom used for meetings, serving instead for storage or living quarters. The building itself is a tangible sign of development effort, but the activity, particularly where it is unfamiliar and not specifically addressed to urgent, locally felt needs, remains outside the villagers' immediate concern, even though they may regard it as desirable.

Through numerous and repeated training sessions CDF has--with considerable success--stressed the importance of conducting frequent regular meetings at the community center to discuss development programs, as well as the maintenance of a permanent office where management of development matters can take place on a continuing basis. These are an integral part of the CBIRD concept. Probably a similar concerted educational effort is necessary in order to create a local demand for, and a sense of personal involvement in, more intensive health, welfare and cultural activities.

Actually the problem is quite complex. There are different voices within the CDF organization itself urging greater emphasis on one or the other kind of project. Different Coordinators have different points of view and, of course, the extent to which they influence the Community Committee's decisions varies in each area. Villages and impact areas are at different stages of development, and the psychological environment also varies from place to place, so that it is extremely difficult for any outsider to judge what combination of projects is best suited and most feasible in a given situation.

In general things are left up to the Coordinator's judgement. He must balance the Committee's expressed wishes against his own conception of integrated and balanced development, or what he believes is necessary in order to comply with CDF's goals or its obligations to funding sources. For example, on Yaksan one of the Coordinator's greatest problems has been the gap between the kinds of projects desired and expected locally (large scale public works) and the varied small scale assistance programs that are regarded as appropriate by CDF. In Sanbuk, where community solidarity in support of CBIRD goals is highest, a medical insurance scheme was organized at the urging of the Coordinator, but it has broken down through lack of popular interest.

Probably the current, somewhat amorphous situation, in which there is a formal delegation of authority to the Committee combined with continuing informal pressure exercised by the Coordinator is as effective as any other system might be in reconciling these opposing points of view. But the compromise solutions are bound to fall short of the ideal, both for the local proponents of concentrating on income-raising projects and for the CDF proponents of giving greater attention to health, nutrition, child care and the status of women.

THE ELUSIVE CONCEPT OF "COMMUNITY"

While the main focus of interest on the part of CDF and of the villagers themselves is development--the actual accomplishment of projects that will improve incomes and the quality of life--it is important also to consider holistically the kind of residential entity, i.e., the social-economic-psychological-spatial environment, within which development can best take place. On the one hand there is the process itself--the dynamic activity that produces desired developmental results. And on the other, there is the social context--a particular set of relationships among local people, their institutions, values and patterns of behavior--that provides a favorable setting for that process. The conceptual difference here is not between economic projects and social welfare projects. Rather it is between concrete developmental activity of all kinds and the small society where it takes place. In other words, it is useful to make a distinction between community and what the community can accomplish. The CBIRD program represents an innovative approach to both aspects of the problem.

Let us consider first the issue of the mini-regional (or multi-village) impact area as a community.* To what extent has CBIRD been able to expand the psychological and behavioral boundaries of residents in the hamlets and clusters of hamlets that make up its impact areas? In Sanbuk it seems evident that there is a broader sense of community beyond village boundaries. It is not, of course, the same closed, exclusive, "we/they" type of solidarity that characterizes most small natural villages where there are tightly grouped clusters of houses; and certainly everyone in the Sanbuk area is not included. Nevertheless, a large measure of cooperative, constructive effort takes place in Sanbuk, not only in the mobilization of labor for carrying out projects but in their planning and direction as well. The management of and participation in other local institutions of a social, administrative, recreational, financial and educational nature also reflects the fact that the social field, i.e., the territorial environment within which farmers are accustomed to share their ideas, work, and visits, and within which they feel comfortable in pursuing their goals, is in fact larger than the single village.

But Sanbuk is exceptional, not only among the CBIRD areas but in Korea as a whole. "Community" is essentially an ideology for those who participate in it. The community's members must not only share common beliefs and goals; they must derive psychological

---

*Community is used here in the sense of a group of frequently inter-acting people who share similar ideals and work together effectively for achieving common goals.

satisfactions from joint participation in work, play, and ceremony.
There must be a common sense of belonging that is stronger than
the rivalry, jealousy, and competition that exists among individuals,
kinship groups, or natural hamlets.

Creating such a working social ideology where it does not
already exist is not easy. Perhaps it is not even possible in the
short run. It is all very well to use such names as Community
Committee and Community Center, or to refer to groups of villages
in the impact areas as a community.* And it is certainly a worthwhile objective to try to foster a sense of community and cooperation
for the achievement of desired goals. But this whole operation--at
least the English-speaking part of it--sometimes seems to involve a
certain amount of self deception. One has the impression that
because the term "community" is used so much, the rhetoric has
taken on a life of its own, convincing the promoters of change that
the desired result is being more fully achieved than may actually
be the case. One can argue, however, that in Korean rural villages
today, particularly those that are developing most rapidly, there is,
in fact, an increase in individual ambition and the pursuit of private
goals compared to the past. Genuine community is being gradually
eclipsed by modernization, just as it has been throughout much of
the industrialized world. Thus, the basis for cooperation is increasingly self-interest, and the basis for effective leadership is
increasingly expertise and demonstrated performance. At the level
of the impact areas Coordinators are fully aware of these social
realities, and the programs are being designed accordingly. Thus,
training, the efficient operation of organizational structures, and
administrative linkages among organizations are crucial. Closely
knit bonds of community, except for such efforts as mobilizing the
labor of a single village, are, although always desirable, less and
less likely to be an integral factor in regional development.

Another essential characteristic of the successful mini-regional
area as exemplified by Sanbuk is that most local residents, whether
they play a leading role or not in the management process, have a
sense of proprietorship--a feeling that the Community Committee,
the Credit Union, the Community Center, and the revolving fund
all are in some degree their own institutions rather than just the
instruments (however welcome) of an outside agency. As a result
there is a qualitative as well as a quantitative upgrading of their
participation in such organizations.

There is a good deal less evidence of community in the Chunsong area, where the program has been going on for the same length
of time. And in the islands where CBIRD was first initiated in
1977, the extension of villagers' sense of mutual responsibility,
territorial loyalty, and focus of cooperative endeavor is still in its
initial stages.

---

*Actually, the word for community in Korean is an esoteric,
technical term used mainly by rural sociologists. It is unknown to
farmers. The Korean for "Community Committee" and "Community
Center" stresses development and welfare rather than community.

It is evidently impossible to pin down the causes of such an elusive psychological trait as community solidarity. The best that can be done is to suggest a set of variables that are related; each community must then be considered in terms of its unique mix of these variables.

Important among these variables, of course, are the *given* characteristics of any particular place--the structural factors that affect cohesiveness and its expression in group activity. Distribution of land ownership, the composition of kinship groups, settlement patterns, ease of transportation, and the quality of local leadership are all significant elements. In both the Chunsong and Wido impact areas those villages where there is a particularly uneven distribution of wealth demonstrate less internal solidarity as well as less desire to cooperate in projects with other communities. In the genuine mountain villages that are outside of but adjoin the Chunsong impact area, most houses are widely dispersed because of the shortage of arable land and steep terrain. In such places cooperation even within a single village is difficult to organize, because few projects can be devised that benefit everyone more or less equally. It is also more difficult to obtain a village consensus, particularly with regard to such projects as electrification or water supply, where the costs of supplying outlying households are much greater than for a single tightly clustered group of dwellings. Topography has an effect also on communication and ease of access, complicating the task of anyone trying to organize cooperative work or participation in other activities. As indicated earlier, these kinds of problems are particularly severe in the island areas.

One of the most crucial variables is the Coordinator's skill and style. It is not only what he does but what kind of person he is--from the villagers' perspective--that makes all the difference. He must be respected, but he must also be liked. One essential ingredient of community is egalitarianism; if the social gap is too great there can be no community. In Korea there are two traditional dimensions or models for personal relationships, the collective or communal and the hierarchical. The Coordinator usually comes to an area with considerable authority, an urban manner, wealth (he controls substantial funds), and education. His relations with high local officials are cordial. The farmer, even the influential farmer, initially accords such a person high status and relates to him in a deferential, subordinate, and somewhat formal manner. Villagers fit naturally into a hierarchical relationship (that of the inferior) in dealing with powerful outsiders; but this is also a way of keeping them outside, of asserting local exclusiveness.

The problem for the Coordinator is to break through the formality and status barrier, so that he can interact on the basis of mutual respect with the local elites. The Coordinator must be popular as a human being, able to relate easily to all kinds of people without being patronizing or paternalistic.

As part of his efforts to instill in influential members of the local population a sense of proprietorship in operating their own local institutions, the Coordinator should stay in the background, boosting the importance and active participation of local leaders. But he must also keep some kind of control over the direction of local initiatives, opposing or somehow mobilizing opposition to impractical schemes. In other words, he must be strong enough to stand up to local interests when the occasion demands it. The ability to keep everything on the right track without antagonizing influential local citizens requires great political skill.

There are some situations, of course, where no amount of skill or good will on the part of the Coordinator can overcome local distrust, at least in the short run. For each impact area there are stories of the jealousies, resentments and hostility engendered during initial stages of the program. It is not yet clear whether some of the problems encountered in the island areas are due to particular states of mind characteristic of isolated communities, to lack of social and political skill on the part of the Coordinator, or simply to the fact that the programs have only been in effect a short time.

No matter how effectively the Coordinator plays his role, or how successfully development projects are carried out, other factors can impede the growth of community feeling beyond village boundaries. Unless there are close social or kin ties linking the villages, or strong common economic interests, it is extremely hard to create a larger sense of community. In the last analysis it also depends on the predominant values and the mood or morale of the local villages making up the impact area. Where many of the influential and wealthy farmers are primarily concerned with furthering their own interests, there is a tendency for them to disengage from close involvement in community affairs and develop independent ties with outside persons and institutions. Or they may try to co-opt the CBIRD structure to further their own ambitions. In such a situation efforts to mobilize support for educational improvement, health care, or recreational events are much more difficult, and the goal of enlarging the community may become unattainable. It seems axiomatic that only where key individuals become personally involved in furthering collective goals is there much chance for success.

CBIRD'S SPECIAL CONTRIBUTION

If we shift our attention away from such lofty themes as abolishing rural poverty, creating harmonious communities, or inculcating participatory democracy in villages and consider instead the CBIRD strategy in terms of its immediate practical goals, we begin to get a clearer idea of its actual accomplishments.

First of all it is widening the social field of farmers and providing the skills and experience they will need in order to survive and prosper in the complex world of commercialized, high technology agriculture. In this connection it is worth noting that in Korea rural development is no longer a matter of jolting farmers out of traditional apathy or conservative agricultural practices. The question is simply how far and how fast rural development will be pushed relative to other sectors of society. A wide variety of services to the farmer such as agricultural extension, credit, storage, distribution, and marketing advice is becoming increasingly available through official channels.

The Saemaul Undong, while centrally planned and administered with the continuing personal backing of the President, has also strongly emphasized the important role of local village leadership in planning and implementing self-help projects. The announced goal has been to transform the consciousness of farmers so that they will recognize the potential benefits of working together for collective community goals. It is not a contradiction to state that strong "top down" bureaucratic pressures have been used to promote enthusiastic "bottom-up" participation. A resemblance to certain mass mobilization strategies in socialist countries, particularly the principle of "democratic centralism" in the People's Republic of China, is probably more than coincidental. On the other hand, the national economic system with which Korean farmers are being more and more tightly integrated is one of free enterprise and competition. As a result, the rewards for efficient agricultural production involving advanced technology are increasing, while incompetent or overly conservative farmers are being driven off the land. And not surprisingly, for the reasons given earlier, the rate of progress in different villages has been quite uneven.

It is in the areas of leadership, the acquisition of relatively sophisticated management skills, and the exploration and utilization of better ties with institutions outside the villages that the CBIRD program is making a particularly useful and important contribution. It supplements the Saemaul Undong in the areas where it is weakest, by providing training in those techniques of integrated rural development that can be practiced by the villagers themselves: systematic long and short range planning, the management of local development organizations, the creation of financial institutions designed to recycle increased income back into the "community" economy, and techniques for obtaining various kinds of outside help from both public and private sources.

To the extent that CBIRD is successful in promoting effective cooperative efforts at the multi-village level, it will enable the traditional cohesive solidarity and mutual interdependence of the village to survive on a larger, more viable scale. In the small, closed, Korean natural community there has always been a great deal of economic and social mutuality. Correspondingly, there has also been an easy intimacy as well as a security and harmony of personal relationships that is expressed constantly in the sharing of work and material goods, generous (often extravagant) hospitality, and frequent informal gatherings. But today a considerable degree of atomization is taking place, as time honored values and customs clustered around such concepts as mutual help, cooperation, and the amicable settlement of disputes give way to the hard driving individualism of the cash crop farmer. As individuals expand and strengthen their connections with outside institutions, ties with their neighbors are weakened. Everywhere there is increased dependence on sources of leadership, capital, know-how, and manufactured goods beyond village boundaries, with the drive for higher living standards taking precedence over most other considerations.

The CBIRD strategy, best exemplified by the Sanbuk area, helps the rural population deal with both of these challenges, the pressing need to expand links with the world outside the village and the threat of commercialized individualism to cooperation. Where successful the CBIRD model can point the way to another alternative direction for rural society: the formation of larger, economically prosperous cooperating social units within which the most important humanistic aspects of traditional rural society can perhaps be preserved against the enormously powerful influences of consumption-oriented materialism and economic individualism. Although the goal of creating genuine multi-village communities may prove somewhat illusory in many instances, the CBIRD approach offers many advantages by enlarging the scale and therefore the effectiveness of self-help and self-management. This permits the Community Committee to undertake more ambitious projects to deal more effectively with local administration, to tap other outside sources of technology and capital, and to train its own leaders in relatively sophisticated management skills.

CHAPTER 9

SOME LESSONS

AND OPEN QUESTIONS

In examining the operational record of CBIRD in search of useful lessons, this report has stressed certain special characteristics of the Korean setting that provide a generally favorable context for rural development, as well as certain other characteristics that place practical limits on the CBIRD approach. Both sets of factors-- positive and negative--need to be kept in view in considering the future potentialities of CBIRD in South Korea and the feasibility of replicating some or all of its special features.

This final chapter recapitulates some of the special contributions the CBIRD program has made in the Korean context and suggests some considerations that will determine its applicability in other countries. It also addresses two outstanding questions of importance to many countries, and a third concerning the survival and future influence of CBIRD in South Korea.

Since 1971 the pace of change in virtually all of South Korea's 36,000 villages has picked up dramatically, as village economies have become more and more tightly integrated with that of the nation as a whole, and as bureaucratic influences on almost every aspect of farm life have deepened. From this standpoint the CDF program must be seen as an effort to fine-tune and accelerate the process in a few carefully selected areas. The rural populations of the CBIRD impact areas are particularly fortunate in that the kinds of benefits, training, and experience they are receiving will have long lasting effects, enabling them to compete more effectively in the materialistic sweepstakes that are now going on in South Korea.

Korean rural development in recent years has taken place under the influence of the Saemaul Movement with its emphasis on paternalistic guidance and material support from above combined with the mobilization of popular cooperative effort under local leadership. CBIRD has supported the Saemaul efforts but has gone beyond them, enabling farmers, fishermen and others in its impact areas to exercise a greater degree of control over the development process. While one general effect of both Saemaul and CBIRD initiatives has probably been to reinforce a realization by these local producers of their dependence on outside institutions and the linkage of their livelihood with the national economy, the CBIRD approach has clearly demonstrated better ways to plan, finance, and direct further progress in accordance with villagers' own goals and needs. It has furnished the multi-village area with a set of institutions and a methodology that enables the local population to make the most of their available resources. Most importantly it provides them with a workable means of acquiring those essential factors of production that are everywhere in short supply: capital, technical know-how, and management skills.

So far, particularly in the mainland impact areas, the CBIRD initiatives have produced impressive results in increased productivity, incomes, and local living standards. On the islands there have been some initial problems and delays, but a wide variety of projects is now being implemented, and given the fact that some of the island programs represent much smaller per capita investment by CDF, the benefits already achieved are significant.

APPLICABILITY OF CBIRD EXPERIENCE
TO POORER COUNTRIES

In a report such as this it is not possible to reach any firm conclusions regarding the extent to which successful CDF programs in Korea are replicable elsewhere. Nevertheless, it seems useful to ask some leading questions that might help to establish a comparative basis for exploring the possibilities.

1) How important is the relatively egalitarian distribution of land ownership in determining the outcome of the CBIRD experiment in Korea?

2) Has the strong demand for agricultural and fishery products from prosperous urban centers been a necessary condition for raising farm income?

3) To what extent does the success of CBIRD's non-formal educational program depend on popular attitudes towards learning?

4) How much has CBIRD depended on the effective operation of local administrative agencies and Korean government inputs in order to achieve its planned goals?

5) To what extent does CDF's concentration on areas with a "good potential for development" account for the program's impressive achievements? Or, conversely, would the CBIRD experience be more relevant for less developed countries if there were greater emphasis on "hard cases"?

There can be no doubt that the first four factors listed above-- the relatively equitable distribution of land holdings, the profitable and expanding markets for agricultural and fishery products, the high value traditionally placed on education and learning in the Korean culture, and the aggressive promotion of rural development by the government--have all contributed importantly to the effectiveness of the CBIRD program. It would seem to follow, therefore, that the absence of any one or combination of these positive factors in another country setting--especially a very low income country with a low economic growth rate--would constitute if not an outright barrier at least a serious impediment to replicating the successful CBIRD experience in South Korea.

As to the fifth question concerning CDF's concentration on areas with a "good potential for development," we can give only a speculative answer. CDF was undoubtedly well advised to choose such promising areas as Sanbuk and Chunsong in which to launch its experiment because it required testing out a complicated and untried approach that would inevitably present sizeable problems and risks even under relatively favorable circumstances.   To have started with the hardest cases could well have doomed the experiment to failure from the outset.   In moving on from these initial areas to the island areas of Wido and Yaksan, CDF did indeed take on some relatively "harder cases." Yet even these areas had a good deal going for them, especially in terms of prospering markets and rising prices for marine products, and the availability of substantial local savings--albeit concentrated in relatively few hands--for reinvestment in development.

There are, however, some much "harder cases" in Korea, particularly isolated mountain villages with only poor to moderate development potential and still lying outside the mainstream of the dynamically growing Korean economy. It is reasonable to suppose that if the CBIRD approach were now to be tried out on some of these truly "hard cases" it would encounter much greater difficulties and would probably have to be modified substantially in certain respects in order to achieve significant results. But the experience thus gained would undoubtedly offer much poorer countries to the south a wider range of useful lessons--both positive and negative--than the present CBIRD experience.

This observation is not intended to imply, however, that the CBIRD approach and the lessons of its experience in South Korea have no relevance to less prosperous countries. On the contrary, it may well be that certain features of CBIRD's strategy and methodologies--for example, its way of dovetailing local planning and implementation with broader nationwide planning and development efforts, its technique of recycling outside grants into local revolving loan funds, and its successful efforts to link rural communities with outside sources of know-how and technical support--may well have considerable applicability to other countries, provided, of course, that they are properly adapted to the quite different circumstances of these countries. Indeed, no one can really know until it has actually been tried.

What is very clear, however, is that CBIRD's unusually favorable environment in South Korea, especially the extraordinary

economic dynamism, cannot readily be replicated elsewhere. Therefore, the expectations of what a modified CBIRD approach might
achieve under much less favorable economic circumstances should be
appropriately modest and realistic. In other words, inflated rhetoric
and false hopes should be studiously avoided.

THREE OUTSTANDING QUESTIONS

The discrepancies noted earlier between CBIRD's more intangible goals--particularly concerning social change and welfare--and
the actual program accomplishments pose a few important unresolved
questions that merit brief review, especially since they apply to
many countries.

1. *Can the Poor Really be Helped?*

It has been pointed out in previous sections that most of the
benefits from CDF investment accrue to middle level and well-off
farmers, and that relatively little can apparently be done to change
this pattern despite the best intentions and efforts on the part of
the CDF staff and Coordinators. In the Korean case it seems evident
that except for outright charity, attempts to help the poorest sector
of the rural population must depend mainly on the trickle-down effect
of generally increased village prosperity. The goals of restructuring
society so as to change the distribution of wealth, and of establishing
a new welfare-oriented mentality among local elites, are simply beyond
the capacities of the CBIRD program--or any other program for that
matter, short of a thoroughgoing political revolution or an ideological
revitalization movement.

The question then inevitably arises; despite the widespread
international consensus on the need to improve the lot of the rural
poor, to what extent is this goal really practicable? Perhaps there
is something wrong with our perceptions of the problems. Have we
taken adequate account of the very solid and durable social/
structural obstacles to the kinds of change that are so widely
regarded as desirable? Or, to put the matter in terms of practical
strategies, is it possible to redistribute wealth or focus efforts
mainly on aiding the poor, while at the same time promoting self-
sustaining rural development? We must conclude here that, in Korea
at least, the answer seems to be no. Further, our assessment of
the CBIRD programs suggests that, regardless of its statements
of basic principles and objectives, SCF/CDF--at the level of actual
operating procedures--has implicitly reached the same conclusion.

Unless a rural society is in a state of chaotic demoralization or
upheaval, which has not been the case in South Korea, an effective
integrated development program must be based on existing traditions,
values, and institutions. It may be possible to modify their operation
in gradual and subtle ways, but if the change agent's commitment
compels him to confront and try to do something all at once about
such intractable problems as the role of women, child-rearing
practices, village authority structures or hierarchies of wealth and
status--all in addition to technical agricultural innovation--then

truly his program's failure is assured. In Korea, at any rate, effective self-help efforts depend on strengthening and improving village institutions and leadership in accordance with generally recognized, traditional standards--not on undermining or radically transforming them. The community worker can never afford to lose sight of the social mechanisms through which people interact and organize their group efforts, no matter how dedicated he may be to certain overriding objectives.

Hard questions must be asked: is the ideal of integrated economic and social development always valid as a working strategy? The CBIRD experience in Korea suggests that this issue should be approached through carefully planned stages, with the major push in social welfare projects coming after effective improvement in the economic sector and after extensive indoctrination through non-formal education. Such an approach reflects two particular characteristics of the Korean context. First, while rural health care is grossly inadequate by Western standards, health problems are not so severe as to impair either village morale or work output. Second, the Korean farmer or fisherman gives highest priority to economic development.

CDF Coordinators and Community Committees have arrived at reasonably successful compromises on this issue in the actual working out of a viable mix of projects in the impact areas. The social welfare effort has been concentrated mainly on women's training, day care centers, and actions to reinvigorate and supplement existing family planning programs. Except for the day care centers, however, the amounts invested have been minor compared to other kinds of projects. And, as has been pointed out before, even with these kinds of projects it is the better educated, more confident, and more aggressive women from economically secure households who receive most of the benefits.

Another lesson here, then, is that if "bottom up" participation and decision-making has any meaning, it is that under the CBIRD approach local leaders will determine the direction that development takes in accordance with their own (and the local administration's) ordering of priorities. The Coordinator has considerable influence on the Committee's deliberations, but any serious effort to alter local priorities would be self-defeating, which is to say that any major and direct effort to improve the lot of the landless and helpless poor will have to wait.

2. *Will Villages Work Together?*

Another major objective of the CBIRD system has been the formation of multi-village communities as the focus for development efforts. Here it is useful to make a distinction between a true sociological community and a set of villages that are able to plan and work together under unified leadership for mutually agreed upon goals. The distinction can be illustrated by differences in the degree of solidarity and the manner in which CBIRD institutions are operated in the different impact areas. Only in Sanbuk does there appear to be a strong and broader sense of community in which

feelings of mutuality and social responsibility--a concern for the
common welfare--go beyond village boundaries to encompass the
whole impact area. The impression is inescapable in Sanbuk that
farmers not only participate energetically, they also take pride in
operating the CBIRD machinery for their own purposes. This same
sense of proprietorship is popularly reflected in the frequent,
everyday use of the Community Center, where, for example, a
steady stream of people conduct their business with the credit union.

In the other CBIRD areas the same general formula is being
followed, and there is widespread and grateful recognition of the
benefits derived from it. But for most people the activities remain
something that is being done for them by outsiders in accordance
with externally imposed rules and procedures. In terms of their
associations, loyalties and economic goals people continue to identify
themselves with a particular village or kinship group. Or, where
such ties are weakened, they are likely to migrate to the city. In
other words, the CBIRD spirit has not yet become an integral, deeply
rooted part of the local sub-culture and social system. The lesson
here would seem to be that while the advantages of larger scale, inter-
village cooperation are self evident, the erosion of village solidarity
and the formation of an expanded rural community is likely to be a
very slow process.

CDF's goal of establishing multi-village development units on a
larger scale is impeded by other factors as well. The idea of the
natural village community as the focus of social life and (now) of
developmental aspirations is deeply ingrained in Korean mentality.
Intimate, long term personal association is regarded as the proper
and natural basis for both rural leadership and cooperative effort.
Accordingly the Saemaul organizers (reportedly including President
Park), while recognizing the importance of planning and coordinated
effort on a regional basis, have continued to emphasize the individual
village, both as the local decision-making unit and as the basis of
labor mobilization. Coordination of larger projects beyond the village
level is regarded as the function of local administration.

Is it likely that the demonstrated effectiveness of the CBIRD
methodology will change official thinking on this issue? On the basis
of the present study it seems highly problematical. The emotional
associations of the village as a social and political unit have been
mentioned above. In addition there are powerful bureaucratic and
political forces influencing the direction of development of rural
institutions. The Korean administration's approach is eminently
pragmatic: 1) any concessions and adaptations to foreign organizations that are necessary in the short run in order to ensure the
continued flow of outside assistance are readily made; 2) there is
a genuine eagerness to learn new techniques and technologies, which
if useful will probably be incorporated somehow in future practices.
In the longer run, however, the prestige, authority, and ubiquity
of Korean governmental agencies will determine the form and manner
of operation of all local institutions.

3. *What are CBIRD's Long Term Prospects?*

Today the social and economic horizons of Korean farmers are
rapidly expanding, and CBIRD projects are accelerating the process.
Local leaders are actively participating in guiding the development of
their communities. But the Korean Government depends on the docile
support of the rural population. It does not look kindly on the formation of any independent, private associations at the local level that
might be in a position to challenge the authority of official agencies
or serve as a rallying point for demands for greater local autonomy.
It would be highly misleading to assume, as some have done, that
the organization of local decision-making for economic development
represents a significant trend in the direction of grass roots political
democracy. Korean tradition, current governmental practice, and
the geo-political situation in Northeast Asia all oppose such a tendency, at least in the immediate foreseeable future.

Thus it seems unrealistic to expect that a set of model or
pilot communities implanted in Korean rural society can eventually
transform that society by example in accordance with a particular
ideal vision. Rather it is the other way around. As CDF phases
out its operation, the model will inevitably be transformed by the
particular conditions and popular attitudes of each area and by the
ubiquitous and growing influence of the bureaucracy.

But even if the present CBIRD model seems unlikely to spread
spontaneously throughout South Korea, will it survive in the
present impact areas after CDF withdraws? Without occasional
capital inputs and at least periodic encouragement and supervision
from the outside, can the CBIRD program sustain itself in anything
like its present form? The answer, in our view, will depend heavily
on whether by then the CBIRD system has achieved a sufficiently
high degree of integration in the sense of being supported and
sanctioned by local values and customs, in addition to achieving the
sense of proprietorship referred to earlier. Given these conditions,
the survival prospects seem promising, but lacking this, there seems
little likelihood that it will be perpetuated after the Coordinator and
his capital are withdrawn.

One promising possibility that merits consideration, even if
it may seem remote at the moment, is that the myon level cooperatives might take over the local CBIRD role of promoting and coordinating integrated rural development. But before this can be
regarded as a serious alternative, there will have to be some drastic
changes in the structural organization and operating style of the
cooperative system, and in the attitudes of its officials. Local
branches of the National Agricultural Cooperatives Federation in
Korea are cooperatives in name only. The parent organization is a
centralized government bureaucracy with a strong "top-down"
orientation. It is extremely powerful, with great resources and
authority in the fields of rural credit, farm input supplies, and in
the collection, storage and distribution of agricultural products.
There have been many changes for the better in its operations as
a result of the Saemaul Movement, but no one believes that it

represents the farmers' views or interests.

At the time of this case study discussions were reportedly
going on at high levels in the Korean Government with a view to
restructuring the cooperative system to achieve a greater degree
of active local participation and greater responsiveness to local
needs. Were this to occur, the national organization would then
play more of an advisory and facilitating role than, as at present,
a strong-handed directive role as executor of government policy.
In such a climate, the seeds of local planning, management and
self-help that CBIRD has planted and nurtured would have a real
chance to thrive. Whether such a vision is utopian or not, it
appears to us that the local cooperative is in fact the logical focus
of integration and the most promising successor to CBIRD.

In any event, there can be little doubt that in the long run
the CBIRD innovations will leave some useful and enduring impacts
on the Korean rural scene. But just what form they will take and
how extensive they will be, only time can tell.

9 IPPA Youth Projects: An Indonesian Experiment in Population Education

Soenarjono Danoewidjojo

EDITOR'S NOTE

This case study examines an experimental youth project of the Indonesian Planned Parenthood Association that was initially inspired by a new "youth program" of the International Planned Parenthood Federation. The case is of interest in its own right but also because it represents an effort to respond to a basic quandary faced by a growing number of voluntary organizations that have been the pioneers of family planning in developing countries. The quandary is: what role should such an organization seek to play after the national government has finally adopted a strong population policy and taken over responsibility for nationwide family planning services?

If the private organization simply goes on doing what it was doing before the government stepped in, it is likely to fade into a marginal participant in the overall national family planning effort. Or worse, it may soon find itself on a collision course with an energetic new government population agency. If in order to avoid such a collision, however, it agrees to confine its program strictly to educational and motivational activities, leaving the provision of clinical services and distribution of contraceptives entirely to government, then the private organization will become divorced from the mainstream of action and may soon lose its credibility and effectiveness.

What other alternative is there? The most promising and potentially useful one, which the International Planned Parenthood Federation has been encouraging its member associations to pursue, is to seek out some important new frontiers to work on where further bold and imaginative pioneering is needed. The most obvious such frontiers are defined by the following five common weaknesses of conventional family planning programs.

First, they have been largely urban-centered and have not reached out effectively to serve the great majority of the population living in rural areas, especially the poorest and most destitute families in greatest need of help. Second, they have preferred to "go it alone", concentrating on their own limited organizational objective of winning "acceptors" while keeping their distance from closely related family improvement services (such as primary health care, nutrition, general maternal and child care, and opportunities for poor women to earn some income) that would make natural allies for gaining broader

635

acceptance of family planning, especially among lower income families. Third, many family planning programs are not even integrated internally; their so-called Information, Education, and Communication components are frequently divorced from one another and from the service and distribution components. Fourth, family planning programs have generally concentrated their efforts on married couples who already have a number of children, neglecting the youth and younger adults who will be tomorrow's parents and whose energies, if effectively mobilized, could add great strength to the family planning movement. Finally, most family planning services have been clinic-based and dominated by the medical profession rather than being community-based with opportunities for local people to participate directly in running the programs.

A variety of innovative efforts by both voluntary and official agencies have been initiated in recent years in an attempt to overcome the above weaknesses, especially in Asia where most governments have already mounted sizeable family planning programs. The unique feature of the Indonesian experiment examined here is that it focuses specifically on rural youth groups in an effort to engage their energies in a broad population education effort directed at out-of-school rural youth (who constitute the great majority of their age group). As so often happens the first time out, this experiment encountered a variety of unforeseen difficulties and was still far short of achieving its original goals at the time of the ICED study. But this is precisely what makes the study of special value to others interested in working with rural youth, for the likelihood is that they too will encounter similar kind of difficulties unless they are forewarned and forearmed.

ICED was very fortunate in securing two able and experienced Indonesian partners to carry out this case study: Mr. Soenarjono Danoewidjojo, former director of PENMAS (the Indonesian national community education program)who was the principal investigator and author of the report, and Mr. S. Sudarmadi of the National Ministry of Education and Culture who served in his private capacity as a special consultant to ICED in helping to organize the study and in making substantial professional contributions. During two visits to Indonesia Dr. Manzoor Ahmed of ICED's staff, worked closely with these Indonesian partners (with whom he had worked extensively on previous occasions) in designing the study and making field visits to project sites. He also assisted in the final editing of the report and contributed an introductory commentary.

ICED is also indebted to Mrs. Sophie Sarwono, Chairman of the Indonesian Planned Parenthood Association, and to Dr. Z. Rachman Masjhur, Executive Director of IPPA, both of whom not only welcomed the idea of an independent examination of this experimental project but cooperated fully in carrying it out; and to Dr. Haryono Suyono, Coordinator of Research and Development for the Indonesian National Family Planning Coordination Board (BKKBN) who gave encouragement to the study and provided ICED with much useful information on the nationwide family planning program.

It should be added that ICED enjoyed full independence in carrying out the project and, along with the author, is solely responsible for the content and conclusions of the present report.

INTRODUCTION*

IPPA'S INVOLVEMENT IN YOUTH

The youth are important in family planning programs as well as in broader efforts to improve the quality of life of rural families because they form close to a quarter of the total population in developing countries and because, as a group, they stand at the threshold of adult roles and responsibilities in the family, the community, and the nation. The youth in developing countries also include large numbers who, at a crucial juncture of life, are especially affected by the deprivation of educational opportunities and the denial of active participation in the process of national development.

Interest of the Indonesian Planned Parenthood Association (IPPA) in youth is traceable to the increased attention of its parent body, the International Planned Parenthood Federation (IPPF), to the youth question. In May 1973 IPPA personnel attended a regional workshop in Singapore for the Southeast Asia and Oceania Region of IPPF on ways of bringing population and family-life education to out-of-school youth. Each national team in the workshop worked on developing a pilot project for its own country. It was here that the outline and concept of the Tangerang youth project took shape.

After elaboration and refinement of the plan outlined at the Singapore workshop, the Tangerang project was implemented in 1975 in two subdistricts of Tangerang district, 25 kilometers west of Jakarta. The planning phase of the project included various steps, such as the identification of out-of-school educational activities for youth in the two subdistricts, the development of appropriate population education curriculum and content, and the selection and training of population education instructors.

The project itself, over a six-month period, and in the course of about 48 hour-long sessions, provided instruction on population matters to 700 youths who were already participants in such programs as Qur'an recital, family life education, scouting, dance lessons, and English lessons.

The original plan, as developed by IPPA participants in the Singapore workshop, was to insert population education components in ongoing vocational skill projects, so as to make population education a

---

* These introductory comments were written by Manzoor Ahmed of the ICED staff.

part of a broader effort to improve the life prospects of underprivileged
out-of-school youth. In practice, apparently because a cluster of appropriate vocational training projects for out-of-school youth located con-
veniently in neighboring villages was hard to find, the project used   as
vehicles other educational programs that had little to do with the economic situation of youths from poor families. In fact, many of the participant youths, particularly those belonging to Boy Scouts and Girl Guides
and some members of the dance and English courses, were students   in
secondary level institutions rather than out-of-school youths.

Recognizing these anomalies in the project, members of an evaluation
workshop (consisting of IPPA personnel and involving outsiders) recommended that in any subsequent expansion of the project illiterate   rural
youths be the target group and population topics be presented in   the
context of a functional literacy approach. Whether the functional literacy approach would have been effective in reaching out and helping youths
from poor rural families (given the uneven record of functional literacy
programs) and whether IPPA could have or should have launched a literacy
program are moot points.

As it happened, after the conclusion of the Tangerang pilot project,
IPPA tried out a new approach of reaching the young people by working with
leaders of youth groups. The unstated assumptions behind this   approach
were that the social dynamics of out-of-school rural youths permitted   the
emergence of leaders or leadership roles, that these leaders or potential
leaders could be identified, and that with appropriate instruction   and
orientation from IPPA these leaders could influence the points of view and
perceptions of their peers. The youth leaders project called for the selection and a two-week training of "leaders," each of whom in turn, would lead
periodic discussion and instructional sessions with peer groups. IPPA would
provide a small financial incentive for a period of twelve months to   the
groups which each group could use in support of its own activities.

We do not know if the underlying assumptions behind the project plan
were justified or not. However, implementation of the project made it
clear that reaching the most underprivileged groups was difficult. In one
of the more successful project locations in the Wonogiri district of West
Java--where visitors interested in the project were often taken--the youth
leaders and the peer groups belonged to cultural, recreational, and sports
organizations of local youth.   These preexisting organizations provided a
base of operation for the selected youth leaders and offered some assurance
that education and information activities might continue after the termination of the IPPA project. Members of these groups were young people who
had a relatively high level of education, many of whom had white collar
employment and generally belonged to "middle-class" families. It appears
that only youths from the relatively better-off families had the inclination or could afford to join the youth activity groups. Members of the
groups were, of course, expected to contact other youths in their respective villages and propagate the population messages to them. Discussion
with members of the groups did not reveal that this was done seriously or
on a broad scale. In any case, it is debatable that these kinds of contact could be very effective. They were at least two steps removed from
IPPA and were likely to have been carried out in a patronizing and somewhat

"didactic" manner, because those outside the groups were not social and cultural peers of the group members and were not participants in the group activities.

Another youth project implemented by the Yogyakarta chapter of IPPA in 1977 attempted to serve indigent girls among the youth by combining training in sewing with population education.   The expectation was that the one-month course would equip the partici-- pants with an income-producing skill and at the same time make them better informed about matters relating to family planning and   family welfare. The courses were over-subscribed and evoked an   en- thusiastic response among young girls in several villages near Yogyakarta. However, the participants, again judged by their edu- cational level and occupational status, were girls from the rela- tively better-off families. The girls attended the instructional sessions in both sewing and population topics, but few acquired sufficient proficiency to be able to earn an income. Moreover, it seems that insufficient attention was given to the question of market demand for sewing skills in the locality. This exper- ience points to the general problems that are faced in attempts to improve the socioeconomic prospects of rural youth from poor families by offering skill training only.

IMPORTANT FEATURES OF YOUTH PROJECTS

The three youth projects have some important characteristics in common that point to both their limitations and their possibili- ties.

1.   The projects focused unambiguously and categorically on education and information for out-of-school youth in both population and family planning topics. The approach was purely pedagogical, employing such paraphernalia as curricula, instruc- tors, instructional sessions, and lectures as distinguished from an action-oriented learning-by-doing approach. The projects were not concerned with the possibility that the youth might play an active role in the national or local family planning activities, or, indeed, in other community development efforts that impinged on the welfare of families or of youths themselves. If the organizers of the projects were aware of existing knowledge about the integrated development approach (and how attitudes and behavior in respect of family planning depended on various socioeconomic factors), there was insufficient recognition of it in the projects. The instruc- tional content did stress the negative consequences of population increase on various aspects of development. The instructional approach also made use of youth groups organized for other purposes to insert the population education content. The aim, however, was the delivery of population messages. The involvement of youth in motivational and educational activities within the context of a family planning (or a broader family welfare) action plan was out- side the scope of the projects.

2.   Each of the projects was planned and implemented on an ad hoc basis that was entirely contingent upon the financial support

that IPPA could get from its parent body. The duration of the operational phase
of the projects ranged from one month to twelve months. In each case there was
a sudden withdrawal of IPPA support and involvement when the project formally
ended. This withdrawal impeded the development of any longer-range strategy and
program approach for youth and affected any possible impact of the projects through
follow-up activities. In situations where some residual activities continued or
some of the activities were adopted by other collaborating organizations, IPPA
failed to maintain a working relationship with them and therefore missed the opportunity to maintain influence and strength.

   3.   In each project the population education component was planned, directed, and managed by IPPA itself. Even when a "vehicle" agency was looked for,
as in the Tangerang project, it was for the purpose of inserting IPPA's population education component into the existing program rather than of making the
collaborating organization a full partner in the effort or of giving it the
responsibility for carrying out the population education part along with other
educational activities. In the other projects that were entirely managed by
IPPA, its role was even more dominant. This dominance of IPPA may have discouraged other organizations, particularly those active in the youth field, from
sharing the responsibilities of population education for youth and may have been
a factor in limiting the potential multiplier effect of the projects.

   4.   As we have noted above, the projects attracted the "middle-class"
and educated sections of out-of-school youth and failed to reach the large
majority of out-of-school youth who are illiterate or semi-literate and belong
to the most disadvantaged socioeconomic groups.

   5.   At an average per capita cost of US$13.50 (US$48,000 for a total
direct clientele of 3,600 young people), the projects must be judged expensive
and impractical when considered in terms of the total needs of the country. This
is a relative judgment that is supported by the fact that the projects for the
most part served the more easily reachable educated, organized, and middle-class
minority and failed to reach the disadvantaged majority whose total number in
the country is close to 20 million.

IMPORTANT ISSUES

   The experience of the youth projects of IPPA raises a number of questions for which clear answers are needed. What really are valid and viable objectives for IPPA in serving the needs of the youth? Who among the youth should
be the prime target groups for youth activities? What is the best approach for
carrying on youth activities? What does the youth project experience of IPPA
say for the future role and functions of IPPA? These are obviously interrelated
questions and one cannot be discussed in isolation from the others.

Valid Objectives

   IPPA has chosen to define its objectives for the youth projects in the
narrowest terms, assigning itself a pedagogical and communication role.   This
appears to be in line with the approach supported by the parent organization,
IPPF.[1] The range of possibilities here is wide and might include projects for
the participation of youth in motivational and educational efforts for the
larger community,in activities designed to improve the economic status of the

---

[1]See IPPF, Working with Youth: Some Out-of-School Approaches to Population,
Family Life and Sex Education, London, 1978. Also IPPF, Reaching Out-of-School
Youth: A Project Planning Handbook for Population-Family Life Education, London,
1975.

youth themselves, or in active roles in more broadly conceived programs
designed to improve the quality of life of disadvantaged familes.   Any
combination of objectives that would be appropriate and feasible for
IPPA cannot be considered independent of the resources and capacities
of the potential target groups. Thus far it would appear that by adopting a narrow pedagogical definition of the purposes of the youth   projects, IPPA has failed to develop an approach that reaches the disadvantaged majority among the out-of-school youth and has   ruled   out a
significant role for itself in promoting an active involvement   of
youth in self-help and community development actions. It needs to be
kept in mind that a pedagogical approach to youth activities that does
not have a direct bearing on the economic situation of the participants
cannot possibly arouse the enthusiasm of the young people from poor
families that are struggling for survival. This observation is amply
borne out by IPPA's own experience.

Priority Targets

        It has been noted in the report that a large majority of the
young people in Indonesia is illiterate or nearly illiterate, having
dropped out of school before acquiring a functional level of literacy
skills. Although it is not documented in the report, it is likely that
these same illiterate and semi-literate youths are also the sons and
daughters of the landless farm laborers, pedi-cab drivers, petty peddlers, and similar groups with extremely low family income. Members
of these groups have no opportunity to benefit from the recent emphasis
that has been placed on population education in formal schools. Nor are
they affected as much by the mass media and the modernizing influences
and values of urban life as those with higher levels of education and
income and a greater awareness of family planning issues. A small
family-size norm is likely to be a part of the cultural milieu that
is shared by the latter groups and from which the disadvantaged
majority is excluded. Population education, as a focus for youth
activities is, therefore, more appropriate to the illiterate and low-
income youth than to those who are more fortunate. Be that as it
may, the purely pedagogical approach is not likely to be effective
in reaching the disadvantaged groups. Even if population education
is the main concern, it must be presented within a broad-based
strategy embracing the active participation of youth in activities
designed to affect their social and economic situation. Although a
case may be made for educating privileged youth in a broad-based
strategy, it should not obscure priorities or distract attention
from the urgent necessity of devising approaches to reach those
who are disadvantaged.

Viable Approaches

        Obviously, a rigidly defined model of youth projects cannot
be recommended; variation in approaches and emphases are acceptable
and necessary even if there is a broad agreement about the main
objectives and the target groups. However, if an integrated activist
approach as opposed to a pedagogic-didactic approach is called for,
certain implications for IPPA, should be mentioned. Given the limited
resources of IPPA, its character as a voluntary organization, and
its basic   mandate   in relation   to population and family planning,

IPPA probably is in no position to launch development projects that
can affect any sizeable number of youths. The best approach for
IPPA is to seek out organizations and programs already engaged in
youth development activities and to collaborate with them by providing inputs which it has the capacity to provide and which will help
the cooperating organizations and programs to achieve common goals.
A good start at collaboration was made by IPPA in the Tanerang
project, although IPPA's input there became more an appendage to the
existing programs than a part of it. This limited attempt at collaboration was abandoned in later projects.

Some organizations and programs with whom IPPA may possibly
collaborate are described briefly in the appendix of this report.
The author has not assessed the effectiveness and performance of these
programs or the compatibility of their objectives and approach with
those of IPPA. This IPPA must do when it seeks collaborative relationships. There are certainly other promising organizations in
the country, particularly voluntary ones, that are not included in
the appendix.

Meaningful collaboration will require IPPA to take a broader
view of its own population objectives--to see them in relationship
to the broader goals of the collaborating organizations and to identify
them with the needs and aspirations of youth. IPPA also has to be
willing to hand over the management of the collaborative effort to
the collaborating organization. IPPA's own limited resources can go
the farthest if it concentrates on such activities as--

    -- working with other organizations in developing new
       ideas and approaches for enhancing the participation
       of the disadvantaged youth in youth activities;

    -- becoming a producer, repository and distributor of
       informational and educational materials on population
       and youth activities for other organizations and
       agencies;

    -- assisting in the evaluation and analysis of programs
       and performances of other organizations and in planning
       and managing improvement in their programs;

    -- becoming a vehicle for the exchange of ideas and
       information, and even mutual collaboration among
       organizations interested in the youth;

    -- supporting experimental projects of other organizations
       which have promise of wide applicability and to provide
       seed money for innovative activities which, if proven
       out, will attract support from other sources.

IPPA's Overall Role

In the light of the above discussion, a general comment or
two may be in order about IPPA's overall role in the context of the

national family planning program. As the report points out, the
national program gives IPPA a circumscribed role mainly in the area
of information, education, and motivation. Since the government
policy is to entrust the BKKBN (National Family Planning Coordination Board) with full jurisdiction and operational control over
family planning activities targeted at the adult population and
BKKBN appears to be quite mindful of exercising this jurisdiction,
IPPA activities in respect of the adult population have to be bound
by the confines of IPPA's assigned role.

     There may be some leeway for IPPA in the area of youth
projects to break new grounds and move in new directions. There are
opportunities for demonstrating the possibilities and problems in
integrating family planning and population activities with other
development activities, and for clarifying the practical implications of "beyond family planning" approaches through supporting
appropriate youth activities. These opportunities can be seized only
if IPPA reassesses its present policies and activities for the youth
and takes note of the important lessons from its past experience.

CHAPTER 2

GENERAL BACKGROUND

THE YOUTH PROJECT OF IPPA

In Indonesia, according to the census of 1971, 61.7 percent of the population are under the age of 25, and 17.1 percent are youth between age 14 and 25 years. It is obvious that the youth, entering the reproductive age and soon taking upon themselves adult responsibilities of parenthood and maintenance of families, must have a sound grasp of population problems and family planning concepts, if they are expected to make sensible decisions about family life problems and family size. The youth who constitute such a large proportion of the population are at a crucial stage of life as far as family planning is concerned.

In line with the long-standing policy and goal of the Indonesian Planned Parenthood Association (IPPA)[1] to make all sections of the community aware of the many implications of population changes and to involve them in population activities, it was decided to launch a pilot population education program for out-of-school youth. The significance of the focus on out-of-school youth is that most Indonesian youths are either not in school, or have never been in school. Recent efforts to introduce population concepts and topics in the school program do not benefit those who have already left school or those who have never enrolled in school. The national family planning program, which of necessity emphasizes services to "eligible couples" and the recruitment of "acceptors" does not specifically cater to the requirements of adolescents and young adults.

The first IPPA youth project, financed by its parent organization, the International Planned Parenthood Federation (IPPF), was launched in eight villages of Tangerang district in West Java in March, 1975. The pilot phase of the project supported by IPPF lasted until

---

[1]Known in Indonesian as PKBI or Perkumpulan Keluarga Berencana.

September, 1975. Subsequently, on the basis of the Tangerang experience, IPPA implemented other projects for youth in different
locations in six provinces during 1976 and 1977. This report of the
IPPA youth activities will attempt to set the youth activities in the
context of the total IPPA program and the national family planning
program, examine the details of the youth activities, and bring out
the lessons learned from the Indonesian experience in the involvement
of youth in programs for improving the quality of life of rural
families.

IPPA - HISTORY, GOALS, AND FUNCTIONS

Perkumpulan Keluarga Berencana (PKBI), or the Indonesian
Planned Parenthood Association (IPPA), was officially established in
December, 1957 with a small group of physicians and social workers as
members of its board. The organization set for itself the goal of
rendering services to prospective as well as married couples in the
form of pre-marital counseling; medical examination, diagnosis, and
treatment of sterility; and planned regulation of pregnancies.

In view of the prevailing sociopolitical situation and public
opinion about family planning at the time, the association had to
restrict itself to activities of a sociomedical nature and provide
services relative to birth spacing as well as overcoming sterility on
a voluntary basis. Birth planning services were mostly given to
women shortly after their confinement (following the postpartum
approach).

Launching extensive open campaigns was hardly feasible because of the opposition of various groups and the lack of government
support. Attempts were made to overcome these constraints by inviting prominent leaders in religion, education, and other fields in
the community to discuss family planning ideas and concepts in a
seminar setting. The family planning seminar held in Jakarta in
1963 was considered by the advocates of family planning to be a
success. Other seminars were held in Bandung, Semarang, Bali, Jogyakarta, and Surabaya. A meeting held in Subang, in the center of a
rubber and tea estate area was attended by about 200 sympathizers.
IPPA soon spread itself outside Jakarta and opened six branches in
Denpasar, Bandung, Surabaya, Semarang, Jogyakarta and Palembang.

Because IPPA as an organization was not entitled to run
family planning clinics, its board members took steps in their personal capacity to establish a Family Planning Service Project designed
to open and run family planning clinics. By 1964, 59 clinics were
reported to be providing family planning services. Twenty-eight
physicians were attached to them as consultants and 60 midwives as
their assistants, while 4,980 persons were registered as regular
visitors to those clinics. In June 1966, when circumstances permitted, the Family Planning Service Project was brought under the
control of IPPA.

By 1967, IPPA, encouraged by the public response to its own
pioneering efforts, began to view family planning, not just as a

necessary health service but as a legitimate means of promoting the economic well-being of the family and the socioeconomic development of the community and the nation. In the "Proceedings of the First PKBI Congress" (1967) it was noted:

> Family planning in the sense of birth control needs to be practised in regions with dense population, while in areas with expanses of land family planning implies birth planning for the sake of maternal and infant health, and family well-being. Furthermore, family planning is one of the avenues for achieving justice and prosperity in society.

This Congress also expressed IPPA's appreciation for the government's family planning policy and indicated the association's preparedness to assist in the government's effort "down to the farthermost corners of the country, in order that the benefits can be enjoyed by all strata of society." In the same year (July 1967) IPPA became a legally recognized corporate body and was accepted as an associate member of IPPF. Two years later IPPA became a full affiliate of IPPF, and therefore eligible for full financial and organizational support from the parent body.

In 1970 the Government instituted BKKBN (Badan Koordinasi Keluarga Berencana, or National Coordinating Body for Family Planning) with its main functions (1) to assist the President of the Republic in deciding government policies on family planning; and (2) to coordinate implementation of family planning programs.

Although BKKBN is nominally responsible only for coordination of family planning services, it has become the implementer of the national family planning program of the government (see below) and has therefore limited the direct role of other agencies, particularly the private ones, in rendering family planning services.

IPPA's main functions, as defined by its charter (and taking into account the national program of BKKBN), are in the field of manpower training, information and motivation, research and evaluation, and (to a limited degree) medical services. As officially set down in the by-laws of IPPA, its functions are to:

-- provide information and education on family planning for the well-being of the family and community;

-- do pre-marital and marital counseling, render assistance in cases of sterility, and for the spacing of pregnancies;

-- render aid in family life education and population education;

-- provide additional training to family planning personnel;

-- assist the government in organizing and supervising the
distribution of equipment and medicines;

-- render, directly as well as indirectly, serviceable
advice for the development of family planning in
Indonesia;

-- assist in a more efficient utilization of new contraceptive methods for tackling population problems;

-- endeavour to make renovations in legal, social, cultural
and other domains in support of family planning programs.

PKBI's organizational set-up parallels the national administrative structure. At the provincial level, there is a chapter
(*daerah*) of the national organization, and a branch (*cabang*), covers a
district (*kabupaten*) or a municipality (*Kota-madya*). By 1977, a
chapter was established in each of the 26 provinces, and over 220
branches functioned throughout the country.

At the national level IPPA is managed by a central plenary
and a central executive committee. The central plenary committee
includes the central officials and representatives designated by provincial chapters. The central executive committee--composed of a
chairman, two associate chairmen, a secretary general and a treasurer--
manages the implementation of IPPA activities and is assisted by an
extensive operational staff, headed by an executive director. The
operational responsibilities of IPPA are divided among the following
bureaus:

-- the Bureau of Information and Motivation,

-- the Bureau of Medical Services,

-- the Bureau of Administration and Finance, and

-- the National Training and Research Center

At the provincial level there are provincial executive directors, who are assisted by heads of divisions, similar in function to
the bureau heads at the central level. The executive committee of
the district level branches generally has to deal directly with the
local projects without the assistance of any executive director or
other full-time personnel.

The Tangerang Project, because of its pilot character, was
managed by a project officer appointed by the central organization in
Jakarta rather than by the district branch. (The project site was
only 25 kilometers away from Jakarta.) The other youth projects
initiated subsequent to the Tangerang experience were managed by the
provincial chapters with the direct involvement of the respective
district branches.

THE NATIONAL FAMILY PLANNING PROGRAM

The national program is directed by the BKKBN (Coordinating Body for Planning), which has established a nationwide organization consisting of 15,000 personnel to implement the program. BKKBN has offices and staff at the provincial, district, and subdistrict levels in the provinces of Java and Bali and provincial offices in the other provinces.

The national program is aimed at dealing with the following main features of the population situation in the country:

(a) the sheer magnitude of population in the country, which has been estimated at 135 million (as of 1976);

(b) the rapid population growth, the annual rate of which has been calculated to be 2.4 percent;

(c) the uneven distribution of population. Java and Madura, constituting 6.9 percent of the total land area of the country, accommodate 64 percent of its inhabitants;

(d) the composition of population, in which the "dependents" under the age of 15 make up 44.4 percent of the population.

The main target population is the poor, mostly farmer, families in rural areas and low income laborer families in towns. Beside clinical services the program is also concerned with informational and motivational tasks.

The PLKBs (family planning fieldworkers) employed by BKKBN at the village level, besides distributing contraceptives, have an important role to play in making the public aware of the disadvantages for both family and society of unplanned parenthood, pointing out the benefits of family planning, and encouraging eligible couples to join in the family planning program. The necessary clinical services are provided through health centers of the Ministry of Health and through clinics run by BKBBN.

The national program for the Second Five Year Plan (REPELITA II, 1974-75 to 1978-79) sets as its goal the intensification of the current family planning program in Java and Bali, especially to extend the community outreach in rural areas; and the expansion of family planning programs outside Java and Bali. It was expected that within the REPELITA II period a minimum target of 8 million acceptors could be achieved, in addition to over 2-1/2 million acceptors already registered in the REPELITA I period (1969-70 to 1973-74).

The number of new acceptors outside Java and Bali was expected to come to one million during the REPELITA II period; emphasis was to be laid on family planning programs in more densely populated provinces like Aceh; North, West and South Sumatra; West Nusatenggara; West and South Kalimantan; and North and South Sulawesi.

Table 1 indicates the progress of program implementation since the initiation of the program in 1969 to 1975.

Table 1

Number of Family Planning Personnel, Clinics and Acceptors

REPELITA Year	Information Officers	Physi- cians	Mid- wives	Assistant Midwives	Clinics	Acceptors (in thous.)
1969/1970	--	421	855	75	727	355
1970/1971	--	556	1,678	580	1,465	1,810
1971/1972	1,930	791	1,758	605	1,861	5,194
1972/1973	4,644	883	1,776	1,143	2,137	10,790
1973/1974	4,780	1,186	2,241	1,959	2,235	13,690
1974/1975	6,639	1,956	3,421	2,657	2,877	15,929

Source: "REPELITA KEDUA" (Second Five Year Plan, Indonesia).

The Presidential decree (No. 8 of 1970) that established BKKBN, gave BKKBN the full authority and responsibility to carry out the national program. (There is also a National Family Planning Advisory Council, with a number of ministers as members, which is expected to give guidance and advice to the National Coordinating Board.) BKKBN is entitled to solicit support for program implementation from relevant governmental agencies at various regional levels (province, district, subdistrict, and village).

It also has the responsibility of working with voluntary organizations involved in family planning activities in orienting and adjusting their programs and goals to the basic national plan and of providing them within certain limits, with financial assistance. One area that BKKBN seems to have found particularly appropriate for collaboration with other government and private agencies is that of population education and communication.

BKKBN and the Department of Education and Culture instituted the National Population Education Project in order to introduce population education in the school curricula and out-of-school educational programs. After an initial probing of the possible approaches, the Ministry of Education in cooperation with BKKBN put into action in 1976 a plan to introduce population themes in the curriculum of secondary schools, to retrain teachers for this purpose, and to fully "assimilate" population education into the national education system.

Another major information and education effort known as the Informal Opinion Leaders (IOL) project is carried out through the IPPA. In this project volunteers who are likely to influence the attitudes and views of fellow community members are recruited in each

locality to serve as speakers and discussion leaders in community
gatherings. The volunteers, in turn, are provided with appropriate
briefing and information through the IPPA organizational network. In
fact, being a channel for information, education, and communication
is seen by the BKKBN as the major role of IPPA within the framework
of the national population program. The youth activities of IPPA,
although on a smaller scale than the IOL project, conform to the
assigned IPPA role in the area of creating awareness and understanding
of population issues among various sections and groups of society.

YOUTH IN INDONESIA

According to the 1971 census, the number of young people in
the 15-24 age group was 20,552,000, or 17.35 percent of the total
population (118,459,845). Projections of 1971 figures indicate a
youth population of over 27 million out of a total population of 140
million in 1977.

The 1971 census also provides data concerning the number of
people, 10 years and older, with various levels of education (Table 2),
but does not provide specific data for the 15-24 age group.

Table 2

Population of 10 years and older, by Area, Sex, Level of Education
(in percentages)

Area and Sex	Number in thousands	No School	Not Completed	Primary School Completed	Jr. High Sch.	Sr.	Acad-emy	Uni-ver-sity
Urban Areas								
Male	7,245	12.5	30.1	30.7	17.4	7.0	1.2	1.1
Female	7,372	31.5	29.2	23.7	10.8	4.1	0.4	0.3
Total	14,617	22.0	29.2	27.2	14.1	5.6	0.8	0.7
Rural Areas								
Male	31,803	33.8	39.2	22.0	3.1	1.9	0.0	0.0
Female	34,006	55.9	28.6	13.6	1.2	0.7	0.0	0.0
Total	65,809	45.3	33.7	17.7	2.1	1.2	0.0	0.0

Table 3

Population within the 15-24 age group, by area, sex,
and education level (in percentages) (1961 Census)

Area and Sex	No. in thous.	No School	Primary School 3 Yrs.	Primary School 5/7 Yrs.	Jr. High Schools	Sr. High Schools	Academy & University
Urban areas							
Male	1,450	14.8	15.6	40.6	21.9	6.5	0.6
Female	1,442	34.8	16.5	30.6	14.1	3.5	0.5
Total	2,892	24.8	16.0	35.6	18.0	5.0	0.6
Rural areas							
Male	5,836	40.8	26.8	27.2	4.6	0.0	0.0
Female	6,771	65.3	19.0	13.6	1.9	0.2	0.0
Total	12,607	54.0	22.6	19.9	3.1	0.4	0.0

The census data of 1961 which provide information about educational achievement of youth showed that 54 percent of the rural youth in the age group of 15-24 had never attended school. Nonattendance was 41 percent among males and 65 percent among females. Among the urban youth, however, one-quarter of the youth did not attend any school. This rate was 15 percent for boys and 35 percent for girls. Census data of 1971 do show that 16 percent of the youth were participating in some form of formal education. They also show that among the youth in the labor force (not enrolled in educational institutions)

a)   849 thousand, or 87 percent of the 972 thousand urban youth belonging to the male labor force, were employed;

b)   383 thousand, or 90 percent of 427 thousand female urban youth in the labor force, were employed;

c)   4.3 million, or 96 percent of the 4.5 million rural youth belonging to the male labor force, were employed;

d)   the analogous figures for the rural females were 2.56 million, or 98 percent and 2.62 million;

e)   in urban areas the male youth labor force made up 22 percent of the whole male labor force, while the female youth constituted 26 percent of the female work force; and

f)   the analogous percentages for rural areas were 20 percent and 23 percent respectively.

CHAPTER 3

ORIGIN AND DEVELOPMENT

OF THE YOUTH PROJECT

HOW IT BEGAN

IPPA had been interested in population education since 1970, especially in programs for out-of-school youth. The Association held several seminars on this subject in 1971, 1972, and 1973; it also participated in domestic as well as overseas seminars or workshops conducted by other organizations or by IPPF. An IPPA-sponsored panel discussion held in January 1972, in which representatives of youth and students' organizations in the Jakarta region took part, was especially concerned with ways and means of involving youth in the solution of population problems.

In May 1973 IPPF held a regional workshop on "Youth-oriented Programs" in Singapore, which was also attended by delegates of IPPA. Following this workshop, IPPA drew up plans for a pilot project to test the feasibility of introducing population education in existing nonformal education courses for out-of-school youth. Eight villages in the Tangerang and Ciputat subdistricts of Tangerang district in the province of West Java--about 25 kilometers west of Jakarta-- were chosen as the sites for the youth project. Existence of a number of youth activities in the locality which would be used as the "vehicle" for providing population education, and proximity to the capital were important considerations in choosing the location of the pilot project.

The courses were expected to continue under their original sponsorship even after the pilot project for population education was concluded, thus permitting the population and family planning education program to continue on a self-supporting basis. A related aim was to assist the local organizations in carrying out population education activities by sharing population education materials, methods, and trained personnel of the project.

Initial Development of the Project

     A project officer appointed by IPPA undertook the respon-
sibility for refining and elaborating the proposal prepared by the
IPPA team that attended the Singapore workshop. Revisions were made
of operational objectives, internal program arrangements, and the
budget estimate.

     The initial preparation phase lasting three months included
the following steps:

    a)   introductory and informatory approaches to germane
        government agencies such as BKKBN, Population Education
        Unit of Ministry of Education, and the district and
        local administration in order to ensure appropriate
        support for the youth project;

    b)   selection of existing learning projects in the locality
        to carry out the population and family planning educa-
        tion program and consultations with their sponsors to
        secure cooperation with those projects;

    c)   selection of instructors-to-be and prospective field
        conductors;

    d)   recruitment of project management and field staff;

    e)   collaboration with Bandung IKIP (Teacher's Training
        Institute) on the development of a training package
        and learning materials;

    f)   training of prospective instructors; and

    g)   printing of learners' source books.

     Only those local learning projects which were locally man-
aged and were running with reasonable efficiency were selected as
the "vehicles" for the IPPA educational program. Other criteria
were that the local project enjoyed the goodwill and support of the
local youth, community, and the local administrative powers. Needless to say the willingness of the sponsoring bodies and the managers
of the projects to participate in the population program was also one
of the prerequisites.

     The local courses which were regarded as suitable "vehicles"
for the population education project were:

    a)   the "Purnama" sewing course in Tangerang subdistrict;

    b)   the Qur'an recital courses in the villages of Sukasari
        and Cipondoh (Tangerang subdistrict), Ciputat,
        Cirendeu and Jombang (Ciputat subdistrict);

c) family life education courses in the villages of
    Karawaci, Sukasari and Gerendang;

d) scouting groups (*Pramuka*) in the villages of
    Sukasari and Rempoa

Afterwards, the local chapter of KNPI (a nationwide youth
organization) also joined in the population education program by
making its English and dance courses available to the Youth Project.

Twenty candidates were selected for training—fourteen of them
to become instructors for population education and six to become field
conductors (of whom two would also function as instructors).

The *camats* (subdistrict heads) of Tangerang and Ciputat and
one *Penmas* (Community Education Directorate of the Ministry of Education) field officer had also been requested to serve as field supervisors.

A lecturer at the Jakarta IKIP was appointed as the part-time
project officer who had the overall management responsibility for the
project. She had experience in population projects through her previous job as Executive Secretary of the Population Education Project
of the government. She was to be assisted by two supervisors (one
from the Muhammadiyah organization and one from IPPA's Bureau of
Information and Motivation).

The content materials (a learning package for the training
of prospective instructors and a manuscript for the learners' source
books) for population and family planning education were prepared in
cooperation with the Population Education Development Institute of
the Bandung IKIP. This task was completed by December 1974.

The two-week instructors' training was conducted in February
1975 at Ciloto, a quiet place with a cool climate in the hills of
Boror district (West Java Province). A detailed description of the
training is given in the next chapter.

Functions and Approaches

After the preparatory phase had been completed, the actual
learning program could begin. Learning sessions took place once or
twice a week, depending on the time schedule agreed on by instructors
and participants. The aim was, however, to get through 48 learning
hours within 24 weeks.

The main topics covered in the program were: demographic
phenomena, population and socioeconomic problems, population and
economic development, population and sociocultural problems, population and the ecology, the development of responsible attitudes towards
family planning and the spirit of self-help in the community.

Instructors used a combination of lectures and group discussion techniques in the presentation of learning content. Active
participation of learners was generated and maintained by task assignments and study tours. Each instructor used whatever techniques were
best suited to the subject concerned, the specific learning group,
and the local conditions in general.

The project as a whole took ten months including the preparatory phase, The implementation of the actual learning program
took approximately six months from March to September 1975.

An evaluation was conducted to assess the effectiveness of
the project in meeting its goals and to judge the project's impact
on students. A workshop was held to consider the implications of
the project's results for the work of IPPA and to consider whether
the pilot project could be used as a model for replication elsewhere
in the country.

SOCIOECONOMIC BACKGROUND

Tangerang district is one of the twenty in West Java province. Bordering on Jakarta City on its east side, it is penetrated
by overland traffic veins from the metropolis to the farthermost
parts of Western Java and across the channel to South Sumatra.

Demographic Data

The district has an area of 1,232 square kilometers and had
a population of 1,066,695 in 1971. The population density of 866
per square kilometer was nearly twice the average of West Java
province (466 in 1971). The eastern parts of the district, including
Tangerang and Ciputat subdistricts where the youth project activities
were located with 1,013 to 2,011 inhabitants per square kilometer,
had strikingly higher density rates than the central and western
parts. The population growth rate in the district (2.5 percent) is
slightly higher than that of the province (2.3 percent).

Means of Livelihood

Data on the distribution of occupations for the whole Tangerang district were not available. The results of a socioeconomic
survey conducted in Serpong subdistrict (near Ciputat) in 1972 may
give us some idea of the distribution of occupations in the more rural
Tangerang areas (Table 4).

Table 4

Occupations of Heads of the Family
in Serpong subdistrict

Occupation	%	Occupation	%
1. Day Labourer	25.8	8. Government employee	3.7
2. Shopkeeper, peddler	19.1	9. Plantation Worker	2.1
3. Farmer	13.3	10. Employee/private busi-	
4. Labourer + peddler	3.1	ness	3.0
5. Labourer + farmer	4.9	11. Entrepreneur	5.6
6. Peddler + farmer	5.7	12. Other combinations	3.8
7. Farmer + other business	1.6	13. Unemployed	8.3

Source: Proyek Serpong-Tangerang U.K.: "Latihan Kerja Ketrampilan dan
Penyaluran Informasi K.B. pada Tenaga Usia Muda di Kacamatan Serpong"
(Vocational Training and FP information for youth in Serpong subdistrict,
 1975).

The use of total land area in Tangerang district is as follows:

```
Wet paddy land (sawah) ...........................64,088 ha
  --with technical irrigation       45,745 ha
  --with semi-technical irrigation   7,500 ha
  --dependent on rain                6,059 ha
  --other types                      2,755 ha
Dry land (tegal)..................................52,678 ha
Plantation estates................................ 5,285 ha
Brackish fishponds (empangs)...................... 4,500 ha
Forests (mostly mangroves)........................   781 ha
                              Total.....128,222 ha
```

Agriculture is one of the main sources of income in the district. In 1973 the 64,088 ha. paddy land yielded 252,024,000 kg. of rice (dry grain), corresponding to an average of 3,932 kg. per ha. This was more than twice the national production average which was 1,714 kg. per ha in 1973. The production of rice, with an average of 236 kg. per capita, taking into account the prevailing consumption rate in Indonesia (120 kg. per capita annually), is plentiful enough to yield a surplus to be shipped to other regions, especially to the neighboring city of Jakarta.

Other agricultural products are ground-nuts, soybeans, maize, sweet potatoes, and casava, while lowland vegetables and fruits are the principal horticultural items. The 5,285 ha under rubber plantations provide low yields, being mostly in a neglected condition.

Animal husbandry includes poultry keeping and the raising of cattle, sheep, pigs, and rabbits. Especially in Ciputat the raising of pedigree fowls has begun to spring up.

A major source of employment is the industries. The textile industry employed 3,168 laborers and the small industries (with a total of 398 enterprises) engaged 2,522 laborers in 1971. The 15,047 home industry undertakings employed 87,584 workers. Besides these, there were people gathering stones, gravel, and sand to supply material for the flourishing building trade in Jakarta.

Regional Development

Based on a regional planning policy, West Java has been divided into seven "development regions," each with its own characteristics and development approaches. The Bogor-Tangerang-Bekasi region (now well known as Botabek area) had been designed to absorb the overflow of the rapidly expanding industries round about Jakarta. The Botabek development region is also to function as a settlement area for industrial workers, supplier of foodstuff, and ecological "buffer" for metropolitan Jakarta. For this latter purpose Botabek has to painstakingly maintain and improve its "green belts." The Botabek area is also subject to a balanced population policy, with targets for "maximum population capacity" and margin for growth for each district that includes immigration and natural growth.

Tangerang district, as a functional part of Botabek, has to subordinate its development program to a certain extent to the above-mentioned regional plan. In view of this constraint the district administration has formulated a geographic development pattern, according to which the whole district has been partitioned as follows:

(a)   settlement and "green belt" area: the subdistricts of Ciputat, Ciledug, Serpong and Tangerang (partly);

(b)   area for industrial development: the subdistricts of Batuceper, Tangerang, Cikupa, Curug and Pasar Kemis;

(c)   main-food supplying area: the subdistricts of Teluk-naga, Sepatan, Rajeg, Mauk, Kronjo, Kresek and Balaraja with technically irrigated lands;

(d)   suppliers of horticultural products (vegetables and fruits): the subdistricts of Legok, Tigaraksa and part of Serpong.[1]

The significance of the subdistricts of Tangerang and Ciputat as industrial workers' settlement and ecology-based development area might have added to the eligibility of these two places as sites of the population education project of IPPA.

Education and Culture

The average educational level of the people in the district was, as in many other parts of the country, relatively low. A size-able portion (53 percent) of the 10-years-and-older population had never attended school; over one quarter (27 percent) had attended but not completed primary school; 17 percent had passed through primary school; nearly 2 percent had reached junior high, and nearly 1 per-cent senior high level education. College graduates made up only 0.12 percent of the inhabitants; and university graduates, 0.05 percent.

The population of Tangerang district is a mixture of a few ethnic groups. Three languages can be distinguished, each of them predominant in certain localities. Sundanese is spoke mostly in the southern subdistricts of Balaraja, Tigaraksa, Cikupa, Curug, Legok and Serpong, and also in the more centrally situated Pasar Kemis and Tangerang. In the northwestern part of the district (Kronjo, Mauk, Kreseg and Rajeg), the local vernacular is Javanese with a Banten dialect. In the eastern subdistricts, bordering on Jakarta town (Ciputat, Ciledug, Batuceper, Teluknaga), and the northern subdistrict of Sepatan, people mostly speak the well-known Jakarta-Malay. Nevertheless, most Tangerang inhabitants can communicate with each other in the Indonesian national language.

Most of the population, 94 percent to be precise, are Moslems. Hindus and Buddhists (about 4 percent) are scattered throughout the district, while Protestants (1.46 percent) and

---

[1]Subdit PMD: "Kebijaksanaan Pembangunan Desa di Kab. Dt. II Tangerang" (Rural development policy in Tangerang district, IInd level administration, 1976).

Catholics (0.88 percent) are concentrated in a few subdistricts, including Tangerang and Ciputat.

The district has three post-high-school-level institutions, (namely: two Islamic universities in Tangerang and Ciputat, and an aviation school in Curug), five senior high schools (two of which are state-owned), five senior high level vocational schools (for commerce, polytechnics, teachers' training and social work), 21 junior high schools (8 of which are state-owned), five secondary-level vocational schools (commerce, home-economics, agriculture, polytechnics and teacher's training), 356 primary schools (7 of which are private; and ten kindergartens. The number of primary school pupils including religious schools was 70,442 and that of their teachers 1,417 in 1974.

Much care has been placed on religious education; there are three religious teachers' training colleges, six secondary level religious teachers' training schools, four *madrasah sanawiyah* (secondary level) and 203 *madrasah ibtidaiyah* (primary level).

In addition, Tangerang district boasts 145 *pesantrens* (Islamic residential learning centers) with 18,315 *santris* (young learners) under the direct guidance and supervision of 177 *kyais* (religious scholars).[1]

Public Health

Health conditions in rural parts of the district are far from satisfactory. The most frequent diseases in the villages are those of the respiratory and digestive organs, skin diseases, acute infections, and nutrition deficiencies. Local outbursts of smallpox, diarrhea, and eye infections have been reported to have occurred occasionally.

Responsible for the health and medical care in the whole Tangerang district is the *dokabu* (district doctor), assisted by a female physician who is specifically in charge of the supervision of mother and child health (MCH) and family planning activities. There are six hospitals in the district: four in Tangerang town (the district civil hospital, a military hospital, a leper asylum and a small private hospital), one at Mauk and one at Curug.

In Tangerang there are two policlinics for MCH care and family planning services, and each of the other subdistricts has a *Puskesmas* (community health center) which also renders general medical, MCH, and family planning services as well. The health center at Ciputat is, however, the only one having a medical doctor. There are also midwifery clinics in most subdistricts. Those health centers not having a physician themselves are supervised by medical staff members from Tangerang, Mauk, or Ciputat. Paramedical and nonmedical personnel of a midwifery clinic consist of a *bidan* (midwife), an assistant midwife, a MCH home visitor, and certain numbers of family planning fieldworkers (varying from one to six).

---

[1]Proyek Pedesaan U.I.: "Gambaran Umum Kabupaten Tangerang" (General Picture of Tangerang District, 1975).

Legok and Kronjo were the only subdistricts having clinics without a *bidan*, and here assistant midwives were responsible for MCH and family planning services. In ten clinics MCH care was done by the MCH home visitor, who was at the same time in charge of the administration of MCH, and often of that of the family planning clinic as well. Only three clinics had a special administrative assistant.

Family Planning

In all the clinics the *bidan*, assistant midwife, and MCH home visitor are expected to take care of the family planning service. BKKBN gives a compensation to the clinics for these services.

Most of the clinics are open daily for general medical care. There are special days fixed for MCH services, often coinciding with conventional "market days." In a number of clinics some days have been appointed for the *bidani*, or the assistant midwife, to accompany the family planning fieldworker on her home visits for family planning service, at least for examination and registration of those who want to become acceptors.

It was found that a great number of acceptors had been motivated by the family planning fieldworkers. Most of these fieldworkers were born and brought up in the region in which they were employed. Having had senior high school education, they underwent, before assuming their tasks as fieldworkers a three weeks' training at the regional IPPA training center in Bogor. In a few subdistricts (viz., Cikupa and Teluknaga) the *dukuns* (traditional birth attendants) also played a role, though minor, as family planning motivators.

CHAPTER 4

FUNCTIONING OF THE YOUTH PROJECT

ORGANIZATION AND PERSONNEL

The Tangerang Youth Project was under the direction of a project officer who, for the successful implementation of his task, was responsible to the Central Board of IPPA. This project officer was assisted by two technical staff members or supervisors in conducting and supervising the execution of the project. The supervisors were to visit the project localities every two weeks and submit a report on the visit to the project officer.

An advisory committee, consisting of the head of the district administration, the chairman of the National Population Education Project, the head of the training division of BKKBN Headquarters, and a representative of the IPPA Central Executive Committee, was to render consultative services and help the project officer in solving operational problems. They were also entitled to attend the project staff meetings and inspect the financial administration of the project.

To ensure regularity in the course of activities, eight field conductors were appointed. They consisted of local officials and representatives of nongovernmental agencies concerned with the local educational process, namely:

   -- two subdistrict heads (Tangerang and Ciputat)
   -- chairman of the Tangerang branch of BKKBN
   -- chairman of the Tangerang chapter of IPPA
   -- one *Penmas* (Community Education) field officer
   -- coordinator of the Qur'an courses
   -- two coordinators (Tangerang and Ciputat) of the PKK
      (Family Life Education) courses

The tasks of the field conductors were to conduct and directly oversee the implementation of the population education program within the several learning courses (Qur'an recital, PKK, sewing, *Pramuka*, etc.). They were also to draw up monthly reports on the progress of operational activities within the learning course they supervised and bring up suggestions for improvements to the project officer. The two subdistrict heads were also responsible for the overall coordination and supervision of the population education activities

in the learning courses within their respective subdistricts. The
field conductors were expected to take part in the staff meetings,
counsel and give guidance to the instructors, and control financial
arrangements within learning groups.

Seventeen instructors were attached to the same number of
learning courses in the two subdistricts, Tangerang and Ciputat,
all of them being under direct supervision of the field conductors.
They had undergone a two-weeks training beforehand and were responsible for educating the learners (i.e., participants of the learning courses) in the various subjects of population education. The
instructors were also to prepare monthly reports on the progress of
their work.

The Tangerang IPPA branch was the local organization which
backed up the project. Its chairman, the district head's spouse,
had made her influence felt in encouraging local power structures
to give their support to the youth project. That the opening ceremony of the project, for instance, could splendidly be held at the
official residence of the district head was a measure of the support given to the project by the district authority and was an
important step in gaining acceptance of the project in the district.

The project officer and one supervisor were graduates in
social and educational studies. The project officer was senior
lecturer at the Jakarta IKIP and had served for many years as
Executive Secretary of PNPK, the national population education project instituted by the Ministry of Education and Culture. In this
last-mentioned function she had had considerable experience in conducting seminars, workshops, and training in population education,
and this was of great advantage to her in the performance of her
task as the manager of the population education project. One of
the supervisors, a graduate of the Islamic Institute, was a lecturer
at the University of Muhammadiyah. He had also had the opportunity
to participate in various seminars and workshops on population
education.

The team of trainers for the instructors' training consisted,
beside the project officer herself, of personnel of the Population
Education Unit at Bandung IKIP, who had beforehand devoted much of
their time in arranging workshops for the development of learning
materials in the field of population education.

Six out of the nine field conductors had joined the two-week
instructors' training course and fully shared various learning
experiences with the other instructor-to-be trainees. The sixteen
instructors, entrusted with the task of conveying population education
to the participants through the various types of learning courses,
had been selected according to the following criteria:

-- they should be put forward by the managers of the
   respective local organizations which conducted the
   local learning courses

-- their appointment as teachers should be approved of by the head of the district, and

-- they should be prepared to participate in the two-week full-time training course for instructors.

There were great differences in the educational background of the instructors. One of them had completed elementary school, five the junior high school and four the senior high school (or their equivalents), while four had graduated from the university with a *sarjana muda* (equivalent to the bachelor's) degree and one with a *sarjana* (equivalent to the master's) degree.

The training of prospective instructors was held from 27 January to 8 February 1975. The training curriculum included such conceptual subjects as policy, strategy, and implementation of population education out of school; relationship between population education and family planning programs; and population growth related to cultural, socioeconomical, and ecological conditions. It included practical subjects on instruction and learning, such as educational approaches in population education out of school, formulation of instructional objectives, methods in the use of audio-visual aids, and evaluation and learning practices.

Interaction between the trainer and the trainee was maintained through lectures, guided discussions, group consultations, and role-playing. The daily time schedule ran for ten hours from 8:00 a.m. until 10:00 p.m., with two hour breaks for lunch and dinner.

THE CLIENTELE

Number of Participants

The clientele for the population education in the project included young people between the ages of 14 and 25. Initially there was a total of 700 participants, consisting of 370 males and 330 females.

They were located in seventeen learning groups or courses:

-- 6 Qur'anic recital groups with 195 learners (116 males and 79 females)

-- 5 Family Life Education home economics (PKK) classes with 185 learners (64 males and 121 females)

-- 3 sewing classes with 155 learners (110 males and 45 females)

-- 2 scouting groups (*Pramuka*) with 44 Boy Scouts and 36 Girl Guides.

-- 1 language study group with 54 participants (43 males and 11 females)

-- 1 dancing group with 31 members (all females)

The number of members in a group ranged from 20 (in one of the
Qur'an classes) to 54 (in the language study group). Their educational background varied from primary to senior high level. Some
learning groups consisted of learners from the same school level;
others, of mixed groups with different educational backgrounds as
shown in Table 5.

The following notes may provide a rough picture of the socie-
tal characteristics of the participants.

Learners in the Qur'an recital classes were relatively young in
age (mostly adolescents)who devoted their spare time under guidance of
the teacher to Qur'an reading and recital. The Qur'an students mostly
came from more conservative Moslem families. These families were prone
to oppose the family planning concept, although recently developed
interpretations of Islamic tenets had opened the way for justifying
and supporting family planning practices.

Participants enrolled for the Family Life Education/home
economic classes were girls and young women who were interested in
household skills such as cooking, needlework, and washing, and family
health subjects such as hygiene, nutrition, and baby and infant care.
They consisted of newly-married housewives and teenagers who were
preparing for their role as housewives.

Those who attended the sewing class in Garendeng hoped to learn
the arts of pattern cutting and machine-sewing and to prepare themselves for the tailoring trade. To this end they were willing to
pay an apprenticeship fee and to pay as well for the material to be
used for cut-out practices. They foresaw the economic prospects of
the tailoring trade in the teeming metropolis of Jakarta.

The youngsters joining the *Pramuka*-group in Sukasari did so in
the context of the extra-curricular program of the Junior High School
they attended. Officially, enrollment in *Pramuka* was voluntary, but
although no credit was to be given by the school staff for participation of pupils in *Pramuka* almost all of the Junior High students
were engaged in the activities of this scouting organization.

The participants in the English language and dancing groups
were members of the government-sponsored KNPI youth organization
and aimed at making the most of their leisure time by engaging
themselves in social, cultural, and recreational activities.

MAIN FUNCTIONS

Learning Activities

The Qur'an recital courses were located in the villages of
Sukasari and Cipondoh (Tangerang subdistrict), Ciputat, Jombang,
and Cireundeu (Ciputat subdistrict). The original learning activities were exercises in recitals of the Holy Script in original

Table 5

Educational Levels of Clientele

	Levels	Types of Learning Groups and their Locations
Same Level	Primary School	Qur'an classes in Sukasari and Cipondoh;
		Family life education classes in Karawaci and Garendeng;
		the dancing group in Sukasari;
	Junior High School	*Pramuka* group in Sukasari
	Senior High School	Qur'an class in Cireundeu
Mixed Groups	Junior, Senior High, and other schools	Family life education classes in Sukasari;
		Language study group in Sukasari;
		Qur'an class in Ciputat
	Primary, Junior, and Senior High School	Sewing classes in Garendeng;
		Qur'an class in Jombang;
		Pramuka group in Rempoa

Arabic, stressing proper pronunciation, articulation, and intonation.
The advanced study of the Qur'an also included translation and expounding of the Divine Revelations.

Population and family planning education were given once a week
to these recital groups. The population topics were related to relevant teachings of religious tenets.

Learning sessions for family life education and home economics
(PKK) took place in the villages Sukasari, Karawaci, and Gerendeng
(Tangerang subdistrict), and Ciputat (Ciputat subdistrict). The
subjects covered in the sessions included hygiene (personal and
environmental), balanced diet, baby and infant care, organization of
household duties, and maintenance of household accounts. The practical lessons included practices in cooking and dressmaking, but in
some cases were extended to the making of productive handicrafts.
Ex-instructors of PKK courses declared that many topics of population
education could be related to some of the PKK subjects. There are,
for instance, obvious connections between birth and death rates and
baby care and personal hygiene, food production and nutrition problems in family; unemployment problems and family efforts in getting
extra earnings; erosion control and home gardening; and pollution and
environmental problems and garbage disposal and sanitation around
home. (See the next section on learning content.)

Three sewing classes had their location at Gerendeng (Tangerang
subdistrict). They belonged to the privately-owned training course
for tailoring, bearing the name of *"Purnama"* (full shining). The training included the usual practices in designing, cutting, and machine-
sewing. Two hours a week were devoted to population and family planning education in each of the three sewing groups.

Scouting exercises were held with the Pramuka assemblies at the
villages Sukasari (Tangerang subdistrict) and Rempoa (Ciputat subdistrict). The Boy Scouts and Girl Guides practiced Morse and
semaphore signaling, knotting, drilling, camping, and other outdoor
activities. Population education sessions, however, were held in
a classroom setting. The instructors attempted to associate the
Pramuka emphasis on the virtues of country life with ecological
aspects of the population problem. The significance of natural
resources for national, regional, and local development, forest
conservation, and pollution control were topics relevant to both
the population education project and the scouting activities.
Migration, as a manifestation of population dynamics, seemed also
to be an inviting subject, since reports on the experimental settling of *Pramuka*-transmigrants from Jombang (East Java) in Lampung
(Sumatra) were already widely known at that time.

At Sukasari (Tangerang subdistrict) the KNPI cultural groups
were engaged in dancing practices and English language study.
Learning activities in population education took place on Sundays
(8:00-10:00 a.m.) and Fridays (2:30-4:00 p.m.) with the dance group,
and on Fridays only (7:00-9:00 p.m.) with the language group. There
were no direct links between the population and family planning

subjects and the dance practices or language studies. The idea was, in fact, merely to make use of the recreational and cultural gatherings as channels for population education.

Content and Methods

Mention has been made of the attempts to relate the population topics with the regular subjects and activities of the various learning groups. The IPPA and IKIP team that prepared the content of the population education project and designed the training sessions for the instructors came up with a wide range of topics and themes which could be selectively emphasized in different groups according to the interests of the groups and the judgment of the instructors. The range of topics included:

1. Population: what we understand by population, causes of population growth, birth and death rates, migration, population density, age groups and population pyramid, Indonesia's "young" population.

2. Population and socioeconomic factors: primary and secondary needs of man, food, housing and clothing, preconditions for family well-being, family needs and family size.

3. Man as producer and consumer: historical development of production modes, relationship between producer and consumer, factors affecting consumers' needs, production and capital formation, necessity of saving and investment.

4. Population growth and production increase: diminution and splitting up of arable land, production factors, intensification of production methods, advantages of a small family size.

5. Population growth and employment: employment opportunities and available manpower, need for relevant skills, urbanization and its adverse consequences, spirit of self-help in community.

6. Population density and employment: inefficient use of land, population density in towns, internal migration (the so-called "transmigration").

7. Population, health and education: population density and shortage of educational facilities, personal and environmental hygiene, population density and health care facilities.

8. Illiteracy and population increase: educational deprivation and its consequences, illiteracy and poverty, the problem of drop-outs, youth delinquency.

9. Religion, culture, and population density: religious teachings on population issues and family planning

concepts, population growth and cultural norms, responsible parenthood, population growth and the social order.

10. Ecology of human life: position of man in the biological
    food cycle, the effect of population increase on this
    biological cycle.

11. Man and natural resources: utilizability of natural
    resources, necessity for its preservation, population
    growth and dissipation of resources.

12. Pollution and erosion: polluted water and air, population
    increase and pollution of the environment, disforestation
    and erosion, consequences of erosion, laying-out of "green
    belts," reforestation.

It was, indeed, a fairly comprehensive curriculum for a six-
month program with 48 session-hours. The coverage of the topics
and the emphasis given to each, of necessity, varied widely for
different topics and different groups.

The instructional methodology was dominated by oral presentation, usually followed by learners' questions. The discussions
were, however, conducted not without constraints and difficulties.
Most of the instructors ascribed those difficulties to the hetero-
geneity of the participants' educational background and knowledge,
shortage of time, and lack of group discipline.

Other educational modes occasionally employed to support the
lectures and discussions were:

-- task assignments
-- study tours
-- visits to local people
-- readings on population issues
-- the writing of essays, and
-- encouragements to save.

Participants were instructed to bring to their classes pictures, articles, and reports pertaining to population and family
planning issues from newspapers and magazines. Some groups were
also assigned the task of collecting population data in the area.
In some cases study trips were made to visit industrial enterprises,
factories, and particularly family planning clinics. Budget limitations and time constraints were, however, reported as impediments
to the study-tour program.

RELATIONSHIP WITH OTHER INSTITUTIONS

The pattern and mechanism of collaboration among government
and nongovernment agencies in Tangerang district, as in other
parts of the country, was not of such a nature that a very close
working relationship could be established. The Tangerang Youth

Project was planned and designed essentially within IPPA. Naturally, various bodies such as BKKBN, PNPK, and other relevant government agencies were consulted; the district administration, in particular, was kept posted about the project and informed of its progress. The project could not have gotten off the ground and continued without the support of the relevant government agencies and the district authorities, but it was a passive approval of the project rather than an active collaboration and partnership.

It goes without saying that the Tangerang Youth Project developed a close relationship with nongovernmental agencies and voluntary organizations that allowed themselves to become the "vehicle" for the IPPA project by letting their learning groups become partners in the project. But nongovernmental agencies other than the "vehicle" organizations seemed to play an insignificant role in the project. One reason for these disparate reactions, advanced by former project personnel, was that a certain amount of financial benefit accrued to the organizations that became direct collaborators as the "vehicle" groups; other organizations who were not offered a financial inducement were apathetic and disinterested, especially because only the "vehicle" organizations enjoyed the financial benefits.

THE IMPACT OF THE PROJECT

The nature of the objectives and expected outcome of the project make it difficult to assess accurately the impact and the results of the project. The expected outcome of the project falls into two main categories:

(a)   increased awareness, understanding, and knowledge about population topics among the participant youths; and

(b)   development of a feasible approach for population education among the out-of-school youth, enhancing IPPA's capacity to carry out such youth activities, and achieving a multiplier effect in terms of population awareness in communities and of the capabilities for effective youth activities among the collaborating organizations.

An opinion survey conducted by the Bandung IKIP evaluation team among the participant youths after the implementation of the project shed some light on how well the first category of objectives had been achieved. An overwhelming majority of the participants held a positive attitude toward the project and seemed to grasp the basic concepts and themes propounded through the instructional sessions. A full 100 percent of the respondents considered population education "very important" or "important" for themselves. Ninety-eight percent of the respondents thought that population problems of the country called for urgent and immediate action, and 38 percent said that population increase in the country caused them personal anxiety. Almost all the respondents (98 percent) felt that everyone should participate in the family planning program. A summary of responses of the participants is given below.

Opinion	Percentage of Respondents Agreeing
Most appropriate age for boys to get married: 25-30 years	59
Most appropriate age for girls to get married: 20-25 years	74
Not in favor of young people marrying under age of 17	91
Children should earn a living before they get married	96
Family planning not contrary to religious teachings	89
Family planning not contrary to social customs	83
Disagree with the opinion that many children would bring more prosperity	57
Intend to encourage their children to practice family planning	66
Expect only three children in their children's family	78
A way out should be found to overcome the adversities of population explosion at present	89
Not feel inferior having only one child	77
Not want to follow the example of families who have more than six children	59
Would not hesitate to practice family planning	77
Fewer children would mean relatively less expenditure for their schooling	91
Fewer children would mean greater chances to acquire well-being for the children	87

To what extent the expected multiplier effect was achieved is even harder to evaluate than the change of attitude among the youngsters. The following points, however, emerge from the Tangerang experience.

1. It is evident that existing organizations and activities involving youth can be utilized as "vehicles" for channeling population and family planning education for youth. In fact, collaboration with organizations that have a range of goals and activities inherently interesting to young people (and responding to their perceived social and economic needs) appears to be the only effective approach for population education among youth. An independent and narrowly conceived population education effort with its own organizational and operational paraphernalia is bound to be expensive and is unlikely to maintain the interest and motivation of the participants.

2. IPPA gained valuable experience in planning and organizing a population education effort for youth and developed a core of people in its own staff and in the collaborating organization (particularly, Bandung IKIP) with experience and expertise in planning, designing, and implementing population education projects for youth. In addition, there was a compendium of content materials

for population education for youth, training materials for instructors, and resource materials for the youth participants. Practical experiences were also gathered in instructional methods and processes, the background and interests of different youth clienteles, and collaboration with voluntary organizations conducting different types of youth programs. This foundation of experience and knowledge was relied upon by IPPA in initiating new youth projects in other parts of the country. (See next chapter.)

3. It stands to reason that the voluntary organizations that had made their learning groups available for the implementation of the population and family planning education project were the most affected by the activities of the project. Involvement in the project helped Muhammadiyah strengthen its information and motivation program for family planning. This program, which is incorporated within the *Majlis PKU* (Council for People's Welfare Development, one of the ten executive councils of Muhammadiyah) is concerned with giving information on family planning, primarily in religiously devout circles of society, which look questioningly at family planning and consequently have strong doubts about the admissibility of contraceptive practices. Religious learning sessions are, therefore, considered among the most suitable for discussions of family planning issues and the underlying population and family problems. Experiences gained in providing population and family planning education to recital groups also proved to be effective, and this led to the launching of several population education projects by Muhammadiyah making use of recital group sessions. The projects were located at Medan (North Sumatra), Jakarta, Bandung (West Java), Klaten (Central Java), Gunung Kidul (Yogyakarta) and Sidoardjo (East Java), and were conducted in cooperation with BKKBN, PNPK and other institutions.

4. It is unlikely that the youth project had any significant direct and immediate effect on family planning practices or acceptor rates in the several communities. The participant youths themselves did not generally belong to the target groups for family planning services and they were not expected to play a role in the provision of family planning services. It is possible, however, that the participation of a group of youths from a community in the project helped enhance the awareness of population issues and family planning measures in the community. Indeed, there are anecdotes of recalcitrant relatives and friends of the participant youths among "eligible couples" being persuaded to adopt contraceptive methods. It is a reasonable speculation that the concentration of a critical number of young adults--conscious, well-informed, and articulate about population issues and family planning practices--in a village community would have, in the long run, a salutary effect on village attitudes towards family planning.

COSTS AND FINANCE

Almost all of the funds needed for the implementation of the Tangerang Youth Project came from IPPF (International Planned Parenthood Federation). The total amount of this aid was US$12,000.

This donation was spent on the principal project activities, such as instructors' training, population education learning sessions, and also for the remuneration of supervisory and administration personnel. Another financial input came from the district administration. This contribution, amounting to Rp.35,000 (about US$90) was used primarily for providing small incentives in the form of writing materials to the learning groups. The management of the "Purnama" sewing class also contributed, especially for the purchase of *batik* dresses to be awarded to participants with outstanding learning achievements.

The budgeted expenditures and the actual amounts spent are shown in Table 6.

Table 6

Expenditures of the Tangerang Youth Project

	Category	Budget Estimate	Actual Expenditure
(1)	Personnel	Rp. 809,000	Rp. 683,250
(2)	Preparatory activities	165,000	77,000
(3)	Instructors' training	1,713,500	1,648,905
(4)	Operational costs of educational program	875,000	987,945
(5)	Learning and administrative equipment	1,267,500	1,377,000
(6)	Evaluation	150,000	165,900
	Total	Rp 4,980,000	4,940,000
		(Approximately US$12,000.00)	

A superficial calculation (that of dividing the total cost of Rp. 4,940,000 by the number of participants, 700), reveals the unit cost per participant to be Rp. 7,057.14, or approximately US$17.50. The above-mentioned cost figures, however, do not include the rental equivalencies of borrowed premises and equipment or take into account the monetary value of services rendered by volunteers. Similarly, there is no account taken of the so-called "opportunity-costs"; i.e., losses for such things as foregone opportunities, earnings, and rentals, on various components, human and nonhuman, of the pilot project. To see the unit cost of US$17.50 in the perspective of the local economy, it may be noted that the annual per capita income in West Java in mid-70's was about US$68 and the monthly cash earning of a rural laborer was in the order of US$25.00.

There are still other considerations which cannot justify a
simple dividing of the total cost by the number of participants in
order to get the unit cost. In the above calculation, overhead
charges like expenses for instructors' training and acquisition
of durable equipment have been regarded as if they were utiliz-
able only for the duration of the pilot project.

The cost structure of any expansion of the Tangerang approach
will certainly be modified in various ways. The initial preparation
and planning costs will, almost by definition, be reduced substantially; similarly the costs involved in the preparation of learning
materials. The fact that the training of Tangerang instructors in
Ciloto, 120 kilometers away from the project locations, by a team
of trainers who came from Bandung suggests that arrangements could
be made to cut travel costs considerably.

As for the actual operational costs of the project (i.e.,
those pertaining to the actual learning activities of participants),
it should be kept in mind that the expenses for incentives, per
diems, honoraria, rentals, and so forth will vary from location
to location. Many of these expenditures will depend on the distance
of the project sites from the headquarters, local conditions,
technical requirements of the operation, personal commitments of
workers, and the availability of free-of-charge resources. Overhead costs at the headquarters will probably show a tendency to
go up with any increase of distance to the project site. Other
costs, such as remunerations for operational services and purchase
of learning materials, will vary, partly depending on the values
of the concerned individuals: whether it is the "modern" busi-
ness-like individualism or the traditional "*gotong-royong*"(mutual
support) view of life that motivates them.

CHAPTER 5

EXPANSION OF THE YOUTH PROJECT

A NEW PROJECT DESIGN

A five-day workshop, held in November 1975 with the participation of IPPA personnel and others concerned with the youth project, examined the implementation and results of the Tangerang Youth Project and the possibility of its expansion. Members of the workshop agreed on the feasibility and desirability of an expansion, beginning with other areas in the Tangerang district itself. However, they felt that the Tangerang project did not reach the illiterate youths, a larger group than the literate youths and also probably in greater need of population awareness. The workshop, therefore, recommended that new youth activities should concentrate on illiterate youngsters, both male and female. The nature of the new projects as envisaged by the workshop was akin to functional literacy courses. The report of the workshop stated that the youth project

> ...should be aimed at raising the standard of life
> of the youth community through the imparting of
> knowledge, and functionalization of reading skills
> in daily life, so as to achieve well being of the
> family and generate acceptance of the small family
> concept as a solution to relevant problems.[1]

More specifically, the objectives suggested were as follows:

(a)   that the learner understand the causes and consequences
      of population growth;

(b)   that he be able to read and write, and make simple
      calculations;

(c)   that he can make his reading, writing and other skills
      more functional in his life.[2]

_____

[1] "Workshop on Tangerang Youth Project" (Report) I.P.P.A.,
Jakarta (1975).

[2] Ibid.

The workshop proposed that the participants be in the age range of 15-35 in order to permit young couples as well as women still in their fertile phase to enjoy the benefit of the project. Variations in the environmental setting for the learning units were to be taken into account by distinguishing among three categories, namely, the coastal fishing village, the industrial area, and the agrarian area.

IPPA, however, did not accept the recommendations of the workshop, shortage of funds and the lack of facilities and personnel being advanced as two main reasons. It appears that launching a functional education program for illiterate youth, even on a limited scale, was considered by IPPA to be too large and difficult a task for its own resources and area of competence.

IPPA's follow-up of the Tangerang project consisted of two types of youth projects, both of which benefitted from the experiences of Tangerang and yet were somewhat different in emphasis and approach. These were (a) a project for involving youth leaders in population education, called the *Biduk Kencana Remaja*, and (b) a project that combined skill training for girls with family life education. We turn to these projects in the following section.

A Modified Expansion Plan

In March-April 1976, six months after the completion of the Tangerang project, IPPA personnel and other collaborators participated in what was called a group meeting on curriculum development. This meeting drew up a modified plan for expanding the youth project.

The main features of this program were as follows:

(a)   approaching youth leaders in out-of-school settings;

(b)   equipping these leadership elements with knowledge and understanding of population problems and utilizing them for propagation of population knowledge and awareness among members of youth groups;

(c)   taking educational and informational activities down to the peripheral level (i.e., remote rural areas);

(d)   avoidance of dualisms in management by taking the implementation of the program in its own hand.

The new program differed from the Tangerang project by its focus on youth leaders as the instrument for propagation of ideas in their own youth organizations, and, in its apparent abandonment of the "vehicle" approach of using existing agencies and organizations.

The new youth program, given the name Biduk Kencana Remaja[1] (Youth Golden Vessel), was planned to be started in May, 1976 in selected locations in metropolitan Jakarta; West, Central and East Java; Yogyakarta and Bali. The successive phases of the program

_____

[1]An acronym formed by taking parts of the words "BIdang kependu-DUKan KEluarga bereNCANA" (the domain of population education and family planning).

implementation were as follows:

(a)   stock-taking of existent youth organizations and
      selection of their leaders for participation in the
      program;

(b)   training seminar for the selected youth leaders;

(c)   evaluation of the training seminar;

(d)   participation of group members in population and
      family planning education activities.

The youth leaders, selected from the respective project
areas, were to undergo a training session for one week. After having
completed the training they were to return to the project localities
to assume their task of propagating among fellow youths in their
communities knowledge and understanding of population problems. The
community youths thus contacted were, in turn, to disseminate their
own understanding and knowledge of population issues to their peers,
at least three within one month. It was expected that in this way
a community outreach could be attained of 5,400 youths per project
area within six months (5 leaders per project area x 60 youths in
two groups x 3 peers per month x 6 months).

The allocation of projects, number of youth leaders to be
trained, site of training, and number of group members to be involved in the program, are indicated in Table 7.

Table 7

Scope of "BIDUK KENCANA REMAJA" Project in 1976-1977

Province	No. of Project Areas	No. of Trained Leaders	Place of Training	No. of Groups	No. of Group Members
Jakarta Metropolitan	1	5	Bandung	10	300
West Java	2	10	Bandung	20	600
Central Java	2	10	Semarang	20	600
Yogyakarta Special Region	1	5	Semarang	10	300
East Java	2	10	Surabaya	20	600
Bali	1	5	Surabaya	10	300
Total	9	45		90	2700

This Biduk Kencana Remaja Program (BKR) was coupled with
another IPPA activity, i.e., the premarriage counseling program.
This counseling program involved the selection and training of three
counselors from each BKR project location. The counselors could

supplement the instructional efforts of the youth leaders and provide necessary information and guidance to youths in the area in need of specific premarital or postmarital advice.

The expenditure for the BKR-*cum*-premarital counseling program had been budgeted as follows:

(a)	Evaluation of youth involvement in family planning	$ 4,838.
(b)	Training seminar for youth leaders	10,299.
(c)	Training-*cum*-workshop on premarriage counseling	4,275.
(d)	Youth leaders' involvement project	8,407.
(e)	Pre-marriage counseling project	3,934.
		$ 31,753.

The case study team have had the opportunity to visit two locations of the BKR project, namely:

(a) Sidoharjo subdistrict in Central Java, and

(b) The Gemblakan-bawah ward in Yogyakarta town.

PROJECT IMPLEMENTATION IN CENTRAL JAVA

The BKR project in Central Java province was implemented in selected subdistricts (*kecamatans*) of two districts, Wonogiri and Sragen.

Ten youth leaders, selected from ten *kecamatans* in two districts mentioned, underwent a one-week training seminar in Semarang, which was designed to prepare the selected youths for communication and information tasks within, as well as outside, the youth organizations in their respective localities.

Criteria and requirements for the selection of trainees were as follows:

(a) age between 15 and 35 (males as well as females),

(b) good health condition (physical and mental),

(c) preferably unmarried and not yet having his/her own family,

(d) being a leader of a youth organization,

(e) initiative, creative abilities, and open-mindedness,

(f) ability in communication and human relations,

(g) sense of social responsibility and interest in population
     problems,

(h) willingness to share, after completing the training,
     knowledge and skills acquired in the training with other
     youths in their localities on an voluntary basis,
     and

(i) willingness to draw up and submit monthly reports on
     their project activities to the local IPPA branch.

The selection was made by the IPPA branch, in consultation
with governmental agencies concerned with youth affairs in the district, as well as the local council of the KNPI (National Youth
Committee).[1]

The curriculum of the residential training in Semarang, which
had been developed by the National Training and Research Center of
IPPA, included two main subject areas:

(1) family planning concepts in relation to the significance
     of small family size for national development,

(2) population issues having a bearing on circumstances in
     the youth's future life.

Of practical importance also was the development of communication skills which would enable the trainees successfully to convey
the relevant ideas and concepts to their groupmates.

After completion of the training the ten selected youths were
assigned one BKR working area each. Each of the two districts had
five working areas, where two youth groups were formed in each. One
group consisted of 30 members.

The trained BKR leaders were called *pembina* (group conductors);
their tasks were mainly to persuade their fellow-members of the following:

-- the importance of small family size as the nation's
    way of life,

-- the need for being alert to the consequences of rapid
    population growth, especially those affecting the
    future of youth,

-- the importance of parental responsibility for the
    pursuing of family well-being.[2]

The *pembinas* were also to encourage the group members to
involve other young people in the communication activities, so that

---

[1]IPPA directions (April 1976).

[2]Ibid.

the pertinent ideas and opinions would be shared widely among the
youth in each community.

Each BKR group member, called *pengganda* ("propagators"), was
to communicate the ideas and concepts to at least three of his peers
within one month. Thus, as noted above, it was expected that within
six months an information outreach of 5,400 youths in each *kabupatan*
project could be achieved.

BKR in Sidoharjo Subdistrict

The BKR activities in one location (the subdistrict of Sidoharjo in Wonogiri district) were coordinated and guided by the head
of the local family planning field team of the national family planning program (BKKBN). This young man happened to be a dynamic individual, devoted to his task as a family planning field agent, and
highly interested in working with local youth. The subdistrict head
(*camat*) of Sidoharjo also was a person who appreciated the significance of youth activities and gave great encouragement and support
to the BKR project and worked closely with the coordinator of BKR.
Together the *camat* and the coordinator constituted an effective
team and were largely responsible for the accomplishments of the
project.

The five youth leaders selected for training from the area
already belonged to informal sports, cultural, recreational, or
social service groups in the locality. The training of the youth
leaders, the cooperation of the *camat* and the local family planning
head, and the availability of a small financial support (Rp. 100.00
per population education session per subgroup) were important factors
that helped in the planning and systematization of the group activities and led to a formalization of the group structure. The active
youth participants in the activities numbered about 200 and were
divided into several subgroups according to the special interests of
the members. Various sports groups included teams in soccer, volley
ball, badminton, and table tennis. Cultural group activities embraced
Javanese and Malay orchestral exercises, *reyog* (traditional horseman
and lion dance), and drum-band. The art of traditional home and
festival decoration were also practiced by one group. Another group
was the *sinoman*, whose traditional job was to render assistance and
services to fellow-villagers at the time of wedding parties, circum-
cision ceremonies, and so on.

Population activities in these groups consisted of two or
three sessions in a month in which the project coordinator (who was
also the local family planning program head) spoke to the sugroups.
Monthly sessions for premarriage counseling were also held for those
who were interested. The group members themselves claimed to have
propagated population messages among youngsters in their respective
villages. The IPPA branch in the district occasionally provided
films and exhibits to be used in the group sessions. The branch,
of course, provided a small subsidy for each instructional session
to each group for the twelve-month duration of the project.

The groups and their multifarious activities, which predated the population project, continued after the official conclusion of the IPPA project and the cessation of the small subsidy. It is likely that the IPPA support and attention, though small in quantity, performed a catalytic role and strengthened the youth groups by supporting the leadership, giving the members practical organizational experience, and bringing to the attention of the local administration the significance of youth activities. The groups also learned to generate resources for themselves by charging small fees for sports events, cultural performances, and social services.

Comments on Sidoharjo BKR

It was difficult for the study team to ascertain the extent of population education that continued after the completion of the IPPA project. The coordinator reported that periodically he took advantage of group gatherings to bring up population topics. The study team had the impression, however, that the enthusiasm for the continuation of population discussion was on the wane among the groups and that the utility and importance of continuous discussion (in a purely information and communication context) among the same participants was not very clear to the group members.

The study team also found that most of the youth participants in the group activities had completed at least primary education and many had completed the higher secondary level. The so-called out-of-school youths in the groups were those who did not go for a higher level of education after completing primary or secondary education. Most of them were employed in various wage-earning occupations (rather than farming) and many had white collar occupations as teachers, clerks, shop assistants and so on. Girls were well represented in the groups. Youths belonging to the lower socioeconomic strata--illiterate or primary school dropout boys and girls belonging to families of landless farm laborers, subsistence farmers, petty tradesmen, or drivers of pedicabs--seemingly were not members of the groups. These youths were probably not excluded by design. The social position of the participants, their interests and life style, and the somewhat exclusive nature of the group activities (cultural and recreational activities requiring certain amount of leisure and even personal expense) did not help the participation of the most underprivileged groups of youths in the project.

PROJECT IMPLEMENTATION IN YOGYAKARTA

The BKR project in Yogyakarta region was located in the Yogyakarta town. This city, in ancient time the capital of a sultanate, is at present the seat of the regional government of the same name.

This city is more densely populated than the country's capital: while the population density in Jakarta in 1971 was 7,726 per square kilometer; Yogyakarta accommodated 10,531 people on the average per square kilometer.[1]

[1]REPELITA II (Second Five Years Plan), Jakarta (1974).

The town is divided into 14 *kacamatans*,with populations varying from 13,000 (kac. Kotagede) to 44,000 (kac. Gondokusuman). Each
kacamatan is partitioned in a number of *rukun kampungs* (urban wards),
each of them headed by a *ketua RK* (ward-boss).

The BKR project in Yogyakarta town had a number of different
locations. Five *rukun kampungs* had been chosen as sites of the project, namely: Suryatmajan, Gamelan, Iromejan, Gemblakan Bawah and
Panembahan. The project was later extended to additional wards, although additional youth leaders were not trained for these wards.

Five young men considered to have met the requirements for
their prospective function as *pembina*,had been trained at the provincial training center in Semarang together with the ten other trainees
from Central Java. After the training they were given the responsibility of conducting BKR activities in one or two *rukun kampungs*.

The Yogyakarta branch of IPPA was in charge of the execution
of the program in the project area. The provincial IPPA chapter,
beside exercising direct supervision, also rendered supporting and
consultative services to the project.

The educational program covered a broad variety of relevant
subjects. Population issues and family planning matters constituted
the core topics, but other youth-related subjects were also included
in the program. The monthly records of the Yogyakarta IPPA branch
had, for instance, made mention of the following topics:

-- mental health among youth
-- the menace of venereal disease
-- addiction to drugs
-- the role of youth in community development
-- upbringing of the young generation
-- youth companionship (between both sexes)
-- early detection of cancer

These topics were presented by physicians, police officers,
and community leaders who served as guest lecturers. IPPA officials
at the provincial level and other competent functionaries occasionally
gave lectures pertaining to family planning and population matters,
such as:

-- economic consequences of population growth,
-- ecological problems,
-- demographic data and their implications,
-- the Islamic view on population matters, and
-- anatomy of human reproduction.

Lectures were usually followed by opportunities to raise
relevant questions. Charts, slides, and filmstrips were used whenever applicable.

Instructional hours were alternated with such recreational
activities as volley ball, table tennis, chess, badminton, folk
songs, and drama performances. The female section of BKR youth were

also engaged in cooking, sewing, flower arrangement and *janur* (young coconut-leaves) decoration practices. There were *arisan* (savings groups in which the proceeds are distributed among members by periodic lottery) gatherings as well, which were held periodically.

The various activities were organized and managed by the lady chairman of the Yogyakarta IPPA branch, who was *ex officio* executive officer of the project. In order to enhance the spirit of solidarity among participants and to maintain a sense of belonging to the BKR movement, friendly gatherings and social meetings were held, occasionally coupled with games and contests. Such events were usually attended by IPPA board members and certain town officials (particularly the ward bosses).

The Yogyakarta BKR project organized, as part of the program, study trips for the youth participants. The trip to Kaliurang in August 1976, for instance, was taken advantage of by paying home visits to study family sizes in community. In December 1977 BKR groups from four locations went on a tour to Sragen, a district in Central Java where a BKR project was being run by the local IPPA. The trip program included discussions (on population and family planning matters) at Taman Jurug, and table tennis, volley ball and soccer matches at Karangmalang (one *kacamatan* town in Sragen district). The traveling BKR groups were accompanied by the head of the social welfare section of the Yogyakarta municipality office, members of the municipal council, IPPA and BKKBN staff, and a few newsmen.

The Yogyakarta project also provided premarriage counseling. But, although PKBI headquarters had already given directions for integrating the premarriage counseling program within the BKR project (with selected group members as counseling clients), there was no regular counseling service program going on in the project area. IPPA staff members in Yogyakarta found that youngsters who did not yet have a definite marriage plan were not interested in attending the premarriage counseling. Instead of providing direct counseling services, the project management, therefore, turned to other approaches such as organizing lectures and discussions, distributing bulletins, and radio programs on premarital topics broadcast by RRI (National Radio Network) on the first Monday of every month.

After the conclusion of the IPPA-sponsored project, funds for honoraria, travel allowances, and back-up material were no longer available. The BKR organization, therefore, had to continue its activities on a self-sustaining basis and to raise funds on its own. For that purpose, a project had been initiated to start a collective tailoring business, by training 25 male and the same number of female BKR participants in the tailoring trade. The sewing machines and other equipment needed were provided by IPPA; two sewing instructors were hired to conduct a regular training course once a week. Mimeographed manuals, liberally illustrated, were provided to the trainees.

The tailoring training was scheduled to run for 14 weeks. Male and female groups were instructed separately, using the same premises and training facilities but on different days.

It was anticipated that products of the prospective tailoring shop would find a ready market in Yogyakarta town itself. Authorities of the municipal office had reportedly undertaken to place orders with the BKR organization for the purchase of uniforms for their office personnel

PLANNED BKR PROJECTS OUTSIDE JAVA AND BALI

IPPA has decided to expand the geographical coverage of the BKR project and has drawn up plans for conducting projects of the same type in North Sulawesi, South and West Kalimantan, and North Sumatra. The objectives, project design, target population, and so forth are to be the same as those for the BKR projects already implemented in Java and Bali.

A slight difference is that in each province there would be only one project area, to be managed by the local IPPA branch, and that each project area would have ten *pembinas* with the same number of working areas. One *pembina* would lead two working groups.

In each working area 60 (2 x 30) members of the working groups would serve as *penggandas* ("multipliers" or propagators), who are expected to propagate population and family planning concepts to 18 (6 x 3) other youths within six months. It is anticipated that, in this way, a community outreach of 10,800 (10 x 2 x 30 x 6 x 3) young people could be attained in each project area.[1] The working groups are to hold meetings four times a month, three times on the main BKR topics and once on the premarriage counseling program.

The project activities were scheduled as follows:

-- training and workshop for premarriage
   counselors   March 1978
-- training seminar for youth leaders
   (BKR)   May 1978
-- implementation of the main program
   of BKR project   July-Dec. 1978
-- implementation of the premarriage
   counseling program   July-Dec. 1978[2]

The total budget estimate for the whole project was $22,724, consisting of $14,542 for training and $8,182 for other educational and informational activities.

---

[1]
IPPA directions (February, 1978).

[2]
Ibid.

SKILL TRAINING AND POPULATION EDUCATION FOR GIRLS

A special project undertaken also under the auspices of the Yogyakarta chapter of IPPA was different from the larger youth involvement effort described earlier in its aim of combining population and family life education with training in sewing for young girls.   The project was planned in recognition of the fact that youths from low-income families, particularly girls, were not attracted to educational projects that did not help improve their economic situation.

The specific objectives of the new project implemented in late 1977 were stated to be the following:

-- to provide information to young girls in rural areas on concepts and methods of family planning;

-- to give them understanding of the relationship between population growth and family and national welfare;

-- to provide them with sewing skill so as to equip them with a proficiency needed for earning a living.

The target groups consisted of four groups of 48 girls each. Thus, 192 trainees from villages in Wonosari district near Yogyakarta were to be included in the project.   Actual enrolment turned out to be 207 girls.

Each group underwent a one-month intensive training course in sewing interspersed by family planning learning sessions.   The four groups were trained successively,   thus making use of the same instructors and sewing machines.   Before performing their respective tasks, the family planning educators and sewing skill instructors had to follow an orientation course themselves for two days.   For the training course six sewing machines were purchased by IPPA and the materials for cut-out and sewing practice were supplied.   The machines would remain the property of IPPA, to be used for similar training programs in other places.

Following completion of the one-month training the trainees were expected to practice their skill, still remaining under the supervision of the project management.   It was hoped that the village administration would help some of the trainees in acquiring working capital for starting sewing shops.

The budget estimate for this project was as follows:

		Rp.
--	Preparatory work	100,000
--	Purchase of sewing machines	300,000
--	Orientation course for sewing trainers and FP-educators	200,000
--	Hiring of two sewing trainers	320,000
--	Honoraria/travel allowance for FP educators	96,000

		Rp
--	Supervisory visits	40,000
--	Honoraria for project management	60,000
--	Purchase of materials for practical training	384,000
--	FP learning materials (inc. AVA)	100,000
--	Stationary and report forms	60,000
--	Translation of reports	40,000

$$\text{Rp.} \quad 1,700,000$$
(equivalent to US$4,150.)

The funds came from IPPF through the national IPPA.

Information collected by a sample survey of 60 trainees by the Yogyakarta IPPA office reveals something of the background of the trainees.

The majority of respondents came from big families: 93.4 percent of their families had more than three children. The numbers of children in the families ranged from 2 to 11, with an average of 6.4, while the mode number was 6 (represented by 20 percent of the families).

The educational levels of respondents were as follows:

	percent
-- not completed primary school	1.7
-- completed primary school	63.3
-- not completed junior high school	3.3
-- still attending junior high school	3.3
-- completed junior high school	21.7
-- still attending senior high school	6.7

The age-range was from 14 to 24, with an average of 18.1 and a mode of 17 years (30 percent of participants). Thirty-five percent of the respondents earned an income from farming and 3 percent were peddlers, while the remaining 62 percent had no earning of their own and depended on their families for support. Seventy-eight percent came from farmers' families and 20 percent had one of the parents as a government employee. A great part (80 percent) of the respondents had enroled after being informed by village officials of the opening of the forthcoming family-planning-cum-sewing course.

Nearly four-fifths of them tried, after having completed the sewing course, to make clothes on their own, whether for other persons (53 percent) or for themselves (27 percent). One-sixth of the respondents decided to seek ways for improving further the sewing skills gained so far.

The study team did not have the opportunity to visit the groups, since the project had already ended at the time of the team's visit. Discussion with concerned IPPA personnel at the Yogyakarta chapter indicated that the sewing courses elicited enthusiastic response from young girls in villages and provided them with an opportunity to get some population and family life education. It was unlikely that a month-long sewing course would give the trainees the proficiency needed to earn an income or that there would be such

demand for sewing skills in the communities as to keep all the
trainees occupied. Moreover, despite the intention of the organizers
of the project to attract members of the underprivileged groups, girls
from the poorest families evidently did not participate. The educational level of the participants and the fact that two-thirds of them
depended entirely on their families for support (unlikely among the
poorest section) support this contention.

CHAPTER 6

CONCLUSIONS AND LESSONS

Creating an awareness and understanding of the population problem and its implications for the welfare and development of the nation among the out-of-school youth and involving them in the national population program is one of the main functions of IPPA. Since 1974, IPPA has been engaged in discovering and developing viable and feasible approaches and methods, consonant with its resources and its role in the national scheme to reach the out-of-school youth population. The experimental Tangerang Youth Project and the subsequent youth leaders project and the skill training project for girls represent the efforts of IPPA to make the large out-of-school youth population the beneficiaries of increased knowledge and understanding of population and family planning issues.

It is clear that the objectives of the youth projects were defined narrowly by IPPA and were confined to the propagation of knowledge and understanding that justify and support the national program for population control. Activities designed to improve the overall social and economic situation of out-of-school youth or projects concerned with the broader goals of rural development with an eventual bearing on the attitudes, values, and behavior of the concerned groups with regard to family planning were seen as outside the scope of IPPA responsibilities. Population education for young people, of course, could not be totally isolated from other aspects of their lives and it was found necessary to utilize the "vehicles" of other activities and organizations to carry the messages of IPPA to the young people. In some instances, activities such as skill-training were sponsored by IPPA to facilitate population education. However, information and communication on population matters remained the goal of IPPA youth projects; other activities and organizations were instruments that served this central goal.

The objectives and strategies of the projects also did not embrace the prospect of any active role of the youth participants, either in the national family planning effort or in broader development activities for the benefit of the community at large. Some multiplier effects of the projects were envisaged, but these were again in terms of communication and information. That is, it was expected that participants would help propagate the message to other nonparticipant youths. The young people were the target of the population education effort so that they could make appropriate personal decisions regarding their family life.

Possibilities were not envisioned of harnessing the human resources represented by the youth for the national population program
and of evolving integrated approaches to family welfare through the
involvement of youth. The youth projects, therefore, have to be
judged and the experiences assessed from the narrow perspective of
population education.

FULFILLMENT OF THE OBJECTIVES

Objectives of the projects in terms of the dissemination of
knowledge and understanding of population issues to the participants
appear to have been achieved. The responses to the questionnaire
survey of the participants in the Tangerang project show that the
participants generally came up with the "desirable" statements.
Responses were not available from the other projects. However, it is
likely that they would not be very different, since the participants
were subjected to the same type of instructional methods and content
and the essential messages were rather straightforward. It has to be
borne in mind that the projects constituted a substantial effort and
commitment of resources to reach a relatively small proportion of
the youth in the country. (The direct financial costs for the three
projects totalled approximately US$48,000 for 3,600 participants.)

The significance of "appropriate" responses of the participants
in terms of their personal behavior, their values, and the eventual
impact on their families is not possible to determine at this stage.
It was also not possible to determine the multiplier effect of the
projects in reaching nonparticipant youths.

LEARNING CONTENT AND METHOD

The "curriculum" worked out for the Tangerang project included
a fairly exhaustive list of topics, which obviously could not be given
a full or adequate treatment within the time limit with the actual
personnel and resources of the projects. Selectivity was obviously
applied and the treatment of the topics certainly varied widely in
different situations. Nor was it necessary to cover the topics
exhaustively. The aim was not to make population experts out of
the young participants but to give them a basic understanding and
awareness of population issues so that they became sensitive to
these issues and were able to make intelligent and informed personal
and collective decisions on these issues.

Experience gained in the three projects seems to indicate that
selection of materials and topics for different groups with varied
interests and educational background needs careful thought and judgment on the part of the organizers. It is not enough to present a
mere laundry list of topics with the selection left to chance. Special
attention must be given to finding ways of relating the topics to the
specific interests and backgrounds of the participants.

A rigid didactic approach often fails to reach the audience,
especially an audience without substantial formal education back-

ground. The "instructors" and "discussion leaders" need ideas, as
well as a supply of materials and teaching aids on interesting ways
of presenting materials and approaches to relating the instructional
themes to the daily life of the learners.

SERVING THE UNDERPRIVILEGED

There was a broad variation in the educational background of
participants in the project. Primary school graduates formed more
than half of the whole clientele, but many had completed junior or
even senior high school. No illiterates and few primary school dropouts were reported to have taken part in the projects. Given the
high rate of nonenrolment and dropout at the primary level in Indonesia, the educational background of the participants clearly shows
that the projects did not reach the underprivileged youth.

Reaching the underprivileged in projects of this sort is difficult. There is, in general, very little access to any type of organized
learning opportunities on the part of people with small incomes and
a low standard of living. Even when they are persuaded to come to
educational programs, there is usually irregular attendance and a
high dropout rate.

IPPA is aware of this problem and has been looking for appropriate educational approaches that will serve a broader range of
clientele, particularly the lowest income group. The initiative taken
at Yogyakarta to combine skill training and population education was
expected to attract the low-income group. As it turned out, even this
combined project could not attract the most underprivileged groups.
The overall social and economic structure imposes almost insurmount-
able constraints on any effort to help the truly indigent and the
destitute. Only a vigorous and well-planned direct attack at the
root of poverty has any chance of being helpful to the destitute.
Whether IPPA can unlock the secret of doing this effectively or whether
it should engage in such efforts are open questions.

COOPERATION WITH OTHER ORGANIZATIONS

IPPA had made a good start in seeking cooperation with private
organizations and governmental agencies in carrying out the Tangerang
Youth Project. This initial step was not followed up in the later
projects which IPPA, itself, attempted to manage and implement through
its branches. The BKR projects, for instance, had no binding relationship with other organizations, although in the initial stages consultations were held with youth organizations like KNPI, and support was
sought from the local administration, BKKBN, and other government
agencies. The project plan was to create informal groups in the
project area which were expected to continue on a self-supporting
basis. It soon became evident that for the groups to exist, they
had to maintain collaboration with existing bodies and agencies in
the area and receive support from the local administration. Therefore, prior to the launching of a community-oriented project, it
will be of advantage to explore possibilities for cooperation and
mutual help with government services, private agencies, and even

business enterprises and individual volunteers. Enlisting the
collaboration of such organizations and individuals opens up various
possibilities, such as getting help in the recruitment of would-be
clients, utilizing relevant expertise, taking advantage of other
human resources, obtaining credit facilities, or at least securing
a favorable position within an established sociopolitical structure.
Penmas (community education), Muhammadiyah, KNPI (national youth
committee), ZPG (student's movement for zero population growth) and
LSD (village social institutions) are examples of these organizations
and agencies. (See Appendix.)

Concerted efforts of the project management with local BKKBN
workers can be of great benefit to the clientele. Besides its coordinating function in family planning programs, BKKBN has the expertise
needed in family planning information and education. The accomplishments of the BKR project in Sidoharjo, as we have seen, are largely
due to the enthusiastic support of the local family planning field
workers.

COMMUNITY PARTICIPATION

The population and family planning education in the Tangerang
Youth Project was implemented according to a scheme worked out in
advance by the technical staff of the project. There was little
participation on the part of the prospective clientele and community
members in planning the program of training for instructors and in
setting out the content, method, and objectives of the project. The
instructors, in turn, conducted the learning sessions in their respective localities following the curricular pattern used in the instructors' training.

It would probably enhance the effectiveness of the project if
the participant youth (and the community concerned with the educational program) could be involved in the planning of learning activities.
The choice of learning content in terms of local needs, the most
suitable time pattern for educational activities, the choice of
working methods to be employed, and other matters could be decided
in consultation with the participating youths. At the very least,
representative members of the community should be brought into the
process of planning and implementing the project.

The BKR project, less rigidly structured, seemed to be in a
somewhat better position to make its clientele active participants
in program planning and management. The responsibility given to
the members of the BKR groups (*penggandas*) to propagate family
planning and population matters to other youths was very likely one
of the incentives to engage themselves in the planning and execution
of various project activities.

FOLLOW-UP MEASURES AFTER TERMINATION OF PROJECT

Experiences with the project clearly show that the sponsoring
agency cannot cut off all connections with the projects at the formal
termination of funding and expect the projects to continue on a

self-sustaining basis. It is always necessary to work out a phased
withdrawal, so that the project can adjust to changed circumstances
and muster the strength to be self-sustaining. In Tangerang and BKR,
as other organizations and established local groups, were already
involved, it should have been possible to arrange for a gradual
phasing out.

Mainly because of the interest and initiative of the *camat* and
the local family planning field agent, the BKR project in Wonogiri
retained its image as a population education project, even after
official termination of IPPA support. Participants preserved their
sense of attachment to the project management and sponsor, although
remunerations and allowances were no longer paid. This situation
probably cannot be replicated everywhere, but it underscores the
importance of advance planning and initiatives to maintain follow-up
links.

Follow-up programs can be carried on in various ways. One
approach would be issuing a periodical bulletin or newsletter; the
editorial staff may consist of the youth representatives themselves,
assisted by ex-project staff members. It will be very useful to
encourage correspondence among readers and editors of the newsletter.
This would ensure a regular feedback from the participants and sustain their interest in population and family planning matters.

APPENDIX

ORGANIZATIONS, AGENCIES,

AND INSTITUTIONS

The following is a description of a number of organizations, agencies, and institutions (in alphabetical order) in Indonesia that are working in the field of community development or nonformal education, some of them involving youth in their programs. These organizations and their programs suggest for IPPA various possibilities of youth activities that can be carried out in collaboration with other agencies in the context of an integrated development approach.

BUTSI (VOLUNTEER RECRUITMENT BODY)

Butsi is an interdepartmental body, with the Minister of Manpower and Internal Migration as chairman, and other ministers (Education and Culture, Agriculture, Foreign Affairs, Health, Industries, Information, Public Works, Religion, and Social Affairs) and the chairman of *BAPPENAS* (National Development Planning Board) as members. This body has the task of recruiting and employing volunteers (for the present, university graduates only) for rural development work.

Volunteers are of either sex with a *sarjana* (master's) or *sarjana muda* (bachelor's) degree and preferably unmarried. They are to serve as volunteers for two years. In one subdistrict a team of five volunteers is posted, but each volunteer usually works in one village. Usually remote villages, far from urban centers, are chosen. Preference is also given to villages involved in the "Applied Nutrition Program," the "Development Area Unit Program" (UDKP), and villages in designated regions for internal migration. A volunteer worker has to serve for at least one year in one village; after that he may stay in the same village or move to another.

Before assuming their tasks in the village, the volunteers have to go through the provincial, district, and subdistrict administration offices successively to be briefed on village development issues and problems. Then they meet the village head and officials they are assigned to assist and conduct a survey on development needs and resources of the village concerned. After that they have to undergo a one-month training in the provincial or district capital.

Butsi volunteers are not intended to serve as specialists or technicians in one or another speciality in development work. They are viewed as generalists who are able to identify various rural development needs and resources. They are to seek technical services and aid from various local extension, education, and information agencies in line with their working plan for the village community. However, volunteers are nevertheless expected to have certain practical skills, such as those of growing vegetables, constructing contour ditches on sloping grounds, and vaccinating chickens. These skills may be helpful to them in maintaining the cooperation of the village people.

The number of *Butsi* volunteer employment since 1969 is as follows:

	Sarjanas	Sarjanas Mudas	Total
1969–1971	30	–	30
1970–1972	46	4	50
1971–1973	60	210	270
1972–1974	30	270	300
1973–1975	8	192	200
1974–1976	..	..	1504

These volunteers have lived and worked in 55,970 villages throughout the country.

INDONESIAN NATIONAL YOUTH COMMITTEE

The *Komite Nasional Pemuda Indonesia* (Indonesian National Youth Committee) or KNPI, sponsored by the government in 1973, strives to involve youth in attaining national objectives in ideological, political, economic, social, and cultural fields.

In the sphere of education emphasis is laid on the participation of youth in literacy work, community learning centers, and also on vocational and cadre training. The scheme for rural community development includes efforts in developing workable relationships with agencies engaged in rural development, initiating youth participation in broadening employment opportunities, and supporting the internal migration program.

The program for family planning is somewhat more elaborate. One of the aims is the augmentation of motivation for family planning among youth—to be attained by conducting orientation courses (at *kabupaten* level), establishing information teams (to be started in Jakarta, with the use of a mobile unit), utilizing existing mass media, and launching a project in 100 villages, starting in West Java. A second aim is the formation of a functional corps of family planning motivators, which involves the coaching of existent motivators as well as the development of new ones.

The cultural program *inter alia* embraces efforts in improving regional culture elements (viz., folk-songs and folklores), and in promoting cultural appreciation among youth groups.

The plan of activities as sketched above was part of the KNPI Four-year Program which was to take effect beginning 1 April 1975. The level of implementation depends on the nature and scope of the different components. Seminars and workshops for development of concepts and overall policies, for instance, are held at the national level. Coaching, training, and orientation courses for "cadres" and leaders of local projects are conducted or managed by provincial or *kabupaten* executive councils (*Dewan Pembina*). Program execution at lower levels is entrusted to "cadre units" in subdistricts (*Kecamatans*), which consist of a number of working groups and "interest groups." The leaders of these groups are in charge of conducting activities in villages through existing youth organizations.

LPUB (INSTITUTION FOR COLLECTIVE ENTERPRISES)

The LPUB, a private voluntary organization, is active in developing collective enterprises with the aim of raising the socioeconomic standard of life and the self-sustaining abilities of low-income population groups. It assists in organizing collective undertakings, identifying problems and potential resources, and strengthening motivation for overcoming these problems collectively.

There are about 315 collective enterprises functioning under the sponsorship of the LPUB. For the development of these collective enterprises, training sessions and workshops have been held in the respective fields of the enterprises. A bulletin entitled "Setia Kawan," is issued periodically to serve as a communication medium among the enterprise units.

This institution is affiliated with a private credit union counseling office, which aims at creating credit cooperatives so as to develop the socioeconomic potentials of the community. The program includes education in fundamentals of cooperatives and leadership training as well.

LSD (VILLAGE SOCIAL INSTITUTION)

In 1969 a government decision was taken to establish a special coordinating sector for all government activities concerned with rural development. This sector, known as "Sector K" is composed of various ministry representatives, with the Minister of Home Affairs serving as chairman and the Director General for Rural Community Development (PMD) as secretary.

This coordinating structure for rural development has been extended to various levels of administration, with each governor, *bupati* (district head) and *camat* (subdistrict head) in charge of coordinating the relevant services or government agencies in his area of jurisdiction. At each level PMD officials serve as secretaries of the interservice rural development group and assist in the coordination work.

The subdistrict (*kecamatan*) has been regarded as the proper administrative unit to be covered by a comprehensive joint development program. Therefore, several subdistricts in each *kabupaten* have been selected to function as project area units. These are the UKDP's (development area units), with the *camat* as chairman and other government services' heads as members.

Within the village community the LSD or *Lembaga Sosial Desa* (village social institution) is viewed as the center for community development activities, and as a vehicle for community organization for the effective use of local government services for village development. It is also a channel for improving communication within the communities themselves and between village people and the various government services.

Rural community development is considered to cover all aspects of village life affecting basic ecomonic and social welfare. Given the number of government agencies and nongovernmental organizations concerned with various aspects of rural development, the role of LSD is considered important in strengthening coordination, in both the planning and implementation of relevant activities, among such agencies and organizations. Some of the special tasks of LSD are: data collecting; pooling of ideas, suggestions, and proposals from village communities; planning rural development programs; and managing implementations.

MUHAMMADIYAH

Since its formation in 1912 Muhammadiyah, a private Islamic organization with a progressive outlook, has been active in the domain of education, health and social services; it is working on the enunciation of codes of individual and community conduct befitting the needs of a developing society.

The central board, which has its seat in Jakarta and Yogyakarta, comprises ten councils (*majlis*). Four out of the ten councils are respectively in charge of:

(a) the execution of educational programs in school and out of school;

(b) the rendering of health and social welfare services in the community;

(c) guidance to members of the organizations who are engaged in economic enterprises and concerned about economic problems in society;

(d) guidance of youth activities.

A sister organization is the *Aisyiah*, composed of women members, and has its own central board. Though autonomous, it has organizational and complementary relationships with Muhammadiyah and

the youth and student activities for girls are coordinated by the
Youth Guidance Council of the principal organization.

Private schools at all (kindergarten, primary, junior and
senior high, and university) levels and Qur'an courses conducted by
Muhammadiyah, among the major activities of the organization, are
widespread throughout the country. The health care program is
carried out through an extensive medical service system, consisting
of 5 hospitals, 73 infirmaries, 298 MCH-centers, 318 polyclinics and
4 dispensaries. A family planning section which is under the same
majlis as that for health, constitutes one of the more important
private family planning units operating under the coordination of
BKKBN.

There are three subsections within the family planning unit,
namely, those for:

a) education, information, and motivation

b) consultation, and

c) clinical services

The first subsection is to provide information regarding
family well-being and planning and enlightenment of Muhammadiyah's
point of view on family planning, particularly to religious leaders
and scholars. The second provides counseling, within the fremework
of religious restrictions and admissibilities, to individual couples
interested in practicing family planning. The third is in charge of
rendering medical and paramedical services for family planning
purposes.

The socioeconomic council of Muhammadiyah is at present in
the process of developing a comprehensive socioeconomic action program
for the organization.

As for the overall organizational set-up, Muhammadiyah has in
certain areas a deeply rooted structure with branches in subdistricts
(*kecamatan*) and subbranches in villages. However, only a limited
part of the sectoral programs (viz., the conducting of Qur'an classes,
kindergartens and primary schools) is being implemented down to the
lowest organizational levels.

PENMAS (COMMUNITY EDUCATION)

Penmas, or *Pendidikan Masyarakat,* a community education system
in Indonesia, is under the jurisdiction of the Directorate General for
Nonformal Education and Sports, which is subdivided into four directorates, i.e., (1) Community Education (*Penmas*), (2) Youth Development,
(3) Sports, and (4) Technical Personnel Development.

At provincial level the *Penmas* office is one of the ten
bidangs (divisions) under the provincial representative of the Department of Education and Culture. At the district level the Office of
Education and Culture has three sections, responsible for conducting

(a) primary and secondary schools; (b) cultural education; (c) *Penmas*, sports and youth development. At subdistrict level the Office of Education and Culture has to coordinate four field staff members, respectively in charge of: (a) primary school education,(b) *Penmas*, (c) sports and youth development, and (d) cultural education.

Penmas has two prominent and related functions: (1) the offering of a core program of basic education, and (2) the facilitation of other learning activities related to locally defined needs. The core program of basic education is formulated according to working principles as outlined in government financial policies and planning schemes. It is manifested in the structured and rather standardized learning activities, such as courses and practical training. Courses in literacy and numeracy, family life education, civics, leadership training, and prevocational skills form the core program supported by printed and other instructional materials. Learning material packages A (for illiterates and nonschool-attenders), packages B (for primary school dropouts), and packages C (for secondary school dropouts and primary school graduates) for basic education are being developed at the national learning center (PKB), while other learning materials are developed through several pilot projects.

The facilitative program involves activities in learning groups organized around specific problems or needs. Assistance is given to the groups in identifying and making maximum use of technical and other resources from varying nonformal education agencies. To support the village level program operation, a number of PKB's or *Panti Kegiatan Belajar* (learning centers) have been established at *Kecamatan* level and more are planned to be established.

THE STUDENT MOVEMENT FOR ZERO POPULATION GROWTH

A number of university students in Yogyakarta, realizing the adverse consequences of rapid population growth, and recognizing the need for a direct involvement of the young generation in effective population control actions, proclaimed the establishment of a Student Movement for Zero Population Growth (ZPG) in 1973.

The movement is aimed at engendering and fostering interest among youth in current population problems, promoting youth participation in population and family planning programs, and introducing the "small family" (with two children) concept as a mode to secure population stability.

Some activities thus far carried on by ZPG are as follows:

   (a)   issue of monthly bulletins (*Warta ZPG*) with free
         distribution,

   (b)   group information meetings,

   (c)   radio broadcasts (through the national RRI network and
         a private broadcasting company),

      (d)   seminars and orientation courses for youth,

      (e)   maintainenance of a library,

      (f)   promotion of population and family planning studies.

The ZPG Movement focuses its activities on the youth sector. In its initial stages it involved high school and university students in its program, but recently it has been giving more attention to youngsters in *pesantrens* (religious learning centers) and out-of-school rural youth.

The movement has its central board located in Yogyakarta and branch secretariats in Surakarta, Semarang, Surabaya, Cirebon, Bandung, Denpasar and Ujungpandang. Up to the present the organization has not spread down to the subdistrict and village level.

10 Working with Tribal People: The Institutes at Kosbad Hill, India

S.H. Deshpande
Vasant Deshpande
Sharad Kulkarni

EDITOR'S NOTE

This study from the State of Maharashtra in India tells the story of two large and highly respected voluntary organizations-- the Agricultural Institute (AI) and the Gram Bal Shiksha Kendra (GBSK)--whose roots go back to the Independence Movement and its humanistic Gandhian principles. These organizations, along with their wider-ranging activities, have been working devotedly for more than 20 years to help their Warli tribal neighbors around Kosbad Hill to extricate themselves from their age-old bondage of exploitation, cultural isolation and dehumanizing poverty. The case study focuses on this particular aspect of their overall programs.

It would be difficult to find anywhere a rural poverty situation more severe or more resistant to change than that of the Warli tribals in the Kosbad area. But it would also be difficult to find in the real world any organizations better suited by commitment and competence to tackle such a hard case. Consequently, anyone concerned with improving the lot of the rural poor in India or any other developing country will find this a highly instructive--if somewhat disquieting-- story.

The story is told by three knowledgeable Indian social scientists: Dr. S. H. Deshpande, Professor of Agricultural Economics at the University of Bombay and author of Problems of Cooperative Farming and numerous journal articles; Dr. Vasant Deshpande, Director of the Nehru Institute of Social Studies at Pune and author of Towards Social Integration: Problems of Adjustment of Scheduled Caste Elite; and Sharad Kulkarni, Director of the Centre for Tribal Conscientiza- tion at Pune and author of numerous articles on tribal problems.

Their research plan was shaped in cooperation with ICED's own Indian staff member, Pratima Kale, during an initial joint visit to Kosbad. Subsequently the authors made further visits to observe various programs in action, to survey and assess the impact of these activities, and to conduct extensive interviews with the leaders, staff members and students of the two institutes and a sample of Warli farmers and other local people.

As social scientists, the authors produced an objective and critic- ally analytical report, notwithstanding their evident sympathy and respect for the two Kosbad Institutes and their leaders, and their

698

*deep compassion for the Warli tribal people. Others may disagree
with some of their interpretations and evaluative conclusions, but
few would deny that they have given us a very substantial and stimulating account.*

*ICED gladly associates itself with the following statement of
gratitude and acknowledgements prepared by the authors themselves.*

> *"We are thankful to AI and GBSK for their unstinted
> co-operation in every way. Particular mention must be
> made of Anutai Wagh, Jayant Patil, Avinash Chaudhary,
> Appa Koske, M.S.Gupte, A.H.Sankhe, Dr.N.V.Modak
> and Appa Amrite. For special interviews we are grateful
> to K.J.Save (author of The Warlis), H.G.Patil (the first
> head of AI), K.M.Chitre (life-long associate of Acharya
> Bhise) and Principal N.G.Joshi (of the R.M.Bhat   High
> School). Mrs. Padmaja Phatak, grand-niece of Tarabai
> Modak, made available to us the manuscript of her Life
> of Tarabai (Marathi). We have relied more on the writings
> of the Nargolkars (Jangalche Raje) and K.J.Save (The
> Warlis), than our references indicate. S.A.Kelkar's
> books, Taraba va Balshiksham (Tarabai and Child Education)
> and Gramin Bal Shikshanache Prashna (Problems of Rural
> Child Education), were equally useful. Prof. Vidyadhar
> Amrite got the maps done. We record our grateful thanks
> to all these. Finally, we must state our deepest appreciation
> of the Warli farmers, students and others without whose
> co-operation our study would have been impossible of
> achievement."*

EDITOR'S COMMENTARY

Two important caveats should be borne in mind in reading this
case study in the interest of keeping a proper perspective and
reaching a fair assessment of the record of the two Kosbad institutes.

First, it should be emphasized that the authors did not attempt to
examine and evaluate the total activities of the two Kosbad institutes
but only that part directly involving the relatively small tribal population in their immediate vicinity. Therefore the findings should not
be misinterpreted as applying to their sizeable outreach activities
that extend throughout the State of Maharashtra and to other parts
of India.

It should be noted with respect to these broader activities that
the Agricultural Institute has earned an outstanding nationwide
reputation for the high quality of its training and research activities
and especially for its wide-ranging promotion of significant agricultural innovations. Its principal, Jayant Patil, for example, was
recently awarded a national prize for innovative work on irrigation
wells. The Gram Bal Shiksha Kendra has similarly earned an outstanding national reputation for its creative and influential work on
preschool children and on nonformal education for older children,
which has had a wide influence through its teacher training activities
and professional publications. Anutai Wagh, its principal, has long
been widely respected--one might even say revered--for her pioneering work and leadership in the field of early childhood education,

especially for disadvantaged rural children. This, in brief, is the broader record of achievement of these institutes against which the findings of the case study should be viewed.

The second caveat concerns the historical roots of these institutions and the contrast between the earlier social and educational reform approach of the Independence Movement and today's broader and more sophisticated "community development" approach. The earlier ideology (which still dominates the strategy of many older voluntary organizations in India) was paternalistic in approach and gave almost exclusive emphasis to education and social improvement as the key to "uplifting" the rural poor. Thus, it gave relatively little attention to attacking the economic roots of poverty or to promoting extensive "community participation"--two elements that have since acquired central importance in contemporary "community development" doctrine, reflecting the deeper understanding that has developed over the years of the causes of poverty, the psychology of the poor, and the basic prerequisites for reducing rural poverty. Not surprisingly, the earlier ideology is often criticized today by Indian rural development experts for being too narrow, unrealistic and paternalistic. Yet most would agree that its dedicated workers deserve great credit for having sensitized the urban educated elite to the vast injustices in the prevailing socioeconomic system, and for creating a political climate favorable to numerous legislative actions and public policies aimed at rectifying these long-standing inequalities and injustices.

It is important to read the case study in the light of this historical perspective so as to avoid the error of judging the performance record of the Kosbad institutes solely in terms of the sophisticated criteria of today's community development thinking. These institutes must be seen for what they are: a blend of the old and the new. Being rooted in the soil of the old social and educational reform movement, they benefit from its considerable strengths and also suffer to a degree from its limitations. But unlike many of the older voluntary organizations, they have broken out of the old mould. The Agricultural Institute, for example, has adopted a strong agricultural development approach, and the Gram Bal Shiksha Kendra has been endeavoring to shed its paternalistic heritage for a more community-based approach; yet neither entirely fulfills the prescription of the modern community development approach.

THE OBJECTIVES AND PROGRAMS

The basic objective of the Agricultural Institute (AI) when it set up its Agricultural School in Kosbad in 1949 was to train modern young farmers, both tribal and nontribal, throughout the Thana District-- a coastal strip north of Bombay stretching 113 kilometers along the Arabian Sea. Gradually AI took on a broader range of training tasks and clienteles covering a much wider geographic area. Today, for example, it runs special training centers for Village Level Workers, tribal youth, village council chairmen and members, ordinary farmers, and applied nutrition workers. In addition it operates two residential primary schools and a middle school, all with a strong agricultural bias.

The Institute has also evolved a wide-ranging agricultural research program that focuses on the ecological potentials of its service area and feeds into its training activities. Its experimental

and promotional activities have included, for example, high yielding
varieties of rice and wheat; the introduction of new fodder grasses,
fruits and vegetables; and improved breeds of milk cows, goats, and
chickens, as well as   bee-keeping.

Although a substantial majority of the Agricultural Institute's
overall clientele is made up of non-tribal farmers, it has for both
historical and locational reasons taken a special interest in the
Adivasi (a general term covering all "Scheduled Tribes" in India),
and particularly in the Warlis who inhabit its immediate neighborhood
and are among the poorest and most disadvantaged of all the tribal
groups in Maharashtra. Of primary interest to this case study is the
multi-pronged Development Program the Institute has been conducting
in several "adopted" Warli villages within a radius of 10 km. of Kosbad
with a total population of some 750 families. A central aim of this
development program has been to introduce a multi-crop, year-round
agricultural system, based on improved irrigation, to replace the
traditional mono-culture system that occupied only the rainy season
and left small Warli cultivators with little food supply or gainful
employment during the long dry seasons. In an effort to break the
critical water bottleneck, the Institute, with substantial financial
aid from international voluntary organizations, constructed 100 dug
wells for selected individual farmers and a number of community wells
to be shared by several farms, at almost no cost to the farmers. It
has also supplied them with seeds, cuttings for fruit tree grafting,
and other supplies, and with training sessions, demonstrations and
extension services to teach them how to apply these improved agricultural and horticultural technologies. On top of all this, the
Institute's own staff and students have frequently done the Warli
farmers' work for them.

As a supplement to the development program, the Institute also
mounted a "Better Living Program". This has included the introduction and promotion of such devices as smokeless stoves, glass roof
panels, sanitary latrines and Gobar Gas plants, all designed to
improve household hygienic conditions and to convert waste into much
needed manure and fuel.

The neighboring Gram Bal Shiksha Kendra (GBSK) is basically
an educational institution whose work has been complementary to the
Agricultural Institute's program. GBSK moved into a virtual educational desert when it came to Kosbad in 1957. Ever since it has
concentrated its efforts primarily on the education and general welfare
of preschool age children, in the conviction that if children born into
dire poverty are to have any real chance in life, they must be given
crucial help in their early formative years. And since its principal
had already made her mark as a creative national leader in preschool
education, GBSK soon became a respected national center for the
training of preschool teachers, especially for Adivasi children, in
other rural areas of India as well.

Inevitably, because of the sparsity and moribund character of
elementary schooling in the Kosbad area, and the almost total non-
participation of Warli children, the GBSK was soon drawn into
primary education as a follow-up to its pre-primary work. Though
the main core of its primary education takes place in regular schools,
some of its most interesting and innovative ventures have been with
"meadow schools" and "night classes" on plantations for working

children unable to attend school, yet anxious to learn.

THE RESULTS

It should be evident even from the above abbreviated sketch of their activities that the two Kosbad Institutes have made a diversified and persistent effort, extending over 20 to 30 years, to uplift their Warli neighbors. The question the case study investigators sought to answer was: What have been the practical results? What discernible impact have all these efforts had on the agricultural practices and productivity of the Warlis; on their traditional beliefs, attitudes and behavior; on the development and upward mobility of their children; on their community cohesion, cooperation and participation; and on the general quality of their family life?

The short answer--which is elaborated and documented in the report--is that there have been significant results, including a number of outstanding individual "success cases"; yet, taken overall, the impact must be judged as disappointingly low, at least in terms of earlier expectations and what one might reasonably have anticipated.

The GBSK's educational work with young children and mothers has clearly yielded some good results. The strong earlier resistance of mothers to permitting their children to attend the creches, balwadis and elementary schools has melted away. Many mothers today are not only willing but anxious to send their children to school, and the children arrive much cleaner than they used to. The attitude toward education has discernibly changed. And some of the children-- though still only a small minority--have climbed further up the education ladder. A number of the teen-agers interviewed, particularly the girls, reflected a new freedom from some of the confining and stultifying traditional beliefs and attitudes of their tribal culture, and a critical view of some of the less constructive behavior of their parents, such as excessive drinking.

Despite these encouraging advances, however, the overall progress has been limited and there is still a long way to go. The old cultural barriers and constraints are still strong; even the educated Warlis still display a lack of self-confidence and a tendency to withdraw. Although GBSK has "reached the poor" and gained their acceptance, it has apparently had little success as yet (though not for lack of trying) in stimulating active community participation and direct involvement in the operation of its activities. It seems particularly significant that although a number of tribals are employed by GBSK as farm workers and office peons, none has ever applied for a position as office clerk and only one among nine elementary teachers is an Adivasi.

Changes on the agricultural front are, of course, more tangible, visible and measurable than with education. The case study investigators conducted a revealing survey of 45 farms run by the only Adivasi farmers actively using any of the 100 individual dug wells referred to earlier. Since they are undoubtedly "above average" farmers in the area, any agricultural revolution that may have occurred would undoubtedly be apparent in their fields. But there has not as yet been any real agricultural revolution. Nor could the case study investigators find much evidence that the innovations under the "Better Living Program" had taken hold. There have been, however, some significant breakthroughs in terms of crop diversification through the adoption by these selected Warli farmers of non-traditional crops--especially various fruits and vegetables that improved their cash incomes.

The investigators concluded, however, that the Agricultural Institute's three-cycle year-round agricultural scheme had not succeeded. For the first (rainy season) cycle most of the 45 farmers, though they had adopted the recommended high yielding rice varieties on a limited scale, were still devoting more than two-thirds of their paddy acreage to the old low yielding local varieties (which yield less than half as much). The wheat that AI had enthusiastically promoted for the next cycle was even less popular, though as indicated above, fruits and vegetables were proving more popular. The adaptation of new types of livestock and sideline activities such as bee-keeping, on the other hand, appeared to have made little headway.

EXPLANATIONS AND POSSIBLE SOLUTIONS

If significant lessons for the future are to be drawn from this rich and lengthy experience, it is necessary to try to understand the causes of both the successes and the failures. This, of course, is the hardest part of such a case study because various causal factors are often so intertwined that it is difficult to sort them out and weigh their relative importance. In the end it becomes a matter of judgment, and frequently there is wide scope for differences of interpretation and opinion.

Thus, for example, the farmers and the AI experts had conflicting explanations for the relatively low impact of the agricultural development program. The farmers explained it largely in terms of adverse technical and economic factors, such as inadequate water supply, the low-moisture retention of their light soils, and the prohibitive cost of the heavy fertilizer applications required for HYVs. The AI experts on the other hand minimized these technical-economic explanations and tended to attribute the low impact primarily to the irrational fears and other idiosyncracies of the Warlis. They dismissed as groundless, for example, the farmers' assertion that "the rains wash away the fertilizer"; they pointed out that AI had always been ready to provide credit for the purchase of fertilizer, that the farmers did not always fully utilize their available water supply, and that AI's theoretical cost calculations demonstrated clearly that the farmers could greatly enhance their income if they adopted AI's recommended innovations. The Warlis, it was said, are good workers but poor farmers; they prefer to work on a large plantation for immediate cash wages rather than cultivate their own small farm more intensively and ultimately realize a larger income.

It is impossible to judge from a distance, of course, where the real truth lies in this particular debate, but it is perhaps worth noting that ICED has encountered quite similar debates between non-tribal small farmers and agricultural experts in numerous other areas, suggesting that it may not be simply cultural idiosyncracies that so often cause the small farmer to reject new agricultural technologies advocated by the experts. Frequently the farmer turns out to have his own rational reasons for treating innovations with extreme caution, usually having to do with his meager resource base, his imperative family consumption needs, the unpredictability of the

weather and market prices, and his very limited capacity to take
risks. It also involves his weighing of available alternatives--such as
spending more hours working his own land in hopes of getting a
possibly larger but postponed income, as against working more hours
on somebody else's larger farm or taking some other available
employment for immediate though meager cash wages. Seen in this
light, the small farmer often more closely approaches "the rational
economic man" than some of the technical experts who advise him.
Their cardinal goal, after all, is increased yield per acre; his is
survival.

This is not to suggest that the inherited cultural traits of the
Warlis (described in the study) were not also an important explana-
tory factor in the relatively low impact of AI's development program.
What seems clear from the evidence is that a wide social distance and
communication gap still persists between the Warlis and the mainly
middle class educated people who seek to help them. Such a gap is,
of course, found in poor villages all over the world, but in the case
of the Warlis it is exceptionally wide because of their long and
continuing (partly self-imposed) cultural isolation. The key problem--
to which the Kosbad institutes (and many others) have evidently not
yet found a satisfactory solution--is how to close this gap. For until
it is closed, or at least substantially narrowed, all sorts of development interventions from the outside are likely to have a disappointing
impact, and all the talk about "community participation" is likely to
have a hollow ring.

In view of the importance of these frequently neglected social
and cultural obstacles to rural development, the authors make a
fundamental point when they suggest that, to be effective, technical
agricultural research should be accompanied by appropriate social
science research. Or to put it differently, he who would help the
poor must first know them, and understand how life looks from
their vantage point. One must also respect their judgment, for the
very fact that they have survived this long under seemingly impossible circumstances suggests that they are not entirely without
wisdom and rationality, even though they may be illiterate and some
of their beliefs, fears, and practices may be baseless and counter-
productive in the light of scientific knowledge.

With respect to the evident lack of "community participation" by
the Warlis in the activities of the two institutes, and their seeming
indifference toward advancing themselves, the authors note that the
approach of the institutes has been strongly paternalistic and that
this may have discouraged a sense of self-reliance. They question,
however, as other observers have before them, whether a more
community-oriented, self-help approach would have been feasible in
the circumstances. Perhaps people must be helped out of the
worst depths of poverty in paternalistic fashion before they are
ready to become their own change agents.

But here the authors encounter something of a chicken-and-egg
dilemma. On the one hand they conclude that education is the only
real means of altering the traditional beliefs and attitudes of the
Warlis and making them self-reliant. Yet on the other hand their
findings suggest that the long and extensive educational efforts of
both institutes, although helpful in other respects, do not seem as
yet to have made any sizeable dent in this respect. Their answer to
this seeming dilemma is that the institutes should give much greater

emphasis to consciousness-raising education that will make the learners--particularly the younger ones--more aware of their socio-economic and political environment, of the basic causes of their exploitation and poverty, of the strengths and weaknesses of their own inherited culture and traditions, and of their own capacity and innate human power to change this environment and their position in it. In advocating more "consciousness-raising" education, however, they caution against a purely agitational approach that can be counter-productive, "to the extent that it makes the clientele believe that all their ills flow from sources outside themselves." They also recognize that the necessary educational approach is at best a long slow process with no quick and dramatic pay-offs.

The authors do not take the position, however, that a purely educational approach will suffice. On the contrary, they conclude that the program objectives of the Kosbad institutes have been too limited in terms of the basic needs, interests and potential motivations of the Warlis, and that even within these objectives the various activities have been too fragmented. They observe, for example, that while each of the innovative devices for improving family living could be justified in its own right, these devices were of only marginal importance to meeting the basic family needs of the Warlis. They suggest instead that AI's agricultural recommendations might have greater acceptance and success accompanied by a primary health care program attuned to the critical health needs and problems of the area. One might also surmise that the Warli mothers would respond with some enthusiasm to well conceived activities designed to reduce their physical burdens, to help them earn some crucially needed cash, and to elevate their status and self-respect.

To ask such a broader and more integrated approach of these two institutes, of course, may be to ask the impossible, for it would confront them with a difficult choice between continuing to concentrate on what they are so unusually well qualified to do, or taking on additional new functions (such as health care, non-farm occupational training, and family planning), which would probably force them to concentrate their attention and limited resources on serving a more limited audience and geographic area. The point is nevertheless an important one for other rural programs, especially newer ones still in the planning or early development stage, or for older ones that may be able to form close partnerships with other organizations capable of rendering complementary family improvement services in the same area.

FOUR BASIC CONCLUSIONS

Viewed in a broad international perspective, the experiences of the Kosbad institutes over more than 20 years reinforce the following important conclusions of wide applicability that have also emerged from other case studies in this series.

First, even the best conceived technical solutions to poverty problems can be thwarted by deep-seated social and cultural factors and by human communication barriers unless effective ways can be found to overcome these obstacles. In other words, in order for beneficial material changes to occur, the perceptions, attitudes and outlook of the people themselves must change. Thus, the diagnosis of rural poverty situations and the successful planning and implementation of corrective measures calls not only for technical expertise in such fields as agriculture, irrigation, health and education but also for the insights of such social scientists as cultural anthropologists, rural sociologists and social psychologists. Thus far, comparatively little use has been made of such social science expertise in attacking the problems of rural poverty.

Second, although rural poverty situations differ considerably from one to another, they almost invariably require a multi-pronged approach addressed to a combination of the basic needs of the individuals, families and communities concerned. A single-sector approach--as for example in agriculture--is likely to be far less effective by itself than as if accompanied by parallel efforts directed at such needs as health, nutrition, maternal and child care, family planning, and off-farm employment. And for each of these efforts to succeed, it must include appropriate educational (i.e., *learning*) components, closely integrated with all other components--which is to say that education should be seen not as a separate "sector" unto itself but as an essential nutrient and lubricant of *all* development activities.

Third, achieving sizeable improvement in rural poverty situations requires fundamental social, economic, cultural and political changes in the local environment. This is a considerably more complex, difficult and time-consuming process than is often assumed, particularly by external assistance agencies that place their faith in neatly packaged, narrowly-focussed three to five year "projects". There is urgent need to find more effective alternatives to this conventional "project approach" in the whole area of rural development.

Finally, voluntary organizations, because of their unique flexibility and capacity to innovate and test out fresh approaches, and because of their potential for attracting able and dedicated leadership and staff who can get close to the rural people and articulate their needs and interests, can be a crucially important supplement to larger scale governmental efforts. But to perform this role most effectively they must (1) have a broad development orientation; (2) be permitted to retain a substantial degree of independent control over their own programs; and (3) receive sufficient *general* and *continuing* financial support from both domestic and international sources--not simply short term "project support" restricted to some limited purpose of special interest to the donor.

CHAPTER 1

THE PHYSICAL AND SOCIAL SETTING

The Agricultural Institute (AI) and the Gram Bal Shiksha Kendra (GBSK) have been working since 1949 and 1957 respectively on Kosbad Hill, situated in a tribal area of Maharashtra (see Map 1). AI's work has extended over research, education, training, extension, and development. Its educational activities, however, include more than purely agricultural education. The principal focus of GBSK's work has been on preprimary and primary education and the teacher training that is associated with both. Work of tribal uplift is only *one* part of AI's totality of activities, whereas it constitutes almost the whole of the activities of the GBSK.

It should be noted that these institutes have been working *in* a tribal area and *for* tribal people. Tribals, of course, are rural people, but they are a special kind of rural people because of the cultural gap that separates them from others. Consequently, they tend to present certain special problems of development, not met with, or not met with to the same extent, in other rural populations. The tribals, officially designated as the "Scheduled Tribes" in India, and called "Adivasi" generally, constitute seven percent of the total population. (See Map 2.) Hence, lessons learned from these tribal programs may have relevance and value for other tribal areas in India or in other countries.

The area in which the two Institutes have been working has had a long history of the worst kind of poverty and exploitation, although in recent years its rigors have diminished. The development problems of part of this area revolve around exceptionally niggardly soil and water resources in a hilly part of the land that raises special problems of its own, although hill agriculture is not exclusively tribal agriculture.

These Institutes are essentially voluntary, and yet they seem to differ markedly from other kinds of voluntary rural development agencies currently working in Maharashtra. The latter generally work on a much smaller scale, in terms of areas or population served. In many cases they are the creations of single individuals with at the most a few local or outside collaborators. They have an accent on "self-less" service which in practical terms means that the workers generally live a simple life and keep their own requirements to a minimum. The Kosbad Institutes' scale of operations is much larger

MAP 1

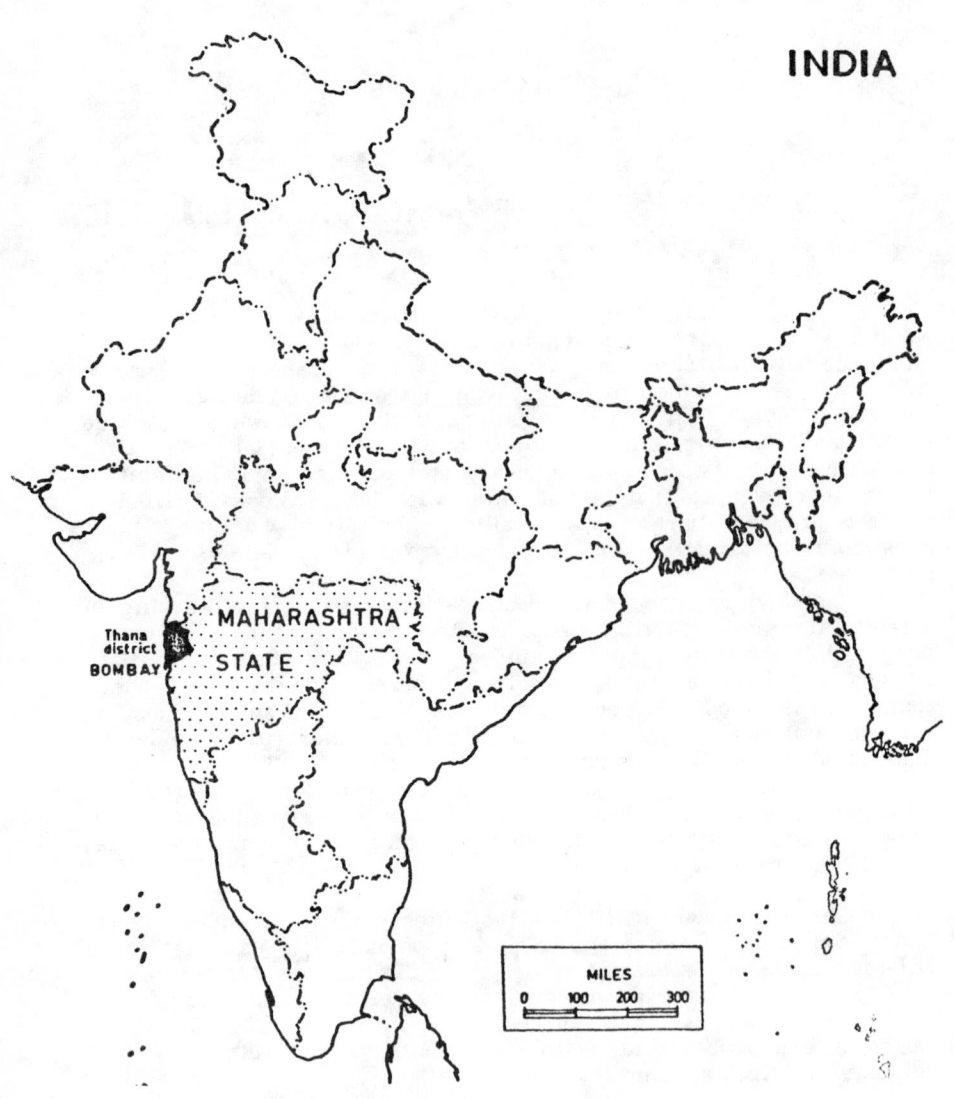

MAP 2

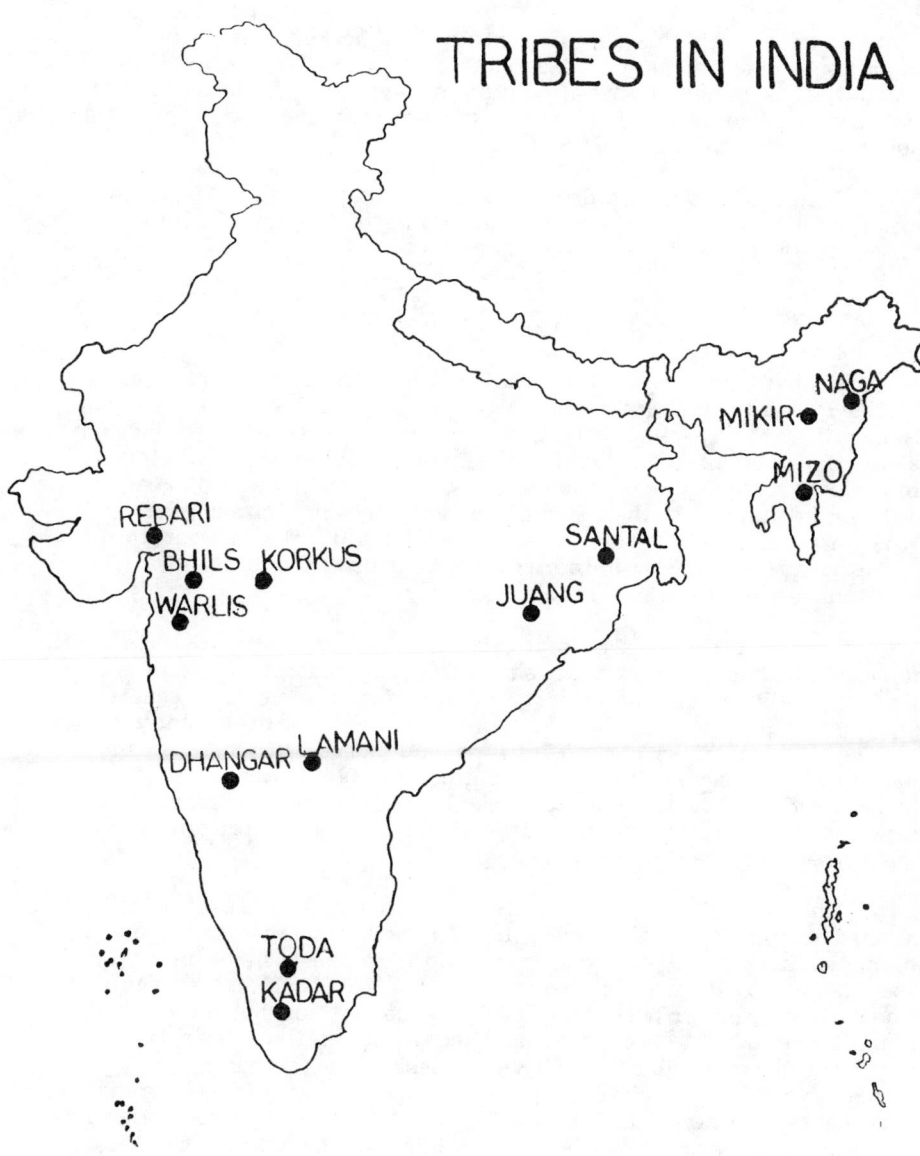

TRIBES IN INDIA

than the average and, being educational institutions subject to
government grant-in-codes, have all the usual organizational trappings, such as differential pay scales, hierarchy of statuses, and
minimum security of service.

Even though this research study can be regarded only as a
beginning, since all potential aspects of the subject have not been
treated, it is believed that its findings have some firmness and
validity because of the fairly long span of time the Institutes have
covered: AI--30 years, GBSK--22 years.

This initial chapter describes the ecology of the geographic
area and the characteristics and conditions of the tribal people
examined by the study.

GEOGRAPHY AND ECOLOGY

Kosbad Hill, from which the Kosbad Institutes operate, falls
in the Dahanu tahsil (sub-district) of the Thana District in
Maharashtra. (See Map 3.) Thana District, lying north of Bombay
along the coast of the Arabian Sea for 113 kilometres, is divided
into three topographical zones: (a) the central portion of the
Sahyadri ranges and their slopes, which is mainly forest area,
(b) the eastern part, mainly paddy fields, and (c) the western
plains along the coast where rice, horticulture, fodder, and
vegetables are grown.

Dahanu tahsil is a coastal tahsil. (See Map 4.) Of the three
topographical divisions mentioned, it has two coastal plains to the
west and hilly areas to the east. The soil of the western coastal
strip is fertile and therefore favorable for horticulture, paddy,
and vegetables. The climate is warm and humid with very small
variations in temperature. The annual rainfall varies from 2000
to 2500 mm. and comes chiefly from the south-west monsoon, June
to September. Underground water resources vary from one area
to another but are generally meager.

The agricultural and forestry potential in the areas around
Kosbad is considerable. Rice soils can facilitate the introduction of
high yielding varieties. A second crop of pulses can be taken on
some lands on the residual moisture in the *rabi* (winter) season.
The hilly terrain with laterite soils is excellent for horticultural
crops such as mango, cashew, and jackfruit; and the grasslands
may be made to produce nutritive grasses. By applying the
silvi-pastoral concept farmers can produce fodder on forest lands,
and the availability of fodder can lead, of course, to meat farming.
The waterlogged areas at the foot of hills can be transformed into
ponds for fish culture. Forest wealth can be utilized for starting
village industries like basket-making from bamboos, cardboard from
coarse grasses, tusser silk from Ain trees, gums, and resins. The
flora can be utilized for beekeeping. The date palm trees can be
tapped for Neera, a nutritious drink, and the leaves can be used
for making brooms and carpets. In the region covered by about

MAP 3

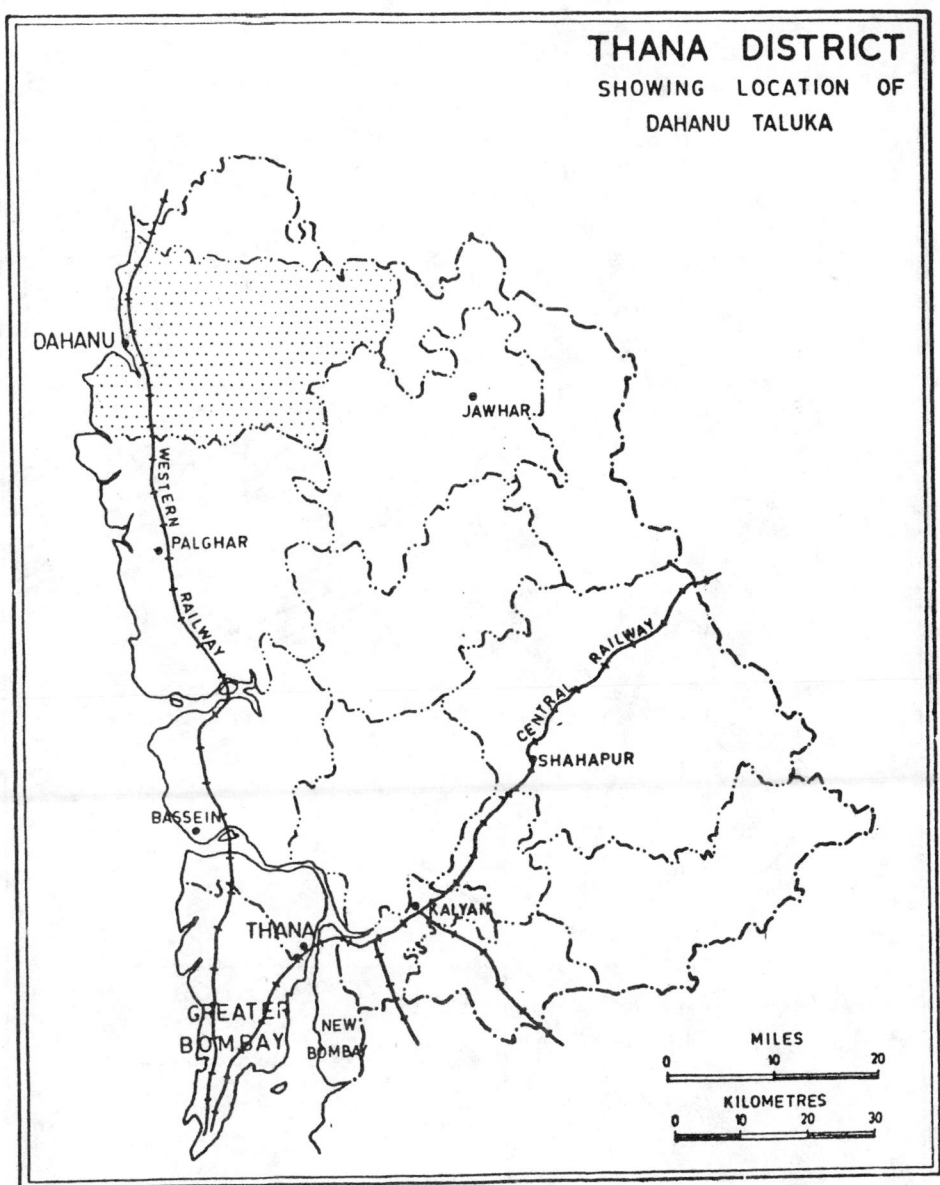

THANA DISTRICT
SHOWING LOCATION OF
DAHANU TALUKA

MAP 4

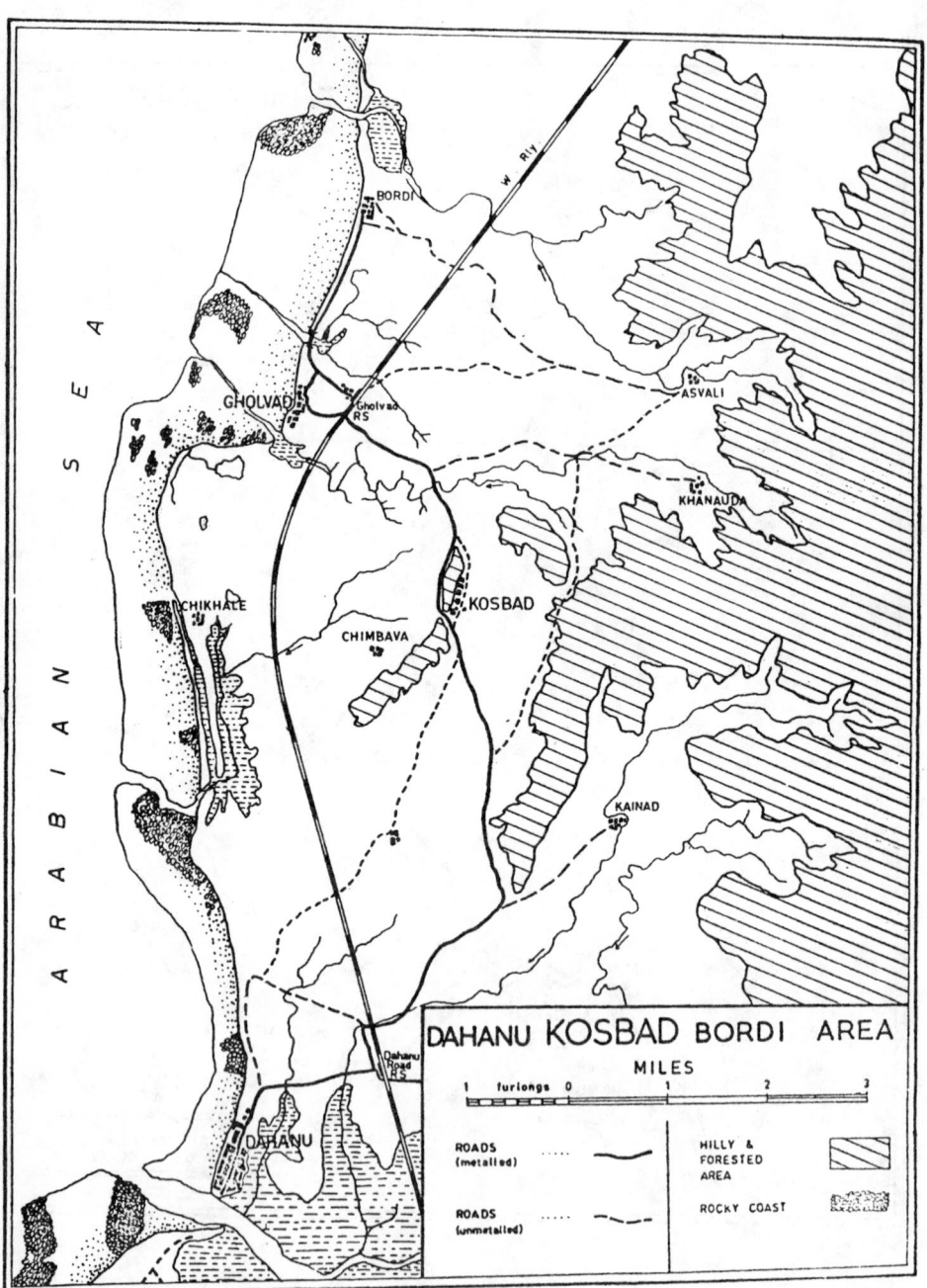

DAHANU KOSBAD BORDI AREA

ten villages around Kosbad there are 10,000 trees of *deshi* (native) mangoes and 20,000 *bor* plants (a native berry). By grafting improved varieties these can be made to produce much larger than normal yields.

On the other hand, there are hardly any mineral resources in the area. Most opportunities for development lie in the direction of exploiting the agri-horticultural lands, grass lands, forests, fisheries, and the subsidiary small industries that are based on these. Water, however, is a critical bottleneck to exploiting these opportunities.

THE TRIBAL PEOPLE
(ADIVASIS) OF MAHARASHTRA

Since both the AI and the GBSK have been working in a tribal (Adivasi) area and in a significant measure for the particular tribes called "Warli," it is desirable at the beginning to provide a brief account of Adivasi life in general and of the Warlis in particular.

The Scheduled Tribes (*i.e.*, Adivasi) population of Maharashtra may be estimated at four million as of 1979 or about six percent of the total state population. Most of them (about 95 percent) live in rural areas.[1] They are, thus, predominantly rural and live for the most part in the hilly areas of the Sahyadri-Satpuda and Gondawan ranges. (See Map 5.)

Most of the Adivasis are small cultivators. About 30 percent of them cultivate less than one hectare, as against 21 percent among the general cultivators. About 64 percent cultivate less than 3 hectares, as against 51 percent among all cultivators in the State.

Most Adivasis live in the hilly areas of the State; lands cultivated by them are less fertile than those owned by nontribals. Most of these lands are devoid of irrigation facilities, and even among those having irrigation facilities the majority have wells that rarely supply water throughout the year.

The economic and technological plane on which the Adivasis live is quite primitive. Division of labor is so meager that the economic structure shows an almost total absence of village industry. The traditional Indian village, however backward, boasts a complement of village artisans supporting the agricultural economy and catering to the consumption and ceremonial needs of the villagers, but tribal villages show little evidence of village crafts. Agricultural implements are generally more primitive than in traditional plains villages.

Adivasis are also educationally backward as compared to non-Adivasis. In the 1971 Census, only about 11 percent of them were

---

[1]The corresponding percentage recorded for the general population of the State in 1971 was 68.

MAP 5

TRIBES IN MAHARASHTRA

recorded as literate, as against 31 percent among the general
rural population. The rate of literacy among Adivasi males was
18 percent, and among females 2 percent. Of the literates among
Adivasis in Maharashtra, only 2.7 percent had completed the
primary stage of education, and only 0.5 percent had completed
the Secondary School Certificate Examination.

The education of Adivasis is far behind that of the general
population. Most primary schools in Adivasi areas are one-teacher
schools. The average number of students in Adivasi areas is 67
per primary school and 260 per secondary school against an average
of 145 and 320 respectively in the non-Adivasi areas. The average
number of students in the primary schools in the State is 12,112
per lakh (per one hundred thousand) population; in the Adivasi
areas it is only 7,626. The average number of students in secondary
schools is 4,230 per lakh of population in the State, whereas in
tribal areas it is only 2,217. The above figures of Adivasi students
must probably be taken with a large pinch of salt; they do not
reflect real attendance. In the State as a whole there are ten
secondary schools per 100,000 population, whereas in Adivasi areas
there is only one secondary school per 100,000 population.

The common characteristics of Adivasi life in Maharashtra, as
in India generally, are their belief in ghosts and witchcraft, their
addiction to drink, a relatively relaxed (by our standards) moral
code regarding sex and marriage, a fondness for song and dance,
a carefree attitude to life, and a pervasive "laziness."

Most Adivasi tribes have suffered greatly as a result of
contact with "civilization": land seizure, exploitation through
tenancy, usury, trading, and forced labor; frequent beatings,
woundings, and torture of the helpless; poverty, malnutrition,
degradation, and virtual slavery. All these have marked their
recent history, and in consequence they entertain a great
suspicion and fear of the outsider and try to withdraw into
themselves.

Most of these traits may be found to exist among the Warlis.

THE WARLIS

General Characteristics

The Warlis constitute slightly less than ten percent of the
total Adivasi population in the State, but they are the largest
Adivasi tribe in the area in which AI and GBSK are working. The
total Scheduled Tribes population in the Thana District in 1971
was 579,538 persons out of the total population of 2,281,664
persons; *i.e.*, between 25 and 26 percent. In Dahanu tahsil, in
which Kosbad is situated, the percentage of the Scheduled Tribes
population to total population was 64.93 in 1971.

The main Scheduled Tribes found in the Thana District are
Warli, Malhar Koli, Thakur and Kathodi; Warlis form the major
group and constitute about 40 percent of the Scheduled Tribes
population of the district.   In the Dahanu tahsil, or taluka,
Warlis form the majority of the Scheduled Tribes population and
also of the total taluka population.   In the villages and padas
(hamlets) around Kosbad they amount to 80 percent. (See Map 6.)

Agriculture has been the main occupation of the community,
followed by forest labor.   The majority of the Warli agriculturists
have been small cultivators, cultivating on an average one hectare
per family.   Many Warlis also work as agricultural laborers on
other people's land.   Small cultivators work as agricultural laborers
to supplement their income, while landless laborers have to depend
entirely upon agricultural and other labor for livelihood.   Some
work in forest "coupes" under forest contractors, and others work
in labor cooperatives.   Trees are felled for a variety of purposes,
some for charcoal, and carried to the place where the charcoal
kiln is situated.   They also manage the kiln and look
after the loading of charcoal into trucks.

In the past some of the Warli laborers were "bonded"; that
is, they had to work in the house and/or on the farm of their
master from whom they had taken loans.   Most of the loans were
marriage loans, and these laborers were called *lagnagadis*
(marriage-debt-laborers).   Their hours of work ranged from 10
to 12 per day and even more in the busy season.   They were paid
a small local measure of paddy, and the wage rate was less than
that for casual laborers.   It took the Warli families years,
sometimes generations, to pay off their "debts" in this manner.
This custom is now reported to be on the wane but is not totally
extinct.

Warlis are even more backward in their education than the
general Adivasi population of the State.   In 1971 literacy among
Adivasis generally (rural and urban combined) was about 12
percent whereas among the Warlis it was only about 8 percent.
About 14 percent males and 2 percent females among the Warli
tribe were recorded as literate in the 1971 census, as against 19
percent males and 4 percent females among the total Adivasis in
the State.   As in education, in other matters also, the Warlis
were and are considered to be the most backward of all the
Adivasis in the State, with the possible exception of the Madias
and Kathodis.

Earlier in this century most of the land in the tracts of
which we speak belonged to the Warlis.   After the opening up of
these areas to outside influences and particularly during famine
years the Warlis began to lose their lands to moneylenders and
others at such absurdly low prices that by the Thirties there
was hardly any Adivasi who could be described as a landowner.
All the land was gobbled up by outsiders, and the Warlis, like
other Adivasis, worked as tenants.   A half-share of the produce

MAP 6

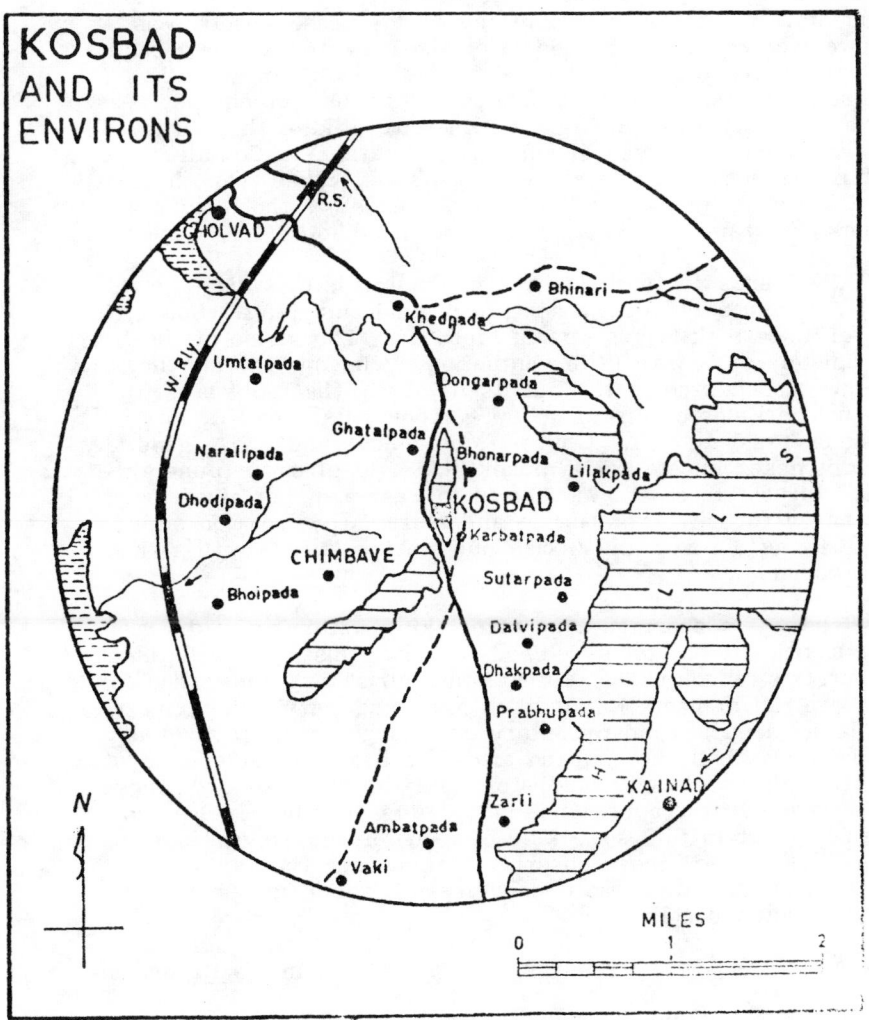

KOSBAD
AND ITS
ENVIRONS

R.S.
CHOLVAD
Bhinari
Khedpada
W. RIV.
Umtalpada
Dongarpada
Ghatalpada
Bhonarpada
Naralipada
Lilakpada
Dhodipada
KOSBAD
Karbatpada
CHIMBAVE
Sutarpada
Bhoipada
Daivipada
Dhakpada
Prabhupada
KAINAD
Zarli
N
Ambatpada
Vaki

MILES
0   1   2

was the prevalent rate of rent; in addition, the Warli family had to
work on the private estate and in the household of the landlord
either for nothing or for very low wages. The Warli family grew
only one kharif crop of paddy producing from 7 to 12 quintals per
hectare. After paying the rent there was little left to subsist on.
According to various estimates and in different areas, from two to
four months of the year were spent in a state of semi-starvation.
A thin porridge (*ambil*) of rice seasoned with a little salt was the
main diet during the lean months, and this had frequently to be
supplemented with jungle roots, leaves of trees, and various kinds
of rodents. At the beginning of the sowing season paddy was
borrowed for consumption, and after the harvest they paid back
up to twice the quantity borrowed. The rates of interest, if
calculated on this basis, ranged from 100 to 200 percent per year.[1]
In grass cutting, tree felling, and charcoal making they received
very low wages and lived in subhuman conditions. Conditions of
the Warli tenants and workers were generally worse than those of
serfs. Physical torture and occasional murder of the Warlis were
not unknown, and Warli women were reported to be freely misused.

The Warlis continue to live in huts made of *kuda* (a sort of
cane) stalks smeared with a mixture of mud and dung. Roofs are
made of large teak leaves strung together. The inside of the hut
is completely dark with little ventilation. The few animals they
have are also housed in the hut itself during the rainy season.
Household articles consist of a few earthen pots, possibly an
occasional brass utensil. Children, both boys and girls, generally
go about naked except for a nicker-like strip of cloth round their
waist. In past times the Warli used to wear a nicker-sized loin
cloth and a turban. Now shorts and shirts are a common sight,
except among old men and women now wear a knee-length sari
and a bodice.

There is a shortage even of drinking water in the dry months,
and sometimes it has to be fetched from long distances. Bathing
is, therefore, infrequent. Women's and girls' hair, unwashed for
days, are full of lice. Malnutrition and unsanitary living give rise
to malaria, diarrhea and dysentery on a large scale. Even today
in many padas half the children are afflicted with scabies and look
terribly undernourished, lackluster, and rickety. As the children
grow, they give the appearance of thriving, partly because they
can roam about to find some kind of food for themselves, partly
because (it is said) they "absorb nutrition from the sunlight."
For "medical" care the traditional Warli institution is the *Bhagat*--
a kind of witch-doctor.

Alcohol is a great scourge. D. Symington in his *Report on*

----

[1]In some areas even today they are reported to be around 500
to 600 percent.

the Aboriginal and Hill Tribes[1] said that the tribals "drink as a race." This is broadly true of the Warlis: a few drops of liquor are poured into the mouth of the newborn baby; a few drops in the mouth is the last gift to the dead. Thus, literally, from the cradle to the grave drinking haunts the Warlis. The Bhagat cannot function without drink; the marriage priestess (*Dhavleri*) cannot perform her rituals without drink; and the tribal council cannot judge cases in the absence of liberal quantities of drink. In short, liquor is consumed extensively in all rituals on all social occasions, and by virtually all Warlis irrespective of age or sex.

In days past the favorite drink was *toddy*, supposed to be nutritious and less inebriating. Now toddy-tapping is legally prohibited except on a license. The Warlis are now increasingly drinking a brew of black *gur* (jaggery or raw sugar) fermented with alum, and numerous illicit stills are said to be operating in Warli houses. This gur-alum concoction is considered to be extremely strong and a serious health hazard.

The Warli Mind

A few sociopsychological characteristics of the Warli, significant from the point of view of his modernization, are mentioned here as important elements in an understanding of him.

A well-known Warli song runs as follows:

> If you are born a Brahmin,
>   You will die writing;
>
> If you become a Marwadi,[2]
>   You will die weighing;
>
> If you become a Chamar[3]
>   You will die making straps and *jotas*[4]
>
> But if you are born a Warli
>   You will be the King of the Jungle.

The proud tone of this song is deceptive; there is hardly anything in an average Warli's life which corroborates, at least on

---

[1]*Report on the Aboriginal and Hill Tribes of the Partially Excluded Areas in the Province of Bombay*, Superintendent, Government Printing and Stationery, Bombay, 1939.

[2]Member of a trading-cum-money-lending caste.

[3]Leatherworker

[4]A *jota* is a leather collar around the neck of a yoked bullock.

a conscious level, the essence of the song. His spiritual world is governed by evil spirits and unkind gods, and his secular world is governed by exploiters in the persons of landlords, moneylenders, traders, police, and civil officers of the government. The Warli has been a slave to all these. No "King of the Jungle," he is a "King of shreds and patches."

Fear is his common characteristic. He seems to be perpetually haunted by it. An anecdote about a tribal community tells of a tribal youth, trying to run away from a government officer on his visit, who, when caught and brought back to the officer, was actually discovered to be a tiger-killer. The "government" is, for the Warli, the quintessence of exploitation, and the Nargolkars[1] have reproduced a lullaby sung by the Warli women at the time of the naming ceremony which asks the child not to be afraid, among other things, of "Sarkar-Darbar"; *i.e.*, government and its paraphernalia. In the face of atrocities exacted upon him, the Warli has hardly ever raised his hand or shown any other sign of resistance. Elsewhere, as the history books tell us, an occasional murder of a moneylender might act as a check on usury; but no instances of this kind were ever reported from the Warli or other tribal areas. In fact, as Symington has reported, the crime rates in tribal areas are among the lowest. These people seem to be the almost perfect examples of what Verrier Elwin has described as "loss of nerve" affecting almost all tribals.

The Nargolkars say that the Warli has no inspiring history. One Warli story tells of a great Warli king of old to whom a Brahmin once came asking for sacred alms. On being asked what his pleasure was, the Brahmin replied, "Land admeasuring a bullock's hide." The king agreed and the Brahmin's "bullock's hide" went on expanding such that it finally enveloped all his kingdom. It is significant, if tragic, that being cheated out of the land is actually the theme of an old folk-tale; indeed, his more recent history is full of such incidents. More significant from the present point of view is the fact that such history can hardly inspire anybody. K. J. Save, author of *The Warlis*, gives a more telling example of the Warli's unflattering self-image by quoting a Warli saying about the origin of the name Warli. "The God created us last and thus finished the rotten business (*pida Warali* in Marathi); therefore we are Warlis."[2]

Probably indicative of this low self-image and also of an absence of a sense of individuality are some of the Warli names: Thinny (*Patlya*) for one who is born thin; Smally (*Barkya*) for one who is born small; Manglya or Mangli for a baby born on a

---

[1] Kusum Nargolkar and Vasant Nargolkar, *Jangalche Raje* (Marathi), Shri Mouni Vidyapeeth, Gargoti, 1955, p. 102.

[2] K. J. Save, *The Warlis*, Padma Publications, Bombay, 1945, pp. 168-69.

Tuesday (*Mangalwar*); Chaitya or Chaiti for one born in the
Chaitra month; and so on. These are almost common nouns rather
than proper nouns, and the lists of names given by the Nargolkars
hardly exceed a page. The widely prevalent custom among all
sections of the Hindu society of naming children after gods and
goddesses is conspicuous by its absence among the Warlis.

Along with most tribal communities the Warlis, too, are
described as "lazy." This laziness is probably a result of varied
factors, not the least of which is the Warli's low level of nutrition
and its inevitable concomitant, a general listlessness. Torpor
induced by liquor would be another factor. Indolence may have
been culturally determined in part through a lack of faith in
human effort in a world ruled by animistic deities and aerial
spirits. According to some observers, racial memories of a hunting
life of old still haunt the Warlis and prevent them from concentrating
on work in a confined area. There is some evidence for this
conjecture. A Warli boy may even today spend hours chasing a
flying bird and trying to kill it with a stone. The Nargolkars
refer to the apparently strange habit of Warli children being
excited over a mouse, chasing it and killing it, shouting war-like
cries. (There is hardly any other game left for them to hunt!)

Associated with the above is the Warli habit of living from
one moment to the next. It is said that he hardly ever thinks of
the morrow, and his pleasures all consist of the immediate rather
than the remote. This is epitomized in a Warli adage, "Catch fish
and drink; the rains are yet far away."[1] When among themselves,
therefore, the Warlis are generally supposed to be of a happy and
cheerful disposition. On almost empty stomachs they can dance the
livelong night to the tune of the *tarpa* (a wind instrument).

The fact that the padas of the Warlis (and other hill tribes)
are somewhat scattered may have been an obstacle to organized
social life. We suspect that the Warlis have few of the associations
ordinarily conjured up in the ordinary Indian villager's mind at
the mention of his village, although this topic is a matter for
further investigation. Another interesting aspect of Warli life
that invites investigation is inter-pada relations, for there is some
evidence to suggest that these are less than cordial if not downright hostile. The reminiscences of Tarabai Modak, the earliest of
those associated with GBSK in Kosbad, record strange occurrences
like that of the children of one pada disappearing from a *Balwadi*
(nursery or kindergarten) when children from another joined it.

Even within the village, in fact even within the family,
observers have suggested a lack of familial warmth. The Warli
family is nuclear in the sense that as soon as the son marries he

---

[1]*Ibid.*, p. 232.

sets up a separate kitchen, if not a separate household. Parents, however old and helpless, it is said, are not properly looked after. Here again, pervasive poverty may be at least part of the explanation, but Banfield's "amoral familism," may be more appropriately descriptive.[1]

An integrating mechanism in any society is a developed language which makes conversation possible. It has been said, unverifiably, that the traditional Warli dialect used to consist of only 300 words. Lack of social life among Warlis, except on occasions of ritual, may owe itself to this deficiency. (The Warli dialect has no script.)

Beyond this, the linguistic handicap may indeed have had an inhibiting effect on the Warli power of thinking. This, combined with the absence of any general intellectual discipline which the inability to count is apt to produce, may have given rise to a native simplicity and innocence that characterizes Warli thinking as it finds   expression in their cosmology, their folk tales and songs, their total Weltanschauung. Harischandra Patil, the first head of AI at Kosbad, has told us one of the ways in which the *Savkar* (landlord-cum-moneylender) used to cheat the Warlis. When a hen laid an egg, the Savkar would offer to buy it for the few *paise* that was its price then, but not take delivery immediately; he would take the full-grown cock or hen a few weeks later saying that the price had already been paid. This, on the one hand, no doubt shows the cunning of the Savkars; on the other, and more important for our purposes, it is a revealing comment on the Warli's innocence bordering on gullibility.

EARLY EFFORTS TO IMPROVE
THE CONDITIONS OF TRIBAL PEOPLE

The Influence of Voluntary Agencies

New influences began to act on the traditional pattern of Warli life from the first decade of the present century. The beginning of ameliorative efforts was made by Christian missionaries. An American Protestant mission, "Church of the Brethren Mission," began running a dispensary in Malyan, near Dahanu, in 1903, and its medical activities gradually expanded. The Mission started schooling activities in 1923, beginning with a rural boarding school for boys with an agricultural and crafts bias. A Catholic mission, "Society of Jesus," started its educational activities in the Umbargaon tahsil (now in Gujarat State) in 1926. The missionaries were thus the pioneers of Adivasi uplift.

The attention of Indians was attracted to tribal areas only in the early Twenties. The Servants of India Society, founded by the liberal leader, G. K. Gokhale, started its tribal uplift work in

---

[1]Edward C. Banfield, *The Moral Basis of a Backward Society*, Free Press, Glencoe, Illinois, 1958.

the Panchmahals district of Gujarat under the dedicated leadership of A. V. Thakkar (or Thakkar Bappa as he was called), and in course of time the work grew to cover many tribal areas in various parts of India.

What attracted the attention and shocked the conscience of the thinking people of the then Bombay State was D. Symington's *Report on the Aboriginal and Hill Tribes* published in 1939. This report exposed in full the mechanics of exploitation and chastised government administration in no uncertain terms. It marked the beginning of a new ethos. After the resignation of the first Congress Ministry in Bombay, the former Prime Minister, Shri B. G. Kher, paid personal attention to the problems of Adivasis in the State and with the help of Acharya Bhise and others founded the Adivasi Seva Mandal in 1940. The Mandal's activities in the Thana District included propaganda among the Adivasis regarding their rights, striving for redress of the injustices done to them, running grain banks, starting schools, giving medical facilities, and organizing cooperative societies of forest labor.

Faint beginnings of a larger social consciousness and awareness of need to come together for solving common problems became apparent when a section of Warlis met together in 1934. According to K. J. Save, representatives of about fifty Warli villages from the coastal and central parts of the Dahanu tahsil held a conference at Waki in that year. It appears from Save's account that the main task the conference performed was to lay down rules relating to marriage. Some of these rules reflect the Warli's desire to bring themselves closer to Brahmanic rites (a very good example of what sociologist, M. N. Srinivas, calls "Sanskritization").

The first flicker of Warli resistance to exploitation was seen in 1944, when author K. J. Save then a Special Officer, Tribals, discreetly asked the Warlis to stop work if they did not get the fixed minimum wage, and this led to a strike of about one thousand Warlis in several villages of the Umbargaon tahsil. This strike, however, was short-lived and, by and large, unsuccessful.

The next, and far more important, step was taken by the Kisan Sabha under the leadership of Communist Party Worker Mrs. Godavari Parulekar, in 1945. Mrs. Parulekar, affectionately called "Godarani" (Queen Goda) by the Warlis, assiduously worked in three tahsils, and for the first time the Warlis gave enthusiastic, wholehearted support. The agitation against landlords, moneylenders, and contractors culminated in police firing in Talwade village in the Umbargaon tahsil. Three Warlis were shot dead and several injured on the 11th of October, 1945. On December 9, 1946, two thousand Warlis marched to Nanivali when another police firing took five lives. The "Warli Revolt" made headlines all over the world. Leaders of the revolt were rounded up, Godarani was served with an expulsion notice, and the revolt soon died down.

---

[1]M. N. Srinivas, *Social Change in Modern India*, University of California Press, Berkeley and Los Angeles, 1966.

Summing up her reminiscences of this period Mrs. Parulekar says,

> After the many battles that the Adivasis had to
> fight to solve their economic problems and to get
> increased wages, their economic condition today is
> better than it was. But it would be wrong to
> assume they no longer starve. The difference in
> their condition has not been so great that they no
> longer need to eat roots and leaves.[1]

She claims, however, that the Adivasi has gained in self-respect and a new self-assertion. To quote the concluding paragraph of her book:

> The main change in the Warli is the awakening of his
> pride and self-consciousness as a human being. His
> manner and deportment reflects the self-confidence
> he has gained out of the knowledge of his strength as
> a member of organization. He has lost his fear and
> his inferiority complex. He has become ambitious.
> He is consumed by a desire to understand world
> politics.... He has begun to desire a better life
> and in order to get it, he is willing to put in any
> amount of effort.... The Adivasi who was afraid
> and could not put two words together in a coherent
> manner now stands on the dais and makes political
> speeches....[2]

Our limited experience suggests that these claims are exaggerated; however, the "Warli Revolt" must be counted a significant event from the point of view of the self-assertion of the Warlis.

Governmental Measures

The government's ameliorative measures have stressed the regulation of tenancy, moneylending, and wages. A beginning in the direction of regulation of tenancy was made by the Government of Bombay in 1939. From then until 1956, when a new and radical amendment to the Bombay Tenancy and Agricultural Lands Act was passed, the provisions of various laws and amendments included, among other things, security of tenure, scaling down rents and voluntary repurchase of land by the tenants. The 1956 "Land to the Tiller" amendment sought to confer land ownership rights on the tenants at a nominal price. Since the objective of the new amendment was to abolish the tenancy system (with a few exceptions) and to substitute owner-cultivation in its place, those who benefited from the law benefited substantially in the sense that they acquired (restricted) property rights in the

---

[1]Godavari Parulekar, *Adivasis Revolt*, National Book Agency Private Ltd., Calcutta, 1975, p. 182.

[2]*Ibid.*, p. 188.

land; those who for any reason (legal or otherwise) failed to
acquire ownership rights suffered substantially because they lost
even the tenancy rights.

In order to improve the conditions of Adivasis working for
forest contractors and plantation owners, minimum wages were laid
down in the Forties; from 1954 the Minimum Wages Act was also
extended to this area.

Since 1947 the government has been encouraging formation of
Cooperative Labor Contract Societies for forest workers. Many
societies, under strict governmental supervision, were reported
to be running well.

Prohibition of alcoholic beverages was imposed on the (then)
Bombay State in 1950 to good effect for a year or so. But gradually implementation became lax and illicit distillation was
generally on the increase.

The educational efforts of the Government of Bombay generally
followed the recommendations made by the Wandrekar Committee
appointed in 1947. The government's policy until then had been
to establish a primary school in every village having more than
1000 population; this was obviously unsuited to the needs of the
Adivasis who lived in very small hamlets. The limit of 1000 was,
therefore, brought down to 500. A few boarding schools were
also established. After a time the concept arose of the "Ashram
Shala" in which a residential school was accompanied by a farm
and/or craft training facilities.

In the early Fifties the "Sarvodaya" scheme was applied to
the Thana District. Under this scheme about 20 to 30 Adivasi
villages in each district were selected for special programs like
agricultural improvement, village industry, education, health,
water supply, and cultural uplift, and a sum of Rs. 4   lakhs
for a period of four years for each such unit was set apart for
this purpose. The Sarvodaya centers were to be run, not by
government administration, but by tested and experienced social
workers mostly belonging to the Sarvodaya movement which was
started by Vinoba Bhave, the famous *Bhoodan* (land-gift movement)
leader.

A few other measures such as grain banks, distribution of
forest lands ("plots") for cultivation, and some facilities for using
forest produce for home use have also been in existence.

Results of Voluntary and Governmental Efforts

The effect of voluntary and government efforts on the
Adivasis, especially the Warlis, have in general been extremely
limited.

The efforts of the Christian missionaries were largely directed to educational and health needs; they did not try to grapple with the underlying economic problems, nor did they strike root among local people because of their proselytizing activities. Efforts of voluntary constructive agencies like the Adivasi Seva Mandal did result in some useful contributions, like legal help, occasional redress of grievances, and the setting up of cooperative societies. But the Mandal's work lacked teeth for two reasons. It avoided confrontation and militancy where it was needed; many of the office bearers themselves came from the exploiting classes, and they constituted the main support of the ruling Congress Party in this area. Mrs. Godavari Parulekar's work was significant in that it aroused the Warli from his age-old torpor and taught him self-respect. But it was purely agitative; its "educational" content was exclusively political. In fact, reports suggest that the Communists ridiculed constructive effort of any kind, including that of curbing drink addiction. Another feature of the Communist movement, according to knowledgeable people in the area, was terror, practiced on the Adivasis.

However, to the credit of the Warli uprising the worst forms of exploitation and atrocities diminished, if they did not disappear altogether. Wages improved. The uprising also proved that the somnolent Warli was capable of being roused and fighting back. At least some Warlis reached a high level of political consciousness and to the extent that self-assertion and belief in human effort (*e.g.*, that the Savkar can be humiliated by organized strength) are also the mainspring of economic development, even political agitation must be given its due importance in the economic context. That the impulse of self-reliance was not directed into economic channels is, of course, another story. It must be remembered, however, that the Communists became one with the Warlis, suffered with them and for them, and were thus able to secure their confidence in much greater degree than other voluntary organizations and political parties.

Moneylending legislation by government has nowhere been a real success and therefore its failure must have been far worse in the Adivasi areas. The "Land to the Tiller" Amendment to the Bombay (now Maharashtra) Tenancy Act was important. It appears that the tenancy system which was the characteristic tenure in these areas has now given way to owner cultivation although, even today, the proportion of tenancy is higher in Adivasi than non-Adivasi areas. But some qualifications are necessary: the lands that the landlords parted with are reported to be inferior, the superior ones being retained for "self-cultivation." There is concealed tenancy in many areas in the wake of the tenancy legislation and the situation is not different here. Possession of land has not led to much improvement in economic conditions because of the moneylenders' hold. Educational efforts have met with little success. It is common in many villages for either the schoolteacher or the children not to turn up. The content and methods of education have been too orthodox and formal without sufficient relevance to the conditions of Adivasi life. As for

the prohibition of alcoholic beverages and other measures of Adivasi
uplift, the general laxity and corruption in government administration has been proverbial.

There have been special programs like the Tribal Development
Blocks. Ashram Shalas (residential primary schools with agricultural and craft bias) have increased in number. Now there is a
special Adivasi subplan with much larger allocations, but its
results have yet to be seen, and many policies are still in a state
of flux.

In any case, government efforts have not kept pace with the
growing population. Since independence, poverty in both absolute
and relative terms is generally considered to have increased in
India. The Adivasi areas are no exception. In fact, what is true
of the larger rural population is likely to be even more true of the
Adivasis. J. S. (Jayant) Patil, head of AI since 1968, tells us
that he sees more disease and poverty today than thirty years ago.

One difference between the other Warli tracts and the area
around the Kosbad Institutes must, however, be noted. There are
many chikoo and banana plantations in the surrounding area that
give year-round employment, and wages today are said to be Rs.
5 or 6 per day for adult workers. During the five years it takes
for the chikoo trees to become ripe enough to yield their fruit,
lily and rose flowers are planted between the rows, and this activity
provides employment for children. (The flowers are plucked in the
early morning around 1:00 a.m., and after the evening meals
the children usually sleep on the plantation and are awakened in
time for the plucking.) Rigors of usury are reported to be less
intense than in other Warli tracts.

It is against this general background of the Warli life and
mind that the educational and other efforts of the Kosbad
Institutes must be seen and evaluated.

CHAPTER 2

EVOLUTION OF THE INSTITUTES

This chapter provides a brief description of the evolution of the AI and GBSK from their early beginnings, with emphasis on the strong moral strain that has characterized them and still, to an extent, sustains them.

THE AGRICULTURAL INSTITUTE
(AI)

The parent body of the AI is the Gokhale Education Society (GES), established in 1917, in memory of Gopal Krishna Gokhale (1866-1915), a leader of the "Moderate" (Liberal) wing in the national independence struggle, an influential statesman and a man of enlightened ideas on social and educational reform. Mahatma Gandhi considered Gokhale his political "Guru." To understand the social reformist aspirations of GES, it is necessary to note that Gopal Krishna Gokhale had himself founded the Servants of India Society in 1905, an organization dedicated to such ideals as the spread of education, service to the depressed classes, famine relief, and Hindu-Muslim unity.   Gokhale was a man of wide influence and prestige, having been a worker of the Sarvajanik Sabha in Poona, Local Secretary of the Indian National Congress held in Poona in 1895, a member of the Bombay Legislative Council (1899-1902), and a member of the Viceroy's Council for twelve years.   The GES was in fact only one of several institutions that were established in the country in the name of Gopal Krishna Gokhale.

One of his admirers was T. A. Kulkarni, a high school teacher in Bombay, whose great compassion for the poor and the unfortunate was a leading attribute of his life; even as a young man he had spent a great deal of time working for industrial workers in the labor areas of Bombay or comforting the inmates of jails. His concern for the disadvantaged was accompanied by a strong interest in agriculture and crafts. He had carried out experiments on fiber development and cattle feed.

The GES is probably the only institution in Maharasthra founded and nurtured by the urban elite that catered at least in part to the educational needs of the rural, backward, and poverty-stricken areas. The history of the GES over the years indicates

that it has given equal attention to both urban and rural areas.
if the first expression of its solicitude for the poor was a high
school in the industrial workers' locality in Bombay, the second was
the establishment in 1920 of what became the Soonabai Pestonji
Hakimji (SPH) High School in Bordi in the Thana District. Through
the combined efforts of T. A. Kulkarni, S. R. Bhise and others,
the Gokhale Education Society was formed. Its constitution,
drafted by the founder of the Trade Union Movement, Shri N. M.
Joshi, was based on the principle of life membership (*i.e.*, members
serving for life and dedicating themselves to the cause of education)
--a practice that had already been established among educational
workers in Maharashtra. As noted above, the GES started its
educational work in 1918 by taking over a proprietary high school
in Bombay later named Dharamsi Govinaji Thackersey High School.
A sign of Kulkarni's interest in crafts was that this high school
was the first institution in India to manufacture spinning wheels
for Mahatma Gandhi.

Another, probably deeper and more pervasive influence on
the further growth and development of GES in the Thana District
was that of S. R. Bhise, or Acharya Bhise, as he was called. As
a young man he came into contact with Kulkarni; and in joining him
in founding the GES, he was asked by Kulkarni to serve in Bordi.
From 1920 until his death in 1969 he spent his life in the service
of GES and of the down-trodden generally. His formal work as an
English teacher and headmaster of the SPH High School in Bordi
formed only a part of his total activity, which covered all the
downtrodden classes in the Thana District. A great Gandhian,
Bhise and his colleagues, including K. M. Chitre, inspired generations of students to take up social work, especially among the
Adivasis. The Adivasi Seva Mandal, founded in 1940, the Forest
Labor Cooperative Societies, experiments in "basic education," and
many other similar movements were launched and nurtured by him.
All in all, a model of self-abnegation, Bhise stood as a towering
figure over the area for about fifty years.

In 1939 the first popular Ministry of the Congress Party was
formed in the Bombay State. Rural development had priority in
its program. In this new atmosphere Bhise started a Rural Development Training Center at Bordi, which gave a certificate course
of one year in Rural Development. The Government of Bombay
subscribed to this idea and extended support to the new venture.
As the GES claims, the Rural Development idea in one of its most
important aspects (*i.e.*, the creation of a multipurpose village-
level worker) actually originated at the Bordi Center. The program,
however, was short-lived. It came to a halt in 1942 when the whole
nation became engulfed in the "Quit India" movement.

The threads were picked up after independence in 1947 when
the time was more propitious for undertaking programs on a larger
scale. To a sense of urgency in the air, there was added an
accumulated fund of ideas and experiences that people wanted to
put into practice. T. A. Kulkarni, who at this time headed the
HPT College at Nasik (started in 1924), took the initiative in

establishing an agricultural institute. By this time, the Government
of Maharashtra had decided to establish one agricultural school in
each district. Taking into account the drive and experience of the
team working at Bordi, the government decided to recognize the
Rural Development Training Center as its official agency in the
Thana District. Thus came into existence the Agricultural Institute
at Bordi in 1947. It may be noted that this is the only instance in
which a private agency was recognized by the government to work
on its behalf. The Institute was soon shifted to Kosbad and started
functioning there from the beginning of 1949.

The first head of the AI at Kosbad was Harishchandra Gopal
Patil, who was S. R. Bhise's student at the SPH High School in
Bordi and whom Bhise had persuaded to study agriculture in spite
of Patil's wish to become a lawyer.   As a young boy, H. G. Patil
was introduced to the study of Adivasi life by Bhise. From 1931
to 1949 he taught agriculture to SPH High School students and
then shifted to head the AI at Kosbad. AI's research, training,
and development activities in the first twenty years was due
mainly to the efforts of H. G. Patil. His memorable contribution
to Indian agriculture was propagation of the Japanese method of
paddy cultivation which he had studied in Japan as a member of an
Indian agricultural delegation in 1951. Kosbad was the testing
ground for the new experiments, and Patil toured almost the
whole of India broadcasting the Japanese method.

In 1968, Jayant Shamrao Patil succeeded H. G. Patil as
head of AI and continues as its leader today.   Jayant Patil, also
a student of Bhise and Chitre at SPH High School, was the son
of Shamrao Patil, a freedom fighter and former Minister of Rural
Development in the Bombay Congress Ministry. Like H. G. Patil,
Jayant Patil was prevailed upon to study agriculture in spite of
his own desire to study law.

Jayant Patil took his Bachelor of Science degree in agriculture
and joined the AI in 1949. Standing first in pursuit of his
M.Sc. degree, he later, as a Fulbright scholar, studied Agricultural
Extension and Horticulture at Kansas State University in the
United States in 1962.   He carried out research on grasses at
the Brisbane University in Australia in 1971, and took up this
same type of research in England in 1976.   In spite of many
lucrative and prestigious job offers, Jayant Patil continues in
his present position which he has   held for the last 29 years,
because he feels his work lies in Kosbad. AI now has a 265-acre
well-equipped farm, and its many thriving activities are largely
due to Jayant Patil's drive and restless energy.

Management and Finances

AI is not an independent institution, but a branch of the
Gokhale Education Society (GES), a registered society and public
trust, with its head office in Bombay. The Society runs several
schools and colleges at different places in Maharashtra. AI is the

only institution of GES, however, which carries on research and
training in agriculture. Two schools at Bordi and Talasari in the
adjacent area impart school training with an agricultural bias.

GES has a board of trustees that looks after the property and
the general management of AI. The schools and colleges are managed
by life members (employees who have been selected to serve for
life, *i.e.*, minimum 25 years). There is also a body called the
"Senate" representing teachers and other employees in the institutions run by the GES; real power is, however, in the hands of
the life members.

Jayant Patil, Principal of the AI and Director of the Krishi
Vigyan Kendra (Agricultural Science Center), is the only GES life
member in Kosbad. He is also the treasurer.

Although the overall authority rests formally with the board
of life members, the AI, especially its Head, can exercise a
considerable amount of initiative.

The AI, in its manifold activities (to be described later)
employs in all 84 persons in different categories. Not all
activities are directed to Adivasi development, but it is a peculiar
feature of the AI that most staff are involved, as and when the
need arises, in activities addressed to the development problems
of surrounding areas. In addition, the trainees and students are
made to participate in these activities. Thus, the total manpower
input going into developmental activities, although not precisely
measureable, is quite large.

The AI has total assets of about Rs. 2.5 million. Its budget
for the year 1977-78 showed total receipts of Rs. 1,964,950,
payments of Rs. 2,092,500 and a deficit of Rs. 127,550. Of the total
receipts of Rs. 2,092,500 the component of government grants
was 1,460,300 or roughly 60 percent.

GRAM BAL SHIKSHA KENDRA
(GBSK)

Strong moral undercurrents are visible in the founding and
growth of GBSK. Its history begins with Mrs. Tarabai Modak
(nee Kelkar), born in 1892 in a Prarthana Samajist family in Bombay.
Prarthana Samaj was a late nineteenth century socio-religio-
reformist movement started by such early graduates of Bombay
University as Justice M. G. Ranade, the Orientalist R. G.
Bhandarkar, Vaman Abaji Modak, and others. Tarabai's father,
Sadashiv Pandurang Kelkar, was the first full-time "missionary" of
the Samaj. He married a widow in days when widow remarriage
was considered taboo and actively opposed. The widow whom he
married belonged to another Brahmin subcaste, and this type of
alliance was also a departure from custom. Sadashiv Pandurang
Kelkar edited the Prarthana Samaj organ, "Subodh Patrika," for
many years and ran a weekly for industrial workers. Uma,

Tarabai's mother, was also far ahead of the contemporary Indian womanhood in general enlightenment and social awareness. Young Tarabai was thus brought up in a uniquely progressive household.

She married into another Prarthana Samajist family, the Modaks, and her husband, K. V. Modak, was a prosperous lawyer in Amraoti. However, the union proved unhappy, and Tarabai left Amraoti in 1923 for Dakshinamoorti near Bhavnagar in Gujarat. Here, under the leadership of Girijashankar (Gijubhai) Badheka, she spent nine years in building up a child education movement that took the form of Nutan Bal Shikshan Sangh (NBSS), founded in 1926. Tarabai and Gijubhai modeled their preschool programs on a combination of Froebel and Montessori, but thoroughly "Indianized" them.

Tarabai came to Bombay in 1936 and started the first preschool center, "Shishu-Vihar," in a middle-class locality. The urge to suit preschool education to the needs and circumstances of the vast masses of poverty-ridden people of India, always dormant within her mind, first found expression in a scavengers' colony in Bombay and finally in the establishment of GBSK as a branch of the NBSS in Bordi in 1945. If Gijubhai can be credited with the "Indianiza-tion" of preschool education, Tarabai can be credited with its "ruralization."

Because Tarabai divided her time between Shishu Vihar and GBSK for the first few years, the main burden of work at Bordi fell on Anutai Wagh. Anutai Wagh had become a widow at the age of 13; she had completed only three years of primary education before her marriage. Later on she completed her primary education at various places and joined the Training College at Pune. After completing the training courses, she joined a primary school at Chandwad in Nasik District as an assistant teacher. She left her job in 1933 and joined the primary section at Hujurpaga Girls' High School in Pune as a teacher. She entered night school and passed her matriculation while working as a primary teacher. Later she acquired a B.A. at Bombay University.

The Kasturba Memorial Trust organized some camps to train women volunteers to run educational centers for children and women. One such camp was organized at Boriwali, a suburb of Bombay, in 1945, where Tarabai was one of the lecturers. Tarabai asked the participants if any of them were ready to work in tribal areas and run a preschool center there. Anutai, tired of a routine teaching job and wanting to do social work in a wider field, volunteered, and this heroic step was the beginning of a remarkable partnership that lasted until Tarabai's death in August 1973.

GBSK's work at Bordi from 1945 to 1957 could be considered pioneering in many ways. During these years it transformed both the content as well as the methods of established preschool and primary education. These will be described later.

While at Bordi, Tarabai and Anutai began to spread their net wider in order to encompass the really disadvantaged classes of society--for Bordi, after all, was a middle-sized township and not representative of the rural areas. About 5 km. from Bordi lived a small group of the Dubla Adivasi tribe, for whose children a Balwadi was started in the year 1952. Here new problems were encountered and new solutions sought. The critical "Vikaswadi" concept (to be discussed later) developed out of the experiences with Dubla children.

However, the inner cravings of Tarabai and Anutai to work in the heartland of poverty and backwardness could not be satisfied by a mere appendage of Adivasi child education. Tarabai, therefore, wound up affairs at Bordi and in 1956 at the age of sixty-four moved to Kosbad "to play the last difficult gambit of my life."

Today on the Kosbad Hill, adjacent to the AI on the north, stand several one-story buildings of GBSK housing a number of its institutions and activities.

Management and Finances

GBSK is not an independent body, but a branch of a national body called Nutan Bal Shikshan Sangha (NBSS), founded by Girijashankar Gijubhai Badheka and Tarabai Modak in 1926. NBSS is a registered body under the Indian laws with its head office in Bombay and several branches all over India. Its main branches where preschool training is given are mainly in Bombay, Kosbad, Bhavnagar and Pune. Shri Morarji Desai, until recently the Prime Minister of India, is the President of NBSS. Anutai Wagh, Head of the GBSK in Kosbad, is its Secretary.

The work at Kosbad is looked after by the GBSK Committee consisting of 21 members, some of whom are actually working at Kosbad. Anutai Wagh is the Secretary of this Committee and Jayant Patil of the AI is one of its members. The paid staff of the GBSK Committee consists of one office secretary and one watchman. Anutai Wagh is the Honorary Director and also the Principal of Bal Sevika Vidyalaya from which she gets her salary.

The GBSK, in its different activities, employs a total of 93 persons. Of these 21 are attached to the primary school and 20 to the Balwadis. The total physical assets of GBSK are valued at about Rs. 520,000. The potential income earning assets are a farm land of about six hectares, a printing press, and buildings rented to staff (which bring in rent in the amount of about Rs. 20,000).

The total receipts in 1976-77 from all activities amounted to Rs. 474,735; expenditures totaled Rs. 577,801, having a deficit of Rs. 103.066--fairly heavy considering the size of the total budget.

Cooperation Between AI and GBSK

The close and cordial relationship between AI and GBSK dates from the latter's inception at Bordi in 1945. In fact GBSK was set up in Bordi because AI's parent body GES had already started its activities there. Similarly GBSK moved to Kosbad partly because AI was already there.

A number of boys and girls who complete their primary education in the GBSK primary school join the AI's secondary school; some of those who pass out from the secondary school join GBSK's Junior College of Education. Some of those trained there man AI's schools. Thus educationally the efforts of the two are complementary.

Physical proximity of the two Institutes on Kosbad Hill naturally leads to constant interaction. GBSK's farm, for example, gets guidance from AI.

CHAPTER 3

THE AGRICULTURAL
INSTITUTE'S PROGRAMS

This chapter describes the activities in which the AI has engaged--and is currently engaging--itself. The AI, started basically as an agricultural training institute, continues to perform this function today. Actually it was never meant, at least formally, to be a development agency for the Adivasis. Nevertheless, a number of factors have given it over the years a strong orientation towards Adivasi development. One is the ideals of the founders to be of service to the downtrodden. The second is the locale, which happens to be in the heartland of the Adivasi area, and the two are not unrelated. Third, although as a training institute the jurisdiction of AI is the whole Thana District, the agricultural problems of the district as a whole are generally similar to the problems of Adivasi agriculture. Finally, it must not be forgotten that the Adivasis constitute about 25 percent of the population of the district.

A brief description of AI's several activities follows. Not all these activities have equal importance in relation to the development needs of the surrounding area, yet each is highly relevant for the reasons mentioned above.

EXPERIMENTAL EFFORTS TO IMPROVE CROPS

Japanese Method of Paddy Cultivation

Inasmuch as rice was the main crop grown in the area, it followed that research should begin with rice. The traditional method of burning the plot used for preparing seedlings involved time and energy and resulted in doubtful gains. In 1951, the Bombay Government sent H. G. Patil, principal of the AI, and two others to Japan to study rice cultivation techniques. The "Japanese Method," subsequently tried at Kosbad, consisted of preparing *raised* seed beds as against *flat* ones, admixing salt water and medicines to seeds before use, using farmyard and compost manure, thin sowing, transplanting in rows, and interculturing with hand hoes. Nothing new was required in the way of equipment--just a new kind of discipline. The new method was profitable (the seed rate was reduced from 20 kgs. to 5 kgs. per acre) and accounted

for a 30-35 percent rise in productivity. Although individual
elements of the Japanese Method, except for the raised seed bed,
were known to Indian farmers, the combination of them created a new
technique that later became popular in most rice-growing regions of
India. Patil, assisted by the Gandhi Smarak Nidhi (Gandi Memorial
Fund), toured the whole of India to propagate the new message.

        In trying the new method on its own farm and inviting farmers
of the region to observe it (selected private farms also experimented
and demonstrated its advantages), the Institute made it clear that
preparation of the raised seed bed was the crucial element. The
raised seed bed was manifestly more beneficial, in that it facilitated
the drainage of water and consequently provided ample scope for
root growth. But convincing the farmers, especially the Adivasi,
of this truth became an overriding concern.

HYVs and Green Manure

        The AI was again the pioneer in the introduction of high
yielding varieties of rice (HYV) in the coastal areas of Maharashtra.
In 1967 it planted IR-8 (initially developed at the International Rice
Research Institute in the Philippines) on one acre and took a
harvest of 25 quintals. The HYVs called for heavy doses of
fertilizers and manures. To fill up the deficiency of organic manure
the AI brought the seeds of a fast-growing leguminous shrub
Glyricidia Maculata from Tamil Nadu and established a plantation on
two acres in 1968. In course of time the enterprise became so
successful that the AI now supplies seeds to the whole of Maharsh-
tra.

Community Nursery

        Because July is the most important month for the full growth
of the rice plant, individual farmers, faced with the uncertainties
of rains, were unable to take advantage of its usual rainfall unless
the transplantation operation were completed earlier, and this
required irrigation which the farmers lacked. Therefore, AI
overcame the difficulty by preparing the seedlings on its own
ten-acre farm under irrigation and thus assured a good quality of
paddy crop. It was one of its important findings that transplanting
by the end of June resulted in approximately 35 percent increase
in production, especially advantageous to Adivasi farmers, some
of the poorest of whom were wont to consume the seed, but not
the seedlings, that AI supplied on a no-profit/no-loss basis.

        The major constraint on this activity was the prohibitive
distances: seedlings cannot be carried more than 5 km. from the
nursery, because of both an absence of roads and means of
transport. The remedy has been to establish nurseries at
different places or to set up seedling banks. After 1972, the AI
opened two more branches at Talasari and Waki.

Adaptation of New Varieties

The next stage was the breeding of seeds more suitable to the climate and other ecological conditions of the region. The situation in the Kosbad region demanded a variety that would mature in the shortest possible period, for two reasons. First, because of low water retention the hilly slopes and uplands are fit only for early maturing varieties; second, and more important, because the tribals and other poor farmers, desperate for food, tend to harvest and consume the longer maturing crops before they are fully mature.

After preliminary experiments, the AI found that the "Blue Belle" variety (obtained from the Beaumont Research Center in Texas) was quite suitable to the region. It matured in about 100 days as against Taichung and IR-8 which takes 120-140 days; moreover, it could be directly sown without transplanting the seedlings, thus saving expense. Experiments were also conducted on a locally developed variety known as "Kosbhat" ("kos" is short for Kosbad and "bhat" means paddy) that matures within 120 days and gives 10-15 percent more yield than Taichung. The research is still going on, the ultimate objective being to evolve a variety that will mature within 60 to 70 days and give a large yield.

Anti-Lodging Device

Lodging[1] of the paddy crop was another problem that drew the attention of the research workers of the AI. This problem was particularly acute in the low-lying areas, receiving large quantities of surface soil, leaves, and animal washings in the running water and consequently becoming overfertilized. The soil thus affected encourages the growth of foliage rather than of grain, as a result, the crop tends to fall on the ground. The traditional way of preventing this, known as *posha*, consisted of replantation and cutting of foliage. But it has its shortcomings in that it diminished yield considerably. After a period of five years Jayant Patil determined that spraying a mild dose of "Two-1 Four-8" on the standing crop, thirty days after transplantation, discourages the growth of foliage, and the crop becomes strong enough to stand till the harvest.

Fodder and Grassland Development

The Thana District has about five lakh acres of grassland which, because of the considerable rainfall and humidity, are good for pasture development. During the past fifteen years, the

---

[1]Falling; wind laying the crop flat on the ground.

Institute has done considerable research work to find suitable grasses. Five kinds that have been successfully identified (1966-1976) and introduced so far are: (1) *Sesbania Grandiflora* (Agasti), a leguminous perennial with 17 percent protein; (2) *Lauconia Gloca* (Goparna or Kubabhul), from tropical America, also a perennial with 27.4 percent protein; (3) *Desmanthus Vigratus* (Dasharath Ghas), with 17 percent protein; (4) *Styloseanthes Humilis*, or "Townsville Stylo" (Shravan Ghas), an Australian legume with 17 percent protein; and (5) *Brachiria Decumbus* (Bharat Ghas), also Australian, with 8 percent protein.

Multiple Cropping

Breaking the monocrop pattern and introducing other crops was another important goal of the research program. Farmers had never thought it possible to grow crops other than paddy. The first task before the Institute was to demonstrate to the farmers that it was possible to grow other crops on their lands.

Wheat, together with green gram, was chosen for experimentation. Many varieties of wheat were brought from different parts of the country as well as from outside India. Mexican wheat was found most suitable, but experiments revealed that important adjustments were necessary to suit the soil and climate conditions of the area. It was found, for example, that the second or third week of November was the most suitable period for sowing; that it was necessary to increase the plant population per acre, since the climate in the region was not as cold as in other wheat growing areas; that this in turn necessitated increasing the seed rate to 60-80 kgs. per acre; that since the soil was sticky, it was necessary to reduce the water quota, and so on. In addition to these technical adjustments, there were other peculiar problems that required solutions of a different kind. For example, it was found that, because all the birds flocked on the wheat growing farms, a special program for crop protection against birds was essential. In spite of all the limitations, the Institute succeeded in demonstrating that 8 to 10 quintals of wheat per acre could be produced.

The third experimental crop was that of summer green gram (*Vaishakhi Moong*), which may be substituted for or grown in combination with chillis or various kinds of vegetables. The Institute has developed two varieties of chilli that mature early and yield 30 percent more. Net income from the chilli crop is said to be Rs. 5000 per acre.

Thus the AI claims to have offered a three-crop cycle to coastal and Adivasi farmers. On a three-acre farm that is well supplied with water, at 1978 prices and costs, the economics worked out roughly as follows:

HYV Rice (30 quintals)	Rs. 3000
Wheat (20 quintals)	Rs. 2400
Green gram or vegetables	Rs. 2000

Straw	Rs. 1000
Value of gross production	Rs. 8400
Less cost of cultivation (at 50%)	Rs. 4200
Net Income	Rs. 4200

If the poverty level for a family in India is drawn at an annual income of Rs. 4000, it is evident that the AI's three-crop cycle can lift irrigated three-acre farmers above it. Breaking the mono-crop pattern, however, depends on making irrigation available. The AI's efforts in this direction will be described later.

Cotton

The AI undertook in 1958 adaptive trials on Laxmi Cotton, a crop until then considered unadaptable to the coastal soils. However, the AI seems to have decided to de-emphasize cotton since the crop does not seem to be suited to the Konkan soils. Whatever cotton is grown now is primarily for training purposes.

Poultry

The AI is on the point of releasing a new breed of poultry birds which it is proud to call "Kosbad Breed." Four English breeds (White Leghorn, Rhode Island Red, Black Australarp, and New Hampshire) are crossed with native breeds to produce a variety that is claimed to have the following attributes: early maturity, greater yield, greater resistance to diseases, greater adaptability to local conditions, and greater acceptability. The original Kosbad breed was white in color; because Adivasis need dark-colored cocks for sacrificing to the gods, a dark-colored breed has been produced.

The Surface Well

A simple piece of research is the surface well (known outside as the Kosbad-type well) developed in 1969. A surface well is a shallow cone-like structure, with a 60 foot diameter and a 16 foot depth. The main purpose of the well is to collect the running rain water and allow its use whenever the rains fail and the crop is in danger of being lost. An incidental benefit is that the running water brings along with it leaves and dung, and the silt thus formed in the well is very useful as manure. About 25 cartloads of good quality manure is obtained every year from each surface well. The cost of construction is between Rs. 700 and Rs. 1000. About 15,000 liters of water are conserved in one well. A simple hand pump, costing approximately Rs. 500, is good for the irrigation of one hectare.

EDUCATION AND TRAINING

The educational centers of the AI are described below in the chronological order of their establishment.

The Agricultural School (Krishi Vidyalaya), Kosbad, 1949

The Agricultural School started at Bordi in 1947 and was shifted to Kosbad in 1949 to train young farmers in Thana District in scientific agriculture.   The school admits 90 boys and offers a two-year program in Agriculture, Animal Husbandry, Fruit Gardening, and so forth.   In addition, such subjects as Cooperation, Public Health, Social Education, Applied Nutrition, and the Working of the Revenue Department are also taught.   There is a heavy emphasis on practical training conducted on the Institute's farm growing food and horticultural crops and accommodating both a dairy and poultry.   Each student   receives a stipend of Rs. 40 per month and two sets of uniforms.   Successful candidates obtain a diploma from the Konkan Agricultural University and become absorbed by the Department of Agriculture of Maharashtra Government, or as Gram Sevaks (Village Level Workers).

Residential Primary School (Ashram Vidyalaya), Kosbad, 1958

About 120 Adivasi boys and girls receive primary education at the Residential Primary School where work experience in agriculture and village crafts is provided.

Mahatma Gandhi Tribal Youth Training Center
(Mahatma Gandhi Adivasi Janata Vidyalaya), Kosbad, 1959

This center is a training school, the first of its kind in India, for young and exclusively Adivasi farmers from five districts: Thana, Kulaba, Nasik, Dhule, and Jalgaon.   No diploma or certificate is awarded, and the students are expected to go back to their farms.   The school offers a long term course of one year and a short term course of four months.   About 160 students are admitted every year.

Panchayat Rajya Training Center
(Panchayat Rajya Prashikshan Kendra), Kosbad, 1962

This center gives short courses of about a week's duration and three-day courses in peripatetic camps to Panchas (members) and Sarpanchas (chairmen) of the village councils.   The courses include village planning, agricultural production, health, Panchayat Law, and social education.   Panchas and Sarpanches from Thana, Kulaba, and Nasik Districts attend them.

An incidental advantage afforded AI by this Center is that through the representatives of local government attending the Center it can keep in touch with developments in these three

districts that have large concentrations of Adivasis.   It can also
propagate its innovations in the process.

VLW Training Center (Gram Sevak Prashikshan Kendra),
Kosbad, 1964

        This center caters to the inservice training needs of Village
Level Workers from six districts of the Bombay division and emphasizes training in agricultural production and extension in its
refresher courses.   One is an "upgraded" course for one year, and
the other a short duration course.

Middle School (Madhyamik Vidyalaya), Kosbad, 1965

        The Middle School at Kosbad has attached to it one boys'
hostel and one girls' hostel.   Agriculture is given an important
place in the program, and for this purpose youth clubs have been
established.   These youth club groups are given projects like
poultry keeping, vegetable gardening, and animal care.

        The students are also trained in social service.   With this
aim in view the school has adopted two padas, Ghatalpada and
Dalvipada, where the students go and help the farmers.   In
Ghatapada there is a community irrigation well serving twelve
families, and students help them with the planting of new seeds
and vegetables.   In Dalvipada they are helpful in the development
of kitchen gardening and horticulture, especially with a view to
improving the Adivasi diet.

Residential Primary School (Ashram Shala),
Social Welfare Center and Seed Production Center,
Waki, 1971

        The school located in Waki, about $2\frac{1}{2}$ km. south of Kosbad,
has an attached farm on a 35-acre plot donated by the government
of Maharashtra where vegetable and fruit seeds are produced.

        The Sydenham College of Commerce and Economics, Bombay,
runs a Social Welfare Center at Waki and provides medical facilities.
The AI gives its guidance to the volunteers of the College.

Applied Nutrition Training (under the VLW Training Center),
Kosbad, 1966

        This training activity of the AI has been organized to help
the Government of Maharashtra run its Applied Nutrition Program
(ANP), which started in 1966 in all the districts.   In each district
two blocks, and in each block ten villages, are chosen.   In each
village three to five acres of land are acquired by the government,
and a well is dug.   Fenced and fitted with pumps, the land is
handed over to the Gram Panchayat (village council) for cultivation

of supplementary foods like carrots, sweet potatoes, tomatoes, and other vegetables. The produce is supposed to be used for schoolchildren and expectant and nursing mothers. Each plot is supposed to become self-sufficient in five years after which government aid ceases. There are nine Gram Sevak Training Centers (GSTC) in Maharashtra, each of which looks after the training needs of surrounding areas. The Kosbad GSTC has two coastal districts (Thana and Kulaba) and two plains districts (Nasik and Jalgaon) attached to it.

The GSTC trains at its headquarters, the principal Gram Panchayat personnel connected with Applied Nutrition Training programs. In addition the GSTC holds peripatetic training camps for other personnel and supplies seedlings to ANP agricultural plots.

Agricultural Technology Center
(Krishi Vigyan Kendra), Kosbad, 1977

This is the latest activity added to the already long AI roster. The funds come from the Indian Council of Agricultural Research and the objectives of the Kendra are to train practicing farmers in practical aspects of agriculture, to train functionaries engaged in agriculture and agro-industries, and to train landless people in agro-industrial occupations. On the whole the functions of the Kendra seem to be the same as have been pursued over the years already by AI, but the additional funds make possible a broader coverage.

A sample of what is done under the Kendra for encouraging grafting of local mango trees with Alphonso variety is as follows:

The Krishi Vigyan Kendra...formulated a course in grafting of mangoes. The course was of one week's duration. One hundred and twenty tribal farmers having mango trees attended. Sufficient practice was given to each of them for acquiring necessary skills in grafting. The Kendra supplied them with budsticks of Alphonso variety. The tools like grafting knife, secateur, and chisel were supplied on loan. The training was so effective that during August to October the trainees carried out over 1500 graftings. Besides, two youths were self-employed as grafters and earned Rs. 600 each.

Nonformal Educational Activities

In addition to the above, several nonformal educational activities are being conducted by AI.

Functional Literacy Classes. In 16 padas classes in functional literacy are held once a week between 12 noon and 2 p.m. Groups of AI staff and students have been assigned to these padas. Lessons are prepared beforehand, cyclostyled, and discussed in a meeting of the entire group of "teachers" every Saturday, and the classes are held every Wednesday. In classes attended by men and women of all ages, emphasis has been on sanitation, personal hygiene, and agricultural improvements.

"Udyan Shalas." On many agricultural and horticultural estates run by rich farmers, children work the whole day and have to go without education. Noting this predicament, some AI workers started evening classes on the estates themselves with the permission of the estate owners. However, the experiment could not continue long because the estate owners later withheld cooperation.

Night Classes. In Dalvi Pada and Brahman Pada classes are held for working girls and boys every night from around 8:30 to 9:30. The children, who are employed plucking lily flowers planted in the chikoo plantations, do their work in the early morning. After class, the children go to the plantation around 10:00 p.m. and sleep there to be awakened around 1:00 a.m.

Mahila Mandals and other Clubs. In all the adopted villages Mahila Mandals (women's clubs), youth clubs, and libraries have been established. Kitchen gardening is taught to members of women's and youth clubs. Mahila Mandal members also get some training in knitting and stitching. These activities are looked after by students of various educational centers of the AI.

TECHNICAL AND LOGISTICAL
ASSISTANCE TO LOCAL FARMERS

Supply Activities

Among the supply activities that the AI organizes, the supply of horticultural crops and seeds is especially important and deserves attention here.

As noted above, the coastal region is deemed suitable for the development of horticulture. The hilly terrain, the humid climate, and the laterite soil are suitable especially for mango, chikoo (*Achrus sapota*), coconut, papaya, and banana plants. To induce farmers to grow these plants is, therefore, one of the important programs of the Institute. As a first step towards this the Institute established a nursery in 1949 with a view to providing seedlings to the farmers.

Chikoo was found to be the most suitable plant for this region. It is a so-called "rolling economy" with year round bearing and gives a steady gross income of Rs. 120 per year per tree for a very long period. About 50 plants can be grown in one acre. With the production cost at roughly half the gross value of the output, the net income per acre per year comes to about Rs. 3000.

Coconut comes next. A ten-year plant yields on an average an annual income of Rs. 150. One acre can accommodate about a hundred plants. Thus gross income per acre will be in the neighborhood of Rs. 15,000 according to AI calculations; with the cost of cultivation at roughly 40 percent, the net income from an acre of plantation would be Rs. 9000. Besides the fruit, the leaves are useful for making carpets and baskets, and for covering huts.

Both chikoo and coconut require irrigation. The AI advises those who do not have irrigation facilities to grow mango and *bor* (a kind of berry) trees, for which AI has developed the most effective and simple grafting and budding techniques. The branches of superior quality plants, such as Alfanso mango and the Ahmedabadi variety of bor, are provided free for the purpose of grafting and budding. A ten-year old mango tree, developed in this way, yields on an average Rs. 200 per year for over sixty years. An acre can accommodate 50 trees. With the cost at 50 percent, the potential net income per acre would be about Rs. 5000. The bor tree, which also does not require irrigation, yields an annual income of Rs. 25. About 50 of these trees can grow on an acre.

Papai (papaya) known as a poor man's fruit, is also being popularized. Its important feature is that it is quick-growing. By preparing seedlings in bamboo baskets the Institute saves about two months' time.

In addition to the above the AI supplies improved chicks and hatching eggs as well as seeds and seedlings of new varieties of rice, improved grasses, and better varieties of vegetables (*e.g.*, onions, brinjals, chillis, cauliflower, tomatoes, soybeans, spinach, beans of many varieties, bottle gourds, snake gourds, and ridge gourds). All these items are priced, but the Adivasis in nearby villages get some items free, or at a low cost.

Extension Channels

AI has only one full time extension worker, but its extension work also involves most of its trainees. The important channels of extension are the following:

(1) New technology and cultivation practices provided to farmers by Middle School students through the medium of their youth club groups. All trainees participate in extension as part of their training.

(2)   Demonstrations on the Institute's farm as well as
      directly on the land of farmers.

(3)   Formal training given to neighboring farmers in very
      short courses. For example, in being introduced in
      the cultivation of chillis, a cash crop, farmers are
      trained in groups for two or three days at a time
      at each critical stage of chilli growth.

(4)   The establishment of credit at banks (a recent service)
      for farmers attending the short courses.

(5)   Provision of extension services to users of community
      and individual wells and to farmers in the "adopted"
      villages.

DEVELOPMENT PROGRAMS

The AI provides special attention to what it calls "adopted"
villages in a radius of about 10 km. They are (1) Kainad (of
which Kosbad is a pada), (2) Waki, (3) Zarli, (4) Chimbave, and
(5) Asawali. The villages and their padas together consist of
about 750 Adivasi families.

The principal development program involves the construction
of wells, which was begun in 1960 but was given special impetus in
1966.

"Community" or Joint Use Wells

The AI has constructed eight community wells for small Adivasi
farmers in six surrounding padas of which seven are functioning.
The well is constructed in a central place in the farm of one
of the beneficiary farmers and about ten or twelve neighboring
farmers having a total acreage of 20-25 acres take advantage of
these wells. The costs of construction, land, leveling, pipelines,
pumps, electricity, and so forth are borne by the AI, which also
manages the distribution of water. The wells are not community
wells in the sense of being owned and operated by the consortium
of small farmers; they are owned by the AI for the *collective use*
of the participating farmers.

Individual (dug) Wells

About 100 wells have been constructed for individual Adivasi
farmers, of which 52 have been fitted with pumps and are in
working condition.

Surface Wells

About 25 surface wells (described on p. 33) have been constructed, but most of these have since been converted to dug wells.

The purpose of these wells, particularly of the community and individual dug wells, is to make multiple cropping possible and help the Adivasi farmer cross the poverty line. Those having wells are helped with all the other aids including the supply and extension services and the nonformal education programs described earlier as well as the better living programs described below.

Subsidiary Occupations. To aid development further subsidiary occupations such as beekeeping, poultry, pisciculture, piggery, and bakery, are encouraged.

EFFORTS TO IMPROVE FAMILY LIVING

The AI has been sensitive to the great need for devices that will improve family living. The following paragraphs describe five efforts that are intended to contribute to better living conditions.

Drinking Water Wells

In fact the AI's well construction program started with drinking water wells, of which five are already in existence. In addition, the AI has recently undertaken an expanded program of construction of drinking water wells in surrounding villages. For this purpose it organizes work camps of about seven to ten days' duration. Members of the AI staff and students of Gram Sevak Training Center, Adivasi Janata Vidyalaya, and Krishi Vidyalaya participate in the work.

Smokeless Stoves

The typical Adivasi hut is without much ventilation and the traditional cooking stove, which ordinarily consists of three stones and firewood, fills the entire hut with smoke that affects the health of the household. The smokeless *chulha* (stove) is a simple cement stove to which a chimney is attached. The model was prepared many years ago by Krishnadas Shah, an expert on rural sanitation. The AI tried to popularize it about six years ago, but the attempt was not very successful. Within the past few months a fresh effort has been made, and the new smokeless stoves called "Magan Chulha" have been constructed in seven Adivasi huts.

Glass Panel Fittings

Just as the Adivasi huts are without ventilation, so are they without much light. The AI has fitted the walls and roofs of eight huts with square glass pieces in wooden frames.

Utilization of Human Waste

To turn human excreta into manure, several innovations
such as low-cost latrines, absorbent urinals, and compost pits are
the subjects of experimentation. These innovations serve both
sanitary and agricultural purposes. The AI has constructed a
"museum" in which various kinds of low-cost, double purpose
toilets are on display.

Gobar Gas Plants

The AI is now making a special effort to popularize the Gobar
Gas Plant, a new application of "appropriate technology" that
utilizes both human and animal waste and provides both organic
manure and gas for cooking and lighting. An additional advantage,
of course, is cleaner surroundings. The Maharashtra Khadi and
Village Industries Board gives a 75 percent subsidy to Adivasis
on the costs of construction and equipment, and the AI ordinarily
meets the other 25 percent as the Adivasi farmers cannot afford even
that. Seven constructions have already been sanctioned by the
Board, and the digging of pits has started in two cases.

To sum up, over the past 30 years the Agricultural Institute
at Kosbad has initiated a wide variety of applied research, education
and training, and direct development activities aimed at improving
the productivity and quality of family life of rural people, ranging
in service areas from clusters of nearby "adopted" hamlets to the
much larger rural areas of five districts. The Institute has
given special attention to assisting the Warlis, but they constitute
only a part of its total "clientele." Although AI is a private
organization it has served many governmental purposes, including
the training and upgrading of Village Level Workers employed by the
State of Maharashtra, and in return it has received substantial
governmental financial support for its various activities. In the
next chapter we will attempt to assess the practical impact of some
of these activities, especially on the lives and living conditions of
the Warlis.

CHAPTER 4

IMPACTS OF THE
AGRICULTURAL INSTITUTE'S PROGRAMS

Because of the bewildering variety of AI's program activities and the diversity of its clienteles, it has seemed best to focus this assessment of results on AI's 'development program," particularly as it applies to the Warlis in the neighboring "adopted" villages and with special attention to the various activities built around the dug wells. This focus has the advantage of bringing the most basic and complex problems of the Adivasi into sharper perspective, and the further advantage of requiring an examination of the effectiveness of important aspects of AI's research, supply, extension and "better living" activities. At the same time, of course, this choice of focus means foregoing any extensive assessment of the impact of AI's numerous activities beyond the Adivasi villages close to Kosbad.

IRRIGATION AND
AGRICULTURAL PRODUCTION

Improved water supply, as noted earlier, is the key to taking advantage of many of the improved agricultural technologies developed and promoted by the AI. In an effort to break this crucial bottle-neck the AI had constructed 100 individual (dug) wells, 25 surface wells and 8 community wells on Adivasi lands in nearby villages. Inasmuch as most surface wells have now been converted into dug wells (only 4 or 5 are still in use), they have not been included in this survey. Thus our assessment of the development program centers on the individual and community dug wells.

Out of the 100 individual wells, only 52 are in working condi-tion; the rest either have no electric connections or, if so, no irrigation equipment.[1] Of the 52 wells that are usable, only 45 are actually used.[2] We are thus left with 45 wells and their users, in

---

[1] These wells were dug in anticipation of a government program for electrification which was later suspended.

[2] Of the seven unused wells, two belong to farmers who have left their villages and migrated to Bombay; two belong to confirmed drink addicts; the other three remain unused because of quarrels over land.

villages containing approximately 750 families or a total population of
perhaps 4,000 to 5,000 persons.

The total operated area of these 45 farmers comes to about
204 acres, of which (1977-78) 127 acres are devoted to paddy (both
traditional and new varieties).[1] Roughly half of this paddy acreage
is irrigated. The land not in rice is partly cultivable (warkas) and
partly devoted to fruit and other trees.

One common complaint of the farmers is the shortage of water;
well-water, in most cases, seems to last only until about the end of
February, thus making it very difficult to support rabi crops in the
dry winter season, prior to the return of the monsoon rains around
June. Many farmers wanted their wells to be dug deeper. When
questioned on this the AI workers pointed out that the neighboring
large estate owners bored their wells deep--sometimes 100 to 150
feet--enabling them to secure more water but at the expense of
Adivasi farmers with shallower wells. It is apparent that as more
and/or deeper wells are dug, the water table will recede further, to
the increasing disadvantage of small cultivators.

It is instructive to see what has happened to the three-crop
cycle recommended by the AI. Although most farmers (43 out of the
45) who are supplied with well water took the new rice varieties
(Jaya, Taichung, and Ratnagiri), of their 127 acres under paddy only
35.5 acres (28 percent) were devoted to these HYVs. On the rest
of their land (91.28 acres, or 72 percent) local low yielding varieties
continue to be grown, despite the fact that the average yield of the
new varieties was about 16.7 quintals per acre as compared to
about 7 quintals for local varieties.

The second recommended crop in the cycle, wheat, which for
a time was enthusiastically promoted by the AI, shows even less
acceptance than HYV paddy. Only 28 farmers planted wheat on
about 25 acres in all. Actually the AI was forced to change its
opinion about the suitability of wheat, which cannot thrive in the
absence of cold weather and ample water or withstand the rust
attacks that have become common. Chillis and sundry vegetables
are replacing wheat under the new AI emphasis. Thirty-one farmers
took vegetables on about 9 acres of land; thirty-six took chilli on
about 8.5 acres. It should be noted that chilli, sown in October
or November, may be repeatedly harvested until May. But here
again, the great limitation is water; chilli requires many irrigations.
But even with scanty waterings until about February, the crop is
profitable and, on the whole, chilli seems to be catching on. It is
also a cash crop and has, therefore, a special appeal.

---

[1]These and following observations have been made on the basis
of an analysis of schedules canvassed with these 45 users, personal
interviews with 16 of them (including an inspection of 14), talks with
officials and workers of the AI, and a few others. Although firm
conclusions are not possible because of only one year's data, the
main problems emerge sharply.

One hardly comes across summer green gram, the third crop in AI's originally recommended three-crop cycle (along with vegetables). Only three farmers took it on a total of 0.5 acres. This scant acceptance obtains partly because the chilli crop is of much longer duration and partly because water is not available in summer. Furthermore, the Adivasis are apparently not accustomed to consuming it.

On the other hand, many farmers use the horticultural innovations—Alfanso mango grafts, papaya, plantains, bor, coconut, chikoo. In fact, fruit trees seem to be very popular. Our 45 farmers together have about 400 mango, 400 chikoo, 550 coconut, 130 bor, 270 guava, 150 banana, and 18 lemon trees—though it was difficult to judge how many of these trees were improved varieties.

On the whole, it may be said that the irrigation program has been only partially successful and the three-crop cycle has not succeeded, mainly because of water shortage. Nevertheless, some change has been achieved by way of diversification of the cropping pattern and the production of nontraditional crops.

It is possible to attempt a rough estimate of the gains enjoyed by the individual well users (who are a small minority of the local Adivasi population). Cash income from the sale of vegetables and fruits has been reported by 40 out of 45 farmers. As many as 16 reported cash incomes exceeding Rs. 300 per year, and 6 of these claimed earnings of more than Rs. 1000 in the year 1977-78. As a result of the construction of wells and change in the crop pattern, 17 farmers report increases in their gross income of more than 50 percent. Nine have more than doubled it.

Increased income has led to improvement in diet, repair of houses, more adequate clothing, and better household utensils. Thirty-five farmers have put up cactus fences. Five have carried out land improvements such as bunding and leveling. Many have been enabled to send children to school.

Inasmuch as most of the wells started operating between 1966 and 1977, it may be said that the gains enjoyed are the result of about ten years' work, which makes the results look pitifully small and well below the income potential projected by AI. It must be noted, however, that the picture would have looked somewhat better if the price of rice had not dropped drastically, from about Rs. 200 to about Rs. 85 per quintal, over the last few years, if input prices had not gone up, and if supplies of chilli, which were a bottleneck, had been greater.

Possibly ten of the 45 farmers could be classified as really "good" in the sense of being comparable in efficiency to industrious farmers in other areas. Their farms are well tended and have a prosperous look. They have most probably crossed the "poverty line." But unfortunately they comprise but a tiny fraction of all the cultivators in the area studied.

Turning from these individual well-users to community wells, we found that only five of the eight community wells are in use. Fifty-four farmers are members of the active community wells but only 29 actually use the water. A study of 16 of these revealed that their total acreage in the command area is 39 acres or roughly 2.5 acres per farmer. In rabi about 16 acres get water, or 41 percent. Each of sixteen farmers has gone in for Jaya on very small acreage; twelve were found to be taking wheat (K-Sona), also on a very small acreage. Because of the small acreage devoted to new varieties, the improvement in yields is marginal. Thirteen take some vegetables like onion and chilli, and all of them have reported cash incomes ranging from Rs. 20 to Rs. 550. Average cash income for the 16 farmers comes to about Rs. 140 per year, which is slight improvement over pre-irrigation days.

On the whole, the available evidence shows that the performance of the community well users has been inferior to that of the individual well users. This is hardly surprising because users of the community wells are the more typical of the area; these wells cater to whatever farmers happen to be in their command area whereas the sample of farmers with individual wells is more selective and could be expected to be more productive.

Further, it must be pointed out that even the above picture is somewhat deceptive, for whatever improvements are visible on the farms is not due entirely to what the farmers themselves have done. The workers, trainees, and the Extension Officer of the AI go round the farms inducing farmers to adopt the innovations and often doing some of their work for them. In the beginning, when the well construction program was taken up, there was great resistance to the idea on the part of the Adivasis, and this resistance was compounded by the propaganda of local vested interests that the Institute was nothing but a new landlord who would eventually take away the land. Now after the construction of so many wells and the work of the AI for over thirty years, the Adivasi's fear of forfeiting his land may be assumed to have vanished; and yet in all these years, as Jayant Patil has told us, no farmer has come forward to ask for a well. Even today very few farmers would come on their own to report a pest attack; the AI people would have to spot it and then induce the farmers to take remedial action, or do it themselves. In the command areas of community wells there are about six farms that are tended not by the owners but by other farmers or the AI itself. Patil himself has wondered how much of AI's work would last if it were to shift elsewhere. In a total of about 100 farmers using both individual and community wells, not more than 15 could be classified as really good farmers, in the sense of their being devoted to their vocation. The slight "breakthrough" that is apparent on the farms is thus somewhat deceptive; the socio-psychological breakthrough bringing about a change in attitudes is meager.

It might be thought that the wells would be uneconomical for these farmers with very small holdings, but in at least this particular

instance this is not the case. According to AI calculations, a well that
costs around Rs. 10,000 (Rs. 12,000 at today's prices) can pay itself
off on a holding of at least five acres, excluding *warkas*. Here the
average holding of paddy land is only about 2.76 acres, but the wells
are practically a free gift to the farmers. Thirty-five wells (and
pumps) were 75 percent subsidized by the Social Welfare Department
of the Government of Maharashtra with the AI financing most of the
remaining 25 percent (the farmer having to pay only Rs. 200 to 300).
Seventeen wells fitted with pumps and pipelines were donated free
by foreign agencies; Community Aid Abroad and Freedom From Hunger
accounted for the currently usable wells. Of the remaining 48 wells,
Oxfam gave 30 and Community Aid Abroad and Freedom From Hunger
gave the rest. It was the idea of Community Aid Abroad to recover
the cost of the wells from the farmers in easy installments and to
create a revolving fund from which further wells could be constructed,
but in no instance has any money come back from the farmer.

REASONS FOR
LIMITED AGRICULTURAL IMPACT

What are the factors that account for this limited impact? The
most striking thing witnessed about the new varieties of paddy, as
noted above, is that although the number of adopters among individual well users is large (93 percent), the coverage in acres is small
(28 percent). In community wells also the number of adopters is
large, but the area covered is small. The reasons given by the
farmers for this small coverage are: (1) many lands are "light";
their moisture-retaining capacity is very low, suitable only for very
early-maturing local varieties; (2) water itself is in short supply;
(3) expenses are prohibitive, especially fertilizer; and (4) the rains
wash away the fertilizer.

The AI workers counter these complaints by pointing out that:
(1) the AI has varieties like Blue Belle and Karjat-184 that are
suitable for light soils, but the farmers do not use them; (2) in
rabi, although water is in short supply, the well can give supplementary irrigation; during kharif (the monsoon period) there is no
technical reason why high yielding varieties (HYVs) should not
be grown on a much larger area; in many cases the available water
is often not sufficiently used; (3) although the AI until recently did
not take much initiative in arranging crop loans through banks,
this service is now being offered; however, the AI had always been
ready to help with fertilizers on a credit basis; and (4) the notion
that the rains will wash away the fertilizer is an irrational fear.

In attempting to explain the real reasons for limited impact, the
AI observers point unerringly to the idiosyncratic Warli attitude.
Important in this context seems to be the average Adivasi's preference
for wage-employment over self-employment (farmers can earn 4 or 5
rupees a day on some of the many estates and plantations in the Kosbad
area). The typical Adivasi, it is said, is a fairly good wage-worker
but an indifferent cultivator; he has no initiative, no desire or ability

to make his own decisions. (A Christian father working in this area for many years suggested that the AI would do well to take over all the Adivasis' farms and employ them as wage earners.) This reluctance to work his own farm intensively may be due in part to the fact that, except for the last twenty years or so, the Adivasi, for several generations, has worked as a tenant under instructions of the landlord rather than as an independent owner-cultivator. AI observers further point out that the Adivasi's faith is in the "immediate"; he prefers a tangible daily wage to a vague expectation of seeing his agricultural investment bear fruit in the distant future.

The drinking habit is generally cited as a further deterrent to increased agricultural productivity, though local observers differ widely in their estimates of the extent of the drinking habit and its effect on agricultural activities. There are two extremes of opinion: one holds that the extent is not such as to seriously hamper agricultural work; the other, that it is great enough to be the main evil. Our own observations suggest that the truth probably lies somewhere in between. Judging from our limited sample we would conclude that at least 15 percent of the farmers are probably drinking so much and so frequently that their agriculture suffers through both the physical and financial effects of drinking.

At a deeper level, there is the "lethargy" and "lack of initiative" of the Adivasi about which frequent complaints are heard. However, one does not know how much of this "lethargy" is caused by drink, undernutrition, niggardliness of nature, absence of faith in human effort arising from a belief in aerial spirits and witchcraft, absence of the "thought for the morrow" (described as a deeply ingrained Adivasi habit of mind), racial memories of the life of hunting, and reluctance to do concentrated work in a narrowly confined area.

As in many other peasant societies, here also any one "getting ahead" in the world often becomes the object of his fellowmen's jealousy. Such an attitude generates social pressures that stand in the way of those few who would like to break new ground. A better farmer may occasionally become the victim of drunken abuse from fellow Adivasis; occasionally his crop may be stolen. Two such specific complaints were heard.

Some Exceptional Success Cases

Although the AI's long and varied efforts to improve the life of the Warlis appear to have had only limited and rather disappointing results, it should be noted that signal success has been achieved in a number of individual cases. For an understanding of the factors involved, a brief description of eight of the best farmers follows:

-- Janu Ravji Dalvi (who takes three crops) is also employed in AI's dairy, his son in the GBSK press, and his daughter in the GBSK Vikaswadi.

-- Barkya Chaitya Ibhad, as well as farming, is employed in the GBSK workshop.

-- Raddhya Kakdya Dhak had the experience of working in Bombay for several years.

-- Babu Udharya Bujad, an agricultural graduate and a trained secondary teacher, is also a first rate self-employed farmer.

-- Govind Lakshman Valvi is educated up to the sixth form and has undergone an agricultural training course of the AI's Janata Vidyalaya.

-- Devji Barkhya Hadal was a worker of the Communist Party for eighteen years and, in connection with Party work, has traveled to Kerala, Madras, and Bengal.

-- Dattatraya Chaitya Varatha has done his Secondary School Certificate examination and obtained the Agricultural School Diploma.

-- Radkya Vadhan has been trained since Balwadi in GBSK and completed the agricultural course of the Janata Vidyalaya. His grandfather had started as a Communist, then come under the influence of Acharya Bhise, one of the founders of the Gokhale Education Society. His father was a carpenter in Bombay. His two sisters, like him, have gone up from Balwadi, been trained, and are now themselves Balwadi teachers.

Three factors seem to characterize these "success cases": (1) substantial educational experience, (2) exposure to the outside world, and (3) experience with nonfarm sources of income. Of these three, the educational exposure appears to be especially crucial. It is not without significance that, against the average Warli literacy rate of about 8 percent, the literacy rate among community well users is 25 percent and among individual well users 65 percent.

IMPACT OF BETTER LIVING PROGRAMS

Better living programs such as fitting glass-panels in the roofs, introducing smokeless stoves, improving latrines, and building Gobar Gas plants do not seem to have caught on in spite of efforts to propagate them. Occasionally smokeless stoves may be seen, but not in use. Improved latrines and other sanitary devices are not to be seen anywhere. Of the eight gas plants planned, two are under construction; therefore nothing can as yet be said about their final acceptance.

On the whole, other development programs concerned with improved living and supplementary income have had a meager response, the reasons for which, as suggested below, seem to be partly economic and partly social.

-- Reference was made earlier in this account to the new white
breed of poultry and the cultural resistance to accepting it.
A dark-colored breed released recently is reported to have
been accepted by four farmers.

-- The Khadi and Village Industries Board has been trying for
the past fifteen years to propagate beekeeping as a subsidiary occupation in this area in cooperation with the AI.
Of the 150 boxes fitted so far, only three have been
acquired by Adivasis. One reason given is that, unlike
the large estate owner, the small farmer cannot guard the
boxes against theft for lack of a watchman. Another
advantage of the large plantation owner is the easy availability of flowering trees within his estate. The Adivasis'
paddy land does not attract honey bees, unless there happen
to be flowering trees or plants in the vicinity.

-- Stylo grass which gives 17 percent protein cannot be grown
unless a separate plot is reserved for it. The Adivasi would
not devote part of his meager paddy land to the production
of grass.

-- The Warlis do not believe in milking cows. Therefore,
although the AI has a dairy in which high-yielding cross-
bred cows are kept, not more than four farmers have
acquired new cows. (There may be other obstacles such
as feed costs and marketing difficulties.)

-- Since 1964 the AI has been trying to encourage the adoption
of stall-fed goats (Bannur variety) which would give good
income to farmers as well as prevent free rummaging that
is destructive of flora and soil. There has been no acceptance of this offer.

-- The planting of mangoes and chikoos, as seen earlier, has
been relatively more popular and probably indicates a
potential for further development. But here too the
collection of small quantities of fruit from a large number
of farmers may present marketing difficulties.

THE EDUCATIONAL PROGRAMS

Nonformal Education

Most important in terms of the general local population, at least
potentially, are certain of the nonformal education programs.

The adult education program in functional literacy, started in
December 1977, covers 16 padas. A visit to two of the classes was
disappointing. At one pada the four adults were drunk. The teacher
was trying to explain to them the care that should be taken with pest
attacks, but it seemed unlikely to have made any impression on them.
A few women were amusedly peeping out to watch the proceedings,

but when an attempt was made to engage them in conversation, they disappeared into the huts. At the other pada nobody was present. These padas, it should be noted, are very close to the Institute: one is less than a half kilometer; the other is so close as to be almost part of the AI campus. Although it would be wrong to generalize from this experience, the indifference and unconcern shown by the Warlis in these instances was obvious.

Our visit to two of the evening classes was more heartening. They were attended by children, more girls than boys, from the age of five to thirteen or fourteen. After their class the children had to spend the night at a private estate to wake up at 1:00 a.m. and go about their duty of plucking lily flowers; yet none of them looked tired. The subjects discussed by the teacher related to personal hygiene combined with reading skill. The children responded to what they learned with enthusiasm.

As observed earlier, Udyan Shala, another evening nonformal program, had to be closed after one or two attempts because of the non-cooperation of the estate owners.

In so far as the lesson planning for these night school programs is concerned, it would appear that the work has been done intelligently and efficiently. Lessons are carefully prepared and circulated in advance. The content is such as to interest the students and convey to them a message. For example, because personal hygiene is a serious problem in these areas, lessons revolving around this theme are important. Because the Adivasi's inability to count or to comprehend weights and measures is a serious handicap, simple corrective measures were among the first lessons of the short-lived Udyan Shala. Letters making up the Marathi word for "weight" were introduced. In another instance words equivalent to "plant a tree" were introduced in a discussion of the importance of planting trees in an area where forests have been indiscriminately cut by the Adivasis for fuel and other needs.

There is also a neat and well-run Balwadi near the AI's campus, some of whose "alumni" have made good, as noted above. Close to the AI's farm in beautiful surroundings, the children play in a specially constructed structure that is open on all sides.

In all the years since its inception the AI has been holding farmers' one-day gatherings, and thousands of Adivasi farmers come to participate and view the AI's innovations. We have no basis, however, for evaluating their practical impact.

From this limited observation of these nonformal education programs it is difficult not to conclude that the lower the age group the AI addresses in its local educational activities for Adivasis, the more effective it is likely to be, especially from the point of view of the keenness of the recipient. One wonders whether the adults are, by and large, a lost generation and whether anything can really be done to give them the enthusiasm and zest of their children in whom there is great hope.

Agricultural Education and Training

Although the focus of this study is on Adivasi development in
the immediate neighborhood of AI, the agricultural education and
training activities addressed largely to clienteles outside this area
deserve brief comment. These, it will be recalled, include:

(1) *The Agricultural School (Krishi Vidyalaya)* that caters to
the needs of students throughout the Thana District;

(2) *The Mahatma Gandhi Adivasi Janata Vidyalaya (Tribal Youth
Training Center)* that serves three districts;

(3) *The Gram Sevak Prashikshan Kendra (V.L.W. Training
Center)* that looks after the needs of the same three
districts as the Tribal Youth Training Center.

(4) *The Pachayati Raj Training Center* that trains officials and
popular representatives of local government authorities
in three districts; and

(5) the *Applied Nutrition Training Program* that caters to
officials from two districts.

Certain facts about the effectiveness of these programs stand
out. First of all, AI has established a reputation for itself as a leading training center. Owing to its pioneering work in many areas of
agricultural development, it has been described by a former Chief
Minister as the "Mecca" of Maharashtra's agriculture. Its attendance
is high and its trainees are widely credited with being good performers.

Second, the fact that AI's Agricultural School is privately
operated gives it an advantage over government schools in terms of
staff continuity; the more experienced faculty members are nontrans-
ferable and hence more stable. For example, Jayant Patil, the
Principal of AI, has been in residence from the beginning (29 years)
and Principal for 10 years. M. S. Gupte, head of the V.L. W.
Training Center, has been on the job for 20 years; Dr. M. V. Modak,
whose concern is animal husbandry, dairly, poultry, and veterinary
problems, has been in his position for 12 years. A. H. Sankhe, who
looks after the adult and other nonformal education programs, has
been associated with the Gokhale Education Society for many years
with a few interruptions, and his close knowledge of and identification
with Adivasi life has made him a particular asset to the Institute.

Third, the fact that the AI has a model farm and its own research
activities makes it the envy of all other institutes. Moreover, in all
AI courses there is a strong emphasis on practical training and direct
involvement in extension work, which cannot be said of many agricultural training institutions. Its effectiveness is further enhanced
by the extensive use of helpful teaching aids such as hand-outs,
folders, and audio-visual aids.

Our limited interviews with students and trainees brought to light the following facts that may or may not be representative. In a meeting with students of the Agricultural School it was clear that the boys wanted to secure salaried jobs which their diplomas might ultimately earn them; none was intent on making a career on his own farm. Students of the Janata Vidyalaya (for tribal youths) were asked if they knew what any of the former trainees were now doing. Of the nine cases they cited, five had taken up jobs away from home and the remaining four continued to cultivate their lands, but in the traditional manner. When asked why modern practices learned at the AI were not carried to the fields, they spoke of the unavailability of irrigation, lack of credit facilities, and corruption in the financing institutions. It also came out that the Adivasi boys coming from four different districts did not benefit equally from the AI's training because of differences in their ecological conditions and crops. Some of the VLWs also said that crops specific to their areas would not benefit much from the training they had received; however they had found the basic agricultural training useful and were happy about it. It must be noted that these comments refer to specific programs and specific aspects and are not offered as a general critique of AI's outward-directed activities, which was beyond the scope of our study.

Our overall impression--admittedly based on fragmentary evidence--is that the AI's agricultural education and training programs reviewed above have probably had a substantially greater impact on the general run of cultivators outside the Kosbad area than on the Adivasi cultivators within AI's immediate vicinity. However, the great diversity in ecological conditions, crop patterns and other features of the different districts served by these various AI programs would appear to be a serious inhibiting factor on their effectiveness. One gets the impression of an overall program that has grown more by accidental accretion than by a process of coherent evolution. Perhaps this is the price that a good quality private institution must inevitably pay when a sizeable portion of its total activities are funded by different government agencies whose needs and interests do not coincide.

MANAGEMENT ASPECTS

The generally low impact of AI's development activities on the neighboring Warlis, as we have seen, may be explained primarily by the extreme poverty conditions and the special socio-cultural characteristics of the Adivasis themselves. It is important to note, however, that AI's own organizational and staffing set-up and its strong preoccupation with agricultural technology *per se* may also be part of the explanation.

The development activities on which our assessment has focused appear to occupy something more than a purely peripheral role; and yet in terms of organizational (and probably financial) resources devoted to it, it suffers by comparison to other activities. It is noteworthy, for example, that the AI has only one Extension Officer

who looks after the work connected with development, and that
there is no separate organizational unit headed by a competent
middle-level officer responsible for planning, coordinating, and
giving impetus to these development activities. The gap between
the Principal of AI and the Extension Officer is a big one, and
the Principal is, of course, a man of too broad responsibilities in
various fields to give single-minded attention to development work.

The decision-making in AI seems excessively centralized, with
large communication gaps between field workers and the higher
authorities, and a lack of adequate procedures for discussion and
proper devolution of authority. The Adivasi themselves evidently
have little if any voice in the formulation of programs intended for
their benefit.

AI's research is largely concentrated on agricultural technology
for improving crops in the coastal areas. While this can be helpful
to farmers, including Adivasi farmers, in these areas, the needs of
those in other areas with different ecological conditions are less well
served. Perhaps more significant, however, has been the lack of
sufficient attention to the practical economic feasibility of the various
new agricultural technologies and innovations recommended by AI
from the vantage point of small farmers with only one to three acres
and a limited water supply. There has been a similar neglect of
research into the economic and social problems of the Adivasi that
evidently constitute serious obstacles to the adoption of new agricultural and other technologies.

Like most other organizations active in agricultural and rural
development, AI lacks systematic record-keeping on the impacts of
its activities, or any system of continuous evaluation that could help
improve the effectiveness of ongoing activities and identify promising
new opportunities.

The AI's overall activities, including in some measure its
development activities, are also handicapped by the fact that the
tenure of a sizeable number of its staff--mainly those working in the
Gram Sevak Training Centre and the Panchayati Raj Training Centre
--hinges on the uncertain renewal of annual government grants.
Such uncertainty and insecurity is bound to affect staff morale.

We have noted these managerial and staff problems not with any
intent to criticize the AI but rather to underscore the kinds of practical handicaps and limitations that almost inevitably plague any
voluntary organization endeavoring to improve the status of the
rural poor.

CHAPTER 5

PROGRAMS AND APPROACHES OF THE
GRAM BAL SHIKSHA KENDRA (GBSK)

The present activities of Gram Bal Shiksha Kendra (GBSK) at Kosbad Hill and surrounding padas are both vigorous and varied. The programs for preschool children were originally intended to follow the Vikaswadi concept; that is, the three preschool activities were combined: a creche for children up to two and a half years, a Balwadi for children of from two and a half to six years and lower classes of the primary for children above six.[1] A happy innovation founded almost by chance is the night school that fills a need for children otherwise occupied by day. Teacher training is served by the establishment of the Rural Bal-Sevika Training Center and the Junior College of Education; hostels are particularly important for inservice teacher training. With the help of UNICEF two types of applied nutrition training are available. A workshop, publication center, and printing press contribute to the need for occupational training, and the Shabari Udyogalaya is a unit for the manufacture and sale of preschool teaching aids. Some of these activities are essentially educational; while others are not. Some are of significance from the point of view of the Adivasi neighborhood, while others are of a more general nature. A description of these activities follows, with emphasis on the problems encountered and the methods used in meeting them.

PROGRAMS FOR PRESCHOOL CHILDREN

The creche and Balwadi start functioning at 8 a.m. and continue until 11:30 a.m. A mirror, combs, soap, and water are kept at the entrance of the Balwadi. The children are required to clean their teeth, wash their hands and feet, and comb their hair before entering. The main emphasis is on the development of the five senses. Individual and group activities are encouraged. All the aids used are made by the Shabari Udyogalaya mostly from material found locally. Thus, children are encouraged to join mud globules, or seeds with

---

[1] At present the children of this age group go directly to the full-fledged primary school, and thus the connection of the primary school with the Vikaswadi has been snapped.

holes perforated in them, into a string, to draw and paint, and to make balls or other toys of clay. Any child can visit the creche in the adjoining room and play with his younger sibling. A child too young for the creche is also allowed to sit with its elder sibling in the Balwadi. An informal homelike atmosphere is deliberately sought.

In the earlier period, the primary school was run during the same hours as the creche and Balwadi. It was a sort of nonformal primary school where children aged six or more who were assigned the duty of looking after their younger siblings were taught reading, writing, and simple arithmetic.

GBSK runs ten Balwadis in the nearby padas of Kainad and other villages. Most of them have creches attached, but children above six years now go to the primary school at Kosbad Hill and so no primary schools are run at these places. All these Balwadis are conducted by women who have been trained in the Bal-Sevika Vidyalaya at Kosbad Hill.

PRIMARY SCHOOL

When Mrs. Tarabai Modak and her group started their work in Bordi, their objective was limited to preschool education. They never thought of opening and running a primary school. They thought that after leaving preprimary school, the children would naturally go to the primary school for education. However, when they saw the condition of the primary school at Kosbad, they realized that most of the tribal children never go to school. It was no use running preprimary schools if the children did not later go to primary schools. The problem of educating tribal children could be solved only if preprimary education and primary education were run simultaneously by GBSK. Therefore, GBSK took over the management of the primary school at Kosbad from the District Local Board in 1956. At that time, it was up to Standard IV. Students were extremely irregular and weak in their studies; the number of students on the roll was 47, with not a single girl student, but the average attendance was only 9.

Strenuous efforts were made to enroll students through house-to-house visits. In the beginning, the students were grouped together irrespective of the form to which they might belong, for their earlier training was so poor that dividing them made no sense. A new method on the pattern of Balwadi was adopted to teach them reading, writing, and arithmetic. Emphasis was laid on dramatization, action songs, and nursery rhymes. The teachers were asked to select lessons that were related to the life of the Adivasi students. This method had some effect in popularizing the school and also in encouraging a regularity of attendance.

Two difficulties were noticed in teaching these students. First, although they learned their lessons and arithmetical exercises with some eagerness, they could not remember what they had learned. (Most of these students were the first in their family to join the school.) However, they had presence of mind, physical endurance, and agility, and it was decided to preserve these qualities of the children.

The second difficulty was that the tribal children were not accustomed to sit at one place and to pay concentrated attention to anything for even an hour or so.

To solve these problems several things were done. Children were allowed   frequent intervals in which to play out of the class, with the teachers taking part. Frequent excursions to nearby hills and forests were arranged. Children were encouraged to collect different things they found in nature. These included beautiful red Gunj seeds, nests of birds, animal skulls and bones, and even dead snakes. These things were kept in a museum which in the course of time became the pride of the school. Certain dead animals were kept in formalin. Children were taught biology, physiology, and other subjects with the help of the objects they had collected themselves. Charts and pictures were prepared and hung in the museum. In this manner students lost the fear of school and developed the faculty of retention. There was a marked improvement in their memory, and the number of students on roll increased year by year. Although the majority were and are Adviasi, the number of non-Adivasi students also increased as the staff of the GBSK and the adjoining Krishi Shikshan Sanstha expanded. This mutual participation helped the Adivasi students to mix with non-Adivasi ones with ease and a sense of equality.

All these efforts had the desired result. The number of students rose from 47 in 1956-57 to 348 in 1977-78, of which 295 were tribal students. The number of girls rose from zero in 1956-57 to 103 in 1977-78.

NIGHT SCHOOL

On the 11th of July 1956, a boy of 14 years approached Anutai and asked to be taught at night since he had no time in the day. This incident led to the night school which started on the 12th with him and a friend. The number of students increased each night and   within   a week the group consisted of ten boys and three girls. The school started at 7:30 p.m. and was over by 10 p.m. every evening. However, most of the boys, particularly the ones coming from a considerable distance, slept on the school premises. Within a few days the number of girls went up to 20. Even some of the girls who attended day school came to the night classes, and most of them spent the night on the school premises.

Whatever changes had been made in the teaching content of the day school had to be made within the limits of the curriculum set by the government. However, the night school was free from these constraints. The living together of the students at night also helped to develop the nonformal character of the night school.

As soon as the night school started, the first program was one
of story-telling. Students were also encouraged to tell stories they
themselves knew. Then there were programs of singing and at times
even group dancing. A group dance called tarpa dance is very
popular among the Warlis, and every girl and boy can take part in it.
The students, however, had a different idea of what a school should
be, and began to demand the teaching of reading and writing.
These subjects were introduced gradually. At first, only the words
they knew were given for writing. They were also taught to write
numbers. Unlike the primary school, the night school had no problem
with irregular attendance. However, as in primary school, the
students learned letters, words, and numbers quickly, but were
quicker in forgetting them. It took a long time for them to remember
what had been taught, but they finally succeeded because of their
own enthusiasm and the untiring efforts of the teachers.

Excursions by these students were also arranged from time to
time, and general knowledge imparted to them through stories, songs,
and small dramatic pieces. There was no formal timetable nor any
set time limit for the completion of any subject or lesson.

Now that Warli parents are ready to send their children to
school despite the cost in loss of their earnings for the family, the
night school is losing its importance. The activity still goes on,
however, and young boys and girls who cannot attend the day school
take advantage of night school.

At present (1978-79), there are 35 students in the night school
at Kosbad. Of these, 17 are studying for the Standard IV examination.
Most of them are above 14 years of age. Occasionally some of those
who are not on the roll also attend the school. Most of the students'
ambition is to pass the Standard VII examination, which is the
final examination for the primary school.

Recently GBSK started operating one more night school at
Dongaripada where GBSK wants to develop a new Vikaswadi complex.
At this night school there are 42 students on the roll but average
attendance is 25.

It should be noted that there are no fees charged in the night
schools, and the teachers receive no remuneration for this additional
work.

WORK EXPERIENCE

One of the prominent features of the primary school is the
occupational training given under the program of work experience.

Work experience is a part of the school curriculum in the State
of Maharashtra. Under this program, students of Standard V onwards
are given training in some productive work. This program is intended
to serve a dual purpose: give the students some sort of elementary
vocational training so that at least some of them can pursue these
vocations later on after obtaining further training and skill, and

secondly, teach the students respect for manual work. How far
these purposes are served by the program in schools all over the
State is debatable. However, GBSK primary school has taken this
program seriously. Actually GBSK started its occupational training
much earlier than the State work experience programs. At the beginning of their work at Kosbad, GBSK workers tried to persuade
children to join the school, but soon they found that the majority
fo children age ten onwards and even less worked to earn some money.
Children of school age used to graze cattle, work in the fields,
collect firewood for their own use or for sale. They did not earn
much, but whatever they earned was necessary for their families,
and school work of any kind seemed to be out of the question.

One of the solutions was the meadow school (discussed later)
but not all children went to look after cattle and so meadow school
could not cater to their needs. In any case, it was decided that
children should be provided some work for three to four hours, and
taught the rest of the time.

In 1956-57, this project got its start by assigning the children
to plucking chillis on the AI farm. The children would study for
three hours in the morning, and the rest of the day they worked in
the field. But since this work was seasonal, children also helped
in constructing GBSK buildings and were paid wages for their work.
GBSK also tried to give some children work on the GBSK farm.
Since these activities could not absorb many children throughout the
year, some children were given the task of collecting firewood from
the nearby forests, but this too had to be given up.

GBSK then tried to teach making bottle covers from paddy
straw in 1959. The work was easy and it was possible to give
continuous employment to Warli children for four hours a day.
GBSK secured orders for these covers from a chemical factory at
Baroda. Children worked for four hours a day and studied for four
hours in the school. The work continued until 1963 when it had to
be stopped because of competition from the traders.

After that GBSK tried to train some boys in carpentry, a
practical training that would provide work throughout the year
and enable them to follow the occupation later. The government's
Cottage Industry Department made arrangements for a two-years
training course. A student trainee received Rs. 10 as a stipend.
The scheme was modified to suit GBSK students by making the course
for a full-time trainee one year in duration and the monthly stipend
Rs. 20. The modification allowed the students at Kosbad to study
in the school for four hours and get carpentry training for four
hours. In 1961-62,   20 tribal boys joined the course, 13 of
whom appeared for the course examination and passed. It was
noticed, by the way, that tribal students had a better sense of
color combination and did their work more skillfully than nontribal
students elsewhere.

After the students completed their carpentry training, GBSK
encouraged them to form a cooperative society which started in March,

1963. At first there were only hand lathes, but now with electrical
lathes various wooden toys, teaching aids for Balwadis, and
even some wooden furniture are made in this workshop.

At present GBSK operates a sort of "earn and learn" scheme
under the program of "work experience." The basic objective is
to reduce the rate of dropouts from Standard V onwards. The results
of this experiment are encouraging, and the rate of dropouts has come
down considerably in recent years. Students are paid for their work
at 25 paise per hour and earn about Rs. 10 per month. Girls stitch
garments and are paid similarly.

TEACHER TRAINING

Rural Bal-Sevika Training Centre

GBSK's attempts to start preschool teacher training date from
the Forties and Fifties at Bordi. At Kosbad a course was started in
1958 under a grant from the Central Social Welfare Board which with-
drew its support in 1960. Now under a grant from the Indian Council
for Child Welfare GBSK has been running the Rural Bal-Sevika
Training Centre since March 1964. The period of training is eleven
months. Every year 50 women workers are admitted to training. Each
worker is given a monthly stipend of Rs. 40. The expenditure on
stipends and teachers' salaries is borne by the Indian Council for
Child Welfare. The trainees are given training in preschool education
and also in games and health care for children up to twelve years.
The applications for training have to come through voluntary institutions, gram-panchayats, and other government or semi-government
organizations, who have to guarantee that they will employ the
trainee at least for three years after the completion of training.
More than 600 women workers have so far been trained at the Kosbad
Centre. It may be pointed out that all such training centers in other
states are run in the capital cities of those states. The center at
Kosbad is unique in that it is the only center run in a village.

Junior College of Education

A training center for primary teachers began in 1957 at Kosbad.
The objective was to train primary teachers to work better in rural
and, in particular, in tribal areas.

Since 1964 GBSK has been conducting a special orientation
and training program for teachers in the center. The object of
this special program is to create motivation and ability to work
in tribal areas. Under this program, special lectures are arranged
on tribal culture and kindred subjects. The trainees are required
to spend fifteen days in a tribal village and run a one-teacher school
there. They also study the working of the Vikaswadi, meadow
school, and night schools run by the GBSK.

In 1968 the primary and preprimary training courses were
merged. In all there are 160 students in this college. There are

five junior colleges of education in Thana district, but only the college
at Kosbad has a preprimary section.

Hostels

GBSK has been running two hostels, one for boys and one for
girls, since 1960. The need to run such hostels arose when GBSK
started a teachers' training center at Kosbad in 1957. The training
center needed a practising school; but because attendance at the
primary school was poor and irregular, GBSK decided to run hostels
for boys and girls to ensure attendance there.

For the first two years, the major problem was to get students
for these hostels. A number of students left within a few days of
joining. The problem was more acute in the case of girls. There
were only four to five girls in the girls' hostel for the first two years.
Later on, however, the number of students began to increase. In
the current year (1978–79) there are 66 boys and 44 girls in these
hostels. Of these about 50 percent are from the tribals and the
rest are from the Scheduled Castes. The District Social Welfare Board
gives a grant of Rs. 45 per boy and Rs. 50 per girl. The additional
expenditure is borne by GBSK. Boys and girls are not charged
a fee.

The hostel work is managed by students themselves. There is
one cook in these hostels. In all other jobs such as cleaning and
serving food groups of students take their turns.

APPLIED NUTRITION TRAINING PROGRAM

Two types of applied nutrition training programs are arranged
by the Gram Bal Shiksha Kendra with the help of UNICEF.

A seven-day training program is conducted at Kosbad from
time to time. The prescribed syllabus for this course is meant
mainly for women volunteers belonging to various women's clubs.
The program consists of lectures on nutrition and about twenty
practical lessons. The trainees also work in the kitchen garden.
Trainees are given information on such subjects as the importance of
nutrition, the concept of a balanced diet, proper methods of cooking
care of children and pregnant women, and the importance of
vegetables and other items in diet. Demonstration lectures are
also arranged.

The second type of program is arranged in ten nearby
villages with the cooperation of the local women's groups. Subjects
are explained with the help of pictures and charts, and lectures
are delivered in simple language. Practical lessons are also
arranged in which women are encouraged to take an active part.
The subjects covered include methods of proper cooking, importance
of nutrition, child care, and general hygiene.

The major differences between the two types of courses are that the first is more intensive and given in seven consecutive days whereas the second is simple and arranged in periodic lectures and practical lessons.

Besides these two programs, the GBSK also holds a ten-day exhibition at a fair 18 miles away from Kosbad.

OTHER ACTIVITIES

Publication Center

The publication center has been running since 1952. Besides the collections of Warli stories and songs, the center has published useful books like *How to Run a Balwadi* and *Meadow School* (both in Marathi). One monthly called *Shikshan Patrika (Journal of Education)* is also published on behalf of the Nutan Bal Shikshan Sangh, the parent body.

Two of the books published by the GBSK in Marathi have been translated into English and published by the Government of India. They are: *Balwadi in Rural Area* and *The Meadow School* by Tarabai Modak.

Printing Press

The press is mainly used for printing GBSK and NBSS publications. During the work at Kosbad, GBSK workers noticed that most of the boys and girls who left their education in the first four classes relapsed into illiteracy as they had no reading materials. It was felt necessary to publish books they could read with interest. The press is also used for this purpose.

Farm

The farm land consists of thirteen acres of which seven are devoted to paddy and six are under orchard. There are 150 mango and 150 chikoo trees. The produce is used partly for consumption at the establishment and partly for sale.

Shabari Udyogalaya

This activity has been started recently for the manufacture and sale of low-cost preschool teaching aids. The unit's production has been in good demand from all over Maharashtra.

Methods and Approaches

In addition to considering what GBSK has done (or sought to do), it is important to review its methods and approaches that stand out markedly and should provide useful lessons to educational workers in other rural areas. A summary account covering the period since the Bordi days is presented below to show how GBSK's unorthodox, imaginative, and flexible approach went on responding in a creative manner to challenges of the local situation.

In Bordi one of the first problems that had to be contended with was that of casteism and untouchability. If Bhangi (scavenger) children came to the school, the other Harijan (untouchable) children would not come; the caste-Hindu children would not be permitted by their parents to mix with the Harijan children. At one time the attendance dropped down to zero. To get over this difficulty the "Anganwadi," frontyard school, was devised. The idea was that if the children did not come to the school, the school would go to them. Small kits of child education apparatus were prepared and the teachers carried them to different localities engaging the children in play. Gradually the caste problem was overcome, the message spread wider, and attendance at the central Balwadi increased.

When children from a long distance could not come to the central Balwadi, a bullock cart was employed to fetch them. These daily journeys to and fro took the form of processions with the beating of cymbals and singing of songs. This made schooling a more joyous experience for the children and increased the awareness of onlookers to what was going on. (This awareness is extremely important, for it must not be forgotten that even in Dadar, a suburb of Bombay, where Shishu Vihar was located, the educated middle-class parents hardly understood the significance of child education in those days. Conditions at Bordi were much worse. The traditional concept of learning was so rigidly fixed in the parents' minds that teaching without slate and pencil, without alphabet and numerals, was considered useless.)

Bordi, after all, was a middle-sized township, and the real Adivasi localities existed on the fringe. In one such area GBSK started a Balwadi for children of the Dulba Adivasi tribe. It was impossible to get hold of exclusively preschool age children here because they were accompanied by their younger and older siblings, since the parents had left the house for work early in the morning and the primary school age children were delegated to look after the younger children. The situation raised a challenge and afforded an opportunity. The answer was "Vikaswadi," alluded to above: a creche for very small babies, a Balwadi for preschool age children, and a primary school for the older ones. The annexing of a creche to the Balwadi was the critical innovation. Because of this arrangement the child could attend the Balwadi and at the same time be near the younger brothers and sisters. This arrangement also satisfied the parents, who would never have trusted their children to independent creches.

In the initial years of the Vikaswadi experiment, mothers used to visit creches to satisfy themselves that their children were not neglected. Never prevented from visiting creches, they were, in fact, encouraged to do so. On festival or other important days mothers were especially invited to Vikaswadi and encouraged to watch the work. The practice of allowing the elder child to visit its younger sibling whenever it liked gave it an opportunity to learn something about child care. This was particularly true in the case of the girls. Adivasi women also unconsciously learned lessons in child care and began to place greater trust in the persons looking after Vikaswadi. This arrangement also led to an improvement in the health of the infants brought to creches. Teachers gave them milk or other nourishing food and administered medicines for simple ailments. Children were kept cleaner than they were in their own homes. The children also heard and saw more things than they would have at home or outside the Vikaswadi. The Vikaswadi thrived later in Kosbad.

The most important aspect of child education in poor countries is the costs that must be sustained. Tarabai and Anutai bent their energies to tackling this problem out of necessity as well as an ideal (in 1945 Anutai's monthly budget for Dubla children's Balwadi was Rs. 3!). Here, too, necessity turned into opportunity.

Tarabai has described the stratagems that GBSK used:

> ...we prepared beautiful works of art from the surrounding trees, leaves, flowers, fruits of the *suru* tree and conchshells and *gunja* seeds.... We found the local potter's method of preparing lumps of mud very novel and we introduced it into our Balwadis. In backward areas people paint pictures on the dung-smeared walls of their huts on occasions like marriage; modelling on this we made small rectangular boards of strips of wood, smeared them with the dung mixture and encouraged children to paint on them with coloured wet mud sticks. Pen and paper being costly we used the ground, the walls, the doors, earthen pots, pans, etc. as bases and prepared variegated colours by mixing *geru* (a red material), lime, yellow earth, etc. Brushes were made by crushing the ends of tender sticks of a *wad* (bunyan) tree.[1]

In a summary form this passage brings out most of the advantages of the new educational aids. They were cheap; they came from familiar surroundings and prevented alienation; they induced inventiveness and explorative ability among children as well as teachers. In certain cases they also helped village craftsmen

[1] Tarabai Modak, *Vees Varshanchi Vatchal* (Marathi; *Review of Twenty Years' Work*); GBSK, Prakashan, Kosbad Hill, 1965, pp. 5-6.

in accordance with Gandhiji's advice to Tarabai in 1949. This practice increased many times in later years at Kosbad, and GBSK now manufactures a number of simple teaching aids for supply to other institutions through its Shabari Udyogalaya.

The Adivasis abject poverty and hunger turned Tarabai's thoughts to ways and means by which the hunger of those children who could not attend school and went in search of things like jungle roots could be quenched. With the aid of the children a small garden plot was cultivated near the the Dubla Balwadi. Tarabai realized that the economic problem was the basic obstacle to any kind of education in the poor communities and this problem remained an obsession with her. One of the things she tried later at Kosbad was the making of bottle covers out of paddy straw which enabled the children to work for a few hours to earn some money and learn during the rest of the time. This activity did not last, however, because the grass traders in the surrounding area found it to be a very profitable proposition. Even today child labor is largely used for such work. This was one of the problems the GBSK could not satisfactorily solve.

Whatever success child education has achieved in this area would have been difficult to achieve without the genuine affection for the down-trodden community and its children, and without a tremendous faith in the work at hand. The difficulties in an area of abysmal poverty and ignorance were such as would have broken anyone's heart. Here Anutai gave of herself in abundant measure. Cleaning girls' hair of lice and applying oil to them, scrubbing the children of dirt and bathing them (sometimes with hot water), applying anti-scabies ointment, looking after and treating sores of malaria-affected children when their parents were away--these were by far the most effective measures of all, and they endeared GBSK to its young clients.

After shifting to Kosbad, another innovation in education was introduced. This was the "meadow school" (*Kuranshala*), conducted for about six months of the year. A number of Adivasi boys and girls above the age of eight were assigned the task of looking after cattle and grazing them in the open fields and pastures. The task was particularly arduous in the rainy season when paddy crops were standing in the fields, and cattle entered these fields unless they were watched carefully. However, in other seasons children were comparatively free after the cattle were taken to open lands. Because it was not possible for these children to attend school, most of them remained uneducated. GBSK hit upon the novel idea of educating them by sending a teacher with them to the meadows and engaging them there in programs that included songs, games of different kinds, and story-telling. There was no classroom, no ringing of bells, no slates or books. Different subjects, such as, elementary arithmetic, geography, language, and hygiene were introduced with the help of natural objects such as flowers, sticks, insects, birds, and stones. This was spontaneous "nonformal" education about which a few words are in order.

In the beginning Anutai and the headmaster of the primary
school went to a meadow and began taking part in the games played
by the children assembled there. This joint participation went on
for some days, and gradually the children began to treat them as
friends. It was then decided to introduce language development and
concepts of measurement (height, length, weight and time), without
in any way imposing anything on them or detracting from their
natural enjoyment of the games. The teachers also insinuated group
programs of cleanliness into the games.

To give them an idea of the passage of time a peg was fixed
in the ground to mark off the tip of the shadow of a tree when they
began their activities. After every hour another peg was fixed,
and the last peg was fixed at 11 a.m. when the activities were over.
Within a few days the children learned to measure time with the help
of measured shadows. Then they were shown a watch and with its
help were taught to read time.

Similarly, concepts of weeks, months, years, length, breadth,
and weight were gradually introduced with the strategic use of
various objects such as stones and sticks and other ordinary objects.

Observation of insects, birds, reptiles, cattle, and trees was
also encouraged. Occasionally, the children were taken to the museum
at the primary school at Kosbad. This museum was mainly stocked
with objects collected by Warli children. It consisted of different
types of stones, dried leaves, branches clay models, dead snakes
kept in formalin, and pictures of different birds.

Children were sometimes brought to the regular primary
school for visits, and occasionally meadow school children were
taught to read and write well enough to join the regular primary
school.

There are no meadow schools now: the night school has partly
met the educational needs of older boys and girls; moreover, large
tracts of land have been bought by plantation owners and the grazing
grounds have receded much farther.

CHAPTER 6

RESULTS OF

THE GBSK PROGRAMS

GBSK's activities, like those of the AI, are of two types: those concerned with the neighborhood and those concerned with outside areas. Inasmuch as visits were necessarily selective, it was impossible to do justice to the latter. Observations of the training programs have also been limited, and therefore the focus here is on the Balwadis (including the central Kosbad Balwadi) and their attached creches, the primary school, and the night school. All of these were visited at least once, interviews were conducted with teachers, workers, and a few boys and girls (past students), and these discussions and impressions were fortified by frequent and extensive talks with Anutai Wagh and her associates. What follows is first a quantitative summary of educational growth and then an impressionistic account of qualitative change based on these visits and meetings.

A QUANTITATIVE REVIEW

The record of GBSK's preschool and school activities is as follows:

In the nine Balwadis started up to 1976, a total of 335 children were on the roll in January 1978. Of these 163 were boys and 172 girls. Of the 335 children only ten were non-Adivasi. If we add about 60 belonging to the two new Balwadis the total strength would come to about 400.

In the three creches run by GBSK there were 87 children in January 1978. Of these 51 were boys, 36 were girls. All except five were Adivasis.

In the primary school at Kosbad there were 348 students in January 1978. Of these 245 were boys and 193 girls. Adivasi boys and girls accounted for 295 of the total 348 students.

In the boys' hostel there were 66 children in January 1978, all of whom were students of the primary school. In the girls' hostel there were four, all of them students of the primary school.

Thus in so far as children's education is concerned, the total strength of students (including those belonging to creches, Balwadis and primary school) in Kosbad and 10 surrounding padas in January 1978 was about 835. Of these 767 were Adivasi. Adding about 25 enrolled in the night school we have somewhat less than 800. This, in substance is a quantitative expression of GBSK's efforts in a place where next to nothing existed twenty years ago.

About 1960, when GBSK had only recently started its work, the educational situation in the seven padas around Kosbad was that seven children were in the creche, six in the Balwadi and 13 in the primary school. This was before the Balwadis and creches in the padas were started and only the central Balwadi, creche and primary school in Kosbad existed. It is against this background that GBSK's success has to be measured. This success is largely due to GBSK's expansion in surrounding padas.

According to a recent survey of 28 villages in the Kosbad region, male literacy is 33 percent. Twenty percent had been to primary school, 11 percent to secondary school and two percent were graduates. Most of these villages are outside the GBSK's (and AI's) sphere of influence. This indicates that in the villages under the direct influence of GBSK (and AI) the percentage of literacy--which has not been taken--must be far greater. This educational change is the combined result of GBSK and AI educational activities; for it must not be forgotten that AI also has its Ashram Shalas, a secondary school, and a Balwadi.

GBSK's two training schools had 219 trainees in 1978, 166 of them women. Since most of them come from outside areas, we have not included them in measuring the educational progress in and around Kosbad.

A record of the work experience program of the primary school and its effects is very revealing. Before it was started in 1975, the proportion of dropouts after the Standard IV was heavy. The work experience program therefore starts from Standard V, and carpentry, farming and stitching (for girls) have been included. In 1975 the program was introduced to Standard V, in 1976 it was extended to Standard VI, and in 1977 to Standard VII. (By this time two groups having completed the full program have passed out of the school.) The dropouts' proportion has, almost by a miracle, dropped down to zero! All the students have joined the AI's secondary school, and special benefit has accrued to the girls, who in general are denied education at all levels more than boys. At the same time as an indication of GBSK's valuable innovation the results of the program also bring out sharply the importance of the economic factor in Adivasi (and poor people's) education.

OBSERVATIONS AND IMPRESSIONS

Turning to qualitative aspects of the results of Adivasi education the following observations seem to be in order:

The primary school now admits children who have had Balwadi training and those who have not. Those who have had the advantage of preschool education are generally more alert and smarter, and they fare better in their examinations.

The GBSK has succeeded substantially in breaking the resistance of children as well as of parents to this early education. Mr. Vasant Patil, the headmaster of the primary school, who has been in Kosbad for twenty years, has said that in the early years children had to be coaxed into attending the school; as soon as they were in, many of them used to jump out of the windows. Now the school-going habit has been formed. Parents who earlier needed a great deal of persuasion now come on their own to enroll their children.   For Balwadis the teachers had to go round collecting the children and clean them; even today some children have to be fetched from some houses because their parents are away at work, but the teachers now say that most are kept ready and clean. Gradually education is taking root. In a *Haldi-kunku* celebration on the Kosbad pada two Warli women were heard making short speeches about how important education is!

A further instance of the spread of the educational message was the request which Anutai Wagh received from two padas (Ghatalpada and Dhakpada) asking her to start Balwadis for each of them on the Padva (Hindu New Year) day. At the opening ceremonies not less than 60 percent of the children were spotted as suffering from scabies; but five months later, at least at Ghatalpada, the scabies affliction seemed much less and the children more cheerful--thanks to Balsevika's efforts.

A process once started achieves momentum. For example, consider how two brothers belonging to the pada, themselves products of GBSK, one of whom is now a holder of a Diploma in Education and a teacher, took the initiative in starting the Dkhakpada Balwadi in their pada. Another example is the experience of the entire Vadhan family. Two sisters, Taya and Sundar, were early entrants in the central Balwadi. They did their primary school and received Balsevika training. Both are now Balwadi teachers. Their younger brother, Radkya, underwent the same process up to primary school and followed with an eleventh-month agricultural course at the AI's Tribal Youth Training Center. [1]   Radkya was followed by a brother and sister through Balwadi and primary school. One revolution of the educational wheel in the Vadhan family has now been completed and another has begun: Radkya's own small daughter, Saroj, has recently been admitted to the Kosbad creche. It seems reasonable to conclude that educational influences, once they enter the family, become self-sustaining.

Six of those who have gone through GBSK's Balwadis or primary school are now trained teachers. Three girls are working in

------

[1]Radkya was included among the eight best farmers described in Chapter 4.

the press in the composing department. One student who attended
GBSK's night school, now the Chairman of the Panchayat Samiti
(tahsil-level) council, helped importantly in setting up the Dongarpada
Balwadi

    Interviews with six Balwadi old boys and girls and others
are revealing about the education of Warlis. Less addicted to drink,
they have not renounced drinking. Many still believe in ghosts and
their evil powers. It would appear that the girls are probably more
promising material than their male counterparts. In the night school
of both the AI and the GBSK, their attendance is better. Their
desire to learn appears to be keener, their readiness to talk,
surprisingly greater. Girls particularly dislike their parents' heavy
addiction to drink. Some girls have given up the Warli type of
sari-wearing and have taken to the modern Maharashtrian fashion,
an innovation that is disliked by their parents and pada-dwellers.
There was one instance in which a school girl strongly urged that
her sick younger sister be taken to the doctor when her parents
insisted on taking her to the Bhagat (witch doctor). In this
particular conflict between the generations it happened that the ailing
girl succumbed to her disease, and this turn of events confirmed the
older sister in her modernist conviction. It is apparent that education
has caused the girls to have more exalted expectations about their
prospective husbands; it is not always easy for them to find suitable
matches.

    In general, even the educated Warlis lack self-assurance.
Although exceptions may be found, they are generally laconic and
diffident. Education, it seems, has not as yet been able to wipe out
this tribal characteristic. For example, an intelligent Warli boy who
secured very high marks in his papers was introduced by his secondary
school teacher who complained that he hardly ever answered any
question put to him in the class. Another top-ranking student of
the Waki Ashram Shala was evidently very nervous and shied away
from the congratulations of visitors who tried to engage him in
conversation.

    The reasons for this diffidence probably lie in the deep-rooted
fear complex mentioned earlier. At least one reason is the feeling
of inferiority the Warli children display when they are identified as
such and shown to guests. Such consternation is probably unavoidable when inquiries are made as to who is Warli, who is Kokna, and
who is Bhil.

    This lack of self-confidence undoubtedly accounts for the
fact that, except in a couple of cases, no local Warli leadership has
come from those attending the two Institutes. One exception is an
MLA who attended the AI; the other is the Chairman of the Block
Council who went through the GBSK night school. This leadership,
again, appears to be conventional, although there are few data on
which to base this observation. One reason may be the cultural
isolation from which the educated Warli seems to suffer. Another
may be the almost total lack of "conscientization" in the educational
content of the Institutes. A third may be the absence of deliberate

efforts to create in the minds of Warli students a respect for some of the desirable features of their own traditional culture.

One serious handicap under which GBSK has been working must be mentioned. After Balwadi, where GBSK has freedom to design the content and methods of its educational programs, the children join the formal stream which is standardized for the entire State. Courses of study, their sequence, contents, textbooks, examinations, are all developed in line with government policy, in which the special needs of Adivasi students are hardly likely to find a place. There is no doubt that, if the GBSK had the freedom to suit the education to the needs of the locale, the children would be far better served.

Management Aspects

Although no formal procedures are laid down, the atmosphere within GBSK is friendly and conducive to free interaction among various categories of workers.

What is lacking is a systematic attempt at self-evaluation. Records of various types do exist, but a purposive documentation and data-collection with a view to assessment, identification of problems, scope for improvement and expansion, etc., are essential. Similarly a follow-up of the careers of old boys and girls would be very useful.

A perpetual problem facing the GBSK is that of finances. Most of the Balwadis and creches are aided either by government organizations or by private agencies (including some foreign ones such as the CAA), but deficits, nonetheless, are burdensome; and in order to make them up, GBSK has to contact donors, stage shows, and publish souvenirs. Under government budget expenses of only Rs. .20 (20 paise) per child per day are allowed for children's snacks in an area where hunger and malnutrition are rampant. These children must first be fed and fed well. Anutai, who will be seventy years old in March 1980, and her colleagues have to do a great deal of running about to collect funds to keep GBSK going in a reasonably effective manner.

In the context of the principal objective of GBSK, three observations occur to the observer.

First, although eleven Balwadis have been activated in Kosbad and its environs in the past twenty years, nothing by way of Balwadi expansion took place in the eleven years from 1961 to 1972 and again from 1972 to 1976.

Second, creches do not exist at all Balwadis. In fact, there are only three creches, attached to Kosbad (central) Balwadi, Dangaripada Balwadi, and Dalvipada Balwadi. The question is raised why they are not attached to the eight other Balwadis.

Third, what has happened to the Vikaswadi concept? Except at Kosbad, it has disappeared, and even in Kosbad it exists in an attenuated form. Kosbad retains the three components, but the primary school is such a big and formal institution housed in a separate building, it is difficult to conceive that an organic relation-ship--as visualized by the pioneers--remains alive among the components. In practice, the Vikaswadi concept seems to have receded into the background, a retreat that, on the face of it, seems unfortunate, considering the vital role it was supposed to play.

No doubt shortage of funds and the pressure of other activi-ties are responsible for these phenomena, and yet they call for a reexamination of GBSK's direction and growth.

CHAPTER 7

A COMMENTARY ON SOME KEY ISSUES

Having surveyed the evolution, activities, and impact of the Kosbad Institutes, we turn now to some critical reflections on the key issues posed to us by the ICED, namely: (1) how well the various program components of these institutes are integrated: (2) the extent to which there is direct community participation in planning and running these activities; (3) the adequacy of the educational inputs; (4) what success the programs have had in actually reaching and involving the poorest families; and (5) the special roles that voluntary organizations can play in rural development.

THE AGRICULTURAL INSTITUTE

Integration

The multifarious activities in which the AI engages itself immediately raise the question   of their relationship with one another.

The AI's origin at Kosbad was in the form of an agricultural school as part of a government program to establish one such school in each district. The AI, naturally, in this capacity, was assigned the work of training agricultural workers for the Thana district. Thus Thana district agriculture should be the main concern of the AI. That this has been so is reflected broadly in the research programs launched. The agricultural potential of the district-- paddy, horticulture, vegetables and grasses--has been what the AI has been mainly trying to develop,and at least technically many of its innovations can be considered successful.

Since the utility of the new methods and practices had to be tested in the field, the training of the trainees of the Agricultural School would have remained incomplete if they had not become acquainted with the field problems. It was, therefore, natural for the AI to directly involve the trainees in the agricultural development of surrounding villages. Thus the development program to which we have paid particular attention has a strong link with the basic, or at least original, objective of the AI. The same, of course, may be said of supply and extension. Because AI needs to know the effectiveness of its research at the field level, it is clear that the main core of its research, its Agricultural School, which

exclusively admits students from Thana district, and its extension
and development programs make up a consistent whole.

This cannot be said, however, about the other training programs.
Through one training center or another the AI has to look after the
agricultural needs of a total of five districts, a responsibility that
has affected the research program to some extent.   For example,
experiments on cotton were primarily impelled through the necessity
of training Jalgaon district trainees of the Adivasi Janata Vidyalaya
and the VLW Training Center. It is also obvious that the training
of non-Thana, or at least non-coastal district, trainees would be
inadequate. Jayant Patil has said that he appealed to the government for the removal of the Jalgaon district from his list of clients,
but to no avail. Being an institute of high repute has its cost;
there are always pressures from the government to do this or that,
even though it may not fit into a coherent pattern.

Located in a tribal area the AI naturally concerned itself with
the problems of the tribals. There were also early stimuli of the
founders, especially those of Bhise, which prompted the AI to
make the downtrodden and poor Adivasis one of its principal concerns.
Technical problems of coastal or Thana district agriculture do not
differ from those of the agriculture of the tribals in this district;
so whatever was useful to Thana district could also be expected to
be useful to the tribals within the district. But dealing with one set
of tribals is different from dealing with another. Their problems
would be common on a sociological and cultural plane, but not
necessarily on the agricultural plane. Bringing together Adivasi
youth from five different districts and several different ecological
zones under the Adivasi Janata Vidyalaya does not seem to result
in substantial benefit for tribal agriculture as such. Thus the
drive towards Adivasis *per se* for their agricultural improvement
seems to lack focus.

Examination of the integration issue has two sides: first, to
see whether the existing activities are purposively linked with one
another; second, to point to other activities which should logically
form part of the total design but are missing. It is to these latter
that we now turn our attention.

On the technological plane one of the objectives of the AI has
been to offer to the small farmers not cultivating more than three
acres per family--and most Adivasis belong to this category--a
technology that would lift them out of their dire poverty. The
pivotal point here was to turn a largely one-season (kharif) agriculture into a year-round enterprise. To accomplish this a constant
source of irrigation is needed. The surface well, one of the earliest
innovations of the AI, does not seem to have made much headway.
The AI itself seems to have gradually turned to dug wells. Of
course, the surface well could serve only as a source of protective
irrigation in dry seasons and could not support a three-crop cycle.
Furthermore, the dimensions of the surface well occupy a substantial
area of a farm that is already small. However, perhaps larger farms
could benefit from such wells--a possibility that would seem to warrant
closer examination.

A further reason for reexamining the potential of surface wells is because the areas dealt with are heavy rainfall but low ground water areas. The nature of the terrain suggests that it would be a great advantage to catch the abundant rain water that otherwise runs down the hills as soon as it falls and leaves the areas totally dry after about four months of heavy showers. Unless appropriate measures are taken the problem of ground water scarcity is going to become steadily more severe.

If rain water or ground water supplies have a limit, then it obviously becomes important also to improve water-utilization techniques in order to insure the most economical use of the available supply. Although we speak as laymen in these matters, this much seems clear: apart from the surface well, developed in 1969, the AI does not seem to have given sufficient attention to irrigation research. If indeed water is the key bottleneck, then it would appear to warrant a high priority in AI's research program.

However, technology alone is not enough when dealing with the Adivasis, or with small subsistence farmers generally. A new technology may look attractive from the limited perspective of an agricultural production expert, but it is important also to examine its attractiveness and feasibility from the broader and quite different perspective of the small farmer. The strongest impression we formed was that the AI has not appreciated the necessity of social science research. For any backward areas, and especially the tribal areas, agricultural problems are deeply embedded in socioeconomic problems and constraints. What will finally click with small farmers or Adivasis depends very much on their social and economic environment and how they perceive their needs, risks, opportunities and alternatives.

Beginning with the economic aspect, we would, for instance, like to know the economic alternatives to paddy cultivation as viewed by the small farmers, which might help explain their meager adoption of the HYVs. If it is true, as reports suggest, that the plantations in the areas around Kosbad afford wage employment at Rs. 5 or 6 a day, then many small farmers may quite rationally find the attraction of wage employment irresistible, purely on the grounds of the relative gains and risks of self-cultivation *versus* wage employment. It is no use simply calculating that HYVs and multiple cropping on a three-acre plot would (under favorable weather and market conditions) give a net income of Rs. 4000; it must also be found out whether wage employment gives as much or more than that without the advance investment, risks and uncertainties involved or the delayed income. Account must also be taken of the fact that the average Adivasi family apparently has substantially less than three acres of good land and poor water conditions for much of the year.

A related question is whether the Adivasis' own land can, by stages if necessary, be converted into mango or chikoo orchards so that he will make even a larger income than what wage-employment yields him, or be in a position to combine wage employment with self-employment in his orchard. This is only an illustration. The main point is that the economic alternatives and risks--seen from the farmer's vantage point--seems lacking in AI's research.

Although wage employment apparently offers a strong competition to self-cultivation in the Kosbad area, it may not constitute the whole explanation of the general Adivasi behavior, because in other areas where competitive income-earning opportunities are not available the Adivasis still resist agricultural innovations. Here again their reasons may in part be rational economic ones, but it would also be desirable to identify non-economic factors that may inhibit modernization.

Once it is understood that Adivasi perceptions and attitudes are basic in any attempt at modernization, AI's educational activities take on a new importance. Although the Ashram-Shalas and the secondary school may seem unrelated to AI's main purpose, they really are not. Our earlier discussion has shown the importance of the educational inputs, especially at the lower age groups. The supplementary occupation programs also seem to fall into place; here again the needs of the trainees cannot be forgotten. In order to learn, many must also earn.

A more critical view needs to be taken of the "better living" program that reflects the "all-sided approach," so popular in rural development efforts in India. This non-integrated approach is little more than a string of loosely-woven programs that find accommodation because in one way or another they "sound good." Undoubtedly AI's attempts to improve family living (smokeless chulhas, glass panels, improved sanitary arrangements) are good in themselves, but if a more rational pattern of living is to be propagated, are these the best items with which to begin?

We suspect that AI could more effectively accomplish its goal of better living if its agricultural and other efforts were accompanied by a medical-cum-family planning service, the absence of which has been a serious lacuna in its totality of effort. Whether run by AI or some companion organization, a low-cost paramedic service with a competent referral system would have many advantages. In the first place acceptability would be greater because the Adivasi, at least in this area, is gradually turning away from the Bhagat. Save described today's Warli attitude as a sort of flitting from the qualified medico to the witch doctors, depending on who delivers the goods, and our own inquiries confirm Save's findings. Secondly, experience elsewhere has shown that AI could undoubtedly establish greater rapport with its clientele through the medium of health services. Finally, such services are a crying need of the area. For example, scabies and other ailments arising from unhygienic conditions and under-nutrition are prevalent; tuberculosis and leprosy are said to be on the increase.

In fact, bad health and low agricultural productivity are undoubtedly closely related to each other in the Adivasi area. For example, at the beginning of the sowing season three health problems converge: food stocks having been exhausted, hence the nutrition level is shockingly low; bad weather and bad water at the onset of the monsoons cause malaria, influenza, and dysentery; and the pressure

of work is abnormally high. It is painfully apparent that physical
efficiency is at a very low ebb at a critical time of agricultural
operations.

Community Involvement

The members of the Adivasi community, so withdrawn, so unready
to be helped, so modest in their aspirations, have shown little impulse
toward community cooperative action and self-help. Or, to put the
matter differently, the AI has not yet discovered the means by which
indifference can be overcome, and it has therefore persisted in a
paternalistic approach to which no reasonable alternative has suggested
itself. Earlier Symington reflecting a similar paternalistic view, had
written that socially and politically the Adivasis were centuries behind
even the intermediate castes of the presidency, and what they needed
most was strong government action both to prevent them from
exploitation and to supply them as fully as possible with their educational, social, and economic needs. To bring one generation gradually
to the general level of their neighbors, he argued, would be enough to
accomplish.

However, on an individual plane as distinct from a community plane
the AI has tried with some success to encourage and assimilate
within itself individual Adivasis, mostly students. It has been helping
deserving secondary school students enter the University. About 12
of its old boys have become agricultural graduates and one has become
a veterinary graduate. Twenty-five girls from the high school have
passed the D.Ed. examination. One Adivasi student has gone in for
the medical course. More important, all four instructors in the
Agricultural School are AI's products and Adivasis. These successes
suggest that if individuals can, through education, be liberated from
the bondage of poverty and inhibiting cultural constraints, then
perhaps there is hope that whole communities of tribal people can be
similarly liberated.

Education

In spite of AI's solicitude for the Adivasis' needs in its many
formal and nonformal educational programs, it seems not to have
appreciated sufficiently that their basic agricultural problem is
rooted in exploitation. Possibly exploitation, in its grosser forms,
no longer exists in Kosbad, but others coming to Ashram Shulas
and the young men from the Bhil, Kokna, Koli Mahadeo, and other
tribes in the Adivasi Janata Vidyalaya have revealed their consciousness of their surroundings. They are ready for subjects wider in scope
than the technical agricultural ones, and this could be consciously
attempted, even in programs supported by government funds. Of
the 160 or so who come and stay together for a year, at least a few
could go back and spread the message of enlightenment and sociopolitical consciousness in their respective areas.

Reaching the Poorest

In research, development, and nonformal education, the emphasis
of AI activities has been on the poor--since all Adivasis are poor. In
formal educational and training activities the emphasis on the poor has
been only partial.

Our assessment of the development program (see Chapter 4) has
revealed two broad conclusions: (1) the AI has not been able as yet
to offer a technology and related services that would make the small
farmer's holding viable, and (2) even a beneficial technique may not
find acceptance for socio-cultural reasons.

The first of these conclusions (as we have noted) is dramatized
by the fact that the well, in the absence of heavy subsidies, is not
an economic proposition to a farmer holding less than five or six
acres of good soil. Although a few smaller farmers may be said to
have crossed the poverty line, this has become possible only because
the wells have not cost them anything by way of capital outlay. The
situation seems to be different for grasses and fruit trees, because
techniques are extremely low-cost. There has been some difficulty
getting small farmers to adopt them, but there is now encouraging
movement and they offer promise which may be further explored.

The second conclusion means that, even where a technique makes
sense in economic terms, it may meet with resistance in irrational
behavioral terms. In short, the problem of reaching the poor in
this area is compounded by two things: smallness and Adivasi-ness.
The latter is probably removable through deliberate efforts to change
attitudes and behavior patterns, especially through formal and nonformal education, but the process is slow with only limited prospect
of immediate returns.

In the debate about poverty and its eradication in India one
(and perhaps a growing) school believes that the conventional methods
of helping the small man, like redistribution of land, tenancy reform,
subsidized credit, extension of cooperation to marketing and agricultural production, small industry, etc., do not really fill the bill.
Most of these have been tried, but they have had little impact--and
not always because of insincerity or inefficiency in implementation.
Generally many of these programs involve subsidies that result in
perpetuating unproductive techniques. Since large, technologically
sophisticated industry has a limited capacity to absorb the unemployed
and underemployed labor, they see the solution in non-farm and
non-industrial employment, *i.e.*, in rural construction works of
labor-intensive kind, preferably with a guarantee of secure employment.
The Government of Maharashtra has had an Employment Guarantee
Scheme functioning for the last four years; but experience suggests
that non-official agencies are necessary to push the program forward
from the workers' end, and here is a new and probably more effective
outlet for the work of voluntary organizations. But it involves work
of a kind to which the AI's objectives, traditions, and methods seem
hardly suited.

Thus, although the AI has a pronounced thrust in the direction of the poor, most of its innovations seem to benefit mainly the larger and non-Adivasi farmers.

An independent corroboration of the poor Adivasis' dilemma was obtained in discussion with the trainees of the VLW Center, many of whom, especially those working in the Adivasi tracts, openly said that it was futile to work for them and that attention should be directed to those who are capable of utilizing new techniques either because of resources or of favorable attitudes.

Around Kosbad employment *is* available, as we have seen, largely because of the fruit plantations. If these could be further expanded, the land would obviously be put to more productive use and income levels would generally rise. In the accomplishment of this three alternatives are open: (1) allowing private land owners freedom to expand; (2) starting larger-scale fruit gardening under government aegis; and (3) organizing small farmers into joint farming societies so that technical hindrances to better land utilization can be removed. Each one of these alternatives has its problems, and a choice among them would have to be carefully made. These, of course, are matters of State policy and mostly fall outside the purview of voluntary agencies and of this case study.

There is, of course, one other option: namely, to leave out of the agricultural development effort the smallest farmers who really cannot be effectively helped because of their small resource base. This would amount to a deliberate decision to exclude the poorest, although the more potentially viable ones among the poor could still continue to be served. This, however, is essentially what is really happening now, though not by conscious design.

A further serious obstacle to involving the poor in development activities is, of course, the drinking problem. The AI seems to have taken it more or less as a fact of life and done little except to address moral invocations. Granted there are no easy solutions, a deeper look into this troublesome problem is needed in order to understand its root causes and to experiment with possible cures. An exchange of experiences and a joint research effort between AI and other organizations facing the same problem elsewhere in India might be rewarding.

Voluntary Organization

As a voluntary organization, AI is the fortunate beneficiary of strong dedication on the part of its workers. Whereas governmental programs have often been administered by personnel lacking the right motivation (especially true in the Adivasi area), the problems of the Adivasis are so complex that unless a large voluntary effort goes into their solution, purely governmental measures will otherwise come to nothing.

In similar vein, the number and variety of activities of AI is
testimony to the innovativeness of voluntary personnel. The extent
to which research and development have been carried bears witness
to deeply motivated voluntary effort.

Be it remembered,however, that many of AI's activities depend
on grants from the government, from whom cooperation and help would
be necessary under any circumstances. This peculiar position has its
advantages; at the same time it has the disadvantage that many times
the AI's choices suffer restriction, not the least in the training programs.
Contrasted with training, the AI's research is entirely unsupported by
government and we find this reflected in the greater freedom and
flexibility with which research is carried on.

The intermediate status of the AI--as a voluntary agency which in
some of its activities is supported by government--also seems to result
in adopting programs of a "safe" type that minimize the risk of stirring
up political criticism and controversy.

GRAM BAL SHIKSHA KENDRA

Integration

In comparison with AI's activities the growth of GBSK activities
appears more organic and cohesive, and is much more concentrated
on the needs of the Adivasi.   Its prime purpose was, and is, preschool
education; but after starting the Balwadi it necessarily had to turn to
the training of preschool teachers to make the movement self-sustaining.
In order to prevent Balwadi-educated children from relapsing into
illiteracy and backwardness, it had to take over and reorganize the
primary school. In order to insure regular attendance at the primary
school the hostels were established. And in recognition of the fact
that the economic problem is a major obstacle to spreading education
and also that education in rural areas should not be divorced from
work experience, the farm and the workshop were given an important
place in the total program.

Given the fact that the Nutan Bal Shikshan Sangh, GBSK's parent
body, was the pioneer in preschool education in Western India, and
that Tarabai Modak was its main pillar after Gijubhai's death in 1939,
GBSK's broader involvement in pre-child education, beyond the
Adviasi and the Kosbad area is understandable. This accounts for
the Publication Center, the editing and publishing of the Shikshan
Patrika and other literature, the printing press, and the Shabari
Udyogalaya. But the GBSK even here has taken care to integrate
these activities purposively with the rest of its programs, for
instance by involving Adivasi boys and girls in their operation. The
night school might seem somewhat unrelated to the main core, but
it arose, after all, in response to the demand of local boys and girls.

The UNICEF-supported applied nutrition training program, to
the extent that it concerns pregnant women and young children, also

fits into the general scheme, but in a slightly more remote fashion. A new activity that the GBSK is contemplating is participation in the massive Adult Education Program that the Government of India has launched. Apart from the doubtful merits of the scheme (in our view), GBSK's involvement in it would seem to be unrelated to its main function and hence could become a counter-productive diversion. We cannot suppress the feeling that as between further expansion of Balwadis and creches (or total Vikaswadi complexes) and the education of adults, the former should have greater priority. In terms of tradition, equipment, and human resources, the GBSK's most effective work lies in child education, in which the opportunities for rewarding service are virtually unlimited.

Community Involvement

What has been said above about community involvement in the context of AI is applicable here. GBSK appears to have had little success in stimulating active community participation and direct involvement in the operation of its activities, but not for lack of trying.

Parental involvement has not only been invited but deliberately encouraged at the creches and Balwadis. GBSK has sought to use the Applied Nutrition Program to bring the Adivasi women closer to its operation. Haldi-Kunku celebrations of women on surrounding padas are one more device to befriend the women and spread the message of the GBSK. Another practice has been to set up a creche at the nearby annual Mahalakshmi fair, attended by thousands of Adivasis, so that the Adivasi women can move about freely and come back in the evening to pick up their children. In its drive towards identification with the people there appears to be a noticeable "feminine" touch about everything that the GBSK does. These efforts have certainly built a trust in GBSK by the Adivasi women and a much stronger appreciation of its educational work than once existed, but this falls short of direct involvement in planning and participating in its activities. The traditional reserve of Adivasi women is still hard to break through.

Insofar as individual Adivasis are concerned, their participation in the activities of GBSK, especially at the higher level of jobs, is very low. All fifteen workers on the farm are Adivasis. Among the office peons all four are Adivasis. In the printing press five out of seven are Adivasis. But among office clerks there is none; in fact, no Adivasi application has ever been received. Among primary school teachers only one among the nine is an Adivasi. None of the staff of the training centers is Adivasi.

Education

Inasmuch as earlier pages comment fully on GBSK's educational approaches and methods, only one point requires further emphasis here, and it touches on the complex problem of "assimilation." On the one hand the Warli must be weaned away from his inveterate and persistent superstition and his primitive religious practices. He must be discouraged from harboring a sense of separate identity and from preserving cultural isolation. But at the same time he must not become detached from his heritage and his fellow men. He must develop his pride, for its source is his own cultural tradition. A balance may be difficult to strike, but it must be struck by dedicated educational effort.

A simple illustration of what we mean is provided by our visit to the night school where we found the teacher giving a lesson on festivals. We interrupted the procedure and asked the students to name some festivals they knew about and some gods and goddesses. In response they named the usual Hindu festivals such as Diwali, Sankranti, and Holi, and familiar Hindu gods and goddesses like Ganesh, Ra, and Maruti. We said jocularly to the boys and girls: "We have come from a far-off place where we never heard the names of these gods and goddesses. Our gods are Bharambha, Vaghaya, Naran Dev, Khalya Dev. Himai Devi...." (all Warli tribal deities). The joke was caught and there was a ripple of laughter in the classroom. When it subsided the children began to vie with one another, naming tribal gods and describing tribal festivals and seemed very pleased.

Reaching the Poorest

Although the difficulties GBSK has undergone should not be minimized, GBSK has been reaching the poorest. Perhaps it is easier to reach them through education than through economic programs of the kind AI has been pursuing. In any event, GBSK had to struggle with indifference, even resistance, to the idea of education, particularly that of child education. It also had to struggle with a deep-seated, pervasive economic problem.

In brief, GBSK has employed the following tools in its struggle: 1) flexible, unorthodox approaches in organizing programs with a considerable element of nonformal education; 2) encompassment of the educational problem from many sides simultaneously: creche, preschool, primary school, meadow school, night school, teacher training, and hostels; 3) continuous effort in combining educational and income-earning activities; 4) efforts to involve parents and other villagers in festivals, functions, and celebrations of various kinds; and 5) unflagging attempts to establish closer relationships and understanding with the general populace.

Voluntary Organization

Voluntary agencies generally have the attributes of dedication, flexibility, freedom to innovate, and informality of procedures. But there are other attributes. In the first place, they are likely to represent the needs of the people more accurately and to serve as conduits from people to the government. In the second place, they serve as an essential part of any genuinely functioning democratic polity by avoiding excessive concentration of initiative and power.

Their possible shortcomings are absence of continuity, smallness of scale, and paucity of means. Like the AI, the GBSK does not belong to the category of the "pure" type of voluntary agency. It has a mixed character, in that it runs certain governmental programs and uses government funds in some of its activities, but for all of this GBSK has generally succeeded in retaining the valuable attributes of a voluntary agency.

CHAPTER 8

SOME GENERAL CONCLUSIONS

This final chapter contains several conclusions and lessons derived from our study of the two institutes at Kosbad that we believe have relevance and possible value for other organizations similarly striving to improve the status of the rural poor elsewhere in India and throughout the developing world.

On the economic and technological plane the fundamental problem of the Adivasis is similar to that of small farmers all over the underdeveloped world. They have too small a resource base, and with existing technology their chances of survival are meager. Given this reality, the question that needs to be seriously considered is whether the main thrust of a poverty removal strategy should be toward helping the small man *on* the farm or *outside* it; and if outside, what real choices are open. We generally agree with the diagnosis of the problem offered by V. M. Dandekar and N. Rath in their book, *Poverty in India*, and with their conclusion that wage employment under government guarantee is the key to the solution. However, modifications will be needed to suit local conditions, and perhaps part-time *agricultural* employment (for example, in orchards under private or public management), rather than relying exclusively on construction works as suggested by Dandekar and Rath, may find an important place in poverty-removal programs in areas such as Kosbad.

If one accepts this view, then it follows that there must be a fundamental reorientation in the conventional thinking, approaches and attitudes of both government and voluntary agencies working in rural areas. The voluntary agencies will have to do three things: first, understand better the problems of their immediate clientele in a larger national perspective; second, press for adoption of viable national and state level policies in order that their own efforts may become more meaningful; and third, change and broaden their objectives and methods of work to suit the requirements of newer but eventually more promising tasks.

Much of the frustration from which voluntary development agencies suffer is attributable to lack of a congenial and feasible development framework. The sphere of voluntary agencies is bound to be small, and they can never be the principal instrument of social and economic change in modern societies; but they can play a special

and very crucial complementary role to government, provided there
is an appropriate national policy and strategy framework within which
to operate. The situation today in India is of a kind in which such a
dynamic national strategy does not exist, and voluntary agencies,
therefore, with all their dedication and idealism, seem to achieve
relatively little. One important task of voluntary rural agencies,
therefore, lies *outside* rural areas, and this consists of generating
pressures for adoption of viable state-level and national policies
for development.

        Given their geographically and otherwise isolated spheres of
action, separate voluntary agencies can achieve very little by way
of generating political or intellectual pressures of the kind required.
What is needed is a forum of such agencies. In Maharashtra such a
forum exists called *Gramayan* (of which all three authors of the
present study are founder-members and members of the executive),
which since 1973 has been trying to perform a variety of functions
to   the   extent   that its meager financial and manpower
resources permit. What Gramayan does is to hold meetings of
representatives of agencies for discussions of mutual problems, and
of governmental policies affecting the poor and Adivasis; to involve
city people (*i.e.*, experts, students and others) in rural development
problems and activities; to publish literature useful for workers; and
to take up projects on its own. Ways and means must be found to
set up organizations like Gramayan and make them more effective.

        As indicated earlier, "smallness" is one aspect of the Adivasis'
total problem; the other is his "Adivasi-ness." In practice this
means that even an economically viable technology may not be
accepted because of social and cultural obstacles.   This applies to
other poverty groups as well. Economists have to be wary about
theories that assume that economic rationality is a universal characteristic of mankind irrespective of the stage of culture to which men
belong. Although our data confirm the importance of the economic
factor, they also underscore the crucial importance of cultural and
social factors. In dealing with Adivasis (and other backward
communities) the latter factors assume supreme importance, and thus
an understanding of them becomes an important prerequisite of
effective developmental effort.

        The problems of the rural poor are magnified in the Warlis.
In sharp contrast to poorer people from the entire coastal areas
who migrate in hordes to Bombay, the Warlis have not been attracted
to urban employment. Even in their own areas they resist change,
no matter how grinding their poverty. Sociological research has not
yet found the key to unlock the secret of the Warli's compelling
attachment to his traditional values and his self-imposed estrangement.
But in a continuing, often frustrating, search and research, it must
be remembered that great strengths inhere in those who would hold
fast to their birthrights and not alienate their traditions.

        It would seem that many social workers, including those working
in the Kosbad area, tend to believe that, once "exploitation" is
removed, the way is clear; and so they direct their energies primarily

to agitational programs. There is no denying that exploitation has long existed and has often been a root cause in the creation and perpetuation of poverty. But purely agitational work can be counter-productive, to the extent that it makes the clientele believe that all their ills flow from sources outside themselves. It would seem that the lesson to be derived here is that constructive activity, even constructive criticism of the poor themselves (which may not make one very popular), is a *sine qua non* of success.

Of course the ultimate answer lies somewhere in continued education--education in its broadest sense as an induced learning activity. It must be made available to all ages, even though the adult generation under study may well be a lost cause. If it is sufficiently appreciated that the basic problem of underdevelopment is a *human* problem (that is, a problem of personality formation), it almost goes without saying that the process must begin and be emphasized with young children and youth--at the most impression-istic stage of life.

Education in new values and attitudes, however, must not result in taking away a person's identity and alienating him from his culture. To strike the right balance between tradition and modernity is always a difficult matter; yet the realization that a balance has to be struck, that every individual's culture must be respected, that his racial pride must not be hurt, will prove a salutory factor in all educational and development efforts.

Index

793

Parasite infestation and con-
trol, (CBFPS) 202, 226,
232
Parulekar, Godavani, 723
Patil, Harishchandra Gopal,
699, 730, 735-736
Patil, Jayant Shamrao, 699,
730-731, 757
Patil, Vasant, 774
Peiris, Devaviraj, 699
Pennappurema, Amara, 508,
510
People's Banks (Sri Lanka),
484
Perakum Shramadana Society,
Sri Lanka, 508
Perera, Daya, 470
Phatak, Padmaja, 699
Physicians
(Savar) 47-48, 85-86, 90,
98
(Lampang) 127, 148-149,
167-168, 191, 194
(Indonesia) 658
training of,
(CBFPS) 213
(BRAC) 369, 387, 391, 392
Pilot projects, 42-44, 310,
468
cost of replication, 181,
183-187
poorest areas not chosen,
613-615
replicability of, 104, 110,
113-116, 194, 542, 613-
615, 629-630
Pitsanuloke Project, Thailand, 118, 122
Planned Parenthood Association of Thailand (PPAT),
196, 217, 219-222, 228,
258, 262
Pongkhan, Khom, 221
Poorest rural families, 12,
14-15, 24, 83-84, 92-93,
105, 117, 134, 203, 215,
217, 220, 234-236, 266,
364, 372, 381, 406, 409,
439-443, 447, 453, 460,
466-467, 472-473, 515

Poorest rural families (cont.)
concentrations of, 478, 615
difficulties in reaching,
413, 510, 595-602, 630-
631
educational approach, 787
See also Gram Bal Shiksha
Kendra
government projects, 538
income producing projects
for, 601, 619
inequality and exploitation
of, 14, 466-467, 473
See also Moneylenders and
land tenure
limits on reaching, 618-619
need for family approach,
13-14
need for organization, 522-
523
need for organizational self-
support, 271
need for quick results, 27
need to test model for, 613-
615
non-farm wage employment,
preference for, 783
ommission from development
training projects, 587,
638, 679, 685, 687
relation to caste structure,
481, 510, 519-520
relation to land tenure, 783
relation to tribal structure,
783-784
resort to crime, 504
strengths of field motivators, 504
success in reaching, 180,
260-261, 370-371, 419, 472
See also Food for Work programs
working with sub groups,
28
Population Council (USA),
229
Population education
Indonesia, 639-643, 665-670,
674-685, 686-688
community participation in,
689

SWRC (continued)
"paraprofessionals," 300, 347, 355
"professional"/farmer partnership, 294-295
"professionals", 300, 347, 355
rural industries and handicraft program, 332-338
"specialists" 290, 300, 306, 310, 328, 347, 355
water development, 327-328
"Social work tradition" (India), evaluation of, 700
influence of paternalism, 704
reaction against, 290, 309
Socio-economic Development Committee (SEDEC), Sri Lanka, 511-513
South Korea, 164, 13-14
Confucion educational values, 603
economic growth, 13, 576
inadequacy of rural health services, 599-601
land reform and development, 14
Office of Rural Development, 606
resistance of traditional rural culture, 616-617
rural economic development, 576, 617, 627
Saemaul Undong (New Community Movement), 524, 526, 530, 535-539, 554, 565, 571, 606, 609, 610, 632
village leadership, 603-604
Sri Lanka, 479-480
economy, 480
geography, 479
history, 479
racial and religious groups, 479-480
rural poverty, 480
Rural Development Department, 484, 502
youth insurrection, 483

Srinivasan, Lyra, x
Srinivas, M. N., 723
Sudama, (an SWRC worker), 308, 315
Sudarmadi, S., 636
Sulla Project (BRAC), Bangladesh, 368-370, 373, 415, 417, 426, 428, 430, 450-457
Sulla Thana Central Cooperative Association, 437
Sulla thana, Sylhet district, Bangladesh, 365, 366, 372, 406
infant mortality, 385
population growth rate, 385
Sumanatissa, Reverend Tunnana, 501
Suvannvejh, Chaichana, 103
Swallows of Sweden, 430
Swedish International Development Authority (SIDA), 12, 99
Sydenham College of Commerce and Economics, Bombay, 741
Symington, D., 723

Talawila Committee for Rural Development (Sri Lanka), 511-513
Talawila, Sri Lanka, 510-513
Tanamalawila, Sri Lanka, agricultural training project, 495
Tangerang district, Indonesia, 637
demography data, 655
education, 657-658
ethnic mix, 657
family planning, 629
means of livelihood, 655-657
religion, 657-658
subordination to regional development plan, 657
public health, 658-659
Tangerang Youth Project, Indonesia, clientele, 622-664
costs and finance, 670-672
courses of study and content, 665-667

Note about the Author

PHILIP H. COOMBS is Vice Chairman and Director of Educational Strategy Studies of the International Council for Educational Development (ICED). His previous positions include: Founding-Director of the International Institute for Educational Planning (IIEP) in Paris; Assistant Secretary of State for International Educational and Cultural Affairs in the Kennedy Administration; Program Director for Education in the Ford Foundation and Secretary of the Fund for Advancement of Education. He has served as consultant to several developing countries as well as the World Bank, UNESCO, UNICEF, FAO and the U.S. Agency for International Development. He also served as a governor of the Institute of Development Studies in Sussex, England.

In his present capacity Mr. Coombs directed, in addition to the present project, two major ICED studies of nonformal education for rural development commissioned by the World Bank and UNICEF. He was senior author of two resulting reports: *New Paths to Learning: for Rural Children and Youth,* and *Attacking Rural Poverty: How Nonformal Education Can Help,* and co-editor (with Manzoor Ahmed) of *Education for Rural Development: Case Studies for Planners.* He is the author of several other works including *The World Educational Crisis* and (with Jacques Hallak) *Managing Educational Costs.*

Mr. Coombs attended Amherst College and did graduate work in economics at the University of Chicago and the Brookings Institution. He then served on the economics faculty at Williams College and Amherst College. More recently he has been a visiting professor at Harvard and Yale.